WITH THEIR BACKS TO TH

WITH THEIR BACKS TO THE MOUNTAINS

A HISTORY OF CARPATHIAN RUS' AND CARPATHO-RUSYNS

Paul Robert Magocsi

Central European University Press
Budapest–New York

Published in 2015
Reprinted in 2016 (with cerrections)
Reprinted in 2017 (with additions)

Central European University Press

An imprint of the
Central European University Limited Liability Company
Nádor utca 11, H-1051 Budapest, Hungary
Tel: +36-1-327-3138 or 327-3000
Fax: +36-1-327-3183
E-mail: ceupress@press.ceu.edu
Website: www.ceupress.com

224 West 57th Street, New York NY 10019, USA
Tel: +1-212-547-6932
Fax: +1-646-557-2416
E-mail: meszarosa@press.ceu.edu

ISBN 978-615-5053-46-7 Cloth
ISBN 978-615-5053-39-9 Paperback

Library of Congress Cataloging-in-Publication Data

Magocsi, Paul R.
  With their backs to the mountains : a history of Carpathian Rus' and
  Carpatho-Rusyns / Paul Robert Magocsi.
    pages cm
  Includes bibliographical references and index.
  ISBN 978-6155053467 (hardbound)—ISBN 978-6155053399 (paperback)
1. Carpatho-Rusyns—History. 2. Europe, Central—Ethnic relations—History.
3. Europe, Eastern—Ethnic relations—History. I. Title.

DJK28.R87M348 2015
943.7'004917--dc23
                        2015004881

For Nadia

For Ever

This book has been published with the generous financial assistance from

Dr. Alex Rovt, New York
The Jackman Foundation, Toronto
The Wasyl Janishewskyj Stipendium, Toronto.

Contents

List of Maps xiv

List of Tables xvi

Introduction xvii

Chapters

1. Carpatho-Rusyns and the land of Carpathian Rus' *1*

Human geography
No shortage of names
Physical geography
A borderland of borders

2. Carpathian Rus' in prehistoric times 15

Earliest human settlements
The Iron Age and the Celts
Early peoples in Carpathian Rus'
The Roman Empire and the Dacians

3. The Slavs and their arrival in the Carpathians 23

The Huns and the displacement of peoples
The origin-of-peoples fetish
Is DNA the reliable way?
The Slavs and Carpathian Rus'
Dwellings of the early Slavs
The White Croats and the Avars

4. State formation in central Europe 33

The Pax Romana and the Byzantine Empire
Greater Moravia
Saints Constantine/Cyril and Methodius
Christianity becomes "our" religion

Who among the East Slavs first received Christianity?
The Magyars and Hungary
Historical memory and political reality
The rise of Poland
Kievan Rus'
The Great Debate: the origin of Rus'

5. **Carpathian Rus' until the early 16th century** 53

The formation of the Hungarian Kingdom
A medieval Carpatho-Rusyn state: fact or fiction?
The Mongol invasion and the restructuring of Hungary
The Vlach colonization
Kings, nobles, and the implementation of serfdom
Poland: administrative and socioeconomic structure
The fall of Constantinople and the decline of Orthodoxy

6. **The Reformation, the Counter-Reformation, and
Carpathian Rus'** 74

The Ottoman Empire in central Europe
The Protestant Reformation
The Catholic Counter-Reformation
Poland and church union
Transylvania and church union in Hungary
The Union of Uzhhorod
Uniates/Greek Catholics: A new church or a return to the old?

7. **The Habsburg restoration in Carpathian Rus'** 88

Rákóczi's "War of Liberation"
Habsburg Austria's transformation of Carpathian Rus'
The Bachka-Srem Vojvodinian Rusyns
Poland and Galicia's Lemko Region

8. **Habsburg reforms and their impact on Carpatho-Rusyns** 97

The reforms of Maria Theresa and Joseph II
Uniate/Greek Catholics and the Enlightenment in Carpathian Rus'
Carpatho-Rusyns become an historical people

9. **The Revolution of 1848 and the Carpatho-Rusyn national
awakening** 107

The multicultural Austrian Empire
Kakania's emperors and kings
What is nationalism and what are national movements?
Nationalism in Hungary

From inferiority to superiority: the transformation of a dangerous complex
Revolution in the Austrian lands and Hungary
The Carpatho-Rusyn national awakening: politics
The first Carpatho-Rusyn political program
The Carpatho-Rusyn national awakening: culture
Did Carpatho-Rusyns really love the Russians?

10. Carpathian Rus' in Austria-Hungary, 1868–1914 129

The Dual Monarchy and Austrian parliamentarism
In search of a Rus' national identity
The national awakening in the Lemko Region
Hungary and its magyarization policies
Magyarization despite the letter of the law
Carpatho-Rusyns in Hungarian politics
Carpatho-Rusyns and national survival
Socioeconomic developments
Was life in pre-World War I Carpathian Rus' so destitute?

11. Carpatho-Rusyn diasporas before World War I 151

Migration to the Srem, Banat, and Bachka
Emigration abroad to the United States
Rusyn-American religious and secular organizations
Rejected Greek Catholics and the "return" to Orthodoxy
"You are not a proper priest"
"Ruthenians" become Uhro (Hungarian)-Rusyns, or Russians, or Ukrainians
Rusyn Americans and international politics

12. Carpathian Rus' during World War I, 1914–1918 167

The end of civilized Europe
World War I in Carpathian Rus'
The war against Carpatho-Rusyn civilians
Magyarization reaches its peak

13. The end of the old and the birth of a new order, 1918–1919 175

National self-determination and socialist revolution
Rusyn Americans mobilize politically
Political mobilization in the Carpatho-Rusyn homeland
Hungary's autonomous Rus' Land
The Ukrainian option
The meaning of Ukraine
Carpatho-Rusyns on the international stage

14. Subcarpathian Rus' in interwar Czechoslovakia,
1919–1938 .... *191*

Czechoslovakia and "Rusyns south of the Carpathians"
Borders and the autonomy question
Carpatho-Rusyn national anthems
Hungarian irredentism
Political life
Socioeconomic developments
Subcarpathian Rus': Czechoslovakia's architectural tabula rasa
Education and culture
Churches and the religious question
Orthodoxy: the jurisdictional problem
The nationality and language questions
The language question

15. The Prešov Region in interwar Slovakia, 1919–1938 .... *219*

Borders, schools, and censuses
The problem of statistics
Carpatho-Rusyns and Slovaks
Socioeconomic developments
Education
The religious question
The nationality question and cultural developments

16. The Lemko Region in interwar Poland, 1919–1938 .... *233*

Poland, its Ukrainian problem, and the Lemko Region
Socioeconomic status of the Lemko Rusyns
Religious and civic activity
The Lemko-Rusyn national awakening

17. Carpatho-Rusyn diasporas during the interwar years,
1919–1938 .... *241*

Romania and Hungary
Yugoslavia—the Vojvodina
The United States
Marriage and property: two sticking points

18. Other peoples in Subcarpathian Rus' *253*

Magyars
Jews
Relations between Jews and Carpatho-Rusyns
Germans
Romanians, Slovaks, and Roma/Gypsies
Russians, Ukrainians, and Czechs

19. Autonomous Subcarpathian Rus' and Carpatho-Ukraine, 1938–1939 269

The struggle for autonomy during the interwar years
Nazi Germany and the Munich Pact
Autonomous Subcarpathian Rus'
From Subcarpathian Rus' to Carpatho-Ukraine
Alternatives to the Ukrainian national orientation
Carpatho-Ukraine's road to "independence"

20. Carpathian Rus' during World War II, 1939–1944 279

Nazi Germany's New Order in Europe
The Lemko Region in Nazi Germany
Carpatho-Rusyns in the Slovak state
Subcarpathian Rus' in Hungary
The apogee of the Rusyn national orientation
Opposition to Hungarian rule

21. Carpathian Rus' in transition, 1944–1945 291

The Soviet Army and Ukrainian nationalist partisans
Rusyn/Lemko Americans and the war in Europe
The Soviet "liberation" of Subcarpathian Rus'
Transcarpathian Ukraine and "reunification"
The act of reunification
Czechoslovakia acquiesces to Soviet hegemony
Why did Czechoslovakia give up Subcarpathian Rus'?
The new Poland and the deportation of the Lemkos: Phase one

22. Subcarpathian Rus'/Transcarpathia in the Soviet Union, 1945–1991 305

Subcarpathian Rus' becomes Soviet Transcarpathia
The Soviet socio-political model
Totalitarian time
Forced collectivization and industrialization
Transcarpathia's new peoples
Revising the past and reckoning with "enemies of the people"
How Carpatho-Rusyns were declared Ukrainians
Destruction of the Greek Catholic Church
Transcarpathia's new Soviet society
Love of the East

23. The Prešov Region in postwar and Communist Czechoslovakia, 1945–1989 321

Postwar politics: the Ukrainian National Council
Population transfers and the UPA

Communist Czechoslovakia according to the Soviet model
Carpatho-Rusyns are ukrainianized
The Prague Spring and the rebirth of Carpatho-Rusyns
Soviet-style political consolidation and reukrainianization
Socioeconomic achievements and national assimilation

**24. *The Lemko Region and Lemko Rusyns in Communist Poland,
1945–1989*** *335*

Poland reconstituted and reconstructed
The deportation of the Lemkos: Phase two
Greek Catholic and Orthodox Lemkos
Lemkos as Ukrainians
Lemko fear and anxiety

25. *Carpatho-Rusyn diasporas old and new, 1945–1989* *343*

Soviet Ukraine (Galicia and Volhynia)
Czechoslovakia (Bohemia and Moravia)
Romania (the Banat and Maramureş Regions)
Yugoslavia (Vojvodina and Srem)
The United States
We want to know who we are

26. *The revolutions of 1989* *355*

Transformation and demise of the Soviet Union
The end of Communist rule in central Europe
Carpatho-Rusyns reassert their existence
One people despite international borders
Proclamation of the First World Congress of Rusyns
The autonomy question again

27. *Post-Communist Transcarpathia—Ukraine* *363*

Unfulfilled political expectations
Ukraine's "Rusyn question"
Carpatho-Rusyns in the international context
Socioeconomic realities
A failed or incomplete national movement?
Traditional religious and secular culture
Protestantism and Carpatho-Rusyns

**28. *The post-Communist Prešov Region and the Lemko Region—
Slovakia and Poland*** *379*

Czechoslovakia's Velvet Revolution
Censuses confirm nationalities
Independent Slovakia and the European Union

Prešov Region Carpatho-Rusyns reaffirm their existence
The Greek Catholic Church: a positive or negative force?
Nationality assertion and assimilation
Codification of a Rusyn literary language
Poland's three Lemko-Rusyn communities
Lemko Rusyns or Lemko Ukrainians?
The Vatra: a symbol of national and political advocacy
The attraction of Polish assimilation

**29. Other Carpatho-Rusyn communities in the wake of the
    revolutions of 1989** *393*
Ukraine
The Czech Republic
Hungary
Romania
Yugoslavia—Serbia and Croatia
The United States
Canada

30. Carpathian Rus'—real or imagined? *407*
Carpathian Rus': a reality or an idea?
Carpathian Rus' beyond Carpathian Rus'
Enemies as friends
A movement of women and young people
Education and national self-confidence

Notes *413*

For further reading *433*
  1. Reference works and general studies
  2. Prehistoric times to the 16th century
  3. The 17th and early 18th centuries
  4. The reform era and Habsburg rule, 1770s to 1847
  5. The Revolution of 1848 to the end of World War I
  6. The interwar years, 1919–1938
  7. International crises and World War II, 1938–1945
  8. The Communist era, 1945–1989
  9. The revolutions of 1989 and their aftermath

Illustration Sources and Credits *477*

Index *479*

List of Maps

1. Ethnographic divisions in Carpathian Rus' 4
2. Carpathian Rus': a borderland of borders 8
3. Geographic features of Carpathian Rus' 10
4. Archeological sites in the Upper Tisza and Lemko Regions 16
5. Central Europe, 5th century 20
6. Central Europe, ca. 750 30
7. Central Europe, 9th century 34
8. Early medieval kingdoms, ca. 1050 44
9. Hungary in the 11th century 54
10. Carpathian Rus', 13th–14th centuries 58
11. Hungary and Poland, 14th–15th centuries 62
12. Central Europe, ca. 1480 68
13. Central Europe, ca. 1570 74
14. Transylvania and Royal Hungary, 17th century 80
15. Austria and Hungary, 18th century 88
16. Austrian Empire, 1848–1849 110
17. Austro-Hungarian Empire, 1867–1914 130
18. Carpathian Rus', ca. 1900 142
19. Southern Hungary, ca. 1900 152
20. Carpatho-Rusyn communities in the United States 155
21. Greek Catholic eparchies in Carpathian Rus' before World War I .. 164
22. World War I in the Carpathians 168
23. Carpatho-Rusyn councils and republics, 1918–1920 180
24. Political claims in Carpathian Rus', 1918–1919 188
25. Carpathian Rus', 1919–1938 192

26. Religious institutions in Carpathian Rus', 1935 .... *226*

27. Magyars and Jews in Subcarpathian Rus', ca. 1930 .... *254*

28. Other peoples in Subcarpathian Rus', ca. 1930 .... *262*

29. Subcarpathian Rus'/Carpatho-Ukraine, 1938–1939 .... *272*

30. Central Europe during World War II *280*

31. Central Europe after World War II *302*

32. Carpatho-Rusyn diasporas after World War II *344*

33. Carpathian Rus' today *364*

34. Vojvodina, Srem, and the Banat today *400*

List of Tables

1.1 Number of Carpatho-Rusyns, ca. 2012 .... *1*

10.1 Carpatho-Rusyns in the Hungarian Kingdom, 1840 to 1910 .... *143*

14.1 Schools in interwar Subcarpathian Rus' *205*

16.1 Nationality composition of the Lemko Region *234*

18.1 Nationality composition of Subcarpathian Rus', 1921 and 1930 .. *253*

23.1 Census data on East Slavs in Slovakia, 1900 to 1991 .... *329*

Introduction

In 2006, I published a small illustrated book titled *The People from Nowhere*. Meant to be a reader-friendly, heavily illustrated introduction to the history of Carpatho-Rusyns, it seemed to fulfill that role not only through the English edition but also through editions in several other languages (Croatian, Czech, Hungarian, Polish, Romanian, Rusyn, Slovak, Ukrainian, and Vojvodinian Rusyn), which made the book accessible to readers in countries where Carpatho-Rusyns traditionally live.

Some readers were taken aback by the title of the book, a light-hearted paraphrase of a statement attributed to the most well-known person of Carpatho-Rusyn background, the American artist and cultural icon of the late twentieth century, Andy Warhol. It seems Warhol's irony, reframed as "the people from nowhere," did not sit well with overly sensitive—and usually recently reborn—Carpatho-Rusyn patriots, who seemed personally insulted that "their" ancestral people might have no real roots and concrete origins like other respectable peoples.

To be sure, *The People from Nowhere* made clear in its very first pages that Carpatho-Rusyns did, indeed, come from somewhere and that they did have a historic homeland which over the centuries spawned a distinct and respectable culture. Aside from its easy-to-read narrative, *The People from Nowhere* fulfilled another important function: it provided the conceptual framework and methodological approach to writing about a people which never had its own state. Many readers got the message about the existence of a distinct Carpatho-Rusyn people and historic homeland (especially critics who do not accept the very premise of the message), but some were still displeased that the text was too short. Brevity, of course, was the point of writing a popular book. The author knew all along that a fuller, more comprehensive history was in the making, and that version is in your hands: *With Their Backs to the Mountains: A History of Carpathian Rus' and Carpatho-Rusyns*.

What is the implication of the metaphor couched in the title of this book? Perhaps an even better title would have been: "no friends but the mountains." But that formulation was already used in a book about the Kurds, also a mountain people who in recent decades have been compared to

Carpatho-Rusyns. The point is that neither of these mountain-dwelling peoples has ever had their own state, and that the various states in which both have lived more often than not have had a negative impact on Carpatho-Rusyn or Kurdish society and culture. In the case of Carpatho-Rusyns, they have through assimilatory pressure since the nineteenth century been pushed gradually back from the lowlands and foothills toward the mountains, and on the northern slopes they have, in the twentieth century, been forcibly driven away. At best, then, the mountains have been a kind of protective shield and refuge in the sense of that turn of phrase used by people who speak of having their back covered.

The book's subtitle suggests two important elements: land and people. As elaborated in the chapters that follow, there is an historic territory in Europe called Carpathian Rus', a concept known to some of its inhabitants even though it is not to be found on most maps past or present. That land has been inhabited in large part, although never exclusively, by Carpatho-Rusyns. On the other hand, there are also Carpatho-Rusyns who have lived—and still live—beyond the territory of Carpathian Rus', whether in neighboring countries or farther away, such as Serbia, the United States, and Canada. Therefore, this book is about Carpathian Rus' the land as well as about Carpatho-Rusyns the people, wherever they may have lived or still live.

With Their Backs to the Mountains began in a manner not atypical of many scholarly books; that is, as a series of lectures for a university course, which were subsequently revised and reformatted into a book. The original lectures were written in the spring of 2010 for a 30-hour course on the history of Carpatho-Rusyns given at the newly established Studium Carpato-Ruthenorum, the first international summer school in Carpatho-Rusyn Studies organized at the University of Prešov in Slovakia. I subsequently used the lectures in a year-long course, titled "The People from Nowhere," taught for the first time in 2011–2012 at my academic base, the University of Toronto in Canada.

It is not surprising, therefore, that the format of *With Their Backs to the Mountains* is somewhat similar to that of a university textbook used in history survey courses. The 30 chapters follow a basically chronological order, tracing historic developments from prehistoric times to the present. A concerted effort has been made to provide a balance between political, socioeconomic, and cultural (especially religious) developments. Also, in keeping with the didactic mode of university texts, many chapters begin by placing Carpathian Rus' in the larger context of the countries which ruled its territory as well as developments within Europe as a whole. Hence, the reader will be exposed to the history, however brief, of Hungary, Poland, the Habsburg Empire, Czechoslovakia, and the Soviet Union, as well as to contextual explanations of larger pan-European phenomena, such as the Reformation and Counter-Reformation, nationalism, and sociolinguistic issues.

In a conscious effort not to interrupt the flow of the narrative, the only footnotes are those which provide sources for direct quotations and statistical data. This means that there are no explanatory footnotes of a definitional or historiographical nature that frequently accompany scholarly texts.

There is, nevertheless, in any survey that covers over two millennia of history, a need to provide explanations for certain terms, events, and social phenomena beyond what is possible to include in a readable narrative. To fulfill that need, I have adopted a practice used in other historical surveys that I previously published. I am referring to the so-called text inserts, which explain certain historiographical problems, elaborate on the contemporary significance of specific past events, and provide the texts of documents or illustrative explanations by other authors, whether scholars, journalists, or belletrists.

For those wanting to know more about a particular aspect of Carpatho-Rusyn history, an extensive section, **For further reading**, is appended. Couched in the form of a bibliographical essay, this section is arranged according to nine sub-sections which basically follow the chronological and thematic content of the book's narrative. Although most of the sources cited are in English, also included are a select number of the best works on a given topic, most of which are in Slavic and other languages of central Europe. The decision to include such works is based on the fact that many potential readers of *With Their Backs to the Mountains* will be in central Europe, where an increasing number of people, in particular younger generations, have at least a reading knowledge of English. Hence, they in particular may be able to make use not only of English-language sources, but also of the often excellent scholarly works in other languages noted in the **For further reading** section.

Geographic place names and to a lesser degree personal names pose a problem for any book dealing with central and eastern Europe. For geographic names I have followed the principles outlined in my *Historical Atlas of Central Europe*, 2nd rev. ed. (University of Washington Press, 2002). Villages, towns, and cities are given in the official language of the state in which they are presently located: Ukrainian for places in Ukraine, Slovak for Slovakia, Polish for Poland, etc. In a few cases where there is more than one form used in a given language (for example, the Ukrainian Mukacheve, Mukachiv, or Mukachevo), I have opted for the commonly accepted local variant, in this case, Mukachevo. In many instances, previous names may appear in parentheses the first time a place as mentioned—Mukachevo (Hungarian: Munkács), Uzhhorod (Hungarian: Ungvár), etc. Names of historic countries, regions, and provinces are given in their common English-language forms—Polish-Lithuanian Commonweals, Galicia, Transylvania, Little Poland, etc.—as found in the *Historical Atlas of Central Europe*. Names of pre-World War I Hungarian counties are given in Rusyn, the districts of Austrian Galicia in Polish.

Personal names and names of organizations are given in the forms found in the *Historical Atlas of Central Europe*; the *Encyclopedia of Rusyn History and Culture*, 2nd rev. ed. Paul Robert Magocsi and Ivan Pop, 2nd rev. ed. (University of Toronto Press, 2005); and *The YIVO Encyclopedia of*

1

Carpatho-Rusyns and the land of Carpathian Rus'

Carpatho-Rusyns have never had their own state, but they have for centuries inhabited a land called Carpathian Rus', which today is found within the borders of Poland, Slovakia, Ukraine, and Romania. Carpatho-Rusyns are also found in other countries, whether in compact communities or in isolation, to which their ancestors emigrated for the most part during the past two centuries. The present-day countries with immigrant or diasporan communities are mostly in Europe: Hungary, Serbia, Croatia, and the Czech Republic; and in North America: the United States and Canada.

TABLE 1.1
Number of Carpatho-Rusyns, ca. 2012[1]

Country	Official data	Informed estimate

Ukraine
  Transcarpathia (773,000)
  resettled Lemkos (80,000)
	10,100	853,000

United States	12,900	620,000
Slovakia	55,500	130,000
Romania	250	35,000
Poland	10,500	30,000
Serbia	14,200	20,000
Canada	—	20,000
Czech Republic	1,100	10,000
Hungary	3,900	6,000
Croatia	2,300	5,000
Australia	—	2,500
TOTAL	**110,750**	**1,762,500**

Human geography

Being a stateless people, it is difficult to determine with any precision the number of Carpatho-Rusyns. According to the most recent official governmental census data, there are 104,000 Carpatho-Rusyns worldwide. Other informed sources suggest that the number could be as high as 1.7 million. (See Table 1.1)

According to linguistic criteria and certain cultural features, Carpatho-Rusyns belong to the Slavic group of Indo-European peoples. More specifically, they are classified among East Slavs because they speak a language which is structurally related to other East Slavic languages: Russian, Belarusan, and most especially Ukrainian. Carpatho-Rusyns have, however, traditionally lived along an ethnolinguistic borderland that intersects with several other related and unrelated languages. These include linguistically related West Slavic languages (Polish and Slovak); an unrelated Romance language (Romanian); and a Finno-Ugric language that is not even within the Indo-European linguistic family (Hungarian).

Spoken and written Carpatho-Rusyn have been influenced in varying degrees by all these languages, which is one of the reasons it is different from closely related East Slavic languages and, therefore, is considered by an increasing number of linguists as a distinct Indo-European Slavic language.[2] Carpatho-Rusyn is generally written in the Cyrillic alphabet, which with the exception of a few letters is similar to the alphabets used in other East Slavic languages. Aside from language, another cultural feature that links Carpatho-Rusyns to other East Slavs is their traditional Eastern-rite Christian religion, which has taken the form of either Orthodoxy or Byzantine/Greek Catholicism.

The historic homeland of Carpatho-Rusyns, referred to in this book as Carpathian Rus', has never existed as a distinct administrative entity; nor has it had independence or, in its entirety, ever had political autonomy. Rather, it is like many other historic regions in Europe—Friesland, Wallonia, the Basque Land, Kashubia, among others—which have functioned as historic homelands in the minds of their inhabitants and in some cases may even be perceived as such by outsiders. The defining feature of these and other historic homelands is that the majority of their inhabitants belong to a distinct people or ethnolinguistic group, whether Frisians, Walloons, Basques, Kashubians or, in the case of this book, Carpatho-Rusyns.

NO SHORTAGE OF NAMES

Carpatho-Rusyns may never have had their own state, but they and their historic homeland have had no shortage of names. Such a phenomenon is not uncommon among many of Europe's peoples, whether they have had their own states, have lost their statehood, or have never had an independent state. The basic problem concerns nomenclature, or how a given people has been called by its own members and by outsiders in the past, and how and when its present ethnonym, or national name, was adopted and accepted as the current norm.

East Slavs inhabiting the Carpathian region have traditionally associated themselves with the name Rus', a concept that has been expressed in formulations such as: the people of Rus' (*rus'ki liudy*), the people of the Rus' faith (*rus'ka vira*), or the nominative forms *Rusnak* or *Rusyn*. The concept of Rus' should not—as is often done in western and even Slavic sources— be confused with the geographic term *Russia* and the ethnonym *Russian*.

Admittedly, the term *Rus'* and its adjectival derivative *Rusyn* are rather vague, since in medieval times Rus' referred to the lands inhabited by all East Slavs (modern-day Russians, Belorusans, Ukrainians, as well as Carpatho-Rusyns). Moreover, the term *Rusyn* (in English: *Ruthenian*) was also the common self-designation for Belarusans and for many Ukrainians until the outset of the twentieth century.

In order to be clear about the specific people that is the subject of this book, we should add a geographic prefix resulting in the ethnonym *Carpatho-Rusyn*; that is, the Rus' people whose traditional homeland is in and near the Carpathian Mountains. It should, therefore, come as no surprise that outsiders writing about the group as well as group members themselves have used terms which refer to geographic location, such as *Carpatho-Ruthenian*, or *Carpatho-Rusyn;* or, if the object is to promote a certain political agenda, *Uhro-Rusyn* (i.e., Hungarian Rusyns), *Carpatho-Russian*, or *Carpatho-Ukrainian*.

Traditionally, the most widely accepted self-designation used by the people themselves was the ethnonym *Rusnak*. This form can still be heard as a self-designation in parts of Carpathian Rus', and it is the formal ethnonym for Rusyns (i.e., *rusnatsi*) living in the Vojvodina and Srem regions of modern-day Serbia and Croatia. Finally, there is another regional term that is of recent origin but that since the early twentieth century has become the primary self-designation among Rusyns living north of the Carpathians in what is today Poland. The term is *Lemko,* or the variant, *Lemko-Rusyn*.

There have also been a whole host of other names applied to Carpatho-Rusyns who inhabit certain areas in Carpathian Rus'. Among the best known of these regional ethnographic terms are Lemko, Boiko, and Hutsul, although there are several others, including Krainiaky, Bliakhy, Dolyniane, and Verkhovyntsi. Some of these terms were not used by group members themselves, but rather by their neighbors or by scholars (especially ethnographers and linguists) seeking to devise a classification schema that might provide some order for their scholarly analyses.

It is perhaps not surprising, however, that scholars disagree about the boundaries between the various Carpatho-Rusyn ethnographic groups. Particularly controversial—among scholars, that is, not among the people themselves—is the farthest eastern extent of the Lemko component of Carpatho-Rusyns. Some scholars (especially linguists) fix the eastern "boundary" of Lemkos between the Wisłok and Osława Rivers on the northern slopes of the Carpathians. Ethnographers tend to push the Lemko boundary a bit farther east to the Solinka River and almost to the

ETHNOGRAPHIC DIVISIONS IN CARPATHIAN RUS'

MAP 1

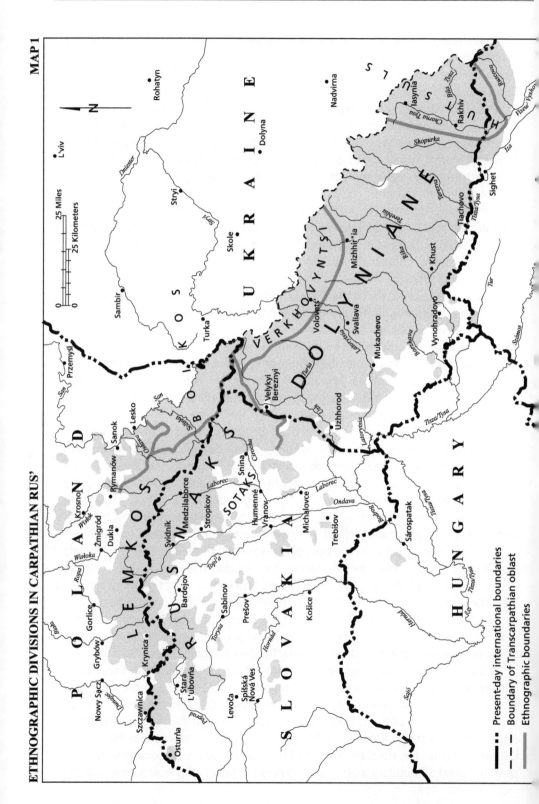

- - - Present-day international boundaries
- - - Boundary of Transcarpathian oblast
——— Ethnographic boundaries

mouth of the San River. Still others push the Lemko boundary southward to include all of the Prešov Region in northeastern Slovakia as far as the Uzh River valley in Ukraine's Transcarpathia/Subcarpathian Rus'.

Aside from the fluidity and vagueness of these scholarly ethnographic constructs, designations such as *Lemko, Boiko,* and *Hutsul* have taken on a political function. Ideologists of pro-Russian and pro-Ukrainian orientation are especially fond of applying the Lemko-Boiko-Hutsul schema to East Slavs living on both the northern and southern slopes of the mountains, thereby "proving" that Carpatho-Rusyns are an extension of either the Russian or Ukrainian nationality. Put another way, for these ideologists, whether civic activists or scholars, there is no Rusyn nationality; rather, there are simply Lemkos, Boikos, and Hutsuls who are ethnographic groups of either Russians or Ukrainians.

The tripartite Lemko-Boiko-Hutsul schema, as applied to East Slavs living on both the northern and southern slopes of the Carpathians, does not, however, respond to reality on the ground. For example, Carpatho-Rusyns on the southern slopes of the mountains have never referred to themselves as either Lemkos or Boikos, while the area inhabited by self-designated Hutsuls is for the most part outside Carpathian Rus'. Only 17 villages on the southern slopes of the mountains (a mere 3 percent of the total number of villages in historic Carpathian Rus') are inhabited by persons who may use *Hutsul* as a self-identifier. On the other hand, the name *Hutsul* has taken on a broader and vaguer meaning. Especially in today's Ukraine it is used as a kind of term of endearment to describe *all* the inhabitants of Ukraine's Transcarpathian oblast, who are viewed with nostalgia as pristine mountaineers that ostensibly embody and preserve the best qualities of traditional Ukrainian culture.

The territorial homeland of Carpatho-Rusyns has also had several names. *Carpatho-Ruthenia, Carpatho-Russia, Carpatho-Ukraine, Rusinia, Subcarpathian Ruthenia,* or simply *Ruthenia* or *Subcarpathia* are among the most common that are encountered in the literature. This book will use the form *Carpathian Rus'*, which suggests both a geographic location (territory in the Carpathian Mountains and its foothills) and the ethnic affinity of the majority population (East Slavic inhabitants whose self-designation, *Rusnak/Rusyn*, derives from the noun *Rus'*).

Since Carpathian Rus' never functioned as a distinct political-administrative entity, how does one determine its boundaries? In short, Carpathian Rus' is where Carpatho-Rusyns have historically lived. One needs to stress the adverb *historically*, since in the course of the second half of the twentieth century the extent of Carpatho-Rusyn inhabited territory has been reduced, either because of physical displacement (both voluntary resettlement and forcible deportation), or because of national assimilation. Therefore, our understanding of what constitutes Carpathian Rus' derives from a historic period before physical displacement and large-scale national assimilation took place.

With that context in mind, the boundaries of Carpathian Rus' encompass a contiguous territory comprised of settlements in which at least 50 percent of the inhabitants (and more often a much higher percentage) described themselves as Carpatho-Rusyns in the censuses of 1900, 1910, and 1921. At that time, there were 1,093 settlements (mostly villages with an average between 300 and 1,800 inhabitants), which could be classified as Carpatho-Rusyn.[3] It is, therefore, conditions during the first two decades of the twentieth century which determine the boundaries of Carpathian Rus' as the unit of analysis in this book. As in historical writing about many European states and historic territories, so too is the concept of Carpathian Rus' as defined above used anachronistically to describe a specific land that before and after the period 1900–1921 may not have been inhabited by a majority Carpatho-Rusyn population or, for that matter, inhabited at all.

Where, geographically, are those villages, and what constitutes the historic territory of Carpathian Rus' in present-day political terms? Carpathian Rus' straddles the borders of four countries, and because of this political reality one may speak of it as divided into four regions: (1) the Lemko Region in present-day southeastern Poland; (2) the Prešov Region in northeastern Slovakia; (3) Subcarpathian Rus', or the Transcarpathian oblast of far western Ukraine; and (4) the Maramureş Region in north-central Romania. It is in these four regions where, until the mid-twentieth century, Carpatho-Rusyns lived in settlements located in a contiguous or geographically connected territory. Like many other historic territories in Europe, Carpathian Rus' has never been ethnically homogeneous. In other words, other groups, including Slovaks, Magyars,[4] Jews, Germans, and Roma/Gypsies among others, have lived in varying proportions in villages throughout Carpathian Rus' where otherwise the majority of inhabitants are Carpatho-Rusyns.

Although Carpatho-Rusyns have traditionally lived in rural villages, they have been drawn to several towns and small cities just to the north (Nowy Sącz, Gorlice, Jasło, Krosno, Sanok) and to the south (Stará L'ubovňa, Bardejov, Prešov, Humenné, Michalovce, Uzhhorod, Mukachevo, Sighet). Until the twentieth century these places had on average only 12,000 to 18,000 inhabitants. Despite their small size, they at least since the outset of the nineteenth century served as the administrative centers for local Austrian Galician districts and Hungarian counties, where buildings housing offices for local government, courts, police, and other civic functionaries (notary publics, lawyers, physicians, newspaper editors) were to be found. Some of these towns had the only secondary schools (*gymnnasia*, seminaries) for Carpathian Rus', as well as the administrative seats of the various churches serving the region. For all these reasons Carpatho-Rusyn villagers and their children would likely at some point in their lives be drawn to these towns, even if only on a one-time basis for a specific purpose.

The towns themselves were a world removed from the rural environment of Carpatho-Rusyn villages. Not only did they have paved (or more likely cobble-stoned) streets and a variety of small shops with goods not available in the village, but the vast majority of each town's inhabitants were of a different nationality and religion. On the northern slopes of the Carpathians those "other" town dwellers were likely to be Roman Catholic Poles; on the southern slopes, Roman Catholic and Protestant Slovaks and Magyars. In earlier centuries Germans were likely to live in the inner core of some towns, while from the nineteenth century all of them included a high number of Jews, who in some cases made up a plurality of the inhabitants. As for Carpatho-Rusyns, those living in nearby villages (nearby implying access by foot or horse-cart) came to these urban centers primarily to trade or to buy manufactured goods, or in a few instances to work at the limited number of jobs that were available, mostly as day laborers or as domestic servants. Gradually, in the course of the twentieth century, political and socioeconomic changes allowed for a greater number of Carpatho-Rusyns to leave permanently their villages in order to settle and work in these and other cities nearby.

Aside from urban areas, there were and still are pockets or islets of rural settlements outside Carpathian Rus', where Carpatho-Rusyns have formed the majority or a significant portion of the population. These islets were—and in some cases still are—located just north of the Lemko Region in southeastern Poland, south of the Prešov Region in eastern Slovakia, in northeastern Hungary, and farther afield in the Banat Region of Romania, the Vojvodina of Serbia, and the Srem in Croatia.

Physical geography

Carpathian Rus' extends about 375 kilometers/232 miles from the Poprad River valley of Slovakia and Poland in the west to the Ruscova/Ruskova River (a tributary of the Vişeu, then Tisza/Tysa) of Romania in the east. This territory, which covers 18,000 square kilometers/7,020 square miles (about the size of the state of New Jersey in the United States) and is only 50 to 100 kilometers/30 to 50 miles in width, encompasses several mountain ranges (mostly the Beskyds) of the Carpathian Mountains and its lower foothills.

A BORDERLAND OF BORDERS

Carpathian Rus' is a borderland of borders. Through or along its periphery cross five types of boundaries: geographic, political, religious, ethnolinguistic, and socio-climatic.

Geographically, the crest of the Carpathian Mountains forms a watershed, so that the inhabitants on the northern slopes are drawn by natural and man-made communicational facilities toward the Vistula-San basins of the Baltic Sea. The inhabitants on the southern slopes are, by contrast, geographically part of the Danubian Basin and plains of Hungary.

Politically, during the long nineteenth century (1770s–1914), Carpathian Rus' was within one state, the Habsburg Monarchy, although it was divided between that empire's Austrian and Hungarian "halves" by the crests of the Carpathians. Since 1918 its territory has been divided among several states: Poland, Czechoslovakia,

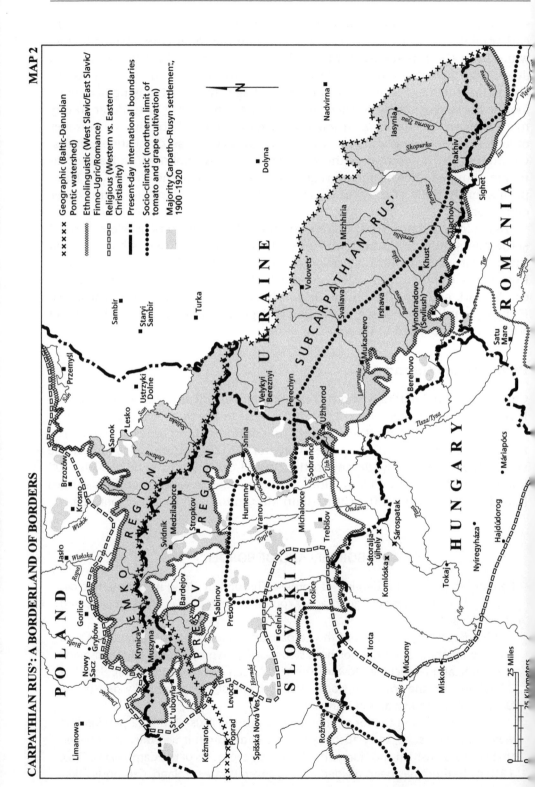

MAP 2

CARPATHIAN RUS': A BORDERLAND OF BORDERS

x x x x x   Geographic (Baltic-Danubian Pontic watershed)

Ethnolinguistic (West Slavic/East Slavic/ Finno-Ugric/Romance)

Religious (Western vs. Eastern Christianity)

Present-day international boundaries

Socio-climatic (northern limit of tomato and grape cultivation)

Majority Carpatho-Rusyn settlement, 1900 -1920

Romania, the Soviet Union, Ukraine, and Slovakia, and for a short period Nazi Germany and Hungary.

Carpathian Rus' is located along the great borderland divide between Eastern and Western Christianity, spheres which some scholars have described as *Slavia Orthodoxa* and *Slavia Romana*. Most of the region's Carpatho-Rusyn inhabitants fall within the Eastern Christian sphere, although they are in turn divided more or less evenly between adherents of Greek Catholicism and Orthodoxy. The religious landscape is not limited, however, to Greek Catholic and Orthodox Christians, since traditionally within and along the borders of Carpathian Rus' have lived Roman Catholics, Protestants (Reformed Calvinists and a lesser number of Evangelical Lutherans), and a large concentration of Jews of varying orientations: Orthodox, in particular ultra-conservative Hasidim, as well as Reformed or Progressive Neologs.

All of Europe's major ethnolinguistic groups converge in Carpathian Rus', whose territory marks the farthest western extent of the East Slavic world and is bordered by West Slavic (Poles and Slovaks), Finno-Ugric (Magyars), and Romance (Romanians) speakers. The Germanic languages have as well been a feature of the territory's culture, since until 1945 ethnic Germans (Spish and Carpathian Germans) and many Yiddish-speaking Jews lived in its towns and cities and also in the rural countryside.

Finally, there is another boundary running through Carpathian Rus', which to date has received no attention in scholarly or popular literature but is nonetheless of great significance. I refer to what might be called the socio-climatic border or, more prosaically, the tomato and grape line. It is through a good part of Carpathian Rus' that the northern limit for tomato and grape (wine) cultivation is found. Whereas south of the line tomato-based dishes are the norm in traditional cuisine, before the mid-twentieth century that vegetable was virtually unknown to the Carpatho-Rusyns and other groups living along the upper slopes of the Carpathians.

The absence of grape and wine cultivation north of the tomato-grape line has had a profound impact on the social psychology of the inhabitants of Carpathian Rus'. A warmer climate and café culture has promoted human interaction and social tolerance among Rusyns and others to the south. By contrast, those living farther north are apt to spend less time outdoors, and when they do interact in social situations the environment is frequently dominated by the use of hard alcohol that in excess provokes behavior marked by extremes of opinion, short tempers, and physical violence. Like all attempts at defining social or national "characteristics," the above assessment is based largely on impressionistic observation and, therefore, is liable to oversimplification. Nevertheless, further empirical research should be carried out to define more precisely the exact location of tomato and grape cultivation, to describe the resultant interregional differentiation in food and drink, and more importantly, to determine how those differences affect the social psychology of the Carpatho-Rusyns and other inhabitants of Carpathian Rus'.

SOURCE: Paul Robert Magocsi, "Carpathian Rus': Interethnic Coexistence without Violence," In Omer Bartov and Eric D. Weitz, eds., *Shatterzone of Empires* (Bloomington and Indianapolis, 2013), pp. 450–452.

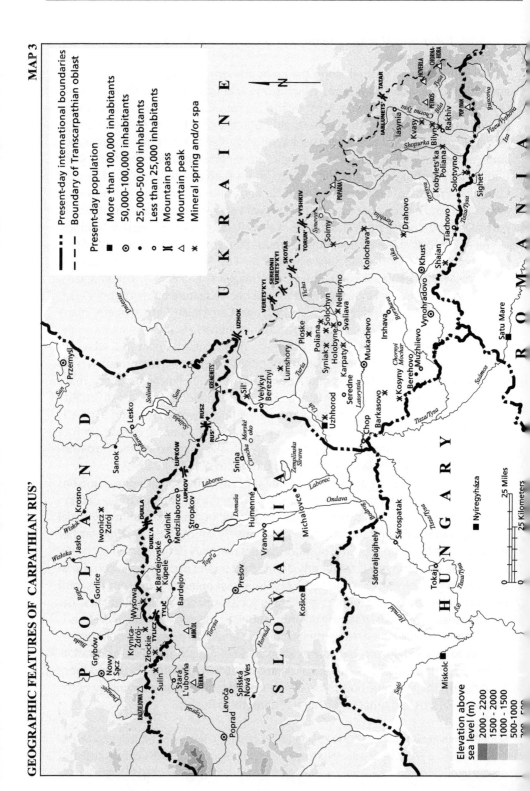

GEOGRAPHIC FEATURES OF CARPATHIAN RUS'

MAP 3

Present-day international boundaries
Boundary of Transcarpathian oblast

Present-day population

■   More than 100,000 inhabitants
⊙   50,000-100,000 inhabitants
•   25,000-50,000 inhabitants
○   Less than 25,000 inhabitants
)(Mountain pass
△   Mountain peak
✳   Mineral spring and/or spa

Elevation above
sea level (m)

2000 - 2200
1500 - 2000
1000 - 1500
500-1000

Since the Carpathian mountain crests form a major European watershed, the rivers in the Lemko Region of Carpathian Rus' (the Biała, Ropa, Wisłoka, Wisłok, Osława, and Solinka), flow northward as part of the Vistula-Baltic Basin. By contrast, most rivers on the southern slopes of the mountains (the Torysa, Topl'a, Ondava, Laborec, Uzh, Latorytsia, Borzhava, Rika, Tereblia, Teresva, Ruscova/Ruskova, and Vişeu) flow directly or via tributaries into the Tisza River, which in turn is part of the Danubian Basin. An interesting exception is the Poprad River, whose source is on the southern slopes of the Carpathians, but which flows northward "across" the mountains and empties into the Vistula-Baltic Basin. This seeming geographical anomaly underscores the fact that the Carpathian Mountains are at their lowest in the western part of Carpathian Rus', something that over the centuries has made communication easy and relations close among Carpatho-Rusyns in the Lemko Region and those in the Prešov Region.

The mountains do get higher the farther one moves from west to east through Carpathian Rus'. In the western areas that straddle the Lemko Region and Prešov Region (the present Polish-Slovak border), the highest peaks are about 1,000 meters, while the several easily accessible passes (Tylicz/Tylič, Beskydek, Dukla/Dukl'a, Palota) are only 500 to 700 meters above sea level. But farther east in Subcarpathian Rus' the mountains are much higher, with several peaks over 2,000 meters in height and with passes (Uzhok, Verets'kyi, Torun'/Vyshkiv, Iablunets'/Tatar) that average between 900 and 1,000 meters above sea level. This geographic factor in large part explains why contact between Subcarpathian Rus' and the adjacent region of Galicia north of the mountain crests has historically been more difficult, resulting in greater isolation of this part of Carpathian Rus' from lands and cultures to the north and east in present-day Ukraine.

The northern ranges (Beskyds, Bieszczady) of the Carpathian Mountains—covered as they are in rich foliage and in general absent of sharp rocky outcroppings—at first glance remind one of the Green Mountains in the state of Vermont. There are, however, some differences. In western Carpathian Rus'—the Prešov Region in Slovakia and the Lemko Region in Poland—the slopes are indeed low and covered for the most part with forests even at highest elevations. Farther east, in Ukraine's Subcarpathian Rus'/Transcarpathia, the mountains may be gradually higher but the forest cover is often less dense. In fact, it is not uncommon to find rounded mountain tops completely denuded of trees. Even the highest mountains with thicker forest cover are frequently interrupted with open spaces at high elevations, the so-called *polonyny* or high mountain pastures. The major reason for the absence of a thick forest cover in the eastern part of Carpathian Rus' has to do with the extensive and unregulated cutting of trees, most especially during the second half of the twentieth century.

Until that time, however, the mountain forests of Carpathian Rus' (mostly beech, oak, fir, and spruce) provided the region with one of its most important natural resources—wood. Other resources included salt (especially in eastern Subcarpathian Rus') and mineral water. Whereas in recent decades salt extraction has ended, the numerous mineral water springs continue to be the basis for a network of spas and health resorts as well as bottled drinking water for domestic consumption and export. On the other hand, there is no significant winter sport industry built around skiing on the mountain slopes that are located within Carpathian Rus'.

The predominant livelihood for Carpatho-Rusyns from early modern times until well into the twentieth century has been agriculture, animal husbandry (in particular, sheep), and forest-related work. Of these three branches of economic activity, small-scale agriculture became the primary livelihood for the vast majority of Carpatho-Rusyns from late eighteenth century. Productivity was always a problem, however, since most of Carpathian Rus'—in particular the Lemko Region, the Prešov Region, and the highlands of Subcarpathian Rus'—is located in what geographers call a hardscrabble belt. This is a landscape characterized by a broken terrain of mountains and hills intersected by river valleys, where crops are sown on limited arable land comprised of sterile soils and a climate marked by excessive cloudiness throughout the year. The higher the elevations, the less favorable are the conditions, so that in the mountains there are generally only two warm summer months (often accompanied by frequent rainfall) while the mid-winter temperatures are well below freezing, sometimes as low as –34° Celsius.

The settlement and field patterns in Carpathian Rus' are typical of those found throughout Europe north of the Alps. Carpatho-Rusyns created so-called street villages, where homesteads were located in a line alongside a single road which more than likely ran parallel to a small river and adjacent tributaries. Such prime location provided a source of water for livestock and for more mundane activity such as washing clothes. The fields were outside the village proper and located adjacent to the river or along low hillside slopes. Generally, the fields were laid out in parallel strips which made it easy to plow in a long single line without the necessity of too much turning, a technique most suitable to the draft animal of choice—oxen. Not only were the strips of land owned or rented by the peasant agriculturalist outside the village proper, they most often were not adjacent to each other. Hence, it was common for a villager to walk to work (usually not more than a kilometer or two) to one or more of his or her strips of land located in various places beyond the village.

Because of the relatively poor soil and limited sunshine that characterized much of Carpathian Rus', only the most hardy grains (rye, barley, oats) and garden vegetables (potatoes, cabbage, beans) could be sown, yet even these yielded only a limited output. The one exception to this agricultural pattern is in the foothills and lowlands of Subcarpathian Rus', just south of its main cities Uzhhorod and Mukachevo. This area is really an extension of the lowland Hungarian plain, where the climate is significantly warmer with long summers and mild temperatures in winter that hover around or above 0° Celsius even during the coldest months (December to February). The favorable climate with its more sunny days and the area's fertile soils have been able to provide not only for the needs of an individual village family, but also to produce surplus yields from the vegetable farms, vineyards, and orchards for sale and extra income. Technically, the area is only partially within Carpathian Rus', since most of the inhabitants have traditionally been—and still are—Magyars, not Carpatho-Rusyns (see Map 1).

In effect, throughout much of their history Carpatho-Rusyns have only been able to practice subsistence farming; that is, to realize a level of crop production that at best can support a single family with little or no real surplus to sell for profit. In order to survive, therefore, most villagers have had to engage in animal husbandry.

The most favored animals of Carpatho-Rusyn herder-farmers have been cows which pasture in and around the village, and sheep which for several cycles each year are driven up the mountains and pastured in the highland *polonyna*. As with agriculture, the products derived from animal husbandry (milk, butter, cheese, wool) have been used to fulfill individual family needs with little or no surplus to sell for extra income.

It is this traditional subsistence-level lifestyle which preoccupied the everyday existence of Carpatho-Rusyns for much of the year, except in the coldest winter months (November to February) when the frozen land was impossible to till. This was a time when handicrafts flourished—weaving and colorful embroidery among females and wood carving and metalwork among males. Activities such as these, often done in common, encouraged singing and recitation of folk tales that remain among the important achievements of Carpatho-Rusyn culture. Whereas peasant parents were not adverse to sending their children to school, they often balked at doing so during the early spring sowing and the early summer and early autumn harvest. It was therefore not uncommon for children, who were needed in the fields, to be frequently absent at the end (April and May) and beginning (September and October) of each school year.

The annual agricultural cycle and the concrete demands of a peasant-based rural society that was concerned primarily with physical survival continued to determine the cultural values of Carpatho-Rusyns even after their socioeconomic conditions began to change slowly in the course of the twentieth century. The gauge for determining the success of an individual remained the same: it was usually associated with one's material and financial achievement. Such attitudes in large measure explain why the group's few leaders in the nineteenth and twentieth centuries found it so difficult to mobilize their Carpatho-Rusyn constituencies to be concerned about such "esoteric" issues as one's national identity, native language, or participation in civic and political life—unless, of course, there might be some concrete material gain that would be accrued from such otherwise unproductive activity.

Two final points about the physical and human geography are worth keeping in mind. The first is that in purely geographical terms, Carpathian Rus' is located in the heart of Europe. In fact, scholars already in the late nineteenth century pinpointed the geographic center of Europe to be just outside the village of Trebushany (today Dilove) along the Tisza River in

2

Carpathian Rus' in prehistoric times

Much of Carpathian Rus', in particular the lands on the southern slopes of the mountains, were in prehistoric times part of a somewhat larger territory which archeologists refer to as the Upper Tisza Region. This includes the area drained by the upper reaches of the Tisza River and its tributaries, which in modern-day terms means the Transcarpathian oblast of Ukraine, eastern Slovakia, northeastern Hungary, and northwestern Romania. Since pre-historic times the Upper Tisza Region functioned as a contact zone connecting the peoples and cultures of the Danubian Basin and Balkan Europe in the south with the inhabitants beyond the Carpathian Mountains to the north, i.e., the Lemko Region in modern Poland.

Earliest human settlements

Thanks to archeological discoveries, mostly in the twentieth century, it is known that the Upper Tisza Region was inhabited as far back as the Eolithic, or earliest period of the Stone Age. In fact, the oldest site of human habitation throughout central Europe and Ukraine, which goes back over one million years, was near the Subcarpathian town of Korolevo along the valley of the Tisza River. The most important development during these prehistoric times came during the Stone Age's Neolithic period; that is, from 5000 to 3000 BCE, when the inhabitants of the Upper Tisza Region evolved from being primitive hunter-gatherers to sedentary agriculturalists. They lived in semi-underground dwellings and were able to support themselves from the crops they grew. Over 200 sites from the Neolithic period have been uncovered in the Upper Tisza Region and have been classified according to various archeological cultures (Kiresh/Kress, Alföld, Bükk, Samosh-Diakovo). It is also from the Neolithic period that the earliest archeological finds have been uncovered in the Lemko Region, on the northern slopes of the Carpathians, in particular in the valleys of the upper Ropa River (Blechnarka, Hańczowa, Uście Gorlickie, Gładyszów, among others). Most of the Neolithic finds consist of stone adzes, flint axes, sickle-like knives, and in the case of the Upper Tisza Region on the southern slopes of the mountains, extensive remnants of decorated pottery.

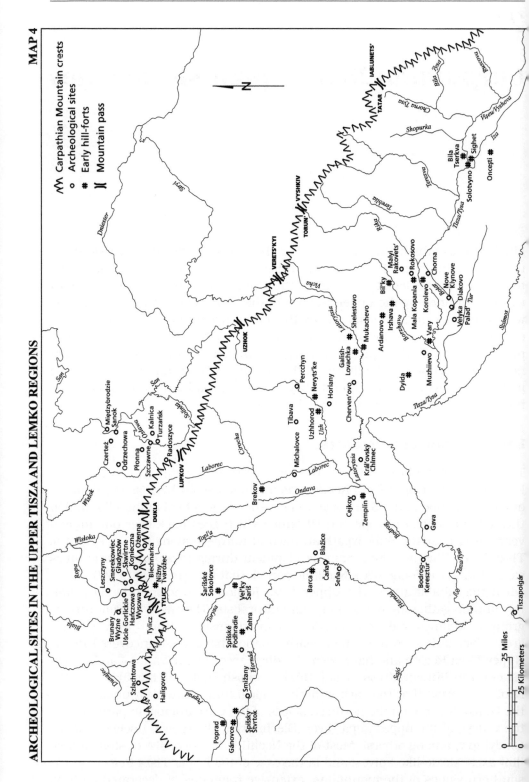

ARCHEOLOGICAL SITES IN THE UPPER TISZA AND LEMKO REGIONS

MAP 4

Carpathian Mountain crests
Archeological sites
Early hill-forts
Mountain pass

The next archeological phase, known as the Eneolithic or Copper Age (ca. 3000–2000 BCE), witnessed the gradual transition from stone to metal implements and also the introduction of cattle-breeding, all of which enhanced the quality of life and longevity of the inhabitants. Those inhabitants also gradually consolidated into clans made up of several families and eventually into larger tribal groups, which began to stake out certain territories they considered their own.

Toward the end of the Copper Age, other Indo-European tribes began to arrive in the Danubian Basin as far as the Upper Tisza Region. They came from the south, in particular from the Balkan peninsula, sometime around 2000 BCE, and they brought with them new and profoundly influential technological changes. What followed was the Bronze Age, which was to last for a thousand years (1900–900 BCE). Familiar with the civilizations surrounding the eastern Mediterranean and Aegean Sea, these Indo-European newcomers from the south introduced into the Upper Tisza Region bronze implements, harnessed horses, and use of the plough in agriculture.

The various cultures identified with the Bronze Age in the Hungarian plain and foothills of the southern Carpathian slopes were the Nyírség (2000–1700 BCE), Otomani (1700–1550 BCE), Wietenberg (1400–1300 BCE), and eventually Stanovo (1200–1000 BCE). The Stanovo culture was best known for its varied and original forms of pottery and agricultural implements subsequently uncovered throughout large parts of central and eastern Europe. The Stanovo dwellers also interacted with peoples on the northern slopes of the Carpathians, with the result that bronze artifacts have been discovered in several Lemko Region villages from the far west (Szlachtowa, Wysowa) to the San River valley in the east (Czerteż, Międzybrodzie). Among the artifacts are those uncovered from are the remains of a settlement at what later became the town of Sanok.

It was not long before the technological advances connected with the Bronze Age promoted the consolidation of one or more tribal groups into unions and the subsequent appearance of hill-forts, later known as *horo-dyshche*, to house the families of the tribal elites and to provide a protected center for trade and small-scale handicrafts (pottery and metal implements). In the Upper Tisza Region, the earliest of these hill-forts were located above the valley of the Hornád River in eastern Slovakia (at Gánovce, Žehra, and Spišský Štvrtok) and in the lowlands near the Tisza River in Subcarpathian Rus' (at Dyida).

Tribal leaders were, not surprisingly, concerned with controlling the agricultural lands surrounding the hill-forts. Such efforts at extending their authority in order to access food supplies from farmers at times caused friction and armed conflict with neighboring tribal unions who may have claimed the same territory. Aside from conflict between local tribal unions, the Upper Tisza Region was always open to new invasions from peoples from the north, south, and east.

The Iron Age and the Celts

This brings us to about the year 800 BCE and the beginning of the Iron Age, which was to last in the Upper Tisza Region until about the middle of the first century BCE. The beginning of the Iron Age was complex and was associated with the arrival of a wide range of invaders from the south (proto-Thracian tribes), the north (tribes connected with the Lusatian culture), and the east (Scythians and Sarmatians). These various tribal groups merged in the Upper Tisza Region to create a new symbiosis, which is described by archeologists as the Kushtanovytsia culture, named after an archeological site near Mukachevo.

The Iron Age Kushtanovytsia culture existed in the Upper Tisza Region from the sixth to third centuries BCE and was characterized by the ability of its inhabitants to smelt iron ore. Iron-smelting allowed for the large-scale production of stronger and more malleable household wares, farming implements, and weapons. Not only did such technological advances contribute to creating favorable conditions for more permanent settlements, they also put weapons into the hands of larger numbers of people, and that both allowed and encouraged increasing conflict and warfare. It is no coincidence, therefore, that during the Iron Age tribal leaders built larger and stronger hill-forts throughout the Upper Tisza Region, specifically near and within Carpathian Rus', ranging from Ganovce, Spišské Podhradie, and Vel'ký Šariš in the west, to Nevyts'ke and Ardanovo in the center, and to Solotvyno, Bila Tserkva, and Sighet in the east.

EARLY PEOPLES IN CARPATHIAN RUS'

300 BCE–60 BCE	Celts
	Teurisci
	Anartii
60 BCE–106 CE	Dacians/Getae
106 CE–250 CE	Costoboci ("free" Dacians), Carpi
250 CE–400 CE	Vandals/Asdingi, Visigoths, Gepids
400 CE–450s CE	Huns, Gepids
460 CE–570 CE	Gepids, Slavs
570 CE–800 CE	Avars, Slavs (White Croats), Onogurs
800 CE–900 CE	White Croats

Accounts of European prehistory refer to the Iron Age with its common technological and social characteristics as being part of the Hallstatt culture. This culture derives its name from a place in modern-day Upper Austria where objects characteristic of the early Iron Age (circa 1100 BCE) were first found. A later phase of the Hallstatt culture, which in the Upper Tisza Region encompasses chronologically the third to first centuries BCE, is known as La Tène culture, from the name of an archeological site in modern-day Switzerland. La Tène culture is primarily associated with tribes known as Celts, who in the mid-fifth century BCE had come into contact with—and were influenced by—peoples of the Mediterranean world (Greeks and Etruscans).

Today most peoples associate Celts with the Irish, Scots, Welsh, Cornish, and Bretons, who live along the far western fringes of the British Isles and Brittany in France. But during the millennium before the Common Era, Celtic tribes inhabited much of Europe north of the Alps. Centered in modern-day western Switzerland and eastern France, they spread westward to the Atlantic coast of France and eastward into Austria, the Czech Republic, and the Danubian Basin of Hungary. Their presence in these regions over two thousand years ago is still remembered by place names, such as Bohemia (from the Celtic tribe Boii) and Carpathian, both of which are of Celtic origin.

About 300 BCE, Celtic tribes (the Anartii and much later the Teurisci) began to make their way into the Upper Tisza Region. They even went further north beyond the low Carpathian ranges into the Lemko Region, where they inhabited a cluster of small settlements in the upper Wisłok and San river valleys. For the next two centuries, these Celts of La Tène culture were the most important inhabitants in Carpathian Rus'. At Novo-Klynovo and at other nearby settlements along the banks of the Botar River, a southern tributary of the Tisza River in Subcarpathian Rus', the Celts built major ovens to smelt iron. Eventually, the largest Celtic settlement was at Galish-Lovachka, two small hills near present-day Mukachevo. It was there that the iron processed in the Botar River valley was transformed into tools, utensils, and weapons and sold to other peoples in the Danubian Basin. Galish-Lovachka may also have been an *oppidum*, the term used by the Romans to describe a fortified town that functioned as a provincial military center, in this case for local Celtic tribal leaders.

The Roman Empire and the Dacians

While the Celts were establishing their control throughout Europe north of the Alps, much more monumental developments were occurring farther to the south in the lands surrounding the Mediterranean Sea. In the course of the first millennium BCE, the city of Rome on the Italian peninsula became the capital of a powerful empire, which by the outset of the Common Era had come to control all the lands surrounding the northern and southern shores of the Mediterranean Sea, from modern-day Spain and Morocco in the west to Turkey, Syria, and Egypt in the east. The northern frontier, or *limes* of the Roman Empire stretched from the North Sea mouth of the Rhine River in the west to the delta of the Danube River as it flows into the Black Sea in the east. During certain periods, however, Roman rule extended beyond this traditional *limes* to include England in the far northwest and the Crimea along the shores of the Black and Azov Seas in the far northeast.

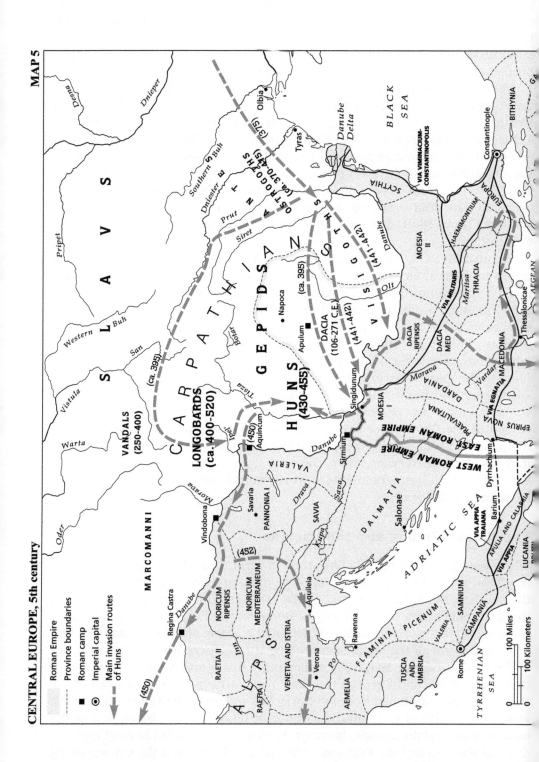

MAP 5

CENTRAL EUROPE, 5th century

Roman Empire
Province boundaries
■ Roman camp
◉ Imperial capital
Main invasion routes
of Huns

Throughout this vast territory, numerous and diverse peoples were exposed to the civilization of ancient Rome, which was characterized by the rule of law; by long periods of economic prosperity and social order; by the development of art, literature, and learning that built upon and refined further the traditions of classical Greece; and eventually by the adoption of Christianity as the state religion. In short, large parts of Europe, northern Africa, and the Middle East were for nearly five hundred years directly or indirectly part of, or drawn into, the Pax Romana—the Roman Order.

Carpathian Rus' was never directly within the Roman Empire, but it did develop certain ties with the Pax Romana, both in economic and, as we shall see later, religious matters. The initial Carpathian-Roman connection was the result of the appearance of a group known as the Dacians. The Dacians were a tribe of Thracians, originally from the southern part of the Balkan peninsula, who about 60 BCE moved northward across the Danube River and the southern ranges of the Carpathian Mountains to settle in Transylvania; that is, in what is today western Romania. Under the leadership of powerful chieftains, who in some sources are referred to as kings, they created a proto-state called Dacia.

In the first century BCE under the powerful chieftain-king Burebista (82–44 BCE), Dacia extended westward to the Danube River in present-day Hungary and southward to the Black Sea coast of Ukraine and Bulgaria. From Transylvania, where they exploited the silver mines and developed a flourishing iron industry, the Dacians expanded northward toward the foothills of the Carpathians in the Upper Tisza Region. They quickly subdued the Celts living there (the Anartii and Teurisci) and drove out or assimilated any survivors. The Dacians under Burebista proceeded to build their own fortified centers at Solotvyno, Mala Kopania, and Bila Tserkva in Subcarpathian Rus' and at Zemplín in eastern Slovakia. These centers were intended to protect the trade routes that ran from north of the Carpathians through their territory and on to the Roman Empire south of the Danube.

More often than not, Dacian relations with the Roman Empire were marked by conflict and extensive warfare, especially during the reign of their dynamic king Decebal (r. 87–106). The Roman-Dacian conflicts culminated with a decisive victory over Decebal by Emperor Trajan at the outset of the second century CE (105–106 CE). Almost immediately the Transylvanian heartland of the vanquished and largely dispersed Dacians was transformed into the Roman province of Dacia. This meant that for nearly a century and a half (formally until 271 CE), the Pax Romana, as represented by the province of Dacia, was on the doorsteps of Carpathian Rus'. That portion of the defeated Dacians who were not captured or subdued by the Romans, the so-called free Dacians (known also by the tribal name Costoboci) went farther north and settled in Carpathian Rus'. There they renewed the old Celtic iron works in the Botar River valley (at Diakovo) and they also built a major pottery-making center in the area around what later became the city of Berehovo. It was these "free Dacians" who before long were able to renew trade between the Upper Tisza Region and the Roman Empire throughout its nearby province of Dacia.

Roman rule north of the Danube depended on the ability of the empire to protect itself against invading warrior tribes. Among these were the Dacians, whom the Romans were eventually able to defeat, although only after extensive investments in money and troops. Against other northern warriors, in particular Germanic tribes, the Romans were ultimately less successful. By the third century CE, Germanic tribes were becoming ever more aggressive, and in 271 they forced the Romans to abandon the province of Dacia. While during the next century the Romans were able to defend their empire along the traditional Rhine-Danube border (*limes*), at the same time Germanic tribes like the Carpi, Vandals-Asdings, and Gepids, as well as the Jazyges of Sarmatian-Iranian origin were able to pass through the Upper Tisza Region and, in the case of the Gepids, to settle more permanently in the Danubian Basin. From there these tribes interacted with the Roman world to the south and west of the Danube *limes* in a relationship that was marked in varying degrees by conflict, alliances, and peacetime trade. This delicately balanced and often precarious situation for the Pax Romana was to change—and decisively so—in 395 CE, the year that marked the first incursions against the Roman Empire of a new warrior people from the east—the Huns.

3

The Slavs and their arrival in the Carpathians

What do the Huns, a nomadic-pastoral people from central Asia, have to do with the Slavic peoples? And, what is the relationship of the Slavs to Carpathian Rus'? About the year 375 the Huns arrived in the steppes of southern Ukraine, where they dispersed the Germanic Ostrogoths living there at the time. The Huns were masterful warriors on horseback who seemed invincible against whichever sedentary and nomadic people, tribal union, and proto-state crossed their path. Fearful of the destructive fate that was likely to befall them from any military encounter with the Huns, Germanic and other tribes hoped to seek refuge by moving westward, crossing the Danube frontier (*limes*), and settling in areas under the protection of the Pax Romana.

The Huns and the displacement of peoples

It was the Huns, then, who set in motion two phenomena beginning in the late fourth and continuing into the fifth century: (1) the so-called displacement, or "wandering of peoples" throughout much of the European continent north of the Danube River; and (2) the further weakening of the Roman Empire which, in turn, was the result of the conflict and instability caused by the Germanic Goths clamoring to settle within its borders. About 375 the Huns destroyed the Gothic proto-state in the Ukrainian steppelands north of the Black Sea, and from there they moved farther westward toward the Roman Empire. By the last decade of the fourth century, the Huns and the Ostrogoths subordinate to them had reached the Roman frontier (*limes*) along the lower Danube River. From there they attacked Roman settlements beginning at Singidunum (modern-day Belgrade) and continuing throughout the Balkan peninsula. In 424–425, Hunnic forces under a chieftain named Ruga turned northward into the former Roman province of Dacia, where they subjected the Germanic Gepids they encountered (see Map 5).

The Huns continued to arrive in the lower Danube valley during the 440s. Under Ruga's successor, a charismatic leader named Attila, the Huns attained after 445 their greatest power. Their main encampment on the lowland plains just east of the Tisza River as it flows into the Danube (near the border between present-day Hungary and Serbia) formed the heart of what some sources refer to as the Hunnic Empire. Attila's domain stretched from the Caspian Sea in the east, through the open steppe and mixed for-est-steppe regions of modern-day Ukraine and southern Russia, and in the west encompassed most of the rest of the European continent north of the Roman Empire's Rhine-Danube frontier (*limes*). This vast territory was at the time inhabited by a wide variety of Slavic and Germanic tribal groups who were subjugated by the small Hunnic ruling and military elite. From their base along the lower Tisza-Danube plain, the Hunnic elite directed attacks in search of whatever precious metals and other luxury items they could extract from the Roman Empire both east and west.

Most of the troops fighting under Attila and his Hunnic generals were drawn from the Germanic (Ostrogoths, Gepids, Heruls) and, in some cases, the Slavic tribes that they had subjugated. The ongoing terror that the Huns inspired throughout much of the Roman world seemed at the time unstoppa-ble. It did, however, come to a rather abrupt end following the death of Attila in 453. Within two years, the Huns left the Danubian Basin and effectively disappeared, with some joining the armies of their former enemy, Rome, and others returning to the steppes of southern Ukraine whence they came.

The power vacuum in the Danubian Basin following the departure of the Huns was filled in the late 450s by the Germanic Gepids. The Gepids had settled in the plains just south of Subcarpathian Rus' two centuries earlier (ca. 269) when the Roman province of Dacia was in dissolution. The Gepids, who reached an accord with the Huns, fought alongside them in cam-paigns throughout Europe. After the death of Attila and the demise of the Hunnic Empire, the Gepids were able to restore their rule from the northern to southern ranges of the Carpathians (modern-day eastern Hungary and western Romania). For over a century (455–567) the Gepid Kingdom, also known as Gepidia, flourished in the plains of Hungary east of the Danube River, including the Upper Tisza Region and Transylvania. The rest of the Danubian Basin west of the Danube River, the area known as Pannonia (present-day western Hungary), came to be settled somewhat later (the mid-520s) by another Germanic tribe, the Longobards.

Among the peoples who were either subjugated by the Huns or who were dispersed in the late fourth century as part of the movement of the peo-ples were the Slavs. Since Carpatho-Rusyns are Slavs, the fate of that Indo-European group is of particular interest. But before turning specifically to developments among Slavs, a few general conceptual matters are in order. These have to do with the question of the origin of peoples and the problem of historical continuity.

The origin-of-peoples fetish

Because humankind is endowed with memory, most individuals have a desire to know where they come from; that is, who are their ancestors? Some also wish to know to which ethnic or linguistic group those ancestors belonged, in order that they may be able to define themselves according to one or more ethnic or modern-day nationality labels. It is interesting to note that states, too, have what could be called a fetish-like concern with origins, something the Ottoman scholar Bernard Lewis has termed "the foundation myth." According to Lewis:

> Most countries and peoples and powers arise from humble origins, and having risen to greatness seek to improve or conceal their undistinguished beginnings and attach themselves to something older and greater. Thus, the Romans, rising in power, felt themselves upstarts beside the Greeks, and therefore tried to trace their pedigree from the Trojans. The barbarian peoples of Europe, ruling over ruins of the Roman Empire, again sought to provide themselves with noble and ancient ancestries, and [they] produced a series of mythical Roman, Greek, or Trojan founders for the various barbarian tribes.[1]

Lewis then goes on to give other examples of historical mythology. One example he does not provide, but which has general relevance for our subject is that of István Horvát. Horvát was a Hungarian historian who, at the very beginning of the nineteenth century during the height of the Romantic era, published a two-volume history of Hungary, in which he unabashedly claimed that the Magyars were associated with most of the great achievements in world civilization (including the building of Egypt's pyramids) and that they were the subject matter of Homer's epics.[2] It is true that by the end of the nineteenth century, and under the impact of the philosophic movement known as Positivism, serious writers removed from their national histories the most extreme examples of self-serving mythology. Nonetheless, many myths still remained, in particular the almost fanatical desire to prove one's present existence by seeking to identify the oldest and most distinguished origins.

Since we know that Carpathian Rus' was never an independent state, the concern with origins has not focused on some political entity, but rather on the ancestors of the people we today call Carpatho-Rusyns. Aside from fulfilling the general human desire to know one's own individual ethnic origins, the questions of where and when a given people has first made its appearance have taken on as well a political dimension. Generations of scholars and patriotic writers have striven not only to determine the earliest appearance of a specific people on a given territory, but also to argue on the basis of historical continuity that they are the supposed ancestors of the nationality or ethnic group living presently on that territory. Therefore, national homelands must have one group which can claim to be the "original," the indigenous, or the autochthonous inhabitants. This indigenous group then proclaims the right to rule a given territory because of its alleged "historic precedence."

One could argue that the concepts concerning the origins of peoples and historical continuity are just that: concepts or intellectual constructs, which have been formulated in modern times by professional scholars or by amateur writers. Hence, they should, at best, be considered hypothetical expla-

IS DNA THE RELIABLE WAY?

In the ongoing search to determine the origins of peoples, including Slavs, among the most recent hypotheses are those based on the results of geogenetic research drawn from the new scientific discipline known as genomics. This research involves DNA (deoxyribonucleic acid), the master genetic molecule that determines what a cell is and does. Samples of DNA taken from blood, hair roots, or placentas found in medieval graves are compared with samples of such matter taken from the present-day inhabitants of a specific territory. Laboratory analysis of the resulting data allegedly can determine the origins of a given modern-day people or individual. Some Carpatho-Rusyn writers, enamoured with these new "scientific proofs," have recently postulated the genetic make-up of present-day Carpatho-Rusyns as being 37 percent Slavic, 25 percent Celtic-Romance-Germanic, 9 percent Adriatic-Balkan, and 8 percent Scandinavian.[a]

The science of genomics is, however, still in its early stages. Much larger DNA samples from the ancient past and present need to be gathered and analyzed before humanistic scholars can hope to make convincing arguments based on genetic evidence. Until that time we are left with often scanty archeological and linguistic data as the main sources for determining the origins of peoples.

[a] Data taken from Dymytrii Pop, "Tsy mav ratsiiu rusyns'kŷi iepyskop Tarkovych, avad' novi aspektŷ v teorii slovianstva," *Rusyns'kyi svit,* VIII [78] (Budapest, 2010), p. 10.

nations of the past, not absolute truths. Put another way, there is no way to be certain about the origins of any given people, and that all arguments about the continuity of peoples or states from earliest times of recorded history to the present are intellectual constructs that can—and more than likely will—be challenged by often equally convincing counter-arguments and alternative intellectual constructs. In that context it would not be amiss to quote the first definition of history found in *Webster's Third International Dictionary*; that is, "a narrative of events connected with a real or *imaginary* [author's emphasis] object, person, or career."[3] With that in mind, the following should be considered only one of several possible versions regarding the origins of the Slavs and their relationship to Carpathian Rus'.

The Slavs and Carpathian Rus'

There exist several conflicting and at times complementary explanations about the origins of the Slavs. Nevertheless, there is today somewhat of a consensus among many—but certainly not all—specialists on this problem that the earliest ancestors of the Slavs, described as proto-Slavs, lived on lands stretching from the northern slopes of the Carpathian Mountains to the marshes formed by the valley of the Pripet River. In modern-day terms this constitutes southern Belarus, western Ukraine, and eastern Poland (see Map

5). The proto-Slavs are said to have been in these territories already in the period about 1200–1000 BCE. They were predominantly a sedentary people living in small settlements along river valleys and supporting themselves by agriculture and animal husbandry, especially cows and in some cases sheep.

DWELLINGS OF THE EARLY SLAVS

Archeological sites from the sixth and seventh centuries reveal a somewhat common pattern for domestic dwellings among the Slavs. The vast majority were so-called sunken structures, that is, dwellings partially dug into the ground, usually less than one meter (three feet) deep. The sunken pit was rectangular in shape and covered by a gabled roof made of wood. Pit sizes ranged from 4 to 25 square meters (14 to 80 sq. feet) with less than 15 square meters (50 sq. feet) being the most common size. This would allow for a family of no more than five persons. The important characteristic of these sunken buildings was a stone oven placed in one of the corners and built directly on the floor.

The stone oven was used for cooking as well as for heating during the long winter months. The partially below-ground dwelling helped provide insulation against the exterior cold. The walls above ground were often of wooden logs filled in with clay and/or reeds. Considering the size of the sunken dwellings and the number uncovered at various archeological sites, these early Slavic settlements from the sixth and seventh centuries were usually located along river valleys and were small in size, consisting of between 50 to 75 inhabitants.

The Slavs also developed a pagan belief system, which despite the diversity and large territorial extent of different tribes had certain common features. Among those features were a series of gods representing various forces of nature: Svaroh the god of heaven; Dazhboh the god of sun; Svarozhych the god of fire; Stryboh the god of wind; Volos the god of cattle, wealth, and the underworld; and Perun, the god of thunder. Among some tribes, especially West Slavs living in areas close to Carpathian Rus', there was a belief in the ultimate "god of all gods," Sviatovit/Sventovyd.

Aside from these gods, who were believed to control the main forces of nature, there were other gods and goddesses like Iarylo, who was connected to the rebirth of spring; Kupalo the god of water, grass, and flowers; Lada, the goddess of love and family; and Mara, the goddess of death. On the darker side were several dangerous supernatural creatures, the best known of whom were the *rusalky*, beautiful female water sprites (allegedly the souls of young girls who drowned themselves or the souls of unbaptized infants) who attracted young men to the water and drowned them.

For the most part, the Slavic pagans did not have any elaborate religious structures, but they did have priest-like figures who intervened with the forces of nature and who performed rituals such as nonhuman sacrifices before various rustic stone or wood-carved statues (idols) representing various gods. Even more widespread were self-proclaimed sorcerers, who convinced many people that through their personal intercession with the forces of nature they could predict the future, influence the weather, help young girls attract boys to fall in love, and heal sicknesses (in particular help barren women to become fertile).

Many beliefs of the pagan Slavs were transformed and retained in the new religion of Christianity when missionaries brought it to central and eastern Europe in the ninth and tenth centuries. Pagan rituals persisted, however, and were adopted to the new faith. This was one of the reasons why Christianity was accepted. While the church did try to suppress pagan beliefs, it had only limited success. The role of sorcerers has in particular persisted and is widespread in both rural and urban areas still in the twenty-first century.

For much of their early history during the first millennium of the Common Era, the Slavs in general lacked their own strong military leaders and, instead, they tended to attach themselves as vassals to more organized tribal groups, in particular those led by nomadic warrior peoples from the east. Sometime during the first century BCE the proto-Slavs began to move out of their original homeland between the Carpathians and the Pripet River valley in several directions, in particular toward the east, west, and south. This brought them into contact with Germanic and Celtic peoples in central Europe, some of whom eventually were assimilated by the Slavs and their way of life. The Slavs also encountered Iranian and Turkic warrior peoples from the east, among whom were the Scythians, Alans, and later the Antes, Croats, Serbs, and Bulgars.

It is important to understand what was meant by the names used or applied to these various warrior peoples. Very often the nomadic Iranian and Turkic peoples from the east, who were given names like Scythians, Sarmatians, etc., by classic Greek, Roman, and later Germanic writers, were actually not one group but rather a heterogeneous mix of peoples of differing cultures and languages. The name for the entire mix, however, was that which represented the military elite, often small in number but strong enough to dominate large areas of mixed nomadic and sedentary populations. For example, the northern Iranian tribe of Scythians, who for nearly half a millennium dominated the steppes of Ukraine and the Crimea, were for the most part comprised of Slavic agriculturalists. Sometimes the Slavic "majority" would assimilate the Iranian and Germanic, or later Turkic ruling tribal elite but, nevertheless, retain for themselves the name of that elite. Hence, the Irano-Alanic Antes, Croats, and Serbs, or the Turkic Bulgars based in central and eastern Europe all bequeathed their names to populations that were already or which became Slavic.

The White Croats and the Avars

Following the disappearance of the Huns in the second half of the fifth century, one of the Iranic nomadic tribes from the steppes of Ukraine known as Croats moved westward. They brought under their control Slavic sedentary agriculturalists and livestock breeders living north of the Carpathians from Galicia westward to Silesia, Lusatia, and parts of Bohemia. The result of this interaction was the formation of a large tribal union (encompassing the Vistulans, Silesians, Lusatian Sorbs, and some Czech tribes) that was referred to in early written sources as the lands of the White Croats and White Croatia. Some scholars believe that by the sixth century the Slavic White Croats (Slavic: *Bilŷ khorvatŷ*) gradually extended their control over Carpathian Rus', at first along the northern slopes of the mountains (the Lemko Region) and then along the southern slopes in the Upper Tisza Region. The origins, ethnic composition, migrational patterns, and the very existence of the White Croats remain a source of controversy, but because of their suspected presence in the Carpathians, many histories of Carpathian Rus' consider the Slavic White Croats to be the earliest ancestors of the Carpatho-Rusyns, in particular the Lemkos.

While the White Croats were establishing a powerful tribal union north of the Carpathians, a new people from central Asia came onto the scene. These were the Avars, nomads of Mongolian or of Turco-Ugric origin, who were part of the large Hunnic domain until they were pushed out of their original homeland in northern Kazakhstan. The Avars eventually made their way to central Europe, and in 568 they entered the Danubian Basin. There they dispersed the Germanic Gepid and Longobard "kingdoms" that had flourished for a century after the demise of the Huns. The Avars proceeded to set up a proto-state known as the Avar Kaganate. From their capital, or *hring*, in the lowlands where the Tisza River flows into the Danube, the Avar rulers or kagans controlled most of the Hungarian plain west and east of the Danube River, as well as Transylvania, and the Upper Tisza Region encompassing eastern Slovakia and Subcarpathian Rus'.

Like the Huns before them, the Avars brought to the Danubian Basin Slavic tribes that they had conquered while moving across the steppes of Ukraine toward the Carpathian foothills. It is as a result of the invasions of the Huns in the fifth century, but most especially of the Avars in the sixth century, that increasing numbers of Slavs settled in the Danubian Basin and the Upper Tisza Region; that is, in Carpathian Rus' on the southern slopes of the mountains. Finally, around the year 700 other Turkic tribes from the east known as Onogurs, who were related to the Bulgars, arrived in the Danubian Basin. Therefore, the Avar Kaganate was composed of a Turkic Avar military elite which ruled over the remnants of Germanic and Romanized peoples already inhabiting the Danubian Basin, as well as more recently arrived Pannonian, Danubian, and Carpathian Slavs and the so-called late Avars—the Turkic Onogurs. Actually, the Slavs were among the most numerous of the tribal groups living in the Danubian Basin at the time, so that in the core of the kaganate there developed a kind of symbiotic relationship in which Slavs served as vassals and armed mercenaries of their Avar overlords.

From the outset of their arrival in the late sixth century, the Avars made several attempts to expand beyond the plains of Hungary. Like previous

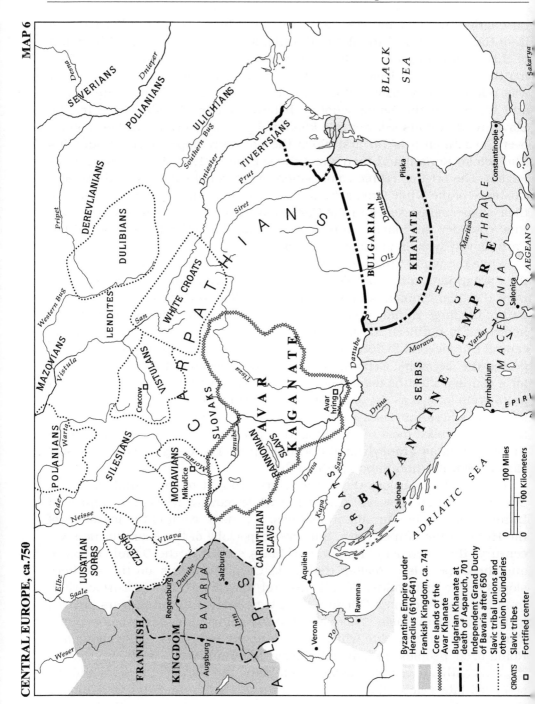

MAP 6

CENTRAL EUROPE, ca.750

Byzantine Empire under
Heraclius (610–641)

Frankish Kingdom, ca. 741

Core lands of the
Avar Khanate

Bulgarian Khanate at
death of Asparuch, 701

Independent Grand Duchy
of Bavaria after 650

Slavic tribal unions and
other union boundaries

CROATS   Slavic tribes

☐   Fortified center

100 Miles

100 Kilometers

nomadic peoples from the north and east, they were drawn to the civilized world of the former Pax Romana beyond the Danube and Rhine Rivers, in particular southeastward into the Balkan provinces of the East Roman (Byzantine) Empire. Beginning in the 580s, attacks by the Avars with their Slav mercenaries against Byzantine lands increased in intensity, culminating in a major attack (eventually beaten back) against the imperial capital of Constantinople in 626. During the conflicts against the Avars in the first decades of the seventh century, the Byzantines allied with the White Croats beyond the Carpathians on the northern flank of the Avar Kaganate. In appreciation of their support, the Byzantine emperor (Heraclius) invited the White Croats to settle along the northern frontier of the empire in what is today Croatia and Serbia. Many White Croats accepted the invitation, bequeathing their name to modern-day Croatia and the Croatians. Other Croats remained behind, however, where they continued to rule parts of Carpathian Rus' on both slopes of the mountains.

Despite the White Croat alliance and reinforcement of the Byzantine imperial armies, the Avars continued their raids throughout the late seventh and early eighth centuries against the empire's territory in the Balkan peninsula. Most of the kaganate's soldiers were actually Danubian and Pannonian Slavs who engaged the Byzantine Empire well into the Balkan peninsula. When the Avar military elite returned home to the Danubian Basin after battle, some of the Slavic soldiers remained behind, and it is in this way that much of the Balkan region, as far south as the Peloponese in the heart of modern Greece, was settled by Slavs during the seventh and eighth centuries.

The Avars were ultimately less successful in their incursions toward the west, where they were blocked by the increasingly powerful Germanic Frankish Kingdom. Under that kingdom's greatest ruler, Charlemagne (reigned 771–814), the Franks destroyed the Avar Kaganate during the last decade of the eighth century. The result was a power vacuum in the heart of the Danubian Basin where the Avar Kaganate was replaced by two new spheres of influence: to the west of the Danube River was Charlemagne's Frankish Kingdom; to the east was the expanding Bulgarian Empire which encompassed the entire valley of the Tisza River including the southern fringes of Carpathian Rus'. Within this power vacuum, in particular along the old Frankish-Avar borderland, the first lasting state structure among the Slavs of the region came into being. That state came to be known as Greater Moravia.

State Formation in central Europe

The ninth and tenth centuries proved to be an important turning point in the history of central and eastern Europe. This is because during that time several state structures came into being, some of which have survived in one form or another until the present-day. For Carpathian Rus', the most important of these new states was Hungary and Poland. But there were other states which also had a direct or indirect impact on the region: Greater Moravia, the Bulgarian Empire, Kievan Rus', and the East Roman or Byzantine Empire.

The Pax Romana and the Byzantine Empire

The previous discussion of the Roman Empire (in Chapter 2) concerned developments in the late fourth and fifth centuries, when the arrival of the Huns in the steppes of Ukraine pushed Germanic tribes westward into the Roman sphere. The arrival of the Germanic tribes provoked military clashes and further political instability, so that the Pax Romana was being shaken to its core. The imperial capital of Rome itself was attacked by the Germanic Visigoths in 410, and just over a half century later the last emperor of Rome was deposed (476). These catastrophic events did not, however, mean the end of the Pax Romana that for centuries had brought political stability and economic prosperity to much of Europe and the Mediterranean world. At least one part of the Pax Romana was to survive for another thousand years in the eastern half of the empire.

Already at the end of the third century CE, the Roman Empire had adopted the practice of rule by two emperors, one for the West based in the city of Rome, and one for the East based in the city of Byzantium. Located along the straits of the Bosporus which separates Europe from Asia, Byzantium was inaugurated as the capital of the East in the year 330 during the reign of the Emperor Constantine. In honor of its founder, Byzantium, the center of the New Rome, was renamed Constantinople.

The border between the West Roman and East Roman Empires was in the Balkan peninsula, running more or less through modern-day Bosnia-Herzegovina (see Map 5). For much of its early existence, the Eastern Roman

MAP 7

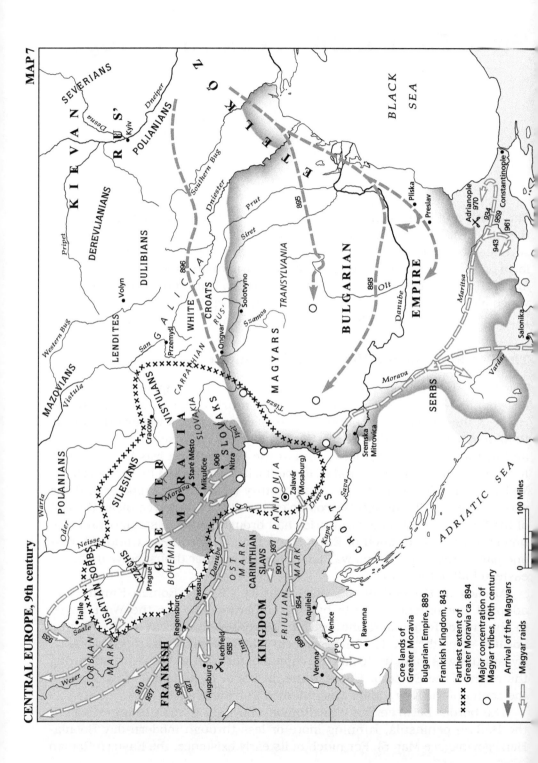

Core lands of Greater Moravia

Bulgarian Empire, 889

Frankish Kingdom, 843

Farthest extent of Greater Moravia ca. 894

Major concentration of Magyar tribes, 10th century

Arrival of the Magyars

Magyar raids

100 Miles

Empire maintained control not only of the Balkan region south of the Danube River (the traditional Roman *limes*), but also of Asia Minor and the Near Eastern Mediterranean lands. Three basic components characterized the Eastern Roman Empire: (1) Roman political tradition—with its heritage of written law and authority centralized in a supreme ruler, the emperor; (2) Hellenic culture—which carried on the tradition of classical Greece and was expressed in the Greek language, not Latin, as in the West Roman Empire; and (3) Christian belief—which used Greek instead of Latin and followed the Eastern, or Byzantine rite that differed from the Latin, or Roman rite practiced in the West Roman Empire. Finally, the citizens of the East Roman Empire always called themselves Romans (in Greek: *romaioi*), and they were called such by outsiders as well (for instance, *Rūm* and *Rumeli* in Turkic languages). Sometime in the Middle Ages, however, European writers began to use the term *Byzantium* when referring to the East Roman Empire. Henceforth, this book will use the terms *Byzantium* and *Byzantine Empire* when speaking of the East Roman world.

As the inheritor and continuer of the Pax Romana, the Byzantine Empire remained a source of attraction for many peoples living beyond its borders, especially in central and eastern Europe. Byzantine influence was especially strong among the Slavic peoples, who by the ninth century were among the most numerous inhabitants in the region. For millennia the Slavs had been vassal-like subordinate peoples who were pressed to fight in the ranks of tribal federations headed by eastern nomadic military elites, such as the Scythians, Alans (Antes), and more recently the Huns and Avars. By the ninth century, however, the Slavs began to form their own political entities.

Greater Moravia

The first of these entities arose along the Frankish-Avar borderlands in the valley of the Morava River in the eastern part (Moravia) of the present-day Czech Republic. There, in the 830s, a West Slav leader (Mojmír) founded a state, which under his successors (Rastislav, r. 846–869, and Svatopluk, r. 870–894) developed into what became known as the Greater Moravian Empire. By the last decade of the ninth century Greater Moravia had come to include what in modern-day terms is the Czech Republic (Bohemia and Moravia), Slovakia, southern Poland (Silesia, Little Poland), as well as parts of Germany (Lusatia) and western Hungary (Pannonia). In the northeast, the Greater Moravian sphere reached as far as Cracow and near Przemyśl along the San River; that is, lands inhabited by remnants of the White Croats on the northern slopes of the Carpathians. Whereas Greater Moravia did not reach quite as far as Carpathian Rus' on the southern slopes of the mountains, it was to have a profound impact on that region and its inhabitants.

Greater Moravian political influence did not go beyond the middle Danubian valley, because to the east an even more powerful state had reached the height of its power in the ninth century—the Bulgarian Empire. Originally based on both banks of the lower Danube River (present-day southern Romania and northern Bulgaria), the Turkic Bulgars, who by this time had been assimilated by the local Slavic inhabitants, created a large state that covered much of the Balkan peninsula and that included as well Transylvania and the Tisza River valley as far north as Carpathian Rus'. The Bulgarians were particularly interested in controlling the salt trade from mines in Transylvania and the Tisza borderland with its rich deposits at Solotvyno.

Even though Greater Moravia had no direct political influence over Carpathian Rus', it did have a lasting cultural impact on the region, specifically in the realm of religion. The ultimate source of Moravia's religious influence was the Byzantine Empire. Ever since the Roman Empire had adopted Christianity as its official state religion—a decision implemented by the founder of Byzantine New Rome, Emperor Constantine—the Church was actively concerned with converting to Christianity the various pagan peoples throughout Europe who resided within and beyond the borders of the former Pax Romana. Byzantium's rulers fully supported the goals of the Church, since Christianization might not only save souls, it could also help secure the empire's borders and enhance trade with its new Christian neighbors.

Between the fifth and tenth centuries, most of Europe's Celtic, Germanic, and Slavic peoples living beyond the northern borders (*limes*) of the old Roman Empire were converted to Christianity. Those conversions were often initiated and carried out by self-sacrificing missionaries from either the Western Latin-oriented Christian Church based in Rome, or by the Eastern Byzantine Greek-oriented Christian Church based in Constantinople. At the same time it was not uncommon for states that had themselves become officially Christian to initiate the conversion process of others either by peaceful or forceful means. Whenever states became involved in this process, political concerns often took precedence over spiritual ones. It is, therefore, not surprising that state-inspired proselytizers representing the Western and Eastern variants of Christianity became rivals in wanting to convert the pagans to their own variant of the faith. Such West-East rivalry was particularly evident in the Church's efforts to convert the Slavs.

Saints Constantine/Cyril and Methodius

For its part the Byzantine Empire was consistently active in trying to forge alliances and maintain peace with its neighbors to the north, among whom the Bulgarians in the nearby Balkan peninsula were the most powerful and threatening. Hence, conversion to Christianity became an integral part of Byzantine diplomacy. In the mid-ninth century, Greater Moravia's rulers sought to enhance their state's political fortunes by seeking an alliance with the Byzantine Empire. Byzantium responded by sending in 863 a diplomatic mission to Moravia headed by two Greek missionaries, Constantine and his brother Methodius. During their mission, which lasted nearly five years (863–867), the Moravians and other Slavs living within Greater Moravia followed their ruler and were converted to Christianity. Aside from conversion, the Byzantine Greek brothers created an alphabet called Glagolitic, and using this alphabet they produced religious texts in a language under-standable to the Slavs. These early texts were based primarily on the spoken language that Constantine and Methodius knew from the Macedonian Slavic speakers in the vicinity of their native Byzantine city of Salonika (modern-day Thessaloniki in northern Greece).

Being talented diplomats as well as linguistic scholars, Constantine and Methodius decided to travel to Rome in 867 in order to report on the results of their mission to the head of the Western Christian Church, at the time Pope Hadrian II. It was also in Rome that they achieved something truly monumental. The pope agreed to their request to recognize Slavonic, alongside Hebrew, Greek, and Latin, as a sacred language, thereby giving it legitimacy to be used in churches to express the word of God.

The subsequent fate of the Slavonic language (and alphabet) was quite complex. Suffice it to say that toward the end of the ninth century the Constantine-Methodian mission was driven out of Greater Moravia, and that their disciples were forced to seek refuge in the Bulgarian Empire, which about the same time (865) was also Christianized by Byzantine missionaries. It was in Bulgaria where the disciples of Constantine and Methodius (Clement and Naum) created a more simplified alphabet for the Slavs, one based on Greek letters. As a mark of respect to Constantine, who had adopted the monastic name Cyril just before his death in 869, the new alphabet was called Cyrillic. In subsequent centuries the Slavonic alphabet written in Cyrillic was adopted by all peoples who accepted Eastern-rite Christianity from Byzantium. Like Latin in the West, Slavonic was a liturgical, not spoken language, used primarily for church matters and only much later for non-religious secular texts. Hence, the language came to be known as Church Slavonic. Since Church Slavonic was to be used by several Slavic and a few non-Slavic peoples, its literary form came to be influenced by the native speech of the various authors and scribes who used it. As a result, there evolved different literary variants of Church Slavonic—Bulgarian, Serbian, Ukrainian, Romanian, Russian, and Carpatho-Rusyn variants, among others.

What is the relationship of all these developments to Carpathian Rus'? Since the White Croats were within the far eastern sphere of Greater Moravia, it is possible that the Slavic inhabitants in or near the Lemko Region became Eastern Christians under Moravian influence. Some writers

CHRISTIANITY BECOMES "OUR" RELIGION

What was the secret to the long-term success of Christianity among Carpatho-Rusyns? Perhaps the best answer to that question comes from John Righetti, a long-time cultural activist and historian in the United States and close observer of Carpatho-Rusyn life in both Europe and North America, who considers the role of the missionaries Constantine/Cyril and Methodius as the crucial factor in explaining Christianity's success.

Coming from a well-to-do family in Thessalonika, a Byzantine port city along the Aegean Sea where Greeks and Slavs lived and worked alongside each other, Constantine and Methodius were fluent speakers of the local Macedonian variant of Slavic. Even more significant for the future work of the Christian missionaries was the fact that they understood the Slavic mindset: the ways Slavs thought about life and death; the important components of their culture; and the relationship to their pagan gods.

This last point was critical. Because of their sensitivity to Slavic culture and its values, when Constantine and Methodius took the message of the Christian Gospel to the Slavs, they did not follow the example of many other missionaries. They did not try to overlay another culture, complete with an alphabet, language, and a new religion; rather, they looked at the cultural context of the Slavs and asked the question: "How can we take their existing cultural values and adapt them to Christianity?"

For their part, how would the Slavs take to a Christian religion that incorporated their own culture? The answer was that they took to it exceedingly well. Why? Because they had to give up very little of their own Slavic belief system in order to accept the Christianity adapted for them by Constantine and Methodius, or more likely by their disciples. So powerful was the "adaptation" approach that to this day many of the practices of the Carpatho-Rusyn Eastern Christian churches are those which their pagan ancestors followed before they adopted to Christianity.

For example, pagan Slavs decorated eggs in the spring and offered them with best wishes to family and friends as symbols of nature's rebirth. As a sign of the coming spring, they exchanged pussy willows plucked from the first bush to "flower" in the Carpathians as soon as the weather started to warm. Decorated eggs and pussy willows were also laid on the graves of ancestors, since a key component of pagan Slavic religion was ancestor veneration. Even today, Carpatho-Rusyns decorate these eggs, called *pysankŷ*, and exchange them on Easter, while the pussy willow is used in place of the palm branch on Palm Sunday, the celebratory day one week before Easter which commemorates the triumphal entry of Jesus into Jerusalem. And many still place willows and *pysankŷ* on family graves.

Christmas replaced an existing celebration at which pagan Slavs honored their ancestors on the winter solstice, the longest night of the year. Carpatho-Rusyns (and many other Slavs) replaced this custom with the Holy Supper, a special meal in which all members of the family should be together, with everything about the event focused on the living family and its connection to ancestors. Some bind the legs of the table together with chains to "keep the family together"; everyone must drink some alcohol from a common cup as a symbolic strengthening of the family; even an extra place is set at the table for Christ to come, although this was originally done so that unseen ancestors could join the meal. Some families still set an extra place for "the ancestors."

Even when the family goes to church for Christmas Eve service, no food is put away, but left on the table to feed the ancestors who may come that night.

Words used within the Carpatho-Rusyn Christian tradition demonstrate the Christian adaptation of former pagan religious practices. A Christmas carol in Rusyn, for example, is called a *koliada,* the first day of the month among the ancient Romans. The Feast of Pentecost, fifty days after Easter, is called Rusalia after the wood and water nymphs (*rusalkŷ*) who were the center of pagan Slavic celebrations in late spring.

Christian saints replaced pagan Slavic gods or, on the commemorative day of a particular saint, they might take on the attributes of a pagan god. For example, St. John the Baptist's Feast Day in the summer fell at the same time as the pagan fertility-and-abundance festival in honor of the god Kupalo. Among Carpatho-Rusyns, St. John the Baptist simply replaced Kupalo, and in some circles his saint's day is referred to as Ivana-Kupalo (John-Kupalo). Analogously, the pagan god of thunder, Perun, was replaced by St. Elijah, who rode to heaven in a fiery chariot. The very word for the Mother of God as a virgin, Diva in Rusyn, is a proto-Slavic word derived from the common Indo-European root word for divinity.

Perhaps the most adaptable Eastern Christian concept for the ancestors of Carpatho-Rusyns was the very idea of "who" was the Church? Among Eastern Christians, the belief has always been that during the service, or Holy Liturgy (meaning "the work of the people"), the Church Militant (those on earth) and the Church Triumphant (those who have already received their reward and are in heaven) come together through the celebration of the liturgy. Imagine Constantine and Methodius explaining to ancestor-worshipping Slavs that when you pray like "we" Christians do, your ancestors come join you in this act!

In hindsight, it is obvious that Constantine and Methodius showed great wisdom in adapting Eastern Christianity to existing Slavic culture. This included allowing the Slavs, as the first of Europe's peoples after the Romans and Greeks, to worship the Christian God in their own Slavonic language. In doing so, they created a form of Christianity that the ancestors of Carpatho-Rusyns embraced passionately. For all these reasons, most Carpatho-Rusyns—whether or not they are active believers—consider Eastern-rite Christianity their "own" religion and an integral part of their identity.

claim that these new Christians came under the authority of a bishop whose eparchy (the Eastern-rite word for diocese) responsible for lands in Galicia north of the Carpathians was reputed to have been founded in 906 with its seat at Przemyśl along the San River.

There are even more ambitious claims for Carpathian Rus' on the southern slopes of the mountains, which throughout the ninth century was within the sphere of the powerful Bulgarian Empire. It seems that in the course of that century, and even before the Constantine-Methodian mission, there were some conversions to Christianity among the inhabitants of the

Danubian Basin, including the Carpathian Slavs. Later church and some secular scholars argued, however, that the main event did not come until 860s, and that it was Constantine and Methodius themselves, or their disciples, who converted the Carpathian Slavs (the putative ancestors of the Carpatho-Rusyns) to Christianity. Some have even argued that the two Byzantine Greek missionaries established an eparchy at Mukachevo in the heart of Subcarpathian Rus'.

WHO AMONG THE EAST SLAVS FIRST RECEIVED CHRISTIANITY?

Most modern-day peoples throughout Europe celebrate the memory of some "national" saint; that is, the person who is believed to have brought the "Christian word of God" to their ancestors. Usually these national saints are religious missionaries, such as St. Patrick among the Irish or St. Rémy among the French, although they may be secular figures, such as Grand Prince Volodymyr/Vladimir of Kiev among the Russians and Ukrainians, or King Olaf I Tryggvason among the Norwegians.

Aside from adopting a national saint, latter-day religious and secular spokespersons have tried to find a specific year, which "their" state or their people can commemorate. More often than not, the date chosen does not represent the exact time of conversion, but rather is a year chosen for its symbolic value. And, of course, the earlier the year, the better. The point is that each Christian people—including Carpatho-Rusyns—has created a conversion myth in an attempt to enhance their own status and prestige among the universal family of Christian faithful.

Among the two largest branches of the East Slavs (modern-day Russians and Ukrainians), the year 988 was designated as the date when the Grand Prince Volodymyr/Vladimir of Kiev adopted Christianity and "converted" en masse the inhabitants of Kievan Rus'. Hence, in 1988 massive celebrations were held among Russian and Ukrainian churches, especially in the diaspora, to commemorate the millennium of the Christianization of Rus', or more precisely—to use the terminology of celebrants—the Christianization of Russia, or the Christianization of Ukraine.

When the Russian and Ukrainian churches invited church jurisdictions derived from the Eparchy of Mukachevo, in particular the Byzantine Ruthenian Catholic Church in the United States, to join in the 1988 celebrations, the proposal to participate fully was respectfully declined. Why? The explanation put forth was the following: churches descended from the Eparchy of Mukachevo already had their celebrations in 1963, when they commemorated the eleventh-hundredth-year anniversary of the mission of Saints Constantine/Cyril and Methodius to the Slavs of Greater Moravia, during which time the East Slavs of the Carpathians were allegedly converted as well. Therefore, Carpatho-Rusyn patriotic writers in the past and present have used this "fact" as another example of their distinctiveness. In short, their argument is that Carpatho-Rusyns received Christianity from the "the Apostles to the Slavs," Cyril and Methodius, over a hundred years before their fellow Eastern-rite Russians and Ukrainians.

There is no clear written documentary evidence to confirm any of these claims, so that they remain, at best, hypothetical speculations. Nevertheless, the modern-day Eastern-rite churches which represent Carpatho-Rusyns continue to claim that their conversion to Christianity dates back to the Constantine-Methodian mission. In other words, the founding date for Carpatho-Rusyns as Christians is said to be the year 863; that is, over a century before the official adoption of Christianity in Kievan Rus' for the larger East Slavic world represented by modern-day Ukrainians, Belarusans, and Russians.

The Magyars and Hungary

As a political entity, Greater Moravia survived only until the first years of the tenth century. Its demise at that time was directly related to events in the east. Sometime in the 890s, the push and pull factors that for millennia characterized the steppelands stretching from central Asia to southern Ukraine prompted the arrival of yet another set of nomadic tribal peoples into the heart of Europe. These were part of a loose federation of Finno-Ugric and Bulgar-Turkic tribes known as Onogurs, from which the name *Hungarian* derives. One of the tribes in the Onogur alliance were the Ugric Magyars, originally based in the southern Ural mountain region, from where they moved gradually westward across the steppes of southern Russia. By the 840s and 850s they were living in the large open steppe of what is today southern Ukraine from the Dnieper River to the delta of the Danube, which they called in their language Etelköz—"the land between two rivers."

Known for their fighting prowess, some Magyar horsemen were engaged by the Byzantine Empire in its ongoing wars with the Bulgarian Empire and by the princes of Greater Moravia in their struggles with the Frankish Kingdom farther west. In this way Magyar mercenaries were already present in the Danubian Basin in the 860s. Attracted by the closer proximity and wealth of central and western Europe—and at the same time being pressured in their steppe homeland Etelköz by another Turkic nomadic tribal union from the east, the Pechenegs—seven Onogur tribes took an oath to unite under the Magyar leader Álmos and to remain loyal to his descendants, in particular his son Árpád. The new tribal federation came to be known as the Magyars.

While Magyar mercenaries continued to serve at various times the Franks, Moravians, and Byzantines, their second most influential of tribal leaders, Árpád, decided to expand into the Danubian Basin on a more permanent basis. Sometime around 894 or 895 he led a large military force together with the six other tribal leaders through the Verets'kyi Pass directly through Carpathian Rus' toward the Danubian plain. In the absence of any protection, the Pechenegs attacked the Magyar tribes and their families who remained in Etelköz (southern Ukraine). Following the brutal Pecheneg massacres to which they were subjected, the surviving Magyar tribes and their families fled en masse westward across the southern Carpathians into

the Danubian Basin. During this second phase of "the conquest," an estimated 400,000–500,000 Magyar evacuees (including 20,000 armed horsemen) arrived on the plains of what is modern-day eastern Hungary and
Transylvania.[1]

It was the first group who came through the Verets'kyi Pass, however,
that subsequently gained legendary proportions in Hungarian culture.
Because the seven Magyar tribes were led by Árpád himself, his route has
ever since come to symbolize the specific manner in which the founders of
the modern state of Hungary carried out the conquest, or "taking possession
of the homeland" (*honfoglalás*). In fact, one thousand years later, in 1896,
the Hungarian Kingdom commemorated its millennium by memorializing
their "founding father" Árpád and the alleged spot in which he entered the
"Magyar homeland" with a monument at the crest of the Carpathians along
the Verets'kyi Pass.

HISTORICAL MEMORY AND POLITICAL REALITY

Carpathian Rus' remains a source of controversy in the historic memory of Hungary
and Ukraine. The source of that controversy is the Verets'kyi Pass on the crests of the
Carpathian Mountains through which the tribal leader Árpád led the Magyar tribes
into the Danubian Basin sometime in the early 890s. One thousand years later,
when the Hungarian Kingdom was at the height of its political power in the modern
era, at first 1895 but then 1896 was designated as the year to hold large-scale celebrations throughout the kingdom, especially in the capital, Budapest, to commemorate the arrival in the Danubian Basin of the Magyars, the so-called *Honfoglalás*
(literally: "taking possession of the homeland"). As the entry way, the Verets'kyi Pass
took on special symbolic value, and it was there where a monument in the form of
an obelisk was inaugurated with great fanfare in 1896.

A quarter of century later, despite the demise of the Austro-Hungarian
Empire, the loss to Hungary of its historic northern lands (Felvidék), and the
onset of Czechoslovak rule in 1919, the monument was left in place, although the
Hungarian-language inscriptions on the obelisk were removed. The inscriptions
were restored in 1939, when Hungary "returned" Subcarpathian Rus'/Carpatho-
Ukraine under its rule and, somewhat remarkably, the Soviet regime which annexed
the region in 1945 left the monument undisturbed. In 1956, however, when
the Soviet Union launched its infamous invasion of Hungary to crush that country's anti-Communist revolutionary uprising, Soviet troops passing through the
Verets'kyi Pass destroyed the monument.

Three decades later, by which time the Soviet Union no longer existed, Magyar
civic organizations, in what was by then the Transcarpathian oblast of independent
Ukraine, launched plans to create a new monument in 1996; that is, on the occasion
of the eleven-hundredth anniversary of the arrival of the Magyars in the Danubian
Basin. The authorities of the Transcarpathian oblast approved the plans for the new
monument and construction began. But some extreme Ukrainian nationalists, in

particular from Galicia and L'viv, opposed the construction of what they considered a "foreign monument on age-old Ukrainian territory." Several Ukrainian "patriots" from Galicia vandalized the construction site. Since, however, the Transcarpathian oblast authorities continued their approval of the project, the monument—in the form of a stylized gateway—was completed and finally inaugurated in 2008.

A somewhat more favorable fate faced another Hungarian historical symbol, the mythological winged-bird called *turul,* which looks like an eagle. When, during the millennium before the Common Era, Magyar tribes were still living in the Ural Mountains on the far eastern edge of modern-day European Russia, legend has it that the mythological mother of the Magyar tribes, a woman named Emese, had a dream in which she was impregnated by the *turul.* The offspring of that miraculous impregnation became the ruling leaders of the various Magyar tribes. Thereafter, the *turul* protected the Magyars from danger and pointed the way westward, where they settled in the steppes of southern Russia and by the ninth century in southern Ukraine. Coincidentally, the mother of the ninth-century Magyar chieftain Álmos was named Emese, who on the eve of giving birth dreamed of a son who would one day be the progenitor of a great royal dynasty. Álmos's grandson was none other than Árpád. Consequently, both leaders were under the protection of the *turul,* which pointed the way that led the Magyar tribes from southern Ukraine farther westward across the Verets'kyi Pass into the Danubian Basin.

In the nineteenth century, Romantic writers revived the *turul* legend in the context of describing the origins of the Magyars. The culmination of *turulomania* came during the millennial celebrations of 1896, when several monuments, each topped by a *turul,* were set up in strategic borderland areas of the Hungarian Kingdom (for example, in what is today Slovakia and Serbia) to protect the northern and southern frontiers of the "sacred homeland" from foreign invasion. One of these monuments—a 10-meter (34 feet) wide plinth (with busts of Ferenc Rákóczi, János Hunyadi, and Ilona Zrínyi) upon which stood a 33-meter (108 foot) high column topped by a large sculptured *turul* with its spread wings—was erected atop Palanok Hill beside the castle of Mukachevo. In 1924, during the period of interwar Czechoslovak rule, the monument was taken down.

Nearly a century later, in 2010, the Ukrainian authorities in Transcarpathia approved the "resurrection" of the monumental column (without the busts on the plinth) with its *turul,* which once again stands atop the Mukachevo castle hill from where it is visible for miles around. Since Mukachevo is located in the center of Transcarpathia/Subcarpathian Rus', and therefore far from the Verets'kyi Pass and from Galicia, the *turul* has been left alone to remind everyone of the historic Hungarian presence in the region.

Medieval Hungarian writers have also contributed to the historical mythology cherished by many scholars and others who write about Carpatho-Rusyns. The best known of these contributions is found in the *Gesta Hungarorum* (The Deeds of the Hungarians), a chronicle compiled in the early thirteenth century by an unknown medieval writer subsequently

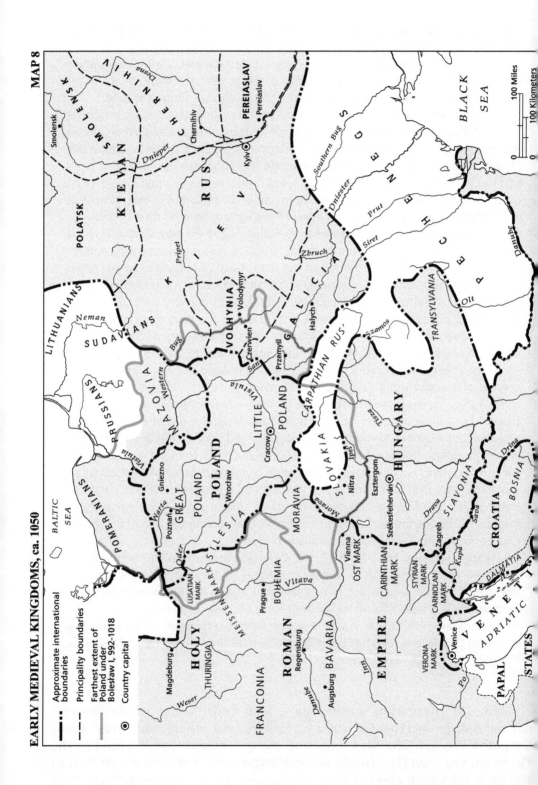

EARLY MEDIEVAL KINGDOMS, ca. 1050

MAP 8

Approximate international boundaries

Principality boundaries

Farthest extent of Poland under Bolesław I, 992–1018

⊙ Country capital

called Anonymous. This "most exasperating and most misleading of all early Hungarian texts"—to quote twentieth-century specialists in these matters—is little more than "a 'toponymic romance' that seeks to explain place names by reference to imagined events and persons."[2] Despite such an assessment, statements in the *Gesta Hungarorum* have been used by politicians in the twentieth century to justify the territorial claims of newly founded or expanding states—ironically, at the expense of modern-day Hungary.

The Carpatho-Rusyn connection has to do with the contention by Anonymous that when the Magyar forces descended from the Verets'kyi Pass they first arrived after great toil (*munka* in Hungarian) at a place they called Munkács (modern-day Mukachevo), and from there they moved westward to capture the castle at Ongvar/Ungvar. There they drove out— and eventually killed—the count (*duca*) of the castle named Loborc. In the minds of Carpatho-Rusyn belletrists writing in the nineteenth and twentieth centuries, the fictional Loborc was transformed into the legendary Prince Laborets', the presumed leader of the White Croat tribal confederation on the southern slopes of the Carpathians, whose center was at a place called Ongvar/Ungohrad, perhaps at or near modern-day Uzhhorod.

Whereas the Laborets' legend remains just that—a legend—there is evidence that the seven Magyar tribes led by Árpád through the Verets'kyi Pass initially settled near Carpathian Rus', on the plain between the Tisza/Tysa and Szamos/Someş Rivers. Within a few years, however, Árpád and the other two heads of the Magyar ruling triumvirate each established his headquarters at various sites west of the Danube in the former Roman province of Pannonia. It is from there that, like the Avars before them, armed Magyar horsemen launched repeated plunderous attacks against the Frankish Kingdom in the west and the Byzantine Empire in the south. (See Map 7.)

The first casualty of these Magyar campaigns was their short-lived ally, Greater Moravia, which collapsed as a state during the first decade of the tenth century. This was also a time when Magyar tribes extended their influence eastward and northward, removing the remaining Bulgarian presence in Carpathian Rus' and neighboring Transylvania. For several more decades the Magyars seemed to have had a free hand raiding various parts of west-central and southern Europe until suffering major defeats inflicted on them by the Frankish Kingdom in 955 (the Battle of Lechfeld near Augsburg) and by the Byzantine Empire in 970 (the Battle of Adrianople).

These defeats forced the Magyar tribal leaders to reassess their situation. In the end, they acted differently from previous invaders who had arrived in the Danubian Basin. While they did cease their aggressive raids against other European states, they did not return to the eastern steppes from where they came. Nor did they disappear by absorption into the local Slavic or Germanic populations of central Europe. Rather, the Magyars decided to remain in the Danubian Basin, and in the second half of the tenth century they began to build a state structure which came to be called Hungary.

The origins of Hungarian statehood are rightly attributed to one of Árpád's direct descendants, a leader named Vajk. Within a few years of succeeding to the leadership of the Magyars, sometime around 995 Vajk converted to Christianity and adopted the new name Stephen. Although at the time many inhabitants, including some Magyar tribal leaders especially in the far eastern regions of the Danubian Basin, were Christians of the Eastern Byzantine rite, Stephen opted for the Western Roman-rite Church, whose pope recognized him in the year 1001 as the first king of Hungary. Roman-rite Christianity (what after 1054 can be called Roman Catholicism) became the official religion of the kingdom, and for his service on behalf of the church he was later canonized by papal decree as St. Stephen.

The rise of Poland

As the Hungarian Kingdom was gradually expanding its control over the entire Danubian Basin, north of the Carpathians a new state formation was coming into being—Poland. This development, led by rulers who belonged to a family called Piast, began in the second half of the tenth century (under Mieszko, r. 960–992) and culminated during the rule of Bolesław I ("the Brave," r. 992–1025), who just before his death in 1025 was proclaimed the first king of Poland. During the reigns of the first Piasts, Christianity was brought to the Polish-ruled lands from the Western Roman-rite Church (966). Bolesław both provided an organizational structure for the Catholic Church and expanded the borders of the realm to the Baltic Sea in the north and beyond the crests of the Carpathians in the south. In the end, these territorial extensions proved to be of short duration, so that under Bolesław's Piast successors Poland's basic sphere of influence remained the lowland plain bounded in the south by the crests of the Sudeten and Carpathian Mountains and in the north by the middle Vistula and lower Warta River valleys with the sporadic addition of territories as far as the Baltic Sea. Within that sphere were several lands, the most important of which were Great Poland/Wielkopolska with its main center at Poznań and Little Poland/Małopolska with its main center at Cracow.

From the early twelfth century Poland remained divided into several principalities, duchies, and independent Mazovia, each of which had its own Piast dynastic line. It was only in 1320 that the lands within Great and Little Poland were reunited under one Piast ruler with Cracow as the seat of the royal coronation and henceforth the capital of the state. During the several previous centuries of internal political division, Poland's borders changed several times. Therefore, Polish rule through the prism of Little Poland's Cracow land/*ziemia* only gradually reached the northern slopes of the Carpathians, where the Lemko Region remained a very sparsely settled transitional borderland adjacent to another political formation in the east—the land of Rus'.

Kievan Rus'

What was "the origin of the land of Rus' . . . and from what source did the land of Rus' have its beginnings?"[3] These phrases are among the opening lines of the most famous medieval Slavic historical text, *The Tale of Bygone*

Years, or the *Rus' Primary Chronicle.* The two questions that arise from those phrases are of crucial importance for an understanding of how the history of Carpatho-Rusyns has been subsequently interpreted by generations of scholars: (1) What was the medieval political entity known as Rus'?; and (2) Who were the inhabitants of that realm that came to be called the people of Rus', or simply the Rus'?

The answer to the question regarding the land of Rus' is relatively straightforward. Sometime in the mid-ninth century (the dates 854 or 860–862 are given in different chronicles), East Slavic and Finnic tribes living in what is today far western Russia and Estonia called upon warrior traders and adventurers from Scandinavia to, as the chronicle says, "come to be prince and rule us."[4] Scandinavian adventure-warriors had been raiding large parts of Europe from Britain and France to the Mediterranean since at least the beginning of the ninth century. These were the people known to western Europe as Vikings or as Norsemen, and who not long after set out across the Atlantic Ocean reaching Iceland and even North America. Nor were these Scandinavians strangers to the east. Since the sixth century they had explored the eastern coasts of the Baltic Sea and by the eighth century had pushed well inland in order to reach the upper Volga River. Descending the Volga, they entered the realm of the Khazar Kaganate, where they were able to gain access to its rich markets filled with products from central Asia and the Middle East.

It is in this context that Scandinavians found it easy to accept the mid-ninth century invitation "to come and rule" over the East Slavs and Finnic tribes east of the Baltic Sea. Added to the names *Vikings* or *Norsemen,* which have remained widespread in western European languages, are the terms *Varangians* and *Rus',* by which the Scandinavians were known in the east. Somewhat like the explorers in search of furs in seventeenth-century North America, the Varangian Rus' set up trading posts along the rivers of northern Russia. Always concerned with finding new sources of trade and access to the lucrative luxury goods from markets in the Middle East, the Varangian Rus' developed a new trade route that bypassed the Volga River and Khazaria, and that allowed for direct access to the ultimate center of cosmopolitan wealth, the capital of the Byzantine Empire, Constantinople. What came into being by the late ninth century was the famous trade route "from the Varangians to the [Byzantine] Greeks." It began at the eastern coast of Sweden (at Birka and Sigtuna), crossed the Baltic Sea, the Gulf of Finland, and via inland rivers and lakes reached the Scandinavian outpost at Staraia Ladoga. From there the route turned southward, passing through another outpost Holmgård (modern Novgorod), and on to the upper Dnieper River, whose course eventually emptied into the Black Sea. As experienced sailors, the Varangian Rus' used the Black Sea to reach their ultimate prize, Constantinople.

It was from these trade routes that the Varangian Rus' gradually extended their control over the local Finnic and more numerous East Slavic tribal groups throughout much of what is today northwestern Russia, Belarus, and Ukraine. Drawn as they were to the south, one settlement along the middle Dnieper River, specifically Kiev, soon became the political as well as commercial center of the growing Varangian Rus' realm. These developments culminated during the reign of the Varangian prince Helgi, known in Slavic sources as Oleg/Oleh the empire builder (r. 880–912), who by the last decades of the ninth century had linked Holmgård/Novgorod in the north with Kiev in the south. He declared himself prince of Kiev, the place he described as "the mother of the towns of Rus'."[5] Because Kiev became the political, economic, and eventually cultural capital, the entire realm ruled by the Varangians came to be known as Kievan Rus'.

For the purposes of understanding developments in Carpathian Rus', of particular importance was the reign of the late-tenth- and early-eleventh-century Prince Volodymyr (r. 980–1015). The reason for his significance has to do with politics and religion. Continuing in the tradition of his Varangian Rus' predecessors, Volodymyr extended the sphere of Kievan Rus' to its greatest territorial extent. Among Volodymyr's acquisitions in the west was the borderland region that later became known as Galicia. After driving out Polish forces, this region—at the time located primarily east of the San River—was brought within the political and cultural sphere of Kievan Rus'. The Rus' principality of Galicia north of the Carpathians included the old White Croat settlement of Przemyśl on the San River and it even stretched somewhat farther west to encompass part of the Lemko Region. The Galician connection established by Kiev's grand prince Volodymyr was to have lasting importance for Carpathian Rus' in centuries to come.

Because of its location, Galician Rus' was periodically the subject of invasions by Poland from the west and Hungary from the south, each of which coveted its territory. By the second half of the thirteenth century, however, Galicia—which in the interim united with a neighboring Rus' principality to form the Kingdom of Galicia-Volhynia—had become a powerful independent state in its own right. Nevertheless, its rulers continued to interact closely, whether in alliance with or in opposition to Hungary.

Examples of such interaction occurred during the thirteenth century, when the king of Hungary Béla IV (r. 1235–1270) granted lands in Zemplyn and Bereg counties to the husbands of his daughters: the defeated pretender to the Galician Rus' principality, Rostyslav (r. 1239) and the long-term ruling prince of Galicia, Lev (r. 1264–1301). Both property transactions were common in medieval society. They might take the form of a lease; that is, a feudal tenure (*leno*) for a limited time frame; or a dowry that a royal daughter brought with her marriage to the ruler of another state. This was the case with Béla IV's son-in-law Lev of Galician Rus', who, on the occasion of his marriage in 1251, obtained the landed estate of Mukachevo in the heart of Bereg county (see Map 10). Such transactions by no means constituted the surrender of territory to a neighboring state, but rather a gift of royal lands by Hungary's king to members of his family. Moreover, those family members were connected to a principality, Galician Rus', which in any case was since 1188 considered by Hungary's kings to be part of their patrimony.

Several centuries later this property transaction was taken out of context and reinterpreted by some reputable historians of the East Slavic world (Hermann Bidermann, Mykhailo Hrushevs'kyi, Stepan Tomashivs'kyi, among others). They assumed that sometime in the early 1280s Lev decided to claim his property and, therefore, annexed not only his estate but the rest of Bereg county, or perhaps even all of Subcarpathian Rus', which allegedly remained part of Galicia between 1280 and 1320. Political ideologists elaborated further, arguing that Carpathian Rus', like Galicia, had once been part of Kievan Rus' and, therefore, someday in the future should be returned (or "reunited with," in the words of Soviet and Ukrainian nationalist ideologists) to the successor states that hoped to rule all the East Slavs—Muscovy/the Russian Empire/the Soviet Union, or an independent Ukraine.[6] Such arguments were indeed used by ideologists of the Russian Empire in the late nineteenth century and once again by the Soviet Union, which in the mid-twentieth century actually realized the "reunification" of Carpathian Rus' with the east (see below, Chapter 21).

The second reason for Volodymyr's importance is that sometime in the 980s—the year 988 is used as the symbolic date—he converted to Christianity according to the Byzantine Eastern rite and then symbolically "baptized" his pagan Rus' subjects, who gradually accepted Eastern Christianity, later designated Orthodoxy, as the official religion of the realm. By the time of Volodymyr's reign, the Varangian Rus' ruling elite had for the most part assimilated into the East Slavic population. As a result of the Christianization inspired by Volodymyr, he initiated a process whereby within a few generations religious and ethnic or territorial identities were fused. In other words, being an East Slavic inhabitant of Rus' and being of the Orthodox faith came to denote the same thing.

This leads us finally to the second question raised in the opening lines of the *Rus' Primary Chronicle*; namely, What did the term Rus' mean? Was it an ethnonym referring to a specific people, or was it only a geographic term describing the lands within a political entity comprised of several peoples, among whom Finnic and Slavic tribes were the most prominent?

THE GREAT DEBATE: THE ORIGIN OF RUS'

The origin of Rus' is a historiographical question that has been hotly debated by scholars and publicists since the eighteenth century. Two basic schools of thought have for the longest time dominated the discussion: the Normanists and the anti-Normanists.

The Normanists basically accept the explanation put forth in the historical account from medieval Kievan Rus' known as the *Primary Chronicle*. The Rus' *Primary Chronicle* relates the tale about an invitation extended by East Slavic and Finnic tribes to Scandinavians called *Rus'*, a name which according to Normanist scholars is derived from *Ruotsi*, the Finnic designation for Sweden, or from *ropsmenn* or *ropskarlar,* Old Nordic terms for seafarers or rowers. The Normanists argue further that it was leaders of these Germanic Scandinavians—Hroerkr/Riuryk, Helgi/Oleg, Ingvar/Igor—who created the polity that came to be known as Kievan Rus'.

By contrast, the anti-Normanists, often incensed at the implication that the East Slavs were incapable of creating their own state and that they needed Germanic Scandinavians to do it for them, respond with arguments about East Slavic tribal unions existing as proto-states before "the invitation." Moreover, the invitation itself was allegedly nothing more than an act by some East Slavic and Finnic tribes who engaged Scandinavians not to rule *over* them, but to work *for* them as military hirelings. As for the term *Rus'*, the Anti-Normanists argue that it comes from the name of an East Slavic tribe (*rosy/rodi*) who lived at time in the valley of the Ros' River, a tributary of Dnieper River just south of Kiev. Thus, Rus' has Slavic, not Scandinavian linguistic origins.

In the second half of the twentieth century, some scholars in North America (in particular the Harvard specialist Omeljan Pritsak) developed the view that the Varangian Rus' did not refer to any specific people, but rather to a band of traders of various ethnic origins who had been plying the North Sea and the Baltic Sea ever since the sixth century. Moreover, the Varangian traders adopted the name *Rus'* from other traders whose base was in the coastal region of Friesland in the present-day northern Netherlands. Moreover, this Frisian-based trading company was closely linked to other trading companies based in modern-day southern France, specifically in the town of Rodez. It is there where allegedly one is to find the "real" origin of the name *Rus'*, and not in Germanic Scandinavia or East Slavic central Ukraine. The irony in all of this is that the present-day inhabitants of Rodez and the immediately surrounding area do call themselves to this day by the French term *rutenois*.

There is one more twist to the story of the origins of Rus' which has direct relevance to Carpathian Rus'. This has to do with the so-called Celtic theory first developed in the 1920s by a Ukrainian émigré lawyer and civic activist (Serhii Shelukhyn) living at the time in Czechoslovakia's capital, Prague. It is true that in the first century BCE, when much of France formed the Roman province of Gaul, the inhabitants of the region around Rodez were called Ruteni. The Ruteni were a tribe of Celts who, as we have seen, lived throughout much of Europe north of the Alps during the three centuries before the Common Era. When the famed Roman general and state-builder Julius Caesar conquered Gaul in 52 BCE, many of the vanquished Celtic Ruteni fled eastward to lands in modern-day Austria that had not yet come under Roman rule. The Ruteni and their descendants remained even after their new homeland was brought into the Roman Empire. In the fifth century, however, when the West Roman Empire was on the verge of collapse under the impact of the Germanic invasions, most of the Celtic Ruteni moved farther eastward, some settling in Carpathian Rus', others moving on and eventually settling in southeastern Ukraine near the Sea of Azov. Among the more inventive tales related to the Celtic theory concerns a leader named Odoacer, allegedly of Ruteni origin, who did not move eastward, but rather joined the Germanic invaders and led the forces which actually deposed the last emperor of Rome in 476.

Some creative writers in present-day Carpathian Rus' have gone so far as to propose a new pantheon of Carpatho-Rusyn national heroes with an even more distinguished pedigree. Hence, alongside the nineteenth-century national awakener Aleksander Dukhnovych, the fourteenth-century Prince Koriatovych, and the ninth-century semi-legendary tribal leader Laborets', Carpatho-Rusyns might consider commemorating as their first "national" hero the conqueror of the Roman Empire, Odoacer.

The historic record suggests that Slavs were living in the Danubian Basin since the fifth- and sixth-century Hunnic and Avar times, and that by the seventh century under the hegemony of the White Croats they inhabited the northern slopes of the Carpathians. There are also archeological and some written sources which reveal that when Christianity first made its way into the Danubian Basin in the ninth century, a number of inhabitants living east of the Danube River and as far north as the Upper Tisza Region of Carpathian Rus' accepted the Byzantine Eastern-rite form of Christianity. These Eastern-rite Christians came to be called by others—and eventually to call themselves—the people of the Rus' faith, or the Rus'. It seems, therefore, that the identifier *Rus'* was present in the Danubian-Carpathian Basin even before later migrants from Galicia and other lands of Kievan Rus' began to arrive in the thirteenth and fourteenth centuries. Therefore, while Kievan Rus' has great significance for developments in eastern Europe, the origins of Carpathian Rus' are to be found first and foremost in Carpathian Rus' itself; that is, among the Slavic inhabitants and the political formations of the Danubian Basin.

Carpathian Rus' until the early 16th century

In order to understand developments in Carpathian Rus' during the medieval period, it is necessary to look at the structure of the two states which came to rule the historic region: Hungary and Poland. When those states were initially formed in the late tenth century, neither had yet extended its sphere of influence to the Carpathian Mountains. That process was to take at least another century.

The formation of the Hungarian Kingdom

The initial stage of state formation was undertaken by Hungary's first king, Stephen I (r. 1000–1038). During the first half of the eleventh century, he expanded the realm from its core in Pannonia west of the Danube River toward the north and east. He also implemented an administrative system based on territorial units, each of which was called the *comitatus* (in Latin)/ *zhupa* (in Slavic languages)/*megye* (in Hungarian), and which hereafter will be referred to as a county. The administrative center of each county was the castle, which also served as the residence of the king's representative, the lord-sheriff (Hungarian: *ispán*, later *főispán*; Rusyn: *zhupan*). The royal lord-sheriff was responsible for commanding the castle's armed retinue comprised of men (*jobagiones castri*) and their families tied to the castle with guard duties. Among the responsibilities of the retinue was to collect taxes; one portion was sent to the king's treasury, the remainder was used to support the castle and county administration. As the king's representative, the lord-sheriff was also responsible for administering royal estates; that is, agricultural lands, forests, and villages that were owned by the king. Gradually, Hungary's kings awarded temporary or permanent land grants to nobles (magnates and gentry), so that alongside royal estates there came into being manorial estates (*dominia/latifundia*) administered and eventually owned by nobles.

At the time of Hungary's first king Stephen I and his successors during the eleventh and early twelfth centuries, the territorial extent of the realm had not yet reached the crests of the Carpathian Mountains. Therefore,

HUNGARY IN THE 11TH CENTURY

MAP 9

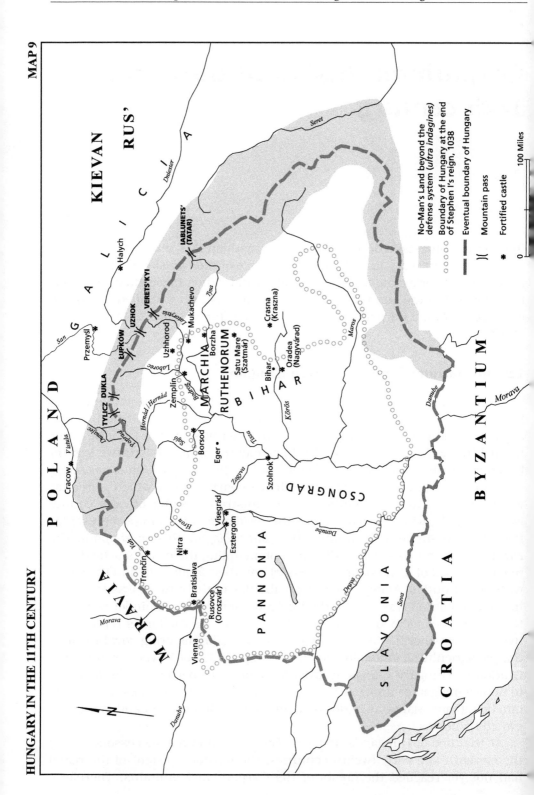

POLAND

KIEVAN RUS'

GALICIA

San

Dniester

Halych

Przemyśl

Vistula

TYLICZ DUKLA

ŁUPKÓW UZHOK VERETS'KYI

Dunajec

Cracow

Poprad

Uzhhorod

Laborec

Mukachevo

Latorytsia

IABLUNETS' (TATAR)

Tysa

MARCHIA RUTHENORUM

Borzha

MORAVIA

Morava

Vienna

Danube

Trenčín

Nitra

Bratislava

Rusovce (Oroszvár)

Váh

Hron

Visegrád

Esztergom

Zagyva

PANNONIA

Drava

Sava

CROATIA

SLAVONIA

Danube

CSONGRAD

Szolnok

Tisza

BIHAR

Satu Mare (Szatmár)

Bihar

Oradea (Nagyvárad)

Crasna (Kraszna)

Körös

Maros

Danube

Morava

BYZANTIUM

Seret

Zemplín

Hornád/Hernád

Bodrog

Borsod

Sajó

Eger

No-Man's Land beyond the defense system (*ultra indagines*)

Boundary of Hungary at the end of Stephen I's reign, 1038

Eventual boundary of Hungary

Mountain pass

Fortified castle

0   100 Miles

N

throughout this period most of Carpathian Rus' on both slopes of the mountains was in a kind of "no-man's land." This was a sparsely inhabited borderland between the Hungarian-controlled plains to the south and the sphere of Poland and Galician Rus' beyond the foothills on the northern slopes of the Carpathians.

A MEDIEVAL CARPATHO-RUSYN STATE: FACT OR FICTION?

The very limited documentary evidence about early medieval Hungary's northern frontier and the no-man's land beyond has not stopped scholars from speculating about what transpired in those territories so long ago. Many histories of Carpatho-Rusyns, beginning in the late eighteenth century, refer to an independent Rusyn principality called *Marchia Ruthenorum,* or the Rus' March, which allegedly existed at the outset of the eleventh century. Is there any basis for believing that such an entity actually existed?

Some scholars have suggested that Hungary's first king, Stephen (reigned 1000–1038), borrowed from the Frankish Kingdom the administrative concept of the *Mark,* or frontier march. The *Mark* was a borderland territory where Frankish rule was at its farthest extent and often named after the people or region it faced but that was beyond the frontier of the Frankish Kingdom, such as the Sorbian Mark, the Ost Mark (the future Österreich/Austria), or the Friulian Mark.

Scholars writing in the nineteenth century uncovered the terms *dux Ruizorum* and *Marchia Ruthenorum,* each mentioned once in medieval documents from Germany and Austria. They assumed that the title *dux Ruizorum,* which appeared in the entry for 1031 in the *Hildesheim Chronicle (Annales Hildesheimensis),* was given by King Stephen to his son Emerich and that it meant the prince of Rus'. The Austrian historian Herman Bidermann, who wrote one of the earliest histories of Carpatho-Rusyns (1862–67), assumed that the term *Marchia Ruthenorum,* which appeared in a late-twelfth-century biography of the bishop of Salzburg (*Vita Chunradi archiepiscopi Salzburgensis*), referred to a territory somewhere on the periphery of Hungary that Bishop Conrad heard about during his mission to that country in 1131. From these two isolated texts, the early-twentieth-century Ukrainian and Czech scholars Mykhailo Hrushevs'kyi and Václav Chaloupecký assumed that the title associated with Emerich in the early eleventh century must derive from his association with a territory called *Marchia Ruthenorum,* the Rus' March (*ruthenische Mark*) or Rus' Land (*Rus'ka Kraina*), although no one seemed to know where it was located. By its very name, the Rus' March should have been somewhere near Hungary's eastern frontier facing the principality of Galician Rus'. Speculation is that it may have been located near Carpathian Rus' (northeast of the Bihar region around Satu Mare/Szatmár in present-day Romania) or, even better for patriotic writers, that it coincided with modern-day Subcarpathian Rus'/Transcarpathia, making it the "first Carpatho-Rusyn state formation."

While some medieval Hungarian sources refer to borderland counties as marches, the little that is known suggests that they were structurally no different from other counties in the heart of the kingdom and not analogous to the system of marches/marks in the Frankish Kingdom. And as for the title of King Stephen's son Emerich as the *dux Ruizorum,* it only appears in the one source from 1131; all other references, including King Stephen's own Testament (*Admonitio*) use the term *dux* without any other attribution.

It is true that Hungary's rulers who succeeded Stephen often hired armed retainers from Kievan Rus' to serve as royal bodyguards—the *Rutheni Regia Majestatis* as they were referred to in contemporary sources. This explains why there are several Rus' placenames that still exist to this day in the Danubian Basin far from Carpathian Rus'. They derive from the presence of these royal Rus' bodyguards who served in areas along what was then the periphery of the Hungarian realm and where they, as veterans in the king's service, were allowed to settle permanently. Among such places are Oroszvár/Oroszfalva/Ruscovce (near present-day Bratislava in far southwestern Slovakia) and Nagyoroszi (north of Vác and the bend of the Danube River in present-day Hungary).

In the end, there is no proof that *Marchia Ruthenorum /Rus'ka* Kraina with its own princes of Rus' ever existed.

On the southern slopes a special defense system, called in Latin documents from the period the *indagines* (Hungarian: *gyepű*), was constructed just north of the castles of Uzhhorod/Ungvár and Mukachevo/Munkács, consisting of logs, ditches, and hedges blocking routes leading into the kingdom. Beyond the defense system (Latin: *ultra indagines*; Hungarian: *gyepűelve*) was the no-man's land where some Carpatho-Rusyns lived in the lowland valleys and foothills. Hungarian rule did finally reach the crests of the Carpathians at the outset of the twelfth century. It was to be at least another hundred years, however, before the county system was systematically installed in Carpathian Rus'. One reason for Hungary's kings deciding to take a more active role in expanding the county system northward was the threat to the kingdom's very existence posed by the Mongolo-Tatar invasion of 1241.

The Mongol invasion and the restructuring of Hungary

The Mongols were the last of the numerous nomadic warriors from the east, who since prehistoric times had periodically invaded central Europe. With massive armies comprised primarily of Tatar soldiers, the Mongols devastated many cities in Kievan Rus' and farther south destroyed the powerful Kipchak/Polovstian tribal confederation which for two centuries had dominated the steppelands of southern Ukraine. Even before the arrival of the Mongols in 1237, thousands of Kipchaks had fled westward where they were greeted as potential allies by the king of Hungary and allowed to settle in the realm where they came to be known as Cumans. Allowing the Kipchaks/

Cumans (sworn enemies of the Mongols) to settle in the Danubian Basin only increased the hatred of Mongol military leaders toward Hungary.

When the Mongol armies, estimated at 100,000 men, set out toward the Danubian Basin, some crossed the Carpathians from the northwest (via Silesia) and others from the southeast (via Transylvania). The main force, however, came through the Verets'kyi Pass—as the Magyar tribes under Árpád themselves had done several centuries before—and entered Subcarpathian Rus' where they destroyed several castles (Khust, Borzha/Vary) that formed part of Hungary's northern defense system. Farther south of Carpathian Rus', at a place called Muhi near where the Sajó River flows into the Tisza, in April 1241 the Mongols annihilated the Hungarian forces sent to defend the kingdom. In the course of the next year they ravaged most of the Hungarian Kingdom, destroying many towns and decimating the population. Later estimates suggest that minimally between 15 and 20 percent of Hungary's inhabitants perished, although in the eastern part of country, including Transylvania and the Carpathian Mountain regions, the percentages of demographic loss were much higher.[1]

Although the Mongolo-Tatar armies abruptly returned to Mongolia in 1242, the devastation they wrought proved to be a lesson not lost on Hungary's king, Béla IV (r. 1235–1270), who survived—if only barely—the invasion. He immediately embarked on a policy to protect the country's northern and eastern frontier along the Carpathians against any future possible Mongol invasion. The defense program took two forms: further implementation of the county administrative system with its castle strongholds and royal towns; and settlement of the mountain highlands with colonists.

Among the first of these new counties was Spish (Hungarian: Szepes), which came into being already in the late twelfth century and encompassed, in part, far western Carpathian Rus'. The reason for Spish's early creation was connected to the influx of German/Saxon colonists, invited by Hungary's kings for their skills in trades, mining, and agriculture. This early colonization by Germanic Saxons resulted in the establishment of towns like Levoča (German: Leutschau) and Kežmarok (Käsmark), which were to retain their German character until the first half of the twentieth century. Other counties in Carpathian Rus', Ung and Borshov, had come into being at the very beginning of the thirteenth century, well before the Mongol invasion. Now, in the post-Mongol period, Borshov was subdivided and replaced by three new counties: Bereg, Ugocha (Hungarian: Ugocsa), and Maramorosh (Máramaros). Farther west, Zemplyn (Zemplén) and Abov (Abaúj) counties were set up during the second half of the thirteenth century. Finally, the last of the counties established in this area was Sharysh (Sáros) in the fourteenth century.

Each county had its administrative center at a castle, some of which were built upon foundations of earlier hill-forts (*horodyshche*) that dated back to prehistoric times. Among these castles stretching from west to east were Spiš, Šariš, Zemplín, Nevyts'ke, Ung/Uzhhorod, Seredne, Munkach/Mukachevo, Kvasovo, Kanko/Sevliush, Nialab/Korolevo, and Khust, around

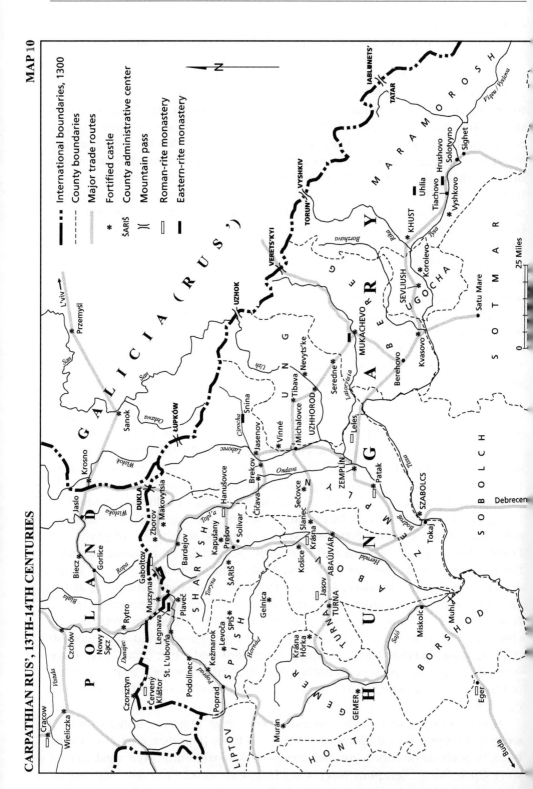

MAP 10

CARPATHIAN RUS', 13TH-14TH CENTURIES

International boundaries, 1300
County boundaries
Major trade routes
Fortified castle
ŠARIŠ   County administrative center
Mountain pass
Roman-rite monastery
Eastern-rite monastery

which in some cases small towns developed. Whereas most of these castles and towns were not directly hit by the Mongol invasion, King Béla IV and his immediate successors replaced what in many cases were earth and timber structures with stronger castles built of stone.

During the post-Mongol reconstruction period, the new and restored towns were either under the direct authority of the king (royal cities) or of the aristocratic landlords. In both cases, urban development was often left in the hands of German colonists, who were invited to settle in the northern lands of the Hungarian Kingdom. Consequently, several of the towns founded in the post-Mongol era that were in or near Carpathian Rus'—Prešov (German: Langdorf), Bardejov (Bartfeld), Mukachevo (Munkatsch), Berehovo (Lamprechtsas), Khust, Tiachovo (Teutsch-Au), and Sighet—initially had a Germanic character. Aside from the German form of their names, often used in official documents, town council meetings may have been conducted in German and artisans (tailors, shoemakers, bakers, cabinetmakers, stonecutters, etc.) were from the late fourteenth century organized in guilds (*tsekhy*) that followed the Germanic model.

The second form contributing to the defense of the northern frontier was population settlement, which also occurred in a somewhat systematic manner. Each landlord, whether the representative of the royal estates of the king, or of the privately owned manorial estates of the nobles, engaged the services of a middleman known as the *sholtys* or *kenez*. His job was to organize the settlement of colonists (*hospites* in the Latin documents). Many of the newcomers who arrived between the thirteenth and sixteenth centuries came from Orthodox Rus' lands north of the Carpathians, in particular from the principality of Galicia, which originally was part of Kievan Rus', but in the mid-fourteenth century was annexed to the Kingdom of Poland.

The *sholtys/kenez* proposed the number of colonists that could settle on the territory of a given landlord, and to encourage settlement the newcomers were often granted exemption from taxes and other duties for initial time periods that ranged from five to twenty years. The settlers were concentrated in villages on both royal and noble-owned lands throughout Carpathian Rus', where most villages date their origins to the period sometime between the thirteenth and sixteenth centuries. The settlers' livelihood was derived from agricultural and forest-related economic activity. Orchards and vineyards were particularly an important source of income on the lowlands and foothills, while in the higher, less fertile mountainous regions animal husbandry (especially sheep), wood-cutting, and stone quarrying were more common types of employment.

The Vlach colonization

Beginning in the fourteenth and continuing into the fifteenth century, there was yet another source of colonization into Carpathian Rus'. This one was from the south. The colonists in question were Vlachs/Volokhs, originally a Romance-speaking people related to Romanians who were sheepherding pastoralists in the mountains of the Balkan peninsula. But what prompted this migration from the south?

For over a thousand years, the Balkan region had been part of the Pax Romana, specifically the political and cultural world of the East Roman, or Byzantine Empire. During the fourteenth century, however, the Byzantines were gradually being pushed out of the Balkans and replaced by the rapidly expanding empire of the Ottoman Turks. The Vlachs, too, were pushed out of their traditional grazing lands by Turkic pastoralists, and therefore they moved farther north into the Carpathians. Some Vlachs eventually reached the northern Carpathians, where they intermixed with Rusyn shepherds and gradually became Slavicized.

Hungary's kings welcomed the Vlach pastoralists and encouraged their settlement in the high mountain areas of Carpathian Rus' and Slovakia. Vlach leaders, known as *voevodas*, negotiated their settlement directly with the king's representatives or with *kenez* middlemen. What evolved was the so-called Vlach Law, which some scholars describe as a variant of German Law. In other words, just as the medieval rulers of Hungary and Poland encouraged people from Germanic lands to settle and develop cities and mining centers, so too did they devise the Vlach Law for those who were skilled at pastoral and agricultural work in mountainous highland regions.

The encouragement took the form of initial tax and duty-free periods, usually ranging from 10 to 20 years. Thereafter, each year they had to pay to the local landlord, whether of the royal estate or noble-owned manorial estate, a portion (usually one-tenth) of their swine, honey, sheep's cheese, and wool, as well as provide horse-drawn labor. Because the Vlachs were by definition mobile, and because they lived in the high mountains where direct governmental control was still limited or nonexistent, the Carpatho-Rusyn and Vlach shepherds were often able to renegotiate their duties, which were decidedly less than those of residents in the lowlands (primarily Magyars) where proprietary serfdom gradually became the norm. Moreover, by this time the term *Vlach* had lost its ethnic connotation, although for the most part it came to be associated with a person of the "schismatic" Eastern-rite Orthodox faith. It is in this sense that the documents from the period use the terms Vlach and Rusyn as synonyms (*Valachus-Ruthenus; Ruthenos seu Valachos*) for persons engaged in animal husbandry and small-scale agriculture.[2] While their duties to local landlords were relatively light, the Vlachs-Rusyns were expected to guard roads and to defend frontier areas, tasks which made them especially valuable to the king. In recognition of their services, one long-reigning Hungarian king, Louis I Anjou ("the Great," r. 1342–1382), began the practice of granting to many Vlachs the title of *nemes* (Rusyn: *niamesh*), which accorded noble social status—albeit of the lowest rank—to residents in communities noted for their military service to the kingdom.

Kings, nobles, and the implementation of serfdom

While the Vlachs and Carpatho-Rusyns in the mountainous highlands managed to retain freedom of movement and other privileges associated with Vlach Law, the peasant agriculturalists in the foothills and lowlands of Carpathian Rus' were gradually being transformed into serfs. Eventually, they became legally attached to the land and its owners. The process of attachment, whether as a proprietary serf "owned" by a landlord, or in the form of an indentured peasant owing duties to the landlord on whose land he or she worked, took many centuries to complete. In large part it was a direct result of the changing relationship between Hungary's royal power invested in the king and its landed aristocratic nobles.

Under the first rulers of the Árpád dynasty, Hungary's kings owned most of lands and forests throughout the realm, over which they had absolute authority. This situation began to change in the first half of the thirteenth century, even before the Mongol invasion, when King Andrew/András (r. 1205–1235) expanded the practice of permanent land grants to the nobles. He also issued a document known as the *Golden Bull* (1222), which guaranteed specific legal rights and economic privileges to the king's servitors who later became nobility. A revised version of the *Golden Bull* (adopted in 1267) extended further the rights of the nobility, especially the most powerful upper stratum known as barons, a small group of figures who with their family offspring controlled in a clan-like fashion most of the country. In effect, the barons and other nobles became partners of the king in determining the country's defense systems. This was also a time when noble representatives from each county (*comitatus*) began to meet annually to discuss their common economic and political interests. This marked the earliest stage in the formation of assemblies which somewhat later (in the 1430s) evolved into a diet made up of nobles from each county as well as barons and other notables who henceforth were to dominate the internal political life and socioeconomic order of Hungary.

As the privileges of the nobles increased, so did the power of the king decline. The low point of royal authority came at the end of the thirteenth century, during the reign of the last descendants of the founding Árpád dynasty. With the exception of the lowland plain, where royal authority still prevailed, most of the rest of the country was divided among the great barons, or oligarchs, who ruled their land holdings as virtually independent entities. During what became known as the oligarchic period in Hungarian history, Carpathian Rus' in the northeastern part of the kingdom came under the control of the Aba and (just to the south) Borsa oligarchic clans. Royal authority was undermined following the extinction of the Árpád dynastic line in 1301, after which the country's nobles decided to invite foreign royalty to rule Hungary. Initially, the choice fell on a distant relative of the Árpáds, Charles/Károly Robert of the Neapolitan branch of the Anjou/Angevin dynasty, which at the time ruled Provence in what is pres-

HUNGARY AND POLAND, 14th-15th CENTURIES   M

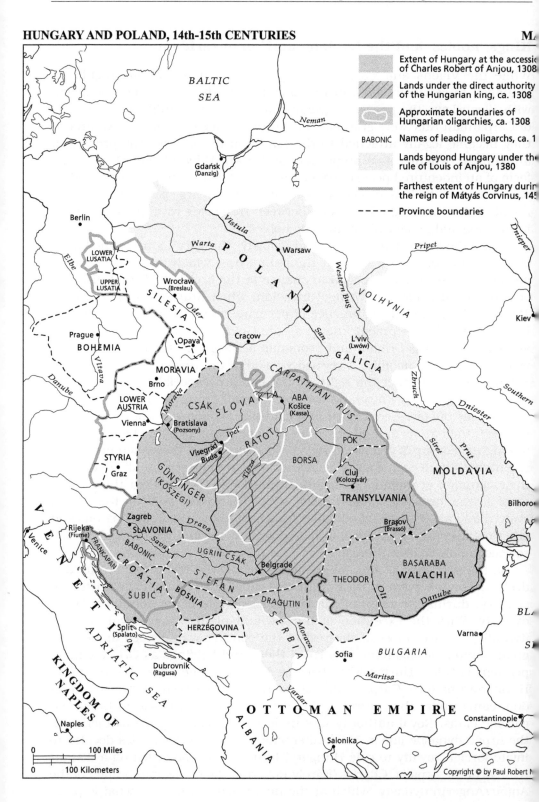

Extent of Hungary at the accessic
of Charles Robert of Anjou, 1308

Lands under the direct authority
of the Hungarian king, ca. 1308

Approximate boundaries of
Hungarian oligarchies, ca. 1308

BABONIĆ Names of leading oligarchs, ca. 1

Lands beyond Hungary under th
rule of Louis of Anjou, 1380

Farthest extent of Hungary durir
the reign of Mátyás Corvinus, 145

- - - - - Province boundaries

Copyright © by Paul Robert M

ent-day southeastern France and the Kingdom of Two Sicilies (Naples and Sicily) in southern Italy.

After several years of unsuccessful efforts against Hungarian noble opposition to establish his claim to the throne, Charles Robert was finally acknowledged as king and crowned as Charles I (r. 1307–1342). Nevertheless, opposition to "foreign" rule continued on the part of Hungary's powerful barons, including those of the Aba/Abadé clan based in Carpathian Rus'. Among leaders who participated in one of the many revolts against the efforts of the "foreign king" to increase royal authority was the lord sheriff of Zemplyn and Ung counties, Petrus/Peter, perhaps of the Aba clan. Centuries later, romantically inclined patriotic historians, without any real proof, claimed that Petrus was of Carpatho-Rusyn origin and that, as Petro Petrovych, he defended "his" people against the encroachments of the king during an uprising in 1315–1316. Eventually, Charles Robert and his Angevin successor Louis/Lajos ("the Great," r. 1342–1382) quelled the oligar-chic revolts, restored royal authority, and expanded the Hungarian Kingdom to its greatest territorial extent. By 1380, Hungary stretched from the Adriatic Sea to the crests of the Carpathian Mountains, at the same time that its king, Louis of Anjou, was ruler of lands farther north and east: Poland (including Galicia) and neighboring Moldavia.

To assist in governing their realm, the Angevin rulers replaced the rebel-lious oligarchs with new barons loyal to them, and at the same time encour-aged settlement of the still sparsely inhabited northern Carpathian border-lands. Among the new noble families loyal to the king who were given lands in Carpathian Rus' were the Czudars, the Perényis, the Rozgonyis, and the Telegdis, who developed the increasingly expanding Makovytsia, Stropkov, Čičvan, and Humenné manorial estates. It is perhaps not surprising that Angevin rulers invited kin from the House of Anjou (the branch based in southern Italy in the Kingdom of Two Sicilies) to help administer their Hungarian realm. The most prominent of the Italian Angevins to find their way to Carpathian Rus' at the outset of the fourteenth century were the brothers, Philippe and Jean Drugeth (De Ruget). The first two Drugeths, who like Hungary's kings were Roman Catholics, were each appointed to the post of palatine, the highest office in the land after the king. They also became the royal lord-sheriffs of Ung and of Zemplyn counties. Eventually these posi-tions became hereditary and, therefore, were to be held by descendants of the Drugeths until the end of the seventeenth century. The Drugeths were also given the manorial estates of Humenné and Ung/Uzhhorod, which by the early fifteenth century were the largest in all of Hungary, encompass-ing 106 villages and 3,200 households, many of which were comprised of Carpatho-Rusyns.[3]

The policy of inviting foreigners to assist Hungary's kings in controlling the realm against the opposition to royal authority by the country's indig-enous nobility was continued by King Sigismund (r. 1387–1437). Although he ruled Hungary for four decades, this dynastic member of the House of Luxembourg was faced with ongoing internal opposition as well as external threats along the country's southern frontier which took the form of attacks by the expanding Islamic Ottoman Empire (see below, Chapter 6).

Among the foreign invitees whose loyalty King Sigismund earned as a result of donations of vast estates and governmental offices was Fedor Koriatovych. Koriatovych was a prince of the ruling ducal family of Lithuania, a powerful state which by the mid-fourteenth century had come to rule most of the lands that had formerly belonged to Kievan Rus'. Koriatovych was at the time ruler of Podolia (recently acquired by the Grand Duchy of Lithuania) and an adherent of the Orthodox Rus' faith. Because of conflict with relatives and rivals for control of lands within Rus' lands of the Grand Duchy of Lithuania, Fedor Koriatovych, as Duke of Podolia, was in late 1393 forced to seek asylum at the court of Hungary's King Sigismund. He accepted the king's offer to become a landlord of the royal estate of Mukachevo in Subcarpathian Rus', which remained in his possession until he died in 1414. As a loyal subject of the Hungarian king, Koriatovych also held at various times the post of lord sheriff of Bereg and Sotmar (Hungarian: Szatmár) counties. In short, Koriatovych was a large Hungarian landowner (referred to in documents at the time as *dominus de Munkach*), whose primary goal was to expand his landholdings and to do so, if necessary, through attacks against neighboring landlords.

Beginning in the late seventeenth century, however, and in connection with legal issues surrounding the fledging Uniate Church, the first of numerous legends about Koriatovych arose. Now he was described as the "Duke of Mukachevo by the Grace of God" (*Theodorus Keriatovich, Dei gracia dux de Munkach*), and as someone who donated large tracts of land "in perpetuity" to the Basilian Monastery near Mukachevo.[4] He was even credited with founding that monastery (to which it was likely that he made monetary gifts) as well as the Krasnŷi Brid Monastery in upper Zemplyn county. He also supposedly erected and fortified the castle of Mukachevo and surrounded the city with walls. By the nineteenth century, folk legends went further still, transforming him into a supernatural hero. One popular folktale relates how, arriving in Subcarpathia, he miraculously received help from St. Nicholas, allowing him to kill a dragon near Monk's Hill (Chernecha Hora), where he then established the Monastery of St. Nicholas. In the words of one historian critical of these legends: "Everything that was important in the past of the Carpatho-Rusyn people began to be ascribed to Fedor Koriatovych."[5]

Despite the more realistic assessment of scholars, in particular Aleksei L. Petrov at the outset of the twentieth century, legends about Fedor Koriatovych persist to this very day. He is still considered by many to be the first prominent figure in Carpatho-Rusyn history, and in recent decades there has been an increase in scholarly publications about him as well as the erection of a life-size statue on the grounds of the Mukachevo castle.

But what did all these developments mean for the vast majority of peasant agriculturalists throughout the Hungarian Kingdom, including that part of Carpathian Rus' on the southern slopes of the mountains? The status of the peasants was, of course, directly related to that of the nobility. After the Angevin dynasty died out in the 1380s, Hungary's nobility, most especially its elite barons, were able to extract from subsequent kings an increasing number of privileges. By the fifteenth century the barons in particular acquired economic wealth and once again political influence at the expense of the prerogatives of the king. As ownership of more and more lands was being transferred from the king (royal estates) to the aristocratic baronial magnates and lesser gentry (manorial estates), increasing numbers of peasants now found themselves living on privately owned lands. This meant a radical change in their legal status. Now they were subject to taxes and labor duties determined by a noble landlord. And, if they had any legal problems, they no longer had access to royal courts but rather had to submit their complaints to local courts dominated by nobles, who, not surprisingly, were concerned primarily with protecting their own material interests.

One of Hungary's greatest rulers of this period, Matthias/Mátyás Corvinus (r. 1458–1490), tried with some success to curb the encroachment by nobles against the peasants. During his reign, the first of several resolutions was issued in 1484 by the Hungarian Diet, according to which "Carpatho-Rusyns (*ruthenos*), Serbs (*rascianos*), Vlachs, and other schismatics [Orthodox Christians]" were exempted from paying the tithe to the Catholic Church, since, as was later explained, they paid duties to their own priests.[6] These privileges of the Vlach Law were, in part, attributed to the protective role of "our king Matiash," who is remembered with fondness and praise in Carpatho-Rusyn folklore and legends.

But Corvinus was an exception. The general trend saw Hungary steadily being transformed into a feudal state in which the peasants were increasingly subordinated to their landlords, whether secular nobles, the church, or the king's estates. As for the nobles, they were able to create a situation in which they were less vassals of the king than figures who shared power (through the Diet) in ruling the state. And as the aristocratic magnates and lesser nobles increased their political, economic, and legal status at the expense of the king, the status of peasants worsened. Discontent with these changing circumstances prompted the first well-documented case of social protest. Beginning in 1492 and continuing for the next few years, a bandit group under the leadership of a Carpatho-Rusyn named Fedor Holovatii attacked the Drugeth estates in the Prešov Region along the borderland north of Humenné and Bardejov and into the Lemko Region north of the Carpathian crests in Poland.

Despite such protests, the legal and socioeconomic power of noble landowners continued to increase until it reached a new stage during the first decades of the sixteenth century. After the death of King Matthias Corvinus in 1490, the Hungarian Diet, which eventually had an Upper House (comprised of magnates, members of the royal council, and other notables) and Lower House (primarily rural nobility and lesser gentry), became the dominant force in the kingdom. It was precisely during this period that the nobility set out to complete the process of curbing the liberties of their peasants. This process went through several stages: peasants were forbidden to testify against nobles in court (1486), then forbidden to hunt (1500), and they were subjected to increasing restrictions on their freedom of movement.

In the midst of these developments a large-scale peasant uprising led by a military leader in the king's service (György Dózsa) broke out in the spring of 1514. The uprising spread throughout the kingdom, reaching Carpathian Rus' (especially Zemplyn county). After the revolt was put down, the nobility quickly took its revenge. In October 1514, Hungary's Diet convened and passed a law which deprived all peasants of their right of free movement and condemned them and their descendents to serve their lords "in perpetuity." Hence, the social stratum known in Latin documents as the *jobagiones,* which were in the early centuries of the Hungarian Kingdom comprised of free persons living on royal estates where they provided both agricultural tasks and military service, were by the early sixteenth century bereft of their freedom of movement and reduced to the status of proprietary serfs.

It is also true, however, that Carpatho-Rusyns and Vlachs (in effect, Rusyns who were shepherds by profession) continued to be exempt from the Roman Catholic Church tithe and that their duties to the landlord were still negotiable. Among such duties were those payable in kind (marten skins, oats, hay), and those which took the form of labor (ploughing, hay-making, harvesting crops). In short, most Carpatho-Rusyns still had a contractual relationship with their landlords and were not yet proprietary serfs.

Nevertheless, proprietary serfdom was to become the norm throughout the Hungarian Kingdom, where landlords gradually were able to reduce and eventually end the privileges associated with the traditional Vlach Law. It was the attempt to end such privileges and impose new duties that increased resentment on the part of Carpatho-Rusyns, some of whom resorted periodically to various forms of social protest, including participation in and support for banditry in the upper mountainous regions.

In 1514, the very same year of the Dózsa peasant uprising, the highly placed royal official István Werbőczi, a member of the lesser nobility from Ugocsa county in Carpathian Rus' (who some writers consider to have been of Rusyn origin), compiled the first Hungarian law code. Known as the *Tripartitum,* it not only provided a corpus of Hungarian customary law, it also described how the nobility was allegedly superior to all other social strata and, therefore, why aristocratic nobles should have exclusive privilege to govern the kingdom. In short, Hungarian society was split into two components: the political nation (*natio Hungarica*) comprised of the aristocracy—magnates, high clergy, and lesser nobility; and the disenfranchised rest of population—peasants and townspeople. The *Tripartitum* (eventually published three years later in 1517) also sanctioned the recent decree of the Hungarian Diet implementing proprietary serfdom, which was to remain in force for the next three and a half centuries, until finally abolished in 1848.

Poland: Administrative and socioeconomic structure

The political and socioeconomic evolution of Poland in many ways resembled that of Hungary. As in Hungary, the power of Poland's kings progressively declined in favor of the increasing political influence of Poland's nobility or *szlachta*, both magnates and gentry. Of particular importance for the Lemko Region of Carpathian Rus' was the territorial expansion of the Polish Kingdom. Blocked in the northern Baltic region by the Teutonic knights, Poland turned its attention to the southeast. During the reign of King Casimir III ("the Great", r. 1333–1370), Polish armies invaded the last independent Rus' principality of Galicia and added that territory to its realm. The annexation was completed in the 1380s; thereafter Galicia, renamed Red Ruthenia (Polish: Ruś Czerwona), was to remain under Polish rule until 1772. It was during that four-century-long period that Poland's ruling elite and its society as a whole became convinced that historic Galicia, located primarily east of the San River, was and should forever remain an integral part of the Polish political patrimony.

Since Poland was officially a Roman Catholic kingdom, that denomination was now introduced and encouraged to find adherents in the otherwise traditional Rus' territory of Galicia, whose inhabitants were of the Eastern-rite Orthodox faith. What developed was a dichotomous social situation: the Polish royal officials, nobles, and townspeople who migrated eastward into Galicia were (as well as polonized local Rus' gentry) mostly Roman Catholics, while the mass of rural peasantry and a dwindling number of nobles and townspeople were Orthodox.

Beginning in the late fourteenth century, all of Poland was administratively divided into palatinates (Polish: *województwa*). Each palatinate was headed by an official called the palatine (Polish: *wojewoda*), who was chosen by the king and who represented royal authority. The palatinates, in turn, were subdivided into lands (*ziemia*), each headed by a *starosta*, or lord-sheriff, also appointed by the king. This administrative structure was extended to the Lemko Region, which itself was divided more or less at the Dukla Pass that marked the border of the Cracow palatinate to the west and the Rus' palatinate to the east. Within these palatinates stretching from west to east were the Sącz, Biecz, Sanok, and eventually Jasło lands (*ziemia*), which encompassed the entire Lemko Region.

When King Casimir III died in 1370 and left no male heir to the throne, Poland's Piast founding dynasty came to an end. As the founding, or national dynasty, the Piasts' hereditary right to rule was never seriously contested. Not so for their successors, however. They were more often than not rulers invited from foreign lands and who were accepted to the Polish throne only if they agreed to grant an increasing number of privileges and prerogatives to the country's nobility. The apogee of noble political influence, as expressed through local noble representative assemblies, or dietines (*sejmiki*) in each of the palatinates as well as in the national diet (*Sejm*) was reached in 1572.

CENTRAL EUROPE, ca. 1480   **MAP 1**

Although before then many of Poland's kings came to the throne by election, the electoral system was not formalized until 1572. Thereafter, all future kings were chosen by the country's nobles in an election whose guidelines were set at a special session (Convocation Sejm) of the national diet which after 1611 met in Poland's new capital of Warsaw.

Along with their increasing political power, Poland's nobility—as in Hungary—was able to acquire large tracts of land and increasing control over the peasant agriculturalists who worked the land. Also as in Hungary, from the end of the fifteenth century an increasing number of restrictions were placed on those peasants who lived on Poland's large manorial estates owned by individual nobles (magnates and gentry) or by the Roman Catholic Church. The restrictions culminated in the 1560s, after which all peasants became proprietary serfs. This meant that they were unable to leave the land and were obliged to render unpaid labor to the lord on whose land they lived.

The manorial system, whereby formerly royal lands held by the king were divided into several large estates (*latifundia*) and given to secular nobles and the church, was introduced into the Lemko Region. The landlords were anxious to attract settlers into the still sparsely settled mountainous areas and, therefore, welcomed newcomers from the Prešov Region just south of the border in Hungary. There the Vlach colonization had been going on for about a century; now it reached the northern slopes of the Carpathians in the fifteenth and most especially sixteenth century, a period from which several Lemko-Rusyn villages date their origins. Some Polish scholars, believing that before this time the region largely was uninhabited, argue that the earliest presence of the Rus' ancestors of the Lemkos is primarily related to the Vlach colonization of the fifteenth and sixteenth centuries. Some Lemko and East Slavic scholars, on the other hand, opt for the theory of population continuity: that the origins of the Lemkos are to be found among the earlier seventh-century White Croat settlers and that the northern Carpathians were already inhabited by Rusyns when the slavicized Vlachs arrived.

Regardless of the question of origins, by the mid-sixteenth century the Lemko Region was divided into manorial estates. The largest number of estates (85 percent) were owned by secular Polish magnates and gentry, among whom the Nawojowski, Stadnicki, Gładysz, and Sienieński families were most prominent. Although the Roman Catholic Church held a very small proportion (5 percent) of lands in the Lemko Region, somewhat unique was the Muszyna Estate. Owned by the Roman Catholic bishop of Cracow, the Muszyna Estate was based in the southwestern corner of the Lemko Region along the border with Hungary. Founded in 1288 it continued to grow in size, so by the late seventeenth century it included two small cities (Muszyna and Tylicz) and 35 villages in which over 90 percent of the inhabitants were Lemko Rusyns. The estate functioned as a kind of semi-autonomous territorial entity with its own courts and military units which were based at the Muszyna royal castle and used to protect the region from foreign invasions (especially Hungary) and to suppress the brigand movement that at times was widespread in the region. Farther east, a similar estate, this one owned by the Roman Catholic bishop of Przemyśl, was based near the Dukla Pass at Jaśliska. Since its establishment in the late fourteenth century, the Jaśliska Estate served not only a defensive borderland function; it was also expected to serve as a catalyst for the possible "return" of the local "schismatic" (Eastern-rite) Lemko-Rusyn population to the fold of the Catholic Church.

As in the Hungarian Kingdom, the Vlach Law freed Rusyn and Vlach (*Rutheni seu Valachi*) inhabitants from having to pay fees or undertake labor obligations for an initial period of 20 to 25 years. Thereafter, the obligations were quite limited—2 to 8 days per year as compared to 52, 100, and even 150 days by the eighteenth century in many other parts of Poland and Hungary. In the context of these conditions, it is useful to be reminded the words of one scholar: that settlement in the mountains was "a call to freedom."[7]

Having become accustomed to such conditions, Vlach-Rusyn peasant-shepherds not surprisingly resented whenever landowners (church or secular) might attempt to increase their rents and labor obligations. Local court cases from the period attest to the efforts (sometimes successful) of villagers to have the increases imposed by landlords rescinded. When legal satisfaction was not possible, however, and especially in times of worsening economic conditions, social unrest would be the likely outcome. Unrest took the form of flight to the high mountainous areas along the Polish-Hungarian border, where small bands of brigands attacked the secular- and church-owned manorial estates. The first wave of brigandage activity, which occurred in the late sixteenth and early seventeenth centuries, was characteristic of the entire northern Carpathian region. At this time, it was brigands like Vasyl' Baius from Leszczyny in the Lemko Region and Vasyl' Chepets' and Andrii Savka from Stebník in the Prešov Region who carried out exploits that were later transformed and remembered in Carpatho-Rusyn folklore as heroic deeds. More often than not, however, these and other brigands simply engaged in common criminal activity.

The fall of Constantinople and the decline of Orthodoxy

One other development during this medieval era was to have a profound impact on Carpathian Rus'. This was related to the very source of Carpatho-Rusyn Eastern Christian religious and cultural life, the East Roman, or Byzantine Empire. Throughout its history the Byzantine Empire faced ongoing problems with defending its eastern borders. Among the frequent invaders from the east were various Turkic tribes of Islamic faith. The most serious of these were the Ottomans, who in the second half of the thirteenth century had broken into western Anatolia (modern-day Turkey), where they set up the basis for what became an Islamic Ottoman state and eventually an empire. From their base in western Anatolia, the Ottomans expanded rapidly, so that during the fourteenth and first half of the fifteenth centuries they came to control all of formerly Byzantine Anatolia and most of the Byzantine provinces in the Balkan peninsula. In effect, they had the Byzantine capital of Constantinople surrounded. In large part, the stimulus driving Ottoman military success came from ideological conviction. The supreme Ottoman secular ruler, known as the sultan, claimed for himself the title of caliph; that is, the office of the figure who was the temporal and spiritual head of the entire Muslim world. As such, the Ottomans led by their sultans had a sacred duty to spread the true "Islamic faith" to "infidel" Christian Europe.

The Ottoman advance reached a major turning point in 1453, when, under Sultan Mehmed II ("the Conqueror," r. 1451–1481), they captured Constantinople. In that fateful year of 1453, after 1,100 often glorious years, the last vestige of the Roman Empire came to an end. The centuries-old original center of Eastern Christianity, Constantinople, became the political and spiritual center of an ever-expanding Islamic state. Eastern Orthodox Christianity, led by the ecumenical patriarch of Constantinople, was immediately reduced from a financially well-endowed official state religion to an outcast and often persecuted faith, whose church was stripped of its previously extensive material resources.

The reduced status of the Orthodox Church after 1453 was to have a negative impact on the many Orthodox peoples in central and eastern Europe who were jurisdictionally under the authority of Constantinople, including Carpatho-Rusyns. At the time the Eastern-rite Christian inhabitants of northeastern Hungary were within the jurisdiction of the Orthodox Eparchy of Mukachevo. This was a monastic eparchy; that is, its elected superiors, or archimandrites, of the St. Nicholas Monastery near Mukachevo were simultaneously bishops. Aside from Mukachevo, other Eastern-rite monasteries at Hrushovo and Uglia in Maramorosh county and at Krasnŷi Brid in Zemplyn county were training grounds for Orthodox priests and cantors. These monasteries also owned large landed estates.

The Ottoman advance did not stop at Constantinople in 1453, nor even at the Balkan peninsula, where territories as far north as the Sava-Danube Rivers and beyond into Walachia and Moldavia were brought under Ottoman control before the end of the fifteenth century. But the Ottoman sultan and the proselytizers of Islam had their sites set on an even greater prize—the Danubian Basin in the heart of central Europe. By the second decade of the sixteenth century the Ottomans were ready to launch new full-scale military campaigns, this time against the Hungarian Kingdom. Their incursions against that state were also to have a profound impact on Carpathian Rus'.

6

The Reformation, the Counter-Reformation, and Carpathian Rus'

The sixteenth century was to bring major changes in the political structure of central Europe. This same period also witnessed profound challenges to the hegemony of the Christian churches, both Roman Catholic and Orthodox, which had dominated and formed European society since the waning decades of the Roman Empire. In short, the sixteenth and seventeenth centuries were characterized by the close interplay of politics and religion, a potent combination that often had a negative and destructive impact throughout most of the continent, including its geographic heartland, Carpathian Rus'.

The Ottoman Empire in central Europe

With regard to secular politics, the biggest changes occurred in Hungary. In August 1526, at the Battle of Mohács, the armies of the Ottoman Empire delivered a crushing defeat to Hungary and its Christian allies. In the course of the battle, dozens of the country's leading dignitaries (magnates and church hierarchs) were killed, and the king himself died while fleeing the battlefield. Hungary found itself at the mercy of the Islamic Ottoman Turks. Their leader Sultan Suleiman I ("the Magnificent," r. 1520–1566) wasted little time, and within three weeks of the Mohács battle the Ottoman forces moved farther north reaching Hungary's capital Buda and even Habsburg Vienna, although capturing neither. Suleiman then returned home, but in 1541 he was back in the heart of the Hungarian Kingdom. This time he captured Hungary's capital and formally annexed most of the Danubian lowland plains that were divided into two districts (the Buda and Temesvar eyalets) of the Ottoman Empire. Beyond Ottoman territory, central Europe's once powerful Hungarian Kingdom was reduced to two separate regions: (1) Transylvania in the east (what is today part of Romania west of the Carpathian crests); and (2) Habsburg Royal Hungary in the northwestern part of the kingdom (present-day Slovakia, western Hungary, and far western Croatia).

In the wake of the king's death at Mohács, who was to succeed him? The surviving Hungarian nobles in Transylvania and Royal Hungary each chose their own candidate. Before the end of the fateful year of 1526, a royal diet

CENTRAL EUROPE, ca. 1570

▬▬▪▪▪ International boundaries	▬▬ Eastern boundary of Holy Roman Empire
▬ ▬ ▬ Boundaries of prinicipalities, duchies, and vassal states	▓ Ecclesiastical states
------ Provincial boundaries	▒ Hapsburg lands
◉ State capital	

Copyright © by Paul Robert Magocsi

0   100 Mi
0   100 Kilomete

(comprised mostly of middle and lesser Hungarian gentry from the eastern part of the country and led by the kingdom's palatine, István Werbőczi) chose in November as their "national" king the Transylvanian prince János Zápolyai. The following month the more powerful nobles, in particular magnates in the western and northern parts of the kingdom, elected as Hungary's king, Ferdinand I, who was of the House of Habsburg. By the sixteenth century, the Habsburgs not only held the title of Holy Roman Emperor, they also ruled a powerful central European state, Austria, with its capital, Vienna.

The subsequent conflict between Hungary's two royal claimants allowed the Ottomans further easy access to most of the country. Aside from their direct control over the central lowland plains, the Ottomans were able to determine the fortunes of Transylvania, which in the 1570s ended its claims to the Hungarian throne and the following decade evolved into a semi-independent vassal state of the Ottoman Empire. Although Hungary's Transylvanian princes were able to create a viable state, whose borders were even expanded northward to include Maramorosh county in far eastern Carpathian Rus', they were in effect subjects of the Ottoman sultan. And because the Ottomans were determined not to allow the two remaining parts of Hungary to unite, the slightest suspicion of any negotiations with Royal Hungary could and did provoke punitive military invasions into Transylvania. It was precisely in the course of these frequent military interventions during the course of the late sixteenth and early seventeenth centuries that villages in Subcarpathian Rus' and as far as the Prešov Region became subject to attacks and destruction on the part of marauding Ottoman soldiers and the cavalry of their Crimean Tatar allies. Memories of these "invasions by the Turks (*Turkÿ*)" are still preserved in Carpatho-Rusyn folklore.

Aside from the territorial division of the Hungarian Kingdom between the Ottoman Empire, Habsburg Royal Hungary, and the Ottoman vassal state of Transylvania, and aside from the rivalry and military conflict between the Habsburg and Transylvanian claimants to the Hungarian throne, to make matters worse these rival political forces were divided by religion. The Islamic Ottoman Empire considered all Christians their mortal enemies (a feeling which was mutually expressed on the part of the Christian states), while the region's Christian powers—the Roman Catholics of Habsburg Royal Hungary and the Protestants of Transylvania—were also irreconcilably divided. It was this potent mix of politics and religion that was to tear what remained of the Hungarian Kingdom even further apart. The ongoing wars between the two rival Hungarian entities—Protestant Transylvania and Catholic Royal Hungary—were to devastate Carpathian Rus' as well.

The Protestant Reformation

In order to understand the complex developments in Carpathian Rus' during the sixteenth and seventeenth centuries, it is necessary to look, however briefly, at developments in the Christian West that were brought about by the Reformation. These changes, moreover, were eventually to have a major impact on the Orthodox Christian East and one of its component parts, Carpathian Rus'. Since the Middle Ages there were forces within Western Christianity that were discontented with what they considered abuses endemic to the Catholic Church as an institution. While reform-minded monastic orders had long been critical of church practices, some religious figures, like John Wycliffe in England and Jan Hus in fifteenth-century Bohemia, went even further. They or their followers founded reformed Christian communities which actually broke away from the Catholic Church. These movements remained limited, however, to certain regions of Europe or lasted for only a specific period of time.

The outset of the sixteenth century brought a new development, however, one in which the ideas of religious reformers were adopted by secular leaders for their own political purposes. In 1517, the year that has come to symbolize the beginning of Europe's Reformation, a Catholic monk living in the German state of Saxony, the university professor at Wittenberg Martin Luther, publicly denounced several practices of the Roman Catholic Church. Luther was criticized by the church authorities, but he refused to recant his views and broke with the Church of Rome. From these protests, Protestantism was born.

The secular ruler of the German state of Saxony, where these events were taking place, embraced what became the Lutheran faith. He then imposed it on all the inhabitants of Saxony, justifying his actions on the principle of *cuius regio, eius religio* (the religion of the ruler is made the religion of the land). The Saxon ruler's act was followed by other secular rulers, so that before long throughout Europe there were "Catholic" states and "Protestant" states. This meant that states which previously may have only clashed over political or economic rivalries, now added a new justification for their actions: they were ostensibly defending the Catholic or the Protestant faith. The result was a period of brutal and often devastating religious wars that raged throughout much of the European continent during the sixteenth and seventeenth centuries.

Luther was by no means the only Protestant reformer. In fact, the entire Protestant movement was characterized by ideological divisiveness among a seemingly endless array of reformers, whose followers created new churches and varieties of Protestantism. Of particular importance for our purposes was Luther's younger contemporary, John Calvin (1509–1564), whose followers known as Reformed Calvinists were initially based in Switzerland. But before the end of the sixteenth century the Reformed Calvinist movement spread to eastern Hungary and Transylvania; that is, to areas immediately adjacent to Carpathian Rus'.

Despite the organizational fragmentation of the Protestant world, the movement did have some common characteristics. One of these had to do with the question of authority. Rejecting the priestly hierarchy of the Roman Catholic Church and any idea that a fellow human being, such as an elected pope, should be considered the "vicar of Christ" on earth, the Protestants argued that the ultimate authority for the Christian faithful was the Bible. Moreover, each individual could communicate with God by reading this holy text. The main job of the Protestant clergy was, therefore, not to administer the sacraments such as communion, but rather to preach and thereby help individuals understand the spiritual significance of biblical texts.

In order to follow these general Protestant precepts, Bibles had to be available; they had to be written in languages understandable to their readers; and, of course, potential users had to be literate. Fortunately for the Protestants, a technological revolution had occurred about 75 years before Luther launched his public protests in 1517. This was the invention of the printing press in 1454. It should, therefore, come as no surprise that the early religious reformers were also linguists (Hus translated the Bible into Czech and Luther into German), and that wherever Protestantism spread it was accompanied by the establishment of printing presses and schools.

The Protestant Reformation reached its height in the sixteenth century, by which time most European states north of the Alps had become officially Protestant or had large Protestant communities within their borders. Among those states was Poland, which, while remaining officially Roman Catholic, did under some of its tolerant kings of the Jagiellonian dynasty allow large numbers of Lutherans, Reformed Calvinists, Bohemian Brethren, and Anti-Trinitarians (Socinians) to function within its borders. In fact, many Polish nobles became Protestants, especially of the Reformed Calvinist variety.

The Catholic Counter-Reformation

The Church of Rome was not, however, about to allow the Catholic faithful to slip from its grasp. During the second half of the sixteenth century (in large part as a result of decisions reached at the Council of Trent, 1545–1563), the Catholic Church launched a counteroffensive against the Protestants which came to be known as the Counter-Reformation. The administrative structure of the Catholic Church was strengthened by establishing a clear line of authority starting with the pope in Rome and extending to archbishops and bishops at the head of each diocese, and through them down to individual priests at the parish level. To maintain contact with particularly problematic regions in Europe, Rome sent papal legates known as nuncios to represent the pope. The papal nuncios resided permanently in countries that were in the front line of the Counter-Reformation, in particular in central Europe.

The Counter-Reformation also adopted the techniques of their Protestant opponents by creating a network of printing presses and establishing schools, in particular seminaries and colleges to educate both the clerical and secular elite and to assure that they would remain intellectually loyal to the Catholic faith. The most active and efficient implementers of this educational counteroffense against the Protestants were members of a new Catholic religious order founded in 1540, the Society of Jesus, commonly known as the Jesuits. The Jesuits arrived in Poland already in 1554, and within a decade they were placed under the royal protection of the king.

Half a century later, the Jesuits were not only in Hungary but in the very heart of Carpathian Rus'. At the invitation of the wealthy and politically influential landowner, Count György III Drugeth – a recent convert to Roman Catholicism – the Jesuits established a community in Humenné (1608). Known for their educational and intellectually persuasive skills, they were called on to staff both the newly founded college/*gymnasium* in Humenné (1613), as well as that same institution when it was transferred in 1640 to Uzhhorod. Among the other Jesuit communities established in Carpathian Rus' were those at Mukachevo, Horiany (near Uzhhorod), and Seredne. The presence of Catholic Jesuits in an otherwise predominantly Eastern Orthodox environment contributed to one of the most influential movements within Carpatho-Rusyn society in the seventeenth century—church union.

Poland and church union

In contrast to the disastrous fate of the Hungarian Kingdom following the 1526 battle of Mohács, Poland in the course of the sixteenth century actually grew stronger and extended its control over a large expanse of territory north of the Carpathians. This was brought about by two unions, a political one in 1569, and an ideological or religious one in 1596.

Ever since the late fourteenth century, Poland had set out to develop closer relations with its powerful eastern neighbor, the Grand Duchy of Lithuania. By the fourteenth century, Lithuania had come to control most of the lands that had been part of Kievan Rus'; that is, the Rus' principalities located in what is modern-day Belarus and northern Ukraine. In 1385, Poland and Lithuania signed an agreement whereby the two countries would be joined in personal union through a common monarch, the first of whom was the Lithuanian grand duke Jogaila. Crowned Władysław II Jagiełło (r. 1386–1434), he became the first of a long line of Polish kings of the Jagiellonian dynasty. Aside from the personal union of Poland and Lithuania, Jagiełło did manage to have the pagan Lithuanians converted to Roman Catholicism. Although the Grand Duchy of Lithuania adopted Catholicism as its state religion, most of its non-Lithuanian East Slavic inhabitants in former Kievan Rus' lands remained Orthodox.

During the sixteenth century, Jagiellonian-ruled Poland was at the height of its political power, and negotiations began with Lithuania (threatened by the growing power of Muscovy on its eastern borders) to bring the two states even closer together. The result was the Union of Lublin signed in 1569, whereby Poland and Lithuania formed a common republic, or commonwealth. The Polish-Lithuanian Commonwealth was henceforth ruled by a common monarch who governed the realm in conjunction with a parliament comprised of noble deputies from both parts of the new political entity. The Grand Duchy of Lithuania continued to exist as a distinct administrative entity, but its entire southern portion (the Rus' territories of modern northern and central Ukraine) was detached and made part of the Polish "half" of the Commonwealth. Hence, as a result of the Union of Lublin of 1569, the Polish Kingdom added to Galician Rus' (which it had already been ruling for nearly two centuries) a very large land mass to the east that was inhabited primarily by an Orthodox Rus' population. Therefore, when the Catholic Reformation spearheaded by the Jesuits was fully underway in Poland, it was faced not only with trying to reconvert Protestants, but also with another question: What should be done with the Orthodox in Lithuania and the eastern lands of the Polish Kingdom (Galicia, Volhynia, and Ukraine)?

From Rome's point of view the Orthodox were "schismatics"; that is, they were in schism, or separated from the pope and the Catholic *communitas*. The separation between Catholic Rome and Orthodox Constantinople had begun in 1054 and became final in the thirteenth century. Nevertheless, Rome did recognize the Orthodox bishops as canonical. In other words, they were properly consecrated by episcopal predecessors going back to apostolic times when the Christian Church was one. Catholics realized that the break between the two branches of Christianity beginning in 1054 was a regrettable reality, but they believed the division could be healed by bringing the Orthodox "schismatics" back into the fold of the "universal Catholic Church." Hence, in contrast to Protestants who needed to be converted, or reconverted "back to Catholicism," in the case of the Orthodox the question was one of reunion. In Poland-Lithuania, the Orthodox bishops and lay leaders themselves also favored bringing the two branches of the Christian flock together, although not at the expense of what they considered subordination to the Catholic pope in Rome. Rather, they looked forward to a union of equals that would include the entire Orthodox and Catholic worlds.

This ambitious goal was not realized, however. Instead, only church and lay figures from Poland-Lithuania were involved. Of the commonwealth's eight Orthodox episcopal hierarchs, six (including the metropolitan-archbishop of Kiev resident in Poland-Lithuania) agreed to enter into communion; that is, to accept church union with Rome. The formal act of church union occurred at the town of Brest, in the southwestern corner of the Grand Duchy of Lithuania in 1596. The result was the formation of what came to be known as a Uniate Church. The newly formed Uniate Church was allowed to retain its Eastern Orthodox rite and traditions (including a married priesthood and the old order Julian calendar), but they now changed their jurisdictional allegiance from the Orthodox ecumenical patriarch in Constantinople to the Catholic pope of Rome. Poland-Lithuania's king immediately recognized the Uniates as the only legal body of Eastern-rite Christians, while those Orthodox who refused to join the union were now part of a church that lost its legal status. Although several decades later, in 1632, the Orthodox of Poland-Lithuania were once again legally recognized, their status in the Commonwealth remained precarious.

This was particularly the situation in the Cracow and Rus'/Galicia palatinates which included the Lemko Region of Carpathian Rus'. The Orthodox inhabitants there were under the jurisdiction of the Eparchy of Przemyśl, whose bishop (Mykhail Kopystians'kyi, r. 1591–1610) was one of those hierarchs who refused to join the church union. Even after his death in 1610, the status of the Eparchy of Przemyśl remained unclear, so that it was not until 1691 that the Orthodox jurisdiction was formally abolished. Thereafter,

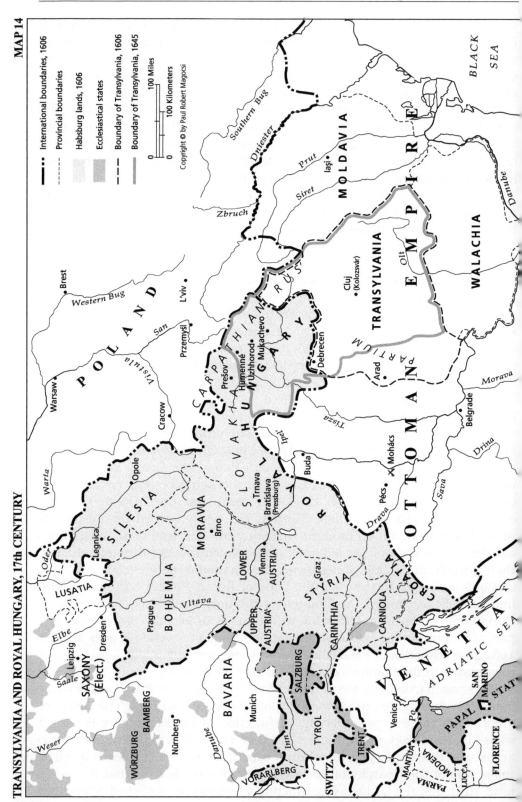

MAP 14

TRANSYLVANIA AND ROYAL HUNGARY, 17th CENTURY

International boundaries, 1606
Provincial boundaries
Habsburg lands, 1606
Ecclesiastical states
Boundary of Transylvania, 1606
Boundary of Transylvania, 1645

100 Miles
0   100 Kilometers
0

Copyright © by Paul Robert Magocsi

BLACK
SEA

Southern Bug

Dniester

Prut

Siret

Iaşi

Zbruch

MOLDAVIA

Brest

Western Bug

L'viv

POLAND

San

Przemyśl

Vistula

Warsaw

Cracow

Opole

Olt

TRANSYLVANIA

Cluj
(Kolozsvár)

WALACHIA

Danube

Morava

CARPATHIAN

Prešov
Humenné
Uzhhorod
Mukachevo

RUS'

HUNGARY

Debrecen

PARTIUM

Arad

Tisza

OTTOMAN

EMPIRE

Belgrade

Drina

Morava

Ipel'

Mohács

Buda

Pécs

Sava

Drava

SLOVAKIA

Trnava

Bratislava
(Pressburg)

Legnica

SILESIA

Oder

MORAVIA

Brno

LOWER
AUSTRIA

Vienna

Graz

STYRIA

CROATIA

LUSATIA

BOHEMIA

Prague

Vltava

UPPER
AUSTRIA

CARINTHIA

CARNIOLA

VENETIA

ADRIATIC SEA

Elbe

Leipzig

Dresden

Saale

SAXONY
(Elect.)

BAMBERG

WÜRZBURG

Nürnberg

Weser

BAVARIA

Munich

Danube

Inn

SALZBURG

TYROL

TRENT

Venice

Po

SAN
MARINO

STAT

PAPAL

FLORENCE

MODENA

MANTUA

PARMA

LUCCA

VORARLBERG

SWITZ.

Warta

Przemyśl became the seat of a Uniate bishop. Nevertheless, Orthodoxy continued to remain entrenched in the Lemko Region, where at the time there were an estimated 120 to 150 Eastern-rite parishes. In effect, it was not until the outset of the eighteenth century that these Eastern-rite parishes finally became Uniate Catholic.

Transylvania and church union in Hungary

The 1596 Brest model of church union was followed half a century later on the southern slopes of the mountains in Hungarian-ruled Carpathian Rus'. At the time, Rusyn-inhabited lands south of the Carpathians were divided between semi-independent Hungarian Transylvania to the east and Habsburg-ruled Royal Hungary to the west. The dividing line of those two spheres was the area between Uzhhorod and Mukachevo, towns which were to change hands several times as a result of an ongoing military conflict between the two rival powers, each of whom claimed to be the legitimate successor to the throne of Hungary. To make matters more complicated, Transylvania's princes had accepted the Reformed Calvinist version of Protestantism, while Habsburg Royal Hungary took on the mantle of defender of the Catholic Church. In the midst of these military and religious conflicts between the Habsburg armies (the *labanc*) and the Transylvanian "rebels" (*kurucz*), many villages throughout Carpathian Rus' were ravaged by either one or other combatants, or by both. Catholic-Protestant religious hatreds did not spare the Uniates and Orthodox, many of whose churches were destroyed, including the Uniate monastery in Krasnŷi Brid which was set aflame and the Orthodox monastery at Hrushovo in Maramorosh county which was razed to the ground and never restored.

Undefended rural villagers were especially hard hit, so that military attacks, disease (cholera epidemics), famine, and flight resulted in an estimated 10 percent decrease in the Carpatho-Rusyn population during the late seventeenth and early eighteenth centuries. Some areas, like the primarily Rusyn-inhabited Makovytsia region in northern Sharysh county (the Prešov Region of present-day Slovakia), suffered a population decline that reached 50 percent.[1] Makovytsia also suffered enormous material destruction, so that between the years 1675 and 1717 the area's livestock decreased dramatically (horses from 618 to 91; oxen from 2,449 to 305; and cows from 2,266 to 279).[2] Since families depended for their very existence on such animals (especially cows), such losses in livestock often meant starvation and even death. Farther east the situation was just as bad, so that during the last decade of the seventeenth century 608 peasant homesteads in Ung county and 157 (out of 237) within the Mukachevo landed estate based in Bereg county were abandoned, not to mention all the inhabitants of seven villages who fled their homes in an effort to find safer ground farther north in the mountainous highlands.[3]

In the midst of these disastrous conditions, Roman Catholic magnates led by the Drugeth family made several attempts to implement church union. The anti-Habsburg Protestant princes of Transylvania were not, however, about to allow their Orthodox inhabitants become part of the Catholic Church. Consequently, when church union was finally proclaimed at the castle of Uzhhorod in 1646, it applied only to those territories owned directly or administered by the Drugeth family: specifically Eastern-rite Christians— for the most part Carpatho-Rusyns—in Sharysh, Zemplyn, and parts of Ung county and its administrative center in Uzhhorod.

Farther east, in Bereg, Ugocsa, and Maramorosh counties, which were ruled by Transylvania and therefore were outside the Habsburg sphere, the Orthodox Church with its episcopal seat in Mukachevo continued to sur- vive. As in the other parts of Christian Europe wracked at the time by fierce religious controversies, Carpathian Rus' witnessed polemics, in this case between Uniate Catholics and Orthodox. The best known polemist was a Uniate priest, Mykhail Orosvygovs'kyi (later given the name Andrella), who "returned" to the fold of Orthodoxy in 1669. For the next three decades, he carried out a spirited campaign through jeremiad-like sermons and writings, which denounced "the lordly lovers of gold" at the Vatican and Rome and their minions in Carpathian Rus' who, he argued, had deceived the people through imposition of the *Unia* (church union). In effect, Orosvygovs'kyi- Andrella's own career path was a reflection of what in later centuries was to be a common characteristic of Carpatho-Rusyn life; namely, while the vast majority of Carpatho-Rusyns remained Eastern-rite Christians, some were Uniate Catholics, others were Orthodox.

One reason that Uniate Catholicism proved attractive to some Orthodox prelates was because of the social and cultural advantages that would accrue to them by association with the Roman Catholic state religion of Hungary and Poland. For instance, when proprietary serfdom was implemented in Hungary at the beginning of the sixteenth century, Catholic priests were exempted, but not the Orthodox "schismatic" priests (*popy*), who were enserfed like their peasant flock. Another factor was related to the Orthodox world as a whole. After the fall of Constantinople in 1453 and the radical decline in the sta- tus of Orthodoxy under Ottoman rule, the Eastern-rite faithful in central and eastern Europe were cut off from the mother church in Constantinople. One result was a general decline in church life, especially in remote areas like Carpathian Rus', where Orthodox priests had no access to formal theological training and in many instances could not even read or write.

THE UNION OF UZHHOROD

"The act that initiated the Union of Uzhhorod in 1646 was ... modest, simple, almost hidden, without any ceremony or juridical and external solemnity."[a]

Considering the importance for Carpatho-Rusyns of the Uniate/Greek Catholic Byzantine Ruthenian Church which the Union of Uzhhorod brought into being, and considering the numerous subsequent references to the union, one may wonder why the event occurred almost without notice. Celebratory grandeur did eventually become the order of the day, but only three-and-half centuries later, when on 26 April 1996 an estimated ten thousand people, including the highest church hierarchs, state officials, scholars, and church faithful from throughout Europe and North America, gathered in Uzhhorod for a three-day series of events to commemorate the union.

But what actually happened back in the mid-seventeenth century? Since early in that century, the powerful pro-Habsburg and pro-Roman Catholic Hungarian aristocratic Drugeth family had attempted to attract its Orthodox subjects and the 600 priests of the Eparchy of Mukachevo to enter into church union with Rome. The culmination of those efforts came on 26 April 1646, when, at the encouragement of the bishop of Mukachevo Vasylii Tarasovych, 63 Orthodox priests living on estates owned by the Drugeth family gathered at the small church on the grounds of the Castle of Uzhhorod. There, in the presence of the Roman-rite Latin bishop of Eger, György Jakusics (the brother-in-law of the recently deceased supporter of church union Count János X Drugeth), the 63 priests made a profession of the Catholic faith. This meant that what became known as the Union of Uzhhorod was accepted by a mere ten percent of the priests in the Mukachevo Eparchy, specifically only those living on the Drugeth manorial estates in the Habsburg-controlled part of Carpathian Rus'—the counties of Ung, northern Zemplyn, Sharysh, Abov, Turna, Spish, and Gemer, which comprise more or less the Prešov Region of modern-day northeastern Slovakia.

The document assumed to have been signed in1646 by the priests who met at Uzhhorod was long lost until finally discovered in 2016. On the other hand, no Eastern-rite hierarch was present, since the Orthodox bishop of Mukachevo was at the time in territory controlled by anti-Habsburg and anti-Catholic Transylvania. No one even informed the pope of the entry of former Orthodox priests from the Mukachevo Eparchy into the universal Catholic Church. Finally, in 1652 the Holy See received information from the primate of Hungary's Catholic Church, the archbishop of Esztergom, who reported on the church union that had occurred six years earlier in the northeastern part of the kingdom. The information forwarded by the primate consisted of a letter, dated 15 January 1652, written by six Carpatho-Rusyn archdeacons to the pope on the occasion of the election of the first Uniate bishop of Mukachevo. The 1652 letter came to be known as the "Document of the Union of Uzhhorod." Because it, too, was lost, latter-day historians were uncertain when the Union of Uzhhorod actually took place, some suggesting various dates between 1646 and 1652. A consensus was eventually reached that favored the 26 April 1646 date.

What was agreed to at the Union of Uzhhorod, other than a profession of the Catholic faith by ten percent (63) of the Eparchy of Mukachevo's priests? The only information that exists comes from over a century later, when in the 1760 several reports were sent to Rome by Hungary's Roman Catholic prelates about the jurisdictional status of the Uniate Eparchy of Mukachevo. Included in a report to the pope, dated 31 March 1767, are the conditions allegedly outlined in the lost 1652 "Document of the Union of Uzhhorod": (1) that it be permitted for us [priests] to retain the rite of the Greek [Eastern Byzantine] Church; (2) that we have a bishop elected by ourselves and confirmed by the [Roman] Apostolic See; and (3) that we have free enjoyment to ecclesiastical immunities.[b]

The last of these conditions proved to be the most challenging, because it depended not on the church but rather on the secular authorities and aristocratic landlords. Some church historians (Antal Hodinka) argue that the chief motivation for accepting church union was not religious in nature, but rather the social and economic emancipation of Eastern-rite priests from servitude to their secular landlords. In fact, several more decades were to pass before the landlords eventually agreed to "emancipate" their Uniate priests. This occurred only after the intervention of the Habsburg emperor, who in 1692 issued a special decree on immunity from feudal obligations.

Considering these complicated circumstances, some historians speak of three church unions that took place among the Carpatho-Rusyns of the Hungarian Kingdom. It may be preferable to speak not of three unions but of three *phases* of the Union of Uzhhorod. The first phase took place at the Castle of Uzhhorod in 1646, but applied only to the counties of Ung, northern Zemplyn, Sharysh, Abov, Turna, Spish, and Gemer. The second phase took place in 1664, when, in Transylvania (by then under the control of the pro-Catholic Princess Sophia Báthory) the union was implemented in the counties of Bereg, Ugocha, Sotmar, lower Zemplyn, and Sabolch. The third phase occurred about 1713, when the future Uniate bishop of Mukachevo (Iosyf Hodermarskyi) succeeded in spreading the union into the county of Maramorosh.

[a] Michael Lacko, *The Union of Uzhhorod* (Cleveland and Rome, 1966), p. 100.

[b] "Document of the Union of Uzhhorod," appended to the 1767 report of the Bishop of Eger to Pope Clement XIII, cited in ibid., p. 108.

In an effort to improve the status of the Uniate Church, Rome appointed in 1690 a Basilian monk of Greek origin, Joseph Decamillis (r. 1690–1706), as bishop of Mukachevo. Despite the still unsettled political status of Carpatho-Rusyn-inhabited lands in Hungary, which was still the site of struggles between Transylvania and Habsburg forces, Decamillis created the basis for an eparchial administrative structure. He also helped to implement the 1692 decree of the Habsburg ruler Leopold I (r. 1657–1705), which assured Uniate priests the same rights and privileges as the Roman Catholic clergy, released them from the juridical authority of the landlord (including abolition of serf duties which they had to fulfill as "schismatic" Orthodox priests), and required manorial lords to provide them with arable lands for use of the parish. Gradually, Uniate parish priests were able to acquire more parcels of land and rent them out to what were to become *their* serf parishioners. The result was that the Uniate clergy gradually became the most well-to-do social stratum in Carpatho-Rusyn society.

Bishop Decamillis also set a new tone for clerical educational standards. He arranged for books to be produced at the Jesuit-run Pázmány University at Trnava in the western part of Royal Hungary (today's Slovakia), whose printshop had previously acquired Cyrillic typefaces. This meant that priests in Hungary's Uniate Eparchy of Mukachevo could be supplied with theologically sanctioned Catholic religious books instead of having to depend on the few "schismatic" Orthodox ones that were available to them until then. It was at Decamillis's initiative that the first books intended specifically for Carpatho-Rusyns were printed (at Trnava): a catechism (*Katekhisis dlia naouki Ouhorouskim liudem,* 1698) and the elementary language primer (*Boukvar' iazyka slaven'ska,* 1699), which for several decades remained the only textbooks available to Carpatho-Rusyn students. Clearly the Uniate Church was well on its way to becoming the most important organized element in Carpatho-Rusyn society.

UNIATES/GREEK CATHOLICS:
A NEW CHURCH OR A RETURN TO THE OLD?

Uniates/Greek Catholics and Orthodox both derive from the same Eastern-rite form of Christianity that traces its roots to the Church of Constantinople in the Byzantine Empire. What, then, makes them different?

Perhaps the most prominent difference has to do with ecclesiastical jurisdiction. The Uniates/Greek Catholics are part of the Catholic world headed by the pope in Rome. The Orthodox are part of a communion of churches, each headed by an ecclesiastical primate (usually a patriarch or an archbishop/metropolitan), who recognizes the symbolic authority of a hierarch known as "the first among equals"—the ecumenical patriarch of Constantinople. The faithful of each church are reminded of this distinction, because in the prayers recited in every liturgy the Uniates/Greek Catholics mention the pope in Rome, while the Orthodox the ecumenical patriarch of Constantinople (modern-day Istanbul in Turkey).

When, in the late sixteenth and seventeenth centuries, a certain number of Orthodox prelates (bishops and priests) in Carpatho-Rusyn and nearby lands inhabited by East Slavs opted to enter into union with the Catholic Church of Rome, they did so with the understanding that they would maintain the particularities of the Eastern/Byzantine rite. Among those particularities were the following: (1) use of the liturgy of St. John Chrysostom and not the Gregorian mass of the Roman-rite church; (2) use of Church Slavonic, not Latin, in the liturgy and in church books; (3) communion partaken by the faithful in two species, leavened bread and wine, unlike Roman-rite Catholic faithful who partake only an unleavened wafer. The Uniates/Greek Catholics were also allowed to maintain other traditions, such as the election of bishops by church councils, a married priesthood, use of the Julian calendar (at the time eleven days "behind" the recently adopted "Western" Gregorian calendar), the absence of organs and any instrumental music in church services, the absence of statuary or any other three-dimensional rendition of the human form, and instead the rendition of saints or other holy figures in two-dimensional mosaics and icons, the latter most prominently displayed on an icon screen (iconostasis) that separated the altar from the congregation in the interior of churches.

Initially, then, there was little outward difference between Uniates/Greek Catholics and Orthodox. Put another way, Uniates/Greek Catholics were more like Eastern-rite Orthodox than Roman-rite Catholics. One doctrinal matter did surface early on, however. This was the so-called issue of the *filioque*. At some point, Roman-rite Catholics accepted the belief recited (or added) to the creed that the Holy Spirit descends from the Father *and* the Son (*filioque*), whereas the Orthodox maintain the traditional view of descent from the Father only.

For most Carpatho-Rusyn faithful these esoteric differences remained just that. They continued to attend the same churches that used the same liturgy in the same language as had been the case before the church unions of Brest (1596) and Uzhhorod (1646) eventually took root in their villages. It is not surprising, therefore, that the Carpatho-Rusyn faithful continued to call themselves *pravoslavni* (Orthodox) long after they had officially became Uniates/Greek Catholics.

Gradually, Roman Catholic influences made their way into Uniate/Greek Catholic churches in ways that were felt at the village parish level. Beginning in the nineteenth century, Western-style pews were added to many church sanctuaries where, following Orthodox practice, none had existed before, and Catholic stations of the cross were depicted on church walls. By the twentieth century, other Roman-rite accretions crept in: some Greek Catholic churches/eparchies switched to the Western Gregorian calendar; icon screens (iconostases) were reduced in size or even removed entirely, "opening up" the altar to the faithful; celibacy for priests was adopted voluntarily or imposed by the Vatican on certain eparchies/dioceses; and the practice of electing a new bishop by fellow hierarchs at church councils was altered, so that the actual selection (from among three candidates proposed by the local secular landlord) was made by the pope in Rome. Clearly, by the twentieth century, the Uniate/Greek Catholic "church-in-between" was becoming increasingly more "Catholic" than Orthodox.

These very trends were what Orthodox polemicists seemed to foresee and to warn against during the negotiations leading up to the Union of Brest (1596) and Union of Uzhhorod (1646) and, in particular, during subsequent decades when Uniatism was gradually replacing Orthodoxy in Carpatho-Rusyn villages. From the very outset—and until this day—the Orthodox world does not recognize the validity of what they consider the uncanonical *uniaty* (in Orthodox vocabulary a derogatory term for Greek Catholics). Hence, at the very end of the nineteenth century, when an Orthodox revival began among Carpatho-Rusyns in the United States and soon after in Europe, its supporters urged Uniate/Greek Catholics "to return to the faith of their fathers"; that is, to Orthodoxy, which had been the only church among Carpatho-Rusyns before the unions of Brest and Uzhhorod.

Uniate/Greek Catholic spokespersons argue that theirs is not a new church created sometime in the late sixteenth and seventeenth centuries. Rather, the church unions of that time were simply healing the "schism" and restoring the one Catholic faith that had existed when, in the ninth century, the "Apostles to the Slavs" Saints Cyril and Methodius, and/or their disciples brought Christianity to the Carpathians. In short, Uniate/Greek/Byzantine-rite Catholics continue to argue that they do not represent anything new, but rather a return to the old.

The Habsburg restoration
in Carpathian Rus'

The three-way conflict for control of the Kingdom of Hungary between Roman Catholic Habsburg Austria, Protestant Transylvania, and the Islamic Ottoman Empire that characterized much of the seventeenth century reached an even greater level of intensity at the outset of the eighteenth century. Some of the fiercest military encounters, especially between the Habsburg and Transylvanian armies, took place in northeastern Hungary and were focused on the monumental castle-fortress of Mukachevo.

Rákóczi's "War of Liberation"

The Rákóczis were one the most powerful magnate families in all of Hungary. The family's various branches had holdings concentrated in the northern part of the kingdom throughout much of the Prešov Region and Subcarpathian Rus'. For example, in 1648 the Rákóczis owned no less than 32 estates throughout Abov, Sharysh, Zemplyn, and Bereg counties, where there were 27,000 serf families representing 100,000 persons living in 56 towns and numerous villages.[1] Those estates were held by Roman Catholic family members in Habsburg-ruled Royal Hungary, as well as by family members (some Protestant) who formed the Rákóczi dynasty of ruling princes (Zsigmond I, György II, Ferenc I, Ferenc II) in Transylvania.

It was in Rákóczi-owned lands both in Austrian-ruled Royal Hungary and in the Ottoman vassal state of Transylvania that opposition to the Habsburgs provided the stimulus for several revolts. The largest of these was the so-called kurucz wars led by Count Imre Thököly. Comprised of politically alienated nobles and discontented impoverished peasants, the height of Thököly's influence came in the early 1680s, when, as "prince of Upper Hungary" under the protection of the Ottoman sultan, the kurucz leader controlled 13 counties in what is present-day central and eastern Slovakia, northeastern Hungary, and Ukraine's Transcarpathia/Subcarpathian Rus' as far east as Khust. The Rákóczis of Transylvania were closely linked to Thököly, since he married Ilona Zrínyi, the widow of Prince Ferenc I Rákóczi. Even after Thököly's defeat and his departure from the country in 1685,

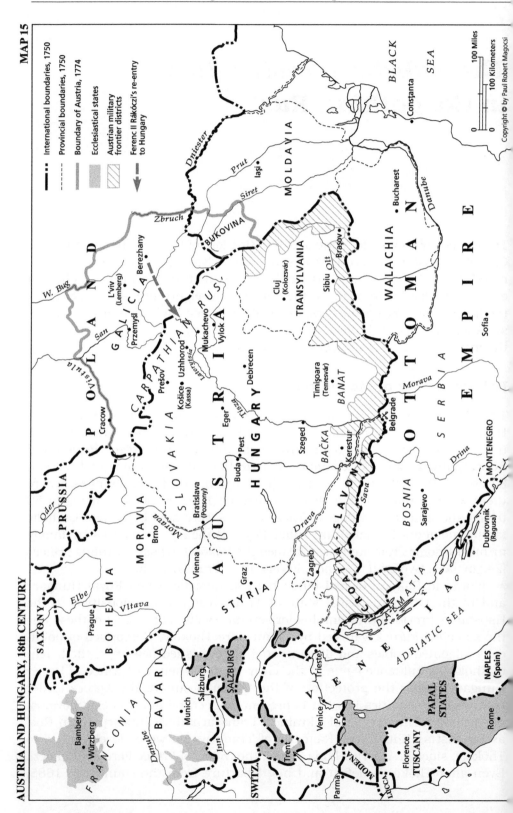

MAP 15

AUSTRIA AND HUNGARY, 18th CENTURY

Zrínyi remained behind with her young son Ferenc at her side, defending the family castle of Mukachevo. When, in 1687, the last *kurucz* stronghold at Mukachevo finally capitulated, the victorious Habsburg ruler Leopold I himself took the young Ferenc under his protection. He entrusted the boy's education to the Jesuits, in order to assure a proper religious (Roman-Catholic) and political (pro-Habsburg) formation. Although things did not work out as the emperor would have hoped, Ferenc was nevertheless to become not only the most famous of all the Rákóczis but one of the most renowned national heroes in all of Hungarian history.

By the 1680s, the fortunes of Habsburg Austria had definitely changed for the better. In 1683, its forces managed to beat back (with the help of Poland) the second and last Ottoman siege of Vienna. This was followed not only by Habsburg victory over Thököly's rule in northern Hungary (1685), but also by the formal return of Transylvania to Habsburg rule (1690), and, finally, by the removal of the Ottomans from central and southern lowland Hungary. According to a treaty signed in 1699 (at Karlowitz/Karlovci) with the Ottoman Empire, Austria was able to reestablish the Hungarian Kingdom's traditional southern boundary along the Sava and Danube Rivers. Already in 1687, Hungarian nobles meeting in the capital of Royal Hungary (Pozsony/Pressburg—modern-day Bratislava in Slovakia) formally recognized the hereditary right of the Habsburgs to the throne of Hungary.

Having driven the Ottomans out of Hungary, the Habsburgs set about to restore their rule throughout the kingdom. Not surprisingly, the kingdom's eastern region, the principality of Transylvania, which had functioned as a semi-independent vassal state during the Ottoman era, was to prove the most difficult challenge. Initially, Austria's military authorities treated the area they had just "liberated" as if it were an enemy land. The civilian population both in the rural countryside and in towns was exploited and persecuted in various ways. A particularly cruel figure was General Antonio Caraffa, a Neapolitan in the service of the Habsburgs, who was appointed Austria's General Commissioner of War. Caraffa was especially brutal toward the Protestant Calvinists in the northeastern part of the Hungarian Kingdom and is remembered as "the butcher of Prešov," where in March 1687 he executed twenty nobles and townspeople and tortured hundreds more on trumped-up charges of an alleged conspiracy against the Habsburgs. For many in Hungary it seemed that their Habsburg "liberators" were worse than their previous Ottoman "occupiers." It was not long before alleged conspiracies were to became real ones.

The next and what was to be the last major uprising against Habsburg rule was led by the Prince of Transylvania, Ferenc II Rákóczi (r. 1704–1711). This greatest of Hungarian national heroes and leader of the country's "war of liberation" was born near Subcarpathian Rus' and raised as a child by his mother Ilona Zrínyi, the legendary defender of the family's castle at Mukachevo during Thököly's *kurucz* uprising. The young Ferenc was, therefore, intimately familiar with the Carpatho-Rusyn peasants who lived nearby and throughout the vast Rákóczi landed estates.

Ferenc Rákóczi, the former ward of the emperor, started his political career as a loyal subject of the Habsburgs. In 1694, at the age of eighteen, he began public service in Royal Hungary as lord-sheriff (*főispán/zhupan*) of Sharysh county with a residence in the city of Prešov. While overseeing the vast Rákóczi family estates in northern Hungary and Transylvania (over a million hectares divided into 20 landed estates, 681 villages, 38 castles, and served by 100,000 peasant serfs), he became aware and sympathized with the plight of the region's impoverished peasantry.[2] Already in 1698 Carpathian Rus' began to experience unrest that for the next decade took the form of increased robber bandit activity in Ung county (led by Ivan Bets), in Maramorosh county (led by Ivan Pynta), and, even more ominous, uprisings among Magyar and Carpatho-Rusyn peasants in Bereg and Ugocha counties. It was also at this time that another high-ranking official, the lord-sheriff of Ung county and inheritor through marriage of the Uzhhorod/Drugeth landed estate, Count Miklós Bercsényi, was himself organizing a conspiracy of lesser nobles to drive out Habsburg rule. Bercsényi convinced Rákóczi to join this new anti-Habsburg conspiracy, although it was soon uncovered and in 1701 both men were forced to flee and seek refuge just north of the Carpathians in Polish-ruled Galicia.

During their otherwise comfortable exile at Galicia's Berezhany castle (where Ferenc pursued a passionate affair with the wife of its lord, the beautiful and politically influential Polish princess, Elżbieta Sieniawska), Rákóczi and Bercsényi continued planning for an uprising against the Habsburgs. Finally, in the spring of 1703, he set out on his historic "return"—along the very route used in the ninth century by the Magyars under Árpád—and crossed the Verets'kyi Pass into Subcarpathian Rus', where he assumed leadership of what came to be immortalized in Hungarian history as the Rákóczi War of Liberation.

Even before the prince arrived in the region, rebels under his banner clashed in early June 1703 with the militia of local pro-Habsburg nobles and were defeated in the "first battle" of the uprising at Dovhe, in the heart of Rusyn-inhabited Bereg county. But then, together with forces under his close friend and ally Count Bercsényi (who also returned from Poland but with hired calvary soldiers), Rákóczi was able to achieve the first victory over Habsburg troops (July 1703) near the lowland Subcarpathian town of Vylok. By the outset of 1704 his forces were able to secure the Rákóczi family castle at Mukachevo and that of Count Bercsényi at Uzhhorod, both places which were to remain the operational centers for Hungary's rapidly expanding anti-Habsburg uprising.

Initially, Rákóczi's "army" consisted of a few hundred armed soldiers and a few thousand Carpatho-Rusyn, Magyar, and Slovak peasants armed only with pitchforks and scythes.[3] But as the uprising spread, it attracted thousands more volunteer fighters drawn from the lower nobility, county castle sheriffs with their armed retainers, and enserfed urban tradesmen. It should not be surprising that these various social groups had different and often conflicting expectations: the noble landlords believed they were fighting for freedom from the Habsburgs and an independent Hungary, while the peasant serfs hoped to be liberated from obligations owed to their landlords. For the moment, however, all were swept up in the euphoria surrounding the persona of the legendary Rákóczi and therefore fought with enthusiasm and determination under his banner, *Cum Deo pro Patria et Libertate* (With God on Behalf of the Fatherland and Freedom).

In the course of the uprising, the Hungarian Diet proclaimed Ferenc II Rákóczi the "Governing Prince" (*Vezérlő Fejedelem*) of Hungary. While he rejected the idea of being elected king, he did agree to the decision of a diet held in 1707 that formally "dethroned" the Habsburg ruler. The well-educated and multilingual prince tried on several occasions to negotiate with the Habsburgs, and he was particularly active on the international diplomatic front, trying to enlist support for his cause from France (King Louis XIV) and Russia (Tsar Peter I). In the end, Rákóczi failed on both the military and diplomatic fronts, and by 1711 his anti-Habsburg struggle for Hungary's independence was over. Ironically, the last stronghold of Rákóczi's War of Liberation to capitulate was the very same place where the uprising had begun eight years before—the family castle at Mukachevo in the heart of Subcarpathian Rus'. It finally fell to the Habsburg forces on 24 June 1711. All of the Hungarian Kingdom was now firmly under the control of the Habsburgs, who were to remain the legal kings of Hungary as well as emperors of the Holy Roman Empire and what later was called the Austrian Empire.

The Habsburg ruler at the time, Joseph I (r. 1705–1711), granted amnesty to the *kurucz* rebels. This meant that the magnates and gentry who participated in the Rákóczi War of Liberation were allowed to return home and retain their manorial estates. But what about the mass of common *kurucz* peasant soldiers, many of whom were Carpatho-Rusyns? They, too, could return to their homes, but they were obliged to become again proprietary serfs owned by the manorial landlords.

Although deceived by Ferenc II Rákóczi's vague and now unfulfilled promises to liberate them from serfdom, Carpatho-Rusyns nevertheless retained a positive image of "their prince" from Mukachevo. Rákóczi himself was said to have referred to Carpatho-Rusyns as *gens fidelissima*; that is, a people most loyal to their prince and, therefore, loyal to Hungary. Thus, for generations to come—and in some circles still today—Prince Ferenc II Rákóczi has remained a symbol of close relations between Hungary and Carpathian Rus' and between Magyars and Carpatho-Rusyns.

With the removal of the Ottomans from the Hungarian Kingdom in 1699 and the victory of Habsburg forces over Transylvania's Prince Ferenc II Rákóczi by 1711, the emperors in Vienna were finally able to turn to the task of reconstruction. Not that Habsburg Austria was left totally in peace. It was engaged in two more wars with the Ottoman Empire (1716–1718 and 1737–1739) and in conflicts with other European powers over questions of royal succession (1756–1763). The difference from the preceding centuries, however, was that these conflicts occurred on territories beyond the borders of the Habsburg Empire. For the rest of the eighteenth century, the lands of the Habsburg realm itself were spared from foreign invasion.

While the Hungarian Kingdom had for nearly two centuries been devastated by foreign (Ottoman) invasions and civil war (Habsburg-Royal Hungary versus Transylvania), it, together with the Rusyn-inhabited lands south of the Carpathians, was to benefit from Austria's efforts at socioeconomic reconstruction. The first step in that process was to deal with—and to replace, if necessary—the ruling elite in the region.

Habsburg Austria's transformation of Carpathian Rus'

Following the defeat of Ferenc II Rákóczi's War of Liberation, the vast manorial estates owned by him and the few other "rebels" who refused the imperial amnesty (among them Miklós Bercsényi's Uzhhorod estate) were confiscated by the Austrian imperial government. The new Habsburg king, Charles VI (r. 1711–1740), reached an accommodation with Hungary's fractious nobility, reasserting all their political, social, and economic prerogatives, including exemption from taxes, unlimited power over their proprietary serfs, and full control over local county administrations. It was at this time that the nobles, satisfied with their status, readapted an older Latin adage about Pannonia to read: *Extra Hungarium non est vita. Si est vita, non est ita* (There is no life outside Hungary. And if there is, it is not really life).

Among the greatest beneficiaries of this political environment were the Hungarian magnates, gentry, and military officers who had remained loyal to the Habsburgs during the *kurucz* and Rákóczi wars. They were able to retain and even extend their landholdings; in Carpathian Rus' this included the Teleki family in Maramorosh county, the Perényi family in Ugocha county, and the Sztáray family in Ung county. The Habsburg authorities also found new landlords, the most prominent of which was the Schönborn family from the central German region of Franconia. In 1728, the Habsburg emperor granted the Chynadiievo estate, formerly owned by the Rákóczis, to the Roman Catholic archbishop of Mainz, Lothar Franz von Schönborn. Within a year he died, and the estate reverted to his nephew, the Roman Catholic archbishop of Bamberg and Würzburg, Friedrich Karl von Schönborn, to whom the emperor gave in 1731 Rákóczi's former Mukachevo estate.

Friedrich Karl revived the Mukachevo-Chynadiievo estate, which was concentrated in the county of Bereg in the center of Subcarpathian Rus'. By the time of his death in 1746, the estate covered nearly 2,400 square kilometers, within which there were 200 villages and 4 towns. Of the nearly 14,000 inhabitants, 93 percent were peasant serfs, mostly Carpatho-Rusyns in the north and Magyars in the south.[4] The Schönborn holdings reflected what had become the standard landholding pattern in Carpathian Rus'. Virtually the entire peasant social stratum resided on privately owned manorial estates with only a small percentage of lands owned by the church (whether Roman or Greek Catholic) and the state.

This period also witnessed an influx of new immigrants. Since almost all towns and many rural villages were bereft of a large portion of their inhabitants as a result of the seventeenth-century wars, the Schönborns invited

German colonists from Bavaria (especially Franconia), who between 1730 and 1750 were settled in several villages surrounding Mukachevo. Unlike the first wave of Germanic colonization, which in the medieval period was directed primarily to royal cities in and near Carpathian Rus', this second wave of Germans (called *Shvabs*/Swabians by the local Subcarpathian population), who arrived in the mid-eighteenth century, went primarily to rural areas. Consequently, many villages around Mukachevo, including some as far north as Svaliava, came to be inhabited primarily or even exclusively by Germans. While Germans living in the towns and cities gradually assimilated and adopted the Magyar nationality, those in the villages retained their German language and identity for the next two centuries until the close of World War II (see Map 28).

The German settlers brought with them new forms of economic management and agricultural practices, which contributed eventually to an improvement of living conditions at least in the central foothills and lowland regions of Subcarpathian Rus'. The local Carpatho-Rusyn and Magyar peasant farmers benefited from these innovations, especially since the Schönborn estate administrators implemented the three-crop rotational system, according to which one portion of arable land was required to lay fallow once every three years. The result was to restore and enrich alternate parts of the land. The German colonists also introduced crops that were new to the region, including corn, tobacco, and, most significantly, potatoes. Before long, potatoes became the basic source of food for Carpatho-Rusyn peasants. Therefore, it is not surprising that still today the most widespread Rusyn words for potato—*krumpli* and *bandurkŷ*—are of German origin. The experience of German colonist farmers also helped to raise the quality of the region's orchards and vineyards and to make possible the production and export of wine and dried fruit to the wider Austrian imperial market. Other activity introduced by the German newcomers to the local agricultural economy included horse breeding in the mountainous areas and small factories to produce beer.

Habsburg Austrian officials were by the eighteenth century supporters of the mercantilist economic theory. Mercantilism called for state intervention, including tariff protections, to encourage and protect domestic industries with the intent to make the empire as a whole self-sufficient. It is in this broader context that the manorial estates in Carpathian Rus' were encouraged to increase agricultural productivity and, as in the case of the Schönborn's Mukachevo-Chynadiievo estate, to establish small-scale industrial enterprises, including iron works (at Shelestovo), metallurgy works (at Frideshovo), glass works (at Velykyi Luh), linen works (at Pidhoriany), a paper mill (at Nyzhnia Hrabivnytsia), and several woodworking, tile, and brick plants. Some of these early, albeit small manufacturing plants formed the basis for enterprises that were expanded in size and productive capacity, especially during the last decades of the nineteenth century (see Chapter 10). Developments such as these dating back to the eighteenth century under-mine the generally accepted view that there was never any kind of industrial activity in Carpathian Rus' until the implementation of Czechoslovak and later Soviet rule in the twentieth century.

What did happen, however, was an increase in socioeconomic dis-parities between different parts of Carpathian Rus'. People in the mostly Rusyn-inhabited higher mountainous areas were indeed reduced to sub-sistence-level farming and poverty-stricken conditions that were made even worse as a result of periodic poor harvests and epidemics in the course of the eighteenth century. Consequently, the status of the mountainous high-landers was a stark contrast to that of the inhabitants living in the foot-hills (mostly Carpatho-Rusyns) and adjacent lowlands (mostly Magyars and Germans), where there were better climatic conditions, improved agricultural technologies and, therefore, greater crop productivity.

The political stability and gradual economic improvements in some parts of Carpathian Rus' were also reflected in the appearance of new sec-ular and religious buildings. The Schönborns expanded the Rákóczi resi-dential palace (1746–1748) in the city of Mukachevo—popularly known as the Bilyi Dom/White House—according to plans of the well-known central European Baroque architect Johann Balthazar Neumann. The Baroque and in some cases neoclassicist styles characterized the new or reconstructed religious and secular buildings, including the Roman Catholic (1762–1766) and Jesuit Collegial (1732–1740) churches in Uzhhorod; the St. Nicholas Monastery complex (1766–1772) near Mukachevo, with its church (1798–1804) designed by Demeter Rácz/Dymytrii Rats'; the church of the Basilian Monastery in Máriapócs (1731–1756); and the Ung county seat/*zhupanat* (1809) in Uzhhorod. There was also extensive building activity in several rural villages, where in the course of the eighteenth century many of the exquisitely modeled churches that still stand today were constructed by local craftsmen using the most readily available building material—wood.

The Bachka-Srem Vojvodinian Rusyns

The eighteenth-century reconstruction efforts carried out in the Habsburg Empire were not, of course, limited to Carpathian Rus'. Of particular concern to the imperial government were the sparsely settled—yet potentially agricul-turally rich—lowland regions in the heart of the Hungarian Kingdom, includ-ing the southern borderland regions along the Sava and Danube Rivers that had only recently been reacquired after the departure of the Ottomans. Among those territories were the Bachka, Banat, and Slavonia (including the Srem), all of which are today divided between Croatia, Serbia, and Romania. In their desire to develop these regions in what at the time was southern Hungary, the Habsburg authorities initiated a major colonization program, bringing in settlers from abroad (mostly from the Germanic Rhineland) and from virtually all the nationalities under its rule to settle and develop these rich agricultural lands.

Among the settlers were Carpatho-Rusyns from villages in what are today eastern Slovakia and northeastern Hungary. In 1745, the first contingent of Carpatho-Rusyns arrived at a settlement called Kerestur located in the heart of the Bachka region. More Rusyns came in the 1750s and 1760s, by which time about two thousand had settled in Bachka Kerestur as well as in the neighboring town of Kucura. The greatest numerical concentration was in Bachka Kerestur, with the result that the village was renamed Ruski Kerestur. These Carpatho-Rusyn settlers described themselves by the traditional ethnonym *Rusnak*, and brought with them their Eastern-rite Uniate Catholic faith, which helped to distinguish them from peoples of other national and religious backgrounds in neighboring Bachka villages. It was also as early as 1757 that Ruski Kerestur got its first elementary school. These factors, plus the virtual absence of intermarriage with neighboring peoples, assured the preservation of Rusyns/Rusnaks as a distinct ethnic group.

Following its reacquisition by the Habsburg Empire in 1699, much of the area in the southern lands of the Hungarian Kingdom initially formed a frontier area called the Vojvodina. Although the area was soon divided into separate Hungarian counties (Bachka/Bács-Bodrog, Srem/Szerem, Torontal), the name *Vojvodina* was restored for official use once again in the twentieth century (see Map 19). Therefore, the Rusnaks living there are known as Bachka-Srem Rusyns or, more often today, as Vojvodinian Rusyns.

Poland and Galicia's Lemko Region

In contrast to the Hungarian Kingdom, where the Habsburg rulers were restoring order and a degree of prosperity, north of Carpathians the Polish-Lithuanian Commonwealth entered a period of sustained crisis that before the end of the eighteenth century led to the state's complete demise. Poland's kings, who never had the kind of power over their subjects that rulers in neighboring states had, were now reduced to the status of virtual figureheads. The traditionally influential Polish nobles (*szlachta*) now reached the height of their political influence in the commonwealth, although the factional quarrels of magnates and gentry among themselves and against the king led to conditions of anarchy during much of the eighteenth century. Matters became even worse following the turmoil in the southeastern, or Ukrainian lands of the commonwealth. The very problematic situation there was the result of three factors: a noble uprising known as the Confederation of Bar (1768–1772); a major revolt by peasants and Cossack-like formations known as *haidamaks* (1768); and the ongoing interference in Polish political life—including the presence of troops—on the part of the Russian Empire.

The Confederation of Bar, whose goal was to remove the Polish king and end tsarist Russian influence in the country, had a direct impact on the Lemko Region. One of the leading "confederates," the noble Kazimierz Pułaski (later General Casimir Pułaski of American Revolutionary War fame), was in 1770 based for a while in the Gorlice district near the Lemko village of Izby. Not only did clashes with tsarist Russian forces occur in the area, but Pułaski's Confederates treated badly the local Lemko Rusyn inhabitants as part of the general Polish aristocratic and Roman Catholic hatred of Russia and of anything to do with Orthodoxy and Eastern Christianity. The negative impact upon Carpatho-Rusyns of Poland's patriotic movement associated with the Confederation of Bar was described in detail a century later in the literary works of the Lemko writer Vladymyr Khyliak.

But as long as Poland still ruled Galicia, its Polish nobles and other landowners (including the Roman Catholic Church) imposed an increasing number of labor duties and taxes on their enserfed peasantry. This was also occurring on the private noble and church-held landed estates which by the seventeenth century had come to control the entire Lemko Region. Some Lemko-Rusyn peasants expressed discontent with the arbitrary rule of their landlords by fleeing to the inaccessible high mountainous areas along the border with Hungary, where they formed small groups known as *opryshkŷ*; that is, robber bandits who periodically attacked and confiscated property from the landed estates. It is from this second wave of Carpathian brigandage during the late seventeenth and early eighteenth centuries that *opryshkŷ* leaders like Vasyl' Baius, Senko, and farther east Ivan Pynta and Oleksa Dovbush carried out their raids against estates on both sides of the Polish-Hungarian border. Already in their lifetimes these figures were transformed into something approaching "national" heroes among Carpatho-Rusyns. After all, for an exploited peasant population that had little or no legal recourse in courts dominated by the same nobles on whose lands they lived, the various mountainous brigands were seen to be fighting for the interests of the socially downtrodden. Somewhat like England's legendary Robin Hood, Carpatho-Rusyn peasants came to believe that "their" *opryshkŷ* robbed from the rich and gave to the poor.

The general anarchic conditions that characterized eighteenth-century Poland were to have their first serious political consequences in the year 1772. The commonwealth's more powerful neighbors to the west, east, and south—namely, Prussia, Russia, and Austria—decided that in the interest of avoiding conflict, each should annex a part of Poland-Lithuania. In what came to be known as the First Partition of Poland, Habsburg Austria acquired in 1772 a large swathe of territory north of the Carpathians stretching from the mouth of the Vistula River in the west to the Zbruch River in the east. This acquisition which eventually included the cities of Cracow and L'viv—and that also encompassed the entire Lemko Region—was formally renamed the Kingdom of Galicia and Lodomeria, or Galicia for short. Hence, for the first time in history, all of Carpathian Rus', on the northern as well as southern slopes of the mountains, was within one state, the Habsburg-ruled Austrian Empire. Just what impact Habsburg rule was to have on Carpatho-Rusyn life, in particular at a time when the empire was headed by enlightened, reform-minded rulers, is the subject of the next chapter.

Habsburg reforms and their impact on Carpatho-Rusyns

In the year 1772, when all Carpatho-Rusyn-inhabited lands were within the Habsburg Empire, that state was headed by rulers who were determined to reform their realm. The dynamic and talented rulers in question were Empress Maria Theresa (r. 1740–1780) and her son Joseph II (r. 1780–1790). Since Joseph became coregent in 1765, many of the reforms after that year were actually inspired and implemented by him. For this reason their reigns, which encompassed a full half century from 1740 to 1790, have come to be known as the era of Theresian and Josephine reforms.

The reforms of Maria Theresa and Joseph II

Both mother and son were enlightened rulers convinced that the good of society as a whole was dependent on the proper functioning of the state. A successful state, in turn, depended on the ability of each inhabitant to serve. In that regard, Emperor Joseph liked to quip that he was simply the first servant of the state. Moreover, the state's inhabitants should know that they are protected by the law and that in order to understand and appreciate the state's function, each inhabitant must be literate. Hence, it is not surprising that the Theresian and Josephine reforms were connected primarily with legal, socioeconomic, religious, and educational matters. Carpatho-Rusyns were to be the beneficiaries of the reforms which were implemented in all of these areas, with the result that Maria Theresa and Joseph II were to be remembered most favorably in Carpatho-Rusyn history.

Ever since the sixteenth century, when serfdom was legalized in Hungary and Poland and later imposed upon certain segments of the rural areas in Carpathian Rus', the status of indentured peasants working on landed estates—but most especially of the proprietary serfs—steadily worsened. The number of work days and duties seemed always to increase, and this almost always happened at the arbitrary will of the landlord to whom the proprietary serf was attached or on whose estate an indentured peasant worked. Interestingly, the only effective defense that peasants had at the time was the possibility that the church would increase the number of holy days on which work of any kind was forbidden. Hence, a whole host of local "holidays," such as the commemoration of the establishment of a parish or the remembrance of a natural disaster (flood, fire, epidemic, etc.), were added to the numerous saints' days and often extended holidays surrounding Christmas and Easter. Church holidays, therefore, came to be appreciated as much for their practical as for their spiritual value. Another result of the arbitrary nature of the feudal system was a general negative attitude toward work that entered the Carpatho-Rusyn social psyche. Work was not something one did to improve one's status, but rather an imposition that one should try to avoid in whatever way possible. After all, an increased work load might improve the resources of the landlord, but not those of the proprietary serfs and indentured peasants.

The reform-minded Habsburg rulers set out to change this situation by adopting decrees to regulate the feudal relations between landlords and serfs. The basic goal was threefold: to fix permanently the number of serf obligations; to forbid—or at least restrict—the arbitrary confiscation by landlords of land allotted to peasants; and, in general, to improve economic conditions so that peasants could pay their state taxes. The most important decree in this regard was Maria Theresa's *Urbarium*, which redefined the property relationship between the landlord and serf by transferring it from the private to the public sphere. Henceforth, lord-serf relations were subject to regulations set forth by the state. Formally decreed at the outset of 1767, the *Urbarium* was gradually implemented in counties where Carpatho-Rusyns lived between the years 1772 and 1778.

Among the most important regulatory features of the *Urbarium* were the following: (1) the size of the peasant plot (Rusyn: *dilets'*; Hungarian: *telek*) was defined, although the size could vary depending on the quality of the soil; (2) house gardens were fixed at a uniform size; (3) peasants were classified as either a "serf with land" or a tenant (Rusyn: *zheliar*; Hungarian: *zsellér*); (4) obligations to the landlord were fixed at 52 or 104 days annually—one day a week of labor (*panshchyna/corvée*) with draft animals (oxen or horses), or two days without draft animals; and (5) specific regulations were issued that concerned other duties, such as the transport of wood and other materials belonging to the landlord, supply of the landlord's manorial residence with firewood, and three days per year of hunting in the forest for the landlord.[1]

Most importantly, the *Urbarium* also guaranteed that peasant serfs, after completing their obligations, had the right to dispose of the rest of their time as they pleased. In other words, an enterprising peasant might find other employment and even transform his obligations into monetary payments. It was also at this time that the state created the village or urbarial commune (Rusyn: *urbarial'na obshchyna*), which consisted of arable fields, pastures, meadows, and forests.

While Maria Theresa's *Urbarium* put some order into landlord-serf relations, it still left extensive power in the hands of the owners and managers of the manorial estates. The size of the peasant plot may have been fixed and protected by the state, but the *Urbarium* did permit the landlord to divide the plot or to allow only a portion of it to be farmed. The landlord was also given the right to require "lazy" peasants to work more than the one or two days per week set out in the decree. Finally, the urbarial village commune was placed under the control of the feudal landlord. Not surprisingly, court records from subsequent decades are filled with lord-serf legal suits and countersuits resulting from the sometimes vague aspects of the regulations set out in the *Urbarium*. It is interesting to note that in order to assure that the regulations became known to the largest possible number of Habsburg citizens, the *Urbarium* was translated and published at state expense into several languages, including Rusyn. This has subsequently provided an opportunity for linguists to analyze the *Urbarium* as an important early published example of a vernacular-based Rusyn literary language.

As part of the efforts undertaken by Habsburg rulers to gain greater control over various aspects of the state, Joseph II turned to the church and the role of religion in general. In particular, he set out to limit the dominant position of the Roman Catholic Church. In 1767, he declared that a papal decree (*bulla*) could not be proclaimed in churches without prior consent from the emperor. Of particular importance was Joseph's 1781 Edict of Toleration, which allowed others to practice their faiths: Protestants (Evangelical Lutherans and Reformed Calvinists), the Orthodox, and Jews. Even within the Catholic Church, Joseph was intent on implementing the principle of equality. For him the various Catholic rites (Roman, Byzantine Greek, Armenian) were equal and, therefore, to be considered "three daughters of one mother" (*drei Töchter einer Mutter*).[2]

Joseph's enthusiasm for equality and rational administrative efficiency also prompted the closing in the 1780s of many "superfluous" monasteries; that is, those which were exclusively contemplative in nature and were not producing something tangible (agricultural products or intellectual activity in the form of education or book printing). Following a papal decree which in 1773 abolished the Society of Jesus, Maria Theresa did the same for the Habsburg realm, where since the Counter-Reformation the Jesuit Order had played such an important role in reestablishing the power and prestige of the Roman Catholic Church. Consequently, all Jesuit colleges, universities, libraries, and churches were confiscated by the Habsburg state. Meanwhile, among Carpatho-Rusyns, over a dozen of the last small Orthodox monasteries and hermitages (*skyty*) that remained in Maramorosh county were closed following the issuance of an imperial decree in 1788.

If the Theresian-Josephine era is not remembered favorably by the Roman Catholic Church and Carpatho-Rusyn Orthodox, for Uniate Carpatho-Rusyns those same decades proved to be a crucial and positive turning point. In effect, the Uniate Church became a respected state-supported institution whose very existence was guaranteed by the Habsburg Empire.

Uniate/Greek Catholics and the Enlightenment in Carpathian Rus'

We last left the Uniate Church at the end of the seventeenth century, when an imperial decree (1692) had "liberated" the Eastern-rite Uniate clergy from serfdom. Consequently, priests were able to improve their socioeconomic status, and the bishop of Mukachevo and several monasteries gradually became important landowners in their own right. The Uniate Church enhanced its landholdings by various means: litigation and court awards to lands it had previously held; grants from the state; donations from individual church members; and purchase. The early decades of the eighteenth century also coincided with the further expansion of the Uniate jurisdiction, following the abolition in 1722 of the last Orthodox eparchy in the eastern regions (Maramorosh county) of Subcarpathian Rus'. Farther west in the Prešov Region, even some villages which had become Protestant/Evangelical Lutheran (Pakostov, Malcov, Ďačov, and Jakubany, among others), or which were originally Orthodox and then Protestant (Závadka, Poráč, Šumiac, Telgart) accepted—or "returned to"—the Rus' faith. Many of these "new" Uniate villages were in the mixed Carpatho-Rusyn and Slovak ethnographic zone in Spish and Gemer counties.

Nevertheless, the Uniate Church was not jurisdictionally independent, because ever since the 1646 Union of Uzhhorod, the bishops of the Eparchy of Mukachevo only had the status of vicar; that is, auxiliary bishop to the Roman Catholic bishops of Eger. This relationship turned out to be problematic, with the result that for much of the eighteenth century Mukachevo's Uniate bishops (Iurii Byzantsii, Symeon Ol'shavs'kyi, and Mykhaïl Manuïl Ol'shavs'kyi, among others) carried out a "struggle against Eger" for jurisdictional independence. A resolution came only with the intervention of the Habsburg state. In 1771, during the episcopate of Ioann Bradach (r. 1767–1772), Empress Maria Theresa issued a decree (approved by Rome) establishing the jurisdictionally independent Eparchy of Mukachevo. That same year, the "apostolic vicar" Bradach was consecrated the first bishop with full episcopal power of the Mukachevo Eparchy. It was also at this time (1773) that, at the request of the Uniate hierarchy, the church's name was changed to Greek Catholic, a designation which was to remain in use until today in Europe and until the mid-twentieth century in North America.

Bishop Bradach died within a year of his consecration; thus, it fell to his immediate successor, Bishop Andrei Bachyns'kyi, to put the new eparchy on a solid financial, administrative, and educational basis. It was during Bachyns'kyi's nearly four decades in office (1773–1809) that the seat of the Greek Catholic eparchy was moved from Mukachevo to Uzhhorod. There he oversaw the construction of a monumental episcopal complex that included the bishop's residence and a library adjacent to the eparchial cathedral housed in the former Jesuit Collegial Church which was provided with an Eastern-rite interior. Bachyns'kyi was particularly concerned with raising the educational and intellectual environment of the eparchy. He supported the central Greek Catholic Seminary (the Barbareum) in the imperial capital of Vienna, while in Uzhhorod he founded an episcopal seminary (1778). He also encouraged priests to set up in each parish an elementary school, which would be staffed by graduates of the newly founded college for teachers and cantors (1794), and he promoted the publication of a primer (*bukvar*) and catechism by Ioann Kutka as textbooks which were made easily accessible in several editions and formats. All these materials were printed in the literary language of the time (vernacular Rusyn heavily influenced by Church Slavonic), which was made the official language of the eparchial administration and educational facilities. Bachyns'kyi also published a Church Slavonic edition of the Bible, and he encouraged priests (Ioann Pastelii, Ioanykii Bazylovych) to write histories of the eparchy and its Carpatho-Rusyns. All these activities brought aspects of Europe's late-eighteenth-century Enlightenment to Carpathian Rus'.

Already during Bishop Bachyns'kyi's lifetime it became clear that the territorially extensive Eparchy of Mukachevo, which covered no less than thirteen counties in northeastern Hungary (comprising 729 parishes and 560,000 faithful), was becoming more and more difficult to administer from one center. Hence, in 1815 it was decided to create a new eparchy by detaching 194 parishes (149,000 faithful) [3] in the western counties—Spish, Sharysh, Abov, Turna, Gemer, Borshov, and the northern part of Zemplyn— of Carpathian Rus' (see below, Map 21). The seat chosen for the new eparchy (formally designated by a papal bull in 1818) was Prešov, where the church that earlier had belonged to the Minorite monastic order was made the Greek Catholic cathedral, and an adjacent building became the episcopal chancellery and bishop's residence. Hence, in the course of the nineteenth century, the cities of Uzhhorod and Prešov, as the seats of separate Greek Catholic eparchies and eventually the location of other civic and educational institutions, became the two major cultural centers for Carpatho-Rusyns on the southern slopes of the Carpathians. The existence of these two eparchies also began a process of gradual regional differentiation between the two parts of Hungarian-ruled Carpathian Rus'—the Prešov Region in the west and Subcarpathian Rus' in the east.

The status of the Uniate Church was also gradually enhanced on the northern slopes of the Carpathians. While Galicia was still part of the Polish-Lithuanian Commonwealth, the Orthodox Eparchy of Przemyśl, which included the Lemko Region, was abolished in 1691. The acceptance of Uniatism by the Orthodox faithful took at least another two decades before it was accepted, a process that was especially slow in peripheral areas like the Lemko Region, where Carpatho-Rusyns continued to call themselves Orthodox (*pravoslavni*), regardless of the fact that they were formally Uniate. Then, in 1772, when Galicia was annexed to the Austrian Empire, the Habsburg authorities improved the status of the church. The Przemyśl Eparchy was one of the two (later three) divisions of the Greek Catholic Metropolitanate of Galicia (restored in 1808). With Austrian financial support, Przemyśl became the home of a Greek Catholic seminary (1780–1783, permanently after 1845), an institute for cantors/parochial school teachers (1817), and an eparchial printshop (1840). In effect, Przemyśl became an important cultural center for the Lemko Region during the late eighteenth and early nineteenth centuries.

The policies of the enlightened Habsburg rulers were especially constructive in the realm of education. In 1777, Maria Theresa issued the *Ratio educationis*. This was a decree designed to implement universal education. Uzhhorod was designated as one of nine educational districts in the Hungarian Kingdom for which there were to be five types of schools. Of great importance was the fact that each of the nationalities was to have schools in which the vernacular, or spoken language, was to be the language of instruction in elementary schools and teacher-training "normal" schools. The imperial authorities made it clear that one of those nationalities was Carpatho-Rusyn. "No one who is familiar with the social conditions in Historic Hungary," to quote the *Ratio educationis*, "can doubt that in the kingdom . . . the seven specific nationalities which are of concern . . . and which differ by their particular languages are: Magyars, Germans, Slovaks, Croats, Ruthenians [including Carpatho-Rusyns], Serbs, and Romanians."[4] In the end, the imperial authorities failed to provide the necessary funds for either the elementary schools or the proposed four-class "normal school" in Uzhhorod, which instead became the responsibility of the Greek Catholic Eparchy of Mukachevo. Bishop Bachyns'kyi was particularly active in this regard, calling on his priests to assure that there was an elementary school attached to each parish. The bishop himself established in Uzhhorod a secular elementary school, a theological seminary (1778), and he placed under the eparchy's administration the *gymnasium* that previously had been operated by the Roman Catholic Jesuit Order until it was banned from the Habsburg realm in the late eighteenth century.

The imperial government was particularly successful in supporting higher-level educational endeavors. In an attempt to raise the theological and general educational standards of future Greek Catholic priests, a General Seminary was established in Vienna at the Church of St. Barbara. Known as the Barbareum, this institution functioned from 1775 to 1784. Half of its 46 places were reserved for seminarians from eparchies serving Carpatho-Rusyn lands: 11 from Mukachevo (Subcarpathian Rus' and the Prešov Region); 6 from Przemyśl (including the Lemko Region); and 6 from Križevci (including the Bačka/Vojvodina region).[5] Even after the Barbareum was closed in 1784, the resident priest at Vienna's St. Barbara Church remained responsible for students enrolled in a new Greek Catholic seminary in the imperial capital (the Stadtkonvikt, 1803–1848), with 81 seminarians from eparchies in Carpathian Rus'. Hence, for nearly a century the St. Barbara Church remained a center where prospective Greek Catholic clergy from all Carpatho-Rusyn-inhabited lands could interact with one another as well as with other students from the empire's Slavic lands studying in Vienna.

For a while L'viv, the Habsburg administrative capital of Galicia, became an important educational center for the training of Carpatho-Rusyn sem-

inarians. Bishop Bachyns'kyi supported both his own eparchial semi-
nary in Uzhhorod as well as the new General Seminary in L'viv (est. 1785).
Another Carpatho-Rusyn, the first rector of the L'viv seminary, Mykhaïl
Shchavnyts'kyi, was instrumental in organizing the Studium Ruthenum,
an educational institute which from 1787 to 1809 helped prepare Greek
Catholic Rusyns to enter the Latin-language University of L'viv. Many of
the teachers and authors of the textbooks for the university-level Studium
Ruthenum were Carpatho-Rusyns (Mykhaïl Dudyns'kyi, Petro Lodii, Andrei
Pavlovych, and Ivan Zemanchyk). Clearly, Carpatho-Rusyns took advantage
of the expanding educational opportunities provided them as students and
teachers during Austria's Theresian-Josephine reform era.

When, at the outset of the nineteenth century, Habsburg policies gradually changed and opportunities for intellectual and professional employment
were less widespread, the more enterprising of this new Carpatho-Rusyn
intelligentsia made successful careers elsewhere. The Russian Empire,
which at the time itself was going through a reform period, was particularly
welcoming to Carpatho-Rusyns. Hence, figures like Ivan S. Orlai, Mykhail
Baludians'kyi, and Petro Lodii were among several who made distinguished
careers in the Russian Empire's educational institutions and its state
administration.

Carpatho-Rusyns become an historical people

Another aspect of the Theresian-Josephine era was the formation for the first
time of a Carpatho-Rusyn historical identity. From this period dates the first
history of Carpatho-Rusyns published in 1749 by a close advisor to Empress
Maria Theresa on educational and legal reforms, the Jesuit priest of Slovak
background, Adam František Kollár. Kollár's history, which appeared in
Latin under the title *Humillium promemoria de ortu, progressu et in Hungaria
incolatu gentis Ruthenicae* (A Homily to Recall the Origins, Development,
and Life of the Rusyns in Hungary), was written to support the demands of
the Eparchy of Mukachevo for jurisdictional independence from the Roman
Catholic bishop of Eger. Kollár's work was clearly designed to enhance the
historic prestige of Carpatho-Rusyns, arguing that they were the indigenous
inhabitants of the Danubian Basin, that they received Christianity in the
ninth century directly from Saints Cyril and Methodius, that they had their
own independent "Rus' principality" in the early Middle Ages, and that the
Eparchy of Mukachevo had existed already in the ninth century.

The interests of the Greek Catholic Eparchy of Mukachevo—this time
purely material interests—were what motivated yet another history of
Carpatho-Rusyns, the two-volume *Brevis notitia Fundationis Theodori
Koriatovits, olim Ducis de Munkacs, pro Religiosis Ruthenis Ordinis Sancti
Basilii Magni, in Monte Csernek ad Munkacs, Anno MCCCLX* (A Brief
Commentary on the Donation Made in the Year 1360 by Teodor Koriatovych,
Former Prince of Mukachevo, on Behalf of the Ruthenian Religious Order
of St. Basil the Great Based on Monk's Hill near Mukachevo). Written by

Ioannykii Bazylovych, who is considered the father of Carpatho-Rusyn historiography, the very title of this work—published in six parts and bound in two volumes between 1799 and 1804—makes clear its practical goal. The work set out to prove that the St. Nicholas Monastery in Mukachevo, of which Bazylovych was long-time archimandrite, had a legal right to certain properties which were allegedly given to the monks by Prince Fedor Koriatovych in the fourteenth-century.

Other histories were also written during this period (by Daniel Babila and Ioann Pastelii), although they remained unpublished, as did five versions of a Church Slavonic grammar compiled by the Basilian monk at the Krasnŷi Brid monastery, Arsenii Kotsak, who undertook this task "so that our miserable Rusnaks will not always be fated to remain simpletons."[6] The culmination of this new trend at writing histories in order to justify the existence and legal rights of Carpatho-Rusyns and their Greek Catholic Church came during the first half of the nineteenth century from the pen of the Uzhhorod priest, Mykhaïl Luchkai. In 1843, Luchkai completed a monumental six-volume *Historia Carpato-Ruthenorum* (A History of Carpatho-Rusyns). Written in Latin, and not published until the second half of the twentieth century, Luchkai's history continued the tradition of glorifying the past of Carpatho-Rusyns, even if most of the claims were in the realm of romanticized mythology.

Responding to the needs of the various educational institutions that existed to serve Carpatho-Rusyns within and beyond their homeland, Luchkai and another contemporary Ioann Fogorashii, each published for Carpatho-Rusyns a Church Slavonic grammar, respectively in 1831 and 1833. The 1830s also witnessed the spread of Pan-Slavism, an ideology that encouraged cultural and political cooperation among central and eastern Europe's Slavic peoples. Among Slavs living in the Habsburg Empire and the Ottoman-ruled Balkans, the movement's adherents called on each Slavic people to learn from the other and, through contacts and cooperation via publications and personal visits, to improve the cultural and civic status of their respective peoples in whichever state they lived. In the Russian Empire, Pan-Slavism—whose supporters were known as Slavophiles—took on a decidedly political and nationalist character that was associated with the tsarist empire's foreign policy goal of expansion into the Balkans and central Europe.

Carpatho-Rusyn intellectuals were also influenced by Pan-Slavism, and in the process they sought to determine their exact position within the Slavic world. The result was a body of writings (some of which were published, while others took the form of correspondence between scholars), which speculated on the relationship of Carpatho-Rusyns with the rest of the Slavic, in particular the East Slavic, world. What, after all, did the terms *Rus'* and *Rusyn/Rusnak* mean? Were the carriers of those ethnonyms—the Carpatho-Rusyns—a branch of the northern Great Russians or of the southern Little Russians (*Malorosy*)? Or were the Carpatho-Rusyns together with Great, Little, and Belorussians part of one Russian people? These questions were discussed in journal articles and in correspondence between Carpatho-Rusyns (Ivan Orlai, Iurii Venelin, Ivan Fogorashii-Berezhanyn) and scholars in the Russian Empire (Mikhail Pogodin, Izmail Sreznevskii, Nikolai Nadezhdin), some of whom even began to visit Carpathian Rus' on research trips during the 1830s and 1840s.

There was another more immediate challenge which faced educated Carpatho-Rusyns, especially those living in the Hungarian Kingdom. Why should they not simply assimilate to Hungarian culture and become Magyars, as the leading Hungarian political activist Lajos Kossuth was proposing in the 1830s and 1840s? This was certainly a tempting option and one which was indeed chosen by many Greek Catholic priests who, in effect, were the only real educated stratum among Carpatho-Rusyns. A few objected to this growing trend, however, in particular a Greek Catholic priest from Prešov, Aleksander Dukhnovych. At the time, Dukhnovych became increasingly concerned with educating his Carpatho-Rusyn flock. In contrast to his predecessors who wrote school textbooks in Church Slavonic, Dukhnovych published in 1847 the *Knyzhytsia chytalnaia dlia nachynaiushchykh* (A Reader for Beginners), the first textbook ever written in the so-called *prosta mova* (plain language), which for the most part was an easily accessible and understandable medium reflecting Rusyn vernacular speech.

It is clear that there was some intellectual and educational activity under-taken during the first half of the nineteenth century on behalf of Carpatho-Rusyn culture. But it was basically carried out by individuals who were often isolated from each other. In effect, no organized and specifically Carpatho-Rusyn civic or cultural life yet existed. All that was to change, however, with the dawn of what became the revolutionary year of 1848.

The Revolution of 1848 and the Carpatho-Rusyn national awakening

The year 1848 is a major landmark in modern European history. In that year revolutions broke out throughout much of the continent, and they were particularly important as a catalyst for political and socioeconomic change in central Europe. The Austrian Empire was deeply shaken by the upheavals of 1848, so much so that it seemed at certain times it would not survive as a state. What was this empire that by the end of the eighteenth century had come to rule all of Carpathian Rus'?

The multicultural Austrian Empire

In one sense, the Austrian Empire was a remnant of the Middle Ages, a time when royal familial dynasties acquired territories as part of their per-sonal patrimony. The family in question was that of the Habsburgs, or more properly, after 1713, the dynasty of Habsburg-Lorraine. Beginning in the late thirteenth century from Germanic territories in present-day Austria, Habsburg rulers based in Vienna along the middle Danube River gradually expanded their realm to the north, south, and especially to the east. Among the most significant of their territorial possessions was the Kingdom of Hungary, which included those parts of Carpathian Rus' (the Prešov Region and Subcarpathian Rus') on the southern slopes of the mountains. The Habsburg acquisition—rather its claim to the crown of Hungary—occurred in 1526, in the wake of the Ottoman invasion into the heart of central Europe. At the time, actual Habsburg control over Hungary was limited to a small strip of territory in the northwest of the kingdom, and nearly two centu-ries passed before imperial Austrian forces would be able to push out the Ottomans, to subdue revolts in Transylvania opposed to Habsburg rule, and finally to gain full control over the Hungarian Kingdom (see above, Chapters 6 and 7).

Although already in 1526 the Habsburgs had added to their long list of titles that of kings of Hungary, the more prestigious title they held was that of emperor of the Holy Roman Empire. That entity was a loose conglomera-tion of mostly small Germanic states that had existed since the Middle Ages.

While it is true that the Holy Roman Empire had limited political power, the title "emperor" carried great symbolic value and clearly enhanced the image of the Habsburgs (who with only one exception continually held the title after 1438) in the context of European dynastic politics.

At the outset of the eighteenth century, the Habsburgs had successfully removed the direct Ottoman presence from the Danubian Basin. This allowed them to consolidate their authority and strengthen the Austrian state through the implementation of wide-ranging reforms, which from the 1740s were implemented by the Habsburg rulers Maria Theresa and Joseph II. But even before Joseph's death in 1790, Habsburg Austria was faced by a new threat, this time from the west, specifically from Napoleonic France. The political upheavals that accompanied the French Revolution of 1789 within a few years had brought to power the ambitious military leader Napoleon Bonaparte. Napoleon was remarkably successful, so that by the outset of the nineteenth century he brought most of continental Europe under the direct or indirect rule of the French Empire. Among his adversaries was Habsburg Austria, which suffered several defeats at the hands of Napoleon's forces, but nevertheless remained for the most part territorially intact.

Napoleonic France did, however, extend its rule over most of the Germanic states of central Europe, and this inevitably had a significant impact on Habsburg Austria. When, in 1804, Napoleon assumed an imperial title that was hereditary, the Habsburgs followed suit. They concluded that the hereditary French imperial model was preferable to their status, which until then was that of elected emperors of the largely symbolic Holy Roman Empire (in any case abolished by Napoleon two years later in 1806). Therefore, the reigning Habsburg ruler proclaimed himself Francis I, emperor of Austria, a title that was to become hereditary among his successors. Consequently, each new Habsburg monarch was crowned at least twice, with the most important coronation occurring first in Vienna as the emperor of Austria, and then in Pozsony/Bratislava (the seat of the Hungarian Diet) as the king of Hungary. It was these two coronations which provided the legitimacy for Habsburg rule.

The threat posed by revolutionary France was finally brought to an end in 1815, following Napoleon's defeat on the battlefield of Waterloo (present-day Belgium) by a grand coalition of Russian, Prussian, British, and Austrian forces. The international peace conference which ended Europe's Napoleonic Era was held in 1815 in the Habsburg capital of Vienna. The choice of this location symbolized the fact that the Austrian Empire was acknowledged as one of the great powers in continental Europe. And, like its victorious allies Russia and Prussia, Habsburg Austria was determined to react quickly and decisively against any French-like anti-monarchical revolutionary ideas—whether real or suspected—that might surface within its borders. This was the birth of the conservative police state, which during the first half of the nineteenth century was best symbolized by Austria's influential chancellor and foreign minister, Prince Clemens von Metternich.

At the close of the Congress of Vienna in 1815, the Austrian Empire was, after the Russian Empire, territorially the second largest state in Europe.

It encompassed what are today the entire countries of Austria, the Czech Republic, Slovakia, Hungary, Slovenia, Croatia, and substantial parts of Italy (as far south as Tuscany), Romania (Transylvania), Serbia (Vojvodina), Poland (west Galicia), and Ukraine (east Galicia, Bukovina, and Subcarpathian Rus'/Transcarpathia). Although the empire functioned as a single political entity, it was internally divided into roughly two components, or "halves." The largest of the two components was the Hungarian Kingdom, a political entity made up of counties, several of which covered the southern portion of Carpathian Rus' (the Prešov Region and Subcarpathian Rus'). The other "half" of the empire was comprised of several lands, or provinces, such as Upper and Lower Austria, Tyrol, Styria, Bohemia, Moravia, Galicia, and Bukovina. In the course of the nineteenth century, the Austrian Empire lost most of its provinces in northern Italy (Lombardy-Venetia, Parma, Tuscany), but added a new one in the southeast, Bosnia-Herzegovina. Although the non-Hungarian half of the empire never had an official name, it was popularly known as Austria. Hence, Carpathian Rus' was divided between the two "halves" of the empire: the Prešov Region and Subcarpathian Rus' on the southern slopes of the mountains were in the Hungarian Kingdom; the Lemko Region on the northern slopes was in Austrian Galicia.

The large territorial expanse ruled by the Habsburgs encompassed a wide variety of peoples, in particular Austro-Germans, Magyars, and Slavs (Carpatho-Rusyns, Croats, Czechs, Poles, Serbs, Slovaks, Slovenes, Ukrainians), as well as Romanians, Italians, Yiddish-speaking Jews, Roma/Gypsies, and Armenians. Such ethnic diversity posed linguistic challenges to the Habsburg administrators. Ever since the Middle Ages, Latin had functioned as the official language in the Habsburg realm, a language that had the advantage of not being associated with any one nationality of the empire. But in the late eighteenth century that situation began to change, when in 1785 Joseph II decreed that German should be the official language for the entire empire. This move prompted the Magyars to propose that the Hungarian language should be used instead of Latin in the Hungarian Kingdom.

The other problem faced by the Habsburg authorities was the increasing spread of nationalism among many peoples of the empire. In many ways nationalism was an ideology that developed in the wake of the French Revolution. The French experience set a pattern whereby political legitimacy no longer rested in a monarchy or other hereditary ruler, but rather in the citizenry; that is, the people or nationality as a corporate entity. Another aspect of nationalism was derived from the writings of German thinkers, especially Johann Gottfried von Herder, who argued that every people throughout the world had its own particular worth and intrinsic value. Herder's views on the role of language as one of the most important and unique cultural values distinguishing a given nationality were particularly influential among the stateless peoples of central and eastern Europe, in particular Slavs living in the Austrian Empire. If, therefore, political legitimacy rested in the people, and if each people had equal cultural worth and

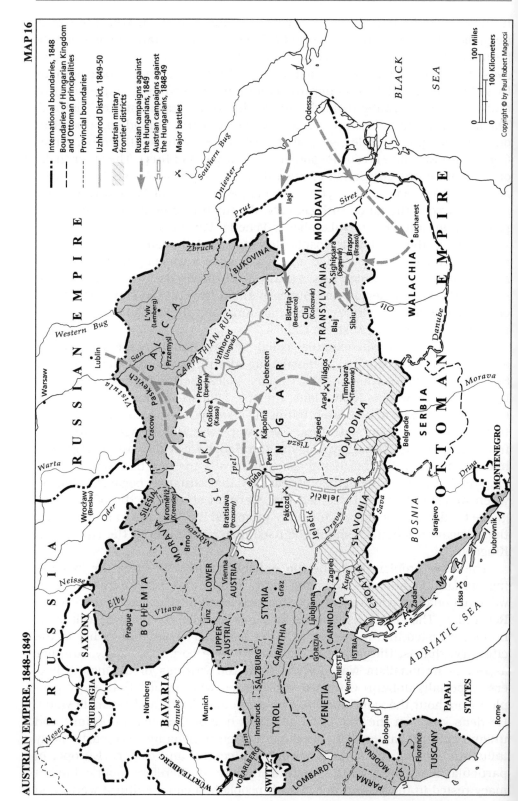

MAP 16

AUSTRIAN EMPIRE, 1848-1849

- ·-··- International boundaries, 1848
- ----- Boundaries of Hungarian Kingdom and Ottoman principalities
- ------- Provincial boundaries
- Uzhhorod District, 1849-50
- Austrian military frontier districts
- Russian campaigns against the Hungarians, 1849
- Austrian campaigns against the Hungarians, 1848-49
- ✗ Major battles

Copyright © by Paul Robert Magocsi

100 Miles
100 Kilometers

KAKANIA'S EMPERORS AND KINGS

In many places throughout Carpathian Rus', especially in small towns and cities, one may still see remnants of the Habsburg Empire. These usually take the form of the abbreviations, *k.u.k.* or *kir. mag.*, which appear on old signs, fire hydrants, and sewage manholes. The abbreviations refer to the titles of the empire's rulers. The status of the Habsburgs as Holy Roman emperors, Austrian emperors, and kings of Hungary, Bohemia, etc. was reflected in the German abbreviation *k.k.* for *kaiserlich königlich* (imperial-royal). After the compromise of 1867, distinctions had to be made between the three levels of government: the crownlands of Austria, the Kingdom of Hungary, and the ministries run jointly by Austria and Hungary.

The older German abbreviation *k.k.* for *kaiserlich königlich* (imperial-royal) was retained, but only for the Austrian "half" of the Habsburg monarchy; a new Hungarian abbreviation *kir. mag.* for *Király Magyar* (Royal Hungarian) was introduced for the Hungarian Kingdom; while the German abbreviation *k.u.k.* for *kaiserlich und königlich* (imperial and royal), implying equality between the two "halves" of the realm, appeared on documents and institutions related to the entire Austro-Hungarian Empire. The Hungarians liked the *k.u.k.* (imperial and royal) formulation, because it allowed them to pretend that the imperial aspect did not apply to Hungary.

It was the ubiquitousness of *k.k.* and *k.u.k.* in the public space that prompted some contemporary writers and commentators—the most famous of whom was the Austrian novelist Robert Musil—to call the Habsburg realm by the somewhat ironic designation *Kakania*.

value, then it followed that those peoples or nationalities should have the right to rule themselves, either in the form of cultural or political autonomy, or perhaps independent statehood. Not surprisingly, therefore, nationalism, whether in its more benign cultural version or its more "revolutionary" political version, was perceived as a threat to the major multinational empires of continental Europe, such as Russia, Austria, and eventually the Ottoman Empire in the Balkans.

Nationalism in Hungary

The Magyars, too, were transformed by nationalism. Although technically they had their "own" state, the Hungarian Kingdom, that entity was at the time largely subordinate to the imperial Habsburg rulers in Vienna. Therefore, when ideas of nationalism and its "liberating" power took hold throughout much of Europe in the first decades of the nineteenth century, activists in Hungary were also inspired by this ideology. In fact, in the 1820s Hungary embarked on what came to be known as its Reform Era, which was intimately connected with two prominent figures, Count István Széchenyi and Lajos Kossuth. Dubbed "the greatest Hungarian," Széchenyi wanted to modernize the economy of the kingdom, but in order to accomplish this

WHAT IS NATIONALISM AND WHAT ARE NATIONAL MOVEMENTS?

Nationalism and national movements are social phenomena that have been the subject of numerous studies that provide a wide range of interpretive explanations. The following provides an overview of how nationalism is understood in this book.

Stated most simply, nationalism is an ideology, which divides humanity into nationalities or peoples, and which argues that the optimal social system for nationalities is when they enjoy complete cultural autonomy and a large degree of political autonomy (self-rule). National ideologists argue that the ideal goal is for a nationality to have an independent state.

And what is a nationality? A nationality (often referred to in English as a nation) is a group of people which is united because they may have one or more of the following six common characteristics: (1) territory (possibly, but not necessarily statehood); (2) language; (3) historical tradition; (4) religion; (5) culture (ethnographic features); and (6) sociocultural values (*mentalité*). Aside from these six common characteristics, which can be considered concrete, observable objective factors, there are also two subjective factors that are important elements in defining a nationality: self-perception and will. What, however, is the interrelationship between these subjective and objective factors?

Many groups of people—often called ethnic or ethnographic groups—also have observable common characteristics. Group members may not realize, however, that they have things in common with each other and, hence, not realize that they belong to a larger national group or nationality. It is the existence of a sufficiently large number of people who perceive themselves as being united that makes the difference between a nationality and an ethnic or ethnographic group. In other words, members of a particular group have to want consciously to belong to a given nationality. Thus, both subjective factors (self-perception and a will or desire) and objective factors (observable common characteristics) are together what determine the existence of a nationality.

With regard to the objective factors and the six common characteristics, it should be noted that the presence or absence of any one characteristic does not in itself determine the existence of a nationality. Some national practitioners have argued that language is the so-called ultimate determining characteristic; that is, each people must have its own distinct language in order to be considered a nationality. One need only think of the Belgians, or Swiss, or Americans, among others (none of whom have their own language) to realize the false nature of the language-equals-nationality equation.

Having defined a nationality, what about national movements and the ideology behind those movements—nationalism? As a historic phenomenon, nationalism arose in Europe during the late eighteenth and early nineteenth centuries. It was in many ways a product of the French Revolution of 1789, in which the people and not the state or its leading representatives—whether a king, prince, or nobility—were held to be the supreme source of political legitimization.

Nationalism could also be seen to have evolved as a reaction to the spread of French dominance throughout Europe, whether in culture or in politics. This was particularly the case in the German lands at the outset of the nineteenth century. Patriotic writers and cultural activists, reacting to the presence of Napoleon's soldiers and to the widespread use of French language and cultural models by the German elite and ruling strata, began to argue that the German language and German culture were at least the equal of French and, as such, should be accorded respect, if nowhere else than in the German homeland.

Of even more general influence were the writings of another German, Johann Gottfried von Herder. A child of the Enlightenment and universalist values, Herder argued that every culture throughout the world had its own particular worth and value. Herder's influence was enormous throughout central and eastern Europe, because he seemed to provide a universally applicable justification for pride in one's own culture, which, in turn, was of great importance for individuals who stemmed from peoples living in countries where their own languages and cultures were unrecognized or even scorned.

While nationalism spread throughout Europe after the French Revolution, its application and goals varied from place to place depending on specific political circumstances. In effect, one can speak of two types or categories of nationalism: (1) state-imposed nationalism emanating from above, and (2) intelligentsia-inspired nationalism emanating from below.

The first category refers to already existing states, whose governments hoped to gain the allegiance of their subjects by trying to convince them that they belonged to a nationality associated with a particular state, such as Great Britain, France, Spain, Russia, or, in the case of Carpatho-Rusyns in the nineteenth century, Habsburg Austria or the Hungarian Kingdom under the scepter of the crown of St. Stephen. Hence, all citizens of those countries, regardless of their ethnic origin, nationality, or language, should declare themselves and be—or become—British, French, Spanish, Russian, Austrian, or Hungarian.

The second category refers to those groups who lived in multicultural states where a language and culture other than their own was dominant. In such circumstances, the group's self-appointed leaders, who came to be known as the national intelligentsia, worked to convince a given group of people that they formed a distinct nationality and as such were deserving, at the very least, of cultural autonomy if not political autonomy, or even better, independent statehood. Since Carpatho-Rusyns were a stateless people, their nationalism was of the intelligentsia-inspired variety.

Two other conceptual matters are worth bearing in mind. The first has to do with what social scientists have recently been fond of referring to as primordialism and constructivism. Traditionally, national ideologists are primordialists; namely, they argue that a national identity was in the blood or, more prosaically, passed on from generation to generation through one's "mother's milk." By contrast, constructivists argue that persons are not born with a national identity. Each person has to learn of his or her belonging to a particular nationality. Before the French Revolution and the beginning of the era of European nationalism, most peoples in Europe may have spoken a distinct dialect, and more often than not they would identify themselves according to a specific religion, a geographic area (city, region, etc.), or as the subject of particular ruler. At various times in the long historic nineteenth century (1780s–1914), activists among the nationalist intelligentsia set out to convince the members of a particular group of their belonging to a larger nationality. In other words, they were constructing an ideology—in this case a national identity— which they then set out to graft onto a group of people, a process which some scholarly analysts have described as creating a kind of "imagined community."

The constructivist project, if you will, was carried out by propagating nationalist ideas via the print media (newspapers and journals), village reading circles, urban-based cultural organizations (libraries, theaters, museums), sports clubs, and, in those cases where the ruling government was favorably inclined, through the educational system. The diffusion of a national identity depended, then, on a network of communication facilities which, in turn, were a function of the degree of urbanization, industrialization, and the general modernization of a given society. In this scenario, access to and control of urban areas became crucial for the success of national movements. This was particularly a challenge for many peoples in central and eastern Europe who lived primarily in the countryside and who comprised only a very small proportion of the inhabitants in towns and cities within or near "their" national homeland.

If the diffusion of national identity was a challenge to peoples without a state, another challenge was the problem of disagreement among the intelligentsia as to just what the proper national identity should be. More often than not among stateless peoples their intelligentsia was divided between factions identifying themselves with different nationalities. This was especially the case in areas like Carpathian Rus', where there were many nationalities. In a sense, the national movement resembled an ideological market place where rival factions propagated their wares. Since no one was born with a fully formed national conscience, then it was possible for an individual to be "nationally constructed"; that is, swayed by one or more of the competing factions. It was, therefore, not surprising to find in Carpathian Rus' individuals from the same indigenous population—whether from the same region, the same village, even the same family—opting to identify themselves as either Carpatho-Rusyns, Hungarians, Russians, Ukrainians, Slovaks, or Poles.

The other conceptual matter to keep in mind is what might be called the phenomenon of multiple loyalties versus mutually exclusive identities. In a sense, having multiple identities is the norm for most individuals in developed and developing societies. In other words, each individual has several potential identities from which to choose: a village, town, city, region, or state of residence; a religious orientation; and a language and/or ethnic group. Certain individuals also have strong loyalties and identify with the university they attended (there was a time when someone from Harvard was indeed different from a graduate of Yale or Princeton, not to mention different from a graduate of a state university), the social clubs to which they belong, the sports teams they support, or with a sexual preference, especially if it is not heterosexual.

In the case of multinational states or empires like Austria-Hungary, certain individuals could feel perfectly comfortable with more than one, what might be called, national identities. Hence, for residents of Carpathian Rus' it was perfectly normal to be both a Rusyn and Hungarian, or a Lemko and Austrian, then, after the close of World War I, a Rusyn and Russian and Czechoslovak, or a Rusyn and Ukrainian, or a Lemko and a Pole. But as the Carpatho-Rusyn movement evolved, some nationalist activists became convinced that in order for the movement to survive, the otherwise natural hierarchy of multiple loyalties or identities had to be replaced by a perceptual framework of mutually exclusive identities. Thus, one should not be Rusyn *and* Hungarian, or Lemko *and* Polish; one should be either one *or* the other, *not* both.

Finally, intelligentsia-inspired national movements can be viewed as going through at least three basic stages: (1) the heritage-gathering stage; (2) the organizational stage; and (3) the political stage. The first stage consists of efforts by individuals to collect the linguistic, folkloric, literary, and historical artifacts of a given people. The second stage is one in which organizations, schools, and publications are formed to propagate knowledge about the cultural heritage that has been collected. The third stage witnesses efforts at participation in political life, often with the intention of obtaining territorial self-rule (autonomy) or independence. During the century and a half beginning in 1848, Carpatho-Rusyns experienced all three stages, although the intensity and success of each varied on the period in which the three "national awakenings" took place: 1848–1867; 1919–1944; or 1989 to the present.

A NATIONALITY

Objective factors	Subjective factors
Common characteristics	Self-perception
territory	Will
language	
historical tradition	
religion	
culture (ethnographic factors)	
socio-cultural values (*mentalité*)	

NATIONAL MOVEMENTS

State-imposed nationalism	Intelligentsia-inspired nationalism
citizenship equals nationality	Multiple loyalties
	Mutually exclusive identities
	Developmental stages
	1. Heritage-gathering
	2. Organizational
	3. Political

he believed it was first necessary to reduce the power of the nobility and its numerous privileges, including its exclusive right of land ownership and exemption from taxes. Kossuth carried the message of reform further, calling as well for the emancipation of the peasantry from serfdom. Kossuth's voice resounded in the Hungarian Diet, where beginning in the year 1832 and for nearly the next two decades he delivered speech after fiery speech and published a popular newspaper (*Pesti Hírlap*), denouncing what he considered the injustices of Austrian imperial rule and even suggesting the possibility of dissolving the union of the Hungarian and Austrian crowns.

Symbolic of the Magyars' demand for greater rights and social transformation was the language question. Latin was still the official language of the Hungarian Kingdom, although already in 1792 Hungarian was made compulsory in schools. Only gradually did Hungarian replace Latin in other spheres of public life. For example, Count Széchenyi caused a sensation, when in 1825 he delivered a speech in the Upper House of the Diet that was not in "civilized" Latin or German, but rather in the "peasant" language—Hungarian. Kossuth was just as adamant in calling for Hungarian to become the state language, a goal that was finally achieved following the adoption of several language decrees between 1832 and 1844.

Since, however, less than half of Hungary's inhabitants were native Hungarian speakers, what should be done with the majority of the kingdom's non-Magyar inhabitants? Whereas Kossuth and Hungary's other liberal reformers were not against the use of other languages in private life, they accepted the new reality: since the 1790s Hungarian entered step by step different areas of public life, so that by 1844 it, in effect, had become the state language and only acceptable medium for official administrative matters and for education. The adoption of Hungarian became a corollary to the view that to be a citizen of Hungary one must be a member of the Magyar nation (*magyar nemzet*) and, preferably, speak Hungarian. These attitudes in the near future were to cause friction among the kingdom's many stateless peoples who themselves were striving for recognition of their own nationalities, languages, and cultures. The concept of the Magyar nation was summed up in a popular slogan: "One country—one language—one nation."[1] The use of a single word, *nemzet*, reflected a deliberate policy intended to fuse two distinct concepts: nation—citizenship in a state; and nationality—belonging to an ethnolinguistic or national group.

FROM INFERIORITY TO SUPERIORITY:
THE TRANSFORMATION OF A DANGEROUS COMPLEX

By the second half of the nineteenth century, the Magyars were the dominant state nationality of the Hungarian Kingdom. This was a time when the authorities of what by then was a self-governing state within the Habsburg realm not only embarked on a policy of national assimilation directed at the kingdom's non-Magyar inhabitants, but also seemed fully confident that their national identity and language were the only cultural features worthy to represent Hungarian society.

Such self-confidence, whether real or pretended, was something relatively new to Hungarian society and its leaders. In fact, Magyars were not only a numerical minority in their "own" kingdom, they—or perhaps more specifically their civic and intellectual leaders—exhibited many of the characteristics associated with most national minorities, a deep-seated inferiority complex.

In the 1830s, when the first modern census was complied by the Hungarian scholar Elek Fényes, the disturbing result was that only 40 percent of the kingdom's population was Magyar. Even after decades of a state supported magyarization policy, it was not until 1900 that a slight majority of inhabitants (51.4 percent) responded that they were Magyars. And, when Hungarian writers and publicists began to speak out about nationality issues, they could not help but remind their audiences that the Magyars, a non-Indo-European Finno-Ugric people in the heart of central Europe, were surrounded on all sides by a "sea" of Slavs to the north and south, Latinate Romanians to the east, and Germans to the west.

There was no shortage of commentary by observers outside Hungary, who pessimistically predicted that the Magyars and their language were destined to disappear. The most popular German-language Austrian playwright of the day, Franz Grillparzer, noted in 1840: "Hungarian has no future. Without links to any other European language and limited to a few million mainly uncultured people, it will never have a public, not to mention the fact that the Hungarian nation has never shown any talent in science or art."[a] None other than the father of cultural nationalism and the defender of the idea that every culture and language has intrinsic value worthy of preservation—moreover, someone who was sympathetic to Magyars— Johann Gottfried von Herder, felt himself compelled to admit in 1791 that "territorially surrounded as they are by Slavs, Germans, Romanians, and other peoples, within a century their [Hungarian] language is likely to disappear."[b]

Such views could not help but make thinking Magyars feel even more insecure. From their perspective, it was the Magyars who were most under threat, not the "national minorities" over whom they ruled. Such an understanding of Hungary's situation galvanized a patriotic response by the early-nineteenth-century reformers István Széchenyi and Lajos Kossuth, whose otherwise liberal views on the need to transform society and enhance the status of the Magyar nationality and Hungarian language were to be transformed in the second half of the nineteenth century into increasingly intolerant state policies directed at the national assimilation of the kingdom's non-Magyar inhabitants. Within large segments of society, the derogatory Hungarian phrase, *A kása nem étel, a tót nem ember* (Porridge is not food, and the Slovak is not a human being), summed up the condescending attitude of most Magyars not only toward the "inferior" Slovaks but also toward the Rusnaks/Rusyns. Consequently, within a generation the Magyar sense of inferiority was transformed into an overly confident sense of superiority, and this was to have very negative consequences for the kingdom's national minorities, not to mention eventual disastrous consequences for Hungary itself.

ª Cited in Paul Lendvai, *The Hungarians: A Thousand Years of Victory in Defeat* (Princeton, N.J., 2003), p. 200.

ᵇ Cited in George Barany, "Hungary," in Peter F. Sugar and Ivo J. Lederer, eds., *Nationalism in Eastern Europe* (Seattle and London, 1969), p. 264n15.

Revolution in the Austrian lands and Hungary

When, in mid-March 1848, revolution broke out in the Austrian Empire, the realm's various peoples reacted in different ways. The Austro-Germans, especially the liberal-minded urban educated professional classes in the imperial capital of Vienna, called for the immediate end of the police state and for the implementation of civil rights to be guaranteed by the adoption of a constitution and by the work of a democratically elected parliament. Austro-German spokespeople also called for the emancipation of the peasants from serfdom. The Hungarians, whose noble-controlled lower house of the Diet had been galvanized throughout the 1830s and 1840s by the passionate rhetoric of the popular leader Lajos Kossuth, wanted to end direct imperial rule and to govern the kingdom through a diet over which "their" Habsburg king would have only nominal authority. Their demands took the form of Twelve Points publicly announced in Pest on 15 March, which henceforth was to be remembered as the symbolic day that launched Hungary's "lawful revolution." The various Slavic peoples and the Romanians, also under the impact of nationalist ideology, wanted to attain some form of political autonomy or, at the very least, cultural autonomy within a restructured empire.

Somewhat surprisingly, the Habsburg authorities themselves reacted quickly, and in a sense they adopted their own "revolutionary" agenda. Already before the end of March 1848, the Habsburg emperor-king, Ferdinand, accepted Hungary's demands to form its own government. As for the "Austrian half" of the empire, in April the Habsburg authorities permitted the convocation in Vienna of an elected constitutional assembly (Reichstag); then, in May, they issued an imperial decree which ended unpaid labor that peasants traditionally owed to their lords, thereby effectively abolishing serfdom. These momentous political and socioeconomic innovations were to have a direct and immediate impact on the Austrian province of Galicia, which included the Lemko Region of Carpathian Rus'. The revolutionary fervor in the spring of 1848 prompted the various peoples throughout the Austrian Empire to make their own demands for some sort of national autonomy or self-rule. The differing and often conflicting demands and interests of the empire's peoples were overshadowed, however, by rapidly changing events in the Hungarian Kingdom.

In that other "half" of the empire, Hungary's Diet, inspired by the rhetoric of Kossuth and other young revolutionary-minded leaders, adopted a whole series of decrees (the so-called April Laws), which among other things abolished serfdom, ended the church tithe, and required the nobility to pay taxes. The proposed future government of Hungary was to be responsible to the elected parliament, whose seat was to be transferred from Pozsony/Bratislava to Pest, and whose lower house was to be made up of members elected by voters who had to own a certain amount of property and/or have a certain level of education as well as an active command of the Hungarian language. Despite such caveats, Hungary's April Laws effectively ended the era of feudalism and changed the status of the vast majority of Carpatho-Rusyns from that of proprietary serfs to free peasants.

The newly radicalized parliament, which created a Hungarian National Guard, refused to provide troops to aid the imperial forces in their efforts to suppress the outbreak of revolution provoked by Italian patriots in the Austrian-ruled provinces of northern Italy. Instead, at the urging of Kossuth, the Hungarian parliament in the summer of 1848 authorized the transformation of the National Guard (*Honvédség*) into a national army. Meanwhile, Hungary's Croats, Serbs, Romanians, and Slovaks had already proclaimed self-governing status and formed military units to defend their interests. The Habsburg imperial government not only allowed, but to a degree even supported, these developments in the hope that they would neutralize the Magyars. On the other hand, Kossuth and the Hungarian parliament were adamant that the territorial unity of the kingdom must in no way be jeopardized. Clashes with the kingdom's non-Magyar nationalities became inevitable, and by September a full-scale battle had broken out between the Hungarian Honvéd Army and the Croats. Since the Croatian forces, led by Count Josip Jelačić, had received authorization for their actions from the Habsburg emperor, Hungary was in effect at war with imperial Austria.

In the midst of these events, and as war was raging between the Hungarians and the Austrian imperial armies, Emperor Ferdinand abdicated and was succeeded in December 1848 by the young eighteen-year-old Franz Joseph, who was duly crowned in Vienna as emperor of Austria. This development provided a convenient excuse for the Hungarians, who declared that they were not legally bound to the new emperor, because he was not—as tradition demanded—crowned as king in Hungary. Meanwhile, hostilities continued, and the Hungarian forces and government were pushed eastward to the town of Debrecen. There, on 14 April 1849, the revolutionaries proclaimed the dethronement of the Habsburgs and elected Kossuth regent for an independent kingdom.

When Austria proved unable to suppress what was now a full-scale war to defend Hungary's independence, the young emperor, Franz Joseph, turned to Russia. He pleaded—literally on his hands and knees, kissing the hand of Tsar Nicholas I—for military assistance in "the holy struggle against anarchy."[2] In June 1849, no less than 200,000 tsarist Russian troops descended on Hungary from the north and east. The main force under Field Marshal Prince Ivan Paskevich entered Austrian Galicia and crossed Carpathian Rus' through the Dukla Pass before reaching Prešov on its way southward to the Danubian Basin. There, together with over 175,000 Austrian imperial troops, they fought the Hungarian national forces until they were finally forced to sur-render near the small village of Világos (today Şiria in west-central Romania) in August 1849. Therefore, it was thanks to the Russian tsar and to Hungary's Slavic and Romanian peoples who remained loyal to "their" emperor that the Austrian Empire was saved and able to remain territorially intact.

The Carpatho-Rusyn national awakening: politics

What impact did the Revolution of 1848 have on Carpatho-Rusyns, in partic-ular on those living in the Hungarian Kingdom? Not unexpectedly, the vast majority of the peasant population remained oblivious to the political and military events about which they had little real knowledge and over which they certainly had no control. The small percentage of Carpatho-Rusyns who did take an interest in civic affairs—mostly Greek Catholic priests and seminarians—for the most part greeted favorably and even enthusiastically the political demands of the Hungarian revolutionaries. As early as March 1848, many students at Uzhhorod's Greek Catholic seminary rushed to join Hungary's newly formed National Guard, and several priests planned to run in the elections to Hungary's new parliament. The enthusiasm of the hour was best summed up by an influential member of the Greek Catholic Eparchy of Prešov, the canon Viktor Dobrians'kyi, whose words reflected what he described as the traditional Carpatho-Rusyn loyalty to Hungary: "Hungarian freedom is dearer than Russian autocracy, and the pleasant atmosphere of Hungary is more attractive than the winters of Siberia."[3]

As it turned out, loyalty to Hungary was to be overshadowed by the activ-ity of canon Viktor Dobrians'kyi's brother, Adol'f Dobrians'kyi, a mining engi-neer who since the 1840s pursued a professional career in central Slovakia. There he participated in civic life and befriended many Slovak national activ-ists. Enthused by the revolutionary events in Vienna and Hungary, Adol'f Dobrians'kyi hoped that the rapidly changing political events would have a positive impact on the Habsburg Empire's Slavic peoples, including his own Carpatho-Rusyns.

In the spring of 1848, Slovaks put forth Dobrians'kyi as the candidate to represent their central Slovak district in the elections to the Hungarian par-liament, but his candidacy was sabotaged by Magyar nobles who managed to have, from their perspective, a more acceptable candidate (a magyarized German) elected instead. Not only was Dobrians'kyi unable to enter parlia-ment, he and his Slovak supporters were accused of Pan-Slavic agitation and threatened with arrest. For the next several months he had to main-tain a low public profile and, therefore, was unable to participate openly in another event of great symbolic importance. That event was the first Slavic Congress, which opened in June 1848 in Prague, where representatives of all the empire's Slavic peoples, except Carpatho-Rusyns, gathered to deliberate their future. Despite the absence of Carpatho-Rusyns, the petition put forth at the Slavic Congress by the Slovak delegation did include several proposals formulated by Dobrians'kyi, among which the very first was that "Slovaks and Rusyns be recognized as distinct nationalities and that they have representation in the Hungarian parliament equal to the Magyars."[4]

Before the end of 1848, Dobrians'kyi moved to Prešov, where together with local Carpatho-Rusyn activists he formulated a political program which was presented to Emperor Franz Joseph in January 1849. Dobrians'kyi hoped that in a restructured Austrian Empire a distinct Rusyn crownland would be created and would unite Hungary's Carpatho-Rusyns with the Rusyns of Austrian Galicia and Bukovina. His proposal was met with enthusiastic support from the Greek Catholic bishop of Prešov (Iosyf Gaganets') and from the Supreme Ruthenian Council in L'viv, which since May 1848 functioned as the main representative organ of the Ruthenians (Rusyns) in Galicia and Bukovina. Although the council in L'viv did not have any representatives from Hungary, Dobrians'kyi met with its leaders from whom he received encouragement, while Aleksander Dukhnovych published a long article in the council's newspaper that stressed the "desired union of all Austria's [and Hungary's] Rusyns into one province."[5]

The imperial authorities in Vienna were less enthusiastic about creating a single administrative unit that would cross the borders of Austrian Galicia and historic Hungary. Nevertheless, they did see in Dobrians'kyi a political ally. Hence, in April 1849 he was appointed civil commissar; that is, imperial Austria's liaison with the advancing tsarist Russian armies invited to help in the Habsburg struggle against the Hungarian revolutionaries. Thus, the most prominent Carpatho-Rusyn activist at the time was enlisted by the very forces which were to crush Hungary's efforts at creating an independent state. The anti-Hungarian position of Dobrians'kyi was to have negative consequences for him personally as well as for the entire Carpatho-Rusyn movement in the future.

As long as the Habsburg authorities were in control of the situation, however, Dobrians'kyi was protected and Carpatho-Rusyn national and cultural interests were promoted. After the Hungarian revolution was defeated, Dobrians'kyi returned to Vienna with a second petition to the emperor in October 1849. This time there was no reference to the Ruthenians/Rusyns of Austrian Galicia and Bukovina. Instead, this second petition called for recognition of the Rusyn nationality in Hungary and for the establishment of a distinct territorial entity where officials would be of Carpatho-Rusyn nationality and where the Rusyn language would be taught in schools and used in the local administration.

THE FIRST CARPATHO-RUSYN POLITICAL PROGRAM

The revolutionary events in the Habsburg Empire that began to unfold in March 1848 prompted Carpatho-Rusyns to formulate their own political demands. A key figure in this regard was Adol'f Dobrians'kyi. In April 1848, he cooperated with Czech and Slovak activists who were planning to hold a Slavic Congress in Prague.

When the congress took place in June of that year, several of the points in a petition submitted by the Slovak delegation included references, at Dobrians'kyi's sugges-tion, to Hungary's Carpatho-Rusyns.

Then, in January 1849, again at the initiative of Dobrians'kyi, Carpatho-Rusyns sub-mitted their own petition directly to Austria's new Habsburg emperor, Franz Joseph. In this petition, Dobrians'kyi made no distinction between the Rusyns of Hungary and the Rusyns in the Austrian provinces (crownlands) of Galicia and Bukovina. The petition called for the unification of "Hungarian Rus' with the Kingdom of Galicia and Lodomeria" to create a new crownland that would include within its borders all the East Slavs (Rusyns/Ruthenians) living in the Austrian Empire. Such a Habsburg Rus' entity would of necessity have to include territory from the Austrian "half" (East Galicia and Bukovina) and the Hungarian "half" (thirteen counties in the northeast) of the empire. Such a territorial entity which would cross historic borders was not, however, acceptable to the Habsburg authorities. Therefore, Dobrians'kyi had to reformulate Carpatho-Rusyn demands.

In the interim, the Austrian imperial government had proclaimed a constitu-tion in March 1849 and defeated the Hungarian revolutionary armies in August 1849, placing the Hungarian Kingdom under the direct rule of Vienna. It was in these changed political circumstances of a renewed neoabsolutist Austrian Empire that Carpatho-Rusyns turned to the Habsburg emperor in the expectation that he would approve a new set of political demands that focused specifically on the Carpatho-Rusyns of Hungary (Subcarpathian Rus' and the Prešov Region). Below are the ten points of the memorandum submitted to the Habsburg Emperor on 13 October 1849 over the signatures of the following Carpatho-Rusyn civic activists: Dr. Mykhailo von Vysanyk, imperial first physician; Adol'f Dobrians'kyi, imperial mili-tary commissar and knight of the [Russian] Order of St. Vladimir; Iosyf Sholtes, priest and advisor of the Greek Catholic Eparchy of Prešov; Aleksander Ianyts'kyi, parish priest of Malcov; Viktor Dobrians'kyi, secretary, notary, and advisor of the Eparchy of Prešov; and Dr. Vintsent Aleksovych, professor of medicine and director of St. Joseph's Hospital in Vienna.

1. We request the implementation of the Constitution of 4 March in all areas where our people live.
2. We request the recognition of the Rusyn nationality (*ruska narodnost'*) in the Royal Land of Hungary.
3. To distinguish our people from neighboring peoples, we propose the following: in those places where there are 15,000 Rusyns living in a compact settlement, even if mixed with a smaller number of other peoples, a separate Rusyn District should be created regardless of the boundaries of existing counties.
4. The Rusyn language (*ruskŷi iazŷk*) should be introduced into schools and govern-ment administration in the following manner: in Rusyn-inhabited areas the Rusyn language should be the language of instruction and a subject taught in elemen-tary schools; in each area where there is a significant concentration of Rusyns, a *gymnasium* should be created as should a Rusyn Academy in Uzhhorod, all at state

expense, and that our youth should be able to complete their studies at the university in L'viv.

In governmental offices in the Rusyn District, preference in hiring should be given to Rusyns by birth, and in general no one should be appointed who is not fluent in the [Rusyn] language.

5. A newspaper (*Vistnyk*) should be created in Vienna to be administered in cooperation with Galician Rusyns and, if necessary, be supported with funding from the state.
6. All forms of discrimination against publications in the Cyrillic alphabet should be lifted.
7. That the salaries of our civil servants, priests, teachers, and cantors be the same as those who hold such posts in other parts of the country.
8. That the Rusyn nationality be given appropriate consideration in appointments to officer ranks in the imperial army as well as in the central government administration in Vienna.
9. That Rusyn chaplains be appointed to those military units in which the majority of soldiers are of the Eastern rite.
10. With regard to peoples of other nationalities living in Rusyn areas and in consideration of mutual respect, all these peoples of other nationality should respect the national distinctiveness of the Rusyn district.

These, in brief, are the demands of the Rusyn people in Hungary.

SOURCE: "Vŷslanstva rusynov uhorskykh v Vidny pred vŷsokym mynysterstvom y Vsesvitlŷm Ieho Velychestva Tronom dilania misiatsa oktobriia 1849," in Mykola Rusynko, *Naukovyi zbirnyk Muzeiu ukraïns'koï kul'tury v Svydnyku*, VI, pt.1 (Bratislava and Prešov, 1972), pp. 70–71.

That same month the Austrian imperial government, which now administered the Hungarian Kingdom directly, divided it into military and civil districts. One of the civil districts was based in Uzhhorod and included the counties of Ung, Bereg, Ugocha, and Maramorosh; that is, Subcarpathian Rus'. As advisor and deputy to the district head, Dobrians'kyi effectively administered the Uzhhorod District, which he viewed as the basis of a future Rusyn administrative entity. In fact, many local officials in the Uzhhorod District were drawn from Carpatho-Rusyn inhabitants; the Rusyn language was introduced as a subject in secondary schools; and trilingual public signs were posted, which included Rusyn alongside Hungarian and German. It is also interesting to note that Carpatho-Rusyns living in counties farther west (Zemplyn, Sharysh, Spish) demanded that they be united with the Uzhhorod/Rusyn District. The view that all Carpatho-Rusyn inhabited lands south of the mountains should be united in one administrative unit was to be reiterated on numerous occasions, most particularly in the twentieth century.

Although the Uzhhorod District was to last only a few months, from October 1849 to March 1850, the desire for some kind of autonomous self-rule was reiterated on several occasions and was to remain part of the

Carpatho-Rusyn political agenda for the next century and a half. More immediately, however, were the Carpatho-Rusyn cultural achievements brought
about during the Revolution of 1848. These were associated for the most part
with another figure, the Greek Catholic priest Aleksander Dukhnovych.

The Carpatho-Rusyn national awakening: culture

Already on the eve of the revolution, Dukhnovych had published in 1847 the
first edition of his elementary school primer (*Knyzhytsia*) in the vernacular
Rusyn language. Two more editions of this popular textbook followed (1850
and 1852) as well as his *Sokrashchennaia grammatika pis'mennago russkago
iazyka* (Short Grammar of the Russian Literary Language, 1853). In order to
propagate these and other publications, in 1850 Dukhnovych established in
Prešov the first Carpatho-Rusyn cultural organization. Known as the Prešov
Literary Society (Lyteraturnoie zavedenie priashevskoe), it functioned for four
years, during which time it sponsored twelve publications, including the first
play in Carpatho-Rusyn literature (Dukhnovych's *Dobroditel' prevŷshaet'
bohatstvo*/Virtue Is More Important Than Riches, 1850) and the first
Carpatho-Rusyn literary anthologies, entitled *Pozdravlenie Rusynov* (Greetings
to the Rusyns, 1850, 1851, 1852). It was in the second of these anthologies
that Dukhnovych's poem "Vruchanie" (Dedication) appeared, a work which
eventually became the national hymn beginning with the famous phrase: *Ia
Rusyn bŷl, iesm' i budu* (I Was, Am, and Will Remain a Rusyn).[6] Even after the
Prešov Literary Society ceased to exist in 1853, Dukhnovych continued his
publication activity, including several histories of Carpatho-Rusyns, an influential pedagogical guide for teachers (*Narodna pedagogika*, 1857), and numerous religious texts, the most popular of which was *Khlīb dushy* (Bread for the
Soul), which by 1877 was already in its eighth edition and which continued to
appear in several more expanded editions until well into the twentieth century.

The sudden increase in publishing activity brought to the fore a challenging problem, that of a standard literary language. Ever since the debates
about the relationship of Carpatho-Rusyns to other East Slavs that began in
the 1820s and 1830s, Dukhnovych was inclined to associate his Carpatho-
Rusyn people with Russia. For instance, he recalled in his autobiography
how "One thing really gave me joy in life, and that was in 1849 when I first
saw the glorious Russian army . . . on the streets of Prešov" on its way to
crush the Hungarian revolution.[7] Dukhnovych and the political activist
Dobrians'kyi were both Russophiles; that is, they considered Carpatho-
Rusyns a branch of the Russian nationality, and they saw the Russian
Empire and its tsar as the best guarantor of the Eastern-rite Christian
faith and ultimately the only force that could save them from the danger of
national assimilation from the Magyars.

Having such convictions, it is not surprising that Dukhnovych,
Dobrians'kyi, and their followers believed that Russian was the most appropriate literary language for Carpatho-Rusyns. In reality, Dukhnovych
believed in the two-language principle: Rusyn vernacular for simple texts

intended for schoolchildren and semi-literate peasants, and literary Russian for more "serious" publications. Hence, the first newspapers published in Vienna in the 1850s and 1860s at the imperial government's expense and intended for the Ruthenians/Rusyns of Austria (Galicia and Bukovina) and Hungary (Prešov Region and Subcarpathian Rus') were in Russian—or more precisely were the best that Carpatho-Rusyns could do to write in Russian, a language they never formally studied.

In the end, all the rhetoric about affinities with Russian culture and language did nothing to change the reality of living in a state in which Hungarian was the official and dominant language for civic affairs and education. Ever since the 1830s, Dukhnovych had been lamenting the almost uncontrollable urge of educated Carpatho-Rusyns to magyarize themselves. In an attempt to reverse this trend, two new national societies were established in which Dukhnovych and Dobrians'kyi were the founders and/or the most active members: the St. John the Baptist Society in Prešov (1862) and the St. Basil the Great Society in Uzhhorod (1866). The primary goal of these organizations was to assist students and seminarians through the publication of textbooks in the Rusyn (or more properly Russian) language and through providing financial support for student dormitories in Prešov and Uzhhorod. These years also witnessed the opening in Uzhhorod of the first Cyrillic printshop in Carpathian Rus' (1863) and the founding of the first newspaper specifically for Carpatho-Rusyns, *Svît* (1867–71).

DID CARPATHO-RUSYNS REALLY LOVE THE RUSSIANS?

In the course of the nineteenth century, a certain portion of the articulate elements—the so-called intelligentsia—in Carpatho-Rusyn society looked with awe and respect on the powerful Russian Empire. They argued that Carpatho-Rusyns were themselves a branch of the Russian people and that they should use the Russian language for educational purposes and cultural discourse in general. Supporters of such Russophile views pointed, in particular, to the allegedly favorable encounter (not necessarily the first) of Carpatho-Rusyns with Russians, when in 1849 tsarist troops crossed into the Hungarian Kingdom to help save the Austrian Empire in its war against Hungary's revolutionaries. But how widespread was this supposed Carpatho-Rusyn affinity with the Russians?

It is certainly true that at the time of the 1848 revolution the prominent Carpatho-Rusyn political and cultural leaders Adol'f Dobrians'kyi and Aleksander Dukhnovych spoke about their "Russian brothers" as saviors from the East. A few decades later, Carpatho-Rusyn activists of Russophile persuasion were still expressing similar views. In an article titled, "The Russian People" (1865), the priest, poet, and publicist Aleksander Mytrak wrote:

> It is comforting to know that aside from us [Carpatho-Rusyns] there exist in the world a people who speak as we do, who pray to God in the same

churches as we do, and whose bravery, wealth, and—thanks to God—cultural level place them now and in the future among the leading peoples.[a]

The revolutionary events two decades earlier, in particular the arrival of tsarist Russian armies as they crossed the Carpathians in June 1849 on their way to crush the Hungarian revolution, were still being remembered with fondness and pride. Another Carpatho-Rusyn priest and poet, Ivan Sil'vai, who was an eyewitness to the 1849 events, claimed that the Carpatho-Rusyns, "upon hearing the Moscovite language, even began to speak with the *Moskali* [Russians] and were able easily to understand each other."[b] Emphasizing the alleged orderly conduct of the tsarist Russian troops, Sil'vai claimed that "our peasants continually helped carry baggage, while smiling children brought to the [army] camp apples, plums, and nuts. . . ."[c]

But did these glowing descriptions by Russophile apologists reflect reality? A perhaps more balanced picture was painted by someone who could not be accused of anti-Russian bias. This was none other than the grandson of Adol'f Dobrians'kyi, Igor Grabar, an accomplished impressionist painter who spent most of his life in the Russian Empire and then the Soviet Union, where he had a remarkably successful career as a historian of Russian art and long-time director of the prestigious Tretiakov Gallery in Moscow. On the eve of World War II, in the darkest days of Stalinist repression, Grabar published memoirs in which he recalled youthful summers in the 1870s on the estate of his grandfather at Čertižné in the Prešov Region:

> When we were kids, our elders tried in every way possible to correct our Ukrainian [read Rusyn] dialect, and to transform our speech into the literary [Russian] language. Particularly active in this regard was my maternal grandfather, Adol'f Ivanovich Dobrians'kyi, a striking and powerful personality who had an incredibly strong influence on me as a child.
>
> Grandfather devoted all his life to the struggle against the magyarization of the Russians [Rusyns] and Slavs in the Austro-Hungarian Empire. He was a fanatical defender . . . and was recognized as the leader of Slavdom in Austria-Hungary—his very name being the symbol of Slavic unity. . . . One should add that for my grandfather and father [Emilian Grabar], the 'Russian idea' was at that time identified with the formula: Autocracy, Orthodoxy, and Nationality [which characterized the reign of Tsar Nicholas I, 1825–1855].[d]

> . . . . . .

> Grandfather, who really loved me, often took me with him to his apiaries, and while collecting honey he told me various stories about the Emperor Nicholas I. . . . All those tales about the Russian troops in Hungary [in 1849] I still recall with sadness, as if in some faraway dreams. But I remember very well my confusion and uncomfortable feeling when, after hearing about these same events from the local Čertižné peasants— whether from eyewitnesses or from children recounting what their parents had told them—I made an unex-

pected discovery. Namely, that the praiseworthy exploits told with such pride by grandfather [Dobrians'kyi] were 30 years later still being cursed by the people of our district. What they recalled were the atrocities committed by Cossacks and *Moskali*. . . . I remember how mothers instilled fear in their children with threats that the *Moskali* were coming. I was terribly baffled by all of this, but I decided not to ask grandfather to explain this strange discrepancy, knowing that he would not tolerate such objections.[e]

[a] A. Mitrak, "Russkii narod," in *Mîsiatsoslov na hod 1866 dlia russkykh Uhorskiia krainŷ* (Uzhhorod, 1865), p. 54.
[b] Uriil Meteor (I. A. Sil'vai), *Avtobiografiia* (1898) (Uzhhorod, 1938), p. 42.
[c] Ibid., p. 43.
[d] *Igor Èmmanuilovich Grabar'* (Moscow and Leningrad, 1937), pp. 15–16.
[e] Ibid., p. 20.

In retrospect, the Revolution of 1848 initiated a period that has subsequently been remembered by historians of Europe as the "Spring of Nations" (or, more properly, nationalities). And this epithet is well deserved, certainly with regard to the many peoples of the Habsburg Empire. In the case of the Carpatho-Rusyns, in particular those in the Hungarian Kingdom, they experienced what in retrospect was their first national awakening. The revolutionary events of 1848–1849 provided a convenient opportunity for an energetic civic leader, Adol'f Dobrians'kyi, to formulate publicly for the first time the idea of a distinct Rusyn nationality. Even if political achievements were limited to a few months of a tenuous autonomy, that experience made an impression and remained in the collective consciousness of educated Carpatho-Rusyn society.

Perhaps even more important were the cultural achievements inspired by Aleksander Dukhnovych, soon to be immortalized as "the national awakener of Carpatho-Rusyns." The first readers, literary almanacs, literary and cultural societies, and national hymn were created by him during this period, while through him and several of his countrymen closer relations were established with the nationally more advanced Slovaks and with Rusyns/Ruthenians north of the mountains in Austrian Galicia. Hence, despite Dukhnovych's claims that the trend toward magyarization had already permeated Carpatho-Rusyn society, the 1860s were to witness the foundation of the first cultural organizations and the first newspaper specifically for Carpatho-Rusyns published in their homeland.

Yet, in another sense, Dukhnovych's long-standing fears were justified. The national awakening had no depth. Unlike other nationalities, Carpatho-Rusyns were thrust into the post-1848 political arena completely unprepared. They had not yet established a clear sense of their own identity, and they were only beginning to form a rudimentary organized cultural base. Thus, what subsequently came to be known as "the first Carpatho-Rusyn national awakening" remained the work of a few individuals, who in the short period of twenty years (1848–1867) were not able to affect the illiterate masses in any significant way.

How then, one might ask, did these leaders achieve the success that they did between 1848 and 1867? The answer is simple. They entered public life at the time when their Hungarian rulers were completely subordinated to Vienna and at a time when the Austrian imperial government felt it advantageous from time to time to give token support and encouragement to Carpatho-Rusyns and other peoples within their realm. This fortunate combination of events was to change after 1867, a year that ushered in a new era in the history of the Austrian Empire.

10

Carpathian Rus' in Austria-Hungary, 1868–1914

The promising beginnings in Carpatho-Rusyn civic and cultural affairs resulting from the Revolution of 1848 were to last for only two decades. The reason that this so-called first national revival came to an end had to do with larger political changes in the 1860s, which saw the transformation of the Austrian Empire into the Austro-Hungarian Dual Monarchy. The two halves of the empire henceforth developed in increasingly different ways, and this had a direct impact on the status of Carpatho-Rusyns. Those living on the northern slopes of the mountains in the Lemko Region benefited from the relatively more tolerant policies of Austrian-ruled Galicia toward its various peoples, while at the same time Carpatho-Rusyns on the southern slopes of the mountains in the Prešov Region and Subcarpathian Rus' were exposed to the increasingly intolerant attitude of the Hungarian government toward its national minorities.

The Dual Monarchy and Austrian parliamentarism

As long as the Habsburg imperial government was in political control of the Hungarian Kingdom, the civic and cultural activity of that realm's non-Magyar peoples was tolerated and, at times, even actively encouraged. By the 1860s, however, imperial Austria was forced in large part by external events (losses in wars with France and Sardinia in 1859 and with Prussia in 1866) to reassess its relationship with Hungary. Direct rule over the Hungarian Kingdom by Vienna was no longer feasible. Hence, after extensive negotiations, the two parties reached a compromise known as the *Ausgleich* of 1867. Implemented the following year, the agreement brought into being the Dual Monarchy. The Habsburgs remained the ruling monarchs as emperors of Austria and kings of Hungary. Also among the common concerns were some economic matters (currency, tariffs), the military, and foreign affairs, whose policies were decided jointly by Austrian and Hungarian representatives of the Dual Monarchy. Otherwise, Hungary was left to govern itself. In a sense, much of what the Hungarian revolutionaries had fought for in 1848–1849 was achieved through peaceful means two decades later with the *Ausgleich*/Compromise of 1867.

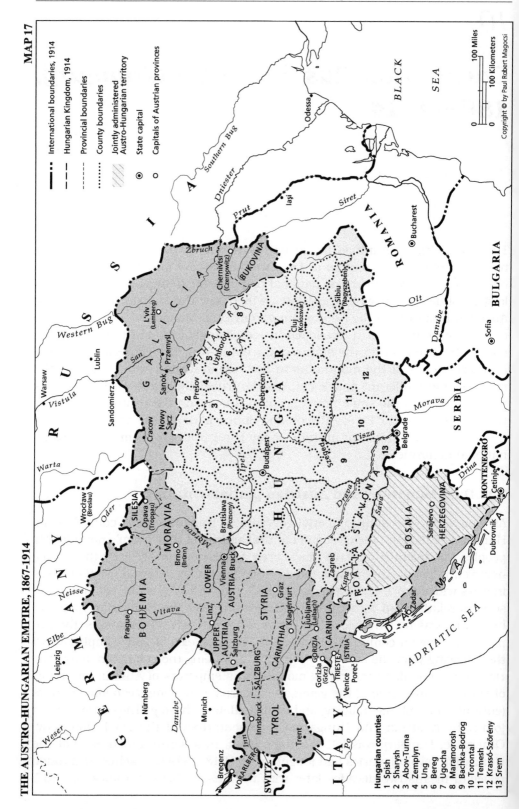

MAP 17

THE AUSTRO-HUNGARIAN EMPIRE, 1867-1914

International boundaries, 1914
Hungarian Kingdom, 1914
Provincial boundaries
County boundaries
Jointly administered
Austro-Hungarian territory
State capital
Capitals of Austrian provinces

100 Miles
100 Kilometers

Copyright © by Paul Robert Magocsi

Hungarian counties
1 Spish
2 Sharysh
3 Abov-Turna
4 Zemplyn
5 Ung
6 Bereg
7 Ugocha
8 Maramorosh
9 Bachka-Bodrog
10 Torontal
11 Temesh
12 Krassó-Szörény
13 Srem

The 1860s also witnessed important political changes within the Austrian half of the empire. This decade, which marked the birth of Austrian parliamentarism and the adoption of a constitution, was to have a direct impact on the province of Galicia, which included one part of Carpathian Rus', the Lemko Region. Beginning in 1861, elected representative bodies were created at the district, province, and imperial level. Every district had its own council (*Rada Powiatowa*), to which some Lemko-Region Rusyns were elected. Each of Austria's provinces had its own diet (German: *Landtag*; Polish: *Sejm Krajowy*), with the one for Galicia based in the provincial capital of L'viv (German: Lemberg; Polish: Lwów). Deputies to the Galician Diet were elected according to the so-called curia system, which allotted to four social strata a specific number of deputies. Since over half of the allotted deputies came from rural communes, the Lemko Region had the possibility to be represented; and it did send deputies to the Galician Diet. In the 1860s and 1870s, a few of those deputies were Carpatho-Rusyns—Seman Trokhanovskii, Mykhailo Starukh, and Petro Kotsylovskii—representing electoral districts that included the Lemko Region.

At the imperial level, the Austrian half of the empire had a bicameral parliament (Reichsrat) in Vienna in which the province of Galicia was allotted a relatively large number of seats in the lower house of deputies (106 out of 516 in 1907). While some Carpatho-Rusyns may have campaigned, throughout this period the Austrian imperial parliament had only one deputy (Volodymyr Kurylovych of Old Ruthenian orientation, born elsewhere in Galicia) elected in 1907 and again in 1911 to represent a district that included the Lemko Region. Regardless of who may or may not have been successful in being elected, the most important point was that the parliamentary structure put in place during the 1860s did allow Carpatho-Rusyns from the Lemko Region to participate directly in Austria's elected bodies at the district and province level.

Also of great significance was article 19 of the 1867 Austrian constitution, which proclaimed that "all peoples of the empire have equal rights and that each has an inviolable right to the preservation and use of its own nationality and language." [1] Therefore, the Habsburg state, at least its Austrian "half," recognized in public life what it called the "customary (*landesüblich*) language" of a given people, which eventually came to mean the vernacular speech of Lemkos and other Rusyns of Galicia.

In search of a Rus' national identity

From the standpoint of the Austrian imperial authorities, they made no distinction between Carpatho-Rusyns in the Lemko Region and the rest of the East Slavic population of Galicia. All were classified as *Ruthenen*, the German form of Ruthenian/Rusyn. On the one hand, it is true that proportionate to their numerical size and in comparison with Galicia's Poles, Ruthenians were underrepresented in the district councils, in Galicia's provincial diet, and in the Austrian imperial parliament. On the other hand, the Ruthenian deputies in the diet and parliament were successful in lobbying for state funds to support education in the native language, and they operated legally within a political system that allowed legally sanctioned Ruthenian political parties, civic organizations, cultural societies, and a wide range of newspapers and other publications. All these factors worked to the advantage of the Carpatho-Rusyns in the Lemko Region when they finally began to mobilize as a civic and national community in the last decades of the nineteenth century.

By that time Galician-Ruthenian cultural life was characterized by a division between three orientations which had markedly differing views on the national identity of the province's East Slavs. The adherents of those national orientations were known as Old Ruthenians, Russophiles, and Ukrainophiles. The Old Ruthenians accepted the view that all the East Slavs were closely related and part of a single Rus' culture that was best expressed through their adherence to Eastern Christianity and the use of a language which they called *ruskii*—basically traditional Church Slavonic with some vocabulary drawn from the Galician-Rusyn spoken vernacular. Despite their cultural association with the larger East Slavic world, the Old Ruthenians were for the most part loyal to the Habsburg Empire. It was the Old Ruthenians who dominated Galician Rus' civic and cultural life during the three decades that began with the Revolution of 1848, and it was with them that Subcarpathian activists from the Hungarian Kingdom identified, as epitomized in the poetic verse of Aleksander Dukhnovych: "Your people beyond the mountains are not foreign to us / for Rus' is one, a single idea imbedded in all our souls."[2]

Galicia's Russophiles, like the Old Ruthenians, also believed in the ethnocultural unity of all the East Slavs. They, however, favored the use of Russian as the appropriate literary language for Ruthenians. They also considered Orthodoxy the "truest" variant of Eastern-rite Christianity and the Russian Empire the best guarantor of the group's national existence, some even looking forward to the day when Galicia would be annexed to the tsarist realm and again be together with fellow East Slavs in one state as—so they argued—had been the case in medieval Kievan Rus'. In turn, Russia's imperial government, the Orthodox Church, and its secular intelligentsia expressed in various ways their concern with what was now referred to as *Zagranichnaia Rus'*, that is, Rus'/Russia beyond the empire's current borders. Russia's neo-Slavism movement helped inspire journalists, editors, and scholars to focus on the plight of their Slavic brethren in the Balkans and in central Europe, most particularly on their "closest relatives," the East Slavs living "under the yoke" (*Podiaremnaia Rus'*) of Austria-Hungary. Such calls did not fall on deaf ears, so that a new generation of Russian scholars (Ivan A. Filevich, Vladimir A. Frantsev, Fedor F. Aristov, and Aleksei L. Petrov, among others) devoted many of their publications to what they called Carpatho-Russians.

Finally, there were the Ukrainophiles, or populists as they were known at the time, who were inspired by the Ukrainian political theorist from the Russian Empire, Mykhailo Drahomanov. During a visit to Austrian Galicia in the 1870s, Drahomanov inspired a group of younger intellectuals (Ivan

Franko, Volodymyr Hnatiuk, Ivan Verkhrats'kyi, and Stepan Tomashivs'kyi, among others), who for the next several decades until the outbreak of World War I in 1914 undertook research projects focussing not only on the Lemko Region and Hungarian Rus' but also on the Vojvodinian Rusyns in Hungary's southern lowlands. Galicia's populist Ukrainophiles stressed national and linguistic differentiation, arguing that the East Slavic peoples—Russians, Belarusans, and Ukrainians—were distinct nationalities, each with its own national language. As for the Ruthenians/Rusyns of Galicia as well as of Bukovina and northeastern Hungary, they were considered a branch of the Ukrainian nationality.

The extensive civic and cultural work of the populists did, indeed, contribute to the increasing success of the Ukrainophile orientation throughout much of eastern Galicia and Bukovina. Nevertheless, during the Austro-Hungarian era down to 1918 as well as for much of the subsequent interwar decades, Carpatho-Rusyn national activists in northeastern Hungary (Subcarpathian Rus' and the Prešov Region) and especially in Galicia's Lemko Region remained primarily inclined toward the Old Ruthenian and Russophile orientations.

The national awakening in the Lemko Region

The earliest organizations designed to serve the cultural interests of Lemko-Region Rusyns were village reading rooms. Beginning sometime in the 1880s, they were set up in separate small buildings or were attached to the local school or parish. The reading room was a place where villagers could find newspapers as well as books and pamphlets about agricultural matters, Austrian civic life, the Rus' historical past, and literary works, all of which were written in Russian or in a language (*ruskii*) close to the Lemko-Rusyn vernacular. The Old Ruthenian-oriented civic and cultural organization known as the Kachkovs'kyi Society/Obshchestvo im. Mikhaila Kachkovskoho was the most active in this regard. Although its central headquarters were in L'viv, the society had several local affiliates, two of which were responsible for the Lemko Region and based in Nowy Sącz and Sanok. It was these affiliates which operated over a hundred reading rooms, so that on the eve of World War I over one-third of all Lemko-Rusyn-inhabited villages had a Kachkovs'kyi Society reading room.[3]

Sanok, which at the time was the main center for Lemko-Rusyn cultural activity, had besides a Kachkovs'kyi Society reading room also a civic center (Narodnŷi Dom). These institutions encouraged the work of a theatrical circle (Dramatychnŷi kruzhok) whose performances in Rusyn were especially popular in Lemko villages. All these Sanok-based institutions, as well as credit and insurance societies which served the practical needs of village agriculturalists, were of the Old Ruthenian or the Russophile orientation.

Another type of organization serving the Lemko Region was the *bursa*. This was a self-governing educational and cultural society, whose main function was to operate dormitories (*bursŷ*) for needy Lemko Region students attending secondary schools located in towns just to the north of the Lemko Region and where Polish was the language of instruction. The first Ruska/ Rusyn Bursa was established in Nowy Sącz in 1898, followed by two others in Sanok (1908) and Gorlice (1908). Aside from providing housing accommodations, the *bursas* sponsored a wide range of programs that promoted Rus' culture (in particular from a Russophile perspective) among young Lemko Region Rusyns who, in their formative student years, found themselves in an otherwise predominantly Polish (and in part Jewish) urban environment.

By the outset of the twentieth century, the Ukrainian national orientation was particularly well developed in Austrian Galicia. Therefore, it is not surprising that Ukrainian-oriented cultural and civic organizations based in L'viv would try to extend their influence to a region and people—Lemko Rusyns—which they considered to be the farthest western branch of the Ukrainian nationality. The most important in this regard was the Prosvita (Enlightenment) Society/Tovarystvo "Prosvita," which set up its first Lemko village reading room in 1893 (in Odrzechowa) and during the decade later formed affiliates in Nowy Sącz, Jasło, and Sanok. Often staffed by Ukrainian-oriented activists from East Galicia, the three affiliates managed by 1914 to set up Prosvita Society reading rooms in 22 Lemko villages, where the Ukrainian language and national ideology were promoted through publications and cultural programs.[4] Ukrainophile activists also established a *bursa* in Nowy Sącz as well as several associations in that city and in Sanok, although their grassroots work in Lemko villages (at least in the period before World War I) did not reach the extent and level of activity carried out by the Ruthenian-oriented Kachkovs'kyi Society.

Despite the best efforts of mentors at the student *bursas* and other civic organizations, the underdeveloped Lemko Region and nearby towns allowed for only very limited career opportunities. For especially talented young people who wished to advance their professional careers, it was necessary to do so in the Polish environment of Galicia's main cities, Cracow and L'viv, the imperial capital of Vienna, or abroad. Even today few people know that several individuals noted for their achievements in late-nineteenth-century "Polish" Galicia were of Lemko origin, among them the Jagiełłonian University professor of chemistry Emilian Chŷrnianskii/Czyrniański, the professor of medicine and founder of the first museum of medicine Valerii Sas-Iavorskŷi/Walery Sas-Jaworski, and the jurist and deputy speaker of the Galician Diet Iuliian Lavrivskii/Lawrowski. Even more common was for natives of the Lemko Region to rise to the highest ranks of the Greek Catholic Church, including two metropolitans of L'viv, Iosyf Sembratovych and Silvester Cardinal Sembratovych, the distinguished church historian and bishop of Przemyśl Iuliian Pelesh, and the L'viv-based theologian Tyt Mŷshkovskii. In contrast to many Carpatho-Rusyn intellectual and professional figures in the Hungarian Kingdom who often—and with enthusiasm—took on a Magyar identity, Lemko Rusyns who worked outside their homeland did not opt to become polonized but rather remained loyal to their Rus' heritage usually in association with the Old Ruthenian orientation.

The last decades of the nineteenth century also coincided with what can be considered the beginning of Lemko-Rusyn belles lettres. Closely linked as they were to Old Ruthenian and Russophile-oriented institutions, most of the poetry and prose writings that appeared on the pages of newspapers and a few individual books were written in the so-called *iazŷchiie*; that is, the Russian language with strong influences from Church Slavonic and the Lemko spoken vernacular. The most prolific writers at the time were Vladymir Khŷliak and Petro Polianskii.

It was not until the appearance of the newspaper *Lemko* in 1911 that authors began to write in the Lemko-Rusyn vernacular. The newspaper's very name suggested that the traditional ethnonym, *Rusnak* or *Rusyn*, should be replaced by the name *Lemko*. Perhaps the reason for the suggested change had to do with the rather vague nature of the term *Rusyn*, which at the time was used to describe all the East Slavs, or Ruthenians of Galicia, including those who were of Ukrainian orientation. Since Ukrainian-oriented individuals used the terms *Ukrainian* and *Rusyn* as synonymous ethnonyms, some national activists in the Lemko Region proposed that they should use another name. Hence, in an effort to distance themselves from fellow Galician Rusyns/Ukrainians, they replaced their traditional ethnonym, *Rusnak/Rusyn*, with *Lemko*, thereby initiating a gradual process of name change in 1911 that was to take another two decades before it was adopted by the population as a whole.

Hungary and its magyarization policies

In contrast to the relatively favorable conditions for national development in Austrian Galicia after 1861, the political environment of the Hungarian Kingdom was much less democratic in nature. Hungary did have its own parliament (*Országgyűlés*) based since 1848 in Pest (after 1873 Budapest) with two chambers: an appointed upper House of Magnates and an elected lower House of Deputies. Members of the lower house were chosen according to a complicated franchise system based on property, taxation, profession/official position, and ancestral privileges. As a result, most peasants and townspeople were excluded from voting. Nevertheless, some Carpatho-Rusyns did become members of the Hungarian Parliament in the last decades of the long nineteenth century, including all Greek Catholic bishops who were automatically members of the parliament's upper house and several secular professionals (usually lawyers) and some clergy who were chosen as deputies to the lower house.

A few of these parliamentarians even spoke out on behalf of Carpatho-Rusyn interests, such as Adol'f Dobrians'kyi, who in the 1860s promoted a program of territorial autonomy for all the nationalities of Hungary, including Carpatho-Rusyns; or Bishop Iulii Firtsak, who in the 1890s managed to convince the government to implement economic reforms in order to improve the status of peasant farmers in the Carpathian highlands. It was more common, however, for elected deputies of Carpatho-Rusyn origin to remain passive (like the future governor of Subcarpathian Rus', Antonii Beskyd) or to support the pro-government parties with which they were aligned.

The status of Carpatho-Rusyns and other nationalities of the Hungarian Kingdom changed radically, and for the worse, in the decades after the Austro-Hungarian *Ausgleich*/Compromise of 1867. Already in 1868 Hungary's parliament enacted a law "on the equality and rights of nationalities." On the one hand, this was a liberal law declaring that each citizen, regardless of his or her national background, was a member of "the indivisible, unitary Hungarian nation [Hungarian: *magyar nemzet*]."[5] Put another way, each individual would be treated equally, but on one condition: that he or she become—or at least publicly identify as—a Hungarian (*magyar*). For centuries, the concept *Hungarian* referred to a civic identity; that is, to any

MAGYARIZATION DESPITE THE LETTER OF THE LAW

In the Hungarian Kingdom as in many countries, the letter and spirit of laws, however liberal, were not necessarily implemented in practice. The contradiction between the spirit and practice of the 1868 national minorities law was already evident during the period from 1875 to 1890, when Hungary's longest-ruling prime minister, Kálmán Tisza, was in power. As head of the Liberal party, Tisza was committed to the national assimilation of the kingdom's non-Magyar peoples, in particular Slovaks and Carpatho-Rusyns.

The late-nineteenth-century atmosphere of magyarization was perhaps best summed up by the distinguished twentieth-century British historian Carlisle Macartney, who, despite sympathy for Hungary, was known and respected for his impartiality.

> ... [T]here were some officials (more than is generally admitted) who continued to treat the non-Magyar public ... sensibly and paternally, even if they did so as the representatives of a Magyar State. Others made it a patriotic virtue to behave worse even than the recognized practice laid down. The conduct of administration and justice were magyarized, down to the lowest level, not only in all internal transactions, but, largely, in the outer services; [consequently], notices to the public, even in purely non-Magyar districts, were in Magyar [Hungarian] only, as were all proceedings in the courts; a defendant could employ an interpreter, but had to pay for his services. The Magyar national culture was treated as the only one deserving respect, or even legitimate, in Hungary; the others were, at best, tolerated contemptuously. Any attempts to cultivate them above the humblest level and even where specifically authorized by the National Law were regarded as potentially or actually treasonable; [they were] always discouraged and, whenever a plausible excuse could be thought up, [they were] forbidden.

SOURCE: C. A. Macartney, *The Habsburg Empire, 1790–1918* (New York, 1969), pp. 722–723.

resident of the Hungarian Kingdom regardless of his or her ethnic origin. Problems arose, however, when *Hungarian* began to be understood as someone not simply of Hungarian speech (*magyar nyelv*) but of Magyar ethnicity.

Although the 1868 law on national minorities made Hungarian the official language of the kingdom, it also provided guarantees for the use of other languages in local administrative matters and for instruction in elementary and high schools. Despite the liberal nature of the law, in subsequent decades its spirit was undermined with the result that non-Hungarian languages were gradually pushed out of use in administrative settings and the school system. Moreover, nationalities as a group or corporate entity were not protected, with the result that national organizations like the Slovak Cultural Foundation (Matica slovenská) were forced to cease operations by the mid-1870s. Whatever organizations that still existed were able to survive only under the cloak of some other purpose, either religious or educational.

This was precisely the case for organizations serving Carpatho-Rusyns, such as the St. John the Baptist Society in Prešov and the St. Basil the Great Society in Uzhhorod. Although these institutions continued some civic and publication activity, the Hungarian authorities allowed their further existence because they were primarily concerned with educational activity: providing accommodations and assisting students and seminarians while they were living in towns that were far from their native Carpatho-Rusyn villages. In contrast to Austrian Galicia and the Lemko Region, where reading rooms propagated national ideals and some form of the Rus' language, there was nothing similar in Carpatho-Rusyn villages in the Hungarian-ruled Prešov Region and Subcarpathian Rus'.

Also in contrast to Austrian Galicia, the Hungarian government initiated in the 1870s a policy of national assimilation. Known as magyarization, its goal was to assimilate as many members of the various nationalities as possible and to transform them into Magyars. Magyarization proved especially successful among that small stratum of the Carpatho-Rusyn population which completed schooling beyond the elementary level. This applied especially to the Greek Catholic seminarians and priests, most of whom enthusiastically welcomed the possibility to speak Hungarian at home and, for all intents and purposes, to act and function as Magyars. The tenor of church life was set by the ruling hierarchy, and several Greek Catholic bishops in both the Prešov and Mukachevo eparchies (Nykolai Tovt, Ioann Valyi, Shtefan Pankovych, Antonii Papp) were among the most avid promoters of magyarization.

The most extreme example of the magyarization fever occurred among that portion of the Carpatho-Rusyn secular intellectual elite which left their provincial homeland for the country's capital of Budapest and other Hungarian cities. There, several were able to make very successful careers as high-ranking state functionaries (Jenő Szabó/Ievmenii Sabov, István Pásztély/Shtefan Pastelii, Oreszt Szabó/Orest Sabov), judges (János Pásztély), artists (Ignácz Roskovics/Ignatii Roshkovych, Ödön Szamovolszky/ Edmund Samovol's'kyi), and university professors (József Illés-Illyasevits/ Iosyf Illeish-Illiashevych, Antal Hodinka/Antonii Hodynka).

Most of these secular figures remained loyal to the Eastern rite of their forefathers (several were sons of Carpatho-Rusyn Greek Catholic priests), but they wanted their church to be more "Hungarian" in spirit. Hence, they were joined by other assimilated Carpatho-Rusyn secular activists in Budapest (Kálmán Demko, Emil Demjanovics, Sándor/Aleksander Bonkáló, among others), who started a movement calling for the replacement of Church Slavonic with Hungarian as the liturgical language of the Greek Catholic Church. Although this was in violation of the Vatican's proscription against the use of vernacular languages for sacred purposes, these Carpatho-Rusyn magyarizers eventually succeeded in their goal.

CARPATHO-RUSYNS IN HUNGARIAN POLITICS

There is a common perception that Carpatho-Rusyns had no experience in politics and government until the onset of Czechoslovak rule after World War I. Such a view was, in particular, promoted by officials and historians of Czechoslovakia who argued—and still argue—that only that country brought after 1919 participatory politics and governmental experience to Carpatho-Rusyns. The historical record suggests otherwise.

Despite the unrepresentative nature of Hungarian political life before World War I, Carpatho-Rusyns were, in fact, either appointed or elected to both houses of Hungary's Royal Parliament. Every Greek Catholic bishop of the Eparchies of Mukachevo and Prešov, beginning with Andrei Bachyns'kyi in 1790 and lasting until the collapse of Austria-Hungary in 1918, automatically held seats in the parliament's upper house. One member of the upper house was a secular figure appointed in 1902 to that chamber for life by the king, the state official Jenő Szabó, son of a Carpatho-Rusyn priest of pro-Hungarian orientation.

No fewer than 21 Carpatho-Rusyns were elected to the lower house of deputies between 1848 and 1910. Nor were all of them passive supporters of Hungarian governmental policies. Among the deputies was none other than the "national awakener of Carpatho-Rusyns," Aleksander Dukhnovych, who served for a short time in 1847–1848 as an appointee of the Eparchy of Prešov. Much more active and outspoken in his criticism of Hungary's policies toward the country's national minorities was Adol'f Dobrians'kyi, who was elected to parliament on three occasions (1848, 1861, and 1867).

Aside from parliamentary deputies, Carpatho-Rusyns also served in the governmental structures of their Subcarpathian homeland, whether as county lord sheriffs/*zhupans,* vice sheriffs, city mayors, or notaries. The political and civic experience gained by parliamentarians, state officials, judges, lawyers, and notaries of Carpatho-Rusyn background in pre-World War I Hungary was not lost on some, such as the state functionary Oreszt Szabó (Hungary's minister for postwar Ruska Kraina), parliamentary deputy Antonii Beskyd (future governor of Czechoslovakia's Subcarpathian Rus') , and the lawyer Miklós Kutka-Kutkafalvy and legal scholar József Illés-Illyasevits/Iosyf Illesh-Illyashevych (future activists in the irredentist movement on behalf of Hungary's efforts to reacquire Subcarpathian Rus').

Already in 1873, the Hungarian government created a Greek Catholic vicariate based in the eastern Hungarian town of Hajdúdorog. Several decades later, in 1912, the vicariate was raised to the status of an eparchy by detaching 162 parishes (mostly from the eparchies of Mukachevo and Oradea) in an area that coincides primarily with present-day northeastern Hungary. Through an interesting ruse that subverted Vatican proscriptions against vernacular languages, these parishes soon began to use only Hungarian in church services. The point is that this entire struggle, which lasted from the 1870s until the eve of World War I, was carried out by avidly pro-Hungarian secular and clerical activists of Carpatho-Rusyn origin, who justified their actions on the grounds that they were not Slavs but rather "Magyars of Greek Catholic faith," whose church should preferably be designated as Hungarian Catholic of the Eastern rite.

Carpatho-Rusyns and national survival

To be sure, not all educated Carpatho-Rusyns favored magyarization and national assimilation, but those in opposition, who were of the generation that promoted the national movement after 1848, were rapidly in decline. Aleksander Dukhnovych himself died in 1865, and while Adol'f Dobrians'kyi lived on until the end of the century, he was effectively removed from Carpatho-Rusyn affairs. Not surprisingly, his Pan-Slavic and Russophile views were unwelcome both to the Hungarian authorities, who succeeded in removing him from his parliamentary seat in 1869, and to the pro-Hungarian Greek Catholic bishop of Mukachevo (Shtefan Pankovych), who forced him to resign from the St. Basil the Great Society in 1871. Dobrians'kyi emigrated eastward and lived for a few years in the Russian Empire. When he did return to the Habsburg realm, the Hungarian prime minister (Kálmán Tisza) succeeded in having him implicated with several Galician Old Ruthenians and Russophiles in a treason trial held in L'viv (1882). Although acquitted, Dobrians'kyi was forced into internal exile, spending the rest of his days in the farthest western edge of the Austrian Empire, in the Tyrolian city of Innsbruck.

Dobrians'kyi's fate was repeated in less dramatic ways by several other Russophile national activists who were forced to take up posts in other parts of the Austro-Hungarian Empire (Kyryl Sabov, Iurii Ihnatkov), or who opted to emigrate abroad and live permanently in the Russian Empire (Viktor Kymak, Mykhaïl Molchan, Emanuïl Hrabar). Among those who remained at home were figures like the newspaper editor and publicist Ioann Rakovs'kyi, the lyrical poets and folklorists Aleksander Pavlovych, Iulii Stavrovs'kyi-Popradov, and Anatolii Kralyts'kyi, the dictionary complier Aleksander Mytrak, the ethnographer and essayist Ivan Sil'vai, and the belletrist and editor, Ievhenii Fentsyk. Following in the footsteps of Dobrians'kyi and Dukhnovych, these figures were Russophiles and sympathizers of Pan-Slavism, who believed that if Carpatho-Rusyns would ever be able to survive in an increasingly magyarized Hungary, they could only do so by associating themselves with the Russian language and Russian culture. And lest one assume that the entire Greek Catholic clergy were magyarizers, it should be pointed out that virtually all the followers of Dobrians'kyi and Dukhnovych were Greek Catholic priests working in isolation in rural villages and more often than not out of favor with their bishop because of their eastern "nationalist" activity.

An alternate view regarding national survival was put forth by a new generation of activists—some but not all of whom were also Greek Catholic priests—who came onto the scene in the 1880s and 1890s. Among them were Laslo Chopei, Ievmenii Sabov, Iurii Zhatkovych, Avhustyn Voloshyn, Hiiador Stryps'kyi, and Mykhaïl Vrabel'. Rather than look to Russia, these activists focused on their own Carpatho-Rusyn culture as a source of pride, and they actively or passively promoted the view that the appropriate language for education and publications should be based on the spoken Rusyn vernacular. These figures believed that one could simultaneously be a Carpatho-Rusyn patriot *and* a loyal citizen of Hungary, views they promoted on the pages of two popular Rusyn-language newspapers that began to appear in the last years of the nineteenth century, *Nauka* (1897–1914), edited by Avhustyn Voloshyn, and *Nedîlia* (1898–1919), edited by Mykhaïl Vrabel'.

In the end, however, all these Carpatho-Rusyn activists, whatever their national orientation, represented but a handful of people fighting an uphill and seemingly futile battle against the overwhelming forces of the Hungarian state and its magyarization policies. Even the benign St. Basil the Great Society, whose main function was limited to publishing an annual almanac, the Rusyn-language newspaper *Nauka* and the Hungarian-language newspaper *Görög katholikus szemle*, was under increasing attack by Magyar and pro-Hungarian Carpatho-Rusyn publicists alike. The pro-Hungarians (or Magyarones) were particularly critical of publications which used the Cyrillic alphabet, since that in and of itself allegedly made the readers susceptible to Pan-Slavic and Russian propaganda. As a result of pressure from pro-Hungarian Greek Catholic bishops, the last Carpatho-Rusyn organization in Hungary, the St. Basil the Great Society, dissolved itself in 1902.

More serious from the standpoint of the survival of any stateless nationality was the school system. Here government policy differed, depending on whether a given school was operated by the state or by the church. The 1868 nationalities law was still in effect, so that instruction in languages other than Hungarian, including Rusyn, was legally possible. Since over three-quarters of schools in Carpatho-Rusyn-inhabited villages and towns were operated by the Greek Catholic Church, the language policy in elementary schools, in seminaries (Uzhhorod and Prešov), and in church-operated teacher's colleges was set by the church hierarchs and their clerical advisors. At the time, most clergy were anxious to be fully accepted in Hungarian society and were therefore not at all opposed to the further use of Hungarian, whether as the sole language of instruction or alongside Rusyn, in bilingual schools. Consequently, it is not surprising that from the 1870s Hungarian became the sole language of instruction in all senior high schools (*gymna-sia*), whether they were run by the state (Uzhhorod, Mukachevo, Berehovo) or by the church (Prešov, Sighet). This was also a period during which the Hungarian government favored establishing state-run elementary schools using the bilingual model and employing teachers responsible to the Ministry of Education. Those teachers, often intimidated by the ministry officials, felt they should stress wherever possible the state language Hungarian at the expense of Rusyn or any other minority language.

As a result of all these factors, the number of elementary schools with Rusyn as the language of instruction declined from a height of 571 (in 1874) to 23 (in 1906). At the same time, the number of Hungarian-Rusyn bilingual schools, which were first introduced in 1880, steadily rose from 246 to 384 in 1904.[6] Aside from the overall increase in the number of the state-run schools, in 1891 the Hungarian language was introduced into preschools (kindergartens), in order that non-Magyar children would be linguistically ready for entry into elementary schools.[7]

Beginning in 1904, the situation changed dramatically. This was connected with what could be considered the culmination of the magyarization process in education. In 1907, Hungary's parliament adopted a school law (*Lex Apponyi*). In effect, Hungarian became the sole language of instruction in state-run schools, since non-Magyar students were required to express themselves in Hungarian already by the fourth year of elementary school. Teachers were now bound by an oath of loyalty to the state: "to encourage and strengthen in the souls of children the spirit of attachment to the Hungarian fatherland and an awareness of being a part of the Hungarian nation."[8] Technically, church-run schools could still offer instruction in a language other than Hungarian, but here too students were expected to be knowledgeable in Hungarian by the 4th grade. To assure that such pedagogical goals were achieved, it was not uncommon that in the curricula for bilingual schools eighteen of the twenty-two hours were conducted in Hungarian. In short, Rusyn and other minority languages felt the full brunt of discrimination that was both encouraged by the state and often implemented—at times enthusiastically—by teachers who were themselves of Carpatho-Rusyn background.

After 1907, there was not a single school in which Rusyn was the sole language of instruction, while the number of Rusyn-Hungarian bilingual schools rapidly declined to a mere 34 in 1913 in which a few hours were conducted in Rusyn.[9] As one magyarized Carpatho-Rusyn activist observed at the time: "In ten years Rusyn youth will be Magyar not only in spirit but also in language . . . . In the Carpathians they will have no relatives because here only Magyars will be everywhere!!"[10]

In the absence of any national organizations, schools, or village reading rooms, in a state that aggressively carried out a policy of national assimilation, and in a situation in which the majority of Carpatho-Rusyn secular- and clerical-educated individuals actively welcomed the possibility to become Magyar, one might expect that the overall numerical size of the group would

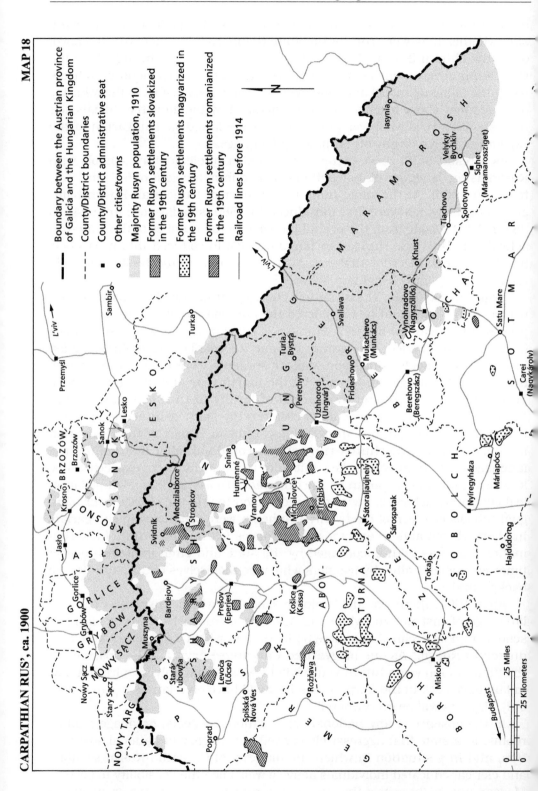

MAP 18

CARPATHIAN RUS', ca. 1900

Boundary between the Austrian province of Galicia and the Hungarian Kingdom

County/District boundaries

County/District administrative seat

Other cities/towns

Majority Rusyn population, 1910

Former Rusyn settlements slovakized in the 19th century

Former Rusyn settlements magyarized in the 19th century

Former Rusyn settlements romanianized in the 19th century

Railroad lines before 1914

decline. It seems, however, as accompanying statistics in Table 10.1 show, that while the number of Carpatho-Rusyns fluctuated, there was a general increase in their number, even during the height of the magyarization efforts being implemented by the Hungarian government.

TABLE 10.1
Carpatho-Rusyns in the Hungarian Kingdom, 1840 to 1910[11]

Year of census	Total number	Number in Subcarpathian Rus	Number in Slovakia
1840	442,900	180,100	203,300
1851	447,400	216,100	113,100
1869	455,000	257,200	183,500
1880	353,200	244,700	88,000
1890	379,800	276,600	96,300
1900	424,800	314,500	84,900
1910	464,300	331,600	97,100

Perhaps it was their very social and educational underdevelopment and their geographic marginality that protected Carpatho-Rusyns from large-scale assimilation. It seems that the most significant decreases took place in the mid-nineteenth century decades before the first state-sponsored census in 1869. The cause for the decline during that period is likely to have been the result of confusion about concepts—that is, one could be of the Rus' faith (*rus'ka vira*) and identify in one census as a Rusyn, but in another as a Slovak or even a Magyar of the Rus' faith. One Czech scholar estimated that between 1850 and 1900, the majority of inhabitants in no less than 176 Carpatho-Rusyn villages claimed Slovak identity and 37 others a Magyar identity.[12]

The other factor contributing to limiting the otherwise increase in the numbers of Carpatho-Rusyns—which might have been greater than it was—is connected to emigration, which by 1880s became an increasingly widespread phenomenon in the Hungarian Kingdom as well as in Austrian Galicia. Emigration was directly related to economic conditions in Carpathian Rus'. On the southern slopes of the mountains, the Hungarian government had during the Revolution of 1848 abolished serfdom; never-theless, the economic status of the peasant farmers at best only margin-ally improved and, at certain periods, even declined. Initially the decline was related to problems of readjustment in the relationship between peasants and their former landlords.

Until the 1848 emancipation, proprietary peasants had free access to the pastures and woods owned by the manorial landlord, a feudal privilege that allowed them to sustain the family cow and heat their dwellings with fire-wood collected in the forests. Now that the feudal relationship with the land-lord was abolished, the government stepped in to regulate the new situation. According to a state patent issued in 1853, two sets of government measures were introduced. One was *segregacia*, according to which a clear distinction was made between the pastures and forests owned by the manorial landlord and those held by the state to which peasant farmers were allowed access. The other measure was the *comasacia/komasatsiia*, according to which arable land allotted for use by peasants was joined together into larger units which were distinct from the lands of the manorial estate. Although intended to improve the status of peasant farmers, when these measures were put into practice in the 1860s and 1870s, the manorial landlords managed to retain the most fertile lands, while the peasants were left with hilly tracts and pastures often far from the village.

By the first decade of the twentieth century, no less than 82 percent of arable lands were owned by the Hungarian state or wealthy magnate families like the Telekis, Schönborns, and Perényis.[13] Meanwhile, most Carpatho-Rusyn peasants had smaller and smaller plots, with 70 percent having less than 10 holds (roughly equivalent to 14 acres) of land, the minimum needed to maintain a subsistence-level existence.[14] Summer seasonal work on the more arable Hungarian lowland plain provided some extra income, but in general peasants were forced to mortgage what little land they owned and to borrow money just to survive. In the end, an increasing number were simply unable to break out of the chronic cycle of indebtedness to creditors (whether landlords or local Jewish innkeepers), while at the same time they were still liable for payment to "their" Greek Catholic Church of the so-called *koblyna*—a tax in kind (grain, straw, wood, etc.), and the *rokovyna*—duties in the form of labor and transport.

To make matters worse, all males were subject to universal military conscription. Even though Austria-Hungary had not been engaged in any wars since the 1860s, the empire maintained an increasingly large standing army made up primarily of recruits from rural areas. Young men were required to do two years of military service, either in the imperial army or in one of the "home" armies (Austria's *Landwehr* or Hungary's *Honvéd*), followed by 9 or 10 years in the reserve. Military service was generally dreaded—even in peacetime—because it placed an incredibly harsh economic burden on young men trying to earn a livelihood and start a family.

Socioeconomic developments

In the absence of war, epidemics, and a relative improvement in health standards throughout Austria-Hungary, the empire as a whole enjoyed a natural demographic increase and people experienced slightly longer life spans during the period between 1870 and 1914. These otherwise positive developments resulted, however, in further strains on the basically subsistence-level agricultural economy in Carpatho-Rusyn villages, which was only made worse by the ongoing tradition of dividing the land among the sons in the family. Ever smaller plots resulted in less productivity and a reduction in the ability to support rural families. Moreover, the Hungarian Kingdom and Austrian Galicia were the least industrialized parts of the Habsburg Dual

WAS LIFE IN PRE-WORLD WAR I CARPATHIAN RUS' SO DESTITUTE?

"Even more backward . . . were the Ruthenians of Upper Hungary. This mountainous region . . . was exploited by Hungarian magnates as a vast hunting preserve. There Ruthenian peasants inhabited clay huts without chimneys, victimized into a state of starvation and alcoholism. Some fasted as often as 250 days per year, while venerating medicine men and won-der-working rabbis."[a]

The foregoing description by an American specialist on Austrian intellectual history was still being repeated as late as the 1970s. It, like many other similar commentaries about pre-World War I Austria-Hungary, suggested that all Carpatho-Rusyn-inhabited lands, especially in the Hungarian Kingdom, were uniformly destitute. No distinctions were made between the status of Carpatho-Rusyns living in remote high mountain villages where conditions were generally quite bad, and those living in the lower foothills and valleys where peasant farmers were often able to produce a surplus harvest and extra income to support their families.

How valid, then, are the many stereotypical accounts of the last decades before World War I with their generalized descriptions of grinding poverty that forced thousands of peasant farmers to emigrate abroad, while at home magyarization policies carried out by a "reactionary feudal" state seemed to threaten the very existence of Carpatho-Rusyns as a distinct Slavic people? The overwhelmingly negative image of Carpathian Rus', especially its regions under Hungarian rule, was to be reinforced by subsequent generations of scholars and publicists, first those who praised interwar Czechoslovakia as the region's "savior" from "dastardly" Austro-Hungarian rule, then by Soviet Marxists who denigrated all aspects of pre-World War I (and pre-1917 Bolshevik revolutionary) Hungarian feudalism. Added to this negative image were the stories of immigrants in North America and their descendants, who were convinced that their parents and grandparents were saved from Austro-Hungarian "oppression" thanks only to the opportunities given them by "democratic" and "freedom-loving" America.

If life in the "old homeland" (*staryi krai*) was all that bad, one might wonder why such a high proportion of Carpatho-Rusyn immigrants (some estimates are as high as 30 percent) returned home *before* World War I. To be sure, Carpathian Rus', like any historic region in Europe, was a land of contrasts. It is true that the high mountainous areas experienced chronic poverty, but villages in the lower elevation foothills and flat plain were able to support peasant families as well as allow and encourage enterprising individuals to increase their income by seasonal work elsewhere.

As for cultural life, there were certainly state- and church-run schools at the elementary, junior high, and senior high school (*gymnasium*) levels, even if the language of instruction was primarily Hungarian. Knowledge of Hungarian was not necessarily a handicap, however, since it did allow sons of Carpatho-Rusyn peasant farmers and Eastern-rite priests to enter—and in some cases to rise to the top eche-lons of—Hungarian civic and cultural life.

And what did those descriptions of Carpatho-Rus' as a cultural backwater actu-ally mean? Carpatho-Rusyn lands were certainly part of what may be considered the periphery or the provinces of the Austro-Hungarian Empire. But then, in the European context of the time (and in many ways still today), the provinces rep-resented everything that was not the capital of a given cultural sphere; in other words, all places beyond centers like Vienna, Budapest, Prague, Paris, or Rome, etc. were considered the provinces.

Lest we assume that Carpathian Rus' was an uncultured, uncivilized, and unknown backwater buried somewhere in the middle of central Europe, it might be useful to know the following. The last decades of the nineteenth century witnessed the grad-ual expansion and architectural transformation of Uzhhorod (Hungarian: Ungvár) with the construction of several apartment and commercial buildings on the south-ern bank of the Uzh River (present-day Petőfi Square), a monumental state-run *gym-nasium*/senior high school in a neo-Renaissance style (1893–1895), an imposing "Great Synagogue" for Orthodox Jews in the Moorish style (1904), and a new neoclas-sical façade for the Greek-Catholic Cathedral Church (1878) which characterizes that structure to this day. While historicism dominated architectural styles in these and other large-scale building projects, such as the monumental neo-Renaissance Bereg county court house in Berehovo (1895) and the French neo-Renaissance and neo-Tu-dor Schönborn Palace at Beregvar north of Mukachevo (1890–1895), at the same time other designers sought to create an indigenous style, which might be considered the Hungarian variant of Art Nouveau/Secessionism, as in the City Hall in Mukachevo (1896) and in three structures in Uzhhorod—the Koruna Hotel (1906), the state-run elementary/junior high school for girls (1911–1912), and the *gymnasium*/high school operated by the Greek Catholic Basilian Order (1911–1912).

Aside from architectural monuments, Subcarpathian Rus' became the center of attention in 1896, the year Hungary undertook a major series of events to celebrate the millennium of the arrival of the Magyar tribes in the Danubian Basin. Hundreds of governmental dignitaries made their way to the region in order to unveil mil-lennial-commemorative monuments at the Mukachevo Castle and at the Verets'kyi Pass, the point where it is believed the Magyars led by their main chieftain Árpád crossed the Carpathians a thousand years before.

Aside from the millennium celebrations, the region became a mecca for some of Hungary's leading creative and performing artists. Simon Hollósy, the founder of the Nagybánya School of Painting, organized annual excursions for painters near the town of Tiachevo. Moreover, Hungary's greatest nineteenth-century painter of historical and patriotic themes, Mihály Munkácsy (b. Michael Leib), was a native of Mukachevo whose civic authorities welcomed their native son in a major public cer-emony in 1882.

This same period, the second half of the historic nineteenth century, also brought Subcarpathian Rus' into the highest levels of musical culture in Austria-Hungary and Europe. The renowned violin virtuoso, Ede Reményi (Eduard

Hoffmann), began performing in the region in the 1860s, while his student, Count Nándor Ploteny, the first violinist in the Hungarian National Theater, hosted at the estate in his native village of Velyki Lazy (just east of Uzhhorod) the world-renowned pianist and composer Franz Liszt. From the 1890s, when Count Plotény was back home encouraging musical culture (and also promoting economic developments among peasants on his Velyki Lazy manorial estate), Hungary's leading modern composer, Béla Bartók, was attending secondary school in the town of Sevliush. It was there that Bartók wrote his first compositions and where he collected the Carpatho-Rusyn folk melodies that were incorporated into some of his later symphonic works. Nor was the region unknown to representatives of "culture for the masses." The world-famous American showman Buffalo Bill (William Frederick Cody) brought his Wild West Show to Uzhhorod and Mukachevo (performing below the castle on Palanok Hill) as part of his 1906 world tour.

The above are only some of many examples that force us to revise and correct the image of pre-World War I Carpathian Rus' as simply a land of downtrodden, exploited, uneducated, and destitute peasants.

[a] William M. Johnston, *The Austrian Mind: An Intellectual and Social History, 1848–1938* (Berkeley, Los Angeles, and London, 1972), p. 355.

Monarchy, and peripheral areas like Carpathian Rus' had only a few industrial enterprises that might provide employment to a significant number of local inhabitants.

In Galicia's Lemko Region, there were a few opportunities to increase one's income beyond the subsistence-level harvests derived from small, family-owned plots. These included: gathering mushrooms and herbs which were sold at good prices in local Carpathian health resorts (Krynica-Zdrój, Iwonicz-Zdrój, Szczawnica, Żegiestów, and Rymanów, among others); working in the forests and open quarries as wood- and stonecutters; doing unskilled manual labor in Galicia's oil industry, which had some wells in the Lemko Region; and traveling as itinerant tinkers (*drotarŷ*) throughout the empire and abroad, or, in at least one village (Łosie), working in the highly profitable cart-grease trade.

On the southern slopes of the mountains in the Hungarian Kingdom, there were—contrary to the generally negative assessment by most subsequent writers about Hungarian rule—some efforts undertaken to improve the region's transportational infrastructure and to introduce industrialization and agricultural reform. Road improvement projects, especially on routes between the larger cities and towns, were initiated by the state. They provided employment to thousands among the local population. The now antiquated Rusyn term for road, *orsag* (actually a calque of the Hungarian word: *ország*, meaning "state") derives from this time.

Even more ambitious were joint Austrian and Hungarian projects to extend railroad lines in order to complete connections between Hungary's capital Budapest and Austrian Galicia's administrative center L'viv/Lemberg. This required the construction between 1870s and 1905 of numerous tunnels and viaducts through Carpathian Rus' in order to cross through four major passes: Lupkov (from Humenné northward to Sanok); Uzhok (from Uzhhorod to Sambir); Skotar (from Mukachevo to Stryi); and Iablunets'/ Tatar (from Sighet to Stanyslaviv). It was the railroad line from Sighet up the Tisza River valley to Iasynia just before the Tatar Pass (completed in 1895) that gradually eliminated the need for raftsmen to transport logs on floating barges for processing in lumber mills downstream. These highly skilled figures and the dangerous work they did, so popular in Carpatho-Rusyn folklore, are visible today only in films shot in the 1920s and 1930s that show the last of the Carpathian raftsmen who actually earned a living from their work as opposed to performing for tourists.

Efforts at industrialization, eventually encouraged by the Hungarian state through tax credits and other incentives, were carried out by the private sector. The metallurgy plant on the Schönborn family estates at Frideshovo near Mukachevo expanded its operations, while at the outset of the nineteenth century a small metallurgy plant was opened in the Ung county village of Turï Remety. Farther east in Maramorosh county there was an already existing metalworks plant in Kobylets'ka Poliana (est. 1774), as well as the salt mines in Solotvyno, which had been exploited since the Middle Ages and which after 1778 were developed more seriously by extending the caverns below and setting up processing mills above ground.

It was not until the last decades of the nineteenth century, however, that a concerted effort was undertaken, with investment from financiers and companies abroad, to exploit the region's forests. The goal was to produce lumber for export to the Hungarian lowlands, as well as to extract industrial chemicals (alcohol, acetate, formaldehyde, etc.) from wood. By the outset of the twentieth century there were 48 factories, most of which employed fewer than 50 workers, as well as sawmills and chemical distilleries that employed between 400 and 500 workers (and in a few cases over a thousand).

The largest of these was the industrial complex at Velykyi Bychkiv, initially developed in 1868 by a Swiss firm. In 1896, with capital from Austrian, Hungarian, and French investors, the firm was taken over by the Klotilda Corporation, which soon became one of Hungary's largest producers of chemicals distilled from wood. Klotilda added to the Velykyi Bychkiv chemical factory (400 to 600 workers) a sawmill and brick factory. Farther west in Ung county, the Bantlin brothers from Konstanz in southern Germany leased in 1889 an already existing chemical factory in Turia Bystra (150 to 300 workers), then in 1893 opened a new distillery plant in Perechyn (420 to 450 workers), both of which were supplied with wood from lumber camps near the villages in the Turia River valley (Remety and Poroshkovo) and from farther north near Chornoholova (800 to 1,200 workers). Somewhat later, in 1908, Budapest investors connected with the Holzhandels Corporation in Vienna opened a large-capacity sawmill in upper Bereg county at Svaliava. With access to lumber from its own mill, a new corporation, Szolyva (the

Hungarian name for Svaliava), opened a major chemical wood distillery, which within a short time employed 1,400 workers.[15]

Also of significance with regard to productive capacity and opportunity for employment, although on a smaller scale and in towns and cities somewhat removed from the Carpatho-Rusyn-inhabited rural areas, were the Mundus furniture factory (900 workers) in Uzhhorod (est. 1882) and the tobacco factory (300 to 700 workers) in Mukachevo (est. 1898). These same cities included several of the region's 16 brick and tile factories, which employed on average between 50 and 75 workers, although the largest plant (300 workers) was in the mostly Magyar-inhabited city of Berehovo. Finally, there were the long-established metallurgical factories and iron works in mostly small villages (12 with a total of 1,000 to 1,300 workers) and the mining complex at Solotvyno (1,100 to 1,200 workers), in the heart of Subcarpathia's primarily Romanian-inhabited area.[16]

Despite the existence of these and other smaller enterprises, at the outset of the twentieth century the total number of steadily employed industrial workers was about 15,600 with about an equal number of part-time work-ers. Together they accounted for only 12 percent of the total workforce in Subcarpathian Rus'.[17] This meant that despite some industrial growth, there were not even remotely enough jobs for the vast majority of Carpatho-Rusyns trying to eke out a livehood from ever smaller plots of land.

In an attempt to improve agricultural productivity and provide meaning-ful employment for rural dwellers, the Greek Catholic bishop of Mukachevo, Iulii Firtsak, in cooperation with a Hungarian official from the Ministry of Agriculture, Ede Egán, helped to initiate the so-called Highlands Program in 1897. This government-funded program was based in Bereg county, where it succeeded in introducing improvements to increase agricultural and live-stock productivity. Based as it was in only some parts of that county, the Highlands Program, despite its good intentions and some successes, proved unable to change to any significant degree the chronic poverty-stricken con-ditions in most highland Carpatho-Rusyn villages. It seemed that the only solution to the sometimes desperate economic plight of rural villagers was to emigrate abroad, in particular to the United States.

11

Carpatho-Rusyn diasporas before World War I

Carpatho-Rusyns were no strangers to migration, especially after the 1848 emancipation from serfdom which released peasants from their landlords. Hence, by the second half of the nineteenth century it was quite common for Carpatho-Rusyn peasant farmers in the Prešov Region and Subcarpathian Rus' to spend six to eight weeks each year working on the lowland plains of Hungary during the harvest season. Nor was work on the Hungarian plains limited to those Carpatho-Rusyns living on the southern slopes of the mountains. Lemko Rusyns also went annually to work as harvesters in Hungary. It was common for groups of 20 to 40 Lemkos from particular villages to travel to Bardejov, where Hungarian agents would hire them for the harvest season. This economic imperative contributed to close cultural, religious, and especially social contacts (including intermarriage) between Lemko- and Prešov-Region Rusyns who, in effect, were oblivious to the fact that they lived on opposite slopes of the mountains and in different "halves" of the Habsburg Dual Monarchy.

Migration to the Srem, Banat, and Bachka

Whereas seasonal migration helped the economic status of families who remained in Carpathian Rus', there were some who decided to settle in the lowland plains of Hungary on a permanent basis. At the turn of the nineteenth and twentieth centuries, several Lemko-Rusyn families moved to the Croatian component of the Hungarian Kingdom, in particular to Slavonia (Slavonski Brod, Lipovljani, Nova Subocka), as well as beyond into the northern areas of Bosnia (in and around Banja Luka and Prnjavor), which had only recently (1878) come under the administration of Austria-Hungary.

Yet another destination in the southern part of the Hungarian Kingdom was a historic region east of the lower Tisza River known as the Banat. Beginning in the 1890s, Carpatho-Rusyns from Maramorosh county in Subcarpathian Rus' and from Spish county in the Prešov Region arrived as farm workers in the Banat, where they found soil much richer than that they left behind in their mountainous homeland. They settled primarily in

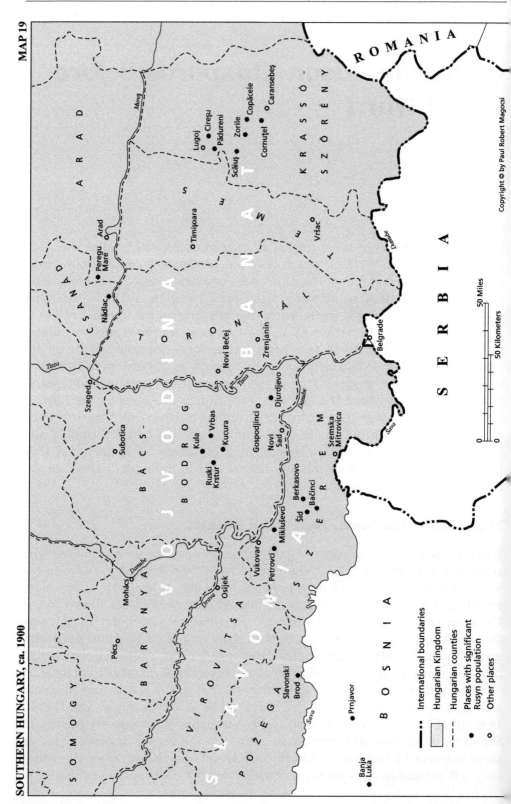

MAP 19

SOUTHERN HUNGARY, ca. 1900

International boundaries

Hungarian Kingdom

Hungarian counties

Places with significant
Rusyn population

Other places

villages like Peregu Mare/Velykŷi Pereg and Nădlac/Velykŷi Lak, which are along Romania's present-day border with Hungary. During the first decade of the twentieth century, Carpatho-Rusyn migration continued, although mostly to the eastern Banat and the foothills of the Southern (Transylvanian) Carpathians, where the newcomers found jobs as forest workers. The heaviest concentration of Carpatho-Rusyn settlement in the eastern Banat was in several villages between the towns of Lugoj and Caransebeş, in particular Zorile/Zgribeshti, Scăiuş/Skeiush, and Copăcele/Kopachele. By 1910, there were about 2,500 Carpatho-Rusyns living in the Banat.[1]

In the end, the most important destination in southern Hungary for Carpatho-Rusyns seeking to improve their economic status remained the Vojvodina, in particular its Bachka region between the Danube and lower Tisza rivers. As already discussed, the first Carpatho-Rusyns had made their way in the mid-eighteenth century to what became Hungary's Bács-Bodrog county, settling primarily in Ruski Kerestur and nearby Kucura (see above, Chapter 7). During the first half of the nineteenth century, migration southward from Carpatho-Rusyn villages located in the Prešov Region and in present-day northeastern Hungary continued. As the population of Ruski Kerestur and Kucura grew, several families in search of jobs and better economic conditions moved to other villages and towns in the Bachka (Djurdjevo, Kula, Vrbas) and farther south beyond the Danube River to Slavonia's far eastern region called Srem (the Hungarian county of Szerém), both in that part which is in present-day Serbia (the villages of Šid, Berkasovo, and Bačinci) and in present-day Croatia (the villages of Petrovci and Mikluševci). By 1910, the number of Vojvodinian-Srem Rusyns in these various communities had reached 15,000.[2]

Vojvodina's Bachka region was geographically part—effectively an unbroken extension—of the Hungarian Plain. This was an area endowed with rich soil and a very favorable climate for agriculture. Consequently, and in stark contrast to the Carpathian Mountain homeland they left (and which they fondly remembered as the Highland/Hornïtsa), the Vojvodinian-Srem Rusyns acquired a considerable degree of economic prosperity that allowed for other kinds of community activity, especially in the winter season. Aside from the elementary school in Ruski Kerestur founded back in the eighteenth century, elementary schools were established in other Rusyn villages throughout the Bachka and Srem.

Because these villages were in relatively isolated, rural areas, they were not subject to the pressures of magyarization that characterized urban life throughout the Hungarian Kingdom and that had such a strong impact on the Carpatho-Rusyn church and secular intelligentsia in cities like Uzhhorod and Prešov. Consequently, in the Vojvodina (Bachka and Srem) from the outset and throughout this entire period, the language of instruction in village schools remained the local Rusyn vernacular which the settlers had brought from eastern Slovakia and northeastern Hungary. It was factors such as these that made educated Vojvodinian Bachka-Srem Rusyns different from their compatriots in the Carpathian homeland. For the most part they did not succumb to magyarization but remained proud of their Rusnak language and cultural heritage. It was from this environment that arose "the father of Vojvodinian literature," Havriïl/Gabor Kostel'nik, who, while still a teenage Greek Catholic seminarian, published in 1904 the first work in the Vojvodinian Rusyn vernacular, a collection of poetry entitled *Z moioho valala* (From My Village).

Emigration abroad to the United States

Neither the seasonal labor migration to the Hungarian plain, nor permanent settlement in the Srem, Banat, and Bachka could respond adequately to the needs of the vast majority of Carpatho-Rusyn peasants in the Carpathian homeland suffering under the increasingly dire economic conditions of the late nineteenth century. Hence, they looked elsewhere—to America.

During the last decades of the nineteenth century, the United States embarked on a massive program of industrialization. Most of the plants and factories that opened their doors were located in the northeastern part of the country. This was an especially favorable area for heavy industry since states like Pennsylvania had huge reserves of coal and iron ore that formed the basis of the steel industry—a major factor in enriching America's rapidly growing economy in the decades before World War I. The factories, mines, and mills required a huge labor force, and to fulfill that need new immigrants were encouraged to make their way to America's shores.

The traditional source of immigration had been northern and western Europe, in particular England, Ireland, Germany, France, and Scandinavia. While these areas continued to supply immigrants, beginning in the 1870s, southern and eastern Europe also became a source—and soon the largest one—of immigrants. American industrialists, in cooperation with shipowners, carried out a comprehensive advertising campaign and created an organizational network that reached into the villages of southern and eastern Europe and that brought from those regions tens of thousands of Italians, Greeks, Poles, Jews, Magyars, Slovaks, and Romanians, among others. It is estimated that between 1890 and 1920 no fewer than 18.2 million immigrants arrived in the United States, and of these 7.5 million were from Austria-Hungary, the Balkans, and the Russian Empire. Among them were Carpatho-Rusyns, of whom an estimated 225,000 came to the United States by the outbreak of World War I in 1914. Whereas a few Carpatho-Rusyn individuals began to arrive as early as the 1860s, it was not until the 1880s and 1890s that substantial numbers arrived.[3]

By the late nineteenth century, leaving Austria-Hungary was from the legal standpoint relatively easy. In the Austrian half of the Habsburg realm, internal passports were abolished (1857), controls at the monarchy's borders were lifted (1865), and every person, unless specifically under court order, had the right to obtain a passport to travel abroad (1867). For Hungary a special law (1903) gave citizens the right to travel abroad—assuming a country would receive them—and they could even do so without an

CARPATHO-RUSYN COMMUNITIES IN THE UNITED STATES

MAP 20

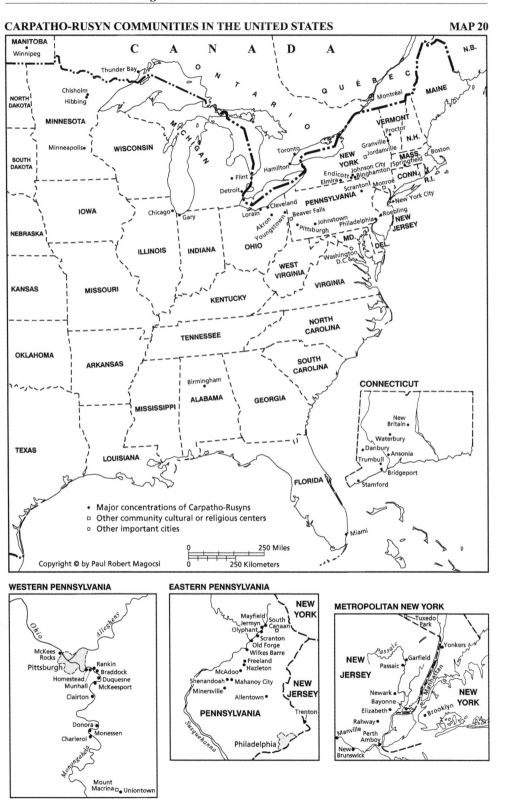

Copyright © by Paul Robert Magocsi

• Major concentrations of Carpatho-Rusyns
□ Other community cultural or religious centers
○ Other important cities

0   250 Miles
0   250 Kilometers

Austro-Hungarian passport. Actually, the highest percentage of emigrants from the entire Austro-Hungarian Empire came from southern Galicia and northeastern Hungary. Aside from Poles, Ukrainians, Slovaks, and Magyars living in those areas there were, of course, Carpatho-Rusyns. In counties like Sharysh, Zemplyn, Ung, and Bereg, from where the highest number of Carpatho-Rusyn immigrants derived, some villages were so severely depopulated that for a while the Hungarian government tried to put a halt to emigration. But since Austria-Hungary had lifted legal restrictions on its borders and issuance of passports, any efforts at restricting emigration were in vain, and the outflow continued unabated.

Initially, most of the immigrants were young males who did not intend to remain permanently in the New World. Not unlike Carpatho-Rusyn migrant laborers on the Hungarian plain, the emigrants abroad intended to work for a few years in America in order to make enough money to return home and buy more land in order to support their families beyond the subsistence level. With such goals in mind, it is not surprising that there arose the so-called sojourner phenomenon. Sojourners were immigrants who worked a few years in America, then returned home for a while before returning again to the New World. In the decades before World War I, migrating back and forth across the ocean was almost as common as was the decision to return home. In fact, before 1914 it is estimated that one-third of all immigrants who came to the United States from southern and eastern Europe returned home permanently.[4]

Nevertheless, the majority of Carpatho-Rusyn immigrants did stay in the United States. Some of the men subsequently sent for their wives and children to follow them; others had from the outset arrived with them together as a family unit. Quick money was, of course, the object, with the result that Carpatho-Rusyn peasant farmers were rapidly transformed into miners and unskilled laborers in heavy industry. Women as well as men found work cleaning public buildings, as domestic servants, operating boarding houses, or in light industrial enterprises (clothing factories, shoe factories, etc.). For most, however, industrial life in the United States was not what they expected. Work in steel plants and coal mines was especially physically demanding and dangerous, leading one immigrant miner to quip: We came expecting to work *in* America, not *under* America.

Carpatho-Rusyn immigrants settled where the mines and factories were, so that by 1910 as high as 79 percent lived in the urban areas of the Middle Atlantic states, in particular Pennsylvania (54 percent), New York (13 percent), and New Jersey (12 percent), followed by Ohio, Connecticut, and Illinois. Pennsylvania was an especially strong magnet because of the large labor pool needed to work in the coal mines in the eastern part of the state and the steel mills in its western part. It is therefore no surprise that because of letters sent to families and friends in Europe, names like Scranton, Hazelton, Homestead, and most especially Pittsburgh became as commonplace as Uzhhorod, Mukachevo, or Prešov in conversations among villagers in the Carpathian homeland.

Although industrial America's work schedule was long—10 to 12 hours a day, six days a week—if the one day of rest happened to fall on Sunday (on which mines and mills otherwise operated), the immigrant worker was, like the vast majority of Carpatho-Rusyns, drawn to church. At the time of their arrival, virtually all Carpatho-Rusyns were Greek Catholics. Moreover, as Greek Catholics they were no different from Rusyn/Ruthenian Greek Catholics living in the Austrian province of Galicia. As we have seen, some of those Galician Ruthenians considered themselves Russians, yet others as Ukrainians (see above, Chapter 10). In fact, these different identities crystallized among peasant-turned-urban dwellers only after they spent some time living in the United States. The point to remember is that Austria-Hungary's "Ruthenian" immigrants, who in the New World later evolved into distinct Carpatho-Rusyn, Russian, and Ukrainian communities, initially functioned together as Greek Catholics.

Rusyn–American religious and secular organizations

There was one problem, however. Until the mid-1880s there was not a single Greek Catholic priest or church in the United States, and even after the first parishes began to be formed, many places where Carpatho-Rusyns lived still did not have their own priests or churches. Thus, the Greek Catholic faithful were forced by circumstance to attend mass in a Roman-rite church and, where possible, they gravitated toward parishes that served fellow Slavic immigrants like Poles and Slovaks. Not content with this situation, some enterprising immigrants wrote to their Greek Catholic bishops in Europe requesting that they send them priests. The first Greek Catholic priest to arrive in America in 1884 (John Volansky) came from Galicia, followed by a few others, including the first one from the Hungarian Kingdom (Alexander Dzubay) in 1889. By 1894, at which time there were nearly two dozen Greek Catholic priests in the United States, all but four were Carpatho-Rusyns from Hungary.

It is important to note that the immigrants themselves, not the Greek Catholic Church in the homeland, took the initiative to invite a priest and establish a parish in America. Hence, in the absence of their own bishop, the immigrant faithful created committees, or councils, made up of lay persons who purchased property and built a church. It was these lay councils which legally owned the churches, and not the bishop. This differed from standard practice in the Catholic world. The question of church ownership was in the future to plague relations between the Greek Catholic hierarchy and the lay faithful.

Even before the establishment of the first churches, another type of organization was created by the early Carpatho-Rusyn immigrants. These were mutual-benefit societies, or fraternal brotherhoods. Newly arrived immigrant workers quickly realized that in the United States neither their employers nor the government (whether at the local, state, or federal level) provided any meaningful social services. In effect, the workers were on their own and with no income should they become ill or maimed. In the worse scenario, should the main breadwinner die or be killed in a work-related accident (not beyond the realm of possibility, especially for miners), his surviving family would receive no compensation. Faced with such American reality, immigrant workers created self-help mutual-benefit societies, the fraternal brotherhoods, to which they contributed a small amount of their wages each week or month. Once a fraternal was established, any member who fell ill, who was injured, or who was killed received a certain amount of money to compensate him or his family. Such fraternal brotherhoods were established in many communities where Carpatho-Rusyn workers lived.

In order to increase their effectiveness, several brotherhoods joined together to create larger organizations. Among the oldest of these, one came into being in 1892, when 14 local fraternals in eastern Pennsylvania joined to form the Greek Catholic Union of Rusyn Brotherhoods/the Sojedinenije greko-kaftoličeskich russkich bratstv. By the outbreak of World War I, the Greek Catholic Union, or Sojedinenije, had nearly 54,000 paying members registered in both adult (758) and youth (354) lodges.[5] The model of bringing together local brotherhoods into a larger union was followed in other communities. Another relatively large organization created by Carpatho-Rusyn workers during the pre-World War I decades was the United Societies of Greek Catholic Religion/Sobranije greko-katoličeskich cerkovnych bratstv. Aside from providing insurance benefits to its members, these and other brother-hoods published in Rusyn newspapers and annual almanacs, which were sent to all members as part of their annual dues. The oldest and largest of these publications was the *Amerikanskii russkii viestnik* (1892–1952), the official newspaper of the Greek Catholic Union.

As their names suggest, the early brotherhoods, while secular in origin, were closely allied to the Greek Catholic Church. Priests were among the members and officers of the brotherhoods, which helped establish and provide financial assistance to individual parishes. Inevitably, the brotherhoods also became involved in church politics.

Rejected Greek Catholics and the "return" to Orthodoxy

The unity that had brought all Greek Catholic Rusyn/Ruthenian immigrants from Austrian Galicia and the Hungarian Kingdom together in the New World quickly dissipated. The divisions, caused by conflicts over religious and national orientation, were frequently made sharper and irreconcilable because of personal antagonisms. The earliest conflicts, however, were caused by religious controversies. As members of the Catholic Church, newly arrived Greek Catholic priests in the United States were required to report to the local hierarch. In the context of the United States, that hierarch was the Roman Catholic bishop of the diocesan territory in which a given Carpatho-Rusyn priest was to function.

For their part, the bishops were part of a larger environment that was increasingly hostile to foreign influences in American life. During the last decades of the nineteenth century, the Roman Catholic Church itself was internally divided by a controversy known as Americanism. One faction, the Americanizers, favored the rapid assimilation of immigrants. Support for such a policy, they believed, would demonstrate Catholic allegiance to American institutions and ideals, which at the time basically reflected White Anglo-Saxon Protestant (WASP) cultural values. The Americanizers hoped to have Catholicism accepted as a legitimate part of the American identity, but in order for this to happen all foreign languages and customs different from the Roman Catholic "norm" had to be expunged.

Added to this was the complete lack of awareness among Roman Catholic bishops in the United States (at the time mostly of Irish descent) that a Catholic rite other than the Roman Latin one even existed. When they were suddenly confronted by immigrants of the Eastern Catholic rite, and when they found out about traditions such as married priests, they were aghast. In some cases, Greek Catholic priests were forbidden to perform their sacramental duties (baptism, weddings) and were not allowed to consecrate the dead in Catholic cemeteries.

One Greek Catholic priest, Alexis Toth, who in 1889 began serving at a parish in Minneapolis, Minnesota, experienced dismissive treatment from the Roman Catholic archbishop of St. Paul, John Ireland. When all efforts at reaching some kind of compromise between the two clerics failed, in 1891 Toth decided to leave the Catholic Church and enter into communion with the Orthodox Church. The only Orthodox Church in the United States at the time was the Russian Orthodox Church in North America, formally an archdiocese of the Russian Orthodox Church in the Russian Empire. Toth, who before coming to America was a professor of canon law at the Greek Catholic seminary in Prešov, justified his decision through legal and historical arguments. The explanation put forth was that he and his parishioners were "returning to the faith of their fathers," that is, the Eastern-rite Orthodox Church to which all Carpatho-Rusyns in Europe had belonged before the Union of Brest (1596) and Union of Uzhhorod (1646).

"YOU ARE NOT A PROPER PRIEST"

The return-to-Orthodoxy movement among Carpatho-Rusyns in the United States and its subsequent presence in the European homeland can, to a large degree, be attributed to a single incident between two headstrong individuals. One was John Ireland, Roman Catholic archbishop of St. Paul, Minnesota, who at the time was a leading figure in the so-called Americanization movement in the United States. This movement was led by Roman Catholic priests who were anxious to have their church fully accepted in "Protestant" America, arguing that Catholics should not be considered any less American simply because their religion differed from the White Anglo-Saxon Protestant (WASP) norm. With such goals in mind, Bishop Ireland was instinctively opposed to any "non-American," non-English speaking Catholics, and certainly those who were not of the "normal" Roman rite.

The other individual was Alexis Toth, an Eastern-rite Catholic priest and professor of canon law at the Greek Catholic Seminary in Prešov, who was very well versed in the history of the churches in union with Rome and their rites and privileges according to Catholic canonical law. In testimony given subsequently (1894) before a county court in Pennsylvania, Father Toth (since 1994 St. Alexis) recalled the fateful meeting he had with Bishop Ireland on 19 December 1889, just a few weeks after he served his first liturgy in America at the Greek Catholic parish in Minneapolis, Minnesota.

I was a Uniate when I came to America. . . . I knew that here in America as a Uniate priest I was to obey the Roman Catholic Bishop of the particular diocese in which I happened to work. The Union demanded this as well as the various Papal Bulls, briefs, and Decretals [sic], as there was no Uniate Bishop in this country.

When I came to Minneapolis, I was there a while, when a Polish priest came up to me and said, 'You better come up with me, I'll introduce you to the bishop of Minneapolis–St. Paul, Bishop Ireland.' This Polish priest was called away to some sick [person], so I went up myself to see him [Bishop Ireland]. I had my priest's clothes on and I introduced myself and showed him my papers. . . .

The place of my appointment was Minneapolis, Minnesota, the province of Bishop Ireland. As an obedient Uniate I complied with the orders of my Bishop, who at that time was John Vályi [of the Eparchy of Prešov], and appeared before Bishop Ireland on December 19, 1889, kissed his hand according to custom and presented my credentials failing, however, to kneel before him, which, as I learned later, was my chief mistake. I remember that no sooner did he read that I was a 'Greek Catholic,' his hands began to shake. It took him fifteen minutes to read to the end after which he asked abruptly— we conversed in Latin:

'Have you a wife?'

'No.'

'But you had one?'

'Yes, I am a widower.'

At this time he threw the paper on the table and loudly exclaimed: 'I have already written to Rome protesting against this kind of priests being sent to me!'

'What kind of priests do you mean?'

'Your kind.'

'I am a Catholic priest of Greek Rite. I am a Uniate and was ordained by a regular Catholic Bishop.'

'I do not consider that either you or this bishop of yours are Catholics; besides, I do not need any Greek Catholic priests here; a Polish priest in Minneapolis is quite sufficient; the Greeks can also have him for their priest.'

'But he belongs to the Latin Rite; besides, our people do not understand him and so they will hardly go to him; that was the reason they instituted a church of their own.'

'They had no permission from me and I shall grant you no jurisdiction to work here.'

Deeply hurt by the fanaticism of this representative of Papal Rome, I replied sharply: 'In that case, I know the rights of my church, I know the basis on which the Union was established and shall act accordingly.'

The Bishop lost his temper. I lost mine just as much. One word brought another; the thing had gone so far that our conversation is not worth putting on record.

SOURCE: *Testimony: Greek Catholic Church et al. v. Orthodox Church et al.,* Court of Common Pleas, Luzerne County, Wilkes-Barre, Pennsylvania, 1894, Vol. I, pp. 235 ff. Cited in Keith S. Russin, "Father Alexis G. Toth and the Wilkes-Barre Litigations," *St. Vladimir's Theological Quarterly,* XVI, 3 (Tuckahoe-Crestwood, N.Y., 1972), pp. 132–133.

Toth did not limit his efforts to the "return" solely of his Minneapolis parish. Armed with the blessing of his new episcopal superior, Toth set out to bring other Greek Catholic parishes into the fold of the Russian Orthodox Church. By 1909, he succeeded in bringing over 25,000 Greek Catholics (mostly Lemko-Rusyn immigrants from Galicia) into the Orthodox fold. In fact, by World War I and for several decades thereafter, the vast majority of members in the Russian Orthodox Church in North America were former Greek Catholics and their descendants from Austria-Hungary. The point is that by the outset of the twentieth century Carpatho-Rusyns in North America were divided between adherents of Greek Catholicism and Orthodoxy.

"Ruthenians" become Uhro (Hungarian)-Rusyns, or Russians, or Ukrainians

Added to differentiation along religious lines were divisions brought about because of regional allegiances and nationality preferences. Whereas immigrants who described themselves as *Rusyn* (in English: Ruthenian) initially joined the same churches and secular organizations, it was not long before friction arose among those who came from the different parts of the Habsburg Empire: Austrian Galicia and the Hungarian Kingdom.

Immigrants from Galicia who did not agree with the policies of the Greek Catholic Union—led almost exclusively by Carpatho-Rusyns from Hungary—broke with that organization and established new mutual-benefit fraternal societies. The Galician "Ruthenians," including Carpatho-Rusyns from the Lemko Region, were themselves divided by national preferences, so that the new organizations they founded in the 1890s had within the next decade come to represent two different nationalities: Russian and Ukrainian. These included the Russian Orthodox Catholic Mutual Aid Society/ Russkoe pravoslavnoe vzaimopomoshchi and the Russian Brotherhood Organization/Obshchestvo russkikh bratstv, comprised primarily of Greek Catholics who "returned" to Orthodoxy; and the Rusyn National Union/ Russkii narodnŷi soiuz, which by 1914 became the Ukrainian National Association/Ukraïns'kyi narodnyi soiuz. Carpatho-Rusyn immigrants from the Lemko Region in Galicia joined and in many cases took up leadership positions in all of the above organizations.

In the midst of conflicts over regional and nationality preferences, America's Greek Catholic Ruthenians got in 1908 their first bishop in the person of Soter Ortynsky. But the joy at finally having a hierarch of their own Eastern rite was short-lived. This was largely because the influential Greek Catholic Union fraternal society was opposed to the new bishop. Their reasoning was twofold: Ortynsky was from Galicia, not Hungary; and, even worse, he seemed to favor the Ukrainian national orientation. One alternative for parishes and priests who were discontent with their "Galician-Ukrainian" bishop was to join the Orthodox Church, whereby they would both "return to the faith of their fathers" and become part of a Russian institution. In effect, the return to Orthodoxy was accompanied by an acceptance that one's nationality was Carpatho-Russian, or simply Russian.

The friction among Greek Catholic immigrants over their regional origin (Galicia versus Hungary) combined with the defections to Orthodoxy (in part a reaction to the alleged Ukrainian orientation of Bishop Ortynsky) so alarmed the Vatican that, when Ortynsky died in 1916, it decided to create separate jurisdictions. One was for Greek Catholic immigrants from Galicia (mostly Ukrainians and Lemko Rusyns who had not become Orthodox), the other was for those from the Hungarian Kingdom (mostly Carpatho-Rusyns, as well as Slovaks, Magyars, and Croats).

Rusyn Americans and international politics

The religious and nationality divisions among Carpatho-Rusyns in the United States were followed closely and were of particular concern to certain states in Europe, where the international political constellation had changed considerably. The former imperial allies, Austria and Russia, which had cooperated so closely to crush the Hungarian Revolution of 1848–1849, had by the late nineteenth century become bitter antagonists and rivals for political influence in central Europe, especially in the Balkans. Tsarist Russia, therefore, would welcome any means to undermine its Austro-Hungarian rival with whom it shared a common border.

The Hungarian government, for instance, through the Austro-Hungarian consulate in Pittsburgh, monitored closely the Greek Catholic Union, which it viewed as an instrument of Pan-Slavic ideology. The authorities in Budapest felt that any cooperation between Carpatho-Rusyns and Slovaks in America might undermine the magyarization efforts of the government in the Hungarian-ruled homeland. On the other side of the religious and political spectrum was the Russian imperial government, which did whatever it could to support the return-to-Orthodoxy movement. The former Greek Catholics were, after all, entering the Russian Orthodox Eparchy of North America, an ecclesiastical jurisdiction within the Orthodox Church of Russia. For instance, Tsar Nicholas II provided funds to support the first Russian Orthodox missionary schools and seminaries in Minneapolis (1897) and in Tenafly, New Jersey (1912). Even the bells in the first Carpatho-Rusyn parish to return to Orthodoxy were a gift from the tsar. (They still hang in the belfry of the Orthodox Church in Minneapolis, Minnesota). It is in this context that seemingly esoteric and even inane religious and national controversies among "Ruthenian" immigrants in the United States took on a particular international interest.

As Carpatho-Rusyn immigrants began to return home, whether on a temporary or permanent basis, they brought with them not only their hard-earned money but also new ideas and convictions about religious and national identity that were formed by their experience in the United States. Among those convictions was an adherence to Orthodoxy. It is perhaps no coincidence that when the return-to-Orthodoxy movement began at the very outset of the twentieth century in the Carpathian homeland, the villages where it first made its appearance were among those where immigrants returned from America: Iza and Velyki Luchky in Subcarpathian Rus'; Becherov in the Prešov Region; and Grab, Wyszowadka, and Długie in the Lemko Region.

In Europe, Carpatho-Rusyn Greek Catholic priests who considered returning to Orthodoxy were helped by a variety of forces. The young Russophile secular activists from the neighboring Austrian province of Bukovina, the brothers Aleksei and Georgii Gerovskii (grandsons of the Subcarpathian Russophile political leader Adol'f Dobrians'kyi), assisted several young Carpatho-Rusyns to be trained in Orthodox monasteries, whether in the Russian Empire (at Dubno, Pochaïv, and Zhytomyr in Volhynia and, in particular, Iablochyn in Podlachia), in Romania (Suçeava), or at the Holy Mount Athos in Greece, where at the "Russian" St. Panteleimon Monastery there were at the outset of the twentieth century no fewer than 20 monks from the village of Iza alone, alongside those from other Subcarpathian villages.

Support for new Orthodox communities also reached Carpathian Rus' by another rather indirect route. So-called "rolling rubles" were sent from organizations in the Russian Empire (the Galician Russian Benevolent Society in St. Petersburg and the Carpatho-Russian Liberation Committee in Kiev) to Orthodox adherents in the United States, who, when returning to their native villages brought back money and publications to help promote Orthodoxy. Among the most popular of these was a brochure, *Hdi hledati pravdu?* (Where to Seek the Truth?, 1894), by the Rusyn-American activist Father Alexis Toth, and the small book, *Bratskii priviet brat'iam i sestram-karpatorussam zhivushchim v predielakh karpatskikh gor i v Amerikie*

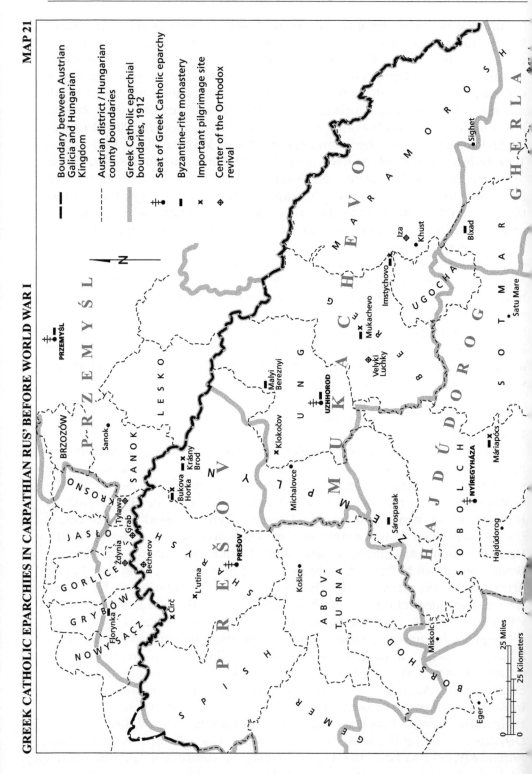

MAP 21

GREEK CATHOLIC EPARCHIES IN CARPATHIAN RUS' BEFORE WORLD WAR I

Boundary between Austrian Galicia and Hungarian Kingdom

Austrian district / Hungarian county boundaries

Greek Catholic eparchial boundaries, 1912

Seat of Greek Catholic eparchy

Byzantine-rite monastery

Important pilgrimage site

Center of the Orthodox revival

(Fraternal Greetings to My Carpatho-Russian Brothers and Sisters Living within the Carpathian Mountains and America, 1893), by Mykhail Sarŷch, a Carpatho-Rusyn convert to Orthodoxy living in the Russian Empire.

Not surprisingly, the Austro-Hungarian authorities became increasingly concerned about what they saw as the Russian threat from the east which was taking the form of promoting conversions to Orthodoxy. Responding to complaints by the Greek Catholic bishop of Mukachevo, the Hungarian government acted quickly. It tried to link conversion to Orthodoxy, which technically was legal, with alleged loyalty to another state (the Russian Empire) which, therefore, could be prosecuted as a treasonous crime. To back up its threat, the Hungarian authorities arrested Orthodox adherents in several villages; then, in 1904, it held the first of two trials in Sighet, the administrative center of Maramorosh county. At this first trial, two dozen Orthodox peasants from the village of Iza were found guilty for having "illegally" transformed their Greek Catholic parish into an Orthodox one.

Despite this setback, Orthodox communities continued to be established throughout Carpatho-Rusyn villages in Maramorosh and Bereg counties. In those two counties, the Hungarian census data for 1910 recorded 1,786 Orthodox, although estimates from the period place the number much higher, at nearly 30,000.[6] Whatever the number, the Hungarian government remained alarmed, prompting the authorities to convene a second trial at Sighet. This one opened in December 1913, and because of its size (initially 180 Orthodox converts were arrested, of which 94 were brought to trial), it attracted widespread international attention. The 94 mostly Carpatho-Rusyn peasants were accused of treason against the state for converting to Orthodoxy. Their conversion allegedly implied that they were taking the first step toward uniting Subcarpathian Rus' with the Russian Empire. After three months of deliberations, the court found 32 of the defendants guilty, including Aleksei Kabaliuk, the prominent Subcarpathian Orthodox proselytizer (who returned voluntarily from the United States to stand in solidarity alongside the accused), and sentenced them to heavy fines and a total of 37 years in prison. Not to be outdone, the Austrian authorities followed suit with a trial in L'viv in the spring of 1914 (March–June), at which the first Orthodox priest to function in the Lemko Region in nearly two centuries, Maksym Sandovych, together with three converts, was accused of spying for tsarist Russia. Although acquitted, Sandovych's freedom was to be short-lived.

The year was 1914, and Russian-Austrian rivalries over the religious orientation of Carpatho-Rusyns were about to be overshadowed by a much more dramatic—and destructive—event, the outbreak of World War I.

Carpathian Rus' during World War I, 1914–1918

August 1914 is a landmark in modern history. Although people did not realize it at the time, that fateful month witnessed a series of events that were to lead to the outbreak of war—the first *world* war. That war was to change the face of Europe and set the stage for another conflict that two decades later would change the face of the world. Ironically, by 1914 most Europeans anticipated, and some even hoped, that war would break out. Few, if any, could have foreseen its consequences. During the next four years, most European countries, as well as the United States, Canada, Japan, and the Middle East, were drawn into a conflict that in the end mobilized an incredible 65 million men, of whom 8.4 million were killed and 21 million were wounded. The statistics boggle the mind. No war until that time had cost so much in human lives.

The end of civilized Europe

In the narrowest sense, the war began in Austria-Hungary after the heir to the throne, Franz Ferdinand, was assassinated in June 1914 by a Serbian nationalist. Serbia at the time was a small country just to the south of Austria-Hungary whose national activists laid claim to what they considered the "Serbian" land of Bosnia-Herzegovina "occupied" by the Habsburgs. In a larger sense, World War I was the result of power politics; that is, diplomatic maneuvering characterized by ever-changing alliances between the continent's "great powers" and smaller states. By the end of the nineteenth century, Europe's great powers included Great Britain, France, Germany, Italy, Russia, and Austria-Hungary. Another power was the Ottoman Empire, but despite its territorial extent it was weak vis-à-vis Europe's other, more modern states. Each of the great powers was afraid that its rivals would take advantage of the weakening Ottoman state; therefore all were willing to come to the aid, at least diplomatically, of the proverbial "sick man of Europe."

At the beginning of the twentieth century there were two rival blocs: the so-called Entente powers comprised of Great Britain, France, and Russia versus Germany, Austria-Hungary, and Italy. Most important for understanding developments in Carpathian Rus' was the fact that Austria-Hungary and

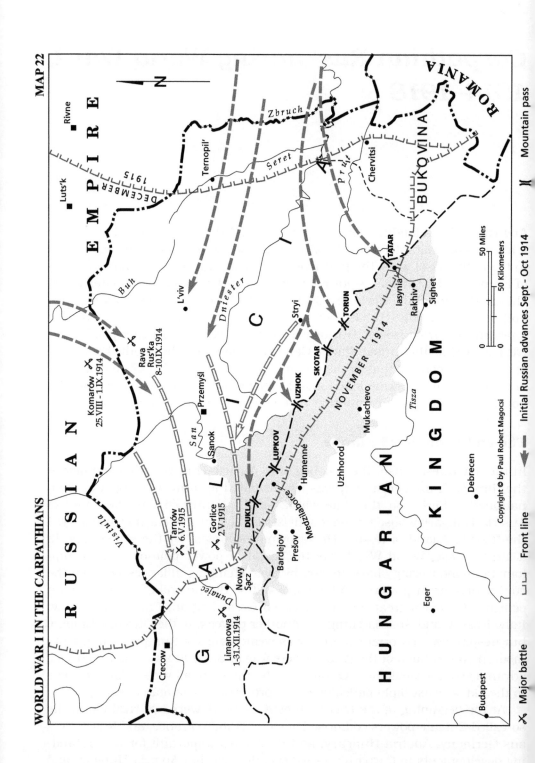

MAP 22

WORLD WAR I IN THE CARPATHIANS

✕ Major battle   ⊔ Front line   ⟵ Initial Russian advances Sept - Oct 1914   )(Mountain pass

Copyright © by Paul Robert Magocsi

Russia, which had been allies during the first half of the nineteenth century, were now in opposing camps. The main reason for the falling-out between these two empires had to do with the so-called Eastern Question; that is, the fate of the Ottoman Empire. Both Austria-Hungary and Russia wanted to increase their political influence in the Balkans, where states like Greece, Romania, Bulgaria, and Montenegro in the course of the nineteenth century struggled against the Ottomans and eventually gained their independence, often with the help of tsarist Russia. Among these smaller states was Serbia, which looked to Russia as its protector and, in turn, was looked upon by Russia as an ally against Austro-Hungarian expansionism.

On 28 June 1914, the heir to the Habsburg throne Franz Ferdinand was assassinated in Sarajevo, the administrative center of Bosnia-Herzegovina, by a Serbian "freedom fighter" (or anti-Austrian terrorist), and that act set in motion a series of events which made war seem inevitable. One month later (28 July), Austria-Hungary did in fact declare war on Serbia, and immediately the prewar great power alliances took effect. Beginning on 1 August it took only a week for most of Europe's larger and smaller states to declare war on each other. Although there were a few subsequent changes in the coalitions, by 1915 the main protagonists were the Allied and Associated Powers (Great Britain, France, Russia, Italy, and eventually the United States) versus the Central Powers (Germany, Austria-Hungary, and the Ottoman Empire).

The two main theaters in the European conflict were the Western Front, where France and Great Britain were pitted against Germany; and the Eastern Front, with Germany and Austria-Hungary pitted against Russia. There were also two southern fronts where Austria-Hungary faced, respectively, Italy and Greece.

World War I in Carpathian Rus'

Galicia and Carpathian Rus' were in the heart of the Eastern Front, and both regions were drawn into the conflict from virtually the very beginning. The conflict in Carpathian Rus' can be divided into three phases: (1) September to December 1914, when tsarist Russian forces took most of Galicia, reaching the Carpathian mountain passes and beyond into the Prešov Region and Subcarpathian Rus' in northeastern Hungary; (2) January to April 1915, when Austro-Hungarian forces launched a massive counteroffensive that contained and in part pushed the Russians back; and (3) May to June 1915, when Austro-Hungarian and German forces drove the Russian armies out of Carpathian Rus' and most of Galicia.

By August 1914, a massive mobilization of the Austro-Hungarian Army together with units of the Hungary's home army (*Honvéd*) brought hundreds of thousands of troops into Galicia in preparation for an attack against tsarist Russia. In the last week of August, Austro-Hungarian divisions did indeed cross the northern frontier and were victorious at the battle of Komarów. Within a week, however, they were turned back by a Russian counteroffensive from the north and east under the overall command of

General Nikolai Ivanov. The counteroffensive proved to be exceptionally successful, so that by the second week of September 1914 tsarist Russian troops captured L'viv, the administrative capital of Austrian Galicia, and began to lay siege to the strategic fortress at Przemyśl along the San River. Although it took another six months (March 1915) before Przemyśl finally capitulated, the main Russian forces decided to bypass the city. Austria-Hungary's troops retreated so rapidly that by the end of September 1914 tsarist Russian armies reached as far west as the Dunajec River. They were finally stopped in December by an Austro-Hungarian victory in a month-long series of clashes remembered as the Battle of Limanowa.

Meanwhile, to the south tsarist troops took control of all the major Carpathian passes and for a few weeks from late September to November 1914 penetrated into northeastern Hungary, reaching as far as Bardejov and Humenné in the west and Sighet in the east. In December the Russians were gradually pushed back out of Hungary. They remained poised near the passes, however, engaging in skirmishes such as those at the Uzhok Pass, which the Russians were able to hold until January 1915. In effect, by the end of 1914, most of Austrian Galicia, including the entire Lemko Region, was in the hands of the tsarist Russian military.

All this meant that the heart of the Danubian Basin was now open to Austro-Hungary's enemy in the east. For their part, Russian strategists believed that the road to Berlin lay through Budapest and Vienna. In other words, their goal of ultimate victory over Germany depended first on crossing the Carpathians and defeating Austria-Hungary.

Fearing the worst, Austria-Hungary's chief-of-staff, Conrad von Hötzendorf, launched a major counteroffensive designed to take back control of the Carpathian passes, relieve the siege of the fortress at Przemyśl, and eventually drive the Russians out of Galicia. The counteroffensive came to be known as the *Karpathenkrieg*, or the Carpathian Winter War, a monumental four-month military struggle that lasted from mid-January to late April 1915. No less than one million soldiers on each side were pitted one against the other in a desperate attempt to secure control of the mountain passes (Dukla, Lupkov, Uzhok, Skotar) in the heart of Carpathian Rus' and the strategically crucial railroad junctions on both sides of the Carpathians (Sanok, Stryi, Medzilaborce, Humenné).

It was during these four months of early 1915 that tsarist troops, largely those of the VIII Russian Army under General Aleksei Brusilov, were based in much of the Lemko Region and Prešov Region south of the mountain passes. In the course of frequent battles and skirmishes, towns like Medzilaborce, Svidník, Humenné and the surrounding Carpatho-Rusyn villages on both sides of the mountains were heavily damaged, including the Basilian monastery at Krasný Brod, which was destroyed. The brutal winter weather and treacherous mountain conditions, with snow already on the ground in early October and temperatures well below zero throughout January and February, took an enormous toll on the combatants. The result? No less than one million dead and wounded on the Russian side and 800,000 on the Austro-Hungarian—gruesome numbers that surpassed losses at the more infamous battles of Verdun and Somme on the Western Front. Hence, the Carpathian Winter War of 1915 has recently been given "the dubious title of the Stalingrad of World War I."[1] In the end, the Austro-Hungarian counteroffensive, whose main intent was to relieve the siege at Przemyśl—which actually fell to the Russians on 22 March—was not only incredibly costly but a military failure!

Confident of their success, the tsarist Russian authorities decided to set up a civil administration as the first step toward the formal annexation of Galicia. Tsar Nicholas II himself visited L'viv in May 1915. By then, he and his advisors were convinced that after centuries of "foreign rule" the ancient "Russian" land of Galicia would once again be part of the patrimony of "Holy Rus'" under the scepter of the tsar of all Rus' (often mistranslated into English as "tsar of all the Russias").

Meanwhile, Germany, shocked by what it considered the military incompetence of its Austro-Hungarian ally just defeated in the Carpathian Winter War, decided to take matters into its own hands. No sooner had Tsar Nicholas II returned home from his triumphal entry into L'viv than Germany's armies, in cooperation with their Austro-Hungarian allies, under-took a counteroffensive. It began in the first week of May 1915 with major victories along a front line between Tarnów and Gorlice, very near the Lemko Region. Before the end of the month, the last of the Carpathian passes (Dukla) was in Austro-Hungarian hands and Russian forces were driven eastward beyond the San River. The fortress at Przemyśl was retaken on 3 June, L'viv on 22 June, and by the end of the month Austria-Hungary was able to restore its rule throughout all of Carpathian Rus' and most of Galicia.

During these early battles and throughout the war, thousands of Carpatho-Rusyn young men served in units of the Austro-Hungarian Army and Hungary's *Honvéds*. In particular, on the Eastern Front, many were cap-tured and forced to spend most of the war years in Russian prisoner-of-war camps. On the southern front they were less fortunate, and thousands died in northern Italy during 12 exceedingly costly but inconclusive battles lasting over a period of two years (May 1915–September 1917) against Italian troops entrenched along the Isonso River.

The war against Carpatho-Rusyn civilians

Back home, the cycle of military advances and retreats by Russian, Austro-Hungarian, and German forces between August 1914 and May 1915 had a very negative impact on large parts of Carpathian Rus', in particular on the Lemko Region in Galicia. There was, of course, much material destruc-tion as a result of fighting during the initial Russian advance into Galicia and northern Hungary, as well as during the Austro-Hungarian counterof-fensive launched at the Battle of Gorlice with the result that several Lemko villages (Tylawa, Bartne, Bodaki, Świątkowa Wielka, Ropica Górna, Krempna, Nieznajowa, and Rozstajne, among others) were partially destroyed.

Even more devastating and with longer-lasting effects than the damage caused directly by fighting was the persecution of Carpatho-Rusyn civilians carried out by the Austro-Hungarian military and Habsburg governing authorities. Already on the eve of the war, Carpatho-Rusyn converts to Orthodoxy were being brought to trial on charges of treason because of their alleged sympathy for Orthodox Russia. The anti-Russian war scare and the actual invasion from the East placed Carpatho-Rusyns in a very precarious situation. Symbolic of the danger was the fate of the Lemko-Rusyn Orthodox priest, Maksym Sandovych. Sandovych was one of the defendants at the spring 1914 L'viv treason trial, who, after acquittal, was released from custody in June 1914. He was rearrested, however, after the outbreak of the war in late August, this time with his entire family, and imprisoned in Gorlice. Within a week, as tsarist Russian forces were rapidly approaching from the east, he was taken out of his cell and shot. As a martyr for the faith, eight decades later in 1994 Sandovych was proclaimed St. Maksym by the Polish Autocephalous Orthodox Church.

There were indeed reports, especially in far eastern Subcarpathian Rus' around Iasynia and Rakhiv, that during the presence of tsarist troops for a few weeks in September and October 1914, local Carpatho-Rusyns welcomed the "Russian enemy" as liberators from Hungarian rule. Another explanation for the persecution meted out by the Austro-Hungarian military and civil authorities was related to the problem of self-identity. The most widespread ethnonym used for Carpatho-Rusyns was *ruskii/rus'kŷi*. In other words, if asked about one's identity, a Carpatho-Rusyn peasant would most naturally respond: *Ia ruskii/rus'kŷi* (I'm a Rusyn) or *Ia bisiduiu/hovoriu po-rus'kŷ* (I speak Rusyn). To the untutored ear of the Austrian or Hungarian soldier, *ruskii/rus'kŷi* (Rusyn) sounded just like *russkii*; that is, Russian. Hence, all Carpatho-Rusyns could be considered to be Russians—the feared and hated enemy! And what was the practical result of this confusion of sounds? As Austro-Hungarian troops ignominiously retreated in September 1914, they frequently shot indiscriminately or executed by hanging hundreds of innocent Lemko Region "Russians" (*ruski*). It was reported that the Hungarian troops (*Honvéds*) serving in Galicia were particularly cruel in expressing their anger against any Lemko Rusyns (*ruski*) who got in their way.

Aside from persecutory acts by Austro-Hungarian soldiers near and along the front lines, the Habsburg governmental authorities carried out persecution in a more systematic manner. Already in August 1914 the Ruska Bursas in Nowy Sącz, Sanok, and Gorlice were closed and their staff arrested. These, however, were only some of the hundreds more persons arrested throughout the Lemko Region during the first months of the war (August and September) on suspicion that they might collaborate with the advancing Russian Army. The arrested had previously been identified in Austrian intelligence reports as members of prewar Russophile-oriented organizations and/or as subscribers to Galicia's Russophile press. As in the Hungarian Kingdom, where Magyarones (pro-Hungarians) willingly denounced fellow Carpatho-Rusyns to the authorities for their presumed sympathy toward Russia and the Slavic East, so too in the Lemko Region were there Lemkos of Ukrainian orientation and Ukrainian patriots from East Galicia ready to inform Austrian military officials about the alleged dangers posed during wartime to the Habsburg Empire by Russophile Lemkos.

Austrian military tribunals passed judgments—often the death penalty—on the arrested. And as for those who were not "legally" executed or lynched on the spot by angry soldiers, they were subsequently deported to an internment camp set up at Thalerhof (Rusyn: Talerhof) in the western Habsburg province of Styria, near the city of Graz. Labeled "Muscophile traitors," no less than 2,000 Lemko Rusyns (some sources say 5,000) from 151 villages were deported to Thalerhof. Among the interned was virtually the entire Lemko-Rusyn intelligentsia, both secular civic activists and priests of the Old Ruthenian and Russophile national orientations. Over 160 died at the Thalerhof camp, mostly from disease and malnutrition, during their nearly three years of incarceration.[2] While it is true that many Lemkos and other Russophile Galician Ruthenians had during the late nineteenth century developed strong cultural sympathies for Russia and some even consciously identified themselves as Russian, until their persecution in 1914 they were for the most part loyal Habsburg subjects. All that changed, however, as a result of Thalerhof. It was fear of returning Habsburg rule that prompted upwards of 10,000 Lemko Rusyns to join the Russian military retreat eastward following the May 1915 Battle of Tarnów-Gorlice. After the war, some of these refugees managed to return home, while many others decided to remain in Russia permanently.

When, in the early summer of 1915, Austro-Hungarian troops and civilian authorities reestablished Habsburg rule in Galicia, more arrests and deportations to Thalerhof took place at the same time that summary executions occurred at the hands of unruly soldiers. The Austrian government also organized two new treason trials, this time in the imperial capital of Vienna, both of which were directed at the most prominent Lemko-Rusyn and Galician Russophile leaders, including lawyers and parliamentary deputies. During the investigatory phase, testimony was gathered from several of Austria-Hungary's leading Ukrainophile political and cultural figures who had little sympathy for fellow Ruthenians who seemed to prefer tsarist Russian to Habsburg Austrian rule. At both Vienna trials completed in August 1915 and February 1917, death sentences were handed down to 17 of the 31 defendants (over half of whom were Lemko Rusyns).[3] The death sentences were eventually commuted to life imprisonment, and following the collapse of Austro-Hungary in late 1918, all were released.

Neither were Carpatho-Rusyns in the Hungarian Kingdom spared the wrath of the authorities. In March 1915, a Hungarian military tribunal in Košice found 800 Carpatho-Rusyn peasants from Bereg, Ung, and Sharysh counties guilty of "cooperation" with the Russian Army, whereas farther east in Maramorosh county 160 were imprisoned without trial.[4] Summary executions were also not uncommon. Hungarian troops, in particular, amused themselves by beating up men, women, and children in Carpatho-Rusyn villages "liberated" after Russian troops retreated. The famous novel by the Czech author, Jaroslav

Hašek, *The Good Soldier Švejk,* includes one such scene of abuse in which the victims are a group of Carpatho-Rusyns near the railroad station at Humenné.

Magyarization reaches its peak

Aside from human suffering and material destruction, the World War I years marked the culmination of the magyarization process that since the 1870s had as its goal the national assimilation of Carpatho-Rusyns and other non-Magyar peoples in the Hungarian Kingdom. During the wartime scare made real by the tsarist Russian occupation of large parts of Carpathian Rus' on both slopes of the mountains, the pro-Hungarian Carpatho-Rusyn intelligentsia, in particular the hierarchy and priests of the Greek Catholic Church, were desperate to distance themselves from anything that might be associated with the "Russian" East. Symbolic of the uncertain and fear-ful atmosphere was a petition adopted as early as April 1915 by a group of Greek Catholic priests speaking on behalf of a so-called people's council that met in the village of Nyzhnyi Verets'kyi in the northern mountainous region of Bereg county. The petition called on the Hungarian government to abolish the term *Rusyn* and, instead, to refer to Carpatho-Rusyns either as "Catholics of the Eastern Rite," or simply as "Magyars."[5]

Already before the war, the Hungarian government had changed many village names from Rusyn to Hungarian. It also passed the laws requiring that newly born children be registered with Hungarian first names and that adults be referred to in official documents only by the Hungarian form of their names. Hence, Ivan suddenly became János, Antonii—Antal, and Shtefan—István. The Greek Catholic bishops of Mukachevo (Antal Papp), Prešov (István Novák), and Hajdúdorog (István Miklósy) went one step further. Meeting in July 1915 with Hungarian government ministers in Budapest, they accepted the government's plan which called for the introduction of the "Western" Gregorian calendar instead of the traditional "Eastern" Julian calendar for use in the church year, and for the replacement of the Cyrillic alphabet by the Roman alphabet (*Latynyka*). The Roman alphabet eventually adopted and based on a complicated Hungarian transcription was worked out by the Prešov seminary professor of Carpatho-Rusyn descent, István Szémán. Within a year, it was introduced into most school textbooks and newspapers. Bishops Novák and Papp formally banned the use of the Cyrillic alphabet in their eparchies and the popular government-sponsored Rusyn-language newspaper also dropped the Cyrillic alphabet, so that *Nedîlia* became *Negyelya* in 1916.

It seemed that the prewar predictions made by some knowledgeable observers that the Carpatho-Rusyns of Hungary would soon all become Magyars were about to be realized. The year 1918 was about to dawn, how-ever, and before its 12-month cycle was completed, the war had come to an end and the Austro-Hungarian Empire itself had ceased to exist. A new era was clearly about to begin and Carpatho-Rusyns were to be among the ben-eficiaries of the enormous political changes that were to transform much of central and eastern Europe.

The end of the old and the birth of a new order, 1918–1919

By 1915, the second year of World War I, the conflict had reached a stalemate. The opposing armies faced each other along fronts which, despite steadily high casualties, did not move in any significant manner. Occasionally there might be an offensive surge by one side, as with the Russian advance during the summer of 1916 that brought far eastern Galicia and Bukovina once again under tsarist control, but within a few months the front lines returned more or less to where they had been before. The year 1917 did bring, however, two events of significance that were to have a profound impact on the outcome of the war. In April, the United States entered the war on the side of the Allies, providing them with military supplies and soldiers that helped reinforce the Western Front. In February and again in October of that year, the Russian Empire experienced two revolutions. The February Revolution toppled the tsar and brought an end to imperial rule; the October Revolution brought to power radical revolutionaries, known as Bolsheviks, who immediately set out to create what they claimed would be the world's first socialist state—Soviet Russia.

National self-determination and socialist revolution

These two developments had important political and military ramifications that were played out in early 1918. In January of that year, President Woodrow Wilson of the United States announced his country's war aims in a 14-point declaration. The declaration proposed the creation of a Polish state and also called for autonomy for the various peoples of the Habsburg Empire. In yet another document Wilson spoke of the right of all peoples for "national self-determination."[1] In other words, each nationality had an inalienable right to govern itself. Wilson's views were adopted by the Allies which meant that among their war aims was the political transformation— although not dismantlement—of Austria-Hungary.

The second development was played out in what after October 1917 became Bolshevik-ruled Soviet Russia. The Bolsheviks were a small but tightly organized socialist party, which called for the overthrow of tsarist and later of parliamentary-style democratic rule in Russia. After they car-ried out a putsch (they called it a "revolution") and took over the reins of government in October/November 1917, they made good on their promise to pull Russia out of the war and to sign a peace treaty (at Brest-Litovsk) with Germany and Austria-Hungary in March 1918. As a result, Germany and its ally Austria-Hungary no longer had to fight along the Eastern Front. This meant that the Central Powers were spared any military threats from Russia, which in any case was soon plunged into civil war between the Bolshevik "Reds" and the so-called "Whites"—all those elements in the for-mer Russian Empire who refused to live in an increasingly dictatorial Soviet state.

The Bolshevik Revolution and Russian Civil War also had an important impact on the tens of thousands of Austro-Hungarian prisoners of war who were released from captivity in late 1917. Among the released soldiers were thousands of Carpatho-Rusyns who witnessed how it was possible to top-ple an imperial regime and take power into their own hands. Ideas about socialism and certainly the end to feudal-like conditions in the Russian Empire, where the Bolsheviks encouraged the confiscation of the property of large landowners, proved to be attractive to young Carpatho-Rusyn sol-diers, mostly of peasant origin. Some even voluntarily joined various armies and partisan units, whether the revolutionary Reds or counterrevolutionary Whites, fighting in Russia's Civil War. Certainly those who returned home in 1918 brought back to Carpathian Rus' convictions about the need for social and political change that they saw was possible from the experience of Russia.

The March 1918 Treaty of Brest-Litovsk signed between Soviet Russia and the Central Powers also recognized the independence of several coun-tries along the western borders of the former Russian Empire. Among those new countries was Ukraine, which was placed under the protection of Germany and Austria-Hungary, and from which the Central Powers began to extract foodstuffs and grain to send to their own starving populations on the home front.

All these factors made it possible for the leading Central Powers, Ger-many and Austria-Hungary, to carry on the war. By the summer of 1918, however, it was becoming increasingly evident that the Allies—now with the direct participation of the United States—were going to be the victors. Nev-ertheless, despite the increasingly weak military position of Germany and Austria-Hungary, both those states remained territorially intact, so that the Habsburg government was able to maintain authority over its empire until the very last weeks of the war. Ever since the imperial parliament was reconvened in May 1917, national activists, at least in the Austrian half of the empire, were able to debate in public various proposals to transform the internal structure of the empire. On the other hand, those activists who favored a complete break with the Habsburgs could only speak out abroad among exiles living and working in Allied countries such as Britain, France, and most especially the United States.

Rusyn Americans mobilize politically

Carpatho-Rusyns were among the many immigrant groups from central and eastern Europe who followed closely military and political developments in their homeland during World War I. Most of their information came from Rusyn-language newspapers that were published weekly, in some cases several days a week, by the various brotherhood societies. While it is true that in contrast to other Slavic immigrants—Poles, Czechs, Slovaks, and Croats—Rusyn Americans began to engage in organized political activity relatively late, in the end they turned out to be even more successful in achieving their goals than were fellow Slavic-American groups who had started earlier. For example, in a comparative assessment of the impact of President Woodrow Wilson's policies on postwar Europe, the respected Slovak-American historian of the Habsburg Empire, Victor S. Mamatey, concluded that "the Ruthenian [Carpatho-Rusyn] immigrants in America did determine the fate of their compatriots at home—a unique case, it appears, of the influence of an immigrant group in America on the political history of Europe."[2]

The first Carpatho-Rusyn immigrants to organize for a political purpose were the Lemkos from Galicia, in particular the Greek-Catholic-turned-Orthodox priest Joseph Fedoronko, and the newspaper editor Victor Hladick, who during the war years was active in the Lemko and Galician Russophile community in western Canada. In July 1917, Fedoronko helped organize in New York City the first congress of the League for the Liberation of Carpatho-Russia/Soiuz osvobozhdeniia Prikarpatskoi Rusi. The League's goal was to unite with a democratic Russia all the Rus' peoples of Austria-Hungary; that is, Carpatho-Rusyns as well as Galician and Bukovinian "Russians." The League promoted this idea until early 1919, by which time it became clear that the cause of democracy in the former tsarist empire was lost, and that a Soviet Russia, which had come into being in the interim and which the immigrant groups opposed, was here to stay.

More representative and eventually more decisive were those Rusyn-American organizations comprised primarily of immigrants from the Prešov Region and Subcarpathian Rus' in the Hungarian Kingdom. In July 1918, the representatives of the largest fraternal brotherhoods, the Greek Catholic Union and United Societies, met in the steel-mill town of Homestead, a suburb of Pittsburgh in western Pennsylvania, to form the American National Council of Uhro-Rusyns. The council, representing specifically Carpatho-Rusyns from the Hungarian Kingdom, adopted a resolution calling for autonomy within the Hungarian Kingdom, or, if borders were to change, to be united with their Rus' brethren in Galicia and Bukovina. Considering subsequent developments, it is interesting to note that this first resolution of the Uhro-Rusyn National Council made no mention of joining with Czechs and Slovaks, whose own immigrant leaders were very active at the time. In the presence of the wartime's most influential "Czecho-Slovak" exile, Tomáš Garrigue Masaryk, they signed in May 1918 what came to be known as the

Pittsburgh Agreement, which guaranteed autonomy for Slovakia in a proposed independent Czecho-Slovak state. Carpatho-Rusyn spokespeople were angered that the Slovaks claimed all of eastern Slovakia, including the Rusyn-inhabited Prešov Region and the city of Uzhhorod, as part of Slovakia in the proposed joint state with the Czechs.

Rusyn-American demands on behalf of their homeland became clarified after the arrival on the scene of Gregory Zhatkovych. Zhatkovych, who held a law degree from the prestigious Ivy League University of Pennsylvania, was at the time an attorney for the General Motors Corporation. Although he was the son of Pavel Zhatkovych, the founding editor of the Greek Catholic Union's influential newspaper, Gregory never played any role in Rusyn-American civic life before the late summer of 1918. From then on, however, he became a decisive figure, especially after the American National Council of Uhro-Rusyns asked him to act on their behalf in promoting their interests with the United States government.

Zhatkovych proved to be remarkably successful in this regard. He drew up a memorandum outlining Carpatho-Rusyn political intentions and, because of connections from his university years, was able to present it in a personal meeting at the White House with President Wilson on 21 October 1918. Zhatkovych's memorandum included three alternatives, but the first and clearly most important one demanded "that our Uhro-Rusyns be recognized as a separate people and, if possible, as completely independent."[3] Other alternatives included unification on the basis of full autonomy with an unnamed neighboring Slavic people or, in the worst case scenario—if prewar borders were to remain unchanged—autonomy within Hungary. Presumably, President Wilson considered a Carpatho-Rusyn independent state unrealistic and proposed instead that Zhatkovych consult with other Slavic political activists.

Zhatkovych acted quickly. Within a few days he met in Philadelphia (at the Mid-European Union, 23–26 October) with the soon-to-be chosen president of Czechoslovakia Tomáš G. Masaryk, with whom he discussed the possibility of including Carpatho-Rusyns within that new state. The expectation was that Carpatho-Rusyns would receive full autonomy in a Czechoslovak federation. At Zhatkovych's initiative, the American National Council of Uhro-Rusyns convened in Scranton, Pennsylvania on 12 November and resolved to seek unity with Czechoslovakia, making clear, however, that the Rusyn-inhabited Prešov Region claimed by Slovaks would be part of an autonomous Carpatho-Rusyn political entity. What became known as the Scranton Resolution was approved by President Wilson as well as by then-elected (in absentia) president of Czechoslovakia, Tomáš G. Masaryk, who suggested that a democratic referendum be held among Rusyn Americans in order to enhance the resolution's legitimacy. In December 1918, 68 percent of Rusyn Americans (through indirect voting by delegates of the leading brotherhood organizations) voted for unification with Czechoslovakia. Interestingly, 28 percent voted for union with Ukraine, but only 2 percent for independence, with even smaller percentages for union either with Russia or Hungary.[4]

Political mobilization in the Carpatho-Rusyn homeland

About the same time that the Rusyn-American communities were reaching specific decisions about their homeland, Carpatho-Rusyns in Europe also began to mobilize politically. Political action was now possible in a situation where Habsburg rule was rapidly disintegrating. During the last days of October, as the new states of Czechoslovakia and Yugoslavia were claiming large blocks of Austro-Hungarian territory, the last Habsburg emperor, Karl I, abdicated, and on 3 November the imperial army signed an armistice of surrender. In effect, the centuries-old Habsburg Empire ceased to exist.

Thereafter, events unfolded in rapid succession. During the first two weeks of November three other states came into existence—Ukraine, Poland, and Hungary—each of which was to have a direct impact on Carpathian Rus'. On 1 November 1918, the day after the last Habsburg emperor abdicated, the Ruthenians/Ukrainians in eastern Galicia declared their independence and in L'viv formed what became the West Ukrainian National Republic. This republic claimed as its territory all the East Slavic/Ruthenian lands of former Austria-Hungary; that is, Galicia east of the San River, northern Bukovina, and all of Carpathian Rus' on both slopes of the mountains. Two months later, in January 1919, the West Ukrainian Republic proclaimed its union with the Ukrainian National Republic based in Kiev, which a year before had declared its independence from Russia. The very day, 1 November 1918, on which Galician Ukrainians declared their independence, they found themselves in armed conflict with local Poles for control of the regional capital of L'viv. Eleven days later, when an independent Poland was proclaimed in Warsaw, its government declared all of Galicia an integral part of its historical patrimony. The conflicting views over Galicia led to a full-scale war between Poland and the West Ukrainian Republic that was to last for the next eight months. Galicia's Lemko Region was, therefore, caught between the conflicting Polish and Ukrainian claims on its territory.

Meanwhile, south of the mountains, anti-Habsburg Hungarian leaders proclaimed an independent republic on 16 November. Although the new republic's government led by Count Mihály Károlyi was liberal in orientation and open to cooperation with the country's many national minorities, it was at the same time determined to maintain the historic boundaries of the Hungarian Kingdom, including all of Slovakia and Carpathian Rus' on the southern slopes of the mountains. This policy was to bring the Hungarian republic into conflict with other states which laid claim to the Carpathian region, in particular Czechoslovakia and Romania.

In the rapidly changing political circumstances accompanying the collapse of Austria-Hungary, Carpatho-Rusyns were also quick to act. Aware of the Wilsonian doctrine of national self-determination, which was believed to be the policy of the victorious Allied Powers, Carpatho-Rusyn leaders in Europe convoked national councils in much the same way that their immigrant brethren had begun to do a few months earlier in the United States.

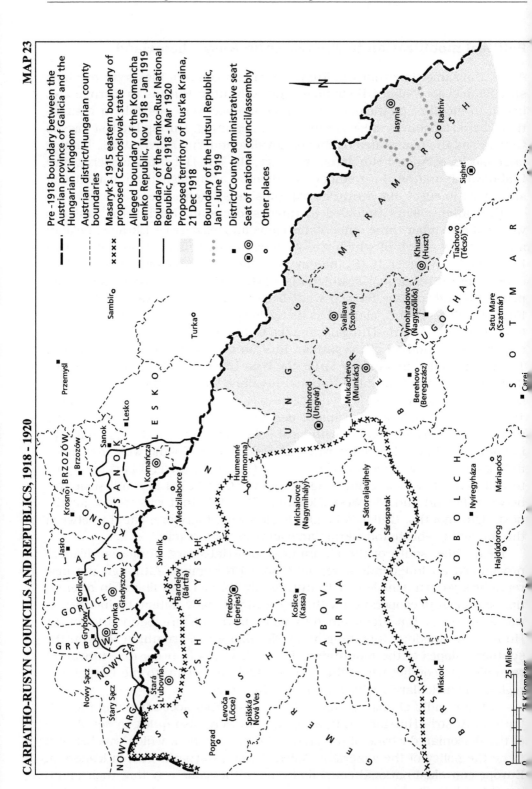

MAP 23

CARPATHO-RUSYN COUNCILS AND REPUBLICS, 1918 - 1920

Pre -1918 boundary between the Austrian province of Galicia and the Hungarian Kingdom

Austrian district/Hungarian county boundaries

Masaryk's 1915 eastern boundary of proposed Czechoslovak state

Alleged boundary of the Komancha Lemko Republic, Nov 1918 - Jan 1919

Boundary of the Lemko-Rus' National Republic, Dec 1918 - Mar 1920

Proposed territory of Rus'ka Kraina, 21 Dec 1918

Boundary of the Hutsul Republic, Jan - June 1919

District/County administrative seat

Seat of national council/assembly

Other places

Also, like the immigrants, the national councils in Europe considered basically the same political options: autonomous self-rule, full independence, or unity either with Russia, Ukraine, Czechoslovakia, or, if necessary, remaining with Hungary. Within the six-month period between 8 November 1918 and 8 May 1919, numerous national councils were established throughout all parts of Carpathian Rus': the Lemko Region, the Prešov Region, Subcarpathian Rus', and the Maramureş Region. In their search for the optimal solution, local leaders were by the outset of 1919 drawn toward four political orientations: (1) unification with Russia; (2) unification with Czechoslovakia; (3) remaining with Hungary; and (4) unification with Ukraine. In two cases, when a given council's desire proved unachievable, it proclaimed an independent state, such as the Lemko-Rusyn Republic in Florynka (December 1918–March 1920) and the Hutsul Republic in Iasynia (January–June 1919). To be sure, none of the Carpatho-Rusyn national councils was acting in isolation; rather, each was influenced by, and trying to maneuver among, the newly formed surrounding political entities that were competing to take control of Carpathian Rus'.

In the Lemko Region, several national councils arose in November 1918; they favored basically two differing political goals. In the eastern town of Komańcza (Rusyn: Komancha), a self-governing executive council was formed, which intended to join the West Ukrainian National Republic. Within less than two months, however, as Galicia's Poles and Ukrainians were engaged in war for control of the former Austrian province, the Polish Army disbanded the Komancha Lemko "republic" in January 1919. Geographically more widespread was the second orientation comprised initially of four councils representing all seven districts in the Lemko Region. On 5 December 1918, delegates from these councils met in the western Lemko Region village of Florynka, where they formed an Executive Council of the Lemko Region, referred to in some circles as the Rus' National Republic (*Russkaia narodnaia respublyka*) and headed by the Greek Catholic priest Mykhaïl Iurchakevych, which coordinated an administration comprised of district-level councils throughout Lemko-inhabited lands from Nowy Targ in the west to Sanok in the east. Initially, the Executive Council hoped to unite the Lemko Region with a democratic Russia. When, however, in early 1919 it became clear that Russia was politically incapacitated by the civil war between the Bolshevik Reds and anti-Bolshevik Whites, the Lemko Rusyns turned instead to their brethren in the Prešov Region with the goal to join them in uniting with Czechoslovakia. Despite the openly stated desire of the Lemko-Rus' leaders not to be part of Poland, the authorities in Warsaw, on the cusp of gaining control of all of Galicia, did not yet intervene directly or try to halt Lemko "separatist" activity.

On the southern slopes of the mountains, Carpatho-Rusyn leaders in the Prešov Region were torn between "uniting with Rus'/Ukraine"—as was proclaimed at a national council held at Stará Ľubovňa on 8 November 1918—or uniting with the new state of Czechoslovakia.[5] Eventually, the faction led by the Prešov lawyer Antonii Beskyd, and in cooperation with Lemko-Rusyn activists from Galicia, formed a national council in Prešov on 21 December 1918. By that time Czechoslovak troops had reached eastern Slovakia, and their presence inspired confidence among the members of the Prešov Carpatho-Rusyn National Council, which in early January 1919 proclaimed openly its desire to unite with Czechoslovakia.

Hungary's autonomous Rus' Land

Meanwhile, the republic of Hungary under Mihály Károlyi was doing its best to maintain the country's historic boundaries along the crests of the Carpathians. The republic's minister responsible for nationalities, the distinguished sociologist and liberal political activist Oszkár Jászi, was quite serious about providing some sort of self-rule for Hungary's minorities. In fact, the Hungarian government did find willing partners among leading Greek Catholic clerics in Subcarpathian Rus'. On 9 November 1918, the priests Petro Gebei (the future bishop of Mukachevo), Avhustyn Voloshyn (the future head of Carpatho-Ukraine), and Simeon Sabov (canon of the Mukachevo Eparchy), convened in Uzhhorod a Council of the Uhro-Rusyn People, which declared that "the Uhro-Rusyn people do not wish to separate from Hungary . . . but expect to receive all the rights that a democratic Hungary intends to provide to all of its non-Magyar peoples."[6]

Convinced that it had the support of local Carpatho-Rusyn leaders, especially those in the influential Greek Catholic Church, the Károlyi government adopted on 21 December 1918 a law (No. 10), which called into existence an autonomous province called Rus'ka Kraina (the Rus' Land). The Hungarian law provided for a Rus'ka Kraina Ministry in Budapest and an administration based in Mukachevo; the latter was to be governed temporarily by an advisory council (Rus'ka rada) of 42 representatives from four counties (Ung, Bereg, Ugocha, and Maramorosh) headed by Orest Sabov and Agoshton Shtefan. Provisions were also made for a Rusyn National Assembly/Rus'kyi narodnyi soim, whose 36 elected members actually convened in early March in Mukachevo. Aside from the above four counties (roughly the equivalent of Subcarpathian Rus'), Rus'ka Kraina was expected to include the Rusyn-inhabited parts of Zemplyn, Sharysh, Spish, and Abov counties in the Prešov Region, although that could occur only after the conclusion of a general postwar peace among the various states to emerge from former Austria-Hungary. In fact, the Károlyi regime never fixed the boundaries of Rus'ka Kraina, which alienated the members of the recently elected national assembly (*soim*).

The Ukrainian option

Hungary's efforts to retain Carpatho-Rusyn lands were challenged not only by pro-Czechoslovak Rusyn activists, but also by local leaders in far eastern Maramorosh county, in particular its Hutsul region. As early as 8 November 1918, Hutsuls under the leadership of Stepan Klochurak met in the large

THE MEANING OF UKRAINE

Ukraine is today the name of an independent state in Europe. With regard to the subject of this book, there are two matters that deserve some explanation. The first has to do with the origin of the name *Ukraine* and how its meaning evolved over time. The second is how the concept of Ukraine has been understood by Carpatho-Rusyns, especially during the period of revolution and political change at the close of World War I.

The name Ukraine (in Ukrainian: *Ukraïna*) is a term of Slavic origin derived from the Indo-European root **krei* "to cut," with the secondary meaning of an edge (*krai*), or borderland (*okraïna*). Some of the earliest medieval written sources among the South Slavs contain terms like *kraj, krajina, krajište;* while in the East Slavic *Rus' Primary Chronicle* the first references to *ukraina* appear as early as 1187 and 1189.[a] The earliest documents from Carpathian Rus', which date from the fourteenth century, also contain the term *kraina*, which in all cases refer to a group of villages that were at the northern edge of settlement, or borderland of Bereg and Zemplyn counties.[b] In these and other medieval sources, the term *ukraina* is never used in reference to a specific territory, but rather in the sense of any undefined borderland.

In the sixteenth century *Ukraina* (in its Polish form) was first used to describe a specific territory encompassing three palatinates (Kiev, Bratslav, and Chernihiv) in what was then the southeastern region of the Polish-Lithuanian Commonwealth. From the second half of the seventeenth century, the term *Ukraïna* was also used by the Zaporozhian Cossacks as a poetic device to symbolize their homeland, whose boundaries waxed and waned depending on political circumstances.

After the demise of Poland-Lithuania between 1772 and 1795, the name *Ukraine* fell into disuse as a term to designate a specific territory. Then, in the early nineteenth century, activists in support of the national revival began to use the term *Ukraine* to designate the land where ethnic Ukrainians ("Little Russians" or "Ruthenians" in official parlance) lived; that is, territory which until 1917–1918 was within the Russian and Austro-Hungarian empires. Only toward the end of World War I and the subsequent revolutionary turmoil that wracked much of central and eastern Europe did *Ukraine* come to be used as the official name for a distinct political entity, whether the Ukrainian National Republic, the West Ukrainian National Republic, the Ukrainian State, or the Ukrainian Soviet Socialist Republic. The latter continued to exist until 1991, when it was transformed into an independent state called simply Ukraine.

Thus, as a term referring to a nonspecific and even ethnically non-Ukrainian territory, the name *Ukraine* dates from early medieval times. As a name for lands inhabited by ethnic Ukrainians, it dates from the nineteenth century. And as a name referring to a state entity, it dates from the early twentieth century.

When did Carpatho-Rusyns first encounter, and how did they understand, the concept of Ukraine? It seems that Carpatho-Rusyns first became seriously aware of Ukraine during their own first national awakening, which began in earnest after 1848. Living at the time within the framework of the Austro-Hungarian Empire,

Carpatho-Rusyn cultural activists in the Hungarian part of that realm interacted quite closely with fellow Rusyn national activists in Austrian Galicia.

The Galician Rusyns were themselves undergoing a national awakening and at the time were divided between at least three national orientations: the Old Ruthenians, Russophiles, and Ukrainophiles. It was the latter who made Carpatho-Rusyn activists aware of Ukraine and the newly emerging Ukrainian literary language which was in the process of being codified in Galicia. But the reaction was not what Galicia's Ukrainophiles expected. The national awakener Aleksander Dukhnovych spoke out in 1863 and set the tone for the majority of Carpatho-Rusyn activists who were to follow him at least until the second decade of the twentieth century:

> I don't understand for what reason you could suddenly change the pure Rusyn language to Ukrainian [*chysta ruskaia mova na Oukraynskuiu*]—as if Galicia were in Ukraine. In Galicia, so far as I know, there is another dialect. . . . Your task should be to awaken Ukraine, so that it would adopt the original script and learn Rusyn grammar. . . . I simply don't understand what attractive force draws Galicia to Ukraine.[c]

Carpatho-Rusyn intellectuals, whether clerical or secular, certainly felt a cultural affinity with the East. But for them the East was the land of Rus'. And whereas Ukraine might also be in the East, it was only within the framework of Rus' that it was acceptable to Carpatho-Rusyns. Ukraine outside the context of a single Rus' (which included in modern-day terminology Russia/Russians, Belarus/Belarusans, and Ukraine/Ukrainians) was unthinkable.

With this cultural context in mind, we might better understand the appearance, albeit occasional, of the name *Ukraine* in the declarations of a few national councils that were formed in late 1918 and early 1919 by Carpatho-Rusyns concerned with their political future. Whatever its political orientation (pro-Hungarian, pro-Czechoslovak, pro-Russian, pro-Ukrainian) and wherever its location (Europe or North America), each national council designated itself with the adjectival form of Rus' (*ruskŷi, russkyi*) but never Ukrainian.

There were, however, a few activists who did favor uniting Carpathian Rus' with Ukraine, whether the West Ukrainian National Republic based in Galicia, or with so-called Greater Ukraine (*Soborna Ukraïna*), whose proponents hoped would encompass all Ukrainian ethnographic lands in the former Russian and Austro-Hungarian empires.

In an effort to make such political goals palatable to the Carpatho-Rusyn public, a few leaders like Emilian Nevyts'kyi at the national council of Stará L'ubovňa (8 November 1918) and Iulii and Mykhailo Brashchaiko at the national congress of Khust (21 January 1919) formulated resolutions and questionnaires, which introduced the term *Ukrainian*, but which at the same time were deliberately vague with regard to terms used for peoples and states. For example, the manifesto issued by the Rusyn National Council/*Russka Narodna Rada* at Stará L'ubovňa spoke only of "our Rus' land [*rus'kii krai*]."[d] In an effort to solicit the views of "the people," the council's organizer E. Nevyts'kyi sent out questionnaires that were careful first to remind rural villagers of their association with the larger East Slavic world:

> We are called Carpatho-Rusyns. Yet we know that beyond the Carpathians live the same Rusyns as us. Their language, traditions, and faith are the same as ours, and for that reason they are our brothers. Together with them we form ethnographically one great multi-million strong people.[e]

It was only in a subsequent questionnaire that Nevyts'kyi introduced the term *Ukraine* as a kind of synonym for Rus'. He called on village priests and schoolteachers to ask "if your villagers want that we Rusyns remain with the Magyars" [i.e., Hungary], or "if our people want to unite with Rus'-Ukraine?"[f] It seems that the number of questionnaires returned by priests and teachers in the Prešov Region was no more than 60 in total.

Somewhat more successful in reaching a larger number of people were the organizers of the Khust national council, who managed to attract 420 delegates (each one allegedly representing one thousand people) from various villages, mostly in the eastern regions of Subcarpathian Rus'. As is evident from the first clause of the council's resolution, the territorial name *Ukrainian* was used unambiguously, although the ethnonym *Ukrainian* appeared only as an equivalent of *Rusyn*:

> The all-national council of Hungarian Rusyns-Ukrainians, from 21 January 1919, declares the unification of all Rusyns-Ukrainians from the counties of Maramorosh, Ugocha, Bereg, Ung, Zemplyn, Sharysh, Spish, and Abov-Torna with Rusyns-Ukrainians living in lands that are part of a Greater Ukraine.[g]

The point is that for most Carpatho-Rusyns before—and even after—World War I, the concept of Ukraine was not differentiated from Rus', which in turn was understood to mean the unified realm of Eastern-rite Christians, regardless whether they were ethnically Russian, Belarusan, Ukrainian, or Carpatho-Rusyn. During the twentieth century, leftist political sympathizers, including Communists in the European homeland and working-class activists in the United States and Canada (especially Lemkos), also understood the concept of Ukraine/Ukrainians in a larger context, one in which Eastern Christian Holy Rus' was in their minds conceptually transformed into proletarian Russia and the Soviet Union.

[a] *Litopys rus'kyi za Ipats'kym spyskom* (Kiev, 1989), pp. 343 and 347.

[b] Aleksei L. Petrov, *Medieval Carpathian Rus': The Oldest Documentation about the Carpatho-Rusyn Church and Eparchy* (1930) (New York, 1998), pp. 60–65.

[c] A. Dukhnovych, "Korrespondentsiia yz Priasheva," *Vîstnyk dlia Rusynov Avstriiskoy derzhavŷ* (Vienna, 1863), No. 11—cited in Kyryl Studyns'kyi, "Aleksander Dukhnovych i Halychyna," *Naukovŷi zbornyk Tovarystva "Prosvita"*, III (Uzhhorod, 1924), p. 92.

[d] *Nauka* (Uzhhorod), 19 November 1918—cited in Ortoskop, *Derzhavni zmahannia Prykarpats'koï Ukraïny* (Uzhhorod, 1924), p. 10.

e Cited from questionnaires reproduced in Zdeněk Peška and Josef Markov, "Příspěvek k ústavním dějinám Podkarpatské Rusi," *Bratislava,* V (Bratislava, 1931), p. 526–527.

f Ibid., p. 526.

g Cited in Ortoskop, *Derzhavni zmahannia,* p. 21.

Subcarpathian mountain village of Iasynia to form a Hutsul National Council. Like the Lemkos in the far northwest of Carpathian Rus', Hutsuls in the far east created a governing administration (with Klochurak as "prime minister") to replace the departing Hungarian authorities and also a self-defense military unit. By January 1919 that unit was about 1,100 strong, comprised of demobilized Austro-Hungarian soldiers from the Hutsul region itself as well as several hundred others who came from Galicia where they were serving with the armies of the West Ukrainian National Republic. The connection with Galicia was significant, since the national council of what was subsequently dubbed the "Hutsul Republic" hoped to unite with the West Ukrainian Republic and become part of a Greater (*Soborna*) Ukraine.

As for the nearby West Ukrainian Republic, which was already engaged in an intense struggle with Polish forces for control of Galicia, it was in no position to assist the Hutsul Republic. Nor did the West Ukrainians wish to clash with Hungary and Romania, both of which claimed authority over Hutsul-inhabited Subcarpathian Rus'. When, in early January, the Hutsul military units moved toward the town of Maramorosh-Sighet, where a national council favoring unity with Ukraine had just completed its deliberations, they were driven back by Romanian troops.

While the Hutsul Republic continued to administer several mountainous villages near Iasynia, yet another national council convened in Maramorosh county, this time at Khust, on 21 January 1919. Under the leadership of two brothers, Iulii and Mykhailo Brashchaiko, the Khust council's resolution proclaimed that "all Rusyns-Ukrainians in Maramorosh, Ugocha, Bereg, Ung, Zemplyn, Sharysh, Spish, and Abov-Turna counties [i.e., Subcarpathian Rus' and the Prešov Region] unite with Greater (*Soborna*) Ukraine." The resolution also expressed the desire that "Ukrainian military forces [presumably from the West Ukrainian National Republic] occupy territory inhabited by the Rusyns-Ukrainians of Hungary."[7]

In the end, neither the Ukrainian nor the Hungarian option had any real hope of success. On the northern slopes of the Carpathians, Polish armies succeeded by June 1919 in driving the West Ukrainian National Republic and its army out of eastern Galicia. The Allied Powers then authorized Poland to occupy that former Austrian province. Although technically the occupation was only on a temporary basis, the Poles immediately proceeded to set up an administration and to treat all of Galicia, including the Lemko Region, as if it were already part of Poland.

As for the Hungarians, they were fully compromised in the eyes of the victorious Allies when, in March 1919, Károlyi's government fell and was replaced by a Bolshevik-style Soviet government headed by Béla Kun. Even Hungary's autonomous province of Rus'ka Kraina based in Mukachevo was in late March transformed into Soviet Rus'ka Kraina. This short-lived experiment marked the first attempt at establishing Communist rule in some part of Carpathian Rus', even though the head (commissar) of Soviet Rus'ka Kraina was a holdover from the Károlyi regime, the decidedly anti-Communist Agoshton Shtefan. Nevertheless, a government council (*uriadova rada*) was elected in early April 1919, and it, together with the already existing national assembly (*soim*), even adopted a constitution for Soviet Rus'ka Kraina within the framework of the Hungarian Soviet Republic. Clearly, all these efforts at self-rule for Carpatho-Rusyns were linked to the political fate of Hungary.

Carpatho-Rusyns on the international stage

In early 1919, when the victorious Allied Powers led by the United States, Great Britain, and France convened a conference in Paris to determine the postwar political order in Europe, one of the major concerns facing the peacemakers was Bolshevik Russia and its proclamations about a socialist world revolution which was slated to spread first to central Europe. Bolshevik predictions seemed to be fulfilled with the appearance of Béla Kun's Soviet Hungary. Therefore, to prevent the further spread of Bolshevik-style revolutions, the Allies authorized and gave military assistance to Czechoslovak and Romanian forces to enter the lands of historic Hungary from the west and from the east.

It was in the context of the offensive against Soviet Hungary that Romanian troops took all of Maramorosh county and in June 1919 dismantled the "independent" Hutsul Republic. By August 1919 Béla Kun's Soviet experiment in the heart of the Danubian Basin was crushed, with the result that two-thirds of historic Hungary's territory was in the hands of other states. The Rusyn-inhabited lands in former northern Hungary were now under the control of Czechoslovak troops (the Prešov Region and western Subcarpathian Rus') and Romanian troops (Subcarpathian Rus' east of Mukachevo).

Carpatho-Rusyn political activists quickly adapted to these new political realities. Those who had favored the Hungarian and Ukrainian options now joined with their compatriots in the Prešov Region and the Lemko Region in support of the Czechoslovak solution. A Rusyn-American delegation headed by Gregory Zhatkovych arrived in Uzhhorod in March 1919 and proceeded to convince local pro-Hungarian sympathizers about the advantages of joining Czechoslovakia. The result was a gathering in Uzhhorod on 8 May 1919 of some 200 delegates who represented the previous councils at Prešov, Uzhhorod, Khust, and the Lemko Region, and who now formed the Central Rusyn National Council. After a week of deliberations, chaired by the former pro-Hungarian supporter, Avhustyn Voloshyn, the Central Rusyn National Council in Uzhhorod declared that it endorsed the memorandum of the Rusyn-American delegation; namely that "Rusyns will form an independent [*nezavysymŷi/nezávislý*] state within a Czecho-Slovak-Rusyn

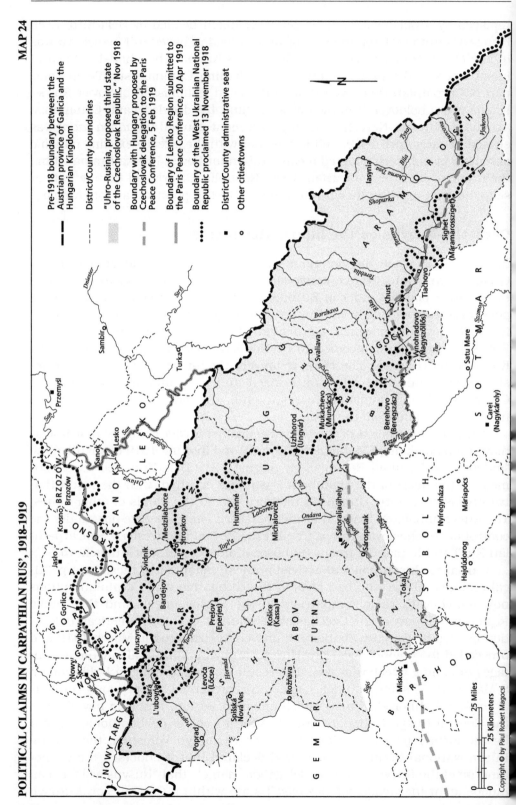

MAP 24

POLITICAL CLAIMS IN CARPATHIAN RUS', 1918-1919

Pre-1918 boundary between the
Austrian province of Galicia and the
Hungarian Kingdom

District/County boundaries

"Uhro-Rusinia, proposed third state
of the Czechoslovak Republic," Nov 1918

Boundary with Hungary proposed by
Czechoslovak delegation to the Paris
Peace Conference, 5 Feb 1919

Boundary of Lemko Region submitted to
the Paris Peace Conference, 20 Apr 1919

Boundary of the West Ukrainian National
Republic proclaimed 13 November 1918

District/County administrative seat

Other cities/towns

Copyright © by Paul Robert Magocsi

republic." [8] The Rusyn-American Zhatkovych was clearly the most authoritative figure at the Uzhhorod gathering, with the result that the Central Rusyn National Council's resolutions reflected his views on what was expected to be a self-governing "Uhro-Rusyn state," whose borders were to be determined by mutual agreement "with representatives of the Czecho-Slovak republic, and which in "all governing and internal matters was independent [Czech: *samostatný*]." [9]

The only losers at Uzhhorod were the Lemko Rusyns. Just a few weeks before, the Lemkos, as part of the pro-Czechoslovak national council in Prešov, submitted a memorandum (together with a map) to the Paris Peace Conference, requesting that the Lemko Region not be separated from Rusyns south of the Carpathians and together with them be made an "autonomous part of the Czecho-Slovak Republic." [10] But the Central Rusyn National Council in Uzhhorod, at the urging of Zhatkovych, rejected the Lemko request to join their brethren in what the Rusyn-American activist called: "Uhro-Rusinia, the proposed third state of the Czechoslovak republic." [11]

To be sure, Carpatho-Rusyn demands were one thing, but political realities could be something else. Czechoslovakia's interest in Rusyn-inhabited lands south of the Carpathians was something very recent, having begun when the country's founding president, Tomáš Garrigue Masaryk, was approached in late 1918 by Carpatho-Rusyn immigrants in the United States. Before that time Masaryk never even considered Carpatho-Rusyn inhabited territory, as evidenced by the eastern boundary line he proposed in 1915 for a future Czechoslovak state (see Map 23). But by 1918 Masaryk's views had evolved and were linked to larger geopolitical concerns in which the soon-to-be president hoped that his small central European country could find solace in having a powerful ally like Russia, whether or not it was ruled by Bolsheviks. With that political constellation in mind, Subcarpathian Rus' seemed an ideal bridge to the east, especially if the borders of Russia or the Soviet Union would ever reach the crests of the Carpathians.

In the interim, Czechoslovakia had to deal with the local Carpatho-Rusyn population, and therefore it did incorporate the basic decisions of the Uzhhorod Central Rusyn National Council as part of its territorial proposals submitted to the international peace conference which was meeting in various palaces just outside Paris during the spring of 1919. The treaty which fixed Czechoslovakia's borders was adopted at Saint Germain-en-Laye on 10 September 1919. This international agreement specified that "the Ruthene territory south of the Carpathians" was to be endowed with "the fullest degree of self-government compatible with the unity of the Czecho-Slovak state." [12] Just what compatibility meant and what was the extent of the "Ruthene territory" being promised self-government were issues that still needed to be clarified. As we shall see, there were no easy solutions to these questions.

As for the eastern boundaries of Czechoslovakia, they were defined by the Treaty of St. Germain and reiterated in the Treaty of Trianon concluded nearly a year later (4 June 1920) with Hungary. All of Slovakia and Carpatho-Rusyn lands south of the mountains were now recognized by the international community as part of Czechoslovakia. Most of Hungary's political and civic leaders were appalled by Trianon, which reduced Hungarian territory to a mere one-third of what it had been within the Habsburg Empire. Over 3.3 million Magyars (31 percent of the total at the time) suddenly found themselves as minorities in states that at best were barely tolerant of them.[13] Almost immediately a political movement began in Hungary known as irredentism; that is, an attempt to get back territories taken away by what Magyars everywhere considered the punitive Treaty of Trianon.

As for the Lemko Region, it together with all of Galicia was initially assigned by the peacemakers in Paris to Poland, but only on a temporary basis. Eventually, however, the Allied and Associated Powers grew tired of the "Galician Question," and in March 1923 they formally recognized all of the former Habsburg-ruled province of Galicia to be a part of Poland. Before the status of Galicia was finally clarified, the Lemko Rusyns, whose request to join Czechoslovakia was turned down in May 1919, managed to maintain a degree of control over their homeland north of the Carpathians for nearly another year. During that time Lemko leaders tried to reach some kind of accommodation with the Polish government. When negotiations broke down, their Executive Council gathered again in Florynka, and on 17 March 1920 formally proclaimed themselves the Supreme Council of the Rus' National Republic of Lemkos under the leadership of Prime Minister Iaroslav Karchmarchyk. The Supreme Council set out to govern the territory it claimed, which was later popularly remembered as the Lemko-Rusyn Republic. The Polish government responded immediately by sending an armed force to disperse the "republic" and establish its own administration throughout the Lemko Region.

The only other part of historic Carpathian Rus' was a small territory that included the town of Sighet (the recent site of a Rusyn national council) and several nearby villages along the northern bank of the Tisza River and its tributaries in far southern Maramorosh county. The decisions at the Paris Peace Conference assigned this small area to Romania.

Hence, following the close of World War I and the disappearance of Habsburg-ruled Austria-Hungary, historic Carpathian Rus' found itself divided by international boundaries and under the rule of three states: Poland, Czechoslovakia, and Romania. There were also scattered and isolated Rusyn-inhabited villages in parts of post-Trianon Hungary and of Yugoslavia (the Vojvodina and Srem, see below, Chapter 17). The subsequent fate of Carpatho-Rusyns was to differ significantly depending on which state they inhabited during the two so-called interwar decades of the twentieth century.

Subcarpathian Rus' in interwar Czechoslovakia, 1919–1938

The postwar political order that formally came into being in the course of 1919–1920 divided historic Carpathian Rus' among three countries: Poland, Czechoslovakia, and Romania. Of the approximately 640,000 Carpatho-Rusyns living in the European homeland at the time, 70 percent (458,000) found themselves within the borders of Czechoslovakia.

Czechoslovakia and "Rusyns south of the Carpathians"

The new state of Czechoslovakia was multinational in composition, a kind of demographic mini-Habsburg Empire. Aside from the Slavic "state-founding" peoples—Czechs, Slovaks, and Carpatho-Rusyns, who comprised together 71 percent of the country's inhabitants (1930)—there were over 3.2 million Germans living in the western "Czech" provinces of Bohemia and Moravia and nearly 700,000 Magyars in the southern regions of Slovakia and Subcarpathian Rus'. Aside from the Czechs, these other peoples had a par-ticular relationship to Czechoslovakia: some (Slovaks, Carpatho-Rusyns, and nearly 190,000 Jews) felt that the country could be theirs if certain demands and expectations were met; others (Germans and Magyars) at best tolerated living in what was tantamount to a foreign country which from their perspec-tive might not even survive as a political entity for very long.

Structurally, Czechoslovakia was a republic with a bicameral central par-liament in Prague, consisting of an elected House of Deputies (*Poslanecká Sněmovna*) and Senate (*Senát*), and a government headed by a president elected for a seven-year term. Only two presidents held office in Czechoslo-vakia throughout the interwar period: the founder of the republic Tomáš G. Masaryk, until 1935, and after that his longtime minister of foreign affairs, Edvard Beneš, until 1938. It is useful to note that throughout central Europe most of the small so-called successor states—those new countries which had been carved out of the old prewar empires—began as parliamentary democ-racies. All with one exception, however, had by the 1930s become authori-tarian dictatorships. The exception was Czechoslovakia, which until the very end of the interwar period maintained a liberal democratic system character-

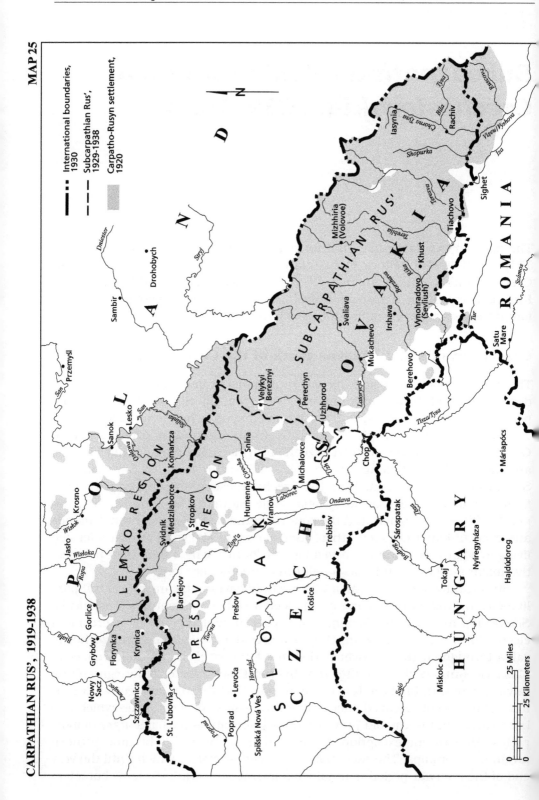

MAP 25

International boundaries, 1930
Subcarpathian Rus', 1929-1938
Carpatho-Rusyn settlement, 1920

ized by representative government and the rule of law. This state of affairs was to have a very positive effect on the country's Carpatho-Rusyns.

The large delegation from the Uzhhorod Central Rusyn National Council, which traveled to Prague in May 1919 to meet with President Masaryk and other officials of the new republic, were filled with high hopes that their voluntary decision to unite with Czechoslovakia was the right one made in the best interests of their people. A leading council member, Avhustyn Voloshyn, later recalled the great faith that was placed in "our Czech brothers"; as he said, "Golden Prague solemnly greeted [and] sincerely cared for the Rusyns, and we returned home with hope for a better future."[1] As we shall see, such hope and faith was perhaps justified, but at the same time, challenged.

Borders and the autonomy question

The challenges resulted from two issues which from the very outset were to sour relations between Carpatho-Rusyns and the central Czechoslovak government, on the one hand, and between Carpatho-Rusyns and Slovaks on the other. One of those issues concerned the yet unspecified borders of "the territory of the Rusyn people [*le peuple ruthène*] south of the Carpathians"— to quote one of the clauses in the 1919 Treaty of St. Germain.[2] According to the Czechoslovak constitution of February 1920, that territory was given an official name, Subcarpathian Rus' (Czech: *Podkarpatská Rus*). The other issue concerned the implementation of autonomy, or "self-government," which was also guaranteed by the international Treaty of St. Germain.

With regard to territory, both the original agreement reached in the United States between Tomáš G. Masaryk and Carpatho-Rusyn immigrants (at Scranton, Pennsylvania, 12 November 1918) and the declaration of Carpatho-Rusyn unity with Czechoslovakia proclaimed in the homeland (Uzhhorod, 16 May 1919) spoke of eight historic counties as comprising the "independent Uhro-Rusyn state": Maramorosh, Ugocha, Bereg, Ung, Zemplyn, Sharysh, Spish, and Abov-Turna. Certainly, the northern portions of Zemplyn, Sharysh, and Spish counties west of the Uzh River were inhabited by Carpatho-Rusyns (see Map 24). But they seem to have been forgotten when the peacemakers in Paris decided to fix the Uzh River as the western boundary of Subcarpathian Rus'; in early 1920, that boundary was enshrined in the Czechoslovak constitution as the provisional border between the two provinces. Protests lodged by Carpatho-Rusyn leaders while they were still in Paris were rebuffed by the Czechoslovak foreign minister Edvard Beneš, who argued that the Slovaks would never agree to any further boundary changes. Slovaks were already discontent, so Beneš claimed, at not having their own border moved even farther eastward in order to include what they claimed was the "Slovak" city of Uzhhorod. Finally, in 1928, when the Czechoslovak republic was administratively reorganized into four provinces, the border between Subcarpathian Rus' and Slovakia was definitely fixed along a line slightly west of the Uzh River; that is, more or less along what is the present-day boundary between Slovakia and Ukraine.

In effect, this meant that throughout the interwar period, Carpatho-Rusyns were to be administratively divided into two provinces. Those living in the former counties of Ung (only that part east of the Uzh River), Bereg, Maramorosh, and Ugocha, numbering 372,000 in 1921, were part of the theoretically autonomous Subcarpathian Rus'; those living west of the Uzh River in western Ung, Zemplyn, Sharysh, Spish, and Abov counties (85,000 in 1921) were part of Slovakia.[3]

This division also affected the legal status of the now administratively divided communities. Carpatho-Rusyns in Subcarpathian Rus' were virtually the state nationality, since language and cultural institutions were considered representative of the area. On the other hand, Carpatho-Rusyns in northeastern Slovakia were only a national minority, whose rights were guaranteed to the degree that they fulfilled the requirements of the other minorities living on "Slovak" territory.

Left with at most only three-quarters of the Carpatho-Rusyn population in Czechoslovakia, the province of Subcarpathian Rus' and its political leadership was also unsuccessful in attaining its other demand—autonomy. Although the Treaty of Saint Germain spoke specifically of the "fullest degree of self-government compatible with the unity of the Czecho-Slovak state,"[4] the extent of that autonomy was not to be decided mutually by both parties but unilaterally by the central government in Prague.

Carpatho-Rusyn expectations regarding self-rule had been established in the fall of 1918 during the initial negotiations in the United States between Masaryk and the Rusyn-American immigrant spokesperson, Gregory Zhatkovych. It is perhaps not surprising that as a United States citizen and lawyer trained in the American political system, Zhatkovych assumed that Subcarpathian Rus' would be comparable to a state in the United States. Czechoslovak reality, however, was to be far from such expectations about self-government.

Both the Treaty of St. Germain and the Czechoslovak constitution did specify that Subcarpathian Rus' should have its own representative diet and governor. As it turned out, however, a diet was never convened, and while a governor was appointed by the Czechoslovak president, his political authority was virtually non-existent. This is because the province's administration was actually directed by a vice-governor (always a Czech), who was appointed by and responsible directly to the central government in Prague.

Because of the conflict over provincial borders and autonomy, the initial political honeymoon between Carpatho-Rusyn political activists and the Czechoslovak government quickly dissipated. In recognition of his contribution to the crucial Czechoslovak cause, Zhatkovych himself was appointed in May 1920 the first governor of Subcarpathian Rus', but within less than a year (March 1921) he resigned in protest over the border and autonomy issues and returned to the United States.

It seemed that the Czechoslovak approach to politics was similar to that of the former Habsburg Empire—procrastination. Prague argued that autonomy could not be implemented in Subcarpathian Rus' because the local inhabitants were not yet mature enough to participate in a modern democratic political process and because many of the local leaders, especially the traditionally influential Greek Catholic clergy, favored or anticipated a return to Hungarian rule. Until a transitional or educative period was completed, Prague would have to rule the region directly. It was not clear, however, how long this transitional period was to last.

Therefore, in 1928, when a revised administrative structure was created for Czechoslovakia, Subcarpathian Rus' did not receive an autonomous diet but rather a provincial assembly comprised of eighteen members (twelve elected and six appointed by the government). The assembly had only an advisory function, since all administrative power remained in the hands of the vice-governor (at the time Antonín Rozsypal), whose title was changed to that of president of the province, whose name was also formally changed to the Subcarpathian Rusyn Land (Czech: Země podkarpatoruská). After Zhatkovych's resignation, other Subcarpathian governors were eventually appointed (Antonii Beskyd in 1923 and Konstantyn Hrabar in 1935), although they remained little more than figureheads whose largely ceremonial functions were, as critics quickly noted, symbolically carried out from an office in the former Hungarian administrative building for Ung county (the Zhupanat), which by then housed the moribund city museum.

CARPATHO-RUSYN NATIONAL ANTHEMS

Nationalist intelligentsias representing peoples without a state, as well as nationality-builders working on behalf of an existing state, have long been aware of the potential for national anthems to provoke in an individual patriotic feelings in times of crisis and to sustain his or her loyalty in times of peace. The *Marseillaise*, composed in 1789 during the early days of the French Revolution, remains the model of inspirational words and stirring music that many other national leaders tried to emulate when composing words and melodies for their own national cause.

When, at the close of World War I, talk of an autonomous territorial entity for Carpatho-Rusyns moved from words to legal reality, the need for a national anthem took on greater relevance. Perhaps it is not surprising that since Carpatho-Rusyns and their homeland always had several names, so too do they have several national anthems.

Virtually unknown in the literature about Carpatho-Rusyn anthems is the first which was composed in early 1919 by the philologist and ethnographer Hiiador Stryps'kyi, for the autonomous province of Rus'ka Kraina, established as part of Hungary in December 1918.

> The Rus' Land has already arisen,
> So that glory and freedom
> For us downtrodden brothers
> Is the fate that now smiles down upon us.

> Our enemies are scattered
> Like dew swept away by the sun,
> And it is we, brothers,
> Who rule our little land.
>
> We lay down our body and soul
> On behalf of our freedom,
> And we, brothers, show to all that
> We are of the family of the Rus' Land.[a]

"The Rus' Land Hymn" (*Himnus rus'ko-kraïns'kyi*), as it was called, was signed by Stryps'kyi's pseudonym, Iador, and accompanied by the dedicatory phrase: "On the occasion of the first concert for Rus'ka Kraina, Budapest, 9 June 1919." It is not known, however, whether there was any music composed for the anthem and if it was performed at the commemorative concert or at any other time.

Much better known is the national anthem composed in May 1919 by Shtefan Fentsyk, otherwise best remembered today as the ambitious Subcarpathian politician from the 1930s and 1940s, who was executed by the Soviets at the close of World War II. Less known is that earlier in his career Fentsyk was a Greek Catholic priest and a trained musician and choral director, who in May 1919 was a member of the Uzhhorod National Council which traveled to Prague to proclaim formally its intention to unite Subcarpathian Rus' to Czechoslovakia. During the long overnight train ride from Uzhhorod to Prague, the creative muses inspired Fentsyk to compose the music for a national anthem set to words of a poem attributed (but still not documented) to the nineteenth-century "national awakener," Aleksander Dukhnovych:

> Subcarpathian Rusyns,
> Arise from your deep slumber!
> The voice of the people is calling you—
> Don't forget your own,
> Our beloved people.
> Let them be free,
> Let them be spared
> Of hostile storms.
>
> Let justice be implanted
> Among the whole Rusyn race!
> The desires of the Rusyn leaders:
> Long live the Rusyn people!
> We all pray to the lord on high
> To preserve and give us a better Rusyn life.[b]

This national anthem was first published by Fentsyk in 1922 and it appeared in several other versions during the interwar years of the twentieth century, although not always using his musical score. It was also performed at most official functions (following the Czech and Slovak national anthems) during these same decades, although it was not legally approved by the Czechoslovak government until March 1937.

At the end of the short six-month period of Subcarpathian autonomy, the one-day republic of Carpatho-Ukraine declared, on 15 March 1939, the Ukrainian hymn, "Ukraine Has Not Yet Perished" (*Shche ne vmerla Ukraïna*), as its national anthem. It is not clear what Carpatho-Rusyn anthem, if any, was performed after the return of Hungarian rule, 1939–1944. Then, during the transitional period of Transcarpathian Ukraine, the Soviet national anthem was adopted already in December 1944. During the subsequent era of Soviet rule, 1945–1991, there was no hymn used in the Transcarpathian oblast of Soviet Ukraine other than the Soviet national anthem, "The Unbreakable Union" (*Soiuz nerushymyi*).

In 1997, the authorities of independent Ukraine (of which Transcarpathia since 1991 was a part) decreed that each oblast should have its own coat-of-arms, flag, and regional hymn. The symbol had been adopted as early as 1990 (the very same one dating back to 1920 and used officially in Czechoslovakia's Subcarpathian Rus'), but the decision on the flag and regional hymn was delayed because of disagreement over the issue between Ukrainian- and Rusyn-oriented deputies in Transcarpathia's regional assembly (*Oblasna rada*). In the end, a compromise was reached that called for the adoption of the yellow and azure-blue Ukrainian colors (on which the "Subcarpathian bear" coat-of-arms was superimposed) for the regional flag, but "Subcarpathian Rusyns, Arise from Your Deep Slumber" as the regional hymn. It is not clear what music, if any, was adopted for the former Carpatho-Rusyn "national anthem," and whether it has yet been performed in any official function of the Transcarpathian oblast of Ukraine.

Aside from national anthems, Carpatho-Rusyns have also a "national hymn." The contrast is somewhat like what exists in the United States, which has an official national anthem, "The Star-Spangled Banner," as well as the popular and much more easily singable hymn, "America, the Beautiful." Analogously, the Carpatho-Rusyn hymn has music sung to the best known poem, "Vruchanie" (Dedication, 1851), of the national awakener, Aleksander Dukhnovych, which begins with the lines that have become, in a real sense, the national credo, "Ia Rusyn bŷl, iesm i budu."

> I was, am, and will remain a Rusyn
> I was born a Rusyn
> I will not forget my faithful people
> And will remain their son.
>
> My father and mother were Rusyns
> As are all my relatives,
> Sisters and brothers,
> And the whole community Rusyn.

My great and mighty people
Are united together in peace,
And with renewed strength and spirit
Are magnanimous to others.

I came into this world under the Beskyds.
The first air I breathed was Rusyn,
It was on Rusyn bread that I was first nourished
And a Rusyn it was who first cradled me.[c]

During Dukhnovych's lifetime, *Ia Rusyn bŷl, iesm i budu* was set to music by someone still unknown. The melody already in the late nineteenth century became popular among Carpatho-Rusyns not only in Subcarpathian Rus' and Dukhnovych's native Prešov Region, but also in the Lemko Region and among Bačka Rusyns in the Vojvodina. In 2007, over a century and a half after it was composed, the World Congress of Rusyns, representing Carpatho-Rusyns in all countries in Europe as well as in North America, adopted "I Was, Am, and Will Remain a Rusyn" (*Ia Rusyn bŷl , iesm i budu*) as the official national anthem of all Carpatho-Rusyns worldwide.

Alongside this all-Rusyn anthem are a few melodies which, because of their popularity, have taken on characteristics of regional anthems: "In the Lemko Region" (*Na Lemkovyni*, with words by Ivan Rusenko and music by Iaroslav Trokhanovskii) for the Lemko Rusyns of Poland; "Brother Rusyns" (*Bratsa Rusini*, with music by Irinei Timko) for the Vojvodinian Rusyns of Serbia; and the "Hymn of Romania's Rusyns" (*Himn rumuns'kykh rusyniv*, with words by Ivan Moisiuk and music by Dragoš Pauliuc) for the Carpatho-Rusyns of Romania.

[a] From the original printed text on display in the Transcarpathian Regional Museum, Uzhhorod, Ukraine, translation by Paul Robert Magocsi.
[b] "Podkarpatskii rusynŷ, ostavte hlybokŷi son"—translation by Paul Robert Magocsi, *Carpatho-Rusyn American*, III, 4 (Fairview, N.J., 1980), p. 4.
[c] Aleksander Dukhnovych, "Vruchanie"— translation by Paul Robert Magocsi, ibid.

Nevertheless, Subcarpathian Rus' held a special juridical status within Czechoslovakia; it was a "state fragment"—to quote one interwar Czech legal scholar who compared it to Canada or Australia within the British Commonwealth.[5] From its very inception, Subcarpathian Rus' was conceived as the Land of Rusyns, whose language had the status of an official medium along with Czech. The province also had its own "national" anthem ("Subcarpathian Rusyns, Arise from Your Deep Slumber," based on a poem attributed to the nineteenth-century national awakener Aleksander Dukhnovych), which was sung on all public occasions, as well as a Subcarpathian Rusyn coat-of-arms, which appeared in official publications, government documents, and on Czechoslovak state symbols. All these factors suggest that Carpatho-Rusyns could certainly be considered, alongside Czechs and Slovaks, as one of the three titular, or state, nationalities of Czechoslovakia.

Hungarian irredentism

One reason for the Czechoslovak government's reluctance to grant autonomy to Subcarpathian Rus' was its concern with Hungary and that country's sustained influence in the region. Hungarian influence was revealed in several ways: the activity and attitudes of pro-Hungarian Carpatho-Rusyns; the presence of a large Magyar population in Subcarpathian Rus'; and the policies of the interwar Hungarian government and irredentist movement directed at recovering lands "torn away" by the Treaty of Trianon.

The prewar community of Carpatho-Rusyns living in Budapest, comprised of several individuals of some influence in Hungary's government and civic circles, were displeased with the fact that they were now cut off from their native homeland by an international border. While the war was still going on, these activists formed in Budapest (August 1918) the Uhro-Rusyn political party. The following year the party submitted a petition to the Paris Peace Conference, which proclaimed that the "Uhro-Rusyn people do not want to be separated from Hungary."[6] Led by Miklós/Nykolai Kutka-Kutkafalvy, József Illés-Illyasevits, and László Balogh-Beéry (pseudonym: Albert Bereghy), the Uhro-Rusyn party was replaced during the interwar years by the Budapest-based Executive Committee of Emigrant Ruthenians, which submitted memoranda to the League of Nations criticizing Czechoslovak rule in Subcarpathian Rus', and worked closely with Hungary's irredentist movement to recover lands lost at Trianon. In Subcarpathian Rus' itself, pro-Hungarian sentiment was most widespread among the highest echelons of the Greek Catholic Eparchy of Mukachevo, including Bishop Antal/Antonii Papp, who in 1924 was expelled from the country for alleged anti-Czechoslovak activity.

The Magyar minority in Subcarpathian Rus' was also considered a threat to political stability in the region, and for that reason its very existence provided the Czechoslovak authorities with another justification for not granting autonomy. As the second largest national group, comprising 17 percent of the population of Subcarpathian Rus', the Magyars (103,700 in 1921) were concentrated in the rural lowlands running along the border with Hungary. As well, they made up a significant portion of the population of Subcarpathia's two largest cities, Uzhhorod (37 percent) and Mukachevo (23 percent).[7] In effect, the Magyars lived on lands that were simply an extension of the Hungarian plain, now separated by the international border between Czechoslovakia and what remained of postwar "Trianon" Hungary. In the Slavic state of Czechoslovakia, the Magyars found themselves in a situation they had never encountered before: they were a minority in their own homeland.

As a national minority, the Magyars did enjoy rights granted all citizens of democratic Czechoslovakia, including education in their native language, a Hungarian-language press relatively free from government control, and elected representatives to local legislative bodies and the national parliament in Prague (see below, Chapter 18). Nevertheless, many Magyars in Subcarpathian Rus', especially their political spokespeople, assumed that

Czechoslovak rule was only temporary and that sooner or later the region would be returned to Hungary.

By the 1930s, local Magyar civic activists were becoming increasingly susceptive to propaganda from neighboring Hungary, whose irredentist rhetoric called for the reacquisition of that country's former northern Highlands (Felvidék); that is, all of Subcarpathian Rus' and at the very least the Magyar-inhabited regions of southern Slovakia. Much of interwar Hungarian society was inspired by the slogan *Nem, nem soha* (No, No, Never), referring to the "odious" Treaty of Trianon which could never be accepted. And just across Subcarpathia's southern border, school children in Hungary began and ended their school class every day by reciting the "Hungarian Credo":

> I believe in one God,
> I believe in the one Fatherland,
> I believe in one divine eternal Truth,
> I believe in the resurrection of Hungary.
> Amen.[8]

It was irredentist threats such as these which prompted Czechoslovakia to reassess the role of its far eastern province of Subcarpathian Rus'. The previous chapter showed that wartime Czech and Slovak political leaders, whether abroad or at home, never expected to have included Rusyn-inhabited lands within their proposed state. When the unexpected actually happened, President Masaryk and his minister of foreign affairs, Edvard Beneš, agreed that Czechs and Slovaks through their state of Czechoslovakia should indeed take care of their Carpatho-Rusyn Slavic brethren, but only until such time that the larger question of Russia and all of the East Slavic lands would become stabilized. By the early 1930s, however, Subcarpathian Rus' took on a new and not unimportant geopolitical significance.

From the very outset and continuing throughout the entire interwar period, Czechoslovakia was surrounded on almost all sides by enemies— Hungary, Poland, and, eventually, Germany. The earliest significant threat was that posed by Hungary, which felt that a profound injustice had been done to it by the Paris Peace Conference's 1920 Treaty of Trianon. To protect itself against the Hungarian threat, Czechoslovakia allied with Romania and Yugoslavia to form the so-called Little Entente. The country's only geographic link with these allies was via Subcarpathia's border with Romania. Thus, the province, which Czech and Slovak leaders had never expected to obtain during the post-World War I repartitioning of Europe, now became an important geopolitical cornerstone of its foreign policy.

Political life

The international environment made it more imperative than ever that the central government in Prague keep a close hold on the administration in Subcarpathian Rus'. It is certainly true that the authorities were never reluctant to prosecute individuals and organizations whose activities were deemed a threat to the state. Nevertheless, Czechoslovakia remained a democratic republic governed by the rule of law. Not only were all citizens, regardless of nationality, treated equally, they could and were by law required to participate in elections at the local, county, and federal level. Subcarpathian Rus' had a fixed number of representatives elected to both the House of Deputies and Senate. And there was no shortage of political parties in the province, ranging from the pro-government Agrarian and Christian Democratic parties on the center and right of the political spectrum to the oppositionist Social Democratic and Communist parties on the far left. There were also political parties, and usually more than one, that served each of Subcarpathia's national minorities: Magyars, Jews, and Germans.

Most political parties in Subcarpathian Rus', including those of the national minorities, were not separate bodies, but rather branches of statewide Czechoslovak parties based in Prague. Even parties that were specific to the region could not hope to have their local leaders elected to Czechoslovakia's national parliament unless they entered into a coalition, or common voting bloc, during national elections. With regard to political parties specific to Subcarpathian Rus', they were all in opposition to the government since one of their main platforms was the implementation of autonomy. The most popular of these oppositional parties were the Subcarpathian Agricultural Union (headed by Ivan Kurtiak), its successor the Autonomist Agricultural Union (later headed by Andrei Brodii), the Carpatho-Russian Workers' Party (headed by Andrii Gagatko and Ilarion Tsurkanovich), and the Russian National Party (headed by Shtefan Fentsyk).

Because of the uncertain political atmosphere in Subcarpathian Rus' during the first few years of Czechoslovak rule (the unresolved provincial boundaries, the yet-to-be convened diet, the presence of Romanian troops occupying the eastern part of the province until June 1920), Carpatho-Rusyns did not participate in the first parliamentary elections of 1921. When, in 1924, the Prague government finally thought the province was ready to participate in the electoral process, the result was a rude shock. Sixty percent of the votes cast were for opposition parties, the Subcarpathian Communists alone receiving 39 percent of the vote. The following year, in elections to the second parliament (1925), the results from the central government's perspective were not much better, with 54 percent of the votes going to opposition parties.[9]

Socioeconomic developments

Whereas discontent with unfulfilled autonomy and the Slovak-Subcarpathian boundary question were issues that motivated part of the anti-government vote, popular discontent was primarily related to economic concerns. Small-scale subsistence farming and animal husbandry remained the mainstay of the Subcarpathian economy. The industrial sector consisted of chemical distilleries and lumber mills from the prewar Hungarian era, some of which (the Klotilda complex at Velykyi Bychkiv) were even modernized and production expanded, as was the rock-salt mine in Solotvyno, before the world economic depression of the 1930s. For the most part, however, industry was not a priority for Czechoslovak government planners. This was because it proved economically more beneficial to export products from the highly industrialized western provinces of Bohemia and Moravia-Silesia to Subcarpathian Rus' than to build new factories in the far eastern province. As for products derived from the region's own natural resources, particularly lumber from the Carpathian forests, businesses in Bohemia and in Moravia-Silesia found it cheaper and easier to import forest products from neighboring Slovakia.

The result was that the vast majority of the Carpatho-Rusyn population—83 percent in 1930—was engaged in agricultural or forest-related work.[10] Shops, taverns, and whatever small-scale factories that existed were for the most part owned and operated by local Magyar and Jewish businesspeople, or by Czechs, who began to arrive in steadily increasing numbers.

Nevertheless, the Czechoslovak government did attempt to improve the economic status of Subcarpathian Rus'. Actually, Prague invested much more than it extracted in revenue from the region. The investments were intended to improve the region's infrastructure through the construction of a hydroelectric system and a network of modern roads and bridges throughout the province in order to accommodate automobiles as well as an airport (1929) in Uzhhorod that handled both domestic and international flights.

An outstanding example of these efforts was carried out in the administrative center of Uzhhorod, which the Czechoslovak government was determined to transform into a worthy "capital" of one of the country's four provinces. An entirely new section of the city (Galago) was conceived by the Czech architect Adolf Liebscher, in which a wide range of administrative buildings and residential areas (with apartment buildings and individual houses) were designed by some of Czechoslovakia's leading architects and urban planners. The new administrative buildings, cultural centers, hospitals, and schools were not limited to Uzhhorod, but were also constructed in other cities and towns throughout Subcarpathian Rus', including single-family residential complexes in Perechyn, Svaliava, Irshava, Sevliush/Vynohradovo, Tiachovo, Solotvyno, Teresva, Rakhiv, and the most ambitious of all in Mukachevo and Khust. Moreover, buildings and other structures (bridges, viaducts, hydroelectric plants) were all built with materials that were meant to last. It is therefore not surprising that today—after another world war and three differing regimes (Hungarian, Soviet, and Ukrainian)—the buildings, roads, bridges, and other infrastructure created by the Czechoslovak regime during that interwar decades are not only still standing but remain the best functioning structures in the present-day Transcarpathian oblast of Ukraine.

In the rural countryside, Czechoslovak governmental agencies promoted new methods of cultivation, introduced better strains of existing crops, and provided educational assistance to farmers and livestock breeders. Moreover, a land reform was introduced in the 1920s, which in Subcarpathian Rus'

SUBCARPATHIAN RUS':
CZECHOSLOVAKIA'S ARCHITECTURAL TABULA RASA

The Czechoslovak government's program to expand the urban infrastructure of Subcarpathian Rus', in particular the province's administrative center Uzhhorod, provided some of the country's leading architects with an opportunity to design and construct buildings in the most modern styles. By the 1920s, Czech architecture had rejected the historicism and organicism (Art Nouveau, Secessionism) that dominated pre-World War I Austria-Hungary in favor of rationality and the idea that a building's form should derive from its function. In particular, "functionless" decorative (read: superfluous) elements should be reduced to the minimum or eliminated entirely. Therefore, functionalism, or what later became known as the International Style, was what Czech architects brought to Subcarpathian Rus' during the interwar years of the twentieth century.

The functionalist approach was epitomized best in Subcarpathia's provincial parliament building (today home to the Transcarpathian Regional Council/*Oblasna rada*) in Uzhhorod (František Krupka, 1936). Other buildings in this style were the Legionaries' Business and Trade/Živnostenský Center (František Krupka, 1929), the Bat'a Shoe Store shopping complex (Josef Gočár, 1920s), and the post office (Josef Gočár, 1932), all in Uzhhorod, and the Children's Hospital in Mukachevo (Jaroslav Fragner, 1926–1928). Some architects preferred allusions to the classical past, giving rise to the so-called Modern Classical Style—with virtually no decorative elements—as in the Rafanda apartment complex (Adolf Liebscher, 1934–1936) and National Bank (František Šramek, 1931) in Uzhhorod, and the Administrative Center in Svaliava (František Krupka, 1930), while others tried to incorporate themes reflective of Slavic folk traditions, such as the residential complex, or so-called Masaryk Colony in Khust (Jindřich Freiwald, 1923–1926), and the Orthodox Church in Uzhhorod (Vladimir Kolomatskii, 1930–1932).

Whatever style they chose, Czech architects saw the far eastern province of their country as a kind of blank slate, a tabula rasa onto which they could experiment with designs and building materials reflective of the ideology of functionalism; that is, the illusion of a psychological break with the past and hopes of a better future in the liberal and democratic republic of Czechoslovakia.

contributed to the breakup of some of the largest estates once owned by the Hungarian nobility. Nevertheless, the practical results of the land reform were limited: only 23,000 hectares/57,000 acres were permanently redistributed to 9,100 farmers, while 20 percent of the land (239,000 hectares/590,000 acres) remained directly or indirectly in the hands of larger landowners.[11] For instance, only one-fifth of the extensive prewar agricultural and forest lands (132,000 hectares/326,000 acres) of the Schönborn family in Bereg county were parceled out to peasant farmers, while most of the rest were "sold" for a symbolic sum and then transferred to the newly established Latorica Company, whose major shareholder was Count Schönborn himself.

The Czechoslovak authorities tried other ways to alleviate the difficult economic situation by encouraging Carpatho-Rusyn farmers in the mountainous highlands to move to the more fertile lowlands in the southern part of the province, but these efforts were for the most part unsuccessful. Hence, by the late 1930s as many as 70 percent of Carpatho-Rusyns still had less than 5 acres (2 hectares) of land, and another 18 percent had between 5 and 12 acres (between 2 and 5 hectares). Such plots were well below the minimum required to support a single family.[12]

This meant that the need to find supplementary work was as acute as ever. But now there was another problem, one brought about by the geopolitical realignment of postwar central Europe. Before World War I, the dire economic status of Subcarpathia's Rusyn rural inhabitants was alleviated by the possibilities for seasonal work on the fertile Hungarian plain or emigration abroad, mostly to the northeast United States. Now, in the postwar circumstances of Czechoslovakia, the new border with Hungary cut off the option of summer work nearby, while United States restrictions on immigration (1921 and 1924) effectively eliminated the American safety valve as a potential source of employment and income.

Other alternatives for permanent immigration were Canada and Argentina, where between 1926 and 1930 nearly 1,800 and 1,200, respectively, may have gone. Closer still was western Europe, where short-term "sojourner" migration was more likely; between 1924 and 1930 about 3,000 persons from Subcarpathian Rus' requested emigration passports, about two-thirds for France, the remainder for Belgium.[13] But this alternative came to an abrupt end, when in 1931 the worldwide economic depression took its toll and eliminated employment opportunities in those countries.

It is true that the western regions of Czechoslovakia, Bohemia and Moravia-Silesia, had a thriving industrial sector, but they were geographically too far away to make it economically feasible for Subcarpathian producers to sell their surplus agricultural products to them. These new realities were only made worse during the economic depression of the 1930s, when mortgage foreclosures, strikes, grain shortages, and starvation became common phenomena.

One other source of discontent was related to the presence of an entirely new phenomenon that appeared in Subcarpathian Rus' during the interwar period—the Czechs. Whereas there were no Czechs in the province before 1919, within two decades they numbered well over 20,000.[14] The Czechs formed a virtual army of civil servants and businesspeople who, together with their families, descended on the province. Not only did they take up jobs in the local administration that may have gone to potential Carpatho-Rusyn candidates, they also took advantage of the law on schools for national minorities. During the 20-year period of Czechoslovak rule, 204 schools with Czech as the language of instruction were opened to serve nearly 21,000 pupils (14 percent of Subcarpathia's total student body by 1938), which included virtually all children of Czech parents as well as an increasing proportion of local Jewish children.[15]

Carpatho-Rusyn displeasure with unfulfilled political promises and worsening economic conditions was translated into ongoing support for oppositional political parties, in particular the Communists. Hence, in 1935, during the last parliamentary elections to take place in interwar Czechoslovakia, as high as 63 percent of the Subcarpathian electorate voted for parties opposed to the government.[16] It seemed that despite the well-meaning efforts and extensive investments of the Czechoslovak government, Subcarpathian Rus' was simply too far away and too underdeveloped for Prague to have been able to make any substantial economic improvements.

Education and culture

It was in the cultural sphere that the Czechoslovak regime made the most marked progress in Subcarpathian Rus'. The contrast could not have been greater between, on the one hand, the prewar Hungarian government, which had little interest in the peripheral areas of the old kingdom other than wanting to magyarize those inhabitants of non-Magyar nationality, and, on the other, the democratic Czechoslovak government, which hoped to improve what it considered the backward cultural level of its fellow Slavs at the eastern end of the interwar republic.

Perhaps the longest-lasting changes occurred in the school system. During Czechoslovak rule, there was a dramatic increase in the number of schools (see Table 14.1). The expansion of the physical plant was accompanied by an increase in the student body, whose number doubled between 1920 and 1938. This development, combined with programs in adult education, reduced the level of illiteracy from over 70 percent in 1900 (near the end of Hungarian rule) to 42 percent in 1930.[17]

TABLE 14.1
Schools in interwar Subcarpathian Rus'[18]

Type	Number of all schools		Number with instruction in "Rusyn"	
	1920	1938	1920	1938
Elementary	475	809	321	469
Junior high (*horozhanka*)	10	52	7	23
Senior high (*gymnasia*)	4	8	3	5
Teachers' colleges	3	5	3	4
Professional/technical	3	5	3	5
TOTAL	**495**	**879**	**337**	**506**

The changes in the language of instruction were even more dramatic. During the last years of Hungarian rule before World War I, there were only 34 bilingual elementary schools, which provided a few hours of instruction in the local Rusyn vernacular. The Czechoslovak regime, however, made a concerted effort to offer instruction in some form of what was referred to as *ruský;* in effect, this meant either Ukrainian, Russian, or the local vernacu-lar. As depicted in Table 14.1, if in 1920 there were over 300 such "Rusyn" schools in all categories, that number increased to over 500 by 1938.

The first long-lasting organizations serving specifically Carpatho-Rusyns also came into being during the interwar period of Czechoslovak rule. The most important were the Prosvita Society/Tovarystvo "Prosvita," estab-lished in 1920 on the model of the pre-World War I Ukrainian organization of the same name in Galicia, and the Dukhnovych Society/Obshchestvo im. A. Dukhnovicha, established in 1923 and reflecting the models and national ideology of Russophile organizations in Galicia. The Prosvita and Dukhnovych societies each constructed its own *narodnŷi dom* (national home) in Uzhhorod, and each was given financial support by the Czechoslovak government. The main instrument through which these orga-nizations disseminated their message was the village reading room, where Subcarpathian peasants could obtain newspapers and books and hear lec-tures. The aim of these grassroots cultural organizations was clear: "In the reading rooms our peasants must first of all be taught that they are Rusyns. The reading room must teach our peasant to love his mother tongue; in short, everything that is Rusyn."[19]

The Russophile and Ukrainophile organizations both increased steadily the number of their reading rooms, although statistics from 1929 and 1937 reveal that the Dukhnovych Society (192 and 297 reading rooms) always had a more widespread network than the Prosvita Society (92 and 253).[20] The libraries in each reading room were stocked with publications produced by each society dealing with a wide variety of topics: agriculture and ani-mal husbandry; civic education; Carpatho-Rusyn history; literature for chil-dren; and belles lettres by local authors and translations from world liter-ature. The Prosvita Society even boasted a first-rate scholarly journal, the *Naukovŷi zbornyk,* whose fourteen volumes published during the interwar years were devoted to various aspects of Carpatho-Rusyn history, language, and culture.

Other aspects of cultural life included a wide range of theatrical, musi-cal, and sports activity that reached large numbers of people in both urban and rural areas. Amateur theatrical circles were connected with many vil-lage reading rooms that provided entertainment to rural inhabitants through plays written by local Subcarpathian authors as well as plays from world literature. The apogee of such activity was reached in 1934, when, with fund-ing from the Czechoslovak government, the professional and permanent Subcarpathian Rusyn National Theater/Zemskii podkarpatoruskii narodnŷi teatr was established in Uzhhorod. Aside from amateur theaters, choirs were also set up in many village reading rooms, some of which had orchestral accompaniment. Semi-professional musical organizations were to be found in the early 1920s in the provincial capital of Uzhhorod, which was home to a philharmonic orchestra/Filharmonia and the Boian Choral Society.

Organized sports (especially soccer) had existed in a few Subcarpathian cities before World War I, but this form of social interaction took on greater importance during the interwar years. Athletic (gymnastic) societies in the form of the Sokol (Falcon) movement first became popular in the early 1920s among the recently arrived Czech administrators and their families. Before long, young Carpatho-Rusyns began to join the "Czech" Sokols (with an estimated 5,000 members in 19 branches by 1935) as well as a similar gymnastic organization, the Carpatho-Russian Eagle/Obshchestvo "Karpatorusskii orel" (est. 1923). As in most European countries, however, football (soccer) was clearly the most popular sport among male children and young men. Regional and national pride was combined with support for the province's own Rus' Sports Club/S. K. Rus', a team that competed successfully throughout Czechoslovakia during the interwar years.

The province even boasted its own school of artists, the Subcarpathian School of Painting. Also known as the Subcarpathian Barbizon, in reference to its large number of landscapes painted outdoors, it included artists like Adal'bert Erdeli, Iosyp Bokshai, and Fedor Manailo, whose works attained a degree of renown both within and beyond Subcarpathian Rus'. In the end, the best known of these creative artists (in terms of the number of people who have seen her work) was the first Carpatho-Rusyn professional sculptor, Olena Shinali Mondych, some of whose life-size statues and busts of famous national awakeners still grace the squares of cities and towns throughout the region.

Finally, a new generation of Carpatho-Rusyns were encouraged by Czechoslovakia's liberal cultural atmosphere to publish literary works that were usually dominated by themes from the Subcarpathian homeland. Several literary and civic affairs journals began to appear (*Karpatskii krai, Karpatskii sviet, Nasha zemlia*), which alongside the annual almanacs (*kalendar'/mîsiatsoslov*) and youth magazines included the works of poets and prose writers, the most popular of whom were Antonii Bobul's'kyi, Vasyl' Grendzha-Dons'kyi, Andrii Karabelesh, Iulii Borshosh-Kumiats'kyi, and Aleksander Markush. All these developments bear witness to a true cultural and national renaissance during these interwar years, which commentators already at the time described as the second Carpatho-Rusyn national awakening.[21]

Churches and the religious question

The cultural sphere was not without its problems, however. One concerned religion and a struggle between churches in competition to attract, or to hold on to, adherents. In the new environment of democratic Czechoslovakia, the traditional predominance of the Greek Catholic Church was quickly challenged by the Orthodox. The result was what some commentators described as a religious war, notably during the 1920s. If, for instance, during the last years of wartime Austro-Hungarian rule there may have been upwards of 30,000 Orthodox adherents in Subcarpathian Rus', after the establishment of a more liberal Czechoslovak regime, their numbers rose dramatically, with 61,000 already in 1921 and nearly doubling to 112,000 in 1930, by which time they represented one-quarter of the province's Carpatho-Rusyn inhabitants.[22]

ORTHODOXY: THE JURISDICTIONAL PROBLEM

In contrast to the Catholic world, whose various ecclesiastical jurisdictions are subordinate to the pope and centralized church institutions based in Rome, Orthodox Christianity is characterized by self-governing national churches. Self-governing status is connected with the existence of an autocephalous church; that is, a body which resolves all internal issues on its own authority. This includes appointment of its own bishops who, in turn, acting through a council or synod, elect their own primate—a patriarch or metropolitan.

Since Christianity in its Eastern-rite form was spread throughout central and eastern Europe from the Patriarchate of Constantinople (New Rome, or Byzantium), the various Orthodox national churches have held the ecumenical patriarch of Constantinople in high regard as the "first among equals." In theory, the various Orthodox churches function together in a "communion of faith" made up of self-governing autocephalous (jurisdictionally independent) churches, all of whom accord primacy of honor to the ecumenical patriarch. Controversy, however, arises at times over process of autocephaly. When a council (synod) of bishops in a given national territory decides to become an autocephalous church, it must obtain permission from the "mother church" of which it is a part. There have been occasions when the autocephalous church comes into being against the wishes of its "mother church" and, having acted on its own, is unable to obtain the blessing of the ecumenical patriarch, with the result that it is considered uncanonical and not accepted by the other churches within the Orthodox communion of faith. There have also been occasions when the ecumenical patriarch does decide to recognize a new autocephalous church, but that it does so in the absence of permission from its mother church; often the result is friction among all churches belonging to the Orthodox communion.

In the wake of the Orthodox revival that took root in the Polish-ruled Lemko Region during the late 1920s, there were no problems on the jurisdictional front in Poland. This is because in 1921 the Polish Autocephalous Orthodox Church had come into being and, without any controversy, got jurisdiction over newly established and existing parishes in the Lemko Region. South of the mountains in the Prešov Region and Subcarpathian Rus', where the Orthodox movement was already well entrenched in the early 1920s, the situation was much more complex. In what was then the eastern region of the new Czechoslovak state, there were potentially three jurisdictions to which Orthodox communities could gravitate: the Serbian Orthodox Church; the Russian Orthodox Church in Exile—the Synod Abroad; and the Ecumenical Patriarchate of Constantinople.

After 1919, many aspects of life in Czechoslovak-ruled Slovakia and Subcarpathian Rus' were still governed by Hungarian law from the pre-World War I Habsburg era. Since 1868, the Orthodox within the former Hungarian Kingdom were legally recognized as being within the jurisdiction of the Serbian Metropolitanate of Sremski Karlovci, which after 1920 became a component part of the Serbian Patriarchal Orthodox Church. Nevertheless, even before the war, when Orthodoxy was spreading throughout the Carpathian region, the movement was driven primarily by prospective Carpatho-Rusyn monks and priests who were trained in monasteries and seminaries in the Russian Empire and at Mount Athos within the lands of the Ecumenical Patriarchate of Constantinople. Therefore, it is not surprising that in 1910 the ecumenical patriarch appointed the Russian Orthodox archbishop of Volhynia and future metropolitan of Kiev, Antonii Khrapovitskii, as his "exarch for Galicia and Hungarian Rus'."

Russian Orthodox influence continued even after the church itself was severely weakened following the Bolshevik Revolution of 1917. This is because a large number of bishops and priests fled from Soviet Russia and settled in various parts of central and western Europe. There they reconstituted what became known as the Russian Orthodox Church in Exile. That institution, first based in Sremski Karlovci, Yugoslavia, continued to be governed by a council or synod, as in pre-revolutionary tsarist Russia; hence, it came to be known popularly as the Synod-in-Exile, or the Synod Abroad. Many priests, monks, and some bishops connected with the Russian Orthodox Church in Exile settled in the new state of Czechoslovakia, where they served parishes and joined monasteries in the eastern part of the country inhabited by Carpatho-Rusyns. Particularly influential in serving the interests of the Russian Orthodox Synod Abroad was the St. Job of Pochaïv Monastery established in 1923 in the village of Ladomirová just outside the town of Svidník in the Prešov Region.

The most important of the three competing Orthodox jurisdictions in the new Czechoslovak state was the Serbian Orthodox Church, which delegated to one of its bishops (Dosifej Vasić of Niš) authority over the new Orthodox parishes—about 60 at the time—in Subcarpathian Rus'. In August 1921, Orthodox priests and monks gathered in the village of Iza to recognize Bishop Dosifej as head of the newly formed Carpatho-Russian Eastern Orthodox Church.

Meanwhile, in the far western Czech lands of the country (Bohemia and Moravia), the Orthodox movement had its own jurisdictional problems. The small community there was split between: (1) converts under the Czech-born Bishop Gorazd (Matej Pavlik, consecrated 1920), who eventually came under the jurisdiction of the Serbian Orthodox Church; and (2) followers of another Czech-born Orthodox adherent, Antonín Jindřich Vrabec, who in late 1922 was consecrated by the ecumenical patriarch as Archbishop Savatij of Prague and All Czechoslovakia. The expectation was that Savatij would became head of an autocephalous Czechoslovak Orthodox Church comprised of three eparchies—Prague, Moravia, and Subcarpathia. For that reason, Savatij delegated a bishop from the Russian Orthodox Church in Exile (Veniamin Fedchenkov) to serve as his auxiliary in the Subcarpathian eparchy.

Czechoslovakia's various Orthodox hierarchs undertook several efforts to overcome the division between the competing jurisdictions, but these ultimately failed. The Czechoslovak government was also involved in these controversies, sometimes giving support to one and then to other of the Orthodox orientations. Consequently, after the mid-1920s, the ever-growing number of Orthodox parishes—with nearly 112,000 faithful by the end of the decade—were divided between those under the jurisdiction of the Serbian Orthodox Church and those under the jurisdiction of the Ecumenical Patriarchate's representative, Archbishop Savatij. The latter's influence was to decline once the Czechoslovak regime decided for its own political reasons (the Serbian Church was in Yugoslavia—a member of the Little Entente) to recognize formally the Serbian Orthodox Church as a legal entity (1929).

For nearly a decade, the Carpatho-Russian Eastern Orthodox Church had no legal status in Czechoslovakia (until 1929) and no permanent resident bishop. Rather, it was headed by Serbian bishops (Dosifej Vasić, Irinej Cirić, Serafim Ivanović, Josip Cvijević), who changed often and were, in effect, present in Subcarpathian Rus' only on a temporary basis. During their absences, the church was adminis-tered by an eparchial council based in Iza and then in Khust that was headed by the respected Subcarpathian archimandrite and "martyr" from the prewar Maramorosh-Sighet trial, Aleksei Kabaliuk. Many Orthodox clerics and laity were displeased with the lack of their own resident bishop, and on several occasions they put forth local Carpatho-Rusyns (including Aleksei Kabaliuk) as possible episcopal candidates.

Finally, in 1931, the Serbian Orthodox Church approved the establishment of the Carpatho-Russian Orthodox Eparchy of Mukachevo and Prešov, appointing as perma-nent resident bishop, yet another Serb, Damaskin Grdanička. Bishop Grdanička was to remain in office until 1938, and during his reign he made Mukachevo the seat of the eparchy and home to a newly constructed and impressive episcopal residence and chancellery. Although the majority of Orthodox parishes (142 in 1938), monaster-ies, hermitages, monks, and nuns in both Subcarpathian Rus' and the Prešov Region were during the Czechoslovak era within the jurisdiction of the Mukachevo-Prešov Eparchy of the Serbian Orthodox Church, there were still a few parishes and priests who remained loyal to the Ecumenical Patriarchate represented in Czechoslovakia by Archbishop Savatij.

The two rival Orthodox jurisdictions continued to exist even after 1939, when Subcarpathian Rus' was reattached to Hungary, although their relative status changed as a result of the new political situation. The Hungarian government was opposed to the presence of a Serbian jurisdiction within its borders, and therefore it favored the idea of creating a jurisdictionally independent (autocephalous) Orthodox church. With that goal in mind, the Hungarian authorities gave their support to Archbishop Savatij, who in early 1939 was able to convince priests in the Mukachevo-Prešov Eparchy under the leadership of the Carpatho-Rusyn Archimandrite Kabaliuk to submit to his jurisdiction. In 1941, the Hungarians deported to Yugoslavia the reigning Serbian bishop (Vladimir Rajić) of the Mukachevo-Prešov Eparchy and placed their hopes on a professor of religion of Don Cossack origin, Mikhail Popov, who the same year was appointed by Archbishop Savatij as administrator for "Greco-Eastern Hungarian and Greco-Eastern Rusyn Church Communities." This was to be the first step toward his becoming bishop for all Orthodox adherents in Hungary. That goal was never real-ized, and instead the Hungarian government recognized the Serbian Orthodox Church and its administrator (Feofan Sabov) as the legitimate representative of the Eparchy of Mukachevo and Prešov.

This remained the situation until the Hungarian rulers were driven out of Subcarpathian Rus' following the arrival of the Soviet Army in the fall of 1944. Almost immediately (November 1944) the leaders of the Mukachevo-Prešov Eparchy (its administrator Feofan Sabov and Archimandrite Kabaliuk) decided that their church be moved from the jurisdiction of the Serbian Orthodox Church to the Russian Orthodox Church—Moscow Patriarchate. The formal transfer did take place following negotiations between the representatives of the Serbian Orthodox and the Russian Orthodox Churches, who met in Moscow in October 1945. In the interim, Archbishop Savatij also transferred his few remaining parishes to the Russian Orthodox Church—Moscow Patriarchate. These events inaugurated a new stage in the jurisdictional status and general development of the Orthodox inhabitants of Subcarpathian Rus' (by then in the Soviet Union) and the Prešov Region (within Czechoslovakia).

The rapid rise of the "return-to-Orthodoxy movement" also created jurisdictional problems. In all lands belonging to the former Hungarian Kingdom, the Serbian Orthodox Church (based in what after World War I became Yugoslavia) had the primary jurisdiction. It is in this church that the most prominent Carpatho-Rusyn Orthodox activist from prewar times, the monk Aleksei Kabaliuk, placed his loyalty. The Serbian Orthodox Church's jurisdictional claims were challenged, however, by an Orthodox activist of Czech origin, Anton Vrabec, who in 1923 was consecrated as Bishop Savatij by the ecumenical patriarch of Constantinople. Consequently, Orthodox parishes in Subcarpathian Rus' were divided between the jurisdiction of the ecumenical patriarch and the much larger number under bishops sent by the Serbian Orthodox Church, which in 1931 created the Carpatho-Russian Orthodox Eparchy of Mukachevo and Prešov for both Subcarpathian Rus' and the Prešov Region. In the end, the Czechoslovak authorities recognized the validity of the Serbian Orthodox jurisdiction.

For its part, the Greek Catholic Eparchy of Mukachevo was obviously concerned with the rapid loss of its members. One immediate result was religious conflict at the village level, where Greek Catholics and newly converted Orthodox—sometimes members of the same family—clashed for control of the village church. If, for instance, the majority of inhabitants in a particular locality proclaimed adherence to Orthodoxy, they would remove the Greek Catholic priest with his family and personal belongings from the parish house and escort them to the end of the village, after which they would immediately invite an Orthodox priest to bless and administer "their" village church. In those cases where the Orthodox formed a minority, efforts to take over the church were met by resistance from the Greek Catholic majority, which led to clashes, intervention by the Czechoslovak police, arrests, and court cases between claimants vying for church property.

The hierarchy of the Greek Catholic Church responded with a missionary campaign in an effort to dissuade any more of its adherents from joining the

Orthodox. Particularly active in these efforts was the Basilian Order made up of monks from Galicia who were likely of Ukrainian national orientation. As a result of these efforts, the number of returnees to Orthodoxy decreased during the 1930s. The Basilians were particularly influential among Greek Catholic youth, since many schools and seminaries were staffed by Basilian male and female teachers.

In part, the religious rivalry was related to the question of national identity. More often than not, individuals who joined the Orthodox Church adopted a Russian national identity. This was in part a reaction to the orientation of the Greek Catholic Church, which initially was dominated by pro-Hungarian elements. By the 1930s, however, the Greek Catholic Church itself changed course and became a bastion of the Rusyn national orientation.

The nationality and language questions

It was, in essence, the issue of national identity and the closely related language question which were the most problematic aspects of Subcarpathia's civic and cultural life. Although these problems had already existed in the nineteenth century, they had been overshadowed by state-imposed magyarization and national assimilation. Now, under the Czechoslovak republic, the local Slavic population and its leaders had the freedom to determine who they were. During the resulting debates, the populace was influenced by émigrés from the former Habsburg Bukovina and Galicia who were either Ukrainophiles (Ivan Pan'kevych and Volodomyr Birchak) or Russophiles (Ilarion Tsurkanovich, Andrei Gagatko, and the Gerovskii brothers). Added to this struggle between Ukrainophile and Russophile intellectuals for the allegiance of the population was a third orientation, the Rusynophile, which argued that the local East Slavs were neither Russian nor Ukrainian, but rather a distinct Carpatho-Rusyn nationality.

What were the differences and similarities, if any, between the three national orientations? Briefly, the Russophiles argued that the inhabitants of Subcarpathian Rus' were part of one Russian people whose homeland stretched from the Poprad River (in present-day eastern Slovakia) to the Pacific Ocean, and that this people was culturally united by an Eastern-rite Christian religion and by the so-called common Russian (*obshcherusskii*) language. Local Ukrainophiles retorted that Carpathian Rus' was actually the farthest western territory inhabited by members of a distinct Ukrainian people, whose cultural and linguistic heritage stemmed from the medieval days of Kievan Rus'. Supporters of the Rusyn orientation at times suggested that the Carpatho-Rusyns were a separate Slavic nationality; usually, however, their ideology did not get much past the stage of negation, i.e., rejecting the Russian and Ukrainian viewpoints for an indefinable something else.

The three national orientations were propagated by a wide variety of newspapers, journals, and literary works. The Russophile position was best revealed in the annual almanacs and brochures of the Dukhnovych Society, in the journals *Karpatsku krai* (1924–25) and *Karpatskii sviet* (1928–38), the newspaper *Russkii narodnyi golos* (1934–38), and the poetry of Andrii Karabelesh and Mikhail Popovych. Analogously, the Ukrainophile position was best seen in the annual almanacs and publications of the Prosvita Society, the journals *Podkarpatska Rus'* (1923–36) and *Uchytel's'kyi holos* (1930–38), and in the literary works of Vasyl' Grendzha-Dons'kyi and Iulii Borshosh-Kumiats'kyi. The least developed of the three orientations, the Rusynophile, did not begin to be expressed with any clarity until the mid-1930s, when the Greek Catholic bishop Aleksander Stoika financed the weekly newspaper *Nedîlia* (1935–38). Under the editorship of the Greek Catholic priest, Emilian Bokshai, *Nedîlia*'s credo was summed up in the following declaration: "We do not need any kind of Ukrainian political ideology, since we would rather be a small drop in a non-Rus' state [i.e., Czechoslovakia] than a nothing in your Ukrainian one! . . . We also do not need to hope for anything from Slavism or Russia, which never intervened to save us when it had the chance."[23]

All aspects of interwar Subcarpathian life were influenced by the presence of these three orientations. School teachers expressed their inclinations toward one or the other of the orientations by using Russian, Ukrainian, or the Rusyn vernacular as the language of instruction in their classrooms. The hiring practices of school directors was often based on the national orientation of a prospective teacher with the result that certain institutions became known as centers for the propagation of either the "Russian" (*gymnasium* in Mukachevo) or the "Ukrainian" (commercial academy in Mukachevo, *gymnasium* in Berehovo) national ideology. Parents were even called upon in 1937 to participate in a referendum in order to determine the most appropriate grammar to be used in schools.

THE LANGUAGE QUESTION

The time when the 'language question' prevailed was the most romantic in the history of Transcarpathia. Just imagine, everywhere in cities and villages, in reading rooms, theaters, government offices and cafés, everywhere, regardless where people met, they talked about the 'language question'. Oh, what times they were! When, for instance, the weather did not change for a long time and people had nothing to say, there was still a good topic for them—the 'language question'.[a]

These words by the satirist Marko Barabolia were written in 1929 and applied to what he called the "Local Governorship" of Subcarpathian Rus'. His description could as well be applied to other regions of Carpathian Rus', at least as a characterization of the Rusyn intellectual elite both before and since Barabolia mockingly put his pen to paper.

Language questions have certainly not been limited to Carpatho-Rusyns; they have been an ongoing concern among many peoples in Europe, even those who had for centuries their own states and national language academies! Hence, even the allegedly most logically planned and carefully guarded national language, French, continues to this day to be debated by members of the Académie française, who among other things, are concerned with the "threat" to their native linguistic patrimony by the all-pervasive force of modern-day English.

Carpatho-Rusyns are no different from any other people in that, to use the most prosaic formula, they speak what they speak. And until they are exposed to formal education (and in many cases even after that experience), what they speak is the so-called vernacular; that is, the oral language learned from their parents and used in their immediate geographic environment (family, town, region). For most people, there is no language question until state authorities or self-designated national leaders propose that their respective citizens need their own *literary* language.

How, then, does one create a literary language? That very notion should remind us of a basic reality: that *all* literary languages are created. In other words, they do not exist naturally in the human environment. The creators of literary languages have often had several options open to them. One option is to adopt an already existing literary language, either a sacred one associated with some centuries-old religious tradition (Hebrew, Greek, Latin, Church Slavonic, etc.); or a modern language already in use as an official medium, which may or may not be related to the dialects spoken by the people for whom the language is intended (Castillian Spanish for the Catalans as a linguistically related example, or English for the Irish as an unrelated example). Another option is to create a new literary language based directly on the spoken dialects. That immediately raises the question: Which cluster of dialects are to be used as the possible basis upon which to build a literary language?; for example, where does Luxemburgisch end and German begin? Then follows another question: From within a given cluster of dialects, which one should be used as the basis for the proposed literary norm? Perhaps only one dialect, and preferably the one spoken by the largest number of individuals and the one which may also be representative of a political center (usually the dialect of a country's capital or its "culturally dominant" region). Or, perhaps the norm should be based on an amalgam of several or all the dialects within a given cluster which would make the literary language more representative of all its speakers.

For nearly four centuries, Carpatho-Rusyns have adopted variants of all the above approaches in their efforts to create a literary language. One, of course, might ask why having a literary language is so important. This is because Carpatho-Rusyns like many other stateless peoples of Europe are spiritual children of the eighteenth-century German philosopher Johann Gottfried von Herder, who posed in his *Letters in support of Humanity* (1783) what subsequently became a famous and often-cited rhetorical question:

Has a people, in particular a culturally underdeveloped people, anything dearer than the language of its ancestors? Therein resides its whole intellectual wealth, tradition, history, religion, and principle of life—its very heart and soul. To deprive a people of its speech is to deprive it of its one eternal good.[b]

Despite our current understanding of nationalities as cultural constructs comprised of many elements, most Carpatho-Rusyn cultural activists in the past and present maintain the position that language is the most important element that defines a people, or that it is, in essence, the very embodiment of a people.

Beginning in the sixteenth and seventeenth centuries, when the first writings by and for Carpatho-Rusyns began to appear in manuscript and then in print, and continuing until the present, the same question has faced all authors: Use some existing literary language, or try to write in a medium that reflects more closely the spoken vernacular? In the seventeenth and eighteenth centuries authors chose both routes, so that we find texts written in the vernacular, alongside some in a liturgical language, whether Church Slavonic or Latin.

In the first half of the chronological nineteenth century, most Carpatho-Rusyn authors used some form of a liturgical language, either Latin or Church Slavonic mixed with a high number of vernacular Rusyn words and grammatical constructs. The latter literary language was referred to as Slaveno-Rusyn. Then, on the eve of the Revolution of 1848, the Carpatho-Rusyn national awakener Aleksander Dukhnovych adopted the so-called two-language principle, which was already popular among many Slavic peoples. In the case of Carpatho-Rusyns, this meant: (1) a vernacular-based language in publications for school children; and (2) Church Slavonic, but this time with borrowings from literary Russian, in publications for educated readers. Already by the 1850s and 1860s, users of the Russian-influenced Church Slavonic thought they were writing in literary Russian as used in the Russian Empire. In fact, in the hands (or pens) of Carpatho-Rusyns, the result was a bastardized variant of Russian mixed with Church Slavonic and local Rusyn dialectisms, something critics called a macaronic jargon (the *iazŷchiie*), and what later more sympathetic authors referred to as the "traditional Carpatho-Russian language." Before the end of the nineteenth century and on the eve of World War I, there were also some efforts to write in a literary language based primarily on spoken Rusyn vernacular.

During the interwar years of the twentieth century, a new language was added to the range of choices: Ukrainian. As with the effort to write in Russian practiced by authors in the second half of the nineteenth century, Carpatho-Rusyns in the first half of the twentieth century had no direct experience with literary Ukrainian. They only gradually became exposed to it through the work of teachers, priests, and other Ukrainian émigrés who settled and found employment in Carpathian Rus' (at the time in Czechoslovakia and Poland). Alongside Ukrainian émigrés were Russian émigrés who undertook similar popular cultural and educational activity. The result were two groups of writers: those who promoted literary Russian, and others who saw literary Ukrainian as the most appropriate language for Carpatho-Rusyns.

The Czechoslovak government pronounced its views on these matters at the outset of its rule in 1919, although its rather inconclusive proposal was to use both Ukrainian and Russian for different levels of schooling. Numerous publications also appeared at this time in vernacular Rusyn, although it was only among the Lemkos in Poland where there was a short-lived attempt in the early 1930s to formulate a literary standard based on the local spoken Lemko-Rusyn vernacular.

During the World War II years, the fate of Russian and Ukrainian language use varied, depending on the political position of the countries which ruled Carpathian Rus' at the time: Nazi Germany (the Lemko Region), Slovakia (the Prešov Region), and Hungary (Subcarpathian Rus', Maramureş Region, and Vojvodina). It was in the largest and most populous of these regions, Hungarian-ruled Subcarpathian Rus', where for the first time a concerted effort was undertaken, with government support, to develop a literary language based on spoken vernacular Rusyn for use in government matters, schools, publications, and cultural life in general. With the end of the war and the onset of direct Soviet rule or influence throughout Carpathian Rus', any ideas about a Rusyn literary language were banned, so that only Ukrainian and Russian were legally recognized as appropriate literary languages for Carpatho-Rusyns. It seemed that the age-old language question was resolved, and in favor of Ukrainian. But then came the Revolutions of 1989, the collapse of Communist rule, a new Carpatho-Rusyn national awakening—and the return of the language question. (see below, Chapter 28)

[a] Marko Barabolia, "Oi stelysia ty, barvinku, na ioho mohyli," *Pchôlka*, IV, (Uzhhorod, 1929), reprinted in Marko Barabolia, *Proekt avtonomiï: tvory* (Uzhhorod, 1991), p. 28.

[b] Johann Gottfried von Herder, *Briefe zu Beförderung der Humanität,* No. 10, in his *Werke,* Vol. VII (Frankfurt am Main, 1991), p. 65.

The result was a victory for the Russian-language grammar prepared under the editorship of the local national activist Ievmenii Sabov (*Grammatika russkago iazyka dlia srednikh uchebnykh zavedenii*, 1924) over the Ukrainian-oriented grammar written by the Uzhhorod *gymnasium* teacher of Galician-Ukrainian origin, Ivan Pan'kevych (*Hramatyka rus'koho iazŷka*, 1922, 1927, 1936).

Other institutions were also drawn into what became known as the language question. Local political parties identified with one, or sometimes two, of the three national orientations: Rusynophile, Russophile, or Ukrainophile. The state-supported Subcarpathian National Theater was rent by the Russian-Ukrainian language controversies until it decided to adopt vernacular Rusyn as its mode of communication on the stage. Young people were also drawn into the fray through participation in either the Ukrainian-oriented Plast scouts or the Russian scouts connected with the Dukhnovych Society. Finally, the region's churches were forced to take a stand on the language question. The Orthodox Church basically used the Russian language in its official communications and in its seminaries, while the larger and more established Greek Catholic Church moved quickly from Hungarian to Rusyn. At the parish level, however, the situation remained as it had always been: the liturgy was chanted in Church Slavonic, whereas homilies, confessions, and other non-liturgical settings were conducted in vernacular Rusyn.

The Czechoslovak administration initially tried to remain neutral in the language and nationality controversies, although its policies at times seemed to favor one orientation over the other—for instance, the Ukrainian over the Russian in the 1920s. By the 1930s, however, it clearly preferred the Rusynophile orientation; that is, the idea of a distinct and, it hoped, a pro-Czechoslovak Carpatho-Rusyn nationality. The first and last governors of the province, Gregory Zhatkovych and Konstantyn Hrabar, also favored the Rusynophile view.

Although Russophilism and Rusynophilism had existed in Subcarpathia's cultural life during the nineteenth century, the Ukrainian orientation did not really make its appearance until the 1920s. But because it was led by capable political and cultural activists (Avhustyn Voloshyn, Iuliian Revai, the Brashchaiko brothers), the Ukrainian orientation before long came to be the most dynamic. Nevertheless, by the end of the interwar period, all three national orientations were exerting more or less equal political and social influence throughout Subcarpathian Rus'. This was the situation in 1938, when Czechoslovakia entered a new stage of its political evolution which was to have a profound impact on national and cultural developments in Subcarpathian Rus'.

15

The Prešov Region in interwar Slovakia, 1919–1938

Carpatho-Rusyns in the Prešov Region of northeastern Slovakia were, like their brethren in neighboring Subcarpathian Rus', citizens of Czechoslovakia. But whereas in Subcarpathian Rus' Carpatho-Rusyns in practice functioned as one of the state nationalities (as did Czechs in Bohemia and Moravia and Slovaks in Slovakia), in the Prešov Region they were a national minority. In other words, Carpatho-Rusyns in Slovakia had no political or administrative autonomy, although as a minority they were guaranteed by the Czechoslovak constitution of 1920 the right to use their native language in public affairs and in publications. Moreover, in villages where they comprised 20 percent or more of the population, educational facilities were provided in their native tongue. These legal principles often met with difficulty, however, when an attempt was made to apply them in practice.

During the interwar years, the history of the Prešov Region was characterized by three developments: (1) political controversy concerning unification with Subcarpathian Rus' and the consequent friction with Slovaks over such related issues as political loyalty, census reports, and language instruction in schools; (2) a poor economic situation that worsened after the worldwide depression of the 1930s; and (3) a cultural renaissance that brought in its wake the problem of finding an acceptable national identity.

Borders, schools, and censuses

The political status of the Prešov Region remained uncertain before 1928. Until that time, a "demarcation line" along the Uzh River separated Slovakia from Subcarpathian Rus'. The final border between the two provinces was to be determined jointly by representatives of both regions. As we have seen, Carpatho-Rusyn spokespeople had maintained from their earliest negotiations with Czech and Slovak leaders in the United States and Europe that the Rusyn-inhabited areas of northern Spish, Sharysh, Zemplyn, and Abov counties (that is, the Prešov Region) should become part of an autonomous Subcarpathian Rus'. Slovak leaders, however, remained completely opposed, arguing instead that territory up to—and even including—the city of Uzhhorod should belong to Slovakia.

The controversy over the Slovak-Rusyn boundary was one of the few issues that united all Subcarpathian politicians. The first governor of Subcarpathian Rus', Gregory Zhatkovych, included demands for unification with the Prešov Region in all his negotiations with Prague officials, and it was their refusal to grant these territories as well as to grant autonomy that led to his resignation in March 1921. Zhatkovych's political rival, Antonii Beskyd, who was a native of the Prešov Region and chairman of the Uzhhorod-based Central National Council, continued to organize meetings throughout Subcarpathian Rus' at which similar demands were made. In Prešov itself, Antonii Beskyd, together with his brothers Konstantyn and Nykolai who were all of Russophile national orientation, established in 1921 the Russian National party (Russkaia narodnaia partiia). That same year the first senator of Carpatho-Rusyn background, Iurko Lazho, was elected to the national parliament in Prague. Lazho's Russophile orientation was explicit: "We demand that our [Carpatho-Rusyn] villages be united with Subcarpathian Rus; and while we are still in the Košice *župa* [an administrative district that included the Prešov Region], the vice-*župan* must be Russian and all the local officials, judges, and notaries must know Russian."[1]

Nonetheless, the drive toward unification with Subcarpathian Rus' received a setback in 1923, when Antonii Beskyd was appointed as the second governor of the eastern province. In return for the governor's post, which he had coveted since the immediate postwar negotiations with Czechoslovakia, Beskyd agreed to tone down his formerly anti-Prague stance and to drop the demand for unification of the Prešov Region with Subcarpathian Rus'.

When, in 1928, the national parliament passed a law dividing the Czechoslovak Republic into four provinces, the formerly "temporary" demarcation line along the Uzh River, with only slight changes, became the permanent provincial boundary between Slovakia and Subcarpathian Rus'. Despite this decision, the Prešov Region's Russian National Party through its organs *Rus'* (Prešov, 1921–23) and *Narodnaia gazeta* (Prešov, 1924–36) continued to demand the fulfillment of one of the main planks of the party's political platform: the unification of all Rusyn lands from the Poprad River (in Spish county) to the Tisza River (in Maramorosh county).

Separated from their brethren in Subcarpathian Rus', the Prešov Region Rusyns were subject to the policies of a Slovak administration. Carpatho-Rusyn interests suffered as a result. This was particularly evident in the school and census policies implemented by the Slovak administration. In 1922, the Ministry of Education in Bratislava instructed its school inspector for eastern Slovakia to adopt a policy whereby Greek Catholic elementary schools, which used Hungarian as the language of instruction before 1919, should now use Slovak. Before 1874 and the onset of Hungary's magyarization policy, there were 246 elementary schools in the Prešov Region, in which the Rusyn vernacular was used.[2] Since the Czechoslovak constitution provided guarantees for minorities, at least theoretically that number of schools should offer instruction in Rusyn. Instead, by the 1923/1924 school year, only 96 elementary schools in the Prešov Region were using Rusyn vernacular.[3] Even President Masaryk was forced to admit, when criticized in petitions submitted to him by Rusyn Americans, that "the statistics actually show that Rusyns in Slovakia do not have a sufficient number of schools."[4]

The low number of Rusyn-language schools was justified by the Slovak administration on the basis of census data. Local officials urged everyone to identify themselves as "Czechoslovak" on census questionnaires. There were two reasons for this. In June and July of 1919, troops from Béla Kun's Soviet Hungary, operating under the auspices of a Slovak Soviet Republic based in Prešov, controlled large parts of eastern Slovakia. In response to this threat, identifying oneself as "Czechoslovak" would be interpreted as loyalty to the new republic. At the same time, local Slovak patriots knew that if Carpatho-Rusyns identified themselves as "Czechoslovaks," then their villages would be classified as such and would, therefore, not be entitled to school instruction in Rusyn as guaranteed by the constitutional guarantees for minorities. For instance, in August 1919, a preliminary census was conducted in Slovakia, but for the two reasons just explained only 81,300 persons claimed to be Carpatho-Rusyns. Actually, that number represented a 16 percent decrease (15,800) in their number compared to the results of the 1910 Hungarian census.[5]

THE PROBLEM OF STATISTICS

Czechoslovakia conducted two censuses, in 1921 and 1930. Both followed the same format providing detailed data on the number, nationality, and religion of the inhabitants in every village and hamlet in the Prešov Region and Subcarpathian Rus'. The statistical results are problematic, however, especially with regard to the nationality category.

In contrast to the pre-World War I censuses of the Hungarian Kingdom, which asked a question about one's "mother tongue"/native language (for some groups a preferred means of gauging national identity), the Czechoslovak census asked a question about nationality. It was not uncommon, however, for a given respondent to confuse the concept of nationality with citizenship. In other words, a respondent would associate national identity with the state in which he or she resided, and not with his or her ethnolinguistic heritage. To make matters worse, Czechoslovak censuses made no distinction between Czechs and Slovaks, but allowed for only one category, "Czechoslovak." In the 1921 and 1930 censuses, many Carpatho-Rusyns, who were pleased about living in a new state, indicated that their nationality was "Czechoslovak." This phenomenon was especially widespread in the Prešov Region of eastern Slovakia, where the number of Rusyns recorded in the Hungarian (1900 and 1910) versus the Czechoslovak (1921 and 1930) census returns varied significantly, even though there was no appreciable natural change in the population of a given village.

Because of the use of the category "Czechoslovak," one can only estimate the number of Czechs and Slovaks in Subcarpathian Rus'. Based on the prewar censuses, and making allowances for natural increases, it seems that the indigenous Slovaks numbered 10,300 in 1921 and 13,200 in 1930, while the Czech newcomers (which may have included some Slovaks as well) numbered 9,500 in 1921 and 20,700 in 1930.

The figures for Jews also vary in Czechoslovak statistics. This is because a person could respond for the nationality question "Jewish" (*židovská*) and for the religion question "Israelite" (*israelské*). The results for the two categories varied, with about 9 percent fewer Jews according to nationality as according to religion in each census. For example, in the 1930 census, among persons of Jewish religion who did not identify with Jewish nationality there were 5,870 who identified as Magyars, 811 as Czechoslovaks, and 708 as Rusyns. Hence it is preferable to use the response for religion (Israelite) to get a more accurate picture of the number of Jews—93,000 (1921) and 102,500 (1930).

Finally, the census category for Carpatho-Rusyns is particularly complicated. The term used in the census reports is *ruská,* which in Czech technically means Russian. The census guidelines explained that *ruská* was a shorthand term within which was included the following responses: Carpatho-Rusyn (*karpatoruská*), Rusyn (*rusínská*), Rusnak (*rusnácka*), Great Russian (*velkoruská*), Little Russian (*maloruská*) and Ukrainian (*ukrajinská*). Consequently, Czechoslovakia's census reports made no distinction between the indigenous Carpatho-Rusyns (clearly the vast majority) and émigré Russians and Ukrainians from the Russian Empire and the former Austrian provinces of Galicia and Bukovina (by that time respectively in Poland and Romania). The number of Russian and Ukrainian émigrés was indeed small—an estimated 3,000 by the 1930s—but they played a significant role in Subcarpathian Rus' as teachers, doctors, lawyers, engineers, clergy, civil servants, and cultural activists. They included both self-declared Russians as well as Ukrainians from what is considered today Ukrainian ethnolinguistic territory in the former Russian and Austrian Empires.

Although the preliminary census of 1919 was roundly criticized by Carpatho-Rusyn leaders, the conditions preceding Czechoslovakia's 1921 "official" census were not much better. That census recorded only 85,600 Carpatho-Rusyns in Slovakia, a figure that was above Czechoslovakia's preliminary census of 1919 (81,300), but well below the last Hungarian census of 1910 (97,100).[6] The efforts of census takers to have Carpatho-Rusyns in the Prešov Region claim for themselves a "Czechoslovak" identity led to a situation in which many villages that were almost entirely comprised of Carpatho-Rusyns (according to prewar censuses) had one segment of its inhabitants listed as "Czechoslovak" and another segment as "Rusyns."

Carpatho-Rusyns and Slovaks

The boundary problem with Subcarpathian Rus' and the census disputes were symbolic of a new phenomenon—a growing friction between Slovaks and Carpatho-Rusyns that was to increase, especially among political leaders, throughout the interwar period. Historically, both peoples had experienced similar socioeconomic conditions within the prewar Hungarian Kingdom and both had suffered equally from the increased magyarization during the second half of the nineteenth century. At the same time, there had been close cultural and political cooperation between the two groups. For instance, the "national awakener of Carpatho-Rusyns," Aleksander Dukhnovych, had been greatly inspired in his work by local Slovak nationalists, while the leading Carpatho-Rusyn political activist, Adol'f Dobrians'kyi, a founding member of the Slovak National Foundation (Matica slovenská, est. 1863), represented Slovak as well as Carpatho-Rusyn interests in the Hungarian parliament (see above, Chapter 9). Finally, in 1919, the Slovak National Council invited Carpatho-Rusyns to join them in the new republic and promised them broad cultural and political autonomy.

The long-lasting friendship and mutual respect between Carpatho-Rusyns and Slovaks broke down quickly after 1919. The specific conditions in eastern Slovakia further complicated matters. Ethnic Slovaks in this region spoke a series of dialects (*spišské, šarišské, zemplínské*) that were substantially different from the Slovak literary standard. Moreover, the Slovak national movement was never very strong in the area, and many local residents felt themselves to be distinct from Slovaks farther west. This feeling of distinctiveness even reached a stage whereby some local activists argued for the existence of a separate Eastern Slovak or *Slovjak* nationality (*vichodoslovenski narod*). For its part, the former Hungarian government supported this development, hoping that doing so would weaken Slovak nationalism. It was in fact with support from the postwar republic of Hungary that in December 1918, an "independent" Eastern Slovak republic was proclaimed in the region's largest city, Košice. The leaders of this movement (headed by Viktor Dvorčak) were quickly dispersed, however, by the Czechoslovak military. Thereafter, the Czechoslovak regime undertook vigorous efforts to "slovakize" the Eastern Slovaks, and that was to have a direct impact on their closest neighbors, the Carpatho-Rusyns.

In their desire to slovakize all or as much of Slovakia as possible, Slovak polemicists filled newspapers with articles denying that there were any Carpatho-Rusyns at all in the Prešov Region of northeastern Slovakia. They argued that the Hungarian government had invented Carpatho-Rusyns in the late nineteenth century in order to weaken Slovak nationalism. And if such traditional Hungarian ideology now being propounded by postwar irredentists in Budapest were not bad enough, the sympathy toward Carpatho-Rusyns expressed by Prague officials and Czech intellectual circles was seen as a deliberate ploy to weaken Slovakia's control over its own eastern regions.

As for those people in eastern Slovakia who continued to call themselves *Rusnaks* (whether ethnic Slovaks or Carpatho-Rusyns), polemicists argued that they did so only because the term *Rusnak* was perceived as synonymous with belonging to the Greek Catholic Church. In the words of one Slovak newspaper: "The people [of northern Sharysh and Zemplyn counties] are our upright Slovaks, who only because of their Greek Catholic faith inadvertently call themselves Rusnaks, [that is, people] of the Rusnak religion. It is teachers who infect them with ideas that they are of Rusyn nationality. This, however, is nonsense, but it happens. . . . There are no Rusyns or Rusnaks here, only Slovaks of Greek Catholic religion."[7] This theme was also expressed by state officials, such as the head (*župan*) of the Michalovce district who declared: "In [historic] Zemplyn county, with the exception of five or six villages in the very north, there are no Rusyns at all."[8] In such an atmosphere, all demands by Carpatho-Rusyn leaders that the Prešov Region be united with Subcarpathian Rus' were rejected outright, and those who suggested such ideas should—in the words attributed to the most influential Slovak leader of the time, the Roman Catholic priest Andrej Hlinka—be "deported in wagons" to the East.[9]

Socioeconomic developments

While relations with Slovaks continued to worsen, the economic situation of the Carpatho-Rusyn population deteriorated as well. Eastern Slovakia and, in particular, the Prešov Region, remained one of the most underdeveloped areas of Czechoslovakia. There were a few lumber factories employing 200 to 500 workers in Medzilaborce and Udavské (near Humenné), and between 1927 and 1929 smaller ones were opened in ten other Carpatho-Rusyn villages. Yet, by 1930, all of these together employed at most only 3.3 percent of the workforce.[10]

As in Subcarpathian Rus', the vast majority of Carpatho-Rusyn in the Prešov Region (89.6 percent in 1939) remained subsistence-level peasant farmers. Their landholdings were small (93.8 percent owned less than 10 hectares per homestead) and were often divided into small plots spread over mountainous and not very productive terrain.[11] The limited agricultural productivity was not enough to support most of the rural inhabitants. The situation was only made worse by the establishment of the Czechoslovak-Hungarian border in 1919, which cut off work opportunities for Carpatho-Rusyns to find seasonal employment as harvesters on the Hungarian plain. And, as in the case of Subcarpathian Rus', the traditional form of relief through temporary or permanent emigration abroad was now largely eliminated because of the United States restrictions in 1924 that were directed primarily against immigrants from eastern and southern Europe. Nonetheless, between 1922 and 1930, just over 6,000 Carpatho-Rusyns from the Prešov Region did manage to get to the United States, while others were able to find work in Canada, Belgium, France, or closer to home in the industrialized regions of Moravia and Bohemia. By the 1930s, however, emigration to these places was also no longer feasible because of the worldwide economic crisis which effectively eliminated the availability of jobs.

The delicate balance between minimal survival and starvation that most Prešov Region Carpatho-Rusyns faced was upset in the 1930s. A bad harvest in 1931–1932 was followed by the impact of the world economic depression. With no hope for supplemental income, many families went bankrupt and mortgage foreclosures became common. In several instances, the officials who carried out this task were met with force by angry peasant villagers and several clashes occurred. The largest of these took place in the northern Zemplyn county villages of Habura and Čertižné (near Medzilaborce) on 13–14 March 1935, where 240 gendarmes had to be brought in to quell the rebellious peasants. Such disturbances further alienated the populace from the Czechoslovak administration and strengthened the appeal of the anti-government political parties, in particular the Russian National Party based in Prešov as well as the Prešov Region branches of the Autonomous Agricultural Union (Avtonomnyi zemledil'skii soiuz) and Communist parties based in Subcarpathian Rus'.

Education

Despite serious problems in the political and economic spheres, there did occur during the interwar period an overall improvement in the realm of culture, in particular schools. Protests by the Russian National Party and the Prešov Greek Catholic Eparchy as well as by the newly founded Rusyn National Committee (Rus'kyi narodnyi komitet, est. 1937) seemed to have had a positive impact on education and the question of language of instruction in schools. In 1931, at the outset of the second decade of Czechoslovak rule, there were only 111 elementary schools in the Prešov Region in which some form of Rusyn served as the language of instruction. Thereafter, the Czechoslovak ministry of education permitted 59 elementary schools, which until then had used Slovak, to use Rusyn instead, while in 43 others Rusyn was introduced at least three hours weekly. This meant that by 1938 there were a total of 213 elementary schools in which Rusyn was either the language of instruction (170) or used for some subjects (43).[12]

What, however, did *Rusyn* mean? As explained above in Chapter 1, the term *Rusyn* (*rus'kyi*) was a rather vague generic concept used to refer to the East Slavic world in general. Carpatho-Rusyn activists in the Prešov Region almost invariably used the term as a synonym for Russian, which they wished to introduce as the language most appropriate for the education of Carpatho-Rusyn youth. Such an understanding of *rus'kyi* (in Slovak: *rusky*) angered local Slovak activists in their own patriotic organizations, in particular the regional branch of the Slovak League (Slovenská liga).

The Slovak League was established in Bratislava in 1920, taking as its model the Slovak League of America created earlier in the century among Slovak immigrants in the United States. Its program was based on "the principle of uncompromising nationalism," with the goal to promote Slovak "national interests within a Czechoslovak" framework;[13] that is, unity but political equality with Czechs. With regard to interwar eastern Slovakia, the Slovak League declared that it did not wish to "create . . . any obstacles to Rusyns and their national interests." Nevertheless, it "was decisively opposed to any efforts to extend the borders of autonomous Subcarpathian Rus' farther westward," and that it adamantly would continue to "protest against

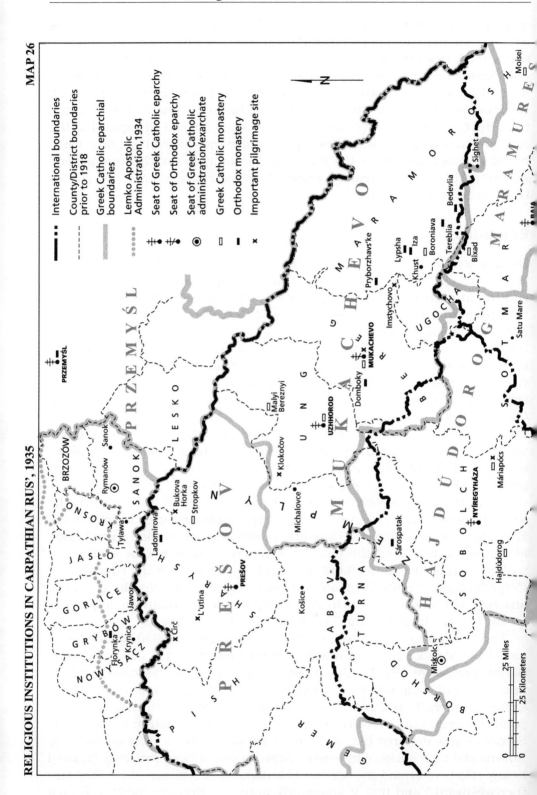

MAP 26

RELIGIOUS INSTITUTIONS IN CARPATHIAN RUS', 1935

International boundaries

County/District boundaries prior to 1918

Greek Catholic eparchial boundaries

Lemko Apostolic Administration, 1934

Seat of Greek Catholic eparchy

Seat of Orthodox eparchy

Seat of Greek Catholic administration/exarchate

Greek Catholic monastery

Orthodox monastery

Important pilgrimage site

Slovaks of the Greek Catholic and Greek Oriental [i.e., Orthodox] faith being declared as Rusyns."[14] And as for schools in the Prešov Region, spokespeople for the Slovak League opposed all demands to remove the Slovak language, arguing that "the establishment of schools with Russian [*russkij*] as the language of instruction indirectly supports a movement that threatens our national and state interests."[15]

Carpatho-Rusyn civic activists nevertheless continued to campaign for more *rus'kŷ* schools not only at the elementary but also secondary level. Particularly successful was a campaign undertaken by the Union of Russian Youth in Slovakia (Ob'iedinenie russkoi molodezhi na Slovakii), which, with the support of the Greek Catholic bishop, Pavel Goidych, resulted in the opening of a Russian-language senior high school (*gymnasium*) in Prešov in 1936. For the first time, Carpatho-Rusyn students from the Prešov Region would not have to travel to Uzhhorod or Mukachevo in Subcarpathian Rus', or attend a Slovak-language *gymnasium* for their secondary education. Prešov's "Russian" *gymnasium* soon became the center where a whole generation of Carpatho-Rusyn intelligentsia was trained in a patriotic spirit.

The religious question

The relatively greater degree of freedom under Czechoslovak rule revived and even exacerbated the long-standing controversies over religion and national identity that for decades had been kept in check by the prewar Hungarian government during its program of magyarization. One indication of the new era was heralded by an increase in the "return-to-Orthodoxy" movement. The little village of Becherov north of Bardejov, which had been the only Orthodox community before World War I, in 1920 received its own priest, a Greek Catholic convert to Orthodoxy from the United States. Soon several families in neighboring villages (Chmel'ová/Komloša, Stebník, Varadka, and Nižná Polianka) also became Orthodox. But the real center of the Orthodox movement was Svidník (at that time Vyšný Svidník).

Svidník's mayor, together with the Carpatho-Rusyn senator in the Czechoslovak parliament, Iurko Lazho, invited an Orthodox émigré monk who fled from Bolshevik Russia, Vitalii Maksimenko, to head the recently founded Orthodox monastery in the nearby village of Ladomirová. Maksimenko was himself from the Orthodox monastery at Pochaïv, formerly in the Russian Empire (after 1919 in Poland), which had a strong tradition of book publishing. Printing and publishing became the main activity at the new Ladomirová Monastery, whose print shop during the interwar years produced a wide variety of Orthodox church books, annual almanacs, a biweekly newspaper (*Pravoslavnaia Karpatskaia Rus'*), and a children's magazine. Actually, Ladomirová—known in Orthodox circles by its Russian name: Vladimirov—became the main source of publications for the Russian Orthodox Church Outside Russia, the so-called Synod Abroad, which remained loyal to the idea of tsarist Russia and was in opposition to the restored Russian Orthodox Moscow Patriarchate, which itself was only surviving with great difficulty in the atheistic Soviet Union. Although the "return-to-Orthodoxy" movement was not as widespread as in Subcarpathian Rus' or in the neighboring Lemko Region, proselytizers inspired by the work of the Ladomirová Monastery did manage to establish by 1935 throughout the Prešov Region over thirty Orthodox parishes with an estimated 9,000 faithful.[16] As in Subcarpathian Rus', the Orthodox Carpatho-Rusyns clashed with their Greek Catholic fellow villagers for control of local church buildings.

Much of the initial success of the Orthodox movement in both the Prešov Region and Subcarpathian Rus' was, in part, a reaction due to local conditions put in place during the era of prewar Hungarian rule. Initially, the Greek Catholic Church was associated with the old Hungarian regime, while Orthodoxy was presented by its supporters as the true church of Rus' and the preserve of the Eastern rite and its traditions which were being threatened by Westernization and Latinization. Also of great importance to poor peasant farmers was the fact that, initially, Orthodox priests did not demand the tithes and labor duties owed to Greek Catholic priests. Moreover, the Czechoslovak government was dominated in the highest ruling circles by a generally anti-Catholic spirit and, therefore, was not about to take the side of the Greek Catholic Church, which, in any case, it felt was infiltrated with pro-Hungarian Magyarone priests.

The Greek Catholic Church was, therefore, caught in the middle of several conflicting forces. The Czechoslovak central government in Prague was unsympathetic; the provincial Slovak administration was trying to slovakize all church-operated Rusyn-language elementary schools; and Orthodox proselytizers were hoping to take over as many local parishes as possible. In this critical period, the Prešov Greek Catholic Eparchy also suffered a leadership crisis. The wartime Magyarone bishop Shtefan/István Novak, like his counterpart in the Mukachevo Eparchy Antal Papp, was opposed to the Czechoslovak republic and already at the outset of 1919 departed permanently to Hungary. The temporary eparchial administrator (Nykolai Rusnak) was also suspected by some of being a Magyarone. The situation only improved after the Vatican appointed Bishop Dionisii Niaradii, a Vojvodinian Rusyn from Ruski Kerestur in Yugoslavia, as the Apostolic Administrator of the Prešov Eparchy. Between 1922 and 1926, Niaradii successfully slowed down the momentum of the return-to-Orthodoxy movement; he appointed émigrés from Polish-ruled Galicia (mostly Ukrainophiles) to fill vacant teaching posts; and he founded the weekly newspaper *Russkoe slovo*. It was not long, however, before Niaradii was criticized by local Carpatho-Rusyn activists as a "foreigner" with pro-Ukrainian tendencies.

The situation of the Greek Catholic Church finally stabilized with the arrival in 1927 of a new apostolic administrator, Bishop Pavel Goidych. A native of the Prešov Region, Goidych was deeply aware of the serious religious and national problems that prevailed throughout the eparchy. In an attempt to correct these problems, he gave material support to several Greek Catholic male and female religious and charitable religious orders throughout the region; he set up the Petra Society in 1927 to help reconstruct churches and to print religious books; he led a concerted struggle against the government for instruction in Rusyn vernacular in elementary schools; and he provided financial support for the newly founded "Russian" *gymnasium* (1936), which was administered by the Greek Catholic Eparchy of Prešov. On the nationality issue, the new bishop followed a middle-of-the-road policy, supporting those activities that favored local culture, while at the same time rejecting the Russophile tendencies of some Carpatho-Rusyn leaders as well as the pro-Slovak pressure of many government officials.

The nationality question and cultural developments

As in Subcarpathian Rus', the religious question was closely interrelated with the problem of national identity. Traditionally, the inhabitants of the Prešov Region identified as Rusnaks; that is, adherents of the Rus' faith (*rus'ka vira*), who beginning in the late nineteenth century were being asked by government officials to identify themselves in national as well as religious terms. While the local intelligentsia urged the people to identify themselves as Rusyns (*rus'kŷ*), the people were not always certain what *rus'kŷi* meant. Some thought it meant belonging to the Russian nationality; others thought it referred to a distinct Carpatho-Rusyn people; while a few argued it was synonymous with Ukrainian. This issue, as in neighboring Subcarpathian Rus', was not limited solely to academic disputes. For instance, Czechoslovak law stated that instruction in schools could be provided in the "mother tongue." The question immediately arose: what should be the literary form of the "mother tongue"—Russian (*russkii*), Ukrainian (*ukraïns'kyi*), or the local Rusyn (*rus'kŷi*) vernacular?

In the Prešov Region, there were basically only two orientations: the Russophile and the Rusynophile, although it was often difficult to distinguish between the two. Both claimed that they were "Carpatho-Russian" (*karpatorusskii*), that they were maintaining the tradition of nineteenth-century national leaders Dukhnovych and Dobrians'kyi, and that they were opposed to the introduction of the "artificial Ukrainian jargon" from Galicia which was being used in many schools in neighboring Subcarpathian Rus'. The Russophiles were initially represented by Antonii Beskyd and his supporters in the Russian National Party, who demanded the introduction of the Russian language into local schools and who supported the idea of one Russian people inhabiting a vast territory—as the popular slogan went—"from the Poprad River to the Pacific Ocean." The Russophile orientation was promoted by cultural and civic organizations like the Prešov branch (est. 1925) of the Uzhhorod-based Dukhnovych Society and the Rus' Club (Russkii klub, est. 1923), which purchased an impressive building on the main street in Prešov and transformed it into the Rus' National Center (Russkii dom).

Most Orthodox priests were of the Russian orientation, and there were also Russophile sympathizers among the Greek Catholic clergy, although Bishop Goidych and some of his priests favored the Rusynophile orientation. Already in 1924, *Russkoe slovo*, the unofficial organ of the Greek Catholic Eparchy, wrote:

If Germans, Czechs, and Slovaks can study the Great Russian language, so the Subcarpathian Rusyn (*podkarpats'kii rusyn*) with a secondary education must more than anyone know the common Russian (*obshcherusskii*) language. But the first duty of Ivan and his wife under the Carpathians is to love and support our local Subcarpathian Rusyn language. Our national local culture, schools, and literature must follow the way of our ancestors—that is, *po-nashomu!*[17]

This attitude was reflected in the first textbooks prepared for the Prešov Region.[18] All of them employed the "traditional Carpatho-Rusyn language"; that is, the local vernacular with many borrowings from Russian and Church Slavonic. The various national orientations were promoted by cultural organizations, all of which had their headquarters in Prešov (primarily a Slovak-inhabited city) but with branches or members in several Carpatho-Rusyn inhabited villages and small towns. The most active of these organizations was the Prešov branch of Subcarpathia's Dukhnovych Society, which in 1933 became a self-governing organization for the entire region. The same year it erected a large statue of Dukhnovych on the main square in Prešov and began the first of the annual national festivals known as Russian Days (*Russkie dni*). By 1937, the Prešov Region Dukhnovych Society had 37 reading rooms throughout the region, many with their own musical and theatrical circles.[19]

In 1930, a small group of leaders led by Dionisii Zubryts'kyi and Iryna Nevyts'ka set up in Prešov a branch of the Ukrainian-oriented Prosvita Society, which was also based in Uzhhorod. The Prešov Prosvita Society published a few issues of a Ukrainian-language newspaper (*Slovo naroda*, 1931–32); however, it did not have any village branches, with the result that the Ukrainophile movement never really took root in the Prešov Region beyond a few members of the urban-based intelligentsia. Other organizations that date from the interwar period included the Union of Russian Women/Soiuz russkikh zhen and the St. Athanasius Society/Obshchestvo sviatogo Afanasiia, which adopted a Russophile or local Rusynophile attitude toward the question of national identity.

A modest renaissance in literature also took place in the Prešov Region during the interwar years. The older generation, best represented by Ivan Kyzak, was joined by new writers (Iryna Nevyts'ka, Dionyzii Zubrytskyi, Aleksei Farynych) and the historian Nykolai Beskyd. A few natives of the Prešov Region, like the Ukrainophile poet Sevastian Sabol (pseud. Zoreslav) and the Russophile playwright Pavel Fedor, lived and published in nearby Subcarpathian Rus'. With the exception of Nevyts'ka, Zubrytskyi, and Sabol-Zoreslav, these and most other representatives of the Prešov Region intelligentsia wrote in "the traditional Carpatho-Rusyn language" (i.e., more or less literary Russian), and for the most part supported the Russophile national orientation.

Despite the fact that Carpatho-Rusyns in the Prešov Region were for the first time in history administratively separated from their brethren in

Subcarpathian Rus', they nevertheless lived in one country and could easily take part in the institutional life and activity farther east. Thus, for example, many Prešov Region activists were members of cultural and civic societies based in Uzhhorod; the region's leading political leader, Antonii Beskyd, was the long-time second governor of Subcarpathian Rus'; and, at least until the 1936 opening of the *gymnasium* in Prešov, many students from the Prešov Region completed their high school education either in Uzhhorod or more likely at the "Russian" *gymnasium* in Mukachevo. It is perhaps no coincidence, then, that among the leading proponents of Carpathian Rus' as a single nationally based territorial unit (including the Lemko Region north of the mountains) was the prolific Prešov Region historian, Nykolai Beskyd. In short, the Czechoslovak regime may have imposed an administrative distinction between the Prešov Region and Subcarpathian Rus', but the Carpatho-Rusyns in both areas remained well aware and continued to function as one people.

16

The Lemko Region in interwar Poland, 1919–1938

The fate of Carpatho-Rusyns in the Lemko Region was dependent throughout the interwar years on the country of which it was part—Poland. That state, in the form of the Polish-Lithuanian common republic (*Rzeczpospolita*), had ceased to exist following the third partition of its territory in 1795. Over a century later, Poland was reborn in the wake of World War I in the form of a second republic, which formally came into being on 11 November 1918.

Poland, its Ukrainian problem, and the Lemko Region

The reconstructed state of Poland was intended to be a democratic republic as outlined by a liberal constitution adopted in March 1921. The constitution provided for a two-chamber legislature consisting of an elected Senate and a House of Deputies (*Sejm*) from which the prime minister, representing the largest political party or a coalition of parties, was chosen. Poland's governmental system also provided for a president elected by the parliament for a term of seven years. The country's dominant political figure was Marshal Józef Piłsudski, whose military exploits during World War I credited him with having made possible the recreation of Polish statehood. In 1926, Piłsudski staged a military coup, and for the next nine years until his death in 1935 he functioned as Poland's supreme leader. In effect, Piłsudski determined the direction of the country's political life, even though the parliamentary structure and office of president remained in place.

Poland was a centralized state in which government policies were implemented by various ministries in the capital of Warsaw. Administratively, the state was divided into palatinates (*województwa*), which in turn were divided into districts (*powiaty*) and rural communes (*gminy*). The Lemko Region was more or less evenly divided between the Cracow palatinate west of the Dukla Pass, and the L'viv palatinate to its east. The districts within these palatinates were almost the same ones that had existed in prewar Austrian Galicia: Nowy Targ, Nowy Sącz, Grybów (until 1932), Gorlice, Jasło, and Krosno in the western half of the Lemko Region, and Sanok and Lesko in the eastern half, from the Dukla Pass to the San River. It is difficult to know the number of Lemkos living in interwar Poland, because government statistics did not record the nationality of the state's inhabitants. Using other criteria based on categories used in censuses (mother tongue and religion), and deleting the Lesko district which was beyond the Lemko ethnolinguistic boundary, one might conclude that the number of Lemkos was in the range of 112,000 (1921) to 130,000 (1931), reaching about 150,000 on the eve of World War II.

TABLE 16.1

Nationality composition of the Lemko Region[1]

Language		Religion	
1921			
Rusyn	103,344	Greek Catholic	112,543
1931			
Rusyn	97,120	Greek Catholic	114,219
Ukrainian	14,462	Orthodox	15,902
	111,182		**130,121**
1935/1936			
		Greek Catholic	127,298
		Orthodox	17,579
			144,877

Like Czechoslovakia, interwar Poland was a multinational state in which an estimated 30 to 35 percent of the population was not ethnically Polish. The largest of the country's national minorities were the Ukrainians, who numbered an estimated 4.4 to 5 million. Most were concentrated in the historic provinces of Volhynia and Galicia east of Buh and the San Rivers. Poland's 1921 constitution guaranteed individuals equality before the law. This meant that persons belonging to a national minority had the right to education in their own language in state schools at the elementary and high-school level, as well as the possibility to operate privately funded schools.

These rights made little impression on most Ukrainians, however. This is because the Ukrainians of Galicia did not consider themselves to be a national minority. Toward the end of World War I they proclaimed on 1 November 1918 an independent West Ukrainian National Republic. This act resulted in an immediate military conflict with the armies of Poland that lasted for the next eight months. Following their defeat in June 1919, most Galician Ukrainians felt that their homeland was being occupied by Poland. It is true that eventually a significant portion of Galician-Ukrainian society, including the Greek Catholic Church, the cooperative movement, and the legal political parties, accommodated themselves to interwar Polish rule. A minority of Galician Ukrainians, especially among young people, did not believe in any kind of political accommodation. These people joined groups, such as the Ukrainian Military Organization (UVO) and later the Organization of Ukrainian Nationalists (OUN), which throughout the entire interwar period carried out an almost uninterrupted underground campaign of sabotage, bombing, and assassinations directed against Polish state property and government officials.

Poland's "Ukrainian problem" inevitably had an impact on the Lemko Region, especially since from the standpoint of Ukrainian nationalist ideology Lemkos were considered a regional branch of Ukrainians. Ukrainian ideology was, in particular, promoted by Greek Catholic priests in the Eparchy of Przemyśl, whose jurisdiction included the Lemko Region. The bishop of Przemyśl at the time, Iosafat Kotsylovs'kyi (incidentally of Lemko origin), was not only a Ukrainophile who opposed Russophile-oriented priests and secular organizations within his eparchy; he was also a "Westernizer," someone who favored bringing the Greek Catholic Church closer to the Roman Catholic "norm." Among the latinizing influences that Kotsylovs'kyi supported were the adoption of the "Western" Gregorian calendar and celibacy for the Eastern-rite priesthood, which he actually introduced in 1924 as a requirement in the Eparchy of Przemyśl. In a very real sense, then, Ukrainians were a problem not only for Poland as a whole but also more specifically for the Lemko Region.

The main goal of the Polish state, of course, was to establish its authority throughout all of Galicia, both west and east of the San River. The authorities in charge of the centralized state were, therefore, not about to tolerate what they considered "separatist" political structures, such as the Lemko Rusyn Republic's independence proclaimed at Florynka in March 1920. Within a week of its declaration, Polish armed forces dispersed the "republic"; then one year later (June 1921) its three leading figures (Iaroslav Karchmarchŷk, Dmytrii Khŷliak, and Nykolai Hromosiak) were arrested and put on trial for anti-Polish agitation. Although all three were acquitted, the trial effectively undermined any efforts at organized Lemko civic and cultural life for at least a decade.

Socioeconomic status of the Lemko Rusyns

Despite the negative repercussions of the trial against the Lemko republic's leaders, some political parties eventually created grassroots organizations in an attempt to attract the Lemko vote in Poland's local, regional, and national parliamentary elections. The most influential of these parties in the Lemko Region was the Russian Peasant Organization/Russka selanska organizatsiia, founded in 1926, which by its very name proposed to represent rural agriculturalists, who actively supported, or at least sympathized with, the view that as *ruski/russki* (the Rus' people) they were part of a common Russian (*obshcherusskii*) nationality whose representative national language should be Russian.

Aside from its views on national orientation, the Russian Peasant Organization was concerned with defending the economic interests of small-scale farmers, the social class to which the vast majority of Lemko Rusyns still belonged. In fact, agrarian issues were the greatest problem facing Poland in general, prompting the country's parliament to adopt between 1919 and 1925 several laws concerning land reform. Church-, state-, and privately-owned estates comprising more than 400 hectares were broken up and distributed to peasant farmers. Despite the large-scale redistribution of land, the status of the peasantry throughout Poland actually deteriorated during the interwar years.

The overall decline in peasant livelihood was particularly felt in the Lemko Region. Together with an increase in population there was a decrease in agricultural productivity, which was the result of trying to farm ever smaller plots of land (further divided and subdivided among male offspring) that were located in climatically unfavorable mountainous terrain. Moreover, because of the new postwar political order, the traditional access for Lemkos to work on the Hungarian plain as seasonal harvesters was now closed off by two international borders (Polish-Czechoslovak and Czechoslovak-Hungarian), as was the possibility of temporary or permanent emigration to the United States, which after 1924 closed its doors to most southern, central, and eastern European immigrants. One outlet, however, was left—Canada. And it was to that country's industrial centers in southern Ontario (Toronto and Hamilton) that an estimated 20,000 Lemko Rusyns emigrated between 1926 and 1930.[2] This same period also saw Lemkos emigrate to South America, mainly to Brazil, Argentina, and Uruguay. Eventually, the Lemko Rusyns assimilated with the larger Ukrainian immigrant communities in those South American countries, although in 1937 a short-lived Lemko Cultural and Enlightenment Society/Kul'turno-prosvityl'ne tovarystvo Lemko was established in Uruguay's capital of Montevideo.

Religious and civic activity

In the European homeland, where there was an absence of any significant organized or cultural activity, the most important development in the Lemko Region during the first decade of the interwar years was the "return-to-Orthodoxy" movement. It began in 1926 in the village of Tylawa (Rusyn: Tŷliava) in the district of Krosno. The reasons for the movement were several: (1) discontent with the latinization influences in the Greek Catholic Eparchy of Przemyśl and with the Ukrainian national ideology of the bishop and of priests assigned to serve in the Lemko Region; (2) the spread of Orthodox propaganda by returning Lemko-Rusyn immigrants from the United States and by Poland's Autocephalous Orthodox Church; and (3) the high cost of pastoral services (baptisms, weddings, funerals) demanded by certain Greek Catholic priests. The "Tŷliava schism," as it was known to the Catholic world, spread rapidly (especially in the years 1926 to 1932), so that by the mid-1930s the number of Orthodox faithful reached about 18,000, which at the time represented about 14 percent of all Carpatho-Rusyns in the Lemko Region.[3] To administer this new community of the faithful, an Orthodox Mission (1932) and then a Lemko Deanery of the Orthodox Eparchy of Warsaw-Chełm (1935) were created.

In contrast to the previous decade, the 1930s witnessed an intensification of civic and cultural activity in the Lemko Region. The Kachkovs'kyi Society reading rooms and several cooperative societies that dated from the prewar Habsburg era were brought under the hegemony of the region's leading political party, the Russian Peasant Organization. In order to coordinate more effectively its activity, that organization created East Lemko Regional and West Lemko Regional subcommittees. Through these regional subcommittees the party hoped to gain the support of Lemko voters at the grassroots level within local cooperatives, reading rooms, and volunteer fire departments. One of the four Ruska Bursas from the pre-World War I era was also finally allowed to reopen in Gorlice (1930), where for the next decade it functioned as a residence for secondary school students and as a Lemko-Rusyn cultural center.

Ukrainian civic and cultural organizations based largely in L'viv also began to promote their national orientation in the Lemko Region, which since the nineteenth century had otherwise been the stronghold of the Old Ruthenian and Russophile national orientations in Galicia. In 1911, during Austrian Habsburg times, the Ukrainian-oriented Prosvita Society set up the Lemko Commission, whose primary goal was to increase the number of reading rooms in the region. Their number continually fluctuated, ranging from 22 on the eve of World War I to a high of 49 in 1929.[4] The Prosvita Society's Lemko Commission also began publishing in Ukrainian a biweekly newspaper, *Nash Lemko* (1934–39), as well as a series of books about Lemko culture and history, the most popular of which were by Iuliian Tarnovych-Beskyd and Frants Kokovs'kyi. These materials were distributed primarily by Ukrainophile teachers and Greek Catholic priests serving in the Lemko Region. Pro-Ukrainian activists also created in 1930 a Museum of the Lemko Region in Sanok, which managed to assemble a significant collection of artifacts representing traditional rural life.

The Lemko-Rusyn national awakening

The first organization based in and designed to serve specifically the Lemko Region was the Lemko Association/Lemkovskii soiuz. Established in Sanok in 1933, its goals were: (1) to create a separate Greek Catholic episcopate for the Lemko Region; (2) to introduce the Lemko-Rusyn vernacular as a language of instruction in elementary schools; and, (3) to provide overall support for Lemko national development and economic welfare. Among the Lemko Association's leading members was Metodii Trokhanovskii, author of the first Lemko-Rusyn language primer (1935) and reader (1936), which for a few years thereafter were used in elementary schools. The Association also published in the Lemko-Rusyn vernacular a weekly newspaper, *Lemko* (1934–39), which among other things promoted the writings of Ivan Rusenko, the most popular and influential national activist, who, because he was generally held in high regard, came to be known simply as "The Teacher." Among Rusenko's best-known poems was "Na Lemkovyni" (In the Lemko Region) which, set to music, was to become the Lemko anthem.

This burst of cultural, literary, and educational activity in the 1930s contributed to the widespread acceptance of the name *Lemko*, which had been introduced to the public at large only on the eve of World War I. The change in ethnonym did not mean, however, that the populace and its leaders lost a sense of belonging to the larger Carpatho-Rusyn nationality. The influential Lemko writer Rusenko made clear the larger national affinity of his people in another poem, entitled "Lemkovyna," in which he spoke of being part of a Carpathian Rus' that stretches east to west "from Tiachevo and Uzhhorod, through Humenné and Prešov . . . and on to Szczawnica . . . through Szlachtowa and Biała Woda as far as Osturňa"; in other words, towns and villages from Subcarpathian Rus', through the Prešov Region, and on to the Lemko Region.[5]

The Lemko Association's goal to create a distinct Greek Catholic eparchy was basically achieved as well. In 1934, the Vatican detached from the Eparchy of Przemyśl all its parishes in the Lemko Region (in the Nowy Targ, Nowy Sącz, Gorlice, Jasło, Krosno, and Sanok districts) and placed them in the Lemko Apostolic Administration, a new church jurisdiction under the direct authority of the pope (see Map 26). Interestingly, the conditions which prompted the Vatican to create the Lemko Apostolic Administration were similar to those which earlier, in 1916, had prompted it to form distinct Greek Catholic jurisdictions for Ruthenians and Ukrainians in the United States. In short, the Vatican felt that it needed to respond to the concerns of the faithful in the Lemko Region who were discontent with the Eparchy of Przemyśl's Ukrainian orientation, a policy which prompted many to leave the Catholic Church and join the Russophile-oriented Orthodox Church.

It is, therefore, not surprising that the new jurisdiction's apostolic administrator, Vasyl' Mastsiukh, and its chancellor, the Lemko historian Ioann Polianskii-Lemkyn, were expected to put a halt to—or at least to reduce— the number of conversions to Orthodoxy caused, in part, by the spread of Ukrainian national ideology. Consequently, they banned the distribution of Ukrainian-language publications from churches in the Lemko Apostolic Administration, removed some Ukrainophile priests, and in general promoted the Carpatho-Rusyn national orientation.

The Polish government's reaction to all these developments was mixed. By the early 1930s, when the Ukrainian movement and the underground Organization of Ukrainian Nationalists was becoming increasingly aggressive throughout eastern Galicia, Poland's policy makers were inclined to support any elements which they believed would contribute to undermining Ukrainianism. Therefore, the non-Ukrainian-oriented Lemkos would seem to be natural allies. In fact, it was Polish government funding that made the establishment of the Lemko Association in 1933 possible. Poland also provided funds to create in 1934 the Lemko Section of the state-supported Commission for Scholarly Research on the Eastern Lands, which was expected to advise the government on Lemko matters. State funding did, in fact, make possible excellent research and publications on Lemko ethnography, language, and anthropology by Polish scholars like Roman Reinfuss, Zdzisław Stieber, Stanisław Leszczycki, and Krystyna Pieradzka. It should come as no surprise that Galicia's Ukrainian leaders strongly opposed institutions like the scholarly oriented Lemko Section, the Lemko Region Affairs Committee of Poland's state Commission for National Minorities Affairs, and the Lemko Apostolic Administration, all of which were considered to be part of an alleged Polish conspiracy to divide and weaken the Ukrainian nationality.

By the late 1930s, perhaps as part of the Polish government's attempts to reach some kind of modus vivendi with its Ukrainian inhabitants, state support for Lemko organizations ceased. Lemko teachers were gradually removed from elementary schools, Lemko-language textbooks were banned from use, and all funds for the Lemko Association were cut off. Clearly, the efforts to create a serious cultural and educational basis for a distinct Carpatho-Rusyn nationality in the Lemko Region were in jeopardy. But as the decade drew to a close, the very existence of Poland as a state was in even greater jeopardy. This is because the year 1939 was to bring to the region an even greater tragedy—Nazi Germany's invasion of Poland and the outbreak of World War II.

Carpatho-Rusyn diasporas during the interwar years, 1919–1938

The political transformation of central Europe after World War I and the redrawing of international borders divided Carpathian Rus'. While Czechoslovakia and Poland included within its borders the largest number of Carpatho-Rusyns, others lived in what was now Romania and Hungary. Finally, farther away were diasporan Carpatho-Rusyns in the new state of Yugoslavia and beyond the ocean in North America.

Romania and Hungary

The closest of these various communities, one that in fact was territorially contiguous with the rest of Carpathian Rus', lived in Romania's Maramureş Region. That community inhabited the southern part of the historic county of Maramorosh (Hungarian: Máramaros; Romanian: Maramureş), which in 1919 was assigned to Romania by the Paris Peace Conference. Included in the Maramureş Region was the former county seat of Sighet, which was the site of a few Carpatho-Rusyn religious and educational institutions, as well as about 15 primarily Rusyn-inhabited villages along the southern bank of the Tisza River and along the valleys of its tributaries, the Vişeu (Rusyn: Vyshova) and Ruscova (Rusyn: Rus'kova) Rivers. Also assigned to Romania at the Paris Peace Conference, but much farther to the south, was the eastern Banat Region, where several villages had a significant percentage of Rusyn inhabitants originally from Carpathian Rus'.

In the northeastern corner of interwar post-Trianon Hungary there were several scattered villages inhabited by formerly Rusyn-speaking Greek Catholics. Already by the second half of the nineteenth century most of the inhabitants in these villages were magyarized, although they remained Greek Catholics and were administered by their own Hungarian Eparchy of Hajdúdorog with its seat in Nyíregyháza. The most important site in this eparchy was the Basilian monastery at Máriapócs, which despite international borders still functioned as a major pilgrimage site for Carpatho-Rusyns from Czechoslovakia (Subcarpathian Rus' and the Prešov Region) who met there annually on the occasion of the 15 August Feast of the Dormition. None of these scattered communities, whether in Romania or Hungary, had any Carpatho-Rusyn cultural or civic institutions during the interwar period. This was not the case, however, for the Carpatho-Rusyn diaspora communities in the Vojvodina and Srem regions of Yugoslavia and those in North America; that is, in Canada and most especially in the United States.

Yugoslavia—the Vojvodina

Among the smaller of all Carpatho-Rusyn diasporan communities were the Rusnaks (their local self-designation), or the Vojvodinian-Srem Rusyns of Yugoslavia. Numbering about 16,000 on the eve of World War I, they lived in compact communities in a few villages located in prewar Hungary's historic counties of Bachka (Hungarian: Bácska) and Srem (Hungarian: Szerém), which together formed an area known as the Vojvodina (see Map 19).[1]

The Vojvodina was one of the most nationally complex regions in all of Europe, although the numerically largest groups living there were Serbs and Croats. It is, therefore, not surprising that at the Great National Council, which was convened in the region's largest city Novi Sad on 25 November 1918, the 757 delegates present voted to join the Vojvodina and Srem to the newly proposed Kingdom of South Slavs—Serbs, Croats, and Slovenes.[2] The kingdom, which was formally established on 1 December 1918, was subsequently renamed Yugoslavia; that is, the state of South Slavs. Among the peoples who voluntarily helped to form Yugoslavia were the "South Slavic Rusyns," as the Vojvodinian-Srem Rusyns were known at the time. Despite their numerically minuscule size, no fewer than 21 of the delegates at the Great National Council in Novi Sad were Vojvodinian Rusyns, and were likely encouraged to participate in the proceedings by the chairman of the council, a Greek Catholic priest named Jovan Chranilović.

Now that they were living in a state ruled by fellow Slavs, the Vojvodinian Rusyns acted immediately to try to improve their cultural and educational status. The large exclusively Rusyn-inhabited village of Ruski Kerestur was to remain the primary base of their activity. In June 1919, at the initiative of two Greek Catholic priests and natives of Ruski Kerestur, Diura Bindas and Mikhailo Mudri, the Rusyn National Enlightenment Society/Ruske narodne prosvitne druzhtvo was established. As the first organization to promote the cultural and educational interests of the Vojvodinian Rusyns, the Enlightenment Society had as its main goal the "publication and distribution of religious, instructional, and entertaining books and brochures, as well as newspapers written in the vernacular Rusyn language."[3]

To enhance its effectiveness, the society purchased a building to house a cultural center (Prosvitni dom, 1932) and it opened a print shop (1936), both in Ruski Kerestur. Faithful to its word, from the very beginning the Rusyn National Enlightenment Society published school textbooks, an almanac (*Ruski kalendar,* 1921–41), and a weekly newspaper (*Ruski novini,* 1924–41). And to assure that the society's publications would be in the vernacular Rusyn speech, they commissioned the prewar "father of Vojvodinian Rusyn literature," Havriïl Kostel'nik (by then a Greek Catholic priest serving far from his homeland in Polish-ruled Galicia) to create a standard grammar which was published in 1923 under the title *Hramatika bachvan'sko-ruskei beshedi* (A Grammar of Bachka-Rusyn Speech).

As in Carpathian Rus', Vojvodinian Rusyn cultural activists had differing views about the appropriate national orientation of their people. One of the cofounders of the Rusyn National Enlightenment Society, Diura Bindas, as well as the author of the first standard grammar, Havriïl Kostel'nik, believed that the Vojvodinian-Srem Rusyns were a branch of the Ukrainian nationality. Others, who were discontent with the Ukrainian orientation, established in 1932 in the Vojvodinian town of Stari Vrbas the Zaria Cultural and Enlightenment (National) Union of Yugoslav Rusyns/Kulturno-prosvitni (natsionalni) soiuz iugoslavianskikh Rusinokh "Zaria". Influenced by the belletrist Evgenii Kochish and the historian Nikolai Olearov, the Zaria society through its weekly newspaper (*Russka zaria*, 1934–41) and annual almanac (*Ruskii narodni kalendar "Zaria"*, 1935–41) promoted the view that the Vojvodinian-Srem Rusyns were a branch of the Russian nationality.

Despite their differing attitudes on the nationality question, the publications of both cultural organizations were all in the Vojvodinian Rusyn vernacular. In fact, the only visible difference in the language used by the two organizations was that the National Enlightenment Society spelled the group's ethnonym with one "s" (*ruski*), while the Russophile Zaria Union spelled it with two "s" (*russki*). Such esoteric differences meant little to the vast majority of the populace, and in particular their children, who, living in isolated rural villages, received their elementary education and continued to use as their everyday language the speech of their parents and grandparents—Vojvodinian (Bachka) Rusyn. Therefore, the Vojvodinian-Srem Rusyns during the interwar years did not experience linguistic assimilation with the dominant language of the state (Serbian), nor were they exposed to the often pedagogically confusing struggles caused by the language question that characterized cultural life and educational institutions in Carpathian Rus'. In short, the Vojvodinian-Srem Rusyns maintained a clear understanding of their identity. They were Rusnaks, and their national language was one and the same *ruska besheda/ruski iazik* spoken at home, in schools, and in public places.

The United States

The Carpatho-Rusyn diasporan or immigrant communities in North America reached the height of their development as a distinct community during the interwar decades of the twentieth century. Immigration to the New World was cut off entirely during World War I. But after the war was over and the international political situation finally stabilized toward the end of 1919 and 1920, immigration resumed and continued at least until the second set of restrictions were put in place by the United States in 1922 and 1924. Most of the Carpatho-Rusyn immigrants during these initial postwar years (over 4,200 alone from Subcarpathian Rus' between 1922 and 1924) represented families joining their menfolk who were stranded in America during the war years and who decided not to return to Europe.[4] Some return immigration did indeed take place and was especially directed toward the new state of Czechoslovakia. The vast majority of prewar immigrants, however, decided to make permanent homes in the United States. Their estimated number during the interwar years was 250,000. A much smaller number lived in Canada, at most about 20,000. Most Carpatho-Rusyns in Canada came from the Lemko Region and arrived during the second half of the 1920s. Others were re-emigrants; in other words, Carpatho-Rusyns who lived and worked first in the United States and then moved north into Canada.

The settlement pattern of Carpatho-Rusyns in the United States remained the same as it had been during the decades before World War I. This meant that the vast majority, nearly 80 percent, were still living in three northeastern states during the interwar years: Pennsylvania (54 percent), New York (13 percent), and New Jersey (12 percent), with most of the rest in nearby Connecticut, Ohio, and Illinois.[5] Coal mines and the steel industry continued to be the primary sources of employment, although the American-born second generation—and this included an ever increasing number of women—worked in light industries (shoe, soap, and cigar factories) or as shop assistants in stores and as waitresses and cooks in diners and restaurants.

Because of their large concentration in specific urban areas, Rusyn Americans were able to maintain a wide range of vibrantly active secular organizations, churches, and even schools. The latter, which were attached to either Greek Catholic or Orthodox parishes as parochial day schools, were popularly known as *ruskî shkolŷ*, a term often translated as "Russian schools." In the *ruska shkola*, children were provided with at least one class in some form of the native language, which more often than not was a corrupted form of Russian intermixed with Carpatho-Rusyn vernacular. This was the language of several grammar books and readers produced in the United States specifically for the *ruskî shkolŷ*.

The largest and most influential Rusyn-American secular organizations remained the brotherhoods, or mutual-benefit societies. As in the early years of immigration back in the 1880s and 1890s, the brotherhoods continued to provide their members with insurance and survivor benefits in case of sickness, work-related accidents, or death. By the interwar years, numerous new brotherhoods representing various religious, national, or regional interests had come into being. The largest, however, remained the Greek Catholic Union of Rusyn Brotherhoods/Sojedinenije greko-kaftoličeskich russkich bratstv. Although based in western Pennsylvania, the Sojedinenije at its height in 1929 had over 133,000 members in 1,719 adult, youth, and gymnastic lodges throughout the United States and some even in Canada.[6] Its official newspaper, the *Amerikanskii russkii viestnik*, appeared three times a week in 40,000 copies per issue. The Greek Catholic Union also published youth (*Sokol Sojedinenija/American Russian Falcon*, 1914–36) and children's (*Svit D'itej/Children's World*, 1917–38) magazines, it sponsored sports clubs and operated an orphanage, and it helped finance the construction of churches and parochial schools. Other brotherhood organizations undertook some of these activities as well, although on a much smaller scale.

The Rusyn-American immigrants and their leaders may have lived in a different country and on another continent, but they were no different from their brethren in the European homeland. It is, therefore, not surprising that the North American community was often preoccupied with the same issues that divided Carpatho-Rusyns elsewhere: religion and the nationality question.

As in Europe, the majority of Carpatho-Rusyns remained deeply committed to their Eastern-rite version of Christianity. The main problem facing immigrants was not only to establish their church as a viable institution, but to do so in the United States where the Catholic Church was dominated by a Roman-rite hierarchy that had little appreciation for—and was often openly antagonistic toward—the Eastern Catholic rite and its traditions. We have seen how already in the 1890s these antagonisms led to the first wave of defections among Greek Catholics to Orthodoxy led by Father Alexis Toth. The interwar years were to be marked by further defections.

The jurisdiction which was responsible for Greek Catholics from the former Hungarian Kingdom was formed as a distinct Ruthenian administration in 1916; then, in 1924, it was raised to an exarchate with a seat in Pittsburgh and a bishop sent from Uzhhorod in the person of Basil Takach. Takach was a capable administrator, who put order into the growing exarchate, but in 1929, after five years in office, he was faced with a new problem. In that year the Vatican issued a decree (*Cum Data Fuerit*) which, among other things, required that all men eligible for ordination to the priesthood must be celibate, and that all church property must be turned over to the bishop. The Vatican had actually issued decrees as early as 1890 and again in 1907 (the *Ea Semper*) requiring that Greek Catholic priests in North America must be celibate, but the decree was ignored. Married priests with their families continued to arrive from Europe, and married men were ordained to the priesthood even by Bishop Takach in the early years of his episcopate. By 1929 the Vatican seemed determined to have its directives enforced and, as a loyal Catholic, Bishop Takach was obliged to comply.

The 1929 decree provoked major protests on the part of many of the exarchate's priests who were backed by the powerful Greek Catholic Union, which in 1932 formed a special Committee for the Defense of the Eastern Rite/Komitet Oborony Vostočnoho Obrjada (KOVO) to coordinate a campaign of criticism against Bishop Takach and the Vatican decree. A few priests, led by Father Orestes Chornock of Bridgeport, Connecticut, not only refused to abide by the celibacy requirement, they eventually broke with the Catholic Church entirely.

In 1936, the group around Father Chornock formed what was called the Carpatho-Russian Orthodox Greek Catholic Diocese of the Eastern Rite Church. The complicated name implied that this was not a new institution, but rather one which maintained the true (*pravoslavny*/Orthodox) form of

Greek Catholicism, which they argued was being undermined by the Vatican and its appointee, Bishop Takach. It is also interesting to note that the leaders of the new diocese did not want to follow the earlier lead of Alexis Toth and join the Russian Orthodox Church of North America. This is because that institution basically dismissed the particular Carpatho-Rusyn religious traditions, most especially the beloved Carpathian plainchant (*prostopinije*) sung by the entire congregation during the liturgy. Rejecting both Catholic Rome and Orthodox Moscow—to paraphrase the rhetoric of the day—the new diocese remained Carpatho-Rusyn in name and practice. Its first bishop, Orestes Chornock, was consecrated in 1938 by the Ecumenical Patriarch of Constantinople into whose jurisdiction the American Carpatho-Russian Orthodox Greek Catholic Diocese (as it later was known) was placed. The seat of the new diocese was in Johnstown, Pennsylvania.

This latest defection from the Greek Catholic Church caused both great personal suffering and legal complications. Many families were now divided between adherents of the Greek Catholic Exarchate of Bishop Takach and the Carpatho-Russian Orthodox Diocese of Bishop Chornock. And to whom did the church buildings, which until 1929 had served one community, now belong? The result was a number of long and costly court cases over church property that were brought before United States courts at the county, state, and federal level. The legal claims and counterclaims were buttressed by arguments about privileges allegedly granted by the Catholic pope of Rome to the Eastern-rite churches going back to the 1596 Union of Brest and 1646 Union of Uzhhorod.

Not unrelated to the church controversies—although a problem which took on a life of its own—was the nationality question. Rusyn Americans from the Hungarian Kingdom had already broken with the pro-Ukrainian Ruthenians/Rusyns from Galicia before World War I. Rusyn-American polemicists rejected what they called Ukrainian separatism, arguing instead that Carpatho-Rusyns were part of a larger Rus' world. But what did that mean? Were they Russians, or were they a distinct Uhro-Rusyn or Subcarpathian Rusyn nationality? Defenders of both orientations, the Russophile and Rusynophile, argued their cases on the pages of publications of the various Rusyn-American fraternal societies throughout the 1920s and 1930s. By the end of the interwar period, the issue was still not decided.

An interesting variant of the nationality controversy arose among immigrants from the Lemko Region. Led by talented journalists and civic activists like Victor Hladick, Simeon Pysh, and Dymytrii Vyslotskii, the Lemko immigrants were particularly concerned with workers' rights and issues related to socioeconomic inequality. Since most of the interwar Lemko emigration headed for Canada, it is not surprising that the group's first organization was established in 1929 in Winnipeg, Manitoba under the name, the Lemko Association of the USA and Canada. Although its headquarters soon moved to Cleveland, Ohio (1931), and then to Yonkers, New York (1939), the Lemko Association maintained several active branches in Canada (especially in Toronto and Hamilton, Ontario) as well as throughout the United States. The association also published newspapers (*Lemko*, 1929–39; *Karpatska Rus'*, 1939–present) and other materials in the Lemko vernacular.

What made the Lemko Association different from most other Rusyn-American organizations was its left-wing political profile. It staged anti-fascist Carpatho-Russian National Congresses in New York City (1936–1939), and in 1940 it helped form a Carpatho-Russian Section of the International Worker's Order. The prolific writer Dymytrii Vyslotskii visited the Soviet Union in 1934, and upon his return and under his influence the Lemko Association became openly pro-Communist, even proposing that Lemkos from the Carpathian homeland as well as immigrants in North America be resettled in the Soviet Union as the best means to resolve the group's national and socio-economic difficulties. The Soviet Union was depicted not only as a worker's state untouched by the sufferings caused by the 1930s depression, but also as a "Russian" state, where the Lemko people would not be subjected to national discrimination and be able to retain their Rus' identity. Consequently, the pre-World War I faith in Orthodox tsarist Russia was transformed into faith in a proletarian Soviet Russia. Not surprisingly, the Communist orientation of the Lemko Association was not appreciated by the majority of religious-oriented Rusyn Americans, let alone by capitalist American and Canadian society as a whole.

MARRIAGE AND PROPERTY: TWO STICKING POINTS

The position of the Roman Catholic Church regarding the status and practices of the Eastern-rite churches in the United States was formulated almost from the very outset of the massive immigration of central Europeans into the new World. A key date was 1890.

In May of that year, the Sacred Congregation for the Propagation of the Faith—the Vatican "ministry" in Rome responsible for matters pertaining to Eastern Catholics—adopted an important jurisdictional principle. Eastern-rite priests and laity who reside outside the boundaries of the churches to which they belong (and this pertained to immigrants in North America) "are subject to the Latin ordinary [bishop or archbishop] of the place where they are staying, especially in Latin [Roman-rite] dioceses."[a] In effect, this meant that Carpatho-Rusyns and other immigrant Greek Catholics were no longer subject to their bishops in the European homeland, but rather to Roman Catholic hierarchs in the United States.

Those hierarchs were, to say the least, not favorably inclined toward their fellow Catholics, albeit of a different rite. A resolution adopted at a meeting of Roman-rite archbishops in Baltimore in the summer of 1890 clearly reflected their negative attitude:

> [T]he presence of married priests of Greek [Eastern] rite in our midst is a constant menace to the chastity of our unmarried clergy, a source of scandal to the laity and, therefore, the sooner this point of discipline is abolished before these evils obtain large proportions, the better for religion, because the pos-

sible loss of a few souls of the Greek rite bears no proportion to the blessings resulting from uniformity of discipline.[b]

The Vatican responded to these concerns by issuing a decree in the form of a circular letter (1 October 1890) from the Sacred Congregation for the Propagation of the Faith addressed to Greek Catholic bishops in Europe. It ordered the return of all married priests in the United States to their homeland and insisted that only celibate priests, or widowers without their children, could go to North America, where such "acceptable" priests would be under the jurisdiction of the local Roman-rite bishop.

However clear the Vatican directives, they were ignored by the Greek Catholic hierarchs in Europe and by Carpatho-Rusyn immigrants, who continued to build (and own) churches in various communities throughout the United States and to invite (and pay) Greek Catholic priests from Europe (almost all of whom were married and with families) to staff them. In an attempt to put some order into the Vatican's relations with America's rapidly growing Eastern-rite churches, Pope Pius X issued an apostolic letter, known as the *Ea Semper* (18 July 1907). On the one hand, the *Ea Semper* responded to the long-standing request of Greek Catholics for their own bishop in the United States; on the other, it stripped the bishop of otherwise standard episcopal authority. Aside from reiterating the opposition to a married Catholic clergy in the United States, the *Ea Semper* decree introduced a new concern: control over church property.

> Article 1. The nomination of the bishop of the Ruthenian [Eastern] rite for the United States is a task fully reserved for the Apostolic See.
>
> Article 2. The bishop of the Ruthenian rite is under the immediate jurisdiction and power of the Apostolic See and is to be overseen by [Rome's] Apostolic Delegate in Washington. Moreover, he is to have no ordinary jurisdiction, but only that delegated to him by the respective bishops of the [Latin-rite] diocese in which the Ruthenians [Carpatho-Rusyn and Galician Ukrainians] reside.
>
> Article 3. The bishop of the Ruthenian rite will be able to visit his parishes provided he has the written permission of the [Latin-rite] bishop. The latter will confer such powers as he deems fit.
>
> Article 4. When the bishop of the Ruthenian rite visits his parishes, he will ask for an account of the property of that parish from the respective priest, and he will see that the priest does not hold in his own name and right items acquired with the help of contributions made in any way by the faithful. . . . Title to such goods shall be either transferred to the local [Latin-rite] bishop as soon as possible or be firmly assigned in any secure and legal fashion approved by the same bishop and thereby remain in support of the parish.

· · · · ·

Article 10. Since there are not yet any Ruthenian priests who were either born or even educated in the United States, the bishop of the Ruthenian rite, in consultation with the Apostolic Delegate and the local [Latin-rite] bishop, will make every effort to establish seminaries to educate Ruthenian priests in the United States as soon as possible. In the meantime, Ruthenian clergymen will be admitted to the Latin seminaries in the area where they were born or in which they are domiciled. But only those who are celibate at present and who shall remain so may be promoted to the sacred orders [priesthood].

• • • • •

Article 17. All priests of Ruthenian parishes in the United States are subject to dismissal at the discretion of the local [Latin-rite] bishop. The bishop of the Ruthenian rite is to be informed in good time. No dismissal, however, should be ordered without serious and fair cause.[c]

Despite Rome's pronouncements, the *Ea Semper's* provisions on priestly celibacy and the transfer of title to church property to the bishop were again ignored. While the number of married priests arriving from Europe may have diminished (especially after the outbreak of World War I in 1914), some Greek Catholic bishops in America responded to the need for clergy by themselves ordaining married men to the priesthood.

Reacting to what seemed like ongoing insubordination within Catholic ranks, the Vatican issued (but did not make public) a new papal decree, the *Cum Data Fuerit,* on 9 February 1929. Among its provisions was a restatement of Vatican policies on property and married priests as well as clarification on two other matters: how bishops are chosen for Eastern-rite churches; and the status of lay organizations associated with, or acting in the name of, the church.

Article 1. The nomination of the bishops is reserved to the Apostolic See.

• • • • •

Article 6. In order to safeguard the temporal goods of the Church, the bishops shall not permit priests of the churches or boards of administrators to possess in their own right goods contributed in any manner by the faithful. They shall insist that the property be held in a manner that makes it safe for the church according to the laws of the various States. They shall issue rules concerning the administration of church property.

• • • • •

Article 12. Until the Greek-Ruthenian Church has a sufficient number of priests educated in the United States, the bishops may through the Sacred Congregation for the Oriental Church ask the Greek-Ruthenian bishops of Europe to send them priests. Priests who are not called by the bishops or sent by the Sacred Congregation, but come to the United States of their own accord, cannot be given faculties by the Greek-Ruthenian bishops in the United States, either for saying Mass, or for the administration of the Sacraments, or for any ecclesiastical work. **The priests who wish to come to the United States and stay there must be celibates.**

· · · · ·

Article 37. **Associations of the faithful of the Greek-Ruthenian rite shall be under the vigilance of the bishops,** who shall name the priest who is to have charge of these associations, in order to avoid any abuses with regard to faith, morals, or discipline. Hence it is praiseworthy on the part of the faithful to join associations which have been formed, or at least approved, by ecclesiastical authority. **The faithful should be on their guard, however, against associations which are secret, condemned, seditious, suspect, or which seek to elude the supervision of lawful ecclesiastical authority.**

Likewise Catholic newspapers, magazines, and periodicals are under the supervision of the bishop, and without his permission priests should neither write in them nor manage them.[d]

When, almost two years later, the *Cum Data Fuerit* decree was made public, it provoked widespread organized and grassroots protest, which resulted in a schism among Rusyn Americans and their Eastern-rite church. One faction abided by the provisions of the *Cum Data Fuerit* and remained within the fold of the Catholic Church; the other (and smaller) faction, in an effort to retain the "true" principles of Greek Catholicism, abandoned the union with Rome and entered into the communion of Orthodox churches. Although the antagonism that marked the early days of these religious disputes is gone, the church schism among America's Carpatho-Rusyns continues to this day.

Whereas the priests and laity of the Byzantine Rite Ruthenian Catholic Church have since 1929 abided by the Vatican's policies on church property and clerical celibacy, the question of a married priesthood has not gone away. In 1990, a new *Code for the Eastern Churches* was approved by the Holy See of the Catholic Church in Rome. It seemed that this matter was finally laid to rest, since the *Code* made clear that "the state of married clerics, sanctioned in the practice of the primitive [Early] Church and in the Eastern Churches through the ages, is to be held in honor."[e] A decade later, Metropolitan Judson Procyk issued the *Particular Law for the Byzantine Ruthenian Catholic Church in the United States,* which also seemed to be clear, allowing "for the admission of married men to the order of the presbyterate [priesthood]."[f] The Vatican, however, was initially reluctant to approve the *Particular Law* and only did so after a clause was added that reiterated celibacy as the "norm" from which "dispensations" might be granted in individual cases at the discretion of the papal authorities in Rome.

More than a century has gone by, during which the controversy over married priests has caused havoc and deep divisions within Eastern-rite churches in the United States. In the end, whereas a married priesthood is recognized *de jure,* in practice ordinations of married men can only occur in exceptional circumstances—circumstances, moreover, that are not determined by the local Byzantine Catholic bishop but rather by the powers that be in Rome.

[a] Letter of the Sacred Congregation for the Propagation of the Faith to the Archbishop of Paris, France, 7 May 1890, cited in Victor J. Pospishl, *Ex Occidente Lex/From the West—The Law: The Eastern Catholic Churches under the Tutelage of the Holy See of Rome* (Carteret, N.J., 1979), p. 24.

[b] Resolutions from the 23 July 1890 Baltimore conclave of Roman Catholic archbishops, cited in G. P. Fogarty, "The American Hierarchy and Oriental Rite Catholics, 1890–1907," *Records of the American Catholic Historical Society of Philadelphia*, LXXXV (Philadelphia, 1974), p. 18.

[c] *Ea Semper* Decree, cited in Paul Robert Magocsi, *Our People: Carpatho-Rusyns and Their Descendants in North America*, 4th rev. ed. (Wauconda, Ill., 2005), p. 28.

[d] *Cum Data Fuerit* Decree, cited in ibid., p. 34.

[e] Canon 373 in *Code of Canons for the Eastern Churches*, Latin-English edition: New English translation (Washington, D.C., 2001), p. 151.

[f] Cited in "Ordination of Married Men in the Eastern Churches," p. 7 (http://byzantines.net/epiphany/ordination.htm).

Those Rusyn Americans who had been actively interested in political developments in the European homeland at the close of World War I continued to monitor the actions of the new states that ruled Carpathian Rus'. The former first governor of Subcarpathian Rus', Gregory Zhatkovych, worked with the Greek Catholic Union, which issued memoranda and other protests criticizing Czechoslovakia for not implementing autonomy in Subcarpathian Rus' as it promised. Rusyn-American organizations also hosted visiting political activists from the homeland—all Russophiles—such as Antonii Beskyd (the future governor of Subcarpathian Rus') in the early 1920s, and Stepan Fentsyk (parliamentary deputy) and Aleksei Gerovskii (Orthodox activist) in the 1930s, to whom funds were given to help support opposition parties in Czechoslovakia. Anti-Czechoslovak feelings among certain Rusyn-American civic activists were so strong that community spokespeople did not speak out against the Munich Pact imposed by the German dictator Adolf Hitler against Czechoslovakia in the fall of 1938, nor against Hungarian irredentist actions which a few months later led to that country's annexation of Subcarpathian Rus'.

Other peoples in Subcarpathian Rus'

Carpathian Rus', like other culturally distinct historic territories in Europe, was never inhabited exclusively by one ethnolinguistic or national group. The focus here is on the only part of Carpathian Rus' which functioned as a distinct administrative unit—Czechoslovakia's eastern province of Subcarpathian Rus'. No less than 38 percent of the inhabitants in that region comprised a nationality other than the numerically dominant one, Carpatho-Rusyns (see Table 18.1).

TABLE 18.1
Nationality composition of Subcarpathian Rus', 1921 and 1930[1]

Nationality	1921		1930	
	Number	Percentage	Number	Percentage
Carpatho-Rusyns	372,500	61.6	446,916	61.6
Magyars	103,690	17.1	109,472	15.1
Jews	79,715	13.1	91,255	12.6
Czechoslovaks	19,775	3.2	33,961	4.7
(Czechs)	(9,477)		(20,719)	
(Slovaks)	(10,298)		(13,242)	
Romanians	10,735	1.8	12,777	1.8
Germans	10,233	1.7	13,249	1.8
Gypsies	425	0.0	1,442	0.2
Others	7,520	1.2	16,285	2.2
TOTAL	**604,593**		**725,357**	

Which peoples lived in Subcarpathian Rus' during the interwar years of 1919–1938? What was their political, socioeconomic, and cultural status, and how did these "other" peoples relate to Carpatho-Rusyns, the national

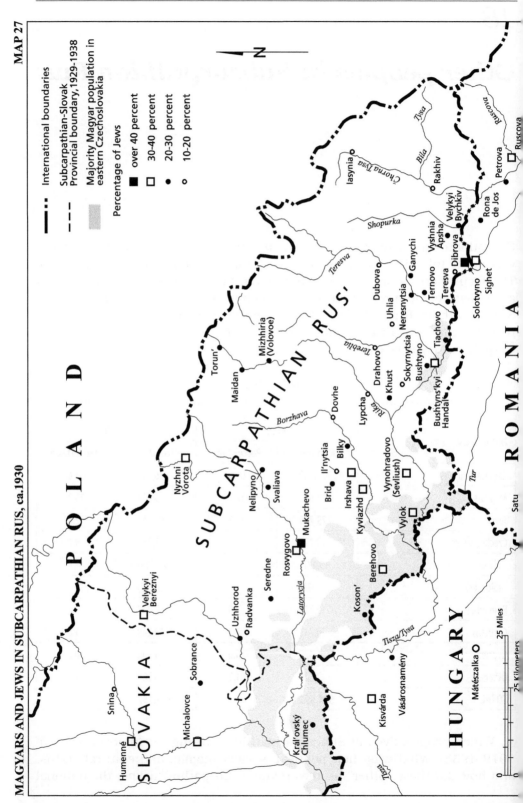

MAGYARS AND JEWS IN SUBCARPATHIAN RUS', ca.1930

MAP 27

International boundaries

Subcarpathian-Slovak
Provincial boundary, 1929-1938

Majority Magyar population in
eastern Czechoslovakia

Percentage of Jews
■ over 40 percent
□ 30-40 percent
● 20-30 percent
○ 10-20 percent

group for whom the province was named? In addressing these questions, most attention will be given to the largest of Subcarpathia's non-Rusyn peoples: Magyars and Jews, followed by some remarks on Germans, Slovaks, and Gypsies/Roma. All these groups can be considered indigenous, or autochthonous peoples, because their forebears lived for several generations, even centuries in Subcarpathian Rus'.

Magyars

Of the 725,000 inhabitants of Subcarpathian Rus' according to the census of 1930, over 109,000 (15.1 percent of the total) identified as Magyars. Most were concentrated in the southwestern part of Subcarpathian Rus', in compact rural villages where they formed generally more than 90 percent of the inhabitants. This area was, in effect, an extension of the lowland plain and nearby Magyar-inhabited villages in Hungary from which Subcarpathian Rus' was separated by the new international border with Czechoslovakia put in place in 1919.

Approximately 23 percent of Subcarpathia's Magyar population lived in urban areas, where they made up a significant portion of the population in the region's largest cities and towns: Mukachevo/Munkács (21 percent), Uzhhorod/Ungvár (17 percent), Tiachovo/Técső (31 percent), and Sevliush/Nagyszöllős (24 percent). The largest of these urban areas was Berehovo/Beregszász, located in the heart of the southwestern lowland plain, where nearly half of the inhabitants (48 percent) declared themselves Magyar.[2] The Magyar population was primarily Western Christian, of whom about three-quarters were Protestant (Reformed Calvinists) and most of the rest Roman Catholic and Greek Catholic. Perhaps as many as 10,000 self-declared Magyars were of Jewish religion, the last of a much larger number of Subcarpathian Jews who had opted for the Magyar/Hungarian national identity before World War I.

The rural component, which accounted for 61 percent of Subcarpathia's Magyars, was engaged in small-scale farming (including truck gardening and fruit cultivation).[3] Concentrated geographically in the region's southwestern lowlands, and speaking a language that was not Slavic or even Indo-European, the rural Magyars interacted mostly among themselves and had limited contact with other peoples in Subcarpathian Rus'. Urban dwellers, on the other hand, who were employed in factories, as independent artisans, and as small retail shop owners (18 percent), or who were in the professions as lawyers, doctors, teachers, and civil servants (21 percent), interacted much more frequently with Jews, Carpatho-Rusyns, and Czech officials. It was the urban Magyars who were most likely to resent their loss of status; that is, what they understood as demotion from their position as the dominant social and cultural group when Subcarpathia was in Austria-Hungary to just another "national minority" in the demonstratively Slavic state of Czechoslovakia—a state, moreover, which favored the region's previously subordinate group, the Carpatho-Rusyns.

Resentment against this change in status is what led Magyars to support political movements that were critical of Czechoslovak rule. Throughout the entire interwar period, the vast majority—sometimes as high as 80 per-cent—of Subcarpathia's Magyars voted for oppositional parties in district, regional, and national elections. Foremost among these was the Communist Party of Czechoslovakia, as well as a coalition of Magyar parties specific to the region, which in 1936 was replaced by a single Hungarian National Party. Consistent voter support allowed for Magyars within both the Communist (József Gáti) and Magyar nationalist parties (Endre Korláth, Ferenc Egry, Károly Hokky) to be elected deputies and senators in all four elections to the Czechoslovak parliament. Although consistently critical of Czechoslovak rule in Subcarpathian Rus', these and other Magyar political activists were careful to avoid speaking openly in favor of the growing irredentist movement across the border in Hungary which was calling for revision of international borders.

Czechoslovakia's constitutional guarantees for the protection of national minorities certainly extended to the Magyars of Subcarpathian Rus', whose cultural life seemed to flourish during the interwar years. Whereas Hungarian-language schools decreased to about one-quarter the number they had been before 1918, communities where the majority of inhabitants were Magyars continued to be served in their native Hungarian tongue, either as the language of instruction for the entire school or in classes set aside for Magyar pupils. By 1938, there were 117 village elementary schools with Hungarian as the language of instruction, and parallel Hungarian-language classes in 30 junior high schools (the so-called *horozhanka* usually located in towns and cities), in the Berehovo *gymnasium* (senior high school), and in the Mukachevo Commercial Academy.[4]

Other aspects of cultural life included a wide range of Hungarian-language newspapers that usually promoted a particular political orientation, a few publishing houses with an albeit limited level of literary production, and a vibrant theatrical scene promoted in large part by the Subcarpathian Hungarian Drama Patronage Society founded in Mukachevo in 1936. Local Magyar activists were active contributors to the Subcarpathian School of Painting, whose head Adalbert Erdeli/Béla Erdélyi was of mixed ethnic background, but certainly of Hungarian cultural heritage. At the more popular level, the Mosaic, later Subcarpathian Hungarian Cultural Society and other societies in individual towns and cities promoted a wide range of events (historic commemorations, evening classes, flower carnivals, annual balls, etc.) that contributed to the preservation of the Hungarian language and group identity. Young people were attracted to gymnastics and soccer sponsored by the Magyar Athletic Club in Uzhhorod, as well as to the scouting movement, for which there was a distinct Magyar section in the Subcarpathian Scout Federation.

Aside from political, cultural, and social activity, perhaps even more important for the daily existence of Subcarpathia's Magyar inhabitants was the autarchic economic policy of the central government in Prague. That policy protected Czechoslovakia's grain producers from potentially cheaper imported foodstuffs. The result was that the wheat-producing areas near Subcarpathia's southern frontier inhabited primarily by Magyars were materially better off than before the war. During the interwar decades, Magyar peasant farmers living on Czechoslovakia's side of the border were certainly more prosperous than their fellow Magyars across the frontier in Hungary. Nonetheless, the reputable British historian of Hungary known for his impartiality, C. A. Macartney, following visits to several Magyar peasant households in the 1930s, reported that the sentiment he frequently encountered was summed up by the statement: "We are better off under the Czechs than we should be in Hungary, but if a vote came, I should still choose for Hungary."[5]

Jews

In stark contrast to the Magyars, Subcarpathia's Jews were less ambiguous in their attitude toward Czechoslovakia. Previously loyal to the Hungarian regime, they quickly adapted to the new reality of Czechoslovak rule.

Although individual Jews had found their way to Subcarpathian Rus' as early as the sixteenth and seventeenth centuries, their numbers remained very small, so that by 1785 there were at most only 2,000 Jews living in the Carpatho-Rusyn inhabited areas of Hungary.[6] Thereafter, their numbers increased dramatically as a result of migration within the Habsburg Empire across the mountains into the Hungarian Kingdom from Austrian Galicia. By 1840, there were 21,600 Jews, many of whom were hired as administrators and other support staff on the large landed estates owned by the Schönborn family in Bereg county. Their numbers continued to rise as a result of further in-migration from Galicia and natural demographic growth (Subcarpathia had one of the highest fertility rates of all European Jewry), so that between 1840 and 1910 the number of Jews increased more than sixfold, to 135,000. Nearly half resided in the eastern county of Maramorosh, with the rest being more or less evenly divided between Bereg, Ugocha, and Ung counties.[7]

The Jews who settled in Subcarpathian Rus' were, like others in central and eastern Europe, Yiddish-speaking Ashkenazim. Somewhat like the region's Christian population, the Jews were divided among different, and often bitterly rival, religious orientations. Although Liberal (Neolog) communities were established in the 1860s in Uzhhorod and in Sighet, the vast majority of Subcarpathian Jews were Orthodox, of whom the ultra-conservative Hasidim were the most prominent. Hasidic Jews were, in turn, divided into devoted followers of a spiritual leader, the *tsadik*, or master and teacher (Hebrew: *admor*), some of whom were reputed to be miracle-working rabbis (Yiddish: *rebbe*). It was not long before Subcarpathian Rus' became home to powerful Hasidic dynasties led by charismatic and often authoritatively domineering *rebbes*.

In contrast to other parts of Europe, over two-thirds of Subcarpathian Jews lived in the rural countryside, where they not only owned land but worked on it themselves as small-scale agriculturalists engaged in fruit-growing, honey-making, and animal husbandry, or were employed as woodcutters and carters. Most were poor, and nearly half their number were illiterate at the outset of the twentieth century.[8] Aside from their native Yiddish, Subcarpathia's Jews communicated easily in Rusyn. It was largely the Jews' socioeconomic status, so similar to that of their Carpatho-Rusyn neighbors, that encouraged equality and mutual respect between the two groups. Pogroms and other organized and spontaneous acts of violence against Jews, common at various times and in most other parts of central and eastern Europe, were absent in Subcarpathian Rus'.

RELATIONS BETWEEN JEWS AND CARPATHO-RUSYNS

Subcarpathian Rus' is considered unique in central and eastern Europe in that the region never experienced any pogroms against Jews. Informed observers and scholars have speculated on the reasons for this seemingly anomalous situation, in particular the generally good relations between Jews and Carpatho-Rusyns. Among the reasons given are economic—most Subcarpathian Jews were poor like their Carpatho-Rusyns neighbors; social—Jews not only owned land but worked on it as peasant farmers and woodcutters; and religious—although of different faiths, both Jews (the Hasidic majority) and Christian Carpatho-Rusyns were God-fearing believers who respected each other for their fervent religious commitment.

Perhaps the best insight into the mutual understanding between Jews and Carpatho-Rusyns is found in the work of the Czech writer, Ivan Olbracht (pseudonym of the Jewish-born Kamil Zeman), in a passage from his most famous novel (1933) about the Carpatho-Rusyn robber bandit, Mykola Shuhai:

> Through centuries of association the Jews and Ruthenians have become used to each other's peculiarities, and religious hatred is foreign to them. True, a Greek [Catholic or an] Orthodox Christian would not for the world consume a milk dish during the fast of Peter and Paul, and a Jew would rather perish than drink any wine that had been touched by a Gentile. But if the Ruthenian pokes fun at the Jew for not eating bacon, for sitting at home with his hat on, and for burning expensive candles to no purpose each Friday night, he laughs at him in all friendliness; and if the Jew scorns the Ruthenian for praying to a man [Jesus Christ] who was put to death in such an unpleasant manner and for venerating a woman [Mary, the Holy Mother]—mind you a woman! [something unheard of for a Hasidic Jew]—he scorns him only in the abstract. They see into each other's ritualistic mystery and religious sorcery just as they see into each other's kitchens and rooms. Should a [Ruthenian] peasant come to a Jewish artisan, who at the moment happens to be conversing with his God, the [Jewish] workman calmly leaves his striped prayer shawl on his shoulders and his phylacteries on his forehead and his left wrist, bids his neighbor good morning, and negotiates at length for the price of repairing the peasant wagon or putting a patch on his sandals or glass in his window. The Almighty is not in a hurry and will wait.

They are interdependent, they visit each other, they owe each other a little cornmeal or a few eggs, or the price of some fodder or the cost of mending the harness. But beware of casting a new idea in their midst, for then at once two types of mind and nervous system [Jewish and Rusyn] will reveal themselves, and the lighting of two clashing gods will flash.

Here we obviously refer only to the poor Jews: artisans, carters, peddlers, and those who live from unknown sources. Insofar as wealthy Jews are concerned ... these are disliked by Ruthenians and Jews alike. The distaste borne by the Ruthenians is one of their several aversions, but the animosity of the poor Jews [toward their wealthy co-religionists] has been sharpened by jealousy into the bitterest hate.

SOURCE: Ivan Olbracht, *Nikola the Outlaw* (Evanston, Ill., 2001), pp. 16–17.

With the collapse of Austria-Hungary in late 1918, and the incorporation of Subcarpathian Rus' into Czechoslovakia, Jewish life was to be significantly influenced by the democratic and secular environment promoted by the new state. During the World War I period, several thousand Jews fled from Subcarpathian Rus', so that by 1921 their numbers decreased to 93,000, only to increase (mainly through fertility) to 102,500 by 1930, at which time they accounted for 14 percent of the province's population.[9] Over one-third still lived in rural areas and over half supported themselves through manual labor (as agriculturalists, livestock herders, carters, and artisans). On the other hand, Jews comprised more than 20 percent of the inhabitants in as many as 37 small towns and cities. They were particularly dominant in places like Solotvyno (44 percent), Bushtyno/Buzhchyns'kyi Handal (36 percent), and Irshava (36 percent). It was the city of Mukachevo (43 percent Jewish), however, with its suburb Rosvygovo (38 percent), which remained the largest community as well as the cultural and spiritual center of Subcarpathia's Jewry.[10] Urban Jews were engaged primarily in trade, as artisans and retail shop owners (including tavernkeepers in small towns and especially in rural villages), and as professionals (doctors, lawyers, notaries, teachers, and civil servants).

In Czechoslovak censuses, Jews were given the option to indicate their nationality as well as their religion as Jewish, with about 12,000 more in each census identifying with Jewish religion than nationality.[11] The government also encouraged secular education, which was gratis in state schools. In the pre-World War I era, a small percentage of the community, especially urban Jews, attended Hungarian-language schools; most, however, received their education at the Jewish *heder* (elementary schools), the *yeshiva* (higher schools, or academies for the study of the Talmud), or the *beis midrash* (houses of religious study for adults). These schools were supported by local Jewish communities, and some, such as the *yeshiva* headed by Rabbi Josef Meir Weiss in Mukachevo, gained a reputation for excellence in Talmudic studies that attracted students from other communities. During the interwar years, the number of Jewish students in Hungarian-language schools and classes declined, as did the number of students in schools with Yiddish and Hebrew as the language of instruction. This is because students from the Orthodox-sponsored Jewish schools began to switch in ever-increasing numbers to state-run Rusyn-language and, most especially, Czech-language elementary and secondary schools.[12] By the mid-1930s, only 3.5 percent of the 19,000 Jewish student population attended the seven Hebrew-language elementary schools and one Jewish *gymnasium* in Mukachevo (a second Jewish *gymnasium* was opened in Uzhhorod in 1934).[13]

Aside from the secular incursion of the Czechoslovak state into traditional Jewish society, the Orthodox majority was challenged by the rapidly growing Zionist movement, which made its first appearance in the Subcarpathian region after World War I. The movement was led by Hayim/Chaim Kugel, a native of Minsk in the Russian Empire, who had gone to study in Prague in 1920 and who arrived in Mukachevo soon after. The Zionists promoted a modern educational program conducted in Hebrew, which was intended to prepare young people for what should be their ultimate goal: emigration (*aliyah*) to Palestine; that is, the ancient Jewish land of Israel (*Eretz Israel*). The Zionists adamantly rejected the Hasidic lifestyle, which they considered to be reactionary and laden with negative superstitions. In response, the Orthodox castigated the Zionists and their institutions, in particular the Hebrew *gymnasium* opened in 1923 in Mukachevo, which the region's most powerful Hasidic *rebbe*, Hayim/Chaim Elazar Shapira, castigated as "a source of heresy and disobedience to our God" and "a danger . . . which every Jew must do his utmost to oppose."[14]

The Hasidic-Zionist conflict spilled over into politics. During the last years of Austro-Hungarian rule, Hungarian-speaking Jews living in Subcarpathia's urban areas were attracted to the left-wing socialist movement. Several played an active role in the 1919 revolution of Béla Kun that created a short-lived Communist regime in Hungary (including Soviet Rus'ka Kraina); subsequently, most joined the International Socialist and Communist parties in Subcarpathian Rus' after the province was united with Czechoslovakia. As supporters of an ideology that espoused atheism, these individuals more often than not rejected—or even denied—their Jewish heritage. Most Subcarpathian Jews, however, remained loyal to their ancestral religious heritage, at the same time that a high percentage continued to vote for the Communist party throughout the interwar years.[15]

The interwar era of Czechoslovak rule in Subcarpathian Rus' encouraged the participation of Jews in political life at the municipal, provincial, and national levels. Initially, Jewish voters were courted by statewide Czechoslovak parties, such as the Agrarian, Social-Democratic, Free Enterprise, and Communist, each of which had branches in the province. As a result, the Jewish vote was split among several Czechoslovak parties as well as Jewish parties. The latter either remained small in size—at best winning seats for its representatives in some municipal elections—or like Subcarpathia's United Jewish party, founded in 1922, within a decade became a branch of the Czechoslovak Jewish party/Židovská strana, which at times cooperated with larger statewide parties or ran independently. For example, the influential Hasidic Rabbi Shapira generally encouraged his followers to vote for the Agrarian party, while the Zionists, with their press organs published in Hungarian (*Zsidó néplap*, 1919–38) and in Yiddish (*Yidishe Shtime*, 1929–38), supported either several smaller Zionist parties or the larger Jewish party. Despite their numerical size, only once, in 1935, did the Jews manage to have their own deputy seated in Czechoslovakia's national parliament—the Zionist Hayim Kugel of the Jewish party, which at the time was in a coalition with the Social-Democrats.

Aside from problems with the Zionists, Subcarpathia's Hasidim were deeply divided by internal conflicts caused largely by personal rivalries among their charismatic and often authoritarian *rebbes*, each of whom felt obliged to defend the interests—and righteousness—of his respective dynasty. Among these were the Spinka dynasty headed by Rebbe Josef Meir Weiss and his son Isaak/Eizik Weiss in Mukachevo and later in Sevliush, and the Sziget-Satmar dynasty led by Rebbe Joel Teitelbaum based in Satu Mare just across the border in Romania. But the most powerful and influential of all Hasidic *rebbes* in Subcarpathian Rus' was Hayim Shapira of Mukachevo.

Backed by the Yiddish-language newspaper *Yidishe Tsaytung* (1927–38), Shapira spoke out with equal vehemence against all who disagreed with his understanding of Judaism: against the non-Hasidic Orthodox for creating a Jewish political party whose very existence was allegedly "contrary to religious command"[16]; against the un-Godly Zionists for creating the secular and, therefore, "heretical" Mukachevo *gymnasium* and youth groups in the rural countryside to infect boys and girls with the misplaced goal of emigrating to Palestine (Eretz Israel); and against all fellow Hasidic *rebbes* who challenged him, including Issachar Dov Rokeah Belz, who eventually was expelled from Czechoslovakia (1922) at the urging of Shapira.

Despite the achievements in education and increased Jewish participation in political life, the Czechoslovak regime was not able to improve in any significant manner the poor economic status of most Jews. Their economic welfare, like that of their Carpatho-Rusyn neighbors, only worsened during the 1930s, following the negative impact of the worldwide economic depression on Subcarpathian society. That same decade also witnessed an increase in the number of small Rusyn- (and Czech-) owned businesses and cooperatives, which challenged the previous Jewish dominance of retail trade. The resultant economic rivalry led at times to boycotts and to criticism in the press. But protests were limited to verbal attacks and, in any case, directed only at Jewish urban shop owners and village innkeepers. The vast majority of Jews continued to live in rural villages, where traditional modes of accommodation continued to exist between the two peoples, symbolized by Rusyns lighting candles and the hearth fire for their Jewish neighbors on the Sabbath, and Jews keeping their shops and market stalls open for the convenience of their Christian customers on Sunday. These humane—some would say idyllic—rela-

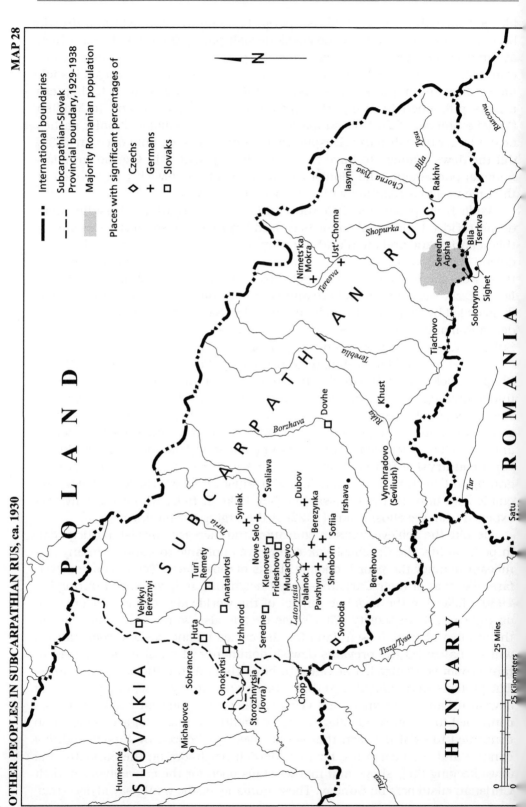

MAP 28

OTHER PEOPLES IN SUBCARPATHIAN RUS', ca. 1930

International boundaries

Subcarpathian-Slovak
Provincial boundary, 1929–1938

Majority Romanian population

Places with significant percentages of

◇ Czechs

+ Germans

□ Slovaks

N

tions were to about to come to an end, however, with the political crisis that struck Czechoslovakia in 1938 and the outbreak of World War II one year later.

Germans

The Germans, known to other Subcarpathians as *Sasy* or *Shvaby*, date back to the medieval period; the ancestors of the interwar community, however, arrived mostly in the course of the eighteenth century (see Chapter 7). Since that time, Subcarpathia's Germans were concentrated in small villages and towns in the heart of former Bereg county just south of Mukachevo and farther north along the Latorytsia River valley near Svaliava. Like Carpatho-Rusyns, a high percentage of Germans (over 3,000) emigrated from the region in the decades before World War I. After 1919, under Czechoslovak rule, their numbers not only stabilized but increased by nearly one-third (10,200 to 13,200 between 1921 and 1930), largely as a result of their fertility and large family units in which 10 to 15 children were not uncommon.[17] Virtually all of Subcarpathia's Germans continued to practice the Roman Catholic faith of their ancestors.

Continuing in the tradition of their forebears who had come to work on the Bereg county estates of the Schönborn family, Subcarpathia's Germans were more or less evenly divided between, on the one hand, rural small-scale peasant farmers and forest rangers, and, on the other, urban dwellers engaged in factories or as civil servants (government clerks, railway employees, teachers, etc.). They made up nearly a quarter of the workers employed in the region's several chemical distilleries and the large tobacco plant and brewery in and around Mukachevo, in all cases holding positions as engineers, technicians, and highly skilled masters.[18]

Unlike the region's Magyars and Jews, Subcarpathia's Germans did not engage in political activity. This is in stark contrast to the large (3.2 million) ethnic German population in the western provinces (Bohemia and Moravia) of Czechoslovakia, which in the 1930s formed the backbone of the increasingly powerful Sudeten German political party (headed by Konrad Henlein) that supported the Nazi ideology of Hitler's Germany. In the mid-1930s, there was an attempt to establish a branch of the Henlein-led party in Subcarpathian Rus', but it attracted little support. It was only after the Munich Pact and the creation of Carpatho-Ukraine that a few hundred Subcarpathian Germans formed in October 1938 the German political party (*Deutsche Partei*) and two months later a German National Council in Khust.

The German minority, which was basically apolitical during the interwar years, did make efforts to sustain its culture and language. As early as 1921, they established the German Cultural Union/Deutsche Kulturverband, which under the influence of a local teacher, Johannes Thomas, was particularly active in urging the local Czechoslovak administration to promote schooling in German. In fact, the number of schools with German as the language of instruction rose from 5 in 1921 to 26 in 1938, by which time there were 8 other schools with classes in German (accommodating a total of over 2,100 students).[19] All these were elementary schools, although in 1933 a German-language high school was opened in Mukachevo.

Romanians, Slovaks, and Roma/Gypsies

In contrast to the Magyar, Jewish, and German minorities, Subcarpathia's Romanians, Slovaks, and Roma/Gypsies did not have any organized community structures. The first two groups, however, were concentrated in a few rural villages, where they formed the majority population: the Romanians (12,800 in 1930) in a few villages along the Tisza River near Solotvyno; the Slovaks (13,200 in 1930) in villages surrounding Uzhhorod and along the border with Slovakia as well as just north of Mukachevo in central Subcarpathian Rus'. There were by the late 1930s four elementary schools (with 2,200 pupils) in which Romanian was the language of instruction,[20] but there were no Slovak-language schools since, as "Czechoslovaks," their villages were assigned Czech-language elementary schools.

The quite small Gypsy community, whose numbers were likely much larger than those given in official census reports (1,442 in 1930), lived in both urban and rural areas, usually in the Gypsy quarter (*tabor*) outside a town or at the beginning or end of a village.[21] In effect, their homes (usually poorly constructed shacks) were distinctly separated from those of the rest of the population. In an effort to encourage Gypsies to adapt to general social norms, the Czechoslovak government passed a law in 1927 which required the relatively small number of nomadic Gypsies to carry an identity card indicating their ethnicity and restricting their settlement in one place to a maximum of three days.

The overall socioeconomic status of the Gypsies was very low. In urban areas, they usually worked as street cleaners or collectors of scrap metal, but they were best known—and appreciated—for their talent as musicians in hotels and restaurants. In villages, they tended sheep and did some forest-related work, but there, too, it was their musical skills which made them an integral and essential presence at weddings and other celebrations of the Carpatho-Rusyn life cycle.

Whereas Gypsy society traditionally did not place any value on formal education, the Czechoslovak authorities were fond of reporting that they had created the first school for Gypsies anywhere in the world. After an unsuccessful effort during the 1923/1924 school year, in late 1926 a Gypsy school was opened in Subcarpathia's administrative capital, Uzhhorod—not surprisingly, on the outskirts of the city near where the Gypsy quarter was located. The teachers and language of instruction were either Czech or Slovak and, in response to the cultural specificity of the student body, much of the curriculum was devoted to music.

Russians, Ukrainians, and Czechs

The most recent of all settlers in Subcarpathian Rus' were the Russians, Ukrainians, and Czechs. Until World War I there were at best only a few individuals from each of these ethnic backgrounds residing in the province. That situation changed radically, especially as a result of the Bolshevik Revolution in Russia in 1917 and the creation of new states at the close of the war. Russians fleeing Bolshevik rule found refuge in various European countries. They were particularly welcomed by the new Czechoslovak state. Most settled in the capital Prague, although several hundred moved eastward in the early 1920s to Subcarpathian Rus'. Their exact number is not known (perhaps about 1,000 by the 1930s), since Czechoslovak censuses did not record them as a separate group, but listed them together with Carpatho-Rusyns.

Several Russian émigrés, especially engineers, were encouraged by the Czechoslovak authorities to go the country's new eastern province, where they were employed in state enterprises, such as hydroelectric and road-building projects. Some also found employment as school teachers or as priests in the rapidly expanding Orthodox Church. For Russian intellectuals, Subcarpathian Rus' was a "Russian land," where they could feel psychologically comfortable, in particular if they could help the local population realize their belonging to the Russian nationality. This was the position of émigrés from the former Russian Empire (Evgenii Nedzel'skii, Petr Miloslavskii, Aleksandr Popov) as well as of civic and political activists from the former Habsburg Austrian provinces of Galicia and Bukovina (Andrei Gagatko, Ilarion Tsurkanovich, the Gerovskii brothers) who believed they were of the Russian nationality. Among the most renowned Russians in interwar Subcarpathian Rus' was the "grandmother of the Russian Revolution," Ekaterina Breshko-Breshkovskaia.

Ukrainian settlers also came from the former Russian Empire, although a larger number were from the neighboring former Austrian province of Galicia, which after 1919 was part of Poland. Like the Russian refugees, the Ukrainians were welcomed by the Czechoslovak government and settled primarily in Prague and nearby towns. And also like the Russians, those Ukrainians who settled in Subcarpathian Rus' felt they were living in their extended homeland and among their "own" people (Carpatho-Rusyns), which they understood to be a branch of Ukrainians. By the 1930s, there were an estimated 2,500 to 3,000 Ukrainians who settled in both the cities and small towns and villages of Subcarpathian Rus'.

The Czechoslovak regime promoted the placement of Ukrainian refugees as teachers in Subcarpathian schools and the provincial educational administration (Ivan Pankevych, Volodymyr Birchak, Andrii Aleksevych, among others). There were also several clergy from Galicia who secured posts as village priests or as seminary and high school teachers in Subcarpathia's Greek Catholic educational institutions. It was these activists who promoted the Ukrainian national orientation among Carpatho-Rusyn youth through their work as teachers, priests, editors, writers, and politicians.

The Czechs, who first began to arrive in Subcarpathian Rus' in 1919, did not come as refugees, but as privileged citizens moving from the western (Bohemia and Moravia) to the far eastern part of their new country. The first wave of Czech in-migrants comprised several thousand civil service functionaries who staffed the state's administration and educational system in

Subcarpathian Rus', as well as gendarmes stationed in small villages to protect the country's borders with Poland, Romania, and Hungary.

In order to strengthen further the province's borders, especially the lowland plain with easy access to Hungary, the central government in Prague
funded a program beginning in 1923 that eventually resulted in ten colonies
throughout Subcarpathian Rus' comprised of Czech farmers from Bohemia
and Moravia. Several were established in exclusively Magyar-inhabited territory east of the railroad junction of Chop, where new villages and hamlets
with Czech-sounding names like Svoboda, Svobodka, and Dvorce attracted
a Czech population which by the 1930s reached 900. Other Czechs continued to arrive in the hope of improving their economic situation by opening
taverns, cafés, and other small-scale businesses in Subcarpathia's towns
and cities, as well as tourist hotels in the more remote northern and eastern mountainous areas of the province. Although it is difficult to know their
exact number (since census reports only recorded them as "Czechoslovaks"),
it seems that by 1930 the number of Czechs in Subcarpathian Rus' reached
20,700 and was to continue to rise during the next decade.[22] About half lived
in the province's largest cities: Mukachevo, Berehovo, and Khust, but most
gravitated to the administrative capital, Uzhhorod.

Many of the Czech newcomers, especially those in the state administration
and civil service, believed that they were coming to help raise the economic,
social, and cultural standards of their fellow Slavs, the Carpatho-Rusyns.
They were nevertheless well aware of the fact that the Subcarpathian environment was different from that which they left, so they set out to create institutions that would remind them of their Bohemian and Moravian homelands. In
this regard, the children of Czech civil servants and rural inhabitants needed
to be educated in their native language. This accounts for the rapid increase
in the number of new Czech-language schools, with over 200 by the 1937/38
school year at the elementary (177), junior high (23), and senior high/*gymnasium* (1) levels, as well as a teacher's training college.[23] Since Czech was the
state's most prestigious language, and alongside Rusyn the official language
of Subcarpathian Rus', parents of other nationalities, in particular Jews, sent
their children to schools with Czech as the language of instruction.

Other institutions set up to fulfill the needs of Subcarpathia's Czechs
included: athletic (gymnastic) societies known as Sokols, with nineteen
branches throughout the province; the Smetana Society to promote the
music of Czech composers; and several new movie houses to show Czech-
language films. There was no shortage of Czech-language newspapers and
journals, some of which were connected with the regional branches of statewide Czechoslovak political parties, in particular *Podkarpatské hlasy* (1925–
38) representing the Agrarian party and *Hlas východu* (1928–33) the Social-
Democratic party. Despite the relatively small size of the community, those
parties often chose Czechs (František Kralík, Josef Zajíc, Jaromír Nečas) to
represent Subcarpathian Rus' in the national parliament.

Throughout the entire interwar period, Subcarpathian Rus' became the
destination for hundreds of thousands of Czech tourists encouraged to vaca-

tion in the pristine mountainous regions of the country's far eastern province by the National Czechoslovak Tourist Club (KČST) and the Friendship Society for Subcarpathian Rus'/Klub přátel Podkarpatské Rusi based in Bratislava. Aside from extensive building projects designed by some of the country's leading Czech architects (see Chapter 14), the pristine natural beauty of Subcarpathian Rus' and its allegedly idyllic Carpatho-Rusyn inhabitants became a source of inspiration for a whole host of visiting Czech creative artists, whether painters (Ludvík Kuba, Václav Fiala, František Foltyń), photographers (Karel Plicka), cinema directors (Vladislav Vančura, Martin Frič), or belletrists (Jaroslav Durych, Jaroslav Zatloukal, Stanislav Neumann, and Karel Čapek, among a whole host of others). Perhaps the most influential of these creative artists was the Czech writer, Ivan Olbracht, who published numerous short stories about the life of Subcarpathian Jews and a novel about the Carpatho-Rusyn brigand Mykola Shuhai (*Nikola Šuhaj loupežník*, 1933). This, more than any other work, whether in its original form as a novel, or its post-World War II offshoots in the form of films, a song revue, or Broadway musical, has immortalized Subcarpathian Rus' and Carpatho-Rusyns in the minds of Czechs to this very day.

The Czech love affair with Subcarpathian Rus' came to an abrupt end in 1938, when developments in other parts of Europe were to change permanently the face of Subcarpathian Rus' and to threaten the very existence of some of its peoples.

Autonomous Subcarpathian Rus' and Carpatho-Ukraine, 1938–1939

Despite the procrastination and reluctance of the Czechoslovak government to fulfill its original promise of autonomous self-rule for Subcarpathian Rus', that question did not disappear from the political agenda of local activists during the interwar years. In fact, the debate about autonomy increased in intensity during the second half of the 1930s.

The struggle for autonomy during the interwar years

The leading local political party which had promoted this issue ever since the 1920s was the Autonomist Agricultural Union headed by Andrii Brodii. It was later joined by the Russian National Autonomist party, established in 1935 and effectively headed by Shtefan Fentsyk. Both parties were supported by Rusyn-American organizations, whether the older Greek Catholic Union, or the Carpatho-Russian Union/Karpatorusskii komitet founded in New York City in 1935 by the Russophile activist, Aleksei Gerovskii. Subcarpathia's autonomist parties also set up branches in eastern Slovakia, since their platforms called for unification of the Prešov Region with Subcarpathian Rus'. Aside from cooperating with several Czechoslovak national parties (including the Sudeten German Party headed by Konrad Henlein) that were in opposition to the Prague government, Subcarpathia's pro-autonomy activists also accepted funds from Czechoslovakia's enemies—from Hungary in the case of Brodii and from Poland in the case of Fentsyk.

Finally, the Central Rusyn National Council, the umbrella-like political organization which back in 1919 had formally united Carpatho-Rusyns with Czechoslovakia, adopted a common position on the autonomy question. The National Council had in the early 1920s split into pro-Russian and pro-Ukrainian factions, but the autonomy question brought them back together. In 1936, the council submitted a constitutional proposal for an autonomous Subcarpathian Rus'. The Czechoslovak government felt that some kind of response was necessary, since the joint Russian-Ukrainian Central National Council represented a very wide spectrum of both pro-government as well as oppositional political forces in the region. The response, however, was far from what local leaders expected. Instead of implementing autonomy, the Czechoslovak government adopted a law (No. 172) in June 1937, which slightly altered the functions of Subcarpathia's governor. The governor was made the formal head of the Subcarpathian Rusyn Land/Země podkarpatoruská and was allowed to recommend laws for the region. In reality, however, the province's Czech vice-governor (by then Jaroslav Mezník) and not its Carpatho-Rusyn governor (Konstantyn Hrabar) remained the most powerful political figure in the region.

Czechoslovakia's ongoing procrastination on the autonomy question resulted in the following scenario. On the one hand, virtually all Subcarpathian political leaders, whether they represented pro-government or oppositional political parties, were alienated by the policies of the central government in Prague. On the other hand, Subcarpathia's rival Russophile and Ukrainophile politicians, as well as factions within those orientations, joined in solidarity with Governor Hrabar to demand that the Czechoslovak government act seriously on the autonomy question. In the spring of 1938, Subcarpathia's leading Russophile (Andrii Brodii, Shtefan Fentsyk, Edmund Bachyns'kyi) and Ukrainophile (Avhustyn Voloshyn, Iuliian Revai) politicians put aside their national differences. This made possible the adoption of a resolution (29 May 1938) issued by the first Russian-Ukrainian Central National Council which called on the Czechoslovak government: (1) "to introduce in the shortest possible time elections to a Subcarpathian autonomous diet (*soim*)"; and (2) "to unite with Subcarpathian Rus' those territories in eastern Slovakia inhabited by Rusyn-Ukrainians."[1] The Subcarpathian demands were supported by a National Committee (*Narodnyi komitet*) created the same month in Prešov under the leadership of two Carpatho-Rusyn parliamentary deputies from Slovakia, Ivan P'ieshchak and Ivan Zhydovs'kyi.

Nazi Germany and the Munich Pact

By 1938, however, Czechoslovakia had to deal with much more serious problems than political discontent in its far eastern province. In fact, before the end of the year, the country's very existence was to be called into question. Ever since the close of World War I, the defeated states which like Germany, Hungary, and Bulgaria managed to survive the conflict, were deeply dissatisfied with the political order created at the Paris Peace Conference. By the 1920s, Hungary was calling for border revisions. In the 1930s, Hungary was joined by what turned out to be an ever greater threat to the postwar European order—Nazi Germany under Adolf Hitler. Caught in the middle of these two irredentist powers, Hungary and Germany, was Czechoslovakia.

Hitler was determined to correct what he and most of the German public felt were the injustices of the Paris Peace Conference's Treaty of Versailles. In the second half of the 1930s, Nazi Germany had adopted a foreign policy, the goal of which was to unite all Germans living beyond the borders of Germany (the so-called *Volksdeutscher*) into what was now being called the Third German Reich. Hitler's first step was directed toward Austria, which in 1918 had been forbidden by the victorious Allies from joining Germany. Two decades later, in March 1938, Hitler simply concluded an annexation pact (*Anschluss*) with Austria, making that country a part of the Third Reich. With Austria secured, Hitler could devote full attention to his next victim—Czechoslovakia.

Hitler's demands on Czechoslovakia were initially limited to only the German-inhabited areas of Bohemia and Moravia, where about three million ethnic Germans lived in what was popularly called the Sudetenland (after a mountain range in this region called the Sudetens). In late September 1938, Hitler invited to the city of Munich his ally, Benito Mussolini of Italy, and the prime ministers of Great Britain (Neville Chamberlain) and France (Pierre Deladier), to discuss what he described as the "Czechoslovak crisis." Since the close of World War I, Great Britain and France were allies of Czechoslovakia, and they ostensibly were expected to come to the aid of that small central European country should it be threatened by its neighbors. Instead, the British and French leaders agreed—with fascist Italy's blessings—that on ethnic grounds Germany had the right to annex the Sudetenland.

Therefore, in what became known as the Munich Pact of 30 September 1938, Hitler's demands were appeased. Large parts of Bohemia and Moravia were awarded to Nazi Germany, which was authorized to begin the occupation the following day (1 October). What remained was a country, which European commentators sardonically described as "rump" Czechoslovakia. In the wake of the Munich Pact and a weakened Czechoslovakia, the central government in Prague conceded to the demands of leaders in the other two provinces of the country—Slovakia and Subcarpathian Rus'—who had been demanding the implementation of autonomy throughout the entire interwar years.

Autonomous Subcarpathian Rus'

On 11 October 1938, the cabinet of the first Subcarpathian autonomous government was appointed by Prague. It was dominated by local Russophile activists under Premier Andrei Brodii. Although Brodii's government lasted only 15 days, during that short time it made clear its ideological stance by criticizing the interwar Czechoslovak regime for its pro-Ukrainian and "anti-Russian educational and cultural policy."[2] It also initiated the process of closing Czech-language schools in Subcarpathian Rus' and undertook propaganda efforts in eastern Slovakia with the goal "to unite all the Russian (*russkaia*) territories in the Carpathians (from the Poprad to the Tysa Rivers) into one unitary, free state."[3] In that regard, Russophile ministers Shtefan Fentsyk and Ivan P'ieshchak (from the Prešov Region) were immediately dispatched throughout eastern Slovakia to organize demonstrations that would show the desire and commitment of the Prešov Region's Carpatho-Rusyns to unite with their brethren in Subcarpathian Rus'.

Premier Brodii and his supporters, frustrated for nearly two decades with Czechoslovak policy toward Subcarpathian Rus', had come to believe that the best chance to achieve autonomy was within Hungary. Now that he was in power, he called for a plebiscite, assuming that a majority of the province's inhabitants (Carpatho-Rusyns and certainly local Magyars) would

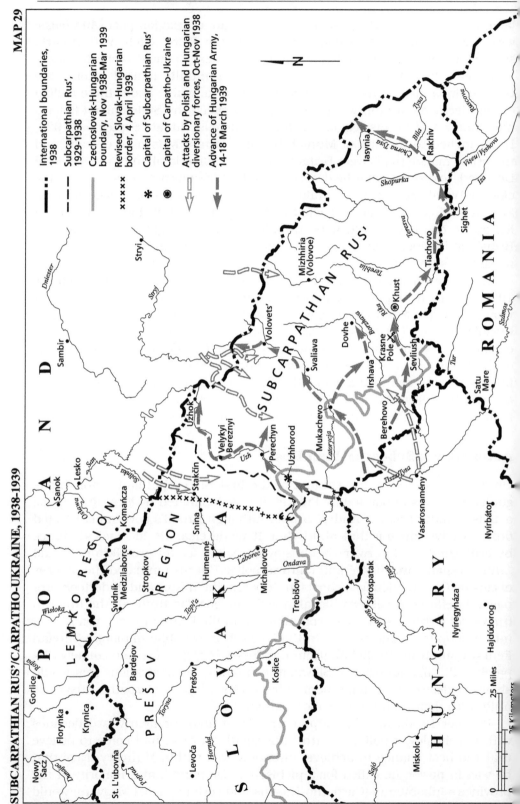

MAP 29

International boundaries, 1938

Subcarpathian Rus', 1929–1938

Czechoslovak-Hungarian boundary, Nov 1938–Mar 1939

Revised Slovak-Hungarian border, 4 April 1939

Capital of Subcarpathian Rus'

Capital of Carpatho-Ukraine

Attacks by Polish and Hungarian diversionary forces, Oct–Nov 1938

Advance of Hungarian Army, 14–18 March 1939

vote to return their homeland to Hungary. Brodii, who since the mid-1930s was being subsidized by the Hungarian government, felt that a favorable outcome from the proposed plebiscite would be a trouble-free way to fulfill Subcarpathian interests and at the same time to achieve Budapest's irredentist aims. These intrigues were exposed by the Czechoslovak authorities, however, resulting in the dismissal of the first autonomous cabinet and the arrest of Brodii. On 26 October, Prague appointed a new government headed by Premier Avhustyn Voloshyn. This began the domination of the Ukrainian orientation in the political life of the autonomous province.

From Subcarpathian Rus' to Carpatho-Ukraine

After less than a week in office, the Voloshyn regime faced its first crisis. The Munich Pact of September 1938 represented only the first phase in resolving what Nazi Germany referred to as the Czechoslovak problem. Germany's most recent ally, Hungary, was to be the beneficiary of the next phase. Less than six weeks after Munich, a conference was held in Vienna (then part of Nazi Germany), where on 2 November 1938 an agreement was reached regarding the further dismemberment of "rump" Czechoslovakia. According to what became known as the Vienna Award, territory was detached from Czechoslovakia's two eastern provinces, for the most part the Magyar-inhabited fringe along the Slovak and Subcarpathian border with Hungary. Among the losses for Subcarpathian Rus' was its administrative center, Uzhhorod, and the province's two other largest cities, Mukachevo and Berehovo. Subcarpathia's autonomous government, now cut off by direct rail communication with the rest of Czechoslovakia, moved hastily eastward to set up its headquarters in the town of Khust. At the same time, most of Subcarpathia's Czech inhabitants—whether government officials, civil servants, and shop owners in urban areas, or farmers settled in the lowland plain—hastily evacuated and returned to Bohemia and Moravia.

Nevertheless, Hungary still remained displeased with the Vienna Award, since the revisionist leaders in Budapest expected to obtain, at the very least, all of Subcarpathian Rus'. Support for such a goal now came from Brodii and Fentsyk, the leading figures in Subcarpathia's first autonomous government who found their way back to Hungarian-ruled Ungvár/Uzhhorod and immediately embarked on a propaganda campaign to gain the rest of Subcarpathian Rus' for Hungary. Bishop Aleksander Stoika as well as other dignitaries of the Greek Catholic Church (Aleksander Il'nyts'kyi, Irynei Kontratovych) also remained in Uzhhorod, and they, too, soon came out in support of "the return" of their homeland to Hungary. Since ranking members of the Greek Catholic clergy were the strongest supporters of the separate Carpatho-Rusyn national viewpoint, that orientation was left without leadership within the reduced territory of autonomous Subcarpathian Rus'. This effectively meant that what remained of Subcarpathian Rus' had an autonomous government and civic society mostly dominated by Ukrainophiles with only a few Russophiles of pro-Czechoslovak political orientation.

Even before the Vienna Award (2 November), which created a mutually accepted Czechoslovak-Hungarian border, the Hungarian government already had plans in place for attacks against Subcarpathian Rus'. In the summer of 1938, Hungary created a special armed force of about 4,000 men that was called the Rongyos Gárda (The Ragged Guard). Its goal was to destabilize international boundaries which throughout the entire inter-war period Hungary was hoping to revise. By the end of August 1938, the Rongyos Gárda was sent to the border of eastern Czechoslovakia, and on the night of 9–10 October launched its first terrorist attack against Subcarpathian Rus'. Attacks were to continue even after the establishment of the new Czechoslovak-Hungarian border in early November.

Nor were such incursions only coming from the south. The government of Poland, which was sympathetic to Hungary's anti-Czechoslovak policy, dispatched army units to attack Subcarpathian Rus' from the north. Known as the secret Łom Operation (Akcja "Łom"), its diversionary attacks against Czechoslovak border posts, bridges, and defensive installations continued throughout October and November 1938.

Aside from the efforts of the Czechoslovak Army's border defense units (SOS) to protect the province from these incursions, the Voloshyn government authorized in early November the creation of the Carpathian Sich Organization for National Defense. Although it was led by pro-Ukrainian activists from Subcarpathian Rus' (Dmytro Klympush and Ivan Rohach), most of the Sich's estimated 2,000 men (of which only 300 to 400 were armed) were actually Ukrainians who began to arrive from neighboring Polish-ruled Galicia. Most were members of the Organization of Ukrainian Nationalists, the underground force which since the 1930s had been fighting a guerilla war against Poland and setting up cells in neighboring countries where "Ukrainians" lived, including Subcarpathian Rus'. These Carpathian Sich volunteers from Galicia saw Carpatho-Ukraine as a modern-day Ukrainian Piedmont, that is, the basis from which an independent Greater Ukrainian state (*Soborna Ukraïna*) would be formed when Poland and the Soviet Union would either be transformed or collapse.

Such seemingly unrealistic political views were for a while given currency by Nazi Germany, which had initiated at Munich the transformation of Czechoslovakia and encouraged the creation of autonomous Slovakia and Subcarpathian Rus'. Beginning in December, members of Voloshyn's government consulted periodically with the Nazi-German government, whether in Berlin, or more often through their newly established consulate in Khust, which helped facilitate economic agreements with Carpatho-Ukraine. For a few months, Subcarpathian Rus'/Carpatho-Ukraine had come to the attention of the international community, since it seemed to be a part of Nazi Germany's plans for the further political transformation of central and eastern Europe.

In legal terms, autonomous Subcarpathian Rus' was formally created by a constitutional amendment adopted by the Czechoslovak parliament on 22 November 1938. Despite the efforts of Ukrainophile activists to change the name of the province, its official designation remained Subcarpathian

Rus' (Czech: Podkarpatská Rus), with the proviso that the alternative name, *Carpatho-Ukraine*, could be used. In fact, the Voloshyn regime only used the alternative form, *Carpatho-Ukraine*, in all its official communiqués. The November constitutional amendment also included a provision which called for elections to a Subcarpathian diet (*soim*) within five months. The proposed diet was to be responsible for passing laws to govern the province and for the final decision on its official name and language.

The future diet was also given a say regarding the controversial issue of the language taught in schools. Nevertheless, it soon became clear that in educational and cultural matters the Voloshyn administration favored and already adopted distinctly Ukrainian characteristics. Although Premier Voloshyn was responsible for education and culture, he delegated these affairs to Avhustyn Shtefan, an ardent Ukrainophile and director of the Commercial Academy in Mukachevo. Mukachevo was already attached to Hungary, so that its schools as well as the various *gymnasia*, trade schools, and teacher's colleges located in other Hungarian-ruled areas of Subcarpathian Rus' had to be transferred to small towns in the north and east of the province. All teachers, directors, and inspectors were required to use the Ukrainian language. The closing of most Czech-language schools that was begun during the Brodii administration was completed. This prompted many Czech civil servants and teachers to begin returning with their families to Bohemia or Moravia.

Most of the newspapers and journals that had existed up until 1938 were discontinued, while the editorial boards of the remaining and new journals were staffed by Ukrainophile personnel. All were published in literary Ukrainian, and all emphasized the Ukrainian character of the autonomous province. Subcarpathia's younger Ukrainophile intelligentsia came out in full force behind the Voloshyn government. Overjoyed at spending his first Christmas in an autonomous Carpatho-Ukraine, Mykola Rishko wrote:

> For centuries we awaited this festive day . . .
> While suffering under enemies in our homes.
> Rejoice my great, invincible people.
> Join in shining ranks
> To greet a holy Christmas in unity
> From the Tysa to the Don and beyond to the Caucasus.[4]

Alternatives to the Ukrainian national orientation

Despite the domination of the Ukrainian national orientation, the Russophiles did not remain inactive. Although the pro-Hungarian activities of Fentsyk and Brodii discredited the Russian national orientation, there were still other Russophile leaders who remained loyal subjects and supported the concept of a federated Czecho-Slovak state. In Khust, a group of 25 pro-Czechoslovak Russophiles met on 14 November 1938 to establish a Central Russian National Council. Its aim was to defend the Russian language and cultural interests in the autonomous province. The council, headed by Vasilii Karaman, Petr P. Sova, and Pavel S. Fedor protested the dismissal of Russophiles from the Provincial School Administration as an example of what they described as the general "Ukrainian terror" and the alleged excesses of the Carpathian Sich which maintained "concentration camps exclusively for *katsapy* [a pejorative term for Russians, used for local Russophiles] and *Moskali*."[5] Unquestionably, one such detention camp was set up as early as 20 November 1938 on orders from Voloshyn at a place called Dumen near the town of Rakhiv. Operated by the Carpathian Sich, Dumen included refugees from Galicia and also local Russophile activists who refused to accept the Ukrainian orientation of Voloshyn's regime.

Another source of discontent was the Orthodox population, most of whose priests (124 in 1938) and faithful were indoctrinated with a love of all things Russian and, therefore, adverse to the Ukrainian ideology of the Voloshyn regime. Whereas the Subcarpathian bishops representing the Serbian Orthodox jurisdiction and the much smaller Constantinople jurisdiction both formally pledged their loyalty to the Voloshyn regime, the traditional Orthodox stronghold in Iza and neighboring villages just to the north of Khust voted en masse against the Ukrainian candidate list in the February elections to the diet (*soim*) and even clashed with the Carpathian Sich and militia in the area.

Discontent came from outside the province as well. In Prague, Subcar-pathian university students of Russophile orientation opposed the use of the name *Carpatho-Ukraine*, while Carpatho-Rusyn immigrant activists in the United States—the vast majority of whom were either Russophiles or Magyarones—sent "protests against the establishment of Ukraine on an immemorial Russian land as ordered by Premier Voloshyn."[6] On the other hand, Ukrainian diaspora organizations (comprised primarily of nationally conscious Ukrainian immigrants from Galicia) lobbied the governments of the United States, Canada, and Great Britain, urging support for "the right of self-determination for Transcarpathian Ukraine" and protesting against the Vienna Award and any further border changes in the region.[7]

Carpatho-Ukraine's road to "independence"

Voloshyn and his cabinet were plagued by increased difficulties with the central government in Prague. The two issues of conflict concerned: (1) the appointment in January 1939 of the Czech general Lev Prchala as a minister in the Khust government; and (2) the fate of many "former Czechoslovak" officials who were released from their jobs, in particular the 820 school teach-ers from the closed Czech-language schools. At the same time, Voloshyn had difficulties with Slovakia's new autonomous government. This was because his pro-Ukrainian supporters, like their Russophile predecessors in the Brodii cabinet, continued to demand the union of Rusyns in the Prešov Region with Subcarpathian Rus'. The goals were the same, even if the rhetoric may have changed, with nationalist spokespeople in Khust predicting "that the Ukrainian flag will fly over the Tatras."[8] Slovakia's autonomous administra-tion based in Bratislava was angered by these claims, even though in strongly

Russophile eastern Slovakia, the previously widespread desire to unite with Subcarpathian Rus' virtually disappeared when it became clear that the Voloshyn government was Ukrainophile, not Russophile in orientation.

Notwithstanding the enormous internal and external difficulties that it faced, the pro-Ukrainian administration in Khust prepared for elections to an autonomous diet. On 12 January 1939, Voloshyn decreed that elections would be held exactly one month later. In an attempt to clarify the internal political situation in the weeks since the establishment of autonomy, all existing political parties were declared invalid and new parties were called upon to submit candidates. One of these new parties, the Ukrainian National Union/Ukraïns'ke natsional'ne ob'iednannia, presented a list of 32 candidates, many of whom were prominent members in various interwar political parties but who were now united under one dominant force—"the idea of Ukrainian nationalism." Other parties which tried to submit candidates were not accepted by the electoral commission, with the exception of the small Nazi-oriented German party/*Deutsche Partei*, which was recently established in an effort to mobilize Subcarpathia's small ethnic German community. In effect, the populace was presented with only one candidate list, that of the Ukrainian National Union.

In response to Fentsyk and Brodii, whose newspapers in Hungarian-ruled Uzhhorod were calling for the union of Subcarpathian Rus' with Hungary, the Voloshyn government argued that upcoming elections to an autonomous diet would be a kind of plebiscite to reveal the attitude of the people regarding the present political situation. The pro-government organ, *Nova svoboda,* stated clearly that voting for the Ukrainian list of candidates meant support not only for the present government of Carpatho-Ukraine but also for the federative alliance with Czechs and Slovaks. In this context, the results of the election (12 February) turned out overwhelmingly positive. The vast majority of voters (92.5 percent) accepted the list of Ukrainian candidates,[9] and on 2 March 1939 the diet (*soim*) of Carpatho-Ukraine held its inaugural session.

Notwithstanding the electoral success registered by the Voloshyn-led government, Carpatho-Ukraine was to be allotted little more than four weeks more of existence. Already by February 1939, it had become evident to many political observers in western Europe that Hitler was only waiting for the right moment to dismantle what remained of Czechoslovakia and to give Hungary the signal to occupy the rest of Subcarpathian Rus'. Internally, the remaining weeks of the Voloshyn administration were marked by increased friction with the central Czechoslovak government in Prague.

In early March, Prague once again reorganized the autonomous Subcarpathian cabinet. And even though Voloshyn was reappointed premier, tensions between Czech and local Ukrainophile leaders increased to such a degree that on 14 March a pitched battle broke out between the Carpathian Sich and Czechoslovak soldiers (mostly Carpatho-Rusyns) stationed in Khust. If that were not problem enough, some radical members of the Organization of Ukrainian Nationalists, displeased with what they considered the indecisiveness of local Ukrainophile leaders, laid plans for a coup to depose Premier Voloshyn. Events elsewhere, however, were to dictate developments and seal the fate of Carpatho-Ukraine.

Hitler decided to liquidate what remained of Czechoslovakia. On 13 March 1939, the premier of autonomous Slovakia, Msgr. Jozef Tiso, was summoned to Berlin and urged to declare Slovakia an independent state under German protection. The following day the Slovak autonomous diet proclaimed its independence. Faced with Slovakia's act, the diet in Khust followed suit and declared Carpatho-Ukraine's independence in the early evening of 14 March. Voloshyn's request that independent Carpatho-Ukraine become a protector-ate of Nazi Germany was rejected. This is because Hitler had already given Hungary his approval (12 March) to invade and annex Carpatho-Ukraine. Nearly 40,000 Hungarian troops began their invasion on 14 March. The Czechoslovak Army stationed in the province initially resisted, but then capitulated that same evening.

The Hungarian forces that continued the invasion on 15 March were divided into three groups: two passed through Uzhhorod and Mukachevo on their way northward toward the crests of Carpathians; the third moved through Berehovo eastward up the Tisza River valley toward Carpatho-Ukraine's capital, Khust. It was along the way toward Khust that on the morning of 15 March the Carpathian Sich, together with some Carpatho-Rusyn soldiers, demobilized from the Czechoslovak Army as well as patriotic young students from the teacher's college in Sevliush, stood their ground at a place called Krasne Pole. Although overwhelmed by the Hungarian forces, Krasne Pole has become in recent years a symbol in Ukraine of heroic sacri-fice on behalf of Carpatho-Ukraine, whose existence, however short, is con-sidered as the embodiment of the Ukrainian national idea in the region.

On the afternoon of 15 March, as Hungarian troops were fast approach-ing Khust, Voloshyn convened the diet (22 of the 32 elected deputies were present) to approve the declaration of Carpatho-Ukraine's indepen-dence proclaimed the night before. As part of the diet's symbolic proceed-ings, Avhustyn Voloshyn was elected president. With no support from Nazi Germany and faced with an ultimatum to surrender from the advancing Hungarian Army, President Voloshyn, his cabinet, and the diet's deputies left the country. That same day, German troops entered Prague, which, together with rump Czechoslovakia's western provinces of Bohemia and Moravia was annexed to Hitler's Third Reich. Among the last orders of the central gov-ernment in Prague were instructions that the Czechoslovak Army units sta-tioned in Subcarpathian Rus'/Carpatho-Ukraine should leave without engag-ing the Hungarian troops. Also departing with the army were any remaining Czechoslovak civil servants and their families.

As for the Carpathian Sich, it was easily dispatched by the advancing Hungarians, although some partisans continued to fight for another month or so in the high mountain areas. In effect, by 16 March, the Hungarian Army had control of Khust, and within two more days it occupied all of Subcarpath-ian Rus'. Such was the end of autonomous Carpatho-Ukraine and its "repub-lic for a day."[10]

Carpathian Rus' during World War II, 1939–1944

It may have taken some time, but the leaders of Britain and France who participated in the Munich Pact of September 1938 eventually realized that the territorial ambitions of Adolf Hitler were not limited to Czechoslovakia. Even his ally in fascist Italy, Benito Mussolini, was enraged at not having been consulted before Germany liquidated what remained of Czechoslovakia on 15 March 1939. Undaunted, Hitler proceeded in the following months to finalize plans for his next conquest—Poland. Poland, however, was much larger than Czechoslovakia, and its armies were poised to resist any attack. Hence, to make his task easier, Hitler did a diplomatic about-face and began negotiations with his hated enemy—Stalin's Soviet Union. The result was a German-Soviet non-aggression treaty, known as the Molotov–Ribbentrop Pact (after the names of the Soviet and German foreign ministers), which was signed on 23 August 1939. A secret protocol of this treaty provided for the division of Poland between Nazi Germany and the Soviet Union in the event of war.

Nazi Germany's New Order in Europe

Hitler, of course, had long planned for such an eventuality, and on 1 September 1939 Germany invaded Poland along a broad front that stretched from the Baltic Sea in the north to the crests of the Carpathian Mountains in the south. In contrast to the Czechoslovak crisis the year before, Great Britain and France lived up to their commitments to Poland and declared war on Germany. World War II had begun.

The British and French declarations of war had no practical impact, so that Poland was left alone to defend itself against Germany's full-scale attack (*Blitzkrieg*) from the west and, as foreseen in the secret protocol of the Molotov–Ribbentrop Pact, a Soviet attack from the east that began on 17 September. Faced with overwhelming and superior military might, the last unit of the Polish Army capitulated on 6 October 1939. Once again, as at the end of the eighteenth century, Poland ceased to exist as a state. The secret protocol in the Molotov–Ribbentrop negotiations provided for a German-Soviet demarcation line originally along the Vistula River but that subse-

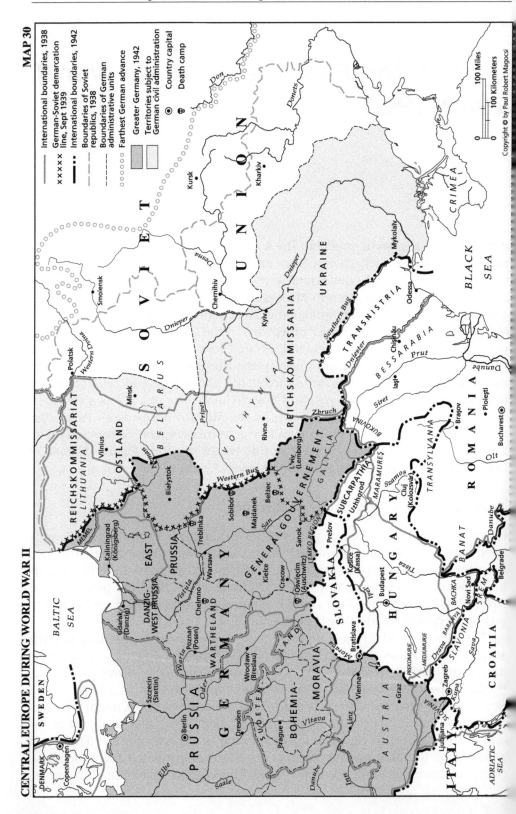

MAP 30

CENTRAL EUROPE DURING WORLD WAR II

International boundaries, 1938

xxxxx German-Soviet demarcation
         line, Sept 1939

International boundaries, 1942

Boundaries of Soviet
republics, 1938

Boundaries of German
administrative units

Farthest German advance

Greater Germany, 1942

Territories subject to
German civil administration

⊚ Country capital

☒ Death camp

100 Miles

100 Kilometers

Copyright © by Paul Robert Magocsi

quently was changed to what is more or less Poland's present-day boundary with Belarus and Ukraine. In the south it followed the San River to its source in the Carpathians. This meant that the Lemko Region fell to the German sphere, while formerly Polish-ruled eastern Galicia (which bordered on Subcarpathian Rus') became part of the Soviet sphere.

During the next several months, Nazi Germany and the Soviet Union proceeded to reapportion among themselves and their allies the territorial composition of central Europe that had been outlined in the Paris Peace Conference at the close of World War I. Actually, Hitler's ally Hungary was to be the first beneficiary of the new order. Within a month after Hungary acquired the rest of Subcarpathian Rus'/Carpatho-Ukraine (15–18 March 1939), it extended its border at the expense of Slovakia, incorporating 74 villages (among which were 36 with about 20,000 Carpatho-Rusyns), almost as far west as the town of Snina (see Map 29).

Then, at the initiative of Hitler himself, a Second Vienna Award (30 August 1940) granted to Hungary north-central Transylvania, including the Carpatho-Rusyn-inhabited Maramureş Region on the southern bank of the Tisza River. Finally, in April 1941, German armies invaded and destroyed Yugoslavia. The Vojvodina west of the Danube River, that is, the Bachka region where Rusyns/Rusnaks lived, was given to Hungary, while the nearby Srem region was given to Germany's ally, the newly independent state of Croatia. As a result of these territorial changes carried out between 1939 and 1941, all the lands of historic Carpathian Rus' were now within the larger sphere of Nazi Germany and its allies: the Lemko Region in Greater Germany itself; the Prešov Region within Germany's ally, Slovakia; and Subcarpathian Rus' and the Maramureş Region (as well as the Bachka) within Germany's other ally, Hungary.

The Lemko Region in Nazi Germany

German-ruled territories of former Poland that were just west of the demar-cation line with the Soviet Union and were organized into an administrative entity known as the Generalgouvernement. The Generalgouvernement itself was subdivided into districts headed by an official (*Gauleiter*) appointed by Hitler. The Lemko Region was within the Cracow district of the Generalgouvernement. Because the Generalgouvernement was itself made an integral part of the Third Reich (Greater Germany), it had a civil administration like other parts of the Nazi state. This meant that everyday conditions in the Lemko Region were better than those in lands farther east that eventually were conquered by Nazi Germany, but were to be ruled as occupied colonies.

East of the demarcation line, that is, in the Soviet zone of former Poland, a national assembly of western Ukraine was convoked in L'viv in late October 1939. Under the protection of the Red Army, the delegates were encour-aged—and they unanimously agreed—to request that their homeland (former Austrian-ruled East Galicia, which in the interwar years was within Poland) be annexed to the Soviet Union. On 1 November, the request was approved by the Soviet central government in Moscow, which assigned the new territorial acquisition of western Ukraine to Soviet Ukraine. Two things resulted from this act: (1) the Soviet Union now shared a border with Hungary, specifically along the crests of the mountains in Subcarpathian Rus'; and (2) Soviet rule led to the almost immediate repression of traditional civic, cultural, and religious institutions in western Ukraine, in particular the Greek Catholic Church. Fearing such repression, an estimated 20,000 Ukrainians, many of whom were national activists, fled westward beyond the demarcation line into Germany's Generalgouvernement, within which was the Lemko Region.

The Nazi German authorities accepted the view that Lemkos were part of the Ukrainian nationality, and to encourage cultural and educational activity in the Generalgouvernement the Ukrainian Central Committee was set up in Cracow under the direction of the Jagiellonian University geographer and Ukrainian civic activist Volodymyr Kubiiovych. Kubiiovych was determined to enhance the status of the Ukrainian national orientation throughout the Lemko Region. Consequently, the Ukrainian language was introduced into all elementary schools, and to train new cadres a Ukrainian teacher's college was established in Krynica. Ukrainian-language technical schools were opened in Sanok and Krynica, as were new branches of the popular-enlightenment Prosvita Society and rural cooperatives. Ukrainian nationalists fleeing from Soviet rule east of the San River demarcation line were welcomed to staff these various institutions in the Lemko Region. Among the Ukrainian refugees from eastern Galicia were several who were given jobs as policemen and as lower-level administrators in the German regime.

Neither the Nazi German government nor the Ukrainian activists were sympathetic to the Old Ruthenian and Russophile activists who had dominated cultural and religious life in the interwar Lemko Region. Consequently, teachers who were not of Ukrainian orientation were removed from schools; the Lemko Association/Lemko soiuz ceased to exist, and the Ruska Bursa in Gorlice, which in 1930 had reopened its doors to students, was closed once again. The Greek Catholic Lemko Apostolic Administration also experienced a radical transformation. In February 1941, a new administrator was appointed in the person of Oleksander Malynovs'kyi. As an active supporter of the Ukrainian orientation, he undertook an active campaign to replace the priests of the Greek Catholic Lemko Apostolic Administration, most of whom were of Old Ruthenian or Russophile orientation, with those of Ukrainian orientation. He was helped in this regard by a major change in the direction of World War II.

On 22 June 1941, Adolf Hitler, disregarding the Molotov–Ribbentrop non-aggression treaty signed two years earlier with Stalin, launched an all-out invasion of the Soviet Union. Within a few months all of Soviet Ukraine came under Nazi German control, and Galicia east of the San River was added to the Generalgouvernement. In the context of the anti-Russian hysteria associated with the invasion of the Soviet Union, the Nazi German authorities, together with the Ukrainians who were working for them, arrested prominent Lemko activists of the Old Ruthenian and Russophile orientation, all of whom were lumped together under the opprobrious Ukrainian term "Muscophiles" (*moskvofily*). Among those arrested were several Orthodox priests and virtually all the leading clerics in the chancellery office and deaneries of the Lemko Apostolic Administration, including the chancellor Ioann Polianskii. Sent to the city of Kielce in former central Poland, they were to remain under house arrest and close Gestapo surveillance until the end of the war. All were replaced by priests of Ukrainian national orientation, so that the Greek Catholic Lemko Apostolic Administration became, in terms of its national identity, no different from the rest of the Greek Catholic Church within the Archeparchy of L'viv in western Ukraine.

The repression directed against large segments of the Lemko Region's secular and religious leadership and their families, not to mention discontent with the increasingly harsh policies of the Nazi police state, prompted many young Lemkos to join the partisan movement. Some Lemkos were to be found in the Home Army/Armia Krajowa, the military forces of the Polish underground state. But because of their generally leftist political sympathies many more preferred to join the Polish Communist underground movement and its military wing, the People's Guard/Gwardia Ludowa. In fact, among the most prominent members of the People's Guard were the Lemko brothers Mykhal and Ivan Donskii, who led a Lemko partisan unit that carried out several successful operations against the Nazi German authorities and the Ukrainian police serving that regime.

Carpatho-Rusyns in the Slovak state

Following the dissolution of Czechoslovakia in March 1939, Carpatho-Rusyns in the Prešov Region found themselves under the control of a Slovak state governed from its capital in Bratislava. The Slovaks had struggled for more than two decades to gain greater autonomy from the Czech-dominated centralized Prague government. Now, they finally had their own state, even if its existence depended on the good will of Hitler's Germany. Slovakia was headed by a president, the Roman Catholic priest Jozef Tiso, who was chosen by a one-chamber elected parliament. Among the deputies were two (Antonii Simko and Adal'bert/Geiza Horniak) who represented the country's Carpatho-Rusyns. The government based in Bratislava was dominated by patriots—in some cases extremist nationalists—whose goal was to slovakize all aspects of the country.

Carpatho-Rusyns in the Prešov Region were especially targeted for discrimination, because after the Munich Crisis they had expressed a desire to be separated from Slovakia and united with Subcarpathian Rus'. Consequently, the Greek Catholic Church and especially its bishop, Pavel Goidych, was accused of disloyalty to Slovakia and of allegedly harboring pro-Hungarian feelings. For instance, in 1939, the president of Slovakia, Msgr. Jozef Tiso, and then in 1940 the minister of propaganda, Šaňo Mach, visited Prešov. On both occasions it is alleged that both Slovak leaders slighted the bishop in public and questioned his loyalty. Also in 1940, a fervent Slovak nationalist, Andrej Dudáš, was appointed to head the administrative district (Šariš-Zemplín *župa*) for all of eastern Slovakia, a post he was to hold for the remainder of the war. Dudáš was convinced that the idea of a Carpatho-Rusyn nationality was little more than a chimera created by the Hungarians, and in 1943 he wrote a book on the subject, concluding that the "so-called Rusyn people (*rusínsky ľud*) in the Carpathian Basin are by origin and character Slovak."[1]

It was in such an atmosphere that Prešov Region Rusyns now found themselves. In early 1939, the Rusyn National Committee and Carpatho-Rusyn National Council were banned, the newspaper *Priashevskaia Rus'* (1938–39) was closed, and the cultural activity of the Dukhnovych Society was restricted. Carpatho-Rusyns were allowed one more deputy (Mykhailo Bon'ko) for a total of three in the Slovak Diet, each of whom was expected to support the government's policy. As a result, the Greek Catholic Church led by Bishop Goidych was about the only institution which could effectively defend Rusyn national interests.

As a result of Goidych's efforts, the Slovak government passed a decree in 1940 making all elementary schools the responsibility of the Greek Catholic Church. This allowed for the continuance of Rusyn-language instruction, and for that purpose four new textbooks were published. The number of Rusyn schools declined to about half what they had been during the inter-war Czechoslovak decades, numbering between only 75 to 80 during the period of the Slovak state.[2] Other cultural activity was even more limited. Slovak administrators wanted to remove Prešov as the cultural center for Rusyns and tried, though unsuccessfully, to have Bishop Goidych's residence transferred from Prešov northward to Medzilaborce. Only one Rusyn-language newspaper was permitted, *Novoe vremia* (1940–44), which like the Greek Catholic school system used the so-called "traditional Carpatho-Rusyn language" (i.e., Russian with local dialectisms) and propagated a Russophile national orientation. Prešov Region authors were generally isolated from each other during the war years, although some cultural activity took place among Carpatho-Rusyn university students in Bratislava through their student club, the Dobrians'kyi Society (Obshchestvo Dobrianskago) and its publications: *Studencheskii zhurnal* (1940–41) and *Iar'* (1942–43).

The economic situation of the mass of Carpatho-Rusyn peasant farmers did not change from what it had been during the interwar years, even though a few thousand went to Germany to earn extra income. Those who remained home were able to take advantage of the arianization laws (September 1941); that is, to receive proprietorship over land and shops taken away from Jews following the adoption by Slovakia of anti-Semitic decrees. Since Slovakia did not suffer any destruction until the last months of the war, some improvements, especially in roads and communications, did take place in the Prešov Region before 1944.

Nevertheless, as in the Lemko Region, so too in the Prešov Region were there Carpatho-Rusyns who became increasingly discontented with what they considered the clerico-fascist Slovak state that had little tolerance for the cultural aspirations of its national minorities. As early as 1943 small uncoordinated partisan units operating in the inaccessible mountainous areas carried out attacks against state property. More organized in nature was the activity of civic and cultural leaders based in Prešov (Dionisii Roikovych, Vasyl' Karaman, Ivan and Petro Zhydovs'kyi, among others), who in Septemeber 1943 established the Carpatho-Russian Autonomous Council for National Liberation/Karpatorusskii avtonomnyi sovet natsional'nogo osvobozhdeniia (KRASNO). Although representing varied orientations ranging from left to right in the political spectrum, what united its members were two goals: to assist Soviet prisoners of war and partisans; and to cooperate with other underground organizations opposed to the Slovak state. Among the latter were organizations which favored the postwar reemergence of a united Czechoslovakia. In that regard, the Carpatho-Russian Autonomous Council expected that Carpatho-Rusyns in the Prešov Region, together with their brethren in Subcarpathian Rus', would be treated as an equal partner with their own autonomy when, after the war, Czechoslovakia would be reconstituted as a federal state comprised of three peoples.

Subcarpathian Rus' in Hungary

The acquisition of Subcarpathian Rus' by Hungary in two stages between November 1938 and March 1939 was considered a major achievement for a country that for nearly 20 years had made border revisionism and territorial irredentism the cornerstone of its foreign policy. Since revisionist propagandists had been promising that under the Hungarian Crown of St. Stephen Subcarpathian Rus' would receive autonomy, the government authorities in Budapest, at least initially, felt obliged to formulate plans for self-rule.

As early as 17 March 1939, Prime Minister Pál Teleki announced that the Hungarian government intended to introduce autonomy in its newly acquired territory. Teleki expected that the proposed Subcarpathian autonomy would serve as a model for other "lost Hungarian lands," which allegedly in the near future would be "returned to the fatherland." The prime minister was supported in his endeavors by the pro-Hungarian Carpatho-Rusyn leaders, Andrii Brodii and Shtefan Fentsyk, who demanded elections to a Subcarpathian national assembly as the first step toward the implementation of wide-ranging political and cultural autonomy.

After nine proposals, the head of Hungary's minority institute at Pécs University submitted a project for autonomy to Prime Minister Teleki, who accepted it as being "true to the idea of the Crown of St. Stephen."[3] The project called for the establishment of the Subcarpathian Voivodeship (Hungarian: Kárpátaljai vajdaság), which was to be ruled by a governor and a 40-member diet. Within the autonomous territory, the Rusyn language (*rutén nyelv*) was to be equal with the state language, although in all Rusyn-language schools Hungarian would be a required subject.

On 23 July 1940, the autonomy bill was finally introduced in the Hungarian parliament. As it turned out, this was the first and last time any serious attempt was made to legalize Subcarpathian self-rule. The Hungarian press in Budapest had from the very beginning expressed reservations, and the military was opposed because it feared that even the slightest semblance of autonomy would be a potential danger to the security of the country. Such an attitude seemed especially convincing after September 1939, when the Soviet Union acquired Ukrainian-inhabited East Galicia and thus acquired a common border with Hungary. Great opposition was also expressed by the so-called "wild" Hungarians—local Subcarpathian Magyars who refused to live in a Carpatho-Rusyn province—and by conservative public opinion in the rest of the country, which was unfavorably reminded of plans put forth back in 1918 for a federated Hungary. In subsequent years, some deputies in the Hungarian Parliament from time to time mentioned the Subcarpathian autonomy issue, but it was never again seriously considered by the government. Carpatho-Rusyn leaders like Andrii Brodii, who naïvely believed that Hungary would grant the region autonomy, reverted to criticizing the Hungarian government as he had criticized the Czechoslovak government during the interwar years. Nevertheless, Brodii together with eleven other Carpatho-Rusyn activists (Shtefan Fentsyk, Aleksander Il'nyts'kyi, Iosyf Kamins'kyi, among others) accepted appointments as deputies and as senators in the Hungarian Parliament.

As for its administrative status, Subcarpathian Rus' was after an initial few months of military rule formally annexed to Hungary on 22 June 1939. Instead of autonomy, the Subcarpathian Territory (Hungarian: Kárpátaljai terület), as it was officially called, or simply Subcarpathia (Kárpátalja), was ruled by a civil administration headed by a commissioner appointed by the head of state, the regent of Hungary Miklós Horthy. Subcarpathia's commissioner (initially Baron Zsigmond Perényi and later Miklós Kozma) was assisted by an appointed 12-member advisory board headed by the Greek Catholic priest, Aleksander Il'nyts'kyi. It is interesting to note that even though the headquarters of the commissioner and civil administration were in Uzhhorod, technically that city and the territory first acquired in November 1938 was not part of the Subcarpathian Territory. In effect, Hungarian Subcarpathia had basically the same reduced territory as did Carpatho-Ukraine in late 1938 early 1939.

Initially, the Hungarian government tried to make a favorable impression on the population by providing various kinds of assistance to Subcarpathia's inhabitants. Hungary's main cooperative society based in Budapest, known as Hangya, set up a network of village cooperatives throughout Subcarpathia, and it is through these that in April 1939 a large sum of charitable funds raised among the Hungarian public was distributed to poverty-stricken peasant farmers in the highland regions (Verkhovyna). The Hungarian government also invested significant sums to provide the local population with employment in public works, in particular the repair of roads in Subcarpathia. The dismantling of Czechoslovakia's border with Hungary also allowed once again for Carpatho-Rusyns to work as seasonal harvesters on the Danubian lowland plains. In the summer of 1939 over

7,500 unemployed and landless Subcarpathian farmers went to lowland Hungary to work, as a result of which they were able to send home 240 railway cars of grain.[4]

At the same time, however, the Hungarian government revised the policy of the Czechoslovak regime and returned to large landowners much of the landed property confiscated from them during the Czechoslovak land reform of the early 1920s. Among the beneficiaries of this policy was Subcarpathia's first commissar, Baron Zsigmond Perényi, whose large estates around his residential manor in Sevliush were returned to the family. Carpatho-Rusyn peasants were not particularly pleased with this partial return to a feudal-like economic system.

The apogee of the Rusyn national orientation

While the Hungarian government did not implement any autonomy or self-government for Subcarpathia, it did permit and even promote a significant degree of cultural and educational activity. Both Hungarian and Rusyn were declared the official languages of Subcarpathia, and most government-sponsored publications and decrees intended for the region were issued in the two languages. The local authorities also made some progress in resolving the language question which had plagued Subcarpathian cultural life during the interwar decades under Czechoslovakia.

At the outset of 1941, government funding allowed for the creation of the Subcarpathian Scholarly Society/Podkarpatskoe obshchestvo nauk, whose primary goal was "to contribute toward the creation of a distinct national identity among Rusyns."[5] Within a few months of the society's establishment, its director Ivan Haraida, a linguist by training, published a grammar that became the standard for a Rusyn literary language that was used in schools and the region's public life. Rejecting both the Russian and Ukrainian orientations, Haraida created a literary form based primarily on the local Subcarpathian Rusyn vernacular. This was the language used in a wide variety of publications put out by the Subcarpathian Scholarly Society, including a literary and cultural magazine (*Lyteraturna nedîlia*, 1941–44), a scholarly journal (*Zoria/Hajnal*, 1941–43), a youth journal (*Rus'ka molodezh*, 1941–44), numerous booklets on a wide range of subjects, and literary works by local authors as well as translations into Rusyn of the classics of world literature.

The Rusynophile-oriented Subcarpathian Scholarly Society in Uzhhorod also published an annual almanac, which included a supplement written in the Vojvodinian Rusyn language. It and other publications were sent to the Vojvodina; that is, to the Bachka (since 1941 part of Hungary), where the Rusyn National Enlightenment Society and the Zaria Cultural Enlightenment Union had ceased to exist after the fall of Yugoslavia in 1941. The Rusyn literary language promoted by the Subcarpathian Scholarly Society was also used in performances of the Uhro-Rusyn Theater in Uzhhorod, which succeeded the Subcarpathian National Theater from Czechoslovak times.

As a result of these developments, the post-1939 Hungarian regime in Subcarpathia provided an institutional basis for the Rusynophile orientation, which until then had been expressed primarily at the individual level. The goal of the various organizations, publications, and school curricula was to convince the indigenous East Slavic inhabitants that they constituted a distinct "Uhro-Rusyn" (Hungarian Rusyn) nationality, whose past history and culture were intimately related to the Hungarian state and the historic realm of the Crown of St. Stephen.

Among Subcarpathian politicians who welcomed the return of Hungarian rule were Andrii Brodii and especially Shtefan Fentsyk who, together with several writers, continued to support the Russophile national orientation and use of the Russian language. For instance, the pro-Russian Dukhnovych Society from the interwar period was allowed to function. Meanwhile, the Ukrainian orientation was banned by the Hungarian authorities, which closed all Ukrainian-oriented organizations, including the Prosvita Society. Prosvita's National Center in Uzhhorod was given to the Subcarpathian Scholarly Society, while its numerous reading rooms throughout the province were either closed or coopted by the newly established Hangya Cooperative Society or the older Russophile Dukhnovych Society. Finally, most of the civic and political leaders who were connected with the period of Carpatho-Ukrainian autonomy were forced into exile, eventually settling in German-ruled Prague or in Bratislava, the capital of the Slovak state.

Opposition to Hungarian rule

But what about the larger number of intellectuals, students, civic activists, and simple peasant farmers throughout Subcarpathia who had become committed to a Ukrainian national identity? Some Ukrainian-language writers adopted the new Rusyn standard and continued to publish with, or even work for, the Subcarpathian Scholarly Society. Then there were young Carpatho-Rusyn males who joined the patriotic Hungarian paramilitary youth organization Levente, or who were drafted into the Hungarian army and even participated in battles on the Eastern Front after Hungary joined its ally, Nazi Germany, in the June 1941 invasion of the Soviet Union.

On the other hand, several younger male and female students still in *gymnasium* (senior high school), especially those imbued with strong Ukrainian national sympathies, expressed discontent with Hungarian rule and were even detained for a while by the authorities. A much larger number, regardless of national orientation (Rusynophile, Russophile, Ukrainophile), were united in their hatred of Hungary, believing that after the war they would be able to live once again in "their" state of Czechoslovakia. Young people, in particular, did not wish to be drafted into the Hungarian Army or the paramilitary youth organization Levente. Over 5,600 (of whom nearly 500 were women) expressed their discontent by fleeing northward across the mountains to what after September 1939 was Soviet-ruled eastern Galicia.[6] To their surprise, they were not welcomed, but considered by the Soviet authorities as spies. Because they crossed illegally into Soviet territory, they were all arrested and sentenced to various terms of forced labor in the Gulag.

After June 1941, when the northern route was closed off by Hitler's invasion of the Soviet Union, the Hungarian security services became increasingly suspicious of any expressions of sympathy toward the East, especially among Carpatho-Rusyn students and youth. Consequently, during the remaining years of the war, hundreds were arrested and questioned about their alleged pro-Ukrainian and pro-Soviet sympathies. The Hungarian regime even held two trials in the summer of 1942 at the Kovner Palace in Mukachevo, where 123 persons were accused of pro-Ukrainian sympathies. In the end, they were all acquitted and released. Tensions continued to rise in 1943 as Soviet armies on the Eastern Front gradually approached the Carpathians, as clandestine radio broadcasts brought news about the activity of the Czechoslovak government-in-exile in London, and as the first partisan reconnaissance groups from the Soviet Union (the Pataky parachute descent in August 1943) reached Subcarpathia. Although the partisan incursions were successfully intercepted by Hungary's military counterintelligence, the country's authorities became increasingly uneasy and responded with more arrests, trials, prison sentences in work camps, and executions.

Finally, much of Subcarpathian society was traumatized by the deportation, between 14 May and 6 June 1944, of virtually the region's entire Jewish population—over 115,000 men, women, and children—to the Nazi German death camps in Auschwitz-Birkenau.[7] Subcarpathian Rus' had never experienced pogroms or any other overt form of anti-Semitic violence, so that the removal of so many friends and neighbors from towns and villages throughout Subcarpathia sent shock waves of fear and uncertainty among Carpatho-Rusyns left behind.

The brutal deportation of Jews in the first half of 1944 changed profoundly the demographic composition of Subcarpathia. By the end of that same year, however, even greater changes were in store, as all of Carpathian Rus' was finally thrust into the battle zones of World War II.

Carpathian Rus' in transition, 1944–1945

Hitler's conquest of Ukraine and other parts of the Soviet Union, as well as his intention to expand Germany's borders ever farther eastward depended on the ability of the German Army (*Wehrmacht*) to continue its success on the battlefield against the Soviet Red Army. What seemed to be German military invincibility came to an end at the outset of 1943. In February of that year, after the incredibly costly three-month Battle of Stalingrad, German forces for the first time were forced to capitulate. The tide of the war had finally turned, and from then on Soviet armies were on the offense advancing slowly but steadily westward. By the end of 1943 they had reached Kiev, and by April 1944 they were approaching the Carpathians. Hungary continued to boast that its fortified Árpád Line along the crest of the mountains was indestructible, but in an effort to be certain that Subcarpathia's population would remain loyal to the Hungarian fatherland, the territory was again placed under military rule headed by a new commissar, General András Wincz.

The Soviet Army and Ukrainian nationalist partisans

The Soviet forces which were moving westward included a large contingent of Carpatho-Rusyns. Actually, they were part of a Czechoslovak unit fighting within the ranks of the Soviet Army. This unit came into existence in a rather strange way. At the end of 1942, military emissaries of the Czechoslovak government-in-exile were able to convince the Soviet authorities to release Carpatho-Rusyns from forced labor camps, where they had been held since fleeing from their Hungarian-ruled homeland back in 1939–1940. The Czechoslovak Brigade (and later, the First Czechoslovak Army Corps), as the unit came to be known, included over 3,000 soldiers from Subcarpathia who initially represented over two-thirds of the total number of soldiers in the unit.[1]

The Soviet struggle to drive the Germans out of Ukraine was further complicated by the large number of partisan units, some of whom were allied and others who were opposed to one or both of major combatants—the German Army and the Soviet Army. One of these units was the Ukrainian Insurgent

Army, which came into being in northwest Ukraine (Volhynia) sometime in 1942. Better known by its Ukrainian acronym, the UPA, this fighting force came to be dominated by followers of Stepan Bandera, head of one of the factions of the prewar underground Organization of Ukrainian Nationalists. It is for this reason that the UPA was also known, especially among its enemies, as simply the *Banderovtsi* (Ukrainian: *Banderivtsi*), or Banderites.

During the last years of World War II, the UPA (Banderites) clashed with both the Soviet and German armies. But they fought even more intensely against Polish partisans and Poland's underground Home Army also active in western Ukraine; that is, in lands like Volhynia and Galicia, which during the interwar years were part of Poland. The struggle between these two bitter opponents was especially costly for the civilian population, since the UPA worked to drive all Poles from their homes in territories that would be part of a future independent Ukraine, while Poland's Home Army and Polish partisan units wished to secure those very same areas—Volhynia and Galicia—which they were convinced must once again remain within a restored postwar Poland. As the fortunes of the UPA struggle waned, its remaining forces retreated westward, eventually finding refuge in the high mountainous areas in Carpathian Rus' during the last months of World War II and the immediate postwar years. Some Carpatho-Rusyns, especially Lemkos, were to be drawn—however unwillingly—into the political and military maelstrom surrounding the UPA (*Banderovtsi*).

As the Soviet armies were moving steadily westward, the question of Europe's postwar political order became an ever-increasing concern for the Allied Powers. The newest member of the Allies was the Soviet Union, whose tenuous relationship with Nazi Germany came to an abrupt end when Hitler launched the German invasion of June 1941. The Soviets were now eligible for assistance from the Allies, which took of war material and supplies primarily from the United States.

Governments-in-exile of former states like Czechoslovakia and Poland also lobbied hard and, eventually, they succeeded in convincing the Allies that each of their respective countries deserved to be reconstructed at the war's end. Consequently, former soldiers and other citizens from those countries were welcomed into the ranks of the British, French, and Soviet armies as individual volunteers or as part of their own national units. One such national unit was the Czechoslovak Brigade/Army Corps formed in the Soviet Union.

Rusyn/Lemko Americans and the war in Europe

On the political front, Czechoslovak political leaders headed by the country's prewar president Edvard Beneš set up in July 1940 a government-in-exile based in London. The Allied Powers—Great Britain, France, the United States, and eventually the Soviet Union—all agreed that the Munich Pact was invalid and that after the war Czechoslovakia was to be reconstituted according to its pre-Munich borders. This meant that Subcarpathian Rus' was again expected to be part of Czechoslovakia. It was with this in mind that the Carpatho-Rusyn lawyer Pavel Tsibere was appointed a member of the London-based Czechoslovak state council-in-exile with the specific function to advise President Beneš about Subcarpathian Rusyn affairs.

Czechoslovak leaders together with Tsibere traveled to the United States, in order to place their cause before the American government and to seek support among the large Rusyn-American community. Gregory Zhatkovych, the former governor of Subcarpathian Rus', not only changed his critical position toward Czechoslovakia, but also convinced his fellow Greek Catholics to join with Orthodox Rusyn Americans and to reassess their attitudes toward developments in the European homeland. In March 1942, representatives of both religious orientations formed in Pittsburgh the American Carpatho-Russian Central Conference, which supported the Czechoslovak option for Subcarpathian Rus'. They expected, of course, that the postwar reconstituted state would be a true federation with full political and cultural autonomy for each of its component parts—the Czech lands (Bohemia and Moravia), Slovakia, and Subcarpathian Rus'. It is interesting to note that already in 1939 the politically leftist Lemko Association set up its own "national committee," which called for the union of all of Carpathian Rus' (by then divided between Nazi Germany and its allies Slovakia and Hungary) with the Soviet Union. After the Soviet Union joined the Allied Powers in late 1941, branches of the Lemko Association in both the United States and Canada in conjunction with the American Carpatho-Russian Congress contributed to the Russian War Relief, raising close to $150,000 for food, clothing, and especially medical supplies destined for the Soviet Army.[2]

As early as the summer of 1941, the Czechoslovak government-in-exile initiated talks with Soviet officials. As contacts between the two parties increased after 1943, Czechoslovak leaders acted on the assumption that Subcarpathian Rus' would remain a part of their postwar country. Since, however, all of central Europe fell within the Soviet military sphere in the Allied war against Nazi Germany, agreement had to be reached on how precisely the Czechoslovak authorities would be allowed to return to Subcarpathian Rus' once the territory was "liberated" by Soviet troops. In effect, everything depended on the Soviet Union and its all-powerful leader, Joseph Stalin.

The Soviet "liberation" of Subcarpathian Rus'

By the summer of 1944, virtually all of eastern Galicia (western Ukraine) was controlled by Soviet armies within what was designated the Fourth Ukrainian Front under the command of Major General Ivan Petrov. On 8 September 1944, General Petrov launched the Eastern Carpathian Offensive with the purpose of crossing the mountains and eventually driving the German and Hungarian armies out of the Danubian Basin. One part the Eastern Carpathian Offensive focused on the Lemko Region and from there into eastern Slovakia. The Soviet armies, together with the First

Czechoslovak Army Corps, met fierce resistance on both sides of the Dukla Pass. Instead of a military operation which the Soviets expected to last one week, the Battle of the Dukla Pass lasted nearly two months until the end of October. The Germans were finally defeated, but only after 150,000 casualties, two-thirds of which were on the victorious Soviet side. Among the casualties were those suffered by troops of the First Czechoslovak Army Corps, including its large Carpatho-Rusyn contingent, which was deliberately sent to this part of the front so that they would not be part of the Soviet units sent to Subcarpathian Rus'.

The other part of the Eastern Carpathian Offensive focused on crossing the five passes into Hungarian-ruled Subcarpathia. German and Hungarian forces behind allegedly "impregnable" fortifications (the Árpád Line) put up little resistance and actually pulled out of Subcarpathia by mid-October. At the same time, the Hungarian civil administration evacuated the region, and on 27 October a Czechoslovak government delegation (headed by František Němec) was allowed to set up its headquarters in Khust under the protection of the Soviet Army. The goal of the delegation was to make contact with local village, or people's, committees in order to set up a Czechoslovak administration and also to seek volunteers to serve in the Czechoslovak Army Corps. As it turned out, neither of these goals was achieved.

This is because real power was in the hands of the Soviet Army, whose own actions on these matters were determined by political emissaries sent by Stalin, among whom were his trusted associate, Lev Mekhlis, and the chief political commissar assigned to the military, Leonid Brezhnev (the future head of the Soviet Union). In essence, Stalin had already decided that, because of its strategic geographical location, Subcarpathian Rus' should belong to the Soviet Union. His reasoning was simple. Control of the region would in the future allow Soviet troops direct access to the Danubian Basin without first having to cross the Carpathians. But because the Soviet Union had during the war accepted the Allied position that Czechoslovakia should be reconstructed according to its pre-Munich boundaries, something needed to be done to show that it was not the Soviets wanting to expand their boundaries, but rather the local population itself which desired unification with its alleged brethren to the east. It is not surprising, therefore, that Soviet advisors sought out among Subcarpathia's inhabitants members and sympathizers of the local Communist party, which had been among the largest political parties in prewar Czechoslovak-ruled Subcarpathian Rus'.

Quite spontaneously, so-called people's committees were formed in virtually every town and village after the rapid departure of the Hungarian administration. These committees were comprised of activists of varying political backgrounds, who at first favored the reestablishment of the Czechoslovak regime. By early November, however, local Communists and other pro-Soviet elements came to dominate the committees, with the result that a movement for union with Soviet Ukraine was now under way.

Of great importance during these weeks was the activity of the reconstituted Subcarpathian Communist party, which held its first conference in Mukachevo on 19 November 1944. Claiming that the inhabitants of Subcarpathian Rus' "belong to the great Ukrainian people," the party conference adopted a resolution which "demanded that historical injustice be removed and that Transcarpathian Ukraine be reunited with Soviet Ukraine."[3] The most important figure at the Mukachevo conference was the Subcarpathian Communist activist Ivan Turianytsia. Although a member of the Czechoslovak government delegation, at the same time he was working secretly with Soviet political advisors. Turianytsia proposed that a national council be convened in order to decide the political future of Subcarpathian Rus'. Most indicative was the choice of words used by Turianytsia. He spoke only about a *Transcarpathian Ukraine* that was to be "reunited" with a Ukraine of which it had never been a part.

Transcarpathian Ukraine and "reunification"

Within a week, on 26 November 1944, no fewer than 663 delegates from committees representing about 80 percent of villages in Subcarpathian Rus' gathered in Mukachevo at what was called the First Congress of People's Committees of Transcarpathian Ukraine. In the presence of 126 guests, including all the generals of the Fourth Ukrainian Front, several political commissars, and agents of the Soviet secret police (NKVD) and military counterintelligence service (SMERSH), the congress began its deliberations, although in effect it held no serious debates. Rather, the delegates were presented with a previously prepared manifesto which expressed a desire "to reunite Transcarpathian Ukraine with its great mother, Soviet Ukraine, and to leave the framework of Czechoslovakia."[4] In the obviously intimidating atmosphere, the delegates unanimously ratified and signed the manifesto.

Until the time came when the Soviet government would accept Transcarpathia's request and reach an agreement with Czechoslovakia (of which

THE ACT OF REUNIFICATION

The manifesto approved by the 663 delegates at the First Congress of Peoples' Committees of Transcarpathian Ukraine on 26 November 1944 and soon after confirmed by 250,000 signatures from the inhabitants of Subcarpathian Rus' remains a source of controversy. The manifesto, with its call "to reunite Transcarpathian Ukraine with Soviet Ukraine," has ever since been hailed by Soviet and non-Soviet Ukrainian historians outside Ukraine—and since 1991 by the independent Ukrainian state—as a legitimate document. Its legitimacy is based on the alleged desire of the local population to leave Czechoslovakia and return to the bosom of "mother Ukraine."

The following eyewitness comments are by a delegate to the 1944 congress, Vasyl Markus. Within a few months of the congress, Markus fled from Soviet-ruled Transcarpathia and eventually emigrated to the United States, where he had a respectable career as a professor of political science. Although he was a strong supporter of the Ukrainian national idea and the "historical justice" of the region's annexation to a Ukrainian state, even if a Soviet one, he has nonetheless left perhaps the fairest assessment of what actually occured during and soon after the gathering in Mukachevo:

The Congress took place on 25–26 November 1944 in the municipal movie theater of Mukachevo under the slogan: 'Long live the reunification of Subcarpathian Ukraine with Soviet Ukraine'. It was in this spirit that speeches were delivered by the mayor of Mukachevo, Nykolai Dragula, who was a Russophile Carpatho-Ukrainian, as well as by the [local] Communists Ivan Turianytsia, Dmytro Tarakhonych, and others. One must admit that from beginning to end the congress and its decisions unfolded like a well-prepared stage performance.

Any divergent opinion was not only rejected out of hand, but eventually brought problems down upon those who spoke out against the trend of the scripted proceedings. Speeches were followed by statements by delegates from different counties, generally in favor of reunification, although some expressed other views about the matter. Among some county delegates arose the suggestion, albeit in a delicate manner, that a plebiscite be held, since 600 non-elected individuals should not be deciding the fate of the homeland. When the organizers of the congress learned of the plebiscite idea, they threatened imprisonment for the several delegates who might have dared to put forth such a proposition.

• • • • •

During the month of December local Communist party committees and village officials received orders to gather signatures in favor of the Manifesto. According to Soviet sources, 250,000 signatures were gathered; that is, a number which represented 50 percent of the region's adult population. Such a figure is not impossible, if one takes into consideration how the signatures were extorted whether by blackmail or duplicity. 'Sign and you will receive fabric for clothing'; or better still, 'Sign on behalf of free land distribution'. Several persons signed more than once, on the street, in public buildings, during meetings, etc. Even elementary school children were forced to sign.

The document then became a kind of constitutional act confirming Transcarpathian Ukraine's reunification with Ukraine. The text was distributed widely in thousands of copies; it was hung in public places; it was cited on numerous occasions; and finally it was the text on which functionaries had to swear their allegiance to the new regime.

SOURCE: Vasyl Markus, *L'incorporation de l'Ukraine subcarpathique à l'Ukraine soviétique, 1944–1945* (Louvain, 1956), pp. 46–47.

according to international law Subcarpathian Rus' was still legally a part), the region was to be governed by a 17-member National Council chosen by the delegates in Mukachevo. Led by the Communist Ivan Turianytsia as chairman and two non-Communist Russophile-oriented civic and cultural activists (Petro Sova and Petro Lintur) as the council's two vice-chairmen, Transcarpathian Ukraine effectively functioned as a semi-sovereign entity during a seven-month transitional period lasting from November 1944 to June 1945.

To be sure, the Transcarpathian National Council had a clear political goal, so that after the Mukachevo gathering in late November events moved rapidly. On 5 December 1944, the council informed the exile Czechoslovak government in London of its decisions and proposed that the Czechoslovak delegation based in Khust leave the province "within three days."[5] In reality, the Czechoslovak government delegation had never been able to establish any effective administration, and in early February 1945 it left for Slovakia, never to return.

Thereafter, the National Council proceeded to make all the necessary internal changes to facilitate Transcarpathia's entry into the Soviet Union. Symbolically, all clocks were put on "Moscow time" (two hours later), and the Soviet national anthem was adopted. During the first months of its rule, the Mukachevo Council nationalized the banks and some industries, and began to distribute land to the peasantry.

Subcarpathia's Orthodox community also adapted quickly to the realities of the new political situation. In early December, an Orthodox delegation went to Moscow to request formally that their church be moved from the Serbian Orthodox to the Russian Orthodox (Moscow Patriarchate) jurisdiction. The delegation also proposed that their homeland be united with the Soviet Union, although not with Soviet Ukraine. Instead, the Orthodox delegation argued that their homeland should become a distinct Carpatho-Russian Autonomous Republic within the Soviet Union. That request was rejected by Stalin, since it would undermine Soviet arguments put forth on the international stage; namely, that the region's "Ukrainian" inhabitants wanted to "reunite" with their historic "Ukrainian motherland."

Czechoslovakia acquiesces to Soviet hegemony

The Czechoslovak government-in-exile did not oppose the developments rapidly unfolding in Subcarpathian Rus'. The position of President Beneš was quite understandable. German and Hungarian forces had still not been driven from the rest of Czechoslovak territory, and only the Soviet armies could achieve this. Furthermore, several Czechoslovak leaders feared that any dispute with Moscow might lead to the loss of Slovakia, about which there was at the time speculation that it, too, might be annexed to the Soviet Union. Ever conscious of these broader issues, the Czechoslovak envoy in Moscow probably best summed up the feeling of Beneš and his government during the winter months of 1944–1945: "Between the Soviet and Czechoslovak governments there was a quiet but clear understand-

WHY DID CZECHOSLOVAKIA GIVE UP SUBCARPATHIAN RUS'?

It is well known that during World War I exiled Czech and Slovak leaders—Tomáš G. Masaryk, Eduard Beneš, Milan Štefánik—who were intent on creating a new state, Czechoslovakia, had no plans to include Carpatho-Rusyns within its borders. Their views on this matter began to change only in late 1918, when at the suggestion of U.S. president Woodrow Wilson, the Rusyn-American leader Gregory Zhatkovych proposed to Masaryk the possibility that Uhro-Rusyns (Hungary's Carpatho-Rusyns) might become part of Czechoslovakia.

Czechoslovak leaders viewed such a possibility in the context of the new state's international security needs. For them the "Little Russian" inhabitants of Carpathian Rus' were, like the Little Russian or Ukrainian problem in general, part of the larger question regarding the future of Russia. To the chagrin of Masaryk, Czechs and Slovaks, who were renowned for their pro-Russian feelings, expected that after the tsarist empire's triumph in the war "a great Slav Empire was to arise with the small Slavonic peoples being linked with Russia," somewhat like "the planetary system in which the planets—the Slavonic peoples—were to revolve around the Russian sun."[a] It is, therefore, not surprising that many Czech and Slovak leaders would feel most secure if their new country were to form a close alliance with a postwar Russian state, although one that preferably would be non-Bolshevik. In the end, the civil war and anarchic conditions that dominated Russia between 1918 and 1920 effectively closed off any political alliance with the east—at least for the moment.

What, then, to do with the Rusyn-American request, backed by the highest levels of the United States government, calling for Carpathian Rus' (at least south of the mountains) to become part of Czechoslovakia? Already by the outset of 1919 Czechoslovakia's negotiators at the Paris Peace Conference, led by the country's Minister of Foreign Affairs Eduard Beneš, convinced themselves and the international peacemakers in Paris that accepting Carpatho-Rusyns and their homeland into Czechoslovakia would be the best solution not only for the region's East Slavic population (downtrodden by centuries of "Hungarian oppression") but also for the country's security needs. In the words of one Czech political commentator who later posed and answered the rhetorical question: "Why were Masaryk and Beneš interested in attaching an autonomous Subcarpathian Rus' to Czechoslovakia? Because of Slavic sympathy? No way. For possible economic advantage? Certainly not. The main reason concerned security (military and political) interests."[b]

While it is true that in the 1930s Czechoslovakia's foreign minister and soon-to-be-president Eduard Beneš spoke of holding onto Subcarpathian Rus' "for the next century," his statement was more of an attempt at self-assuring rhetoric than a reflection of strategically sound statesmanship.[c] Most Czechs and Slovaks at the time who thought seriously about their country would probably have agreed with one of the country's leading specialists on Subcarpathian Rus', Karel Kadlec, who as early as 1920 wrote: "we are only holders of a foreign deposit [Subcarpathian Rus'], which we will have to give up some day."[d]

But give up Subcarpathian Rus' to whom? To the one foreign power in which Czechoslovak leaders had since the World War I era placed their hopes—Russia? Certainly by the 1930s the Russian world was stabilized, even if it was in the form of the Soviet Union under a dictatorial Bolshevik leader Joseph Stalin. Yet for tiny Czechoslovakia threatened at the time from the west by another dictator, Nazi Germany's Adolf Hitler, and by antagonistic neighbors to the north and south, Poland and Hungary, the Russian east once again seemed the country's only salvation. It is, therefore, no surprise that as early as October 1939, when Czechoslovakia no longer existed and just two days after Soviet armies invaded Poland, the then exiled President Beneš informed the Soviet ambassador in London that after the war "we [a restored Czechoslovakia] must become direct [territorial] neighbors of the Soviet Union. This is one of the things we learned from Munich. The question of Subcarpathian Rus' will be decided between us somewhat later, and we certainly will reach a mutually acceptable solution."e

Traumatized by the September 1938 Munich Pact and the betrayal of Czechoslovakia by its western allies Great Britain and France, Beneš was determined not to jeopardize future Czechoslovak-Soviet relations. Throughout the war years he operated on the assumption that Subcarpathian Rus' would be part of a restored Czechoslovakia and that it would share a common border with his Soviet ally which, in the interim, would have reincorporated East Galicia into Soviet Ukraine. These assumptions were confirmed in all talks that Beneš had with Soviet officials. Therefore, it came as a great surprise to him when, in late 1944, the Soviet position changed.

Beneš was upset, however, not because his country was about to lose Subcarpathian Rus', but because he felt personally slighted at not having been told earlier: "If they [the Soviets] had wanted Subcarpathian Rus'," Beneš lamented to his personal secretary, "they could have told me. I never would have wanted to hold on to Subcarpathian Rus' at the expense of our Russian friendship."f Hence, it is no surprise that in his talks in Moscow with the Soviet Ministry of Foreign Affairs, Beneš quite easily agreed to an agenda that was based on the following understanding of developments 25 years earlier at the close of World War I: since "Carpatho-Ukraine was in effect separated [by Polish-ruled Galicia] from Soviet Ukraine, [and] in order that it not fall to Hungary, it was necessary to annex it to Czechoslovakia. Prague, however, considered the annexation of Carpatho-Ukraine to Czechoslovakia as a kind of mandate; it never believed that the question of Carpatho-Ukraine was definitely decided. . . . Whereas [Czechoslovakia's] president is not authorized to decide this by himself, there is no fear that the Czechoslovak people would be against our giving up Carpatho-Ukraine."g

Historians have ever since tried to explain Czechoslovakia's loss of Subcarpathian Rus' to the Soviet Union. Was it because Stalin and Soviet officials were being duplicitous in their dealings with Beneš during the war years? Was it because the November 1944 Congress of People's Committees in Mukachevo was a sham and the result of pressure by Soviet security services upon the local inhabitants to demand "reunification with Mother-Ukraine"? Was it because a non-elected provisional parliament in Prague was acting against the will of the people when it approved the June 1945 Czechoslovak-Soviet Treaty of secession?

Whatever excuse for Czechoslovakia's actions one may wish to believe, the fact remains that during the first half of the twentieth century most Czechoslovak political leaders and policy makers consciously or unconsciously assumed that Subcarpathian Rus' must sooner or later be returned to where they assumed it belonged, the East, whether in the form of Russia, or of Ukraine, or what eventually happened—a "Russian"-ruled Soviet Ukraine. Put another way, regardless of the international situation at the close of World War II, Czechs and certainly Slovaks did not have the political or moral will-power to demand that wartime agreements be upheld and that Subcarpathian Rus' remain within a restored Czechoslovak state.

It is perhaps because of these deeply seated attitudes that many subsequent general histories and discussions of interwar Czechoslovakia, whether written by Czechs or by foreign specialists of the country, provide little or no information about Subcarpathian Rus' and Carpatho-Rusyns. Certainly, there are some Czechs who nostalgically remember through direct experience or through tales told by parents the eastern region of their former pre-World War II country. For the most part, however, present-day Czech and Slovak societies are unaware or indifferent to the fact that Subcarpathian Rus' was once part of Czechoslovakia and that it should be considered an integral part of their common country's historical heritage.

[a] Thomas Garrigue Masaryk, *The Making of a State: Memories and Observations, 1914–1918* (New York, 1927), p. 15.

[b] Ivo Ducháček, "Jak Rudá Armáda mapovala střední Evropu: Těšínsko a Podkarpatsko," *Svědectví,* XVI [63] (New York, Paris, and Vienna 1981), p. 545.

[c] Edvard Benesh, *Promova pro pidkarpatorus'kyi problem i ioho vidnoshennia do chekhoslovats'koï respubliky* (Uzhhorod and Prague, 1934), p. 45.

[d] Karel Kadlec, *Podkarpatská Rus* [published speech delivered in Prague to the Society for State-Building, 21 April 1920] (Prague, 1920), p. 26.

[e] Eduard Beneš, *Memoirs of Dr. Eduard Benes: From Munich to New War and New Victory* (Boston, 1953), p. 139.

[f] Eduard Táborský, *Prezident Beneš mezi Západem a Východem* (Prague, 1993), p. 215.

[g] Notes of the meeting of the Soviet and Czechoslovak delegations at the Kremlin in Moscow, 21 March 1945, in Ivan Vanat, *Materialy do istoriï Ukraïns'koï Narodnoï Rady Priashivshchyny* (Prešov, 2001), document 9, pp. 45–46.

ing that no conflict should be allowed to occur over Subcarpathian Rus'."[e] Consequently, Czechoslovak leaders began to convince themselves that Subcarpathian Rus' was not of central importance to their cause. For his part, Stalin informed Beneš in January 1945 that the "Soviet government has not forbidden, nor could it forbid, the population of the Transcarpathian Ukraine from expressing its national will . . . although [in the end] the issue can only be settled by [signing] a treaty . . . just before or after the end of the war with Germany."[7]

Stalin's strategic views on central and eastern Europe were governed by two principles: that the boundaries of the Soviet Union must be extended farther westward; and that countries along its new western borders must be allies in case of any future conflict with Germany. To achieve these goals, the Soviet Union needed to obtain the acquiescence of its wartime Western allies on the border question and to strengthen the Communist parties in each of the countries just beyond its future western borders. During the war Stalin met twice with Prime Minister Winston Churchill of Great Britain and President Franklin D. Roosevelt of the United States at conferences in Tehran (November 1943) and at Yalta (February 1945). It was at Yalta that the Allies agreed specifically to the postwar boundary between Poland and the Soviet Union and where the Americans and British accepted the likelihood that most of the countries of central Europe—including all of Carpathian Rus'—would fall under the sphere of Soviet political influence.

When the war in Europe ended following the capitulation of Germany on 8 May 1945, the Soviet Union could turn its full attention to the question of borders with its western neighbors, including two which had a Carpatho-Rusyn population: Czechoslovakia and Poland. On 29 June 1945, the Soviet Union and Czechoslovakia signed a treaty according to which Subcarpathian Rus'/Transcarpathian Ukraine was ceded to the Ukrainian Soviet Socialist Republic.

The new Poland and the deportation of the Lemkos: Phase one

The victorious Allied Powers agreed during their wartime deliberations that Poland, which was brutally wiped off the map in the fall of 1939, should be reconstituted. Its borders, however, were to be changed in a radical manner, almost as if the entire country had been "picked up" and moved westward. Poland's prewar eastern regions (Polish: *kresy*), which were inhabited primarily by Ukrainians, Belarusans, and a smaller number of Lithuanians, were annexed to the Soviet Union and assigned to the Ukrainian, Belarussian, and Lithuanian Soviet republics. From the Soviet point of view, they were not annexing but simply reuniting territories they first took in September 1939, when together with Nazi Germany they destroyed Poland. Among those territories was western Ukraine (formerly Polish-ruled eastern Galicia). The new Soviet-Polish border followed quite closely the so-called Curzon Line (proposed by a British diplomat back in 1920), which ran southward along the Western Bug River and then southwestward toward the crests of the Carpathian Mountains to a point near the source of the San River. This meant that the historic Galician Rus' cultural centers of Przemyśl and Sanok, together with the entire Lemko Region, were assigned to postwar Poland.

In compensation for its losses in the east, the Allied Powers meeting at the postwar Potsdam Conference (July 1945) agreed to give Poland territories that before the war had been part of Germany and inhabited primarily by Germans: Silesia and Pomerania in the west as far as the Oder and Neisse Rivers, as well as the former free city-state of Danzig (renamed Gdańsk) and

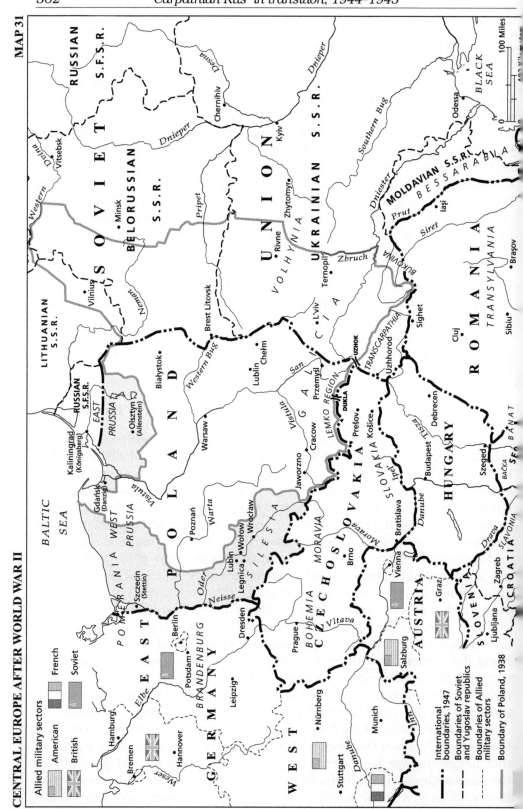

MAP 31

CENTRAL EUROPE AFTER WORLD WAR II

Allied military sectors

American   French

British   Soviet

International
boundaries, 1947

Boundaries of Soviet
and Yugoslav republics

Boundaries of Allied
military sectors

Boundary of Poland, 1938

BALTIC
SEA

RUSSIAN S.F.S.R.

LITHUANIAN S.S.R.

RUSSIAN S.F.S.R.

EAST PRUSSIA

Kaliningrad
(Königsberg)

Vilnius

Minsk

BELORUSSIAN S.S.R.

Vitsebsk

Western Dvina

Desna

Dnieper

RUSSIAN S.F.S.R.

Chernihiv

Kyiv

Dnieper

SOVIET UNION

Pripet

UKRAINIAN S.S.R.

Rivne

Zhytomyr

VOLHYNIA

Southern Bug

Dniester

MOLDAVIAN S.S.R.

BESSARABIA

Odessa

BLACK
SEA

Gdańsk
(Danzig)

POMERANIA

WEST PRUSSIA

Szczecin
(Stettin)

Vistula

Olsztyn
(Allenstein)

Białystok

Brest Litovsk

Western Bug

Lublin

Chełm

San

Przemyśl

L'viv

Ternopil'

Zbruch

BUKOVINA

Prut

Siret

Iaşi

ROMANIA

TRANSYLVANIA

Braşov

Sibiu

Cluj

Sighet

Uzhhorod

UZHOK

TRANSCARPATHIA

DUKLA

LEMKO REGION

GALICIA

Cracow

Jaworzno

Vistula

Warta

Poznań

POLAND

Warsaw

Lubin

Wolów

Legnica

Wrocław

SILESIA

Oder

Neisse

Odra

EAST GERMANY

BRANDENBURG

Berlin

Potsdam

Leipzig

Dresden

Elbe

Hamburg

Bremen

Hannover

Weser

WEST GERMANY

Nürnberg

Munich

Stuttgart

Danube

BOHEMIA

Prague

Vltava

MORAVIA

Brno

CZECHOSLOVAKIA

Morava

SLOVAKIA

Bratislava

Prešov

Košice

Ipeľ

Debrecen

HUNGARY

Budapest

Danube

Szeged

BAČKA

BANAT

Tisza

Vienna

AUSTRIA

Graz

Salzburg

Drava

SLOVENIA

Ljubljana

Zagreb

CROATIA

SLAVONIA

0   100 Miles

a part of East Prussia. These territories were referred to in official Polish sources as the *Zieme Odzyskane,* or Recovered Lands, a designation which implied that in early medieval times they had been inhabited by Slavs (and alleged ancestors of modern Poles) until forcibly driven out as part of the Germanic "push to the East" (*Drang nach Osten*). Technically, the lands east of the so-called Oder-Neisse Line were assigned by the Allied Powers to Poland on a temporary basis until a peace treaty with Germany could be signed. As it turned out, that did not occur until 1991, almost half a century later!

Changing borders was one thing, but what about people of a given nationality who suddenly found themselves living in a state other than "their own"? What, therefore, should be done with the hundreds of thousands of Poles in the western regions of postwar Soviet Ukraine and with the tens of thousands of Ukrainians and other East Slavs in the eastern regions of postwar Poland? And what about the smaller number of Czechs in western Ukraine (Volhynia) and the Carpatho-Rusyns in postwar Czechoslovakia (northeastern Slovakia)?

By the end of World War II, policy makers throughout Europe, not to mention other parts of the world, became convinced that one way to avoid future conflict was to solve the problem of national minorities by moving populations. The ideal situation would be one in which ethnolinguistic boundaries would coincide with political (state) boundaries. With this in mind, the Communist governments of Poland and the Soviet Union signed an agreement in September 1944 that provided for the mutual exchange of populations between those two countries. This basically meant that Poles from what was now the western regions of the Soviet Union would be resettled to Poland, while East Slavic peoples in Poland (Russians, Belorusans, Ukrainians, and Carpatho-Rusyns) would be resettled to the Soviet Union.

Consequently, between November 1944 and September 1946, some 80,000 Lemko Rusyns were resettled in Soviet Ukraine. During the spring and summer of 1945, over 6,500 Lemkos were sent to far eastern Ukraine, to the industrial Donbas region near the border with Soviet Russia.[8] Confronted with the very difficult material conditions in a culturally alien and climatically windswept open-steppe environment, many Lemkos soon left the Donbas region in the hope that they could leave the Soviet Union and return to their Carpathian homeland. Because of the border controls, they made it only as far as Soviet-ruled East Galicia, where they joined thousands of other newly arriving Lemkos who were allowed to settle in Ternopil', L'viv, and mostly in small rural towns to the south and east of those two cities. In effect, most of the central and eastern parts of the Lemko Region were depopulated, although anywhere from 25,000 to 35,000 Lemkos managed to remain in postwar Poland, mostly in the western part of the Lemko Region.[9]

On a much smaller scale, but following the same principle that was aimed at making ethnoliguistic and political borders coincide, were the provisions outlined in the Czechoslovak-Soviet treaty of June 1945. It is true that most Czechs had left Subcarpathian Rus' when that region was annexed to

Hungary in 1938–1939. But those Czechs who somehow managed to remain in Hungarian-ruled Subcarpathia throughout the war years, as well as the region's indigenous Slovaks, were offered the possibility of *optatsiia;* that is, the option to return to their ancestral homeland. Soldiers who fought in the Czechoslovak Army Corps and who were natives of Subcarpathian Rus' were also given the option to settle in postwar Czechoslovakia. About 25,000 persons requested to leave Soviet Transcarpathia, although in the end only 4,000 or so were allowed to do so.[10] The efforts to resettle people across the new borders as well as within countries were to continue for a few more years, but that is part of the story of post-World War II Carpathian Rus'.

Subcarpathian Rus'/Transcarpathia in the Soviet Union, 1945–1991

Between the years 1945 and 1991, the largest part of Carpathian Rus', the province known as Subcarpathian Rus', was an integral part of the Soviet Union. During the nearly half century of Soviet rule, the political, socioeconomic, and cultural life of the region, officially called the Transcarpathian oblast of the Ukrainian Soviet Socialist Republic, was profoundly transformed.

Subcarpathian Rus' becomes Soviet Transcarpathia

Among the first goals of the Soviet regime was to determine and secure the borders of Transcarpathia. Basically, Transcarpathia's territory coincided with that of Subcarpathian Rus' when it was part of Czechoslovakia before the Munich Pact of 1938. The Czechoslovak-Soviet Treaty of June 1945 did outline a few modifications along the province's western boundary with Slovakia, after which it became an international border between the Soviet Union and Czechoslovakia. Among those modifications was the small salient just west of Uzhhorod which was given to Czechoslovakia in return for the major rail junction of Chop farther to the south (see Map 25). For the next half century, Chop became the main entry point to the Soviet Union for passenger and freight railway traffic to and from the capitals of central and south central Europe—Prague, Bratislava, Budapest, and Belgrade. To impress travelers arriving at this gateway to the Soviet world, in the 1950s a monumental railroad station in a pompous style, which some have dubbed "socialist Baroque," was constructed in the otherwise sleepy provincial village of Chop.

It is interesting to note that in February 1945, the same month Soviet troops appropriated the railway junction of Chop, farther east in the town of Sighet, delegates from 17 Carpatho-Rusyn villages in the surrounding Maramureş Region formed a national council. In the presence of the chairman of the Transcarpathian National Council, Ivan Turianytsia, the delegates at Sighet signed a memorandum requesting that the Maramureş Region—Carpatho-Rusyn-inhabited villages south of the Tisza River—be united with Transcarpathian Ukraine. The Sighet memorandum was sent to

Moscow, although Stalin rejected it. The region remained part of Romania as it had been before World War II. The Maramureş incident at Sighet is one of the rare examples in which the Soviet Union refused an offer to expand its boundaries.

Nor were the slightly revised borders of Subcarpathian Rus'/Transcarpathia just lines on a map. The region, now part of the virtually "sacred Soviet fatherland," needed to be protected against any possible future invasion from the West. Already in November 1945, a barbed wire fence with watchtowers was constructed along the border with Czechoslovakia not only as a deterrent to some imagined invasion from the imperialist West, but more realistically as a deterrent to the large number of Carpatho-Rusyns who might opt to move westward, not to mention residents from other parts of the Soviet Union who looked for any opportunity to leave the Stalinist "paradise." Transcarpathia's southern borders with Hungary were also "protected" with barbed and electrified wire fortifications.

Finally, in July 1947, the Soviet government in Moscow decreed that all of Transcarpathia was henceforth a "restricted zone of the highest level."[1] This meant that the region was rapidly transformed into a militarized zone, with heavy installments of army weapons and eventually rockets. Internal movement for local residents was restricted, and there were even border checkpoints along all the Carpathian mountain passes connecting Transcarpathia with the rest of the Soviet Union. Ironically, these checkpoints along the crests of the mountains continue to exist to this day within independent Ukraine.

The Soviet socio-political model

What was this Soviet Union to which historic Subcarpathian Rus', renamed Transcarpathia, now belonged? The Soviet Union was born out of the Bolshevik Revolution of 1917, although it did not formally come into being until December 1922. The new Soviet state was federal in structure—a union of national republics of which there were initially 4, then eventually 15, in number. Each of these republics was allegedly "national" in that it was named after a so-called titular nationality. The titular nationality referred to the group which in most (but not all) cases formed the majority of inhabitants. Administratively, the national republics were subdivided into oblasts: some national republics, aside from oblasts, also had autonomous republics and autonomous regions within their borders. Each of the republics had its own government and at certain times in Soviet history they even had the theoretical right to secede from the union. At the highest level of the state was the bicameral Congress of Soviets (later Supreme Soviet), the country's supreme legislative organ, which, together with the Soviet government, were both located in Moscow.

Each of the administrative divisions within the Soviet Union, from the village, city, district (raion), oblast, and republic level to the "national" All-Union level had its own council or soviet. Deputies to each council were chosen in elections, in which each Soviet citizen of voting age was compelled to vote. The electoral ballot, however, contained the name of only one candidate accompanied by the admonition: "Citizen! Make Your Choice." Because the Soviet Union considered itself an egalitarian worker's state, only one party, the Communist party of workers, was necessary. Because each Soviet republic had its own party, members from Transcarpathia were registered in the Communist party of Ukraine. Although the vast majority of deputies in each of the councils at these various administrative levels were Communists, there were a few non-party deputies as well.

The other guiding principle of Soviet society was centralization. Despite the eventual existence of 15 national republics and several autonomous republics and regions, all were subordinate to the central government and its ministries in Moscow. The policies of the government and its ministries were, in turn, determined by the All-Union Communist party. The All-Union authorities also directed the so-called command economy that was instituted in 1928. In other words, economic policy for the entire Soviet Union was determined by central ministries in Moscow according to guidelines and production quotas that were formulated in so-called five-year plans. There was no free enterprise; hence, all factories, transportation systems, power plants, banks, and shops in the service sector (restaurants, beauty parlors, barber shops, tailors, etc.) were owned by the state.

All land was also owned by the state, as a result of which agriculture was carried out on large state farms (Russian: *sovkhozy*; Ukrainian: *radhospy*), or on the more widespread collective farms (Russian: *kolkhozy*; Ukrainian: *kolhospy*). The state and collective farms came into being as a result of a policy of forced collectivization that was instituted throughout the Soviet Union in 1929. Peasants were now employed as farm workers on land that in many cases had once been their own, but which they were forced to turn over to the state. In Soviet Ukraine, forced collectivization was carried out in an often brutal and bloody manner culminating in the artificial Great Famine (*Holodomor*) of 1933 that claimed at the minimum 4.5 million lives. Henceforth, peasants were not allowed to leave "their" collective farms, so that in a sense they were transformed into what might be called "socialist" serfs. For their labor they received payment-in-kind; that is, a portion of the harvest instead of money. During the period of Stalinist rule, which lasted until Stalin's death in 1953, retired peasants did not even receive an old-age pension and had to work throughout their "retirement" years. In postwar Soviet Transcarpathia, such realities were glossed over by Communist agitators during their propaganda campaigns to convince the inhabitants of Subcarpathian Rus'— as well as potential Carpatho-Rusyn resettlers from postwar Poland and Czechoslovakia—about the alleged advantages of living in the Soviet Union.

In January 1946, Transcarpathian Ukraine, headed by its National Council, was formally abolished, with the result that the region became an oblast like any other in the Soviet Union. About the same time, the Communist party of Transcarpathian Ukraine was also abolished (December 1945) and transformed in to a regional/oblast branch of the republic-wide Communist party of Ukraine. The party branch was expected to make Transcarpathia's

TOTALITARIAN TIME

As early as 5 November 1944, in anticipation of Soviet rule, the city council of Uzhhorod adopted Moscow Time (two hours ahead of Central European Time). This seemingly benign act had profound implications for the everyday lives of most people in Subcarpathian Rus'/Transcarpathia, as recalled by Magdalena Lavrincová, at the time the young daughter of Vasyl' Zozuliak (who later returned with his family to the Prešov Region in Czechoslovakia, where he became a well-known Ukrainian writer and civic activist). In the words of the adult Magdalena:

I remember how I was awakened from a deep sleep. A weak lightbulb was flickering in our room, while outside was the darkest night. It was the end of September 1945, and my oldest sister had just begun first grade at the elementary school in Uzhhorod. 'Sonia, my dear daughter, get up. You've got to be in school before eight o'clock. And if you're not on time, they'll punish you and also us, your parents.'

A fear of decrees issued by the state authorities dominated everything and everybody. And it affected even tender school-aged children. Fear overpowered everyone; in fact, fear was one of the most basic components of the repressive Soviet system. 'Why does my sister have to get up so early? It's still night time, isn't it?'—I asked still asleep.

But mother gave me no answer. . . . In the end my sister got up, even though she, too, was half asleep. Mother helped her get dressed, and the both of them—obviously on an empty stomach—set out into the pitch-black night.

Years later I came to realize that throughout the entire Soviet Union—this enormous land mass that covered one-sixth of the entire planet—Moscow time was the standard everywhere [in European Russia, Belarus, and Ukraine]. So, if in Moscow itself children began their classes at 8:00 a.m., that moment had to be the same in lands that may be two, even three thousand miles away. To be sure that included the western regions of the Soviet Union, including Ukraine's Transcarpathian oblast, even though it might be the deepest night. That was my first experience with the inhumanness of the Muscovite ruling authorities.

SOURCE: Magdalena Lavrincová, "Detstvo na Podkarpatskej Rusi," *Podkarpatská Rus*, XXII, 2 (Prague, 2012), p. 10.

political, socioeconomic, and cultural life conform to the rest of Soviet society. Ukraine's central Communist party authorities did not trust the locals, however. Consequently, during the second half of 1946 no less than 68 percent of the members of the former Transcarpathian Communist party, accused of "being spoiled by bourgeois ideology," were purged. In their stead, ideologically reliable Communist cadres were brought in from central and eastern Ukraine.

The changes did not even spare Ivan I. Turianytsia, the local Communist who had implemented Transcarpathia's reunification with the Soviet Union. In 1948, he was removed from his position as first secretary of the regional party. Only now could the region's Communist party functionaries be trusted with transforming Transcarpathia into a Soviet land.

Forced collectivization and industrialization

As a predominantly agricultural area, the land question had historically been of greatest importance to the majority of its inhabitants. Hence, the National Council of Transcarpathian Ukraine issued a decree in February 1945; that is, already during the pre-Soviet transitional period. It provided for the confiscation of the large landed estates reconstituted under the war-time Hungarian regime. Those and other confiscated lands (nearly 53,000 hectares) were then distributed to over 54,000 peasant households (about 37 percent of the total in the region).[2] The region's land-hungry peasants were overjoyed with this process, which clearly endeared the new, albeit transitional, regime to a significant portion of the region's peasant farmers.

Their joy turned out to be short-lived, however, because, beginning in late 1946, the oblast authorities undertook what had previously been done in Soviet Ukraine during the early 1930s—collectivization of the land. Communist agitators were sent throughout Transcarpathia to convince (by using force, if necessary) peasant farmers to turn over their land to the collective farm. The process did not occur without difficulty. Well-to-do peasants labeled with the opprobrious term *kulak* (Ukrainian: *kurkul'*) were forced—through increased taxes and the confiscation by the state of a high portion of their produce—to give up their land. There were protests against collectivization (at the village of Uhlia in 1948; and in Irliava, Turï Remety, and Dobron' in 1949), but the authorities reacted swiftly, even arresting and sentencing to forced labor village women who thought they might have been spared punishment because of their gender. An estimated 2,200 peasant farmers, whether or not they were classified as *kurkuls/kulaks*, were sentenced to terms ranging from 8 to 25 years of forced labor and were deported to camps in the eastern and northern regions of the Soviet Union that were part of a penal system known as the Gulag.[3]

Collectivization continued, so that by the end of 1948, there were 371 collective farms in Transcarpathia accounting for 41 percent of arable land.[4] Collectivization was even introduced into the high mountainous regions, where the population was engaged primarily in animal husbandry, not farming. The villagers living there now became "collectivized shepherds." By May 1950, the collectivization process was completed.

Since collectivized agriculture was subordinate to the overall Soviet command economy, it became subject to the whims of central policy makers in faraway Moscow. In the second half of the twentieth century, especially during the decade when the All-Union Communist party first secretary Nikita Khrushchev was in power (1956–1964), the Soviet central government initiated experiments in the agricultural sector which state planners were convinced would be successful. For instance, between 1955 and 1965 Transcarpathia was subjected to a campaign to transform the oblast into "a land of orchards and vineyards," for which a total of 98,000 hectares were to be planted.[5] Not only were these unrealistic goals never met, but overall production actually decreased. Then, 20 years later, between 1985 and 1987, most of the vineyards that still existed were torn up during an All-Union anti-alcohol campaign launched by the reform-minded head of state at the time, Mikhail Gorbachev. There was even an attempt in the early 1950s to cultivate tea and citrus fruits, which obviously could not survive despite the relatively mild climate of the Transcarpathian lowlands.

Somewhat more successful was the industrial sector. Soviet policy makers invested in existing and now state-owned lumber mills, chemical factories, and food-processing plants which were expanded and provided with the latest advances in Soviet industrial technology. Among the largest of the enterprises was the tobacco factory in Mukachevo and the salt works in Solotvyno, both of which dated back to the nineteenth century. Whether or not these and the many smaller enterprises could have survived in a free-market economy, they were certainly able to function in the large state-driven Soviet economic system. Even more importantly, they provided steady employment to large sectors of a society like Transcarpathia, which traditionally had been able to provide its inhabitants with, at best, only a subsistence-level existence based on small-scale agriculture and animal husbandry.

There were, nonetheless, some ambitious individuals who were well aware of Transcarpathia's long-standing migratory labor tradition, in which peasant farmers had for decades supplemented their livelihood by engaging in seasonal labor on the plains of Hungary or by undertaking longer work stints in the mines and factories of the northeastern United States. Although these avenues were all closed because of strict Soviet border controls implemented after World War II, a new source of employment was the vast Soviet Union. It was not uncommon, therefore, for thousands of Transcarpathian residents—Carpatho-Rusyns and, in particular, members of the region's small Romanian minority—to work for a few months each year at difficult construction sites in the Russian north and in Siberia, where they earned large sums of money that provided their families relatively comfortable lives in the Transcarpathian homeland.

Transcarpathia's new peoples

Another aspect of the Soviet transformation was connected with the profound demographic changes that took place in Transcarpathia during the second half of the twentieth century. There was an overall increase in the number of inhabitants in the oblast, rising from nearly 776,000 in 1946 to over 1.2

million in 1989.[6] Particularly noticeable was the population increase in urban areas like the oblast's administrative center Uzhhorod, whose pre-War World II population of 26,000 increased fivefold to 117,000 by the end of the Soviet period in 1989. Analogously, the oblast's second-largest city, Mukachevo, more than tripled in size from 26,600 to 84,000 during the same period.[7]

The nationality composition of Transcarpathia's population changed as well. In September 1944, when the Soviet Army crossed the Carpathians, 5,100 Subcarpathian Magyars fled their homes to seek refuge in Hungary and nearly 2,500 ethnic Germans fled to their ancestral Austria and Germany.[8] As discussed in Chapter 20, the vast majority of the prewar Jewish inhabitants (over 100,000) were killed during the 1944 Holocaust. About 15,000 to 20,000 managed to survive and return home, but between 1945 and 1947 most left Transcarpathia permanently, whether fleeing before the Soviets closed the border in September 1945, or soon after by legal means as part of the Czechoslovak-Soviet agreement which gave Jews the option to emigrate to postwar Czechoslovakia.[9] Even before Transcarpathia became part of the Soviet Union, the Soviet military and security services interned by December 1944 nearly 15,000 males between the ages of 18 and 50. Virtually all of the internees were of Magyar and German nationality and, as such, they were subject to punishment because of their alleged association with the wartime fascist enemies, Germany and Hungary. The arrests of Subcarpathian Magyars continued into July 1945, by which time about 30,000 were sentenced to forced labor camps in eastern Ukraine and Siberia. Although amnestied in 1955, an estimated 5,000 never returned to Transcarpathia, having died while in internment or as a result of the harsh conditions in Siberia where most work camps were located.[10] Among Subcarpathia's smaller ethnic German community, a Soviet decree passed in January 1946 authorized the deportation to western Siberia of entire families totaling 2,000 persons.[11]

In turn, large numbers of Ukrainians and Russians were sent to Transcarpathia, where they found employment in the expanding industrial sector, in the military, and in the ranks of the local Communist party and oblast government administration. By 1989, there were an estimated 170,000 Ukrainians from neighboring Galicia and from other parts of Soviet Ukraine, as well as 49,000 Russians living in Transcarpathia.[12] The newcomers settled primarily in the oblast's largest cities, Uzhhorod and Mukachevo, where they were accommodated in hastily and poorly built architecturally nondescript apartment blocks. Despite the predominance of ethnic Ukrainians among the newcomers, many of them used Russian as their language of communication. This, combined with the fact that Russian was the language of prestige throughout the Soviet Union, transformed Transcarpathia's urban areas, where formerly Hungarian and Yiddish were the dominant languages, into an environment in which Russian was the primary language of communication.

Another factor concerned the degree to which the Ukrainian and Russian in-migrants remained divorced from the social context of Transcarpathia in which they found themselves. They spoke neither Rusyn nor Hungarian, the languages of the majority rural population, and they did not own their own homes or belong to a family network based in the region's villages. And while many of these Ukrainian and Russian in-migrants may have attained good positions in the oblast's administrative, industrial, and military sectors, they were always—and in many ways still are—considered newcomers (*novopry-buli*) and, therefore, outsiders by the indigenous local Carpatho-Rusyns and Magyars.

Ever since the Bolshevik revolution of 1917, the Soviet ideal was to break with the past and create a new society that would not be hindered by any historical baggage. Whether or not these ideals still existed in the post-World War II era, Soviet policy makers were determined to undermine traditional modes of existence and cultural values in their newly acquired territory of Transcarpathia.

Revising the past and reckoning with "enemies of the people"

The very first step was to clarify the national identity of the majority population. Formally, it was the Transcarpathian Ukrainians who, in 1944, requested "reunion" with the Ukrainian motherland, and it was on those grounds that the Soviet Union justified the annexation of Subcarpathian Rus' from Czechoslovakia. But what should be done with the vast majority, the indigenous East Slavs who still identified themselves as Rusyns, not Ukrainians? As long ago as 1924, the Moscow-based Communist International (Comintern) declared the East Slavic inhabitants of Czechoslovakia, regardless what they called themselves (Rusyns, Carpatho-Russians, Rusnaks), to be an integral part of the Ukrainian nationality. Moreover, Ukrainian ideologists—be they Soviet Marxist or nationalist—argued that the name *Rusyn* was simply an older equivalent of the modern ethnonym *Ukrainian.*

HOW CARPATHO-RUSYNS WERE DECLARED UKRAINIANS

Long before Soviet rule was established in Subcarpathian Rus', the Communist party developed a clear position on the nationality question. There were two phases of the process of ideological clarification, which took place between 1924 and 1926 in what might be called the international and regional context of the Communist movement.

In June–July 1924, the Fifth Congress of the Communist International (Comintern) took place in Moscow. At this gathering of Communist parties from various countries worldwide, the Comintern discussed specifically the "Ukrainian question." Its resolution on the "Nationality Question in Central Europe and the Balkans" declared not only that the "Ukrainian question is one of the most important nationality questions in central Europe," but that, regardless of the particular form it takes "in Poland, Romania, and Czechoslovakia [Subcarpathian Rus' and the Prešov Region], it is nonetheless part of one Ukrainian nationality question that requires a common revolutionary resolution for all these countries."[a] The Comintern's 1924 resolution also "unanimously called on the Communist parties of Poland, Czechoslovakia, and Romania to promote the unification of Ukrainian-inhabited territories in those countries—previously torn away by the imperialists—with the Soviet Workers' and Peasants' Republic [the Soviet Union]."[b]

The second phase of ideological clarification regarding the nationality question took place at the seventh conference of the 24th Committee, or Transcarpathian regional branch of the Czechoslovak Communist party, which met in Uzhhorod in December 1926. In November 1924, Subcarpathia's Communists had approved the resolutions of the Comintern's Fifth Congress and acted on its nationality guidelines. As the Subcarpathian Communist Ivan Mondok later reported to the Czechoslovak Communist party: "It is true that [before 1924] we did not have a clear understanding of the Ukrainian question. . . . We in western Ukraine [Subcarpathian Rus'] did not know who we were. Are we Russians [Rusi], are we Rusyns, are we rus'kyi with a soft sign?—in a word, we did not know who we were."[c]

Awareness of being Ukrainian eventually took hold among Subcarpathia's Communists, if only gradually. If, for instance, at the 1924 Comintern Congress, Subcarpathia's delegate, Comrade Vasilev [Ivan Lokota], spoke on behalf of "the Subcarpathian Russian [prikarpatskii] proletariat,"[d] and if until that time the regional party newspaper Karpatskaia pravda was published in a mixture of Russian and local Rusyn vernacular, in the course of 1925 the party and its published organs began to use literary Ukrainian and refer to the region's inhabitants as Ukrainians.

The new position of Subcarpathia's Communists was spelled out in a resolution of the December 1926 party conference titled, "The End of the 'Language' Question." Nothing could be clearer than the very opening lines of that resolution:

> We are part of the Ukrainian people. We speak the same language, with only some small variants, as the 40-million-strong Ukrainian people. The entire scholarly world recognizes this. . . .
>
> The national name we have used until now, rusyn/rus'kyi, was for a long time used as well in Galicia, Bukovina, and Bessarabia until it was dropped at the beginning of this [twentieth] century. Among us, however, it was artificially retained by the Hungarians and now again artificially by the Czech bourgeois regime in an effort to divide us in spirit from our family of fraternal Ukrainian workers and peasants. . . .
>
> In the future we will call our homeland by its justifiably proper name; from now on we will not call it Subcarpathian Rus', but rather Transcarpathian Ukraine.
>
> We, Transcarpathian Ukrainians, must now completely rid ourselves of the name Rusyn. . . . And, even more so, we should no longer use the [adjectival] form rus'kyi, because that is the same as russkii, which means Russian or Muscovite; in no way is it our name, which is Ukrainian. . . .

Actually, for us there is no 'language question.' This is because it's clear to us that we are Ukrainians.[e]

[a] *Pravda* (Moscow), 27.VIII. 1924—cited in *Shliakhom Zhovtnia: zbirnyk dokumentiv*, Vol. II (Uzhhorod, 1961), doc. 23, p. 55.

[b] Ibid., pp. 55–56.

[c] Protokol V. řádného sjezdu Komunistické strany Československa (sekce Komunistické Internacionály), pp. 139–140—cited in Ivan Bajcura, "KSČ a ukrajinská otázka," in Olena Rudlovchak and Mykhailo Hyriak, eds., *Z mynuloho i suchasnoho ukraïntsiv Chekhoslovachchyny* (Bratislava, 1973), p. 11.

[d] *Piatyi Vsemirnyi Kongress Kommunisticheskogo Internatsionala: stenograficheskii otchet*, pt. 1— cited in *Shliakhom Zhovtnia*, doc. 22, p. 53.

[e] "Kinets' 'iazykovoho' pytannia?," *Karpats'ka pravda* (Uzhhorod), Nos. 47, 48, 49 (1926)—cited in Mykola Skrypnyk, "Natsional'ne vidrodzhennia v suchasnykh kapitalistychnykh derzhavakh na prykladi Zakarpats'koï Ukraïny," *Prapor marksyzmu*, No. 1[2] (Kharkiv, 1928), pp. 225–226.

Armed with the Communist party's unambiguous views on this matter, the Soviet regime in Transcarpathia simply declared that the region's indigenous East Slavic inhabitants were all Ukrainians. Hence, in 1946, when the first census was taken and people were asked about their nationality (a required identity label in Soviet identity cards), anyone who answered "Rusyn" was recorded as "Ukrainian." In effect, after 1946 the Carpatho-Rusyn nationality ceased to exist in Soviet Transcarpathia. Anyone who might continue to use that identity label was considered an opponent of the guidelines governing the new social order and, therefore, was a potential or actual anti-Soviet counterrevolutionary.

The decisive manner in which the Soviet authorities were prepared to back up their ideological views became evident in the way that all non-Communist civic, cultural, and religious activists were treated. In December 1944, the Transcarpathian National Council set up a special tribunal to pass judgment on individuals who were in any way connected with the defeated "fascist" regimes that had recently ruled the region; that is, Hungary and even before that, Carpatho-Ukraine. A special tribunal, or people's court, was set up in Uzhhorod and authorized to pass only two judgments on the accused: ten years of hard labor, or death. Actually, many Carpatho-Rusyn activists who served in the Hungarian regime did not leave the region at the war's end, believing that as with previous regimes, whether Habsburg, Czechoslovak, or Hungarian, they could reach some kind of accommodation with the new rulers. They learned quickly how the Soviet regime was differ-ent. In May 1946, several "collaborators," including the well-known prewar and wartime Carpatho-Rusyn politicians Andrii Brodii and Shtefan Fentsyk, were given the death sentence and promptly executed. Those leaders who did not remain in the region, in particular officials from autonomous Carpatho-Ukraine, were hunted down by Soviet counterintelligence agents (SMERSH) operating in Czechoslovakia (Prague and Bratislava), forcibly brought back to Soviet territory, and imprisoned. Some, like the premier of prewar autonomous Subcarpathian Rus' and the president of Carpatho-Ukraine, Avhustyn Voloshyn, died in prison before beginning to serve their term.

Destruction of the Greek Catholic Church

Another symbol of the past, which from the Soviet perspective needed to be eliminated, was the Greek Catholic Church. In 1946, the Soviet authorities outlawed the Greek Catholic Church in neighboring eastern Galicia. The technique used there was to cooperate with the Russian Orthodox Church by convening a church council (*sobor*) in L'viv. No bishops were present, but the 216 Greek Catholic priests who were there (only 9 percent of the total) proclaimed their intention to break with Catholic Rome and return to the bosom of Orthodoxy. It is interesting to note that the chairman of the L'viv church council and the leading figure promoting the return to Orthodoxy was Havriїl Kostel'nik, the Greek Catholic priest originally from the Vojvodina, who for his previous work is considered the founding father of the Vojvodinian Rusyn language and literature. All of Galicia's Greek Catholic bishops and those priests who did not attend the church council and who refused to become Orthodox were arrested and sentenced to long terms of hard labor in the Soviet Gulag.

In Transcarpathia, the technique for liquidating the Greek Catholic Church was slightly different. In late 1944, when the Soviet Army was in control of the region, local Orthodox agitators succeeded within a year in transforming as many as 60 Greek Catholic parishes into Orthodox ones. The Orthodox were helped by the Red Army in driving out the Greek Catholic priest and his family from villages, particularly in the eastern part of Subcarpathian Rus'. A more organized campaign was set in motion by the Soviet authorities. They made several attempts, but were unable to convince the head of the Greek Catholic Eparchy of Mukachevo, Bishop Teodor Romzha, to break with Rome. Hence, another approach to the problem was set in motion. While returning from a visitation to some of his parishes, a "traffic accident" was arranged, and although the bishop survived and was brought to a hospital in Mukachevo, he was poisoned by a secret police agent (in the guise of a nurse) a few days later on 1 November 1947. In the following months the secret police (NKVD) put increasing pressure on the eparchy's Greek Catholic priests to renounce their faith. Most refused, although about one-third did join the Orthodox Church, including the well-known historian who was also active in cultural life during the wartime "fascist" Hungarian regime, Irynei Kontratovych.

In January 1949, agents of the Soviet security service informed the acting administrator of the Greek Catholic Eparchy of Mukachevo that it must cease functioning. From that moment the church was declared illegal; its remaining priests (128) and Basilian monks and nuns were arrested; and all church and monastic property confiscated. The state parceled off many church buildings to secular institutions (many churches were turned into cinemas, sports centers, or storehouses) and it "loaned" others—including the Greek Catholic Cathedral Church in Uzhhorod—to the Orthodox Church for its religious purposes. As for the local Orthodox Eparchy of Mukachevo-Uzhhorod, until then within the jurisdiction of the Serbian Orthodox Church, it was accepted into the jurisdiction of the Russian Orthodox Church (Moscow Patriarchate), which became the only Eastern-rite religious body legally permitted to operate within the Soviet Union.

In effect, during the first five years of Soviet rule (1945–1950), the three traditional pillars of the Carpatho-Rusyn people were taken away from them: their national identity, their land, and their Greek Catholic Church. Moreover, all this was being done during the last decade of rule under the supreme Soviet ruler and "savior" of the fatherland in the war against Nazi Germany, Generalissimo Joseph Stalin. Despite—or perhaps because of—his enhanced status both at home and abroad, Stalin was more paranoid than ever, with the result that Soviet society remained a totalitarian police state dominated by fear and suspicion throughout all walks of life. No wonder that in provincial areas like the military zone of Transcarpathia, local residents were psychologically traumatized and stunned into silence as they saw their traditional society being taken away before their very eyes.

Transcarpathia's new Soviet society

Having gotten rid of the old, it was essential that Soviet society create something new—cadres of citizens who would be loyal to the state. The most effective way to do this was through the school system and, secondarily, through adult education. All the former cultural institutions, regardless of national orientation, were closed (the Russophile Dukhnovych Society and the Rusynophile Subcarpathian Scholarly Society) or, in the case of the Ukrainophile Prosvita Society, not allowed to reopen. Beginning in August 1947, even the libraries in the reading rooms of these societies and elsewhere were stripped of their books which were destroyed because of association with previous "bourgeois regimes." Laws were adopted making it a crime to keep such books in private libraries.

On the other hand, thousands of new titles printed in tens of thousands of copies were sent from other parts of the Soviet Union, while state-owned publishing houses and printshops in Transcarpathia itself produced new titles (1,400 by 1970, with an average printing of 13,600), all in accordance with Soviet Marxist ideological guidelines.[13] In effect, no literature could be produced—or even read legally—without the prior approval of the Communist party and its censors. Several Communist-party and Communist-youth-organization newspapers at the oblast and district (raion) level were published with large circulations (Zakarpats'ka pravda alone had a daily circulation of 130,000). The Communist "spiritual" message was also conveyed through the most favorite medium of Lenin, the founder of the Soviet state. This was the cinema. By 1967 there were no less than 816 facilities showing films throughout Transcarpathia.[14] In a somewhat more systematic fashion, a wide range of night schools and study groups were created to teach the adult population the Communist principles on which "their" worker's state was based.

Of particular importance for the diffusion of Soviet ideology was the school system. Within the first five years of Soviet rule, the regime nearly doubled the number of elementary, elementary/secondary, and middle-level schools (from 445 in 1944 to 852 in 1950), and it established several new institutions specializing in music, the arts, and technical subjects (electronics, metallurgy, forestry, and agriculture).[15] A major achievement was the establishment in 1945 of the first higher-level institution of learning in the history of Subcarpathian Rus'/Transcarpathia, the University of Uzhhorod, initially with faculties in history, philology, medicine, and biology. Soviet investments in a whole host of schools at various levels did, indeed, provide opportunities for a large segment of Transcarpathia's inhabitants to acquire a higher education in their homeland. A not-insignificant number of graduates went on to make successful professional careers at distinguished universities and research institutes in Moscow, Leningrad, Kiev, and other major centers of the Soviet Union.

The language of instruction in Transcarpathia's schools was Ukrainian, with Russian as a required second language. At the University of Uzhhorod, mostly Russian was used in lectures and exams. As for the local Rusyn language, it was non-existent in the school system, although Rusyn vernacular remained the common spoken language in rural villages. Whereas the younger generation had a passive knowledge of the spoken language, they learned nothing about their local Carpatho-Rusyn culture. All students may have been familiar with the great Ukrainian and Russian writers Taras Shevchenko, Ivan Franko, and Aleksander Pushkin, but they were taught next to nothing, if anything at all, about the national awakener of Carpatho-Rusyns, Aleksander Dukhnovych, or about other Carpatho-Rusyn writers and cultural activists.

LOVE OF THE EAST

Despite the geographic location of Carpathian Rus' in the heart of central Europe and the inclination of its intellectuals to be drawn to the cultural centers of the former Austro-Hungarian Empire and its successor states—Budapest, Vienna, Prague, and Cracow—Carpatho-Rusyns have been drawn to the East. There are many reasons for this: the affinity of their spoken dialects with other East Slavic languages (Russian and Ukrainian, in particular), the rituals and belief system of their Eastern-rite Christian faith, which is similar to that of other East Slavs; and the somewhat mystical belief in the power of Russia or the advantages of unity with an independent Ukraine as the only means to preserve their unique Carpatho-Rusyn culture— and possible economic survival—in the face of the Westernizing influences and economic exploitation by non-Rus' states under whom they have been forced to live for centuries.

Beliefs such as these are what permeated the worldview of many Carpatho-Rusyns in the twentieth century and even beyond until today. Political inexperience prompted many Carpatho-Rusyns to believe that they could find salvation in the East, epitomized in the twentieth century by the world's "first worker's state," the Soviet Union, which itself claimed to be the successor to the "progressive" aspects of Russia and Russian culture and language. It is, therefore, not surprising that some Carpatho-Rusyns, who otherwise derived from a deeply faithful Christian environment, became staunch supporters of a new faith—that of revolutionary social change coming from the East. For them the East meant Russia and Ukraine, often confusingly merged as the new revolutionary—and eventually Communist—Holy Rus'.

Eventually, some—although not all—Carpatho-Rusyns became aware of the shortcomings of their naïve faith in the East. More often than not, their discovery of what the East was really like came at great existential cost, as revealed in the following recollections of a Subcarpathian Communist "true believer."

Now that I am in my 74th year, memories of the past keep recurring. When I was a child, my father was working in the United States from 1912 to 1920. Thanks to God, not only did he return home, but he brought dollars with him. He bought a bell for our village church, more land, cattle, and sheep for our homestead, and he began to farm. Of the 11 children born into our family, only 4 survived—the death of children was quite common in those days.

We four surviving sons were all good at school, two of us finishing the *horozhanka* [junior high school] and two graduating from *gymnasium* [senior high school]. . .

During elections to the Czechoslovak parliament [1924, 1929, 1935], father always chose column four; that is, he voted for the Communists. This is because we read various brochures by [local Communist leaders Ivan I.] Turianytsia, [Oleksa] Borkaniuk, and [Ivan] Lokota. For instance, Borkaniuk's booklet, *What Does the Soviet Union Mean to Us?*, provided a shiny and colorful picture of the Stalinist paradise.

Then, in 1939, one of my brothers, followed in 1940 by another [fled from our Hungarian-ruled homeland] and crossed the border into the Soviet Union. . . . Instead of paradise, they were met by arrest, interrogation, torture, and a sentence of three-years' imprisonment in the Stalinist Gulag. We back home knew nothing about this.

Then came the "liberation" [by the Soviets in 1944]. I, as the youngest son, volunteered to join the Soviet Army. After the war was over I learned that one of my brothers [released from the Soviet Gulag], who had fought in the Czechoslovak Brigade, was killed in battle at Bila Tserkva [in central Ukraine], while the other [also released from the Gulag], who was in General Svoboda's Czechoslovak Army Corps, was parachuted into Slovakia [in 1944] to participate in the partisan uprising there. After the war, he remained in Czechoslovakia, having had enough of Stalin's paradise. There he completed university studies in Brno, went on to earn a doctorate, and eventually became a professor. Meanwhile, [at home in what was now Soviet Transcarpathia], our father was in 1947 declared a *kulak* and sentenced to seven years in prison.

I myself was able to finish university and began to work [in Soviet Transcarpathia] as a teacher. Nevertheless, all those years I was haunted by the fact that I was the son of a *kulak*; that is, an enemy of the people. Perhaps I have spoken too much about the story of only one family, my own. But, believe me, there were many such families in [Soviet] Transcarpathia, some of whom met an even more tragic fate.

SOURCE: Matfei Shchadei, "Chyim ahentom buv Oleksa Borkaniuk" (For Whom Was Oleksa Borkaniuk an Agent), in Vasyl' Belei, *De i iak pomer Ivan Lokota* (Mukachevo, 2009), p. 8.

In fact, Soviet policy makers engaged local Communist ideologists to par - ticipate in a campaign begun as early as 1948 to demonize the entire range of nineteenth-century Carpatho-Rusyn national awakeners (A. Dukhnovych, A. Pavlovych, I. Sil'vai, A. Dobrians'kyi, and others). These figures were henceforth branded as "members of the reactionary class and instruments of Vatican obscurantism."[16] It was also common practice to remind the public through the media and in countless indirect everyday encounters about the superiority of the allegedly more progressive recently arrived Russian and Ukrainian administrators and intelligentsia, in contrast to the ideologically conservative and even retrograde "locals." Not surprisingly, then, symbols of local pride such as the national anthem ("Subcarpathian Rusyns, Arise from Your Deep Slumber") and the national hymn ("I Was, Am, and Will Remain a Rusyn") were banned from all publications and public performance. In the words of one local historian who in those years was himself an active Communist propagandist:

> ... all political, economic, and ideological means were used to integrate Transcarpathians into the Ukrainian world—and from there into the all-Soviet social world—with the ultimate goal to eliminate among the indigenous [Carpatho-Rusyn] population its particular genealogical ori- gins and respect towards its ancestors, traditions, customs, and home- steads that had been cultivated for centuries. . . . Within one or two generations a good portion of the local inhabitants (especially among the educated) became marginalized and lost any awareness of their own regional history and ethnic [Carpatho-Rusyn] identity.[17]

To be sure, students were being exposed already in elementary school to courses in regional studies (*kraieznavstvo*), and public life was filled with performances by hundreds of amateur folk ensembles and even a profes- sional song and dance ensemble in Uzhhorod that promoted Carpatho- Rusyn folk culture. But all of this was presented as "Transcarpathian"; that is, a regional variant of Ukrainian culture. Even those who wanted to distinguish themselves from the rest of Ukraine, did so by referring to vague descriptors like the "Transcarpathian people," even the "Transcarpathian language," or simply *po-nashomu* (in our own way). If aware at all about anything Carpatho-Rusyn, a "Transcarpathian" would be quick to respond that it was something from the past. And in a Soviet political environment that was ever suspicious of previous regimes and previous national labels, such a past should best be forgotten.

The Prešov Region in postwar and Communist Czechoslovakia, 1945–1989

In contrast to Subcarpathian Rus', which was spared any substantive destruction during the advance of the Soviet armies, the Prešov Region was part of the zone in which the two-month long and very costly Battle of the Dukla Pass took place. During September and October 1944, many Carpatho-Rusyns had to be evacuated, and several villages in the area north and east of Svidník were severely damaged. Despite their defeat in the Dukla Battle, it took at least two months before the German forces, with their Slovak allies, were driven out of the region. The city of Prešov itself was not in Soviet-Czechoslovak military hands until mid-January 1945.

Postwar politics: the Ukrainian National Council

As soon as the administrators of the Slovak state fled before the advancing Soviet-Czechoslovak forces, village and town councils were formed to take on local government functions throughout the Prešov Region. On 1 March 1945, representatives of these councils met in the city of Prešov, where they established the Ukrainian National Council of the Prešov Region (Ukraïns'ka narodna rada Priashivshchiny). This was the first time the name *Ukrainian* was used in the title of any Prešov Region organization, almost all of which before that time favored the ethnonym *Russian* (*russkii*). The decision to call this council "Ukrainian" reflected the dominant role played by Communists and pro-Communist sympathizers in the local councils. The Czechoslovak Communists were simply following the guidelines set by the Comintern back in 1924: that the East Slavic inhabitants of the Prešov Region and all of Carpathian Rus', regardless what they may have called themselves, were Ukrainians, and that any other national orientation should be disregarded.

The Ukrainian National Council also reiterated the long-standing position of Carpatho-Rusyn political and civil activists in the Prešov Region: unification with their brethren in Subcarpathian Rus' or, as it was already being called, Transcarpathian Ukraine. Actually, the desire for unity with Transcarpathian Ukraine began already in late 1944. Just three days after the First Congress of Peoples' Committees proclaimed in Mukachevo (26

November 1944) its intent to unite Transcarpathian Ukraine with Soviet Ukraine, a group of Prešov Region activists who happened to be in Uzhhorod at the time formed a Provisional National Council of Prešov and Russian [sic] Ukrainians. The council's proclamation expressed "only one wish: to annex to their free motherland—Transcarpathian Ukraine—all of Prešov Ukraine [the Prešov Region in Slovakia] as well as the Lemko Region in Galicia."[1] By the outset of 1945, several activists were going through villages in the Prešov Region, urging the local Carpatho-Rusyn inhabitants to express a willingness and desire to unite with Transcarpathian Ukraine.

This activity culminated at the 1 March 1945 founding meeting of the Ukrainian National Council in Prešov. The council sent telegrams to the Soviet Union's supreme leader Joseph Stalin, thanking him for the sacrifices of the glorious Red Army that liberated their land from "the German fascist yoke" and expressing the hope that "the day will soon come when age-old historical injustice will be overcome and the great Ukrainian people will be re-united within one state."[2] The Ukrainian allusion was made more specific in the council's other telegram to the first secretary of the Communist party of Ukraine, Nikita Khrushchev: we are "turning to you with the request that, when the question of Transcarpathian Ukraine is resolved, to remember that in the Prešov Region there also live Ukrainians, who in terms of national composition and culture are blood brothers of the Transcarpathian Ukrainians."[3] The Prešov council's proceedings also acknowledged the request of the Lemko Worker's and Peasant's Committee north of the mountains in Gorlice and its desire to be united with the Prešov Region and Transcarpathian Ukraine. It is not without significance that the Prešov Region Ukrainian National Council did not consider it necessary to inform the Czechoslovak government of its actions.

Not unexpectedly, the statements calling for unification with Transcarpathian Ukraine worried Slovak leaders, who urged their Rusyn brethren in the Prešov Region to remain within Czechoslovakia, where they would be guaranteed full rights as a national minority. The Czechoslovak option became, in effect, the only feasible alternative for the Prešov Region. As Khrushchev himself later recalled in his memoirs: "Representatives from some region in Slovakia inhabited by Ukrainians even came to Kyiv to ask me to unite their land with Soviet Ukraine,"[4] and were deeply dissatisfied when told this would not be possible. Finally, in late May 1945, the Prešov Ukrainian National Council declared its intention to support the new Czechoslovak government headed by the country's prewar president, Edvard Beneš, but only on the condition that political and cultural autonomy be granted.

The restored Czechoslovak state under President Beneš was intended to be a parliamentary democracy, similar to the interwar first republic, in which several political parties would compete to form a government. With this goal in mind, elections were held in May 1946 to the restored Czechoslovak parliament. Although in the Czech lands (Bohemia and Moravia) the Communist party garnered a majority of the vote, in Slovakia it received only 30 percent of the vote as opposed to the Democratic party, which garnered twice as much (62 percent).[5] In the Prešov Region, there was a Rusyn-Ukrainian branch (Rusko-ukrajinská sekcia) of the Democratic party with its own Russian-language newspaper, *Demokraticheskii golos* (1945–48). Whereas a slight majority of Carpatho-Rusyns (50.1 percent) voted for the Democratic party, a significant proportion (45.8 percent) voted for the Communists.[6]

Despite being an electoral minority in Slovakia, the Communist party was nonetheless the most influential political force in the country. Consequently, following the 1946 parliamentary elections, the Communist leader, Klement Gottwald, became prime minister. Moreover, the country's democratically ori- ented President Beneš, seemingly still traumatized at his country's "betrayal by the West" at the 1938 Munich Pact, reoriented Czechoslovakia's foreign policy toward the Soviet Union. This could not but help raise the pres- tige of Czechoslovakia's Communist party. In effect, the Democratic and Communist parties were locked in a battle for control of the country, with the result that during the immediate postwar years Czechoslovakia was vir- tually paralyzed by an ongoing series of internal political crises. External events also did not seem to bode well for the country. Backed by the pres- ence of the Soviet Army, Czechoslovakia's neighbors—Poland to the north and Hungary to the south—had already become Communist countries ruled according to the Soviet model. It seemed only a matter of time before Czechoslovakia would follow suit.

Meanwhile, in the Prešov Region, the Ukrainian National Council (in which Communists and their sympathizers were playing an increasingly influential role) continued to act as if it were the only legitimate represen- tative of the Carpatho-Rusyn populace. Since the council abandoned its demand to unite with the increasingly pro-Soviet Transcarpathian Ukraine, its members argued that at the very least Carpatho-Rusyns should be granted autonomy within Czechoslovakia. In 1947, Carpatho-Rusyn civic activists submitted two proposals to the Slovak government in Bratislava: one calling for personal-cultural autonomy, the other for territorial auton- omy.[7] Both proposals were rejected.

On the other hand, the Ukrainian National Council was successful on the cultural front. It helped to organize a Ukrainian National Theater (Ukraïns'kyi narodnyi teatr), a publishing house (Slavknyha), a school board (Referat ukraïns'kykh shkil), and a youth organization (Soiuz molodi Karpat), and it continued to publish the influential newspaper, *Priashevshchina* (1945–52). Despite the names of these various bodies, all publications, theatrical per- formances, manifestos, and so forth were in Russian, not Ukrainian. The educational system in the Prešov Region was also considerably expanded, so that by the 1948/1949 school year it comprised 51 kindergartens, 275 elementary schools, 41 *horozhanky* (elementary/junior high schools), and 4 *gymnasia* (senior high schools).[8] In all schools, Russian, not Ukrainian, was the language of instruction. In effect, the problem of national identity remained unresolved. Newspapers and organizations may have called them- selves Ukrainian, but they used Russian for written communication and educational instruction. Meanwhile, the majority of the populace identified itself as Rusyn, or even more often by the local ethnonym, *Rusnak.*

Population transfers and the UPA

Two other developments during the transitional postwar years had a direct impact on the Prešov Region. Within the general context of demographic engineering or forced population transfers, a policy adopted by many countries in Europe (3 million Germans were expelled from Czechoslovakia and 3.2 million from Poland), in July 1946 Czechoslovakia and the Soviet Union signed an agreement on "repatriation" and mutual population exchange. This set in motion what came to be known as the Volhynian Operation/*Volynská akce,* whereby the approximately 40,000 Czechs living since the mid-nineteenth century in the former province of Volhynia (now in Soviet Ukraine) would be exchanged for an equivalent number of Ukrainians, Russians, and Belarusans living in Czechoslovakia.

Because an equivalent number of people were not to be found among these groups, the Czechoslovak authorities, aided by Soviet propagandists, turned to the Carpatho-Rusyn population (now called Ukrainians) in the Prešov Region of northeastern Slovakia. Considering that the region had been heavily damaged by the war and that its mountainous terrain was never able to support adequately its rural population, some Carpatho-Rusyns were easily convinced by tales about rich agricultural lands waiting for them should they decide to resettle in the Soviet Union. By May 1947, when the Volhynia Operation was completed, over 10,000 Carpatho-Rusyns from the Prešov Region (2,665 families) opted to be exchanged for Czechs from the Soviet Union. In the end, just over 8,100 were voluntarily resettled in the Volhynian region of northwest Soviet Ukraine, mainly in rural areas around the town of Rivne.[9] In stark contrast to most other resettlement actions occurring at the time throughout central and eastern Europe, the Prešov Region exodus was entirely voluntarily. Nevertheless, within a few weeks of their arrival in the Soviet Union, many of the Carpatho-Rusyn *optanty*—or those who opted, as they were known—realized that they had made a mistake and wanted to return home. But it was too late. No one left Stalin's Soviet Union.

The other matter that complicated postwar conditions in the Prešov Region was the presence of the Ukrainian Insurgent Army, or UPA. This underground military force, which from 1943 fought on the territory of former eastern Poland against the German and Soviet armies and Polish partisans, had not yet surrendered. It was held up in the inaccessible mountain areas along the postwar borders of Poland, Czechoslovakia, and the Soviet Union; that is, in the very heart of Carpathian Rus'. The UPA was most active in Poland in 1945 and 1946, at which time some of its units crossed over into the Prešov Region. There they hoped to solicit support from the local Carpatho-Rusyn population which, from the perspective of the UPA, was Ukrainian. While their efforts were not met with success, the Czechoslovak authorities, in particular the Communist-controlled Ministry of the Interior, nevertheless remained suspicious about the possibility that "bourgeois-na-tionalist" activists among the Prešov Region's Carpatho-Rusyns might become instruments of the UPA's efforts to undermine Communist rule and Soviet influence in the region.

Communist Czechoslovakia according to the Soviet model

The generally unstable political conditions in Czechoslovakia became clar-ified in early 1948, when in February the Czechoslovak Communist party led by Prime Minister Klement Gottwald carried out a *putsch* and took over the government of the country. Within a few weeks of the "February Revolution," President Beneš resigned, and under Gottwald Communist-ruled Czechoslovakia set out to build a socialist society according to the model, and frequently at the direction, of the Soviet Union. It was not long before profound political and social transformations took place throughout the country, three of which were to have a profound impact on the Carpatho-Rusyns in the Prešov Region: (1) collectivization; (2) de-catholicization; and (3) ukrainianization. These developments occurred more or less simultane-ously between the years 1949 and 1953.

As in other Soviet-influenced central and eastern European countries, Czechoslovakia's new leaders accepted the Leninist-Stalinist principle that centralized state planning was the most efficient way to organize the econ-omy. Thus, industry, public services, and retail stores were nationalized and agriculture collectivized. When collectivization in the agricultural sector began in 1949, it soon became clear that Carpatho-Rusyn peasant farmers were for the most part unwilling to give up their land voluntarily to the collective. Using political and social pressure (including arrests), local Communist party activists led the drive toward collectivization. But opposition by the peasantry together with the general ineffectiveness of large farming operations in moun-tainous regions slowed the process, so that after a decade (that is, by 1960) only 63 percent of farmland in the Prešov Region was collectivized.[10]

Much quicker was the process of the de-catholicization. As in most other matters, Czechoslovakia followed the lead of the Soviet Union, where the Communist party ideologists had accepted the view that the Greek Catholic Church was little more than a Vatican-inspired tool used since the late six-teenth and seventeenth centuries to latinize the Eastern rite and eventually to catholicize the originally Orthodox Eastern Slavic (Rus') peoples. Following the Soviet precedent in western Ukraine (Galicia), where the Greek Catholic Church was already abolished in 1946, Czechoslovakia's Communist author-ities, in cooperation with the local Orthodox clergy, arranged a church coun-cil in Prešov on 28 April 1950. The result was the liquidation of the Greek Catholic Eparchy of Prešov.

Greek Catholic priests were given the opportunity "to return" to the Orthodox Church, but in the end only 103 (39 percent of the eparchy's total of 265) actually did so. Of those who refused—among whom were several who initially signed the manifesto issued by the 1950 church council—some ceased their priestly activity, 65 were arrested and sentenced to various terms of imprisonment, and others went into hiding.[11] Arrested already on the eve of the April 1950 church council, nearly one year later Bishop Pavel Goidych was brought before a court, which in effect was a political show trial broadcast live on radio throughout Czechoslovakia. The object was to impress—and frighten—listeners. The popular bishop, otherwise known for his defense of Carpatho-Rusyn cultural interests and of persecuted Jews during World War II, was found guilty of anti-state activity, including having allegedly had contact with the UPA and with local Ukrainian "bourgeois nationalists." He was sentenced to life imprisonment. All Greek Catholic lay people, should they wish to continue in the faith, had to become Orthodox.

Meanwhile, the Communist authorities gave encouragement to the Orthodox. A cathedral church was built in Prešov, and in the same city an Orthodox seminary was opened. All the former 241 Greek Catholic, together with the existing 19 Orthodox, parishes were reapportioned into two eparchies, Prešov and Michalovce, which initially were placed under the jurisdiction of the Russian Orthodox Patriarchate of Moscow.[12] In November 1951, however, the two Prešov Region eparchies were "released" from the jurisdiction of Moscow in order to become part of the newly created Autocephalous Orthodox Church of Czechoslovakia.

Carpatho-Rusyns are ukrainianized

The long-standing unresolved question of national identity among the Prešov Region Rusyns was also settled by administrative procedure. Although the Carpatho-Rusyn population had since 1945 been officially referred to as Ukrainian, it was Russian (as during the interwar years) which remained the language of instruction in schools and the medium for newspapers and cultural life. While the intelligentsia felt itself to be Russian, the mass of the rural populace continued to refer to itself as Rusnaks (*rusnatsi*). The local intelligentsia, dominated by Russophiles, continued to conflate the popular ethnonym *rus'kyi* (Rusyn) with the term *russkii* (Russian), while those government officials and civic leaders who accepted the new Communist order used the ethnonym *Ukrainian* to describe the group. Frustrated by the ongoing terminological confusion, Carpatho-Rusyn delegates at a regional conference of the Slovak Communist party held in Prešov in 1950 lamented: "Five years after the war and we still don't know who we are: Russians, Ukrainians, or Rusyns. This is shameful."[13] Once again, following the Soviet model in Transcarpathia, it was decided that only a Ukrainian identity and cultural orientation would be permitted. Ukrainian was already introduced into Russian schools as a subject in 1949; then, in June 1952, the Slovak Communist party in Bratislava decreed that Ukrainian should be used in all schools of the Prešov Region. The following year it became the language of instruction for all subjects.

The change was sudden, with no preparations either in the pedagogical or general social sphere. Russophile-oriented teachers had to "ukrainianize" themselves or lose their positions, while the local populace was expected to identify as Ukrainian. Most of the recently established postwar organizations, whether or not they were Russophile in orientation, were liquidated between 1949 and 1952, including the Ukrainian National Council, its Russian-language newspaper *Priashevshchina*, the Ukrainian School Board, the Union of Carpathian Youth, and the Slavknyha publishing house. Only the Ukrainian National Theater and state-run radio programming remained, although their presentations henceforth were required to be in Ukrainian, not Russian.

Some voices were raised against the administrative introduction of ukrainianization, but such critics (mostly among Russophiles) were either silenced, released from their jobs, or imprisoned. Those who spoke out against the new policy, including the most fervent Russophiles who denied the very existence of a Ukrainian nationality, were paradoxically labeled with what had become in Communist Czechoslovakia the dangerous epithet of "Ukrainian bourgeois nationalist."

To promote the new Communist-approved national orientation, a non-political and acceptably socialist organization was created in 1951—the Cultural Union of Ukrainian Workers in Czechoslovakia/Kul'turnyi soiuz ukraïns'kykh trudiashchykh ChSSR (KSUT). Its object was "to provide Ukrainian workers with national consciousness and pride, and to instill in them both an awareness of belonging to the great Soviet Ukrainian people and of realizing the ideal of Czechoslovak socialist patriotism and proletarian internationalism."[14] To fulfill those tasks, KSUT began publishing a weekly newspaper (*Nove zhyttia*, 1952–present), a monthly magazine, (*Družhno vpered*, 1951–98), and a literary, historical, and public affairs journal (*Duklia*, 1953–present). KSUT also organized numerous lectures and cultural programs throughout the Prešov Region; it supported (by 1963) 242 local folk ensembles; and it sponsored annual drama, sport, and folk festivals, the largest of which was held annually since 1956 in the small town of Svidník. Aside from KSUT's activity, Czechoslovakia's Communist government provided funds to establish a Museum of Ukrainian Culture (est. 1956), a Department of Ukrainian Language and Literature (est. 1953) at the Prešov branch of Šafárik University, and the Dukla Ukrainian Song and Dance Ensemble/Pidduklians'kyi ukraïns'kyi narodnyi ansambl' (est. 1956) as part of the Ukrainian National Theater in Prešov.

In order to staff the new network of Ukrainian educational and cultural institutions, the Prešov Region's intelligentsia—the vast majority of whom were Russophiles—had to be retrained. This meant that they had to become nationally conscious Ukrainians *and* socially conscious Marxists. Not all local activists were willing or able to manage the transition. In part, they were replaced by nationally conscious Ukrainian activists from Subcarpathian Rus', who had come to Czechoslovakia just before, during, or immediately after the war, and who were to play a direct or indirect role in Prešov Region cultural affairs. Among these also were Subcarpathian Russophiles, who transformed themselves into Ukrainians.

To assure the future success of the Ukrainian national orientation, a few younger Prešov Region intellectuals (some of whom had begun their career as Russophiles) were sent to Soviet Ukraine's capital of Kiev in order to supplement their education. Already by the 1960s, the Prešov Region had a talented native-born group of Ukrainian-oriented cultural activists, among whom were belletrists, actors, theatrical directors, teachers, and scholars in various disciplines (history, language, and ethnography). Within a few decades of Communist rule, government-sponsored experts were proudly proclaiming that, thanks to the guidelines and the practice of "socialist internationalism," the nationality question among the Prešov Region's "Ukrainians" ceased to exist.[15]

Despite such optimistic claims and ongoing substantial funding from the Czechoslovak government to support the cultural development of its Carpatho-Rusyn minority, the results at the grassroots level were meager. The rapid introduction of ukrainianization, which accompanied the liquidation of the Greek Catholic Church and collectivization of land holdings in the early 1950s, created unfavorable conditions that encouraged national assimilation. As one villager later recalled:

> Today, I am like that dumb sheep. I don't have anything. I had my own [Greek Catholic] God, you took him from me. I had my own [Rus'] nationality, but you took that away, too. I had a little piece of land, even that you took. Everything that I had you took.[16]

Consequently, many people concluded that if they could not identify as Rusyns and have their own *rus'ki* schools, it would be better to be Slovak than Ukrainian.

The process of national assimilation was most graphically revealed in the census figures and in school statistics. Since the late nineteenth century, when census takers began to ask the inhabitants of the Prešov Region to indicate their nationality, the basic choices were between, on the one hand, Rusnak/Russian/Rusyn/Ukrainian, and on the other, identifying with the state nationality: Czechoslovak/Slovak or, before World War I, Hungarian. The following table reveals that there was initially a gradual and then sharp decline in the number of Carpatho-Rusyns in the Prešov Region during the twentieth century. The decline was most evident in censuses taken during the period of Communist rule (1950, 1961, 1970, 1980), when only a Ukrainian identity was permitted.

At the same time, and again particularly during the second half of the twentieth century, there began a steady decline in the number of schools which taught some form of language that was representative of the local culture—whether Rusyn vernacular, literary Russian, or literary Ukrainian. For example, in 1948, 275 elementary schools had Russian as the language of instruction.[17] After the change to Ukrainian, parents themselves began to demand that their village schools use instead Slovak as the language of instruction. As a result, within a single decade the number of elementary

TABLE 23.1
Census data on East Slavs in Slovakia, 1900 to 1991[18]

Year of census*	Number in all Slovakia	Number in Prešov Region
1900	84,906	–
1910	97,114	–
1919	81,332	–
1921	85,628	–
1930	91,079	–
1940	85,991/61,270	–
1950	48,231	40,446
1961	35,435	33,333
1970	42,239	36,115
1980	39,260	31,368
1991	32,408	29,782

* The figures for 1900 and 1910 refer to "mother tongue"; all the rest to "nationality" and include persons who responded either Rusyn, Russian, or Ukrainian. There are also data from 1991 for mother tongue: 49,099 Rusyn and 9,480 Ukrainian.

schools with Ukrainian as the language of instruction declined from 245 in 1955 to only 68 in 1966. Also, between 1948 and 1966, the number of junior high schools declined from 41 to 3 and the *gymnasia* (senior high schools) from 4 to 1.[19] By the mid-1960s, the pro-Ukrainian intelligentsia had come to realize that the government-approved Ukrainian nationality policy was largely a failure and that before long they might have no constituency to serve. This was the situation in the Prešov Region when, in 1968, Communist Czechoslovakia embarked on a period of reform known as the "Prague Spring."

The Prague Spring and the rebirth of Carpatho-Rusyns

In January 1968, Alexander Dubček, the new chairman of the Communist party of Czechoslovakia, set out on a bold experiment. He and a group of reformers within the Communist party wanted to loosen political controls, to decentralize the economic structure of the country, and in general to introduce democratic change. In short, the reformers hoped to create a new Czechoslovakia where socialism would prevail but "with a human face." All individuals and groups were called upon to participate in the reform movement.

Although Carpatho-Rusyns had fared better than any other national minority in Czechoslovakia since World War II, they nonetheless had many complaints, especially with regard to their lack of political equality with Czechs and Slovaks which had been promised them during the war. In an effort to improve the status of Carpatho-Rusyns, the Cultural Union of Ukrainian Workers (KSUT), taking advantage of the Prague Spring's liberal atmosphere, called for a national congress to be held no later than May. The goal was to reconstitute the postwar Ukrainian National Council that was dissolved in 1952. Because the Prague Spring had brought an effective end to censorship, KSUT's weekly newspaper, *Nove zhyttia*, was soon filled with articles demanding political, economic, and cultural autonomy for Carpatho-Rusyns. The idea of political or territorial autonomy, however, went against both the Communist principle of centralized rule as well as against the general Slovak conviction that no part of Slovakia should have any special administrative status based on nationality or any other criteria. Thus, the proposed national congress was abruptly called off on direct orders from the Slovak Communist party presidium in Bratislava.

Lack of success in the civic and political realm was, in part, compensated by some achievements in the sphere of religion. In June 1968, the Greek Catholic Church, which had been outlawed since 1950, was legalized again. The institution was not, however, able to resume its historic role as a unifying force for Carpatho-Rusyn interests. This is because it became immediately embroiled, on the one hand, with the Orthodox over the use of church buildings and, on the other, with the Slovak-oriented clergy within its own ranks over what vernacular should be used and from what national group the new bishop should come. The property issue was particularly problematic. Who had a right to use the Eastern-rite churches—the Orthodox who held them since 1950 or the Greek Catholics who had owned the churches before that year and now wanted them back? This thorny issue was resolved by the mechanism of a plebiscite. Among the first symbolic steps of the plebiscite was the return of the Prešov eparchial cathedral church to the Greek Catholics in July 1968. In the course of the next year, plebiscites were held in about 210 parishes; only 5 opted to remain Orthodox. In the end, the Communist authorities, not wishing to see the virtual demise of Orthodoxy, recognized the existence of 205 Greek Catholic and 87 Orthodox parishes.[20]

While there were peaceful transfers of property from the Orthodox to Greek Catholics, there were also several cases marked by assaults and the forced removal of the Orthodox parish priests, breaking down church doors, disruption of services, and in at least one instance the death of a Greek Catholic curate. The situation was made even more ominous in that most of the plebiscites were carried out after 21 August; that is, in the presence of Soviet armed forces throughout the country. While it is known that some Orthodox priests garbed in sacred vestments greeted Soviet troops as "liberators and defenders of Orthodoxy,"[21] unfounded rumors soon began to circulate according to which the Orthodox had supposedly "invited" the Soviets and that it was them, in the post-invasion environment, who were spreading rumors about the Greek Catholics as "anti-socialist counterrevolutionaries."

As for the Greek Catholics, their last bishop, Pavel Goidych, had died in prison in 1960. His auxiliary and successor, Vasyl' Hopko, who had been released from confinement a few years later, was finally allowed to return to Prešov in 1968 and lead the process of restoring the eparchy. His return did not sit well with pro-Slovak elements within the church, however. Supported by Slovak sympathizers in the Vatican, and especially émigré Slovaks in Canada, the pro-Slovak faction vowed that no bishop of Carpatho-Rusyn background should ever again head the Greek Catholic Eparchy of Prešov. Consequently, the Vatican relieved Bishop Hopko as acting head of the eparchy (in December 1968) and instead placed it under an administrator of Slovak background, Monsignor Ján Hirka. For the next two decades, the eparchial authorities under Hirka were able to restore the Greek Catholic Church, although services in most churches, including the estimated 75 parishes in Rusyn villages, were slovakized. This meant that the Church Slavonic language traditionally used in the liturgy and the spoken Rusyn vernacular used in the non-liturgical parts of the service (homilies, announcements, printed materials) were both gradually phased out and replaced by Slovak.

Other demands made during the Prague Spring centered on the perennial question of national identity. Meetings, letters, and newspaper articles reflected a widespread popular desire to do away with the "artificial" Ukrainian orientation promoted by the "little band of intellectuals" and to bring back "our own Rusyn schools" and cultural leaders.[22] The people were once again officially referred to as *Rusyn*—a term which had been forbidden in public discourse since the introduction of ukrainianization in 1952. Symbolically, the proposed national council was to be called the Council of Czechoslovak Rusyns (Rada chekhoslovats'kykh rusyniv).

The almost daily meetings and fervent discussions during the eight months of the Prague Spring were suddenly interrupted on 21 August 1968, when more than half a million troops from the Warsaw Pact countries led by the Soviet Union invaded Czechoslovakia. For several days the country was deprived of its leadership which was arrested, brought to Soviet Transcarpathia, and from there flown to Moscow. When Dubček and his associates were allowed to return home, the program of democratization undertaken by Czechoslovakia's liberal Communist leaders during the Prague Spring was slowed down and, before long, was completely ended. In the Prešov Region, plans to hold a national congress of Czechoslovak Rusyns were again postponed after the Warsaw Pact invasion and then permanently cancelled. Discussions about national identity did continue for a few more months, and among them were proposals to introduce the Rusyn vernacular instead of Ukrainian for some publications. In the end, however, none of these proposals was ever realized.

Besides the shock of the Soviet-led invasion and the ongoing religious and nationality quarrels, the Prague Spring also brought for Rusyns an increase in friction with Slovaks. The Slovak press and certain organizations (in particular the revived Slovak Cultural Foundation/Matica slovenská) were critical of Rusyn-Ukrainian political and cultural demands and even accused the group as a whole of collaboration with the Soviets. Some Slovaks went so far as to suggest that all Rusyns be deported to Soviet Ukraine.

It is true that throughout Czechoslovakia at the time it was common knowledge that one of the Communist "traitors" suspected—and later confirmed—of having invited the Soviets to invade the country was Vasil Bil'ak, the first secretary of the Slovak Communist party. Bil'ak had lived in a Czech-language environment in Bohemia since the age of 12. He was, however, born in a Prešov Region village and, following official guidelines, described himself as a Ukrainian. Because of his well-known pro-Soviet sympathies, Czech and Slovak public opinion attributed such attitudes to his national origin. By association, therefore, all Carpatho-Rusyns in the Prešov Region were suspect of being pro-Soviet sympathizers.

Soviet-style political consolidation and re-ukrainianization

In an atmosphere of fear and uncertainty, Carpatho-Rusyn villagers tried to overcome the social stigma attached to them and to compensate with expressions of loyalty to Czechoslovakia. This took the form of demanding more Slovak schools for their children. By 1970, the numbers decreased to 41 elementary schools and to 4 *gymnasia* in which there were sections using Ukrainian as the language of instruction.[23] Despite a campaign by cultural activists on the eve of the 1970 census (in which people for the first time in Communist Czechoslovakia were allowed to identify themselves as Rusyn but nonetheless be recorded as Ukrainian), just over 36,000 persons in the Prešov Region responded that they were either Rusyn, Ukrainian, or in a few cases Russian.[24]

At the outset of 1970, the inspirational leader of the Prague Spring, Alexander Dubček, was replaced as head of the Czechoslovak Communist party by Gustav Husák. Under Husák, loyalty to the Soviet Union was the new imperative, and with the active help of the Carpatho-Rusyn Vasil Bil'ak (by then the influential Communist party secretary responsible for foreign policy and ideology), he introduced a policy of "political consolidation" in order to purge Dubček and all other active and passive supporters of the Prague Spring from Czechoslovakia's Communist party.

Many throughout the country lost their jobs, including some of the most vocal reform-minded activists in the Prešov Region (the chairman of KSUT, Ivan Matsyns'kyi, and the writers and publicists Iurii Bacha, Mykola Mushynka, and Mykhailo Shmaida). These and others were also expelled from the Ukrainian Writer's Union and forbidden to publish for periods that in some cases lasted two decades. Nonetheless, other Ukrainian-oriented cultural activists continued to function, several belletristic and scholarly books and serial publications continued to appear throughout the 1970s and 1980s, and Ukrainian cultural institutions—KSUT, the Ukrainian museum in Svidník, and the Ukrainian department at the university in Prešov—maintained about the same level of activity with even greater financial backing than they had before 1968. The rigid Ukrainian nationality policy, however, made these organizations as ineffective as ever in the effort to stem the tide of assimilation that steadily threatened the very survival of Carpatho-Rusyns in the Prešov Region.

Socioeconomic achievements and national assimilation

Aside from political, cultural, and nationality problems, the government of Communist Czechoslovakia since 1948 made certain progress in raising the general standard of living of the Prešov Region. For the first time, a communications network was established, making the region accessible to the rest of the country through bus transportation that reached most villages. Symbolic of Soviet-inspired modernization was electrification begun in 1957 and completed for every Carpatho-Rusyn village within four years.[25]

The almost exclusive dependence on agriculture was also altered. Beginning in 1956 and the introduction of Czechoslovakia's Soviet-style Second Five-Year economic plan, several factories and mills were built in small towns throughout the Prešov Region: Stará Ľubovňa (machine and tool works, textile), Orlov (building materials), Bardejov (shoes, glass, and porcelain), Svidník (clothing), Stropkov (electronics), Medzilaborce (machine and tool works), Krásny Brod (building materials), and Snina (machine and tool works). Carpatho-Rusyns were also attracted to employment opportunities in factories located farther south in primarily Slovak-inhabited cities (Sabinov, Prešov, Humenné, and Michalovce), while just west of Košice the massive East Slovak steel works began operation.

This expansion of industrial development within and near the Prešov Region drastically changed the social structure of Carpatho-Rusyns. By 1970, only 30 percent of them were engaged in agriculture and forestry, and another 24 percent in non-industrial pursuits (probably related to agriculture), while 27 percent worked in industry and 10 percent in the building trades.[26] In spite of such changes, the average income of Carpatho-Rusyns, while it improved beyond what it was before, stood in 1968 at almost two-fifths below the all-Czechoslovak average.[27] Realization of these differences forced many young people with ever-rising economic expectations to emigrate permanently, whether to nearby Slovak cities or farther westward to the northern industrial region of Moravia, where wages were much higher. Such out-migration, which continued unabated from the 1950s, resulted in labor shortages on farms and zero, or below-zero, population growth rate in many Carpatho-Rusyn villages throughout the Prešov Region.

By the 1980s, the future of Carpatho-Rusyns as a distinct national minority in Czechoslovakia looked bleak. This was the result of the Communist government's official nationality policy of ukrainianization, of socioeconomic changes, and of assimilation with Slovaks. Despite the administrative and often intolerant aspects of government policies, too much emphasis should not be placed on the state-imposed change in nationality orientation as the exclusive explanatory factor in the decline in the number of people willing to identify as Rusyns or as Ukrainians. Much of the explanation also lies in the social mobility that accompanied the improved economic status of the group during the last four decades of Communist rule. In effect, economic backwardness and geographic isolation, which traditionally characterized Carpatho-Rusyn social space, were no longer factors that could, as in the past, "protect" the language and identity of Carpatho-Rusyns from what turned out to be the indirect cost of modernization—national assimilation.

Since the 1950s, all Prešov Region villages, even remote mountainous ones, were connected with daily bus routes to lowland Slovak cities. This made commuting for shopping, work, and, eventually, permanent settlement quite easy and inexpensive. Gradually, most Carpatho-Rusyn villages became little more than havens for older people. The young rarely stayed, so that village schools, regardless of language of instruction, became unnecessary. Many were closed for lack of pupils, and in those that remained, by 1988 there were only 22 schools with fewer than 1,500 students in which Ukrainian was the language of instruction.[28] In effect, Carpatho-Rusyn villages in the Prešov Region were literally dying out or, in several instances, destroyed in order to make way for more "productive use" such as reservoirs.

For those Carpatho-Rusyns who found work in the cities farther south, the social setting they encountered was purely Slovak. The linguistic and cultural environment that promoted national assimilation was encouraged further by the advent of television, whose broadcasts were exclusively in Slovak or Czech. Moreover, national assimilation was enhanced by several other factors: (1) by the similarity of the Slavic dialects spoken by Carpatho-Rusyns and neighboring East Slovaks; (2) by the similarity in religion among many East Slovaks who, like Carpatho-Rusyns, were Greek Catholic; and (3) by the continuance of a traditional pattern of intermarriage in which more often than not Slovak became the dominant medium in ethnically mixed households. Thus, while Communist Czechoslovakia's policy of industrialization in eastern Slovakia brought concrete improvements in living standards throughout the Prešov Region, these achievements, in turn, contributed to undermining the status of Carpatho-Rusyns through what became a "natural" trend toward social mobility and slovakization. This seemed to be the rather bleak future for the Carpatho-Rusyns of Slovakia when, suddenly, the year 1989 dawned on central and eastern Europe.

The Lemko Region and Lemko Rusyns in Communist Poland, 1945–1989

The Lemkos are unique among all of Europe's Carpatho-Rusyns in that they hold the dubious and unenviable distinction of having been removed from their homes and settled permanently elsewhere. In essence, within a few years after World War II came to an end, the traditional Lemko Region—that is, lands where for centuries the dominant population and culture was Carpatho-Rusyn—ceased to exist. The reasons for this state of affairs had to do with international factors and, in particular, the policies of the state in which Lemko Rusyns once again found themselves—Poland.

Poland reconstituted and reconstructed

As discussed above (Chapter 21), the immediate post-World War II years were characterized by a belief among leaders in many European states, including the Allied Powers, that population exchange was a legitimate and effective way to eliminate the national minority problem that was considered a major cause of the recent world conflict. No country in Europe experienced the degree of demographic transformation as did Poland. Virtually all of pre-war Poland's 2.7 million Jewish inhabitants were killed in the Holocaust, as were a comparable number of ethnic Poles in the course of World War II. Subsequently, in postwar Poland about 3.2 million Germans were by 1947 expelled from the Recovered Lands in the west and north, while 1.7 million Poles arrived from Soviet territory in return for over half a million Ukrainians, Belarusans, and Lithuanians, who were resettled eastward.[1] Despite these massive shifts in population, which were basically completed by 1947, postwar Poland still included within its borders several national minorities. Their percentage of the total population, however, was very small, at most 2 to 3 percent.[2]

Aside from boundary changes and population transfers, postwar Poland had a new political system. As early as July 1944, a Communist-dominated Polish provisional government was formed with the backing of the Soviet Union. The provisional government, initially based in the eastern Polish town of Lublin, was ready to take control of the country as soon as the Soviet

Army drove the German forces west of the Oder-Niesse line, which finally occurred in mid-April of 1945. The new Communist-ruled state was eventually (1952) named the Polish People's Republic. Following the model of the Soviet Union, Communist Poland nationalized all privately owned enterprises, introduced a command economy, and in part collectivized agriculture. The policies of the centralized government were determined by the Polish United Worker's party, often in close collaboration with Soviet advisors.

The deportation of the Lemkos: Phase two

Among the relatively small number of inhabitants of non-Polish nationality left in the country after the postwar population transfers were Lemko Rusyns. We have already seen (Chapter 21) how in "Phase one" between 1944 and 1946, on the basis of a Polish-Soviet agreement, about two-thirds of the Lemko Rusyns (about 80,000 persons) were resettled eastward to Soviet Ukraine. Nonetheless, there remained an estimated 25,000 to 35,000 still living in their ancestral villages located mostly in the western areas of the Lemko Region.

On the one hand, Communist Poland formally adopted the Soviet principle of non-discrimination and support for the cultural aspirations of national minorities. And, also following the Soviet model, all Carpatho-Rusyns—and that included Lemkos—were considered part of the Ukrainian nationality. On the other hand, Communist Poland's policy makers considered Ukrainians, like Germans, to be among the wartime enemy peoples. In any case, they favored the goal of transforming Poland into an ethnically homogenous state inhabited primarily, if not exclusively, by Poles. How, then, to achieve what were in essence contradictory goals: tolerance for national minorities and efforts at creating Polish ethnic homogeneity?

In the case of the remaining Lemkos, a solution seemed to present itself in the form of the UPA, or Ukrainian Insurgent Army. The remaining forces of the anti-Soviet and anti-Communist UPA had by 1945 found refuge in the Carpathian Mountains, mostly in the eastern areas of the Lemko Region. The UPA tried to undermine the establishment of Poland's Communist regime in the region, and in that regard they hoped to stop the resettlement of Ukrainians and Lemkos to Soviet Ukraine. Polish security forces fought several skirmishes against UPA units, but were unable to drive them out of the region until early 1947, when they were assisted in their efforts by Soviet and Czechoslovak Army units. The UPA was finally removed from southeastern Poland. Some units fled across Czechoslovakia to the western zones of Germany; others moved eastward into Soviet Ukraine. There they continued to engage Soviet security forces until the early 1950s, when the last remaining fighters were either shot or arrested and sent to the Soviet Gulag.

The concerted military efforts against the UPA provided the Polish authorities with a convenient excuse to rid the southeastern corner of the country of its remaining Lemko and Ukrainian inhabitants. No fewer than

20,000 Polish army troops were sent to the region to carry out the so-called Vistula Operation (*Akcja Wisła*). Within just over three months (28 April to 12 August 1947), an estimated 155,000 people, of whom about 35,000 were Lemkos,[3] were forcibly evacuated from their homes (often with a few hours' notice) and resettled mostly in the southwestern (Lower Silesia) and west-central (Lubuskie) areas of postwar Poland that had only recently been "recovered" from Germany. Even though over 7,300 managed to avoid the forced deportation, the Vistula Operation, remembered as the Lemko "Road to Calvary," effectively put an end to the centuries-old Rus' character of the Lemko Region.[4]

As a result of the earlier "voluntary" resettlement eastward to Soviet Ukraine and now the forced deportation of 1947, no less than 47 Lemko villages were totally bereft of inhabitants and ceased to exist.[5] Houses and churches were left to decay, and within a few years they crumbled and were overrun by vegetation and trees. The remaining 125 or so other Lemko villages were resettled by Poles (and even some Gorale mountain folk) from nearby areas in southeastern Poland. Whatever their origin, these newcomers had no sense of pride or respect for the Lemko villages they were given. They chose the best houses and land, leaving the rest to decay. Moreover, during the long winters it was easier to gather firewood by tearing down a nearby house, barn, or church than by felling trees in the forest. Thus, by the early 1950s, the material and cultural vestiges of the Rus' past in the Lemko Region were (with the exception of cemeteries) largely obliterated.

Most Lemkos were traumatized by the deportation process. Driven by gunpoint from their homes, the deportees were forced to wait several weeks before arriving in their new homes, and during that time hundreds of deportees (including Lemkos) were removed from the transports and arrested. Nearly 1,200 Lemkos were interned at Jaworzno, part of former Nazi Germany's Auschwitz concentration camp complex, where several died.[6] When the deportees finally reached their destinations in Lower Silesia and Pomerania, the authorities settled them in small towns and villages, making sure that Lemkos—as well as Ukrainians—would not comprise more than 10 percent of the population in any given locality. For example, the 168 families (690 persons) from the Lemko Region village of Florynka were dispersed to no less than 42 different localities in western Poland. In Lower Silesia, by 1948 the largest concentrations of Lemkos were in three towns just west of Wrocław: Wołów (2,545), Lubin (2,427), and Legnica (2,068)[7] (see Map 31).

Some Lemkos, however, refused to live "abroad" (*na chuzhyni*)—the abroad here meaning western and northern Poland. Some even tried to return to their Carpathian homeland, although until the mid-1950s they were almost always turned back. One outstanding exception was the world-renowned naïve painter Nykyfor (Epifanii Drovniak). After deportation in 1947, he returned home, but was again deported. He returned twice more until finally allowed to remain in his native town, the popular resort of Krynica-Zdrój.

Beginning in the 1950s, an increasing number of individuals finally managed to gain official permission from government authorities to return to their native villages. They could not regain, however, their old homes—now occupied by new Polish owners—and were forced to build new ones, often on the outskirts of the village. Despite such difficulties, by the late 1990s an estimated 6,000 (perhaps 10,000) Lemko families managed to return to their Carpathian homeland.[8] This, of course, was only a fraction of the 140,000 individuals that had lived in the Lemko Region on the eve of World War II.

Greek Catholic and Orthodox Lemkos

Like the Soviet Union and Czechoslovakia, Communist Poland also had to deal with the Greek Catholic Church. Its task was made much easier than in the other countries, because of the unique conditions related to the depopulation of the Lemko Region. Poland's Communist authorities accepted the Soviet view that after the L'viv Church Council (Sobor) of 1946 the Greek Catholic Church legally ceased to exist in historic Galicia, which included lands in post-1945 Poland that had been under the jurisdiction of the Eparchy of Przemyśl and since 1934 part of the Lemko Apostolic Administration. Based on such a premise, the Polish government issued decrees which first nationalized Greek Catholic Church property (1947) and then legitimized the seizure (1949) on the grounds that it belonged to "juridical persons" whose "existence and activities lost their purpose as a result of the resettlement of their members to the Soviet Union."[9] As a result of these decrees, the Greek Catholic Church in Poland was "delegalized."

Consequently, after 1947, the Lemko Greek Catholic Apostolic Administration (with its 129 parishes and about 130,000 faithful as of 1943) ceased to exist.[10] Church property in the depopulated Lemko-Rusyn villages was left to decay and eventually disappear. In those Lemko villages resettled by Poles, former Greek Catholic churches were often appropriated by the Roman Catholic Church, in a few instances given to the Orthodox Church or, in the case of wooden ones, simply abandoned until torn down by local residents who used what remained of the structures for firewood.

Lemkos living in western Poland were not about to give up their religion. The Orthodox faced little problem, since the Polish Autocephalous Orthodox Church remained a legal religious body and set up new parishes in Lower Silesia and Pomerania where there were large concentrations of Lemkos and Ukrainians. Then, in 1983, a new Orthodox Eparchy of Przemyśl-Nowy-Sącz, with its seat in Sanok, was created to administer parishes (33) serving primarily those Orthodox Lemkos who managed to return to their Carpathian homeland.

The situation for Greek Catholics was more complex. While the church as an entity or corporate body remained "de-legalized," individuals were allowed to form parishes, but only if they were attached to existing Roman Catholic ones. By the late 1980s, about 70 parishes were formed, mostly in Lower Silesia and Pomerania, as well as a few in the Lemko Region.[11] All were under the jurisdiction of Poland's Roman Catholic Church and were administered in conjunction with a special delegate from the Vatican responsible for Catholics of the Eastern rite. Since the majority of Poland's Greek Catholics were ethnically Ukrainian, it was that language which was gradually introduced into the liturgy, a transition that was basically completed by the 1980s.

Lemkos as Ukrainians

The Ukrainian factor had a particularly negative impact with regard to the relationship of Lemkos to the larger Polish society. Even though the vast majority of Lemkos (especially those who remained in the western Lemko Region after the first resettlements of 1945–1946) neither provided assistance nor were even near UPA units, they were lumped together with Ukrainians in the minds of Poles among whom they lived. In this context it is important to note that Poland had a long history of military conflict with the Zaporozhian Cossacks of Ukraine that dated from the sixteenth century. Ongoing tensions and mutual hatred between the two peoples continued into the twentieth century during the Polish-Ukrainian war for control of eastern Galicia after World War I and the underground war between Polish and Ukrainian partisans that began in the summer of 1943 and continued until the closing months of World War II. This most recent conflict, which was still fresh in the minds of many people in postwar Poland, was particularly brutal toward the civilian population, resulting in the death of an estimated 50,000 Poles (and perhaps another 10,000 Ukrainians) in the region of Volhynia alone.[12] After eastern Galicia and Volhynia were annexed to the Soviet Union, many Poles who resettled to postwar Poland from those regions lost family members in the most recent conflict and, as a result, they harbored strong antipathy toward Ukrainians in general.

LEMKO FEAR AND ANXIETY

The need for Lemkos in postwar Communist Poland to distance themselves from anything associated with the East in order to accommodate and, hopefully, lose oneself in the "Polish" West was best expressed by Iaroslav Horoshchak, a Lemko-Rusyn cultural activist who was born and raised in western Poland where his parents were forced to resettle in 1947. Horoshchak released to the public a revealing memoir-like account (under the pseudonym Iaroslav Hunka), in which he recalled what it was like growing up as a youth in Communist Poland. The following are excerpts from his 1985 brochure published in Polish under the title, *Łemkowie-dzisiaj* (The Lemkos Today).

I do not remember at all when I learned that I was a Lemko.

· · · · ·

For a very long time I knew nothing about ourselves. At home they said that we were Lemkos simply in the ethnic sense, yet at the same time there prevailed a strange sort of attraction to Rus' (as a whole), which automatically spread to us, the children. Father sometimes said that he used to give his nationality as Rusyn.

· · · · ·

Those Lemkos who are scattered throughout Poland are slowly succumbing to assimilation (as it is so nicely called, isn't it?).

· · · · ·

It is sad to look at those Lemkos who choose the "undignified but convenient" way out. They are afraid of their own shadows! They change their first and last names (like one man who had changed his name twice, to Bazyli and Wacław, although Poles still called him Vasyl'). They no longer speak Lemko even at home. They are also teaching their children only Polish, for which, however, they achieve the exact opposite of what they wish. In the end, Poles despise them instead of respecting them (always mindful of their own several-million-strong Polish diaspora abroad which is expected to—and does—preserve its national identity within a foreign environment). At the same time, fellow Lemkos look down with pity on those who are so desperately trying to become Polish. Couples who are in such mixed Polish-Lemko marriages are isolated from both groups of "mixed people," who seem to think they are "being assimilated." Yet, at times, when the Lemko speech of their parents is heard, it grates so unpleasantly on their ears. It could happen at a baptism party, where hearing a Lemko song will gnaw at one's insides. And then, as the pain of guilt from trying to run from one's own culture arises, one tries to soothe own's soul by drowning in alcohol.

SOURCE: Jarosław Hunka, *Łemkowie—dzisiaj,* "For Internal Use of the Student Circle of Beskyd Mountain Tourist Guides" (Warsaw, 1985), pp. 2 and 11.

For most Poles, the Lemkos that they encountered in the western Recovered Lands of "their" postwar country were simply a regional variant of the hated Ukrainians. It is for these reasons that many Lemko parents refused to send their children to the few Ukrainian-language minority schools that were eventually opened by the Polish government. The response of young Lemkos, in particular, was to conceal their ethnic identities, to avoid as much as possible any association with the East, to speak Polish, and, if possible, to inter-marry with Poles. In effect, they wanted to become Poles.

The generally oppressive atmosphere in Communist Poland began to change somewhat after 1956. A year later, a government-sponsored organization was created, the Ukrainian Civic and Cultural Society/Ukraïns'ke sotsio-kul'turne tovarystvo (USKT). From its base in Warsaw and branches throughout the country, the society's main goal was to promote Ukrainian culture and language, which it did through the support of amateur folk ensembles, lectures, and popular publications, including the weekly Ukrainian-language newspaper, *Nashe slovo*. All these activities were funded by the Polish government, which considered the Civic and Cultural Society as the "official" representative of the Ukrainian national minority (and that included the Lemkos) and as the only legitimate spokesperson for the group's interests.

In fact, several Lemkos were initially among the leading activists in the Ukrainian Civic and Cultural Society, whose newspaper *Nashe slovo* contained a special section called the "Lemko Word," later the "Lemko Page" (*Lemkivska storinka*), written in the Lemko-Rusyn vernacular. There were also efforts to create a separate Lemko civic organization, but these were not successful because, as Communist Poland's chief party ideologist (Aleksander Sław) stated: "Every citizen ... has the right to declare his national preference; he must, however, choose only from those identities recognized as 'nationalities.' And in this regard one must point out that there is no Lemko nationality."[13] At most, the authorities permitted the creation in 1959 of a Section for the Development of Lemko Culture within the framework of the Ukrainian Civic and Cultural Society. Headed by Mykhal Donskii (a decorated World War II Polish partisan leader) and Pavel Stefanovskii, the Lemko Section promoted cultural activity directed specifically at Lemko communities in western Poland. When, in 1965, these two activists requested once again government approval for the creation of a distinct Lemko organization, they were accused of "separatist tendencies," they were dismissed from the Lemko Section, and then replaced by other Lemko activists willing to accept the official Ukrainian orientation.

In line with Polish governmental policy, there appeared a number of Lemko cultural activists who, whether out of conviction or political necessity, identified as Ukrainians. Others, however, preferred to avoid altogether any discussion of the nationality question. Such a carefully neutral position was adopted by the Lemkovyna Song and Dance Ensemble, founded in 1969 under the artistic direction of Iaroslav Trokhanovskii. Although it functioned only on a sporadic basis in the 1970s and 1980s, the ensemble's concerts proved to be extremely popular and helped to boost pride and a greater respect toward the ancestral Carpathian culture among the younger generation of diasporan Lemkos born or raised in a Polish environment.

An entirely new form of cultural awakening was the Vatra (Bonfire) phenomenon. This was a loosely organized gathering of young Lemko enthusiasts with no government support—and surprisingly no intervention by the authorities—who met over a weekend each summer to hear concerts, lectures, and other entertaining activities, all with the underlying purpose of teaching people about Lemko-Rusyn culture and history. The relaxed atmosphere was not unlike that at the Woodstock-style rock festivals happening a decade before in America, although instead of drugs and sex to enhance the music, Lemkos and their Polish sympathizers got high on discovering their ancestral culture to the accompaniment of late-night drinking and folk-singing bouts. The first of the Vatras was held in 1983 on a hillside between two mountain villages in the heart of the Lemko Region. By the second half of the 1980s, what became an annual event was drawing anywhere between 4,000 and 8,000 participants. This was a true grassroots movement whose participants understood and welcomed the idea that Lemko-Rusyn culture and language were both a source of individual pride as well as something worthy of preservation for future generations.

Carpatho-Rusyn diasporas old and new, 1945–1989

The border changes and population exchanges that characterized the immediate post-World War II years created new Carpatho-Rusyn diasporas, while
at the same time the political transformation in Soviet-dominated central
Europe altered the status of the older diasporas. Among these new and older
diasporas were Carpatho-Rusyns living in six countries: Ukraine (Galicia
and Volhynia), Poland (Silesia, Lubuskie, and Pomerania), Czechoslovakia
(Bohemia and Moravia), Romania (the Banat and Maramureş), Yugoslavia
(the Vojvodina and Srem), and the United States. The new Carpatho-Rusyn
communities found in western Ukraine and western Poland came into being
as a result of events connected with the closing months of World War II. This,
as we have seen, was the result of two phases of deportation between 1944
and 1947 of the entire Lemko-Rusyn population from its Carpathian homeland and its transformation into two diasporas: one in Soviet Ukraine, the
other in western Poland (see Chapters 21 and 24).

Soviet Ukraine (Galicia and Volhynia)

The first and larger of these two Lemko-Rusyn diasporas was that in western Ukraine, which initially consisted of 80,000 or so Lemkos resettled over
a two-year period (October 1944 and September 1946). They were settled in
various parts of eastern and southern Ukraine (Luhans'k, Donets'k, Kherson
oblasts, among others), although the largest numbers went initially or were
subsequently resettled in villages and small towns in the eastern half of the
historic province of Galicia just north of the Carpathians; that is, in Soviet
Ukraine's L'viv, Ternopil', and Ivano-Frankivs'k oblasts.

Much is known about the Lemkos who managed to remain in Poland,
and in particular about the negative attitudes of Poles toward them after
resettlement in the western regions of that country. By contrast, and for
the longest time, little was known about the postwar fate of the Lemkos in
Soviet Ukraine. As a result of memoiristic accounts that have recently been
made public, it turns out that the reception accorded Lemko newcomers on
the part of the local Ukrainians of Galicia was not much better. Despite the

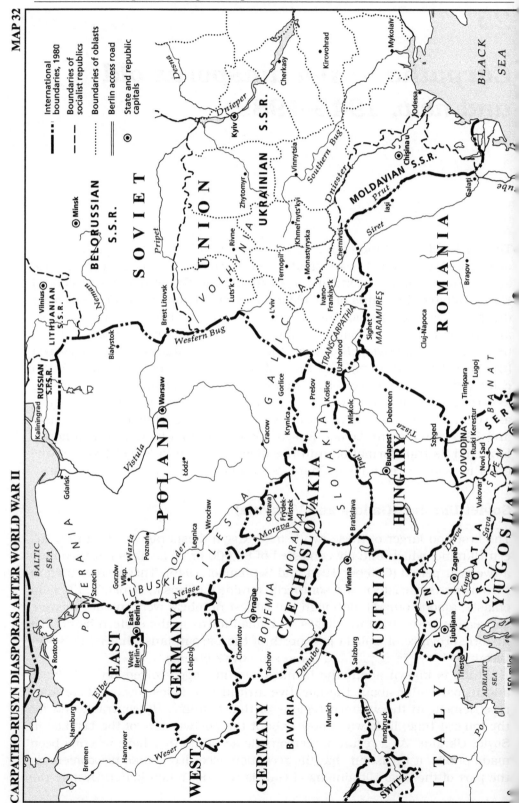

MAP 32

CARPATHO-RUSYN DIASPORAS AFTER WORLD WAR II

International boundaries, 1980

Boundaries of socialist republics

Boundaries of oblasts

Berlin access road

⊙ State and republic capitals

long-standing rhetorical argument that Lemkos are an ethnographic branch and integral part of the Ukrainian nationality, it was not uncommon for the Ukrainians in postwar East Galicia to denigrate Lemko traditions and, in particular, their vernacular speech. If these people are really Ukrainians, why are they not like us? Such Galician-Ukrainian attitudes were summed up by the commonly heard phrase: "We don't need these Lemko strange intruders" (*Lemko-zaid nam ne treba*).[1]

It took at least two decades for the Lemkos to adapt to the Soviet environment and to begin to overcome the stigma attached to them by their neighbors. Sometime in the 1970s, a few individuals initiated activities whose goal was to restore a sense of pride toward Lemko culture and to preserve some elements of the ancestral heritage for their offspring who were born and acculturated in Soviet Ukraine. Although the distances were not all that great (Ternopil' is about 340 kilometers from Krynica, in the heart of the Lemko Region), the Lemkos of Ukraine were totally cut off from their ancestral homeland. Because of stringent Soviet border controls (applicable against "fraternal" Communist countries like Poland), they were not even permitted to visit the Carpathian villages where they themselves or their parents were born.

As part of the effort toward cultural renewal, folk music was the first aspect of traditional culture that was promoted in Ukraine. This became possible following the creation of the Lemkovyna Choir in 1969 in the village of Rudne near L'viv and of the remarkably successful concert and recording career of the Baiko Sisters, whose repertoire since as early as 1953 was comprised primarily of Lemko folk songs. Also, a small number of Lemko intellectuals working in L'viv began to publish popular and scholarly studies about their people (Ivan Krasovs'kyi, Petro Kohut) and to create artistic works, in particular wood sculptures (Vasyl' and Volodymyr Odrekhivs'kyi, Andrii Sukhors'kyi), based on Lemko themes. In keeping with official Soviet nationality policy, all these activities were carried out with the understanding that Lemkos were a regional group of Ukrainians.

A smaller and virtually unknown post-World War II Carpatho-Rusyn diaspora in Ukraine were the *optanty*. These were the 12,000 or so Carpatho-Rusyns from the Prešov Region, who in 1947 voluntarily opted to be resettled in the Volhynia region (around Rivne) in the northwestern corner of Soviet Ukraine (see Chapter 24). From the very outset, their experience was wrought with difficulties. The negative reception they encountered in Volhynia on the part of the Soviet authorities and the local Ukrainian population, not to mention the wartime devastation in that part of Ukraine which itself was barely recovering from a famine in 1946–47, were factors that prompted most of the Prešov Region newcomers in Soviet Ukraine to demand their immediate return to Slovakia. Petitions sent to the Soviet and Czechoslovak authorities were, however, rejected out of hand, and those individuals who organized attempts to return home were branded "bourgeois nationalists" and/or "traitors." Several of the "ring leaders" were arrested by the Soviet secret police and deported to forced labor camps in the Gulag. In the 1960s, a few of the discontented "Volhynian" Rusyns were allowed to settle in Soviet Transcarpathia, which was at least near Slovakia. Nevertheless, by 1989 there were still about 8,000 of the *optanty* (settlers) living in Volhynia.

It is interesting to note that the Prešov Region diaspora in Soviet Ukraine never identified as Ukrainian. In fact, most individuals adamantly argued that they were of Slovak nationality, which, they assumed, would justify their right to return to Slovakia. Beginning in the mid-1960s, a small but steady number of *optanty* were allowed to return to Czechoslovakia. Once again, these *re-optanty* (that is, those who "opted a second time") were faced with difficulties, this time when they attempted to return to their native villages in the Prešov Region, where their former neighbors expressed dissatisfaction with these unexpected "immigrants from Russia" in their midst. As a result, most of the *re-optanty* moved to towns and cities in eastern Slovakia, where they largely assimilated into Slovak society. Among the most famous of the *re-optanty* was the then one-year-old child who grew up to become the renowned National Hockey League star player, Peter Bondra. Other *re-optanty*, who as youngsters in Ukraine attended Ukrainian- or Russian-language schools, found positions in various cultural institutions in the Prešov Region, especially in the Ukrainian National Theater, the Dukla Ukrainian Folk Ensemble, the Cultural Union of Ukrainian Workers—all based in Prešov—and the Museum of Ukrainian Culture in Svidník.

Czechoslovakia (Bohemia and Moravia)

Three distinct Carpatho-Rusyn diasporas came into being after World War II in the western regions of Czechoslovakia (present-day Czech Republic). The first of these was formed as a result of the general policies of the Czechoslovak government. Both before and after the Communists came to power in 1948, that government was anxious to repopulate the peripheral areas of Bohemia and Moravia; that is, the so-called Sudetenland from which nearly three million Germans were expelled in 1946–1947. Carpatho-Rusyns from the Prešov Region were among those welcomed to settle, for example, in the industrial regions of northern Moravia, more precisely the Czechoslovak part of Silesia, where they found employment in the large-scale industrial enterprises located in towns like Ostrava and Frýdek-Místek. Smaller numbers found similar factory work in the towns of northern and far eastern Bohemia.

Another group of Carpatho-Rusyns in the western regions of Czechoslovakia were returnees from post-World War II Communist Romania. Back in the nineteenth century, Carpatho-Rusyns from the Prešov Region (mostly from the villages of Kamienka and Jarabina in Spish county) and from Subcarpathian Rus' (Maramorosh county) had moved to the lowlands of the southern Hungarian Kingdom (see Map 19). One of those areas was the eastern Banat, which after World War I was annexed to Romania. After World War II, in what was by then Communist-ruled Romania, these Banat Carpatho-Rusyns, who had nearly a century before left the Prešov Region (which in the interim had become part of Czechoslovakia), were given the opportunity "to return home." Instead of settling in their ancestral villages in the Prešov Region, the receiving authorities assigned them to former German-inhabited areas in the western regions of Czechoslovakia. Of the approximately 550 Banat Carpatho-Rusyns who arrived between 1947 and 1949—and who by that time identified themselves as Slovaks of the Greek Catholic faith—the majority (87 families) were settled in the town of Chomutov in northern Bohemia, the remainder (21 families) in southern Moravia along Czechoslovakia's border with Austria.[2]

Yet another group of Carpatho-Rusyns from Romania were nearly 500 persons from the hamlet of Văgaş and village of Tarna Mare (Rusyn: Ternavka) in former Ugocha county near the post-1945 border with Soviet Ukraine.[3] This group was resettled in several small villages of far western Bohemia near the town of Tachov along Czechoslovakia's border with West Germany.

The post-World War II Carpatho-Rusyn diaspora in western Czechoslovakia, whether the newcomers from the Prešov Region or resettlers from Romania, did not establish any organizations. Other than their adherence to the Greek Catholic Church, they did not function as a community during the period of Communist rule. Consequently, most adapted to their Czech surroundings, and after intermarriage they and their offspring assimilated fully to Czech culture and identity.

Romania (the Banat and Maramureş Regions)

In Romania, there were still two territorially distinct communities of Carpatho-Rusyns. Not all who lived in the Banat region (especially those who originally came from Maramorosh county, now in Soviet Transcarpathia) could return to their ancestral homeland. Consequently, there were by the 1970s still about 10,000 living in a few dozen communities throughout the Banat, whether in villages where they formed a significant proportion of the inhabitants (Cireşu/Cheresne, Copăcele, Cornuţel/Kornutsel, Dragomireşti, Zorile, among others) or in the region's main towns of Lugoj (especially the Pădureni suburb) and Timişoara (see Map 34).

There was an even larger group of Carpatho-Rusyns in post-World War II Romania living in several villages of the Maramureş Region. Technically, the Maramureş Rusyns were not a diaspora, since they had lived for centuries in lands—along the upper Tisza River and its tributaries, the Vişeu (Rusyn: Vyshova) and Ruscova (Rus'kova) Rivers—that were territorially contiguous with the rest of Carpathian Rus'.

The Maramureş Region, which was annexed to Hungary in 1940, was returned to Romania at the close of World War II. The restored government of Romania was dominated by the Communists, so that the country, like its immediate neighbors, became a political satellite of the Soviet Union. Since Romania's Communist authorities also adopted Soviet guidelines with regard to the nationality question, Carpatho-Rusyns were classified as a branch of the Ukrainian nationality and treated as an integral part of the larger

Ukrainian national minority. Consequently, Sighet (Romanian: Sighetul Marmaţiei), which remained the cultural and administrative center of the Maramureş Region, became home to a Ukrainian-language secondary school (*lycée*) to which children who completed elementary schools in the area's surrounding Carpatho-Rusyn villages were sent. The approximately 30,000 inhabitants (1966) in 17 rural villages of the Maramureş Region continued to speak their native Rusyn vernacular, although they were classified by the authorities and for the most part considered themselves Ukrainians.[4]

Also, as in the neighboring Soviet Union, Communist Romania abolished the Greek Catholic Church in 1949, imprisoning priests and bishops who refused to break with Rome and join the Orthodox Church. Since most of the Carpatho-Rusyns in the Maramureş Region as well as in the Banat were Greek Catholic, they and their parishes after 1949 were forcibly converted to Orthodoxy.

Yugoslavia (Vojvodina and Srem)

The one major exception among all Carpatho-Rusyns in post-World War II Europe was the community in the historic Vojvodina (Bachka) and Srem regions of Yugoslavia. Like Czechoslovakia and Poland, Yugoslavia was reconstituted as a state after World War II, and like those two states it came under the rule of the Communists. After 1948, however, Communist Yugoslavia broke with the Soviet Union and eventually maintained political neutrality between the Soviet-dominated East and the free-market capitalist West. On the other hand, Yugoslavia was the only Communist-ruled country in central Europe that adopted the Soviet administrative model; that is, a union of national republics and autonomous regions.

This decentralized structure—albeit under the careful control of the Communist party headed by the country's wartime hero Marshall Josef Broz Tito—was to have a positive impact on the country's various peoples, including the Rusyns/Rusnaks of the Vojvodina and Srem. Communist Yugoslavia was a federation divided into six national republics. The largest of these republics, Serbia, created within its borders in 1946 two autonomous regions, Vojvodina and Kosovo. Most of the towns and villages where the Bachka and Srem Rusyns/Rusnaks lived (Ruski Kerestur, Kucura, Djurdevo, Šid) were in the Vojvodina and therefore within the Serbian republic. A few Srem villages (Petrovci, Mikluševci) near the city of Vukovar were within the Croatian republic (see Maps 32 and 34).

Since Tito-led Communist Yugoslavia was not a political satellite of the Soviet Union, it did not feel obliged to adopt Soviet guidelines, such as those regarding nationality and religious matters. Therefore, the Vojvodinian-Srem Rusyns/Rusnaks were not classified as Ukrainians and the Greek Catholic Church was not abolished. This meant that the majority of Yugoslavia's Rusyns/Rusnaks remained Greek Catholics whose parishes were within the jurisdiction of the Eparchy of Križevci with its seat in Croatia's capital of Zagreb.

As a result of the generally tolerant attitude of the Yugoslav government toward the country's various peoples, Vojvodinian Rusyn culture flourished. In the village of Ruski Kerestur, the traditional center with the largest concentration of Rusyns/Rusnaks (5,600 in 1948), a publishing and print shop, a weekly newspaper (*Ruske slovo*), and a senior high school (*gymnasium*) were all established within the first year after the end of the war. During the next decade, a literary and cultural journal (*Shvetlosts*, 1952–present), a children's magazine (*Zahradka*, 1947–present), and an annual almanac (*Narodni kalendar*, 1957–present) began to appear as well as regular radio broadcasts (1949–present). All of these activities were carried out in the Vojvodinian Rusyn language.

By the 1960s, Novi Sad, the provincial capital of the autonomous Vojvodina region, became the base for most Rusyn cultural activity, including an Institute for Publishing Textbooks (est. 1965), a media company (Ruske Slovo Publishers, est. 1968), a Rusyn-language program on state television (est. 1975), and a lectureship (est. 1973) at the University of Novi Sad. A decade later, in 1981, the lectureship was transformed into a *katedra*, that is, a full-fledged Department of Rusyn Language and Literature, which at the time was the only university-level institution in the world devoted to instruction and research on Carpatho-Rusyn topics and the training of teachers to staff the region's Rusyn-language schools. The department's teaching associates produced an updated literary standard for Vojvodinian Rusyn (by Mikola Kochish in the 1970s) and they published a wide range of dictionaries and textbooks for use in schools and cultural institutions. The smaller community in Croatia had its own organization based in Vukovar, the Union of Rusyns and Ukrainians, which from the early 1970s published a popular educational and public affairs magazine (*Nova dumka*, 1971–present).

Despite the enormous growth in cultural and educational activity—all carried out in the Vojvodinian Rusyn language—many of the region's intellectual leaders were inclined toward the Ukrainian national orientation. In other words, they believed—following the tradition of the "father of Vojvodinian Rusyn literature" Havriïl Kostel'nik—that Yugoslavia's Rusyns/Rusnaks comprise the farthest western branch of the Ukrainian nationality. At the same time, whether out of conviction or practical necessary, they did not try to introduce literary Ukrainian, but rather enhanced the Vojvodinian Rusyn vernacular to the status of a sociologically complete language and a respectable medium to express the group's cultural and educational aspirations.

The Ukrainian orientation was indirectly supported by Communist Yugoslavia. This was the result of that country's particular approach to its nationality question. Yugoslavia's policy makers devised—somewhat on the Soviet model—a three-tier hierarchy to categorize its peoples. The highest level comprised "nations" (Serbs, Croats, etc.), who had the right to their own republics. Then came "nationalities," which were accorded a wide range of cultural and civic support even though they did not live in their own "mother country" (*matična zem*), such as Croats in Serbia or Serbs in Croatia. Finally, there were ethnic groups without a "mother country" (Bunjevač, Gypsies, etc.), who were classified as "national minorities" with only a limited degree of governmental support for cultural activity.

In 1974, when the autonomous status of the Vojvodina was substantially increased (in many ways the region became almost the equivalent of a national republic), the Rusyns/Rusnaks were given the possibility to become a nationality instead of a national minority. To do so, however, they needed a "mother country." The group's leading intellectuals suggested Ukraine be the mother country. The suggestion was accepted, and having fulfilled the necessary "theoretical" criteria, the Rusyns/Rusnaks (Ruthenians in official Yugoslav publications) became one of the five nationalities of the Vojvodinian autonomous region. Vojvodinian Rusyn was designated one of the official languages of the Vojvodina (into which all laws and government publications had to be translated); increased funding was given to the Rusyn nationality for its cultural and educational affairs; and the Vojvodinian Rusyn language appeared on all public signs on institutions of the autonomous government.

The economic status of the Vojvodinian Rusyn population, numbering 19,300 (as opposed to 5,000 Ukrainians) in 1981, also improved during Communist Yugoslav rule.[5] A major food-processing plant helped to provide full employment to the inhabitants of Ruski Kerestur and surrounding areas. And for those Rusyns who wished to increase their incomes, they were allowed to migrate as seasonal laborers to western European countries, in particular West Germany. Yugoslavia's Communist authorities not only permitted its citizens to work abroad—something unimaginable for people in the Soviet Union and all its satellite countries—they even encouraged the phenomenon. The government's reasoning was simple: the "guest workers" (as they were known in West Germany) sent back to their families "hard currency" in the form of hundreds of thousands of German marks which helped Yugoslavia's own economy.

The United States

Numerically, the largest diaspora after 1945 continued to be, as before, that of Carpatho-Rusyns living in North America, particularly in the United States. The group's many secular organizations and differing Eastern-rite church jurisdictions—in many cases dating back to the pre-World War I era—continued to function. They steadily lost their national character, however. The reasons for this change had to do with developments in the European homeland as well as a new attitude among secular and religious organizations toward the national identity of their Rusyn-American membership.

Still during World War II, Rusyn Americans expressed concern with the fate of their brethren in the European homeland. At least for a while that concern continued, so that in 1945 leaders in the Greek Catholic Union mutual-benefit society convened at their headquarters in Munhall, Pennsylvania, a Carpatho-Russian Congress. The congress drafted a petition which it submitted to the United States government and to the newly founded United Nations, protesting against the annexation of Subcarpathian Rus' to the Soviet Union and its implementation of ukrainianization. It turned out that the Munhall petition, as well as a few subsequent protests (1951 and 1964) on the part of Rusyn-American organizations, had no real impact on developments in the European homeland, even though they did coincide with American foreign policy, which during the "Cold War" was increasingly critical of Communist rule and Soviet expansionism.

It was also during the Cold War years that the tradition of close contact between Rusyn Americans and their family and friends in Carpathian Rus', whether through letters or personal visits, virtually came to a halt after the Soviet Union and its Communist satellite countries put a stop to travel and even postal contact of its citizens with the "capitalist West." In effect, Rusyn-American organizations no longer had any political role to play, and the community as a whole was cut off from the European homeland. Furthermore, during the Cold War, which lasted well into the 1980s, Communist-dominated media in Europe described most Rusyn-American organizations as enemies of socialism, while in turn American society was increasingly suspicious of people within the United States who traced their origins to lands ruled by the feared "Russian Commies." Such attitudes only encouraged further the otherwise natural tendency of younger people of Carpatho-Rusyn ancestry to adopt and assimilate fully into American society and to reject the language and eventually any association with the European Carpathian homeland of their parents and grandparents. Symbolic of this change was the gradual introduction of English into the previously vibrant Rusyn-American press.

Among the most active proponents of Americanization was the Greek Catholic Exarchate of Pittsburgh, which in the 1960s was raised by the Vatican to the status of a metropolitan province with three, and eventually four eparchies (Pittsburgh, Pennsylvania; Passaic, New Jersey; Parma, Ohio; and Van Nuys, California). The church was now formally called Byzantine Catholic, and if the name *Rusyn*—in English *Ruthenian*—was used at all, it referred to the Eastern-Catholic rite and not to any particular ethnic group. English eventually replaced Church Slavonic in the liturgy and Rusyn vernacular in homilies, while some priests (with the approval of their bishops) removed the traditional Eastern-rite icon screens (iconostases) that separated the altar from the congregation and added Roman-rite accretions, such as stations of the cross. All this was done in an effort to make their churches more like the general Catholic norm; that is, to make them seem more American.

The Russian Orthodox Church in North America, the jurisdiction which had absorbed the pre-World War I large-scale "return" of Greek Catholics to Orthodoxy led by Father Alexis Toth, went through its own version of Americanization. In 1970, the Russian Orthodox Church in North America became jurisdictionally independent and was renamed the Orthodox Church in America. The church's intellectual leadership and its episcopal hierarchs (many of which were of Lemko-Rusyn ancestry) actively set out to de-ethnicize the church. This meant not only opening it up to all Americans, but most especially rejecting its past association with Russians, Carpatho-Rusyns, or any specific East Slavic ethnic group. The only jurisdiction that formally maintained some relationship with its member's specific Carpatho-Rusyn ancestral heritage was the American Carpatho-Russian Orthodox Diocese based in Johnstown, Pennsylvania. But it, too, insisted on using the descriptor *Russian*, which only further confused and alienated many young people, who preferred to be Americans just like everyone else—and certainly not be associated with the ultimate enemy of the United States: the "Commies" in the Soviet Union and its satellite countries.

The most extreme example of misplaced identities and national orientations was that adopted by the Lemko Association. Ever since the 1930s, the Lemko Association had not only adopted the Russophile viewpoint that Carpatho-Rusyns were, like all East Slavs, part of a larger Russian nationality, it also remained pro-Communist in political orientation. Whereas such views were tolerated during World War II, a time when the Soviet Union was an ally of the United States, they were no longer acceptable during the Cold War period and America's renewed obsession about the seemingly imminent dangers of Communism. Because of its Communist Russian orientation, the Lemko Association alienated itself from its members' American-born children, so that by 1980 it had dwindled down to only a few hundred members. By contrast, the patriotically American and increasingly de-ethnicized Greek Catholic Union with its over 40,000 members had by the end of the 1980s evolved into a financially successful insurance company with assets of over 100 million dollars.[6] Nevertheless, at the same time that the Greek Catholic Union attained stability and financial solvency, it showed little commitment to the Carpatho-Rusyn ancestral heritage of most of its members.

WE WANT TO KNOW WHO WE ARE

The ethnic revival in the mid-1970s that was connected with the bicentennial celebrations in the United States and the ethnic revival, or "Roots" movement, also had an impact on some Americans of Carpatho-Rusyn background. The motivation behind such interest was best summed up in the editorial to the first issue of the *Carpatho-Rusyn American* quarterly magazine, written in 1978 by its founding editor, at the time a Ph.D. candidate at Columbia University, Patricia A. Krafcik. Embued with memories of her grandmother and a nostalgic longing for an ancestral homeland never seen, she wrote "The Story of Anna":

One day in 1914, sixteen-year-old Anna Bujdoš embraced her mother warmly and kissed her tear-stained cheeks and lips. Then, clutching a small bundle of belongings and food, she took her place on the back of an open horse-drawn cart and let her legs swing down over the side in rhythm with the cart's rocking movement. Tears stung her eyes as the cart pulled away from her village. Ruská Vol'a. She gave a last long look at the humble wood and white-washed house, the rolling mountains in the distance, and at her mother waving and calling out 'Come back soon!' Come back soon—but in her mother's strong face, Anna read a different message: if my life has been hard, God grant that you make yours better. Live now not for me, live for yourself, your children, and your grandchildren.

At this moment of departure, however, Anna needed the comfort of knowing that she would return. After a long journey across an ocean, she would meet her own people in New York and New Jersey (these were still only strange place-names to her), find work, and then take her income back home to help her family. All this at sixteen years of age? To me now, her granddaughter, this seems inconceivable, but it seemed perfectly possible to Anna and to thousands of young men and women like her. To them this was an adventure, pursued, of course, not without some apprehension. But the whole world lay out there!

· · · · ·

Like the majority of young people, Anna never did return to her village. The years passed, and her mother's silent words—Make a better life for yourself and your children—became her inspiration. In the new land, she met and married a young man from a neighboring village in the old country, Mykhailo Cherkala, who still dreamed of the green hills and the wild mountains brimming with legends of wonderful bandit-heroes who protected the Rusyn people from the demands of unscrupulous rulers not of their own blood. . . . But Mykhailo also shared Anna's dream of a better life. And the new dream was stronger than the old.

· · · · ·

Their daughter Anne married an American Marine officer. And from this marriage—from thousands of such marriages—has emerged the third generation on American soil. And now, secure in our being Americans, we dream again of the mountains, the secret streams, the bandit-heroes of the native land of our Annas and Mykhailos.

But our interest in ethnicity is not limited to dreaming. Now we can explore Rusyn ethnicity in academic surroundings, by observing and recording those traditions to which our people still cling in this country and in the old country, and by studying the language of our parents and grandparents. The Rusyn cultural heritage is rich and varied. It is a precious possession which we can preserve by sharing it with each other. Let us, the young people, together with our parents and our grandparents dedicate this publication to that endeavor.

SOURCE: *Carpatho-Rusyn American*, I, 1 (Fairview, N.J., 1978), p. 2.

Destructive and costly rivalries between various Eastern-rite church jurisdictions, confusing explanations about the identity of a small ethnic group without its own independent state, and the generally negative association of East Slavs in America with the Cold War Communist enemy were all factors that by the 1970s had led to the virtual end in the United States of any community that could be defined as specifically Carpatho-Rusyn. In an attempt to overcome what could only be characterized as ethnocultural nihilism, a small group of recent university graduates of Carpatho-Rusyn parentage, with no allegiance to any existing religious or secular organization, formed in 1978 the Carpatho-Rusyn Research Center. In one sense, the center was responding to the so-called ethnic revival, or "Roots" movement that had taken hold throughout American society in conjunction with the 1976 bicentennial celebration of the United States. In 1978, the Carpatho-Rusyn Research Center began publishing a quarterly magazine (*Carpatho-Rusyn American*), distributing scholarly but reader-friendly publications, and organizing conferences and lectures. All these activities had a clear goal: to explain to Americans of Carpatho-Rusyn descent as well as to the American public-at-large that Carpatho-Rusyns are not Russians, or Ukrainians, or Slovaks, or anything else, but rather a distinct Slavic nationality.

Some segments of Rusyn-American society responded to the message about the cultural and national distinctiveness of their ancestral heritage and began to establish folk ensembles and dance groups in various parts of the northeastern United States. Nevertheless, this hesitant ethnonational awakening stimulated by the "Roots" movement in the 1970s unfolded in isolation. This is because the European homeland was still ruled by Communist regimes which continued to ban the very idea that Carpatho-Rusyns might be a distinct nationality. All this seemed to suggest that Rusyn Americans—at least those who had some sense of their unique ancestral heritage—were the "last of the Mohicans" speaking on behalf of a people that no longer existed in its place of origin, Carpathian Rus'.

Then, as now, one should avoid making assumptions about the future based on present conditions. With hindsight we now know that the realities of the 1980s ended with the year 1989, which set in motion the radical transformation of central and eastern Europe. What was seemingly gone forever—the Carpatho-Rusyn people—was like a phoenix to be revived in the wake of the Revolutions of 1989.

The revolutions of 1989

The year 1989 was a major turning point in the history of Carpatho-Rusyns as it was for all of the states and peoples of central and eastern Europe. For nearly half a century since the close of World War II in 1945, the entire region was under the hegemony of the Soviet Union. This meant not only direct Soviet rule in the Transcarpathian oblast of Soviet Ukraine, but also its indirect and often decisive influence in Czechoslovakia, Romania, and Hungary. Throughout the postwar decades, political influence emanating from Moscow was implemented by the ruling Communist parties in each of the Soviet Union's central European satellite countries. Soviet economic influence was carried out through a union known as Comecon (the Council for Mutual Economic Aid), whereby the command economies of the satellites were integrated with each other and in large measure dependent on direction from the Soviet Union.

By the last quarter of the twentieth century it had become clear that the Soviet economy—and therefore the integrated economies of its central European satellites—were not expanding. Moreover, the general standard of living throughout the region was at best stagnating, if not declining. While there were sporadic efforts at economic reform, most especially in Hungary and Poland, the kind of serious political as well as economic restructuring that was needed proved to be impossible until change first came in the Soviet Union. No one, however, expected such change to occur in the foreseeable future.

Transformation and demise of the Soviet Union

In 1985, the Soviet Communist leadership, faced with its own country's increasingly problematic economy, elected as general secretary of the All-Union Communist party Mikhail S. Gorbachev. He was determined to strengthen and preserve the Soviet Union, but to do so he and a group of innovative advisors determined that it was necessary to restructure the Soviet economy and to open up its society to new ideas. These goals were summed up by two programmatic concepts: *perestroika*, meaning restructuring; and *glasnost'*, or openness, which implied a willingness to listen to public criticism about how the country was being run.

As part of the proposed "new face" of the Soviet Union, Gorbachev set out to change its relationship with the United States and the "capitalist" West from one of confrontation to one characterized by negotiation and even cooperation. It was this radical transformation in Gorbachev's foreign policy that led to a profound change in the Soviet Union's relationship to its satellite countries in central Europe. Confident in their new relationship with the West, the Soviet reformers felt secure enough to decide that its satellite countries could, henceforth, make whatever political and economic changes they felt necessary without fear of intervention from the Soviet military. In essence, the Soviets unilaterally relinquished their control of central Europe.

The end of Communist rule in central Europe

The impossible suddenly seemed possible. By 1989, Poland and Hungary led the way toward ending the exclusive role of their respective Communist parties and began to decentralize their command economies. In October, East Germany's Communist government fell, and that country immediately set upon a path that within less than a year resulted in the reunification of Germany.

Among the last countries in the region to accept change were Czechoslovakia and Romania. On 17 November 1989, a massive demonstration in Czechoslovakia's capital of Prague set in motion a series of events throughout the country that subsequently came to be called the Velvet Revolution. Without any serious resistance, the Czechoslovak Communist rulers who had controlled the country for four decades stepped aside and were replaced by intellectual dissidents. Foremost among the dissidents was Václav Havel, who in late December 1989 became the country's elected provisional president. All the restrictions of what was now being called the totalitarian era—censorship, closed borders, arbitrary arrests, and the domination of the Communist party—came to an end. Czechoslovakia's new leaders were determined to overcome all aspects of the totalitarian past and to return their country to the family of democratic European nation-states. Havel himself became a world celebrity in Western political, intellectual, and cultural circles, since he seemed to embody the tradition of humanism that in an earlier era had made Czechoslovakia a respected state under its founding philosopher-president, Tomáš G. Masaryk. Thus, to the revolutions of 1848, 1918, and 1948 was added the year 1989. From now on, all references to life in Czechoslovakia would be determined by that date: totalitarianism (*totalitá*) before 17 November 1989; democracy since then. Even the form of the country's name was altered, so that the new spelling, *Czecho-Slovakia*, might somehow reflect the equality between the Czech and Slovak lands that comprised the federal republic.

In the same month, December 1989, when Czechoslovakia's peaceful (or "soft") Velvet Revolution brought Václav Havel to the country's presidency, farther south in another Soviet satellite, Romania, political change was to occur in a much more violent manner. Romania's feared and hated inter-nal secret security service, the Securitate, was not about to give up control to that country's democratic forces. Fighting broke out between the secret police and demonstrators that ended only when Romania's long-time Communist dictator Nicolae Ceauçescu and his politically influential wife were assassinated during the last days of 1989. Romania's government was now in the hands of anti-Ceauçescu democratic forces and former Communist functionaries.

In the Soviet Union itself Gorbachev's reforms took some time before they reached all areas of the country, including Soviet Ukraine. This is because soon after his ascent to power in 1985 Gorbachev faced strong and consistent opposition from conservative elements in the Soviet Communist leadership. They were aghast at what they considered radical policies which seemed to weaken the country both internally and externally. Among Gorbachev's strongest critics was the conservative-minded head of the Communist party of Ukraine, Volodymyr Shcherbyts'kyi. Finally, in September 1989, Shcherbyts'kyi was replaced by a more reform-minded leader, while in early 1990 the Communist party throughout the Soviet Union was forced, with Gorbachev's blessing, to relinquish its monopoly on power. From that moment political developments in Soviet Ukraine were directed not only by the Communists, but also by non-Communist Ukrainian nationalist groups united in an umbrella organization called the People's Movement of Ukraine, better known by the Ukrainian word for movement: Rukh. Both the Communists and Rukh were represented in Soviet Ukraine's parliament (Verkhovna Rada), which in July 1990 declared the country a sovereign state. This meant that Ukraine would manage its own internal affairs, although still remaining a part of the Soviet Union.

The other country where Carpatho-Rusyns lived, Yugoslavia (which had not been a Soviet satellite), was still ruled by its federal and republic-level governments dominated by members of the Yugoslav Communist party. The Serbian republic, however, made what turned out to be an ominous decision: in 1989 it abolished the autonomous status of the Vojvodina and Kosovo regions. That move set in motion a series of events provoking a major political crisis that culminated in 1991, when several of the country's republics (Slovenia, Croatia, Macedonia, and in early 1992 Bosnia-Herzegovina) seceded from the Yugoslav federation. In effect, Communist Yugoslavia ceased to exist, although its former federal government tried to hold on to power over the only republics (Serbia and Montenegro) which remained within the now drastically reduced country.

What, however, did these revolutionary changes sparked by the events of 1989 mean for the various countries of central and eastern Europe where Carpatho-Rusyns lived during the post-World War II Communist era? In general, all the countries which experienced a change in regime (reduced Yugoslavia, or Serbia-Montenegro being the exception) set up multiparty representative governments with a presidential office and parliament chosen in free elections. The new liberal-oriented governments in virtually all the region's countries made serious attempts to overcome the shortcomings of the Communist past by lifting censorship, releasing political prisoners, allowing freedom of religion, and opening their borders to allow their citizens to travel abroad. The proverbial Iron Curtain was literally torn down as freedom had come to millions of citizens. Although each country addressed the problems of its economy differently, they all rejected the command economic system of the Communist past and instead allowed for privately owned businesses to be established and for lands held in collective and state farms to be returned to their former owners.

Carpatho-Rusyns reassert their existence

Carpatho-Rusyns reacted very quickly to the enormous political and social changes prompted by Gorbachev's reforms in the Soviet Union and the Revolutions of 1989. At first glance, such a reaction seemed surprising, considering the fact that under Communist-ruled regimes since World War II nowhere, except in Yugoslavia, did Carpatho-Rusyns exist as a legally recognized nationality with their own organized civic and cultural life.

The first Carpatho-Rusyns to act were the Lemkos in Poland, and they did so even before the Revolutions of 1989. Since the early 1980s, Poland's Lemko Rusyns had been gathering, if only on an annual basis, at summertime weekend retreats called Vatras (see above, Chapter 24). By the end of that decade, the Vatra held in the Carpathian homeland had already become a setting for debates between, on the one hand, those Lemkos who considered themselves a distinct nationality (perhaps, but not necessarily related to other Carpatho-Rusyns) and, on the other, by those Lemkos who believed they were a regional branch of the Ukrainian nationality. In April 1989, the supporters of the distinct Lemko-Rusyn orientation established in the Silesian town of Legnica, an important center of Poland's Lemko diaspora, the Lemko Society/Stovaryshŷnia Lemkiv, under the chairmanship of a young diasporan Lemko, Andrei Kopcha. Before the end of the year, the society began to publish as its official organ, a magazine called *Besida* (1989–present) in the Lemko-Rusyn vernacular.

In the course of 1990, activists in three other countries also established civic and cultural organizations. In February, the Society of Carpatho-Rusyns/Tovarystvo karpats'kykh rusyniv came into being in Uzhhorod, Ukraine under the chairmanship of the city's chief architect, Mykhailo M. Tomchanii. The society initially attracted a wide spectrum of some of the leading civic activists, educators, and creative artists in Soviet Transcarpathia who wished to see their native Carpatho-Rusyn culture revived and recognized in Ukraine. A few months later, in Yugoslavia, the Rusyn Cultural Foundation/*Ruska matka*, an organization that had existed for a few years just after World War II, was reconstituted with its seat in Ruski Kerestur, the heart of the Vojvodina. While Rusyn institutions had existed and even flourished in Communist Yugoslavia, the Rusyn Cultural Foundation was intended to be a community organization that would defend Rusyn interests without having to depend solely on government funding and, therefore, possible ideological control. The foundation was, in particular, opposed to those intellectuals who, while using the vernacular language in their publications, nevertheless argued that the Vojvodinian Rusyns were a part of the Ukrainian nationality.

In Czechoslovakia, within one week of the Velvet Revolution that on 17 November 1989 had toppled the Communist regime, a few activists in Prešov (led by Aleksander Zozuliak) established a body called the Initiative Group of Czecho-Slovakia's Rusyn-Ukrainians for Reconstruction/Initsiatyvna hrupa rusyniv-ukraïntsiv ChSSR za perebudovu. The goal of the Initiative Group was to resolve the nationality question among Carpatho-Rusyns and to replace the Communist-era Cultural Union of Ukrainian Workers (KSUT) with an organization that would promote the Carpatho-Rusyns as a distinct people and not as a branch of the Ukrainian nationality. As early as January 1990, KSUT dropped the Communist-era epithet "workers" and reconstituted itself as the Union of Rusyns-Ukrainians of Czecho-Slovakia/Soiuz rusyniv-ukraïntsiv Chekhoslovachchyny (SRUCh). Almost immediately controversies arose within the organization between supporters of a distinct Rusyn national orientation and those who were Ukrainian in orientation. Eventually, the Rusynophiles left SRUCh and established in Medzilaborce the Rusyn Renaissance Society/Rusyns'ka obroda, which was formally constituted on 17 November 1990; that is, on the first anniversary of Czechoslovakia's Velvet Revolution. Before the end of the year, the Rusyn Renaissance Society, under the chairmanship of the Prešov theater dramatist Vasyl' Turok, began publishing an illustrated magazine (*Rusyn,* 1990–present) and a few months later it launched a weekly newspaper (*Narodnŷ novynkŷ,* 1991–present), both of which appeared in the local Rusyn vernacular.

Regardless of country of location, the ideological message of each organization was the same and based on the following four principles. (1) Carpatho-Rusyns form one people or nationality (*narod*) and, with the exception of Yugoslavia and the resettled groups in western Poland, live as the indigenous population in the valleys of the Carpathians where their ancestors settled as long ago as the early Middle Ages. (2) Carpatho-Rusyns are not a branch of any other nationality, whether Ukrainian, Russian, Polish, or Slovak, but rather a distinct fourth East Slavic nationality. (3) As a distinct nationality, Carpatho-Rusyns need to have their own codified literary language based on spoken dialects. (4) In all countries where Carpatho-Rusyns live, they should enjoy rights accorded all national minorities, including use of the Rusyn language in newspapers, radio, television, and, most important, as a medium of instruction in schools.

One people despite international borders

Aside from establishing civic and cultural organizations within individual countries, the incipient post-1989 Carpatho-Rusyn movement quickly realized the value of cross-border cooperation. No one at the time considered seriously the creation of a Carpatho-Rusyn state, although accusations of this kind were directed at the movement by its pro-Ukrainian antagonists. In other words, most Carpatho-Rusyn cultural activists accepted the fact that historic Carpathian Rus' was divided among four countries and that such political reality was not likely to change. In order to compensate for these territorial divisions, however, some kind of interregional, or "international" Carpatho-Rusyn organization seemed to be the solution. Hence, the idea of a world congress was born.

The original intent of the congress initiators to meet in Soviet Tran-scarpathia was not possible; thus, the first World Congress of Rusyns took place in Medzilaborce, Slovakia, in March 1991. The congress attracted over 200 delegates led by the chairmen of each of the recently founded Car-patho-Rusyn organizations in Poland, Slovakia, Ukraine, and Yugoslavia, as well as the head of the already existing Carpatho-Rusyn Research Center in the United States. There were even representatives of the pro-Ukrainian orientation who were present at the congress and who were allowed to speak out against what they considered this unfortunate manifestation of "Rusyn separatism." The presence of Ukrainophiles had little impact on the two-day world congress, which overall was characterized by an atmosphere of excite-ment and even euphoria. After all, this was the first time in history that Car-patho-Rusyns from five countries and two continents met to hear about the

PROCLAMATION OF THE FIRST WORLD CONGRESS OF RUSYNS

We, representatives of Rusyns who live in the Czech and Slovak Federal Republic, the Socialist Federal Republic of Yugoslavia, the Polish Republic, the Carpatho-Rusyn regions of the Soviet Union, and the Rusyns who reside in the United States and Canada, have met at the First World Congress of Rusyns in Medzilaborce, Czechoslovakia.

Freedom and democracy have become the basis of the political and social life of eastern Europe and have provided an opportunity for self-determination and a worthy life for our people who live in the East Carpathian region and in other coun-tries of the world.

We Rusyns have always supported the cultural heritage of our ancestors. We admire the inspiration and enlightenment found in the works of our national poets Aleksander Dukhnovyč and Aleksander Pavlovyč, as well as other leaders who have striven to preserve our ethnic distinctiveness and identity.

The nationality policy of the totalitarian regimes in eastern Europe after World War II has caused tragic consequences for the destiny of the Rusyn people. We wit-nessed the forcible attempt to liquidate the Rusyn language, the cultural and reli-gious traditions of our ancestors, and to falsify history.

We appreciate and respect the attempts of the Ukrainian people to build democ-racy and to pursue a free and unfettered development. However, we declare that the

Rusyns are not a part of the Ukrainian people but rather an independent and distinct people.

We are thankful to the authorities of the Czech and Slovak Federal Republic and the Socialist Federal Republic of Yugoslavia for their help in promoting the free development of our people. We appeal to the authorities of the Soviet Union and the Ukrainian Soviet Socialist Republic to respect the national rights of Rusyns in Subcarpathian Rus' [Soviet Transcarpathia]. The Rusyn people will stand tall and decide independently their place within the family of free nations in the international community.

Medzilaborce, Czechoslovakia
24 March 1991

SOURCE: *Carpatho-Rusyn American,* XIV, 3 (Pittsburgh, 1991), p. 9.

past and present situation of their people and to consider joint projects to improve the future status of Carpatho-Rusyn culture and language.

The very existence of the world congress convinced its participants—and eventually the governments of the countries in which they lived—that Carpatho-Rusyns did exist and that they were a force with which the region's post-Communist states would have to contend. Subsequent congresses were to be held every two years in a different country, and within a few years Carpatho-Rusyn communities from several other states were added as permanent members: the Czech Republic, Hungary, Canada (together with the United States representing North America), Romania, and Croatia (alongside Serbia, which replaced the former Yugoslavia). The first World Congress and most other organizations that were subsequently founded in the various countries where Carpatho-Rusyns lived stressed that their main concerns were cultural in nature; that is, recognition of Carpatho-Rusyns as a distinct nationality; codification of a Rusyn literary language; and use of that language in schools, publications, and media.

The autonomy question again

In Ukraine's Transcarpathian region, however, where nearly three-quarters of Carpatho-Rusyn in Europe lived, expectations went beyond the merely cultural. First of all, Transcarpathia's Rusyns did not consider themselves a national minority, but rather the "autochthonous" or indigenous majority population. Secondly, they argued that the autonomous status of the region, first as Subcarpathian Rus' within interwar Czechoslovakia and then as Transcarpathian Ukraine during the last months of World War II (November 1944 to June 1945), was abolished by the Soviet Union in violation of international law. Therefore, Transcarpathia's indigenous Rusyns felt they had legal precedence to demand that a "republic of Subcarpathian Rus'" be restored within Ukraine, regardless what political form that country would adopt.[1] The local oblast authorities in what was still Soviet Transcarpathia even encouraged these expectations. In the fall of 1990, the elected Regional Council (*Oblasna rada*) in Uzhhorod appointed a commission of experts to study the autonomy question. The commission came back with a recommendation calling for autonomy.

Meanwhile, political events in the Soviet Union as a whole were changing rapidly. Conservative elements in the All-Union and in several republic-level Communist parties were profoundly discontent with the reforms implemented by Gorbachev and with the demands for sovereignty and even independence being announced by some of the union republics. Such displeasure culminated in August 1991, when a small group of malcontented leaders in Moscow tried to remove Gorbachev and thereby to avoid the further disintegration of the Soviet state. The attempted coup failed, although the immediate result was that some republics, like Ukraine, proclaimed on 21 August 1991 that it was henceforth an independent non-Soviet state. In order to legitimize this move, Ukraine's parliament in Kiev proposed that a national referendum on independence, in conjunction with presidential elections, be held on 1 December 1991.

The last few months of 1991 also witnessed increasing political activity in Ukraine's Transcarpathia, where the regional authorities as well as the Society of Carpatho-Rusyns (together with the region's other national groups, in particular the Magyars) campaigned on behalf of autonomy. There were even proposals among some segments of the public that Transcarpathia might be better off within the borders of another country, such as Czechoslovakia or Hungary. In an attempt to obtain some consensus on this matter, an agreement was reached with the central authorities in Kiev to add another question on the 1 December referendum, in which the population would be asked whether Transcarpathia should be accorded "the status of a special self-governing (*samouprava*) administrative territory as a legal subject within independent Ukraine."[2] The results of the referendum revealed that a substantial majority (78 percent) voted in favor of self-government, while at the same time 92 percent of the region's voters approved the status of Ukraine as an independent state. For the next few weeks Gorbachev made a desperate attempt through political negotiations to preserve in some form the Soviet Union. His efforts failed, and on 31 December 1991 the Soviet Union ceased to exist.

Transcarpathia's Carpatho-Rusyn activists initially welcomed these developments, because they expected their demands to reinstate "autonomy" were about to be realized within the framework of an independent Ukraine. The next chapter will investigate to what degree their expectations were justified.

Post-Communist Transcarpathia—Ukraine

The referendum of 1991 and the emergence of an independent Ukraine brought hope to Carpatho-Rusyn activists in Transcarpathia/Subcarpathian Rus' that in a future autonomous province which they were promised the nationality question would be resolved. Moreover, hopes were high that the self-governing region would more effectively be able to manage the inevitable challenges of moving from the Soviet-style state-owned and state-directed command economy to some form of a free-market economic system. The first disappointment came with the autonomy question.

Unfulfilled political expectations

In late November 1989, just one week before the 1 December referendum and Ukraine's presidential elections, the head of the national parliament (Verkhovna Rada) and candidate for president, Leonid Kravchuk, traveled to Uzhhorod to meet with the local Transcarpathian administration and its elected Regional Assembly (Oblasna rada). As the leading presidential candidate, who as it turned out did win the elections one week later by a comfortable majority (58 percent), Kravchuk declared that should the referendum question on autonomy be approved, self-government would be implemented in Transcarpathia within a few months, that is, by the spring of 1992. The fact that no less than 78 percent of eligible voters did cast their ballot in favor of self-government and that the country's president-elect favored the idea only increased the expectations of autonomy supporters.

During the next few weeks after the 1 December referendum, no fewer than four carefully worked out proposals for autonomy were published, including the "official" one calling for a "special self-governing administrative territory" that was submitted by Transcarpathia's Regional Assembly to the central authorities in Kiev.[1] The decision on implementation was within the authority of Ukraine's national parliament (*Verkhovna Rada*), but it simply refused to authorize any kind of self-rule for Transcarpathia. When President Kravchuk was confronted with requests as to why his pre-election promise regarding self-rule was not being implemented, he blamed it on the national parlia-

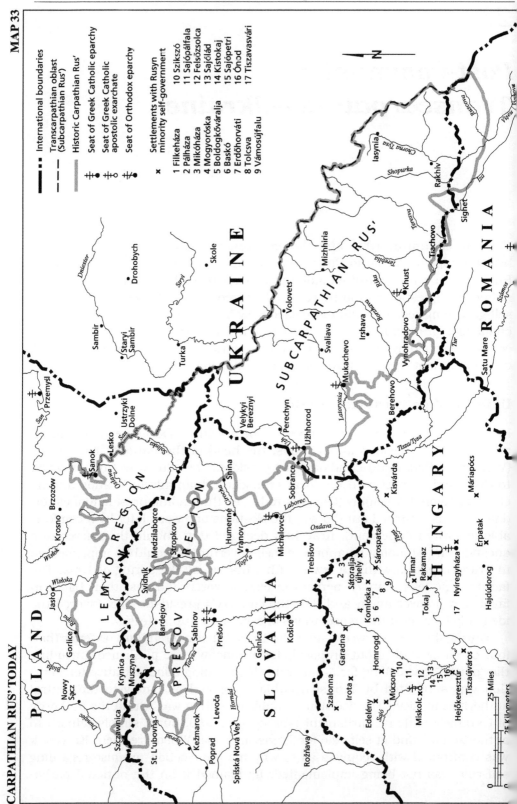

CARPATHIAN RUS' TODAY

International boundaries
Transcarpathian oblast (Subcarpathian Rus')
Historic Carpathian Rus'
Seat of Greek Catholic eparchy
Seat of Greek Catholic apostolic exarchate
Seat of Orthodox eparchy

Settlements with Rusyn minority self-government

× 1 Filkeháza
2 Pálháza
3 Mikóháza
4 Mogyoróska
5 Boldogkőváralja
6 Baskó
7 Erdőhorváti
8 Tolcsva
9 Vámosújfalu
10 Szikszó
11 Sajópálfala
12 Felsőzsolca
13 Sajólád
14 Kistokaj
15 Sajópetri
16 Ónod
17 Tiszavasvári

ment. From the standpoint of the Subcarpathian autonomists, it was simply Ukrainian "nationalists" and "extremists," especially from neighboring Galicia, who were opposed to any kind of special status for Transcarpathia. Their opposition in part reflected the general position of the Ukrainian authorities which did not consider Carpatho-Rusyns, in terms of language and ethnicity, as anything distinct from the rest of the ethnic Ukrainian population.

It is also important to note that the question of autonomy, or self-governing status, applied to Transcarpathia as a whole, not simply to its Carpatho-Rusyn inhabitants. For example, during the debates about this issue in 1990, local Magyar spokespeople were among the most adamant supporters of autonomy, while ethnic Ukrainians who had arrived in the region after World War II, most especially from neighboring Galicia, as well as local Ukrainian-oriented Transcarpathians, were strongly opposed.

Nevertheless, in the wake of Kiev's refusal to implement the December 1991 referendum results, Transcarpathia's Rusynophile civic activists, in particular those in the Society of Carpatho-Rusyns, continued to press the autonomy question. Numerous petitions were sent to Ukraine's government, to its national parliament, and also to the European Parliament and the United Nations. When these failed to elicit any results or even a response, activists in the Society of Carpatho-Rusyns, by then led by a professor of biochemistry at Uzhhorod University, Ivan M. Turianytsia, formed in 1993 a "provisional government" for what was called "the republic of Subcarpathian Rus'." The "republic" had its own self-appointed cabinet led by "prime minister" Turianytsia, which was waiting in the wings to govern "Subcarpathian Rus'" whenever Ukraine would capitulate to its demands.[2] Although nothing concrete ever came of this affair, the Carpatho-Rusyn problem did reach the attention of the media in central and western Europe, as well as in Russia and the United States, all of which prompted a response from Ukraine's government. That response took the form of a call to its own experts to investigate the matter and to formulate appropriate policies to deal with what was now dubbed the "Rusyn question."

Not unrelated to the issue of possible self-rule for Transcarpathia was the question of the very structure of the new Ukrainian state. After four years of independence, the country's legislators were still unable to adopt a constitution, and during the seemingly unending debates on this matter, it was not clear whether Ukraine would become a centralized state like France, or a federal state like Germany or Austria. Should the federal option be adopted, then it seemed likely that "autonomous" Transcarpathia could be one of the state's component parts. When, however, a constitution was finally adopted in June 1996, Ukraine became a centralized state with a president elected by popular vote for a seven-year term and a one-house elected national parliament (Verkhovna Rada) whose largest party (or bloc of parties) had the right to nominate the prime minister. The lines of authority between the president and prime minister were insufficiently clarified and were to remain a bone of contention in Ukrainian political life.

Although back in December 1991 referenda were held in two regions of Ukraine regarding self-rule, only one, the Crimea, was given that status in the form of an autonomous republic. The rest of the country remained, as in Soviet times, divided into oblasts, one of which included Transcarpathia. Each oblast continued to have its own elected representative body, the Regional Assembly (Oblasna rada), which was responsible for initiating legislation applying to the region itself as specified by the central government. Each oblast was also given a governing administration, whose head—popularly known as the governor—was appointed by the president. It is through the oblast's governor and his administration that Ukraine's authorities in Kiev are able to implement presidential authority and policies throughout the country.

Ukraine's "Rusyn question"

When, in 1996, Ukraine adopted a constitution for a centralized state, this effectively meant shelving the issue of Transcarpathian autonomy. Ukraine's central authorities in Kiev could now turn to the other aspect of the "Rusyn question"—national identity. This aspect of the question, however, had a larger context. The Ukrainian government was well aware of the officially recognized status of Carpatho-Rusyns in neighboring countries and of the views and activity of the World Congress of Rusyns. Kiev also followed closely the demands for recognition of Carpatho-Rusyns as a distinct nationality, which were formulated by several organizations in Transcarpathia and submitted in the form of petitions to the United Nations, the European parliament, and the government of Ukraine itself.

On the other hand, pro-Ukrainian activists from Transcarpathia (Pavlo Chuchka, Oleksa Myshanych) and from neighboring countries like Czechoslovakia (Mykola Mushynka, Iurii Bacha) and Poland (Volodymyr Mokryi) had since the Revolution of 1989 been publishing brochures, newspaper articles, and media reports denouncing what they called "political Rusynism." This nefarious phenomenon, so they said, was the work of a few "intellectually misguided" or "politically opportunistic" individuals "paid" and, in some cases led by Carpatho-Rusyn "protectors" in North America (especially the University of Toronto Professor Paul Robert Magocsi).[3] The coordinated work of all these groups—to create a "non-existent" Rusyn nationality—was considered little more than a thinly disguised camouflage to detach Transcarpathia from Ukraine and unite it with either Hungary or Czechoslovakia. The large Ukrainian nationalist diaspora in the United States and Canada, a force toward which independent Ukraine's government paid a significant degree of deference, also joined in the denunciations against the Carpatho-Rusyn movement, calling on the Ukrainian authorities to rid their state of the dangers of "political Rusynism."

The basic Ukrainian understanding of this matter remained the same as it had been when first formulated by patriotic Ukrainian scholars and nationality builders in the late nineteenth century. That understanding was based on two principles. The first was that the East Slavic inhabitants living in the Carpathian region were subdivided into three ethnic groups—Lemkos, Boikos, and Hutsuls. These three groups allegedly lived on both the northern and southern slopes of the mountains and that they, as evident by their language and ethnographic characteristics (material and spiritual culture), comprised an integral part of the Ukrainian nationality. (See Chapter 1, text insert, No Shortage of Names).

The second principle had to do with nomenclature; namely, that the ethnonym *Rusyn* (including the local variant *Rusnak*) was an older form of the name *Ukrainian*. In other words, all Rusyns, including those who used the self-identification *Lemko*, were Ukrainians. Convinced of the scholarly validity (*naukova pravda*) of these two principles, outspoken Ukrainian ideologists—as well as much of the public-at-large within Ukraine itself and, most especially, the Ukrainian diaspora in North America—automatically assumed the following: that all efforts, whether by individuals, organizations, or states (such as interwar Czechoslovakia, Poland, and World War II Hungary) "to create" from Rusyns a distinct nationality were simply politically inspired attempts to undermine Ukraine as a state or, worse still, to deny that Ukrainians themselves were a distinct nationality. The latter view had, in fact, been actively promoted by Russophile-oriented Carpatho-Rusyn activists in Europe and North America before World War II.

It is in this larger context that in October 1996 the president of Ukraine (by then Leonid Kuchma) accepted the policy recommendations of a governmental ministry, which were outlined in a ten-point document titled: "Plan for Resolving the Problem of Ukrainians-Rusyns."[4] The "Plan," which by its very name and content recalled Stalinist-like Soviet practice, called on Ukraine's government to undertake a concerted effort to reinforce the Ukrainian national idea not only among the East Slavic inhabitants of its Transcarpathian region but also among inhabitants in neighboring countries—Slovakia, Poland, Romania, Hungary, Serbia, and Croatia—who might call themselves Rusyn but who should be made to know that they are Ukrainian. In effect, the government of Ukraine was poised to launch a campaign against the Carpatho-Rusyn movement both within and beyond its borders.

Like many other decrees and programs announced by the government of independent Ukraine, its Plan to resolve the "Rusyn question" was given only haphazard support. Nevertheless, the resolutions were never rescinded by the government which continues, in effect, to take the position that a Rusyn nationality and language "has never existed, does not exist, and will not exist"—ironically, the very same phrase used by the Russian imperial government in the late nineteenth century to deny the existence of the "Little Russian" language and "Little Russians" (Ukrainians) as a distinct nationality.[5] For example, during preparations for the 2001 census, organizations in Transcarpathia submitted petitions to the Ukrainian government demanding that an individual should have the right to indicate that he or she is of Rusyn nationality. The authorities never provided a clear answer, either positive or negative, and census-takers who went to each household did not have any guidelines on this issue. Despite the unfavorable environment during the collection of census data, just over 10,090 persons in Transcarpathia responded that they were Rusyns, although the authorities reported them as "an ethnographic group of the Ukrainian ethnos."[6] Yet even those results were not reported in national census publications, so that Rusyns did not appear on the list of Ukraine's over 130 statistically recognized nationalities. In other words, Carpatho-Rusyns did not exist in Ukraine.

Carpatho-Rusyns in the international context

Ukraine's position on non-recognition of Carpatho-Rusyns, and the directives in its 1996 "Plan" calling for diplomatic intervention on this issue with neighboring countries which do recognize Rusyns, provoked ongoing concern among Carpatho-Rusyn communities outside Ukraine as well as among spokespeople for the governments of other countries where they live. Parliamentary representatives, in particular from countries like Slovakia, the Czech Republic, Hungary, and even the United States, frequently expressed disagreement with Kiev's refusal to recognize Carpatho-Rusyns and, in particular, its seeming interference in this matter outside the borders of Ukraine. The United Nations Committee on the Elimination of Racial Discrimination was even more specific, issuing a public statement (October 2006), which "recommends that the State party [of Ukraine] consider recognizing Ruthenians [i.e., Carpatho-Rusyns] as a national minority."[7] The United States government has also weighed in this matter. Ever since 1999, its State Department *Country Reports on Human Rights* has listed the call by "Rusyns (Ruthenians) . . . for status as an official ethnic group" in Ukraine.[8]

Ukraine's Orange Revolution, which in early 2005 brought a Western-oriented and allegedly democratic president to power in the person of Viktor Iushchenko, in particular turned the international spotlight on Ukraine and its internal problems, including the "Rusyn question." The United States special envoy to Ukraine during the "Orange Days," Senator John McCain, subsequently sent a letter which, in consideration of the "substantial scholarly support for the distinctiveness of the Rusyn people and language," called on President Iushchenko to recognize this fact and, hopefully, "give them all appropriate consideration."[9] The Committee for the Elimination of Racial Discrimination within the framework of the Council of Europe (to which Ukraine is a signatory), expressed in 2006 its concern "about the absence of official recognition of the Rusyn minority [in Ukraine] despite its distinct ethnic characteristics."[10] Even the Secretariat for Human Rights of the National Parliament of Ukraine, that is, the country's ombudsman, issued several appeals to its own government to recognize Rusyns as a distinct nationality.

Whereas opposition to recognition of Carpatho-Rusyns on the part of Ukrainian nationalist forces within the country and among the Ukrainian diaspora was as strong as ever, President Iushchenko was at the same time under international and domestic pressure to address this matter. Perhaps it was such pressure, combined with the advice of the highly influential presidential advisor and native of Transcarpathia Viktor Baloga, that resulted in a strange development. By the outset of the twenty-first century, the vast majority of deputies in Transcarpathia's Regional Assembly (*Oblasna rada*) remained opposed to the "Rusyn question" and to any kind of recognition. Moreover, in the wake of the Orange Revolution, virtually all deputies were supporters of the Ukrainian nationalist coalition which still dominated the government in Kiev. Despite the seemingly otherwise unsympathetic political environment, on 7 March 2007, Transcarpathia's Regional Assembly voted by an overwhelming majority (71 in favor, 2 against, 2 abstentions) to recognize Rusyns as a distinct nationality on the territory of its competence, that is, Transcarpathia, and also to request that the national parliament in Kiev do the same for all of Ukraine.[11]

Emboldened by the Regional Assembly's March 2007 decision on nationality recognition, Transcarpathia's Carpatho-Rusyn community activists, led by the dynamic and charismatic Orthodox priest in Uzhhorod, Dymytrii Sydor, revived the autonomy question. Claiming that Ukraine's refusal to grant nationality recognition is tantamount to "ethnocide against the Rusyn people," the so-called Diet of Subcarpathian Rus'/Soim podkarpatskykh Rusynov (headed by the priest Sydor) and the National Council of Subcarpathian Rusyns/Narodna rada podkarpatskykh rusynov (headed by the physician and Regional Assembly deputy Ievhen Zhupan) issued a declaration (15 December 2007) calling for the immediate implementation of a Rusyn "self-governing national-territorial entity." The declaration also called upon "the European Union and Russia to protect and guarantee the resolution of the 'Rusyn question' in the spirit of international legal norms."[12] Half a year later, these two organizations convened a European Congress of Subcarpathian Rusyns (June 2008), which in October formally proclaimed "the renewal of Rusyn statehood in the form of a Republic of Subcarpathian Rus',"[13] to take legal effect on 1 December 2008.

In the end, nothing came of all these somewhat pompous declarations with their, at times, overblown threats directed at the Ukrainian state. Particularly provocative, however, was the presence at the Rusyn "congresses" in Transcarpathia of Russian nationalist activists from other parts of Ukraine (especially the Crimea), as well as the decision of the participants that their "republic" be "under the international control of the European Union and Russia."[14] Any mention of the latter was sure to anger the Ukrainian government and national patriots, always concerned about Russian interference in Ukraine's internal affairs. The Carpatho-Rusyn declaration also provoked widespread interest and favorable reaction in the Russian media, while at the same time a negative response of the more moderate World Congress of Rusyns, which condemned the actions of the Transcarpathian "extremists" as a political provocation that would set back the Carpatho-Rusyn cause.[15]

Socioeconomic realities

While it is true that since 1989 the politically loaded questions like autonomy and national identity were high on the agenda of Transcarpathia's Carpatho-Rusyn activists (working mostly out of Uzhhorod and Mukachevo), the vast majority of Transcarpathia's Carpatho-Rusyn inhabitants exhibited little

interest and, in many cases, were totally indifferent to such "political" matters. Their concern—as had been for centuries the primary concern of their
parents, grandparents, and ancestors—was economic survival. In short, the
collapse of the Soviet Union and Communist rule may have brought political
freedoms, the possibility to travel abroad, and the promise of democratically
elected representative institutions, but in the economic realm the collapse of
the Soviet order was simply disastrous.

During the Soviet era, the traditional agricultural and livestock-raising
economy of Transcarpathia was significantly transformed. For example,
more than 300 new factories were built between 1946 and 1990, and no
less than 40 percent of these were set up in the agriculturally unproductive
high mountainous regions.[16] And while many of these factories would never
survive in a free-market, profit-driven economy, they could be and were sustained by the Soviet Union's centralized command economic system in which
the state guaranteed the purchase of the goods produced. Most importantly,
the factories provided jobs for large numbers of people who otherwise would
be unemployed.

Another aspect of Soviet rule was the creation of a generally well-equipped
and staffed medical system throughout the region. The result was an
improvement in health standards, which, combined with the traditional desire
of Carpatho-Rusyn parents to have several children and the arrival of tens of
thousands of in-migrants from other parts of the Soviet Union (an estimated
120,000 between 1946 and 1970 alone), resulted in a veritable demographic
explosion. Hence, if at the close of World War II and the onset of Soviet rule
there were 755,000 inhabitants in Transcarpathia, by the end of the Soviet
era those numbers had nearly doubled, to over 1.2 million.[17] Yet even the
industrialization efforts of Soviet planners could not resolve the age-old problem that characterized Subcarpathian Rus'/Transcarpathia—insufficient natural resources to support the local population—with the result that an estimated 200,000 people were forced to leave the region between 1947 and 1991
in search of work and residence in other parts of the Soviet Union.[18]

With the end of the command economy and state support in post-1991
independent Ukraine, most factories in Transcarpathia, in particular in the
remote highland areas, simply collapsed within a few years. Ukraine's central
and regional authorities tried to attract foreign investment, and indeed several so-called joint ventures were set up; that is, foreign companies provided
capital to restore existing factories or build new ones staffed by local management and workers. However, problems with property law and an inequita-
ble tax system in Ukraine, combined with widespread corruption, limited the
amount of foreign investment in Transcarpathian industry. All these factors
resulted in a catastrophic economic situation, with disastrous consequences
for the region's inhabitants. If, for instance, in the last year of Soviet rule
(1991) there were only 2,500 persons out of work, a decade later that number had sky-rocketed to 360,000, about 50 percent of the workforce.[19]

Labor migration to the East was no longer feasible, since the rest of
Ukraine had its own economic woes, while Russia was now a foreign coun-

try whose post-Communist economy had also not yet turned around. The desperate Transcarpathian population, this time females as well as males, sought work on a semi-permanent basis by going West, to nearby Hungary, Slovakia, most especially Prague in the Czech Republic, and to as far away as Portugal. Thus, for the vast majority of Transcarpathia's Carpatho-Rusyns, their lives in independent democratic Ukraine have taken a decided turn for the worse. Since their overwhelming concern is to figure out how to survive economically and to support their families, even at the cost of accepting menial jobs at home or abroad, they have little time for anything else, and certainly not for "esoteric" and financially unproductive matters like autonomy or the nationality question.

A failed or incomplete national movement?

What, then, has been achieved by the Carpatho-Rusyn movement in Transcarpathia in the nearly two decades since the end of Soviet Communist rule? Certainly, the general democratic environment of independent Ukraine has allowed for the creation of Carpatho-Rusyn organizations and the unrestricted publication of books and other materials. All this, moreover, has been happening despite the fact that at least until 2007 Carpatho-Rusyns as a group were not officially recognized. Nevertheless, most of the Carpatho-Rusyn organizations established since 1991 have not engaged in cultural activity designed to raise awareness in the population that it comprises a distinct nationality. Instead, the small number of individuals who have joined Carpatho-Rusyn organizations became convinced that as a group they must first attain political autonomy for their homeland and only after that address cultural and identity issues.

There were, to be sure, many organizations in Transcarpathia going back to Soviet times whose primary concern was cultural preservation. Among these were the wide network of amateur and professional folk ensembles, not to mention the expanded educational system, all of which during Soviet times and in independent Ukraine accepted and promoted the official view that the indigenous East Slavic inhabitants were Ukrainians. Another important organization was the church. While under the officially atheist Soviet state, the church lost much of its previous influence over the populace, especially in Transcarpathia's ethnically mixed urban areas, in post-1991 independent Ukraine there was a marked revival of interest in religion and a steep rise in church attendance.

Traditional religious and secular culture

It was common knowledge that before its destruction in 1949, the Greek Catholic Church was closely linked to the nationality question and identity of the local Carpatho-Rusyns. In fact, at certain times in the nineteenth and twentieth centuries, individual Greek Catholic priests and hierarchs were in the forefront of the Carpatho-Rusyn national movement. In September 1989, during the waning days of Soviet rule, the Greek Catholic Church was legally reconstituted. It slowly but gradually regained some church property from the Orthodox and increased its membership, whether as a result of some Orthodox returning to Greek Catholicism or the attraction to its ranks of younger generations who had never attended church.

The expectation of some people that the Greek Catholic Eparchy of Mukachevo might somehow assist the Carpatho-Rusyn revival was not realized, however. Almost immediately the eparchy became internally split between hierarchs and priests who wanted it to be Ukrainian in orientation (with use of Ukrainian language in the liturgy and sermon) and those who, by default, preferred to maintain the local national orientation and traditions (including a Church Slavonic liturgy and sermons in Rusyn vernacular).

Another aspect of local tradition was connected with the jurisdictional status of the Eparchy of Mukachevo. Generally eparchies/dioceses are components of a larger church province that customarily (although not always) coincides with state boundaries. Therefore, all the Greek Catholic eparchies on the territory of present-day Ukraine could theoretically be within the framework of one metropolitan province, in this case the Ukrainian Greek Catholic Major Archdiocese of Kyiv-Halych. On the eve of World War II, however, the Vatican had approved plans to create a distinct metropolitan province for the Ruthenian Catholic Church in the former Czechoslovakia based on the two existing (Mukachevo and Prešov) and one new (Khust) eparchies. Until those plans would be realized—and as it turned out they never were—the Mukachevo Eparchy would remain directly under the jurisdiction of the Vatican. This was its status when the eparchy was legally restored in 1989 on the eve of the collapse of the Soviet Union.

Within a few years after Ukraine became independent in 1991, some Ukrainian-minded Greek Catholic activists, often inspired by former atheist and newly born Ukrainian nationalists, argued that there should be only one Greek Catholic jurisdiction on the territory of Ukraine. Consequently, clerical and lay traditionalists in the Eparchy of Mukachevo who wanted to leave things the way they were—a jurisdictionally distinct Ruthenian Catholic Church directly responsible to the Vatican—were accused of Carpatho-Rusyn "separatism." The Vatican authorities reviewed this matter in 2007 and decided, at least for the foreseeable future, to maintain Mukachevo's jurisdictional status (*ecclesia sui juris*) distinct from the rest of the Greek Catholic Church in Ukraine. Nevertheless, the new hierarchs of the Greek Catholic Eparchy of Mukachevo have striven to accommodate to the general Ukrainian environment of Transcarpathia, so that in the end the restored Greek Catholic Church in Ukraine's Transcarpathia provides no formal support to the Carpatho-Rusyn movement.

The situation among the Orthodox is even more complex. The church in Transcarpathia remained within the jurisdiction of the Moscow Patriarchate; moreover, after the collapse of Communist rule, the region was not welcoming to other Orthodox jurisdictions (the Ukrainian Autocephalous and Kiev Patriarchal churches) that were decidedly Ukrainian in national orientation

PROTESTANTISM AND CARPATHO-RUSYNS

Carpatho-Rusyns have traditionally been adherents of Byzantine Eastern-rite Christianity, and much of the narrative in this book has revealed the intimate inter-relationship of Carpatho-Rusyn society and culture with the Orthodox and Greek Catholic churches. The religious revival that took place in Subcarpathian Rus'/ Transcarpathia following the disintegration of the Soviet Union and Communist rule in 1991 was not, however, related only to the Orthodox and Greek Catholic worlds.

Just after the collapse of Communist rule (1993), there were 1,210 registered religious communities in Transcarpathia, a number which had risen to 1,755 by the outset of 2013. While the relative and absolute number of Orthodox and most espe-cially Greek Catholics has risen during these two decades (together they make up 65 percent of total registered communities), the proportion of communities associ-ated with some form of Protestantism has remained the same, at 22 percent.[a] While it is true that aside from the Magyar-dominated Reformed Church (113 communi-ties) most of the other "Protestant" communities are small in size and with member-ships that continually fluctuate, there is no question that Protestantism has estab-lished an increasingly visible presence throughout post-Communist Transcarpathia, especially in larger towns or cities.

Several Greek Catholic and Orthodox priests viewed this situation with alarm and often spoke out against the dangers of these various "sects," which they believed threatened to undermine the traditional religious heritage of Carpatho-Rusyns. Very often the rhetoric of traditional religious leaders blamed this "danger-ous" situation on Protestant institutions based in western Europe and, in particu-lar, the United States. These were suspected of providing large sums of money to proselytize among the allegedly naïve and susceptible Eastern-rite faithful or for-merly non-religious individuals seeking some kind of spiritual stability in the rapidly changing social and cultural environment throughout much of central and eastern Europe, including Transcarpathia. More often than not, the proselytization was not carried out through traditional means, such as preaching at emotionally charged evangelical-style religious gatherings. Instead, more indirect techniques were employed and couched in social programs (including soup kitchens serving free meals) and English-language courses for young people who at the time were eager to learn about—and perhaps emigrate to—the West.

Despite the displeasure of some Orthodox and Greek Catholic priests and lay-people toward what they considered a phenomenon brought to the region for the first time by American evangelical preachers after the fall of Communism, Protestantism is hardly new to the region. In fact, the first Protestant community was established as early as in 1540 in the town of Khust, just a few years after Martin Luther posted on the doors of the cathedral in Wittenberg (1517) his "revolutionary" theses, which protested against abuses in the Catholic Church. The first Protestant community in Khust was soon followed by others in the southern regions of Subcarpathian Rus', primarily among the local Magyar inhabitants and, to a lesser degree, among the region's ethnic German townspeople. Subcarpathia's earliest

Protestants were for the most part not followers of Luther, but of the other influential sixteenth-century religious reformer, John Calvin, who is considered the founder of the Reformed variant of Protestantism.

Protestantism itself is a somewhat vague concept that today is used to describe a variety of sects, which often differ widely in their belief systems and, in some cases (Unitarians, Jehovah's Witnesses), may have only a tenuous relationship to basic Christian religious precepts. Moreover, there are significant differences between mainline Protestant churches (Anglican, Presbyterian, Lutheran, Anabaptist), which date back to the sixteenth-century Reformation, and those founded much later in the nineteenth or twentieth centuries. With regard to the Carpathian world, mainline Protestantism took hold for the most part among neighboring peoples: Reformed Calvinism among the Magyars of Subcarpathian Rus', and Evangelical Lutheranism among urban Germans and Slovaks in towns in and near the Prešov Region.

Because of the close association of religion with a particular ethnic group (Orthodoxy or Greek Catholicism among Carpatho-Rusyns; Protestantism among Magyars and Germans; Roman Catholicism among Germans, Slovaks, and Magyars), each Christian religious community in Subcarpathian Rus' lived in relative spiritual isolation from one another. There were some exceptions, however, when Protestant secular authorities interfered directly in the life of the Orthodox and Uniate/Greek Catholic churches. This was particularly the case in the seventeenth and early eighteenth centuries, when much of Subcarpathian Rus' was part of Protestant-ruled Transylvania (see above, Chapter 6).

It was not until the twentieth century, however, that Protestantism began to make serious inroads into Carpatho-Rusyn society. This occurred, in particular, during the interwar period of Czechoslovak rule, although not because of any expansion on the part of mainline churches (Reformed Calvinist, Evangelical Lutheran). Rather, it was because of the proselytization by missionaries promoting alternative variants of Protestantism—Baptists, Adventists, and so-called Free Christians.

The earliest and best organized of these groups were the Baptists, who are noted for their practice of adult baptism, rejection of certain dogmas and sacraments of other Christian churches, and emphasis on free interpretation of the Bible. They reject ecclesiastical hierarchies that are characteristic of most mainline Eastern- and Western-rite Christian churches, and instead are helped in their individual understanding of the Bible by a presbyter (the rough equivalent of a priest or pastor), who heads Baptist congregations, each of which is effectively self-governing.

The Baptist movement made its appearance in Subcarpathian Rus' already under Austro-Hungarian rule during the first decade of the twentieth century, in particular among some of the region's Magyar inhabitants. After World War I, Baptist congregations began to include Carpatho-Rusyns, whose leaders were helped in their missionary work by the Evangelical Baptist Union of Czech Brethren based in Prague. The regional center of the Baptist movement was in the town of Velykyi Bychkiv in far eastern Maramorosh county, where in 1933 the Unity of Subcarpathian Brothers/Iednota podkarpatskykh brativ was set up to encourage further missionary work.

Even less structured than Baptist congregations were the so-called Free Christian/Svobodni khrystiiany, or Bible readers. The first such community was established in 1920 in the village of Kliucharky in Bereg county, and from there the movement spread to several other Carpatho-Rusyn villages around the city of Mukachevo and to other parts of Subcarpathian Rus'. It is interesting to note that, in the case of both the Evangelical Baptists and Free Christians, the most important missionary work was conducted in interwar Subcarpathian Rus' by immigrants who returned home from working abroad, whether France (Ivan Frantsuk) or the United States (Petro Semenovych).

Ever since the sixteenth-century Reformation, the basic principle of the Protestant movement has been a belief in the authority of the Bible and the right (even duty) of each Christian believer to read and interpret Biblical scripture for him or herself, although under the guidance of the Holy Spirit and with the help—but not dictate—of religious leaders (elected pastors and presbyters, or self-appointed "leaders"). On the far end of this "Protestant" spectrum were the Jehovah's Witnesses, whose origins date from the 1870s in the United States (Charles Taze Russell of Allegheny, Pennsylvania). The movement, fostered by the Watchtower Bible and Tract Society and its publication, *Watchtower Awake,* is centered on a belief in the second coming of Christ and the preceeding Battle of Armageddon, which allegedly has already begun. Jehovah's Witnesses have no ministers and no churches, but meet in buildings called the Kingdom Hall. Because of their rejection of all governments (and refusal to serve in the military), they have experienced various forms of persecution in virtually every country where they are found, including the United States where they originated. It is not certain whether there may have been some Jehovah's Witnesses (Russelistŷ) in Subcarpathian Rus' during the interwar years, but there is evidence that they existed during the return of Hungarian rule to the region after 1938–1939, in particular among the region's ethnic Magyar inhabitants.

Relative to the dominant Greek Catholic and Orthodox churches, and the Reformed Calvinist Church (mostly among Subcarpathia's Magyars), the number of individuals within the overall population of Subcarpathian Rus' who were associated with some form of Protestantism was always small. On the other hand, the movement was well represented among Carpatho-Rusyns. Hence, in 1946, the recently established Soviet regime reported that of the 1,600 Evangelical Baptists and 700 Free Christians organized in a total of 81 communities, all but 11 of those communities were comprised of Carpatho-Rusyns.[b]

During the Soviet period it was not only the Greek Catholic Church which became a target of persecution on the part of the officially atheistic government. Because its members were almost all Magyars, the Reformed Calvinist Church was branded by association with "fascist Hungary," which had just been defeated and driven out of Subcarpathian Rus'. Consequently, in 1947 the Soviet government refused to recognize the church's newly elected administrator (István Györke, subsequently arrested and sentenced to hard labor in the Gulag), and instead helped to find a candidate who was more malleable to the Communist rulers.

Whereas the officially atheistic Soviet state did allow religious organizations to function, they could do so only with permission granted by legal decree. In that context, the authorities favored bringing the various Protestant groups together; if united in one organization, they could more easily be monitored and controlled by the government. The authorities hoped to include the mainline Reformed Church as well, but the active refusal of Magyar pastors to join in the unification process was successful, so that the church was left to function as a distinct religious body.

For other "Protestant" groups the model to follow was that of the All-Union Council of Evangelical Christians established in 1944 in the Soviet capital of Moscow. Two years later "the act of union of all Free Christian communities in Transcarpathia with the All-Union Council of Evangelical Christians and Baptists" was proclaimed at a council in Mukachevo, which consequently allowed these groups "to be registered together according to the laws of the Soviet Union."[c]

It is not surprising, considering the independent-minded thrust of Protestantism, that a certain number of Transcarpathian Baptists, Free Christians, and other Evangelicals refused to recognize what, from their perspective, was a government-imposed amalgamation of their communities. Those who refused to join the 1946 Mukachevo act of union were subject to persecution. These included unauthorized groups like the Bible-reading Brethren or Eastern Brethren/*Skhidni braty*, who dated from the interwar years, as well as the Seventh-Day Adventists, whose communities began to expand after World War II during the early Soviet period. Among the illegal "underground sects" (*sektants'ke pidpillia*) which felt the full brunt of Soviet persecution were the Jehovah's Witnesses. Beginning in 1947, a concerted campaign was undertaken to uncover Jehovah's Witnesses in various places throughout Transcarpathia (Solotvyno, Rakoshyno, Kobylets'ka Poliana, and elsewhere), who were then arrested and sentenced to terms ranging from 5 to 25 years. Among their "crimes" were the following: acting as enemies of the Soviet state, refusal to vote and serve in the military, and possession of anti-Soviet (that is, religious) publications.

Both before and during Soviet times, most Protestant "sects" used Russian-language religious texts and listened to "sermons" in Russian. This was likely because of the easier access to Russian-language Bibles and other literature going back to the pre-World War I Russian Empire and, in particular, to the work of international organizations like the British and Foreign Bible Society, which since 1804 had published several editions of Russian-language Bibles. Even in the United States, where a few Carpatho-Rusyn immigrants founded in the early 1920s a Bible-reading community based in Proctor, Vermont (with branches in Connecticut and New Jersey), their main newspaper *Prorocheskoe svietlo* (*The Prophetic Light,* 1921–53), appeared in "Russian" (actually a mixture of Russian, Church-Slavonic, and Carpatho-Rusyn dialects).

The predominance of the Russian language remains characteristic of the various Baptist and Evangelical sects, which have been given a new lease on life following the collapse of Soviet rule. Independent Ukraine, which itself has struggled to implement democratic rule since the country's establishment in 1991, has maintained a generally liberal policy and has registered without much difficulty a wide range of non-mainline "Protestant" groups. Whereas the Ukrainian government has been tolerant of these communities, their adherents have frequently been the brunt of criticism in sermons by Orthodox and Greek Catholic priests. They are even more often the target of negative comments from fellow Transcarpathians who are suspicious of what they believe are "secretive" and, therefore, suspicious sects, whose adherents practice "strange" rituals that are unacceptably different from the Eastern- or Western-rite Christian "norm."

Although Protestant sects are today an integral part and a social reality in Transcarpathia's urban and rural areas, their adherents have for the most part not become involved in the Carpatho-Rusyn national revival. There are some exceptions, however. Those exceptions even include some descendents of Carpatho-Rusyns in the United States. For over a decade toward the end of the twentieth century, the head of the fundamentalist Christian sect, the Worldwide Church of God and the publisher of the influential religious magazine, *The Plain Truth*, was Joseph W. Tkach. The son of Carpatho-Rusyn immigrants from the Prešov Region, Tkach was anxious to proselytize in the former Soviet Union; the first place his church began its work was in 1992 in Ukraine's Transcarpathia, where, as the church's official newspaper reported, "the somber crowd listened with great interest" as the preacher from America "spoke about Mr. Tkach's Rusyn roots."[d]

Even more ironic is the following little-known fact: the initiator of the First World Congress of Rusyns in 1991 was Rudolf Matola, a native of the village of Kliucharky, which had a Free Christian Bible-reading community going back to the 1930s. Matola not only was the stimulus behind the convocation of the Rusyn World Congress, but as a Subcarpathian Evangelical Protestant of long-standing, he published a large-scale history of the church (*Ystoriia tserkvy*, 2005) in his personal variant of the Rusyn language.

[a] The figures for 1993 are based on the sociological research data reported in Ivan Myhovych, *Relihiia i tserkvy v nashomu kraï* (Uzhhorod, 1993), pp. 84–85; the figures for 2013 are data confirmed by Ukraine's Ministry of Culture and reproduced in Serhii Fedaka, *Z istoriï khrystyianstva na Zakarpatti* (Uzhhorod, 1993), pp. 11–13.

[b] Oksana Leshko, "Protestants'ki hromady Zakarpattia u 30-kh—40kh rr. XX st.," in *Naukovi zapysky Uzhhorods'koho universytetu: Seriia istorychno-relihiini studiï*, Vol. I (Uzhhorod, 2012), p. 77.

[c] Cited in ibid., p. 78.

[d] *The Worldwide News* (Pasadena, Calif.), 6 October 1992, p. 2.

Transcarpathia's Orthodox priesthood is, therefore, trained in and maintains contact with the Orthodox world of the Moscow Patriarchate, where Russian is considered the language and culture of prestige. There are, nonetheless, a few Orthodox priests who play an active role in Carpatho-Rusyn affairs, the most prominent of whom is Dymytrii Sydor, who, aside from his controversial political activity, has managed to design in the Russian style and to oversee the construction on a main square in Uzhhorod the largest cathedral-size Orthodox church in all of central Europe.

Because of the political preoccupation of most Carpatho-Rusyn activists, cultural work remains very underdeveloped in Ukraine's Transcarpathia. In contrast to most other countries where Carpatho-Rusyns live, since 1991 there has been no Rusyn-language newspaper published in the region other than sporadically (lasting at most for a year or so). In essence, there is no Carpatho-Rusyn press in Transcarpathia, other than a few issues funded by specific political parties on the eve of national elections.

This is not to say that there have been no cultural achievements. These, however, have been the result of individual initiative, such as the monumental two-volume Rusyn-Russian dictionary by Igor Kercha, Rusyn-language literary works by a few authors (Volodymyr Fedynyshynets', Ivan Petrovtsi), and a few issues of a scholarly and public affairs journal (*Rusnats'kyi svit*, 1999–2008). Again, in contrast to Poland, Slovakia, and Serbia, where the Carpatho-Rusyn communities are much smaller, in Transcarpathia there have been efforts but no success in creating a generally accepted grammar as the basis for a standard Rusyn literary language.

Among the most systematically organized cultural efforts have been those undertaken by the Valerii Padiak Publishing House, which since the year 2000 has published nearly a hundred volumes in Rusyn and other languages (primarily Ukrainian and Russian) that promote various aspects (historical, linguistic, literary, ethnographic) of Carpatho-Rusyn culture. For the past few years there has also been a so-called Sunday school program, that is, extracurricular classes—usually taught in Rusyn by teachers in state schools—with courses about Carpatho-Rusyn history and culture. The popular Sunday school program depends entirely on funding from the Carpatho-Rusyn diaspora in North America. Despite such support, the 24 to 40 classes that have been in existence since 2004 (with a high of 860 students in 2008) are hardly able to respond to the needs of a Carpatho-Rusyn population in Ukraine's Transcarpathia, which some suggest could number as high as 773,000.[20] In the end, "the third Carpatho-Rusyn national revival," which certain commentators have used as an epithet to describe developments since the Revolutions of 1989, has witnessed only limited success in post-Communist Ukrainian-ruled Transcarpathia.

The Post-Communist Prešov Region and the Lemko Region—Slovakia and Poland

The fate of Carpatho-Rusyns in the "western half" of historic Carpathian Rus' following the Revolutions of 1989 was dependent on the policies of the countries in which they lived: Czechoslovakia and Poland. Despite the differences between the post-Communist experience of these two countries, which in turn was to have an impact on the evolution of the movement for national emancipation and self-awareness, Carpatho-Rusyns on both sides of the Czechoslovak-Polish border were in the end to be brought closer together than they had ever been in the twentieth century, at least since the pre-World War I days of Habsburg-ruled Austria-Hungary.

Czechoslovakia's Velvet Revolution

The Velvet Revolution, Czechoslovakia's version of the upheaval of 1989, not only brought an end to Communist rule, it also set in motion a series of events that within a few years brought an end to the very country itself. Ever since Czechoslovakia had come into being in 1918, its governments were faced with the problem of power-sharing between the country's two largest nationalities, Czechs and Slovaks.

Basically, Czech leaders were comfortable with a centralized state, while the Slovaks preferred a federal structure in which their part of the republic would govern itself. These contrasting views, which continued into the post-1948 Communist era resurfaced during the "Prague Spring" of 1968. In an effort to assuage the Slovaks, who were among the leading figures in the 1968 reform period, the country was structurally transformed into a federal state, henceforth comprised of the administratively distinct Czech Socialist Republic and Slovak Socialist Republic. The Communist principle of centralized rule did not, however, provide Slovakia in any meaningful way with self-rule. Consequently, in the post-Communist era after 1989, the country's new leaders were faced with the task of trying to readjust the relationship between the two parts of what from April 1990 was called the Czech and Slovak Federated Republic. In effect, the country had three governments: the Czech Republic government; the Slovak Republic government; and the Czecho-Slovak federal government.

Even though Carpatho-Rusyns in Slovakia's Prešov Region played no part in the controversies about federalization, they did have the advantage of being able to address their concerns and requests for support from either the Slovak government, the Czecho-Slovak federal government, or both. These multiple options worked in their favor with regard to one event that during the early post-Communist years was to be of crucial importance for the future status of Carpatho-Rusyns. That event was the census of March 1991.

Censuses confirm nationalities

Since 1968, the ethnonym *Rusyn* was again recognized in Czechoslovakia as a legitimate self-descriptor, although it was considered a synonym for Ukrainian. Therefore, in censuses conducted during the last decades of Communist rule (1970 and 1980), persons who might have responded *Rusyn* were recorded as *Ukrainian*. But what was to happen in the democratic environment of post-1989 federal Czecho-Slovakia, which was headed by the liberal-minded former dissident and now president of the country, Václav Havel?

According to generally accepted human rights principles—to which the Havel-led post-Communist Czecho-Slovakia ascribed—each individual should have the right to determine and to declare publicly his or her own nationality and to be recognized as such by the authorities. Nor was the right to self-identity of importance only to the individual. The numerical size of the national group as a whole had some very important practical implications. This is because it was almost inevitable that the amount of governmental financial support for each of the state's national minorities would be based on the size of the particular group. Pro-Ukrainian activists in the Prešov Region wanted only one group—which they called "Rusyns-Ukrainians"—to be recorded in the published census data. Pro-Rusyn activists, on the other hand, took what they felt was the liberal democratic position that individuals should not only have the right to identify but also to be recorded as *either* Rusyn *or* Ukrainian.

In the end, the Czecho-Slovak federal authorities (some of whose advisors were sympathetic to the view that Carpatho-Rusyns have the right to be considered a distinct nationality) decided in the 1991 census to report the two groups separately. The results in the nationality category were just under 17,000 Rusyns, nearly 14,000 Ukrainians, and 1,600 Russians.[1] Even more significant were the results on the question of native language: 49,100 persons indicated Rusyn versus only 9,500 Ukrainian.[2] Clearly, these figures proved that there was indeed a Carpatho-Rusyn community concentrated in northeastern Slovakia. The question remained how the governmental authorities were going to deal with the reality of one ethnoliguistic group whose members opted to identify with two different nationalities: Carpatho-Rusyn or Ukrainian.

Actually, the situation was a bit more complex. There were still some Carpatho-Rusyns who held the conviction—embedded in them by their education in the 1930s and 1940s—that they were of the Russian nationality.

Such Prešov Region "Russians" were decreasingly smaller in number, and it is likely that a significant proportion of the Russian respondents on the census were not locals, but rather recent immigrants from Russia or ethnic Russians from eastern Ukraine. Among persons of Carpatho-Rusyn heritage, much more numerous were individuals who, on census questionnaires, either confused citizenship with nationality or consciously opted to identify as Slovaks. As we have seen, the number of Carpatho-Rusyns in the Prešov Region had declined by three-quarters between 1910 and 1991 (see above Chapter 23, Table 23.1). The longstanding phenomenon of national assimilation and the question of how to attract "Slovaks" of Carpatho-Rusyn ancestry back to the fold became issues of even greater concern than the tendency of some group members to identify as Ukrainians or as Russians.

Independent Slovakia and the European Union

It was not long before the Prešov Region's Carpatho-Rusyns would have to rely on dealing with only one government. This is because the debates about the administrative relationship between Czechs and Slovaks finally ended with the replacement of Czecho-Slovakia as a country and the birth, on 1 January 1993, of two new independent states: Slovakia and the Czech Republic. Slovakia became a republic headed by a president elected by popular vote for a five-year term, and with a one-chamber parliament whose largest party, or coalition of parties, designated the prime minister to form the ruling government.

Initially, the government of independent Slovakia continued the liberal democratic direction of the 1989 revolutionary era and tried to provide equal financial support for the cultural activity of both pro-Rusyn and pro-Ukrainian organizations. This situation changed at the very end of 1994, however, when after several interruptions the Slovak nationalist leader Vladimír Mečiar returned as prime minister, a post he was to hold for the next four years. During that time Slovakia provided much less funding to its national minorities (on average only one-quarter of what the previous short-lived governments provided) and, in practice, it favored the Ukrainian over the Rusyn orientation in the Prešov Region.[3] The country's political situation turned around again in late 1998, when a coalition government (under Prime Minister Mikuláš Dzurinda, of part Carpatho-Rusyn heritage) came to power. The Dzurinda government, with a new post of deputy prime minister for human and minority rights (held by an ethnic Magyar, Pál Csáky) as well as the new president Rudolf Šuster (of Carpathian German heritage), was much more favorable to the country's national minorities in general and was more balanced in its attitude toward the Rusyn national orientation and its civic and cultural organizations. The government's efforts to improve relations with the country's national minorities (especially the politically influential Magyars and socially problematic Roma/Gypsies) was in part motivated by wide-ranging internal reforms undertaken as Slovakia prepared for entry into the European Union.

Accession to the European Union, which finally took place in May 2004, had both a positive and negative impact on Carpatho-Rusyns. On the one hand, Slovakia's Prešov Region Rusyns were no longer separated from their closest brethren, the Lemko Rusyns in Poland, which also entered the European Union in 2004. On the other hand, while border controls between Slovakia and Poland eventually disappeared, pressure from the European Union required that Slovakia reinforce its borders with Ukraine. The relatively easy flow of cross-border traffic that characterized the 1990s began to end at the outset of the twenty-first century as a result of an increase in restrictions that made it more difficult to maintain contacts between Carpatho-Rusyns in the Prešov Region and Ukraine's Transcarpathia. Some cynical, albeit perceptive, commentators quipped that the democratic European Union had created a new "Iron Curtain" along the eastern borders of Slovakia and Poland with Ukraine.

Despite the sometimes negative aspects of Slovakia's internal political policies, Carpatho-Rusyns in the Prešov Region began to make considerable progress during the last decade of the twentieth and outset of the twenty-first centuries. The progress was the result not only of Slovak government funding, but also because of the commitment of a small but effective group of Carpatho-Rusyn activists working in the media, publishing industry, schools, and cultural institutions, in particular the theater.

Prešov Region Carpatho-Rusyns reaffirm their existence

At first, the group's interests were represented by only one organization, the Rusyn Renaissance Society/Rusyns'ka obroda. On 17 November 1990, the first anniversary of the Velvet Revolution, the society held a plenary session at which it spelled out a set of goals whose achievement was to govern the direction of the Carpatho-Rusyn movement in Slovakia's Prešov Region for the next two decades. Its four basic goals were: (1) to have the concept of a distinct Rusyn nationality officially recognized in Czecho-Slovakia; (2) to codify a literary standard for publications in the Rusyn language; (3) to have Rusyn introduced as a language of instruction, at least in the first four years of elementary school in all villages inhabited by Rusyns; and (4) to have Ukrainian cultural and educational institutions carry the name *Rusyn* and to direct their attention primarily to the inhabitants and culture of the Prešov Region.[4] During the following two decades, all four of these goals were achieved in whole or in part.

Already in 1990, the professional Ukrainian National Theater in Prešov was renamed the Alexander Dukhnovych Theater (after the nineteenth-century Carpatho-Rusyn national awakener), and within a few years its repertoire was performed exclusively in Rusyn. About the same time, the extremely popular and professional Dukla Ukrainian Folk Ensemble changed its name to PULS (actually, the Slovak acronym of its original name) and removed most non-Rusyn dances and songs from the repertoire. These same years also coincided with intense linguistic work by two Prešov University faculty (Iurii Pan'ko and Vasyl' Iabur). Their efforts resulted in the publication of several standard language texts and the gathering of civic leaders and Slavic scholars from Slovakia and abroad in the country's capital of Bratislava to celebrate the formal announcement of the codification of the Rusyn language (27 January 1995). This announcement laid to rest skeptical opinion in Slovak political and civic circles that Carpatho-Rusyns did not have their own language. More importantly, it paved the way for instruction in schools and for the use in state-supported media (especially radio) of what was henceforth referred to as the *Rusyn language.*[5]

The efforts to promote the Rusyn language and national orientation were contested by the pro-Ukrainian intelligentsia and their organizations. Consequently, Slovak government policy makers were frequently at a loss with regard to deciding which orientation to support. In the end, the government opted to support both, accepting the local reality that from one ethno-linguistic group (representing individuals from the same region, the same village, and in some cases from the same family) there existed two nationalities: Carpatho-Rusyn and Ukrainian. Hence, the state-run radio station based in Prešov and later Košice was authorized to broadcast separate Rusyn-language and Ukrainian-language programs.

Schools in which some classes from the Communist era were taught in Ukrainian still continued to operate, while new Rusyn-language classes, following the adoption of a state-approved curriculum, were allowed to function in Slovak-language schools if a certain percentage of parents requested them. Because of the voluntary nature of the program and the reluctance of parents to have their children learn a language which, they believed, had little "practical" value, Rusyn-language classes were opened in only a handful of schools. In only one case (the village of Čabiny in 2005) was Rusyn introduced not simply as a subject but as the school's language of instruction. Technically, therefore, there was—and still is—only one Rusyn elementary school in Slovakia.

Much more successful has been education at the university level. The existing Department of Ukrainian Language and Literature—originally intended to serve the higher educational needs of the local Carpatho-Rusyn population—was left intact at Prešov University. Then, in 1999, the university created a Rusyn-language section, which six years later was transformed into the Institute for Rusyn Language and Culture, whose primary task is to train prospective teachers for elementary schools and to promote scholarship and publications about Carpatho-Rusyns.

Meanwhile, the Rusyn Renaissance Society continued to pressure government authorities to change the name and the orientation of the state-supported Museum of Ukrainian Culture in Svidník, whose excellent permanent displays and archival holdings dealt almost entirely with Carpatho-Rusyns. A change from Ukrainian, whether in name or policy, never took place, so that in the end the Slovak government decided to create another institution, the Museum of Rusyn Culture. Alongside the Ukrainian and other museums representing national minorities, the Museum of Rusyn Culture has operated since 2007 in Prešov as part of the statewide Slovak National Museum.

The Greek Catholic Church: a positive or negative force?

From the standpoint of Carpatho-Rusyn cultural interests, one area remained problematic—the Greek Catholic Church. In the wake of the Revolution of 1989, the status of the church was greatly enhanced. With its 259 parishes and 208,000 faithful (1990), it remained the largest religious body among the Prešov Region's Carpatho-Rusyns.[6] Already before the end of 1989 the Vatican gave full authority to Jan Hirka as resident bishop of the Eparchy of Prešov; then, in 2008, the eparchy became the seat of a metropolitan church for Slovakia with eparchies in Prešov, Košice, and Bratislava. At the same time, however, its hierarchs transformed the Greek Catholic Church into a Slovak institution, by replacing Church Slavonic with Slovak in the liturgy and homilies and by assigning Slovak-speaking priests to many villages where the majority population is Carpatho-Rusyn. The slovakization policy provoked criticism by the Rusyn Renaissance and other civic societies as well as discontent on the part of some patriotic Rusyn-oriented priests and laity.

In many ways, the post-1989 era seemed to be a return to the past. In the nineteenth century, a small group of patriotic priests were faced with the overwhelming threat of magyarization favored by their own Greek Catholic hierarchs; now, at the end of the twentieth century a new generation of patriotic Carpatho-Rusyn priests (Frantishek Krainiak, Iaroslav Popovych, among others) have felt obliged to resist the slovakization of the Prešov Greek Catholic hierarchy (led by Bishop Ján Hirka and his successor, Ján Babjak). Convinced of the close relationship between religious practice and the preservation of one's ancestral heritage and national identity, these priests revived the pre-Communist-era Carpatho-Rusyn religious organization, the St. John the Baptist Society, and they have produced for the faithful a wide variety of publications (religious books, annual almanacs, magazines), including the four books of the New Testament Gospel, all translated into the Rusyn vernacular.

Nationality assertion and assimilation

This wide range of what one might call cultural reclamation activity produced results that, in a sense, could be quantified. In 2001, the second census since the Revolutions of 1989 was conducted in Slovakia. Somewhat unique for central Europe was the government's policy of actively encouraging its citizens through a widespread pre-census media campaign to identify with their ancestral culture, whether or not it was Slovak. In other words, Slovakia's authorities were making it clear that all the inhabitants of the country, despite differing ethnolinguistic or national backgrounds, were equally Slovak citizens. The question for Carpatho-Rusyn activists was whether their cultural work since the Revolution of 1989 had any impact on stemming the tide of national assimilation, which had led to a steady decrease in the number of Carpatho-Rusyns during the period of "imposed" ukrainianization and "voluntary" slovakization that had characterized the four decades of Communist rule in Czechoslovakia.

In the end, the results of the 2001 census were more positive than even Carpatho-Rusyn enthusiasts as well as skeptics (including pro-Ukrainian critics of Rusynism) had predicted. The number of persons who responded that their nationality was Rusyn increased, in comparison to the 1991 figure, by 40 percent (to 24,200), while the mother tongue (native language) response was up by 12 percent (to 54,900).[7] A decade later, in the census of 2011, the number of persons who responded *Rusyn* to the nationality question increased once again, this time by nearly 39 percent to 33,500. Those identifying with the Rusyn mother tongue increased slightly to 55,500. During these same two decades, 1991 to 2011, the number of persons identifying as Ukrainian declined by 47 percent in both categories (down to 7,400 for nationality and to 5,700 for mother tongue).[8]

Despite such positive developments in the number of Carpatho-Rusyns, national assimilation has remained a matter of concern for civic activists in Slovakia's Prešov Region. The trend toward depopulation of villages that steadily increased during the last decades of Communist rule has continued, as young people in search of employment move away permanently to Slovak towns near the Prešov Region and to urban centers in other parts of Slovakia. Many intermarry with spouses of Slovak or other nationalities and only rarely are they able or willing to pass on their ancestral Rusyn language and heritage to their offspring who are born and fully acculturated in a Slovak environment. Carpatho-Rusyn villages, many of which are today the preserve of older people, are almost all experiencing demographic decline, with several having fewer than a hundred inhabitants. Local village schools continue to close for lack of pupils and several Greek Catholic and Orthodox parishes are served by visiting priests who are only able to serve liturgies on a weekly basis. Even in those villages where an elementary school may still exist, parents remain reluctant to request that Rusyn be taught, so that throughout Slovakia's Prešov Region there are at most only a dozen schools where students receive formal instruction in the language of their ancestors, and even that consists of only a couple of hours per week. Therefore, what exists is a discernable contrast between the relative vibrancy of the national movement among intellectual leaders residing in towns and cities and the rather passive—at times even negative—view of the rural residents toward what they are told is "their" Carpatho-Rusyn heritage.

The organizational strength of the Carpatho-Rusyn movement in the Prešov Region has, however, made Slovakia after 1989 the natural site for international, or interregional coordination. Hence, the headquarters of the World Congress of Rusyns was set up in Prešov and that body's official organs (*Rusyn* and later *Holos Rusyna*) are published in the same city and at Slovak government expense. The first and second international congresses of the Rusyn language (1992 and 1999) were also held in Slovakia. It was at the first of these that the general principles for creating a Rusyn literary language (or languages) were agreed upon and eventually followed by scholars and writers in all countries where Carpatho-Rusyns live.

CODIFICATION OF A RUSYN LITERARY LANGUAGE

After the political changes brought about by the Revolutions of 1989, Carpatho-Rusyns in all countries proclaimed the need, as a distinct nationality, to have their own codified literary language based on the spoken vernacular. But what specific spoken vernacular? In other words, which spoken dialect, or amalgam of dialects, should serve as the basis of a new codified literary norm?

These kinds of questions are not easily resolved and, moreover, are questions which have faced patriotic intelligentsias among other nationalities as well. In an attempt to arrive at a linguistic consensus that would also be acceptable to the people for which a given literary language was being formulated, the intelligentsia representing a particular European people decided to discuss—and hopefully resolve—these matters at so-called language congresses. Among the earliest of such congresses were those convened for the Dutch language in Belgium (1849), followed by congresses for Catalan (1906), Yiddish (1908), Belarusan (1926), Ukrainian (1927), and Turkish (1932), among others.

Leaders in the post-1989 Carpatho-Rusyn national revival also felt that a language congress was necessary to resolve the problems they faced in trying to create a Rusyn literary language. Aside from purely linguistic issues, their goal was made more complicated by the fact that Carpatho-Rusyns lived in at least five different states. That experience, lasting nearly half a century after World War II, had a marked impact on the Rusyn spoken language in each of those countries.

In an attempt to address such challenges, a "working language seminar"—which before long was referred as the First Congress of the Rusyn Language—was convened in November 1992 in a spa resort near the town of Bardejov in northeastern Slovakia. Present were writers, journalists, scholars, and cultural activists from Carpatho-Rusyn communities in Poland, Slovakia, Ukraine, Hungary, Yugoslavia, the United States and Canada, as well as professional linguists, Slavists, and language planners from several other countries. After two days of deliberations, the following twelve-point resolution was adopted:

(1) Participants in the seminar concluded that the Rusyn language should be codified on the basis of the spoken vernacular in each of the regions where Rusyns live (Subcarpathia, Lemko Region, Prešov Region, and Vojvodina).

(2) In order to achieve this goal the participants considered of greatest importance: (a) to create dictionaries of specific and general content; and (b) to publish Rusyn grammars on the basis of the selected linguistic data.

(3) It is of great necessity to prepare a historical grammar of the Rusyn language.

(4) The literary language of each region should be formed on the basis of the dominant dialect.

(5) Literary works should be developed that make use of the new lexical and grammatical norms.

(6) The new linguistic norms should be introduced into the school system and public life.

(7) A theoretical and practical language institute should be created.

(8) In the process of codification there should be close cooperation with Slavic scholarly institutes in all countries.

(9) The graphic system (alphabet) for the Rusyn language is Cyrillic.

(10) Each region should prepare a bibliography of current works in Rusyn.

(11) A coordinating commission for the Rusyn language created at the seminar will continue to meet periodically.

(12) The participants of the seminar expressed the conviction that the codification of the Rusyn literary language will be a long process whose success will be determined by usage in daily life.[a]

Since the 1992 congress, two others have been held (1999 in Prešov and 2007 in Cracow). The original conceptual principles still guide linguistic work, and most of the goals set out in the 1992 resolutions have been achieved. The only addendum is that Carpatho-Rusyns in Hungary have recently (2011) decided to codify a fifth variant of the Rusyn language.

[a] Cited in the *Carpatho-Rusyn American,* XV, 4 (Pittsburgh, Pa., 1992), p. 5.

Poland's three Lemko-Rusyn communities

The situation of Carpatho-Rusyns, or more specifically Lemkos, in post-Communist Poland is more problematic. One of the main challenges that has faced Poland's Lemko Rusyns is the fact that the group remains geographically dispersed among three areas: the Lemko Region in the far southeastern corner of Poland, and two other regions at the opposite ends of the country: Lower Silesia in the southwest, and the Lubuskie palatinate in west-central Poland along the border with Germany. Even within each of these areas Lemkos do not live in any large concentrations but are dispersed throughout several villages and towns in which they form a very small minority among the country's dominant population—Poles.

In an attempt to reach these geographically dispersed communities. Poland's first Lemko-Rusyn organization, the Lemko Society/Stovaryshŷnia Lemkiv, embarked on a program of grassroots cultural activities carried out both in southwestern Poland (the Lemko Amateur Theater at Legnica) as well as in the Lemko Region (the International Biennale of Lemko-Rusyn Culture at Krynica). Several other reestablished or newly formed organizations which came into being in the early 1990s focused their programs on the region where their headquarters were based, whether in the Lemko Region (the Museum of Lemko Culture in Zyndranowa and Ruska Bursa Society in Gorlice), in Lower Silesia (the Kychera Song and Dance Ensemble at Legnica), or in Lubuskie (the Association of Lemko Culture at its Lemko Tower center at Gorzów Wielkopolski).

As in neighboring Slovakia, the success of these Lemko-Rusyn organizations depended on two factors: the dynamic work of individuals, in this case the civic activist Andrei Kopcha, the poet Petro Murianka-Trokhanovskii, and the scholar Olena Duć-Fajfer; and the willingness of the Polish government to provide funding. In contrast to Slovakia, however, the post-Communist government of Poland initially provided no funding for Rusyn-oriented Lemko organizations. While not denying individuals the right to identify themselves as Lemkos or as Lemko Rusyns, the authorities generally continued to maintain the pre-1989 Communist position that Lemkos were a branch of Poland's numerically much larger Ukrainian national minority.

It is likely that the position of the governmental authorities in this matter was influenced by Poland's foreign policy goals. Post-Communist Poland was committed to establishing strong ties with its newly independent neighbor to the east, Ukraine. Consequently, Poland's policy makers were reluctant to alienate nationally patriotic elements in Ukraine, who adamantly argued that the Lemkos of Poland, like other East Slavic inhabitants (Boikos and Hutsuls) of the Carpathians are "ethnographic (sub-ethnic) groups" of the Ukrainian nationality. Ukraine's position was spelled out in 1999, when, as a member of the Council of Europe, it was required to provide formal clarification on this matter. While not denying that some of its citizens preferred to identify themselves as Rusyns or as Lemkos, its report to fellow European Council members stressed that "the overwhelming majority of representatives of these ethnic groups identifies itself as Ukrainians."[9]

While Poland was reluctant to irritate Ukraine's sensibilities on the "Rusyn matter," Lemko-Rusyn activists continued to lobby for recognition and financial support, which they finally began to receive in 1995. The sums were initially small, but by 2006 Lemko-Rusyn organizations received over 2.6 million złoty, placing them eighth (just after Jews) with regard to the amount of funding received by Poland's 14 recognized national minorities.[10]

It was in this changed atmosphere of increasing governmental support that the Lemko Society/Stovaryshŷnia Lemkiv created a Committee on National Education to promote the codification of a Lemko variant of the Rusyn language. The society published several textbooks culminating with the appearance of a standard grammar in the year 2000 (co-authored by a Lemko-Rusyn school teacher Miroslava Khomiak and the Polish linguist Henryk Fontański), whose appearance marked the formal codification of the Lemko-Rusyn language. As early as the 1991/1992 school year, classes in Lemko Rusyn were introduced first in two and then three schools in the Lemko Region, although they received no government funding. In 1999, however, Poland's Ministry of Education approved a curriculum for Lemko Rusyn to be taught at the state's expense at both the elementary and *gymnasium* (high school) levels. While the number of schools with Lemko-Rusyn classes increased (by the 2004/2005 school year there were 20 elementary- and 13 *gymnasium*-level classes spread throughout the Lemko Region, Lower Silesia, and Lubuskie), the number of students remained minuscule both at the elementary (164) and high school (109) level.[11] In order to train Lemko teaching cadres, a Lemko-Rusyn Philology Program was established (2001) at the Pedagogical University in Cracow.

Lemko Rusyns or Lemko Ukrainians?

As in neighboring Slovakia, these and other efforts to establish an institutional base for Lemko-Rusyn culture were opposed by certain activists of Lemko origin who argued that they—and the group as a whole—are part of the Ukrainian nationality. Alongside already existing Ukrainian organizations in Poland, the pro-Ukrainian Lemko activists created in 1990 the Union of Lemkos in Poland/Ob'iednannia Lemkiv v Pol'shchi with its base in Gorlice, a town near the Lemko Region. Symbolically, the Lemko Society (Stovaryshŷnia) emphasized its national orientation by membership in the World Congress of Rusyns, while the Union of Lemkos (Ob'iednannia) became a founding member of the World Federation of Ukrainian Lemko Organizations, based in the United States.

The rivalry between the supporters of these two organizations—the Rusynophile Stovaryshŷnia and Ukrainophile Ob'iednannia—for the allegiance of Poland's Lemkos was first evident at the annual summer Vatra Festival held in the Carpathians. The organizers of the festival, which began in 1983, were of Rusyn orientation, but by 1990 it was being run by the Union of Lemkos (Ob'iednannia). Consequently, the midsummer weekend gathering was rapidly transformed into an ostentatiously Ukrainian event at which participants from Ukraine—including at one year's festival the president of Ukraine, Viktor Iushchenko—were prominent guests. Since that time the original pro-Rusyn organizers revived their Vatra among the Lemko diaspora. It is held in the Silesian village of Michałów and has remained a Rusyn-oriented event sponsored by the Lemko Society (Stovaryshŷnia).

The pro-Rusyn Lemko Society (Stovaryshŷnia) and the pro-Ukrainian Union of Lemkos (Ob'iednannia) also competed with each other in an effort to obtain property that had once belonged to the community. One example was the building originally owned by the Ruska Bursa in Gorlice, which was confiscated by Nazi Germany in 1939, coopted by the Communist Polish authorities after the war, and eventually given to the city. Some members of the Lemko Society established in 1991 the Rusyn-oriented Ruska Bursa Society, which was allowed to hold language classes and other cultural events in the building. After a long court battle with the city of Gorlice and challenges for ownership lodged by the pro-Ukrainian Union of Lemkos, the Rusyn-oriented Ruska Bursa Society gained exclusive ownership of the building in 2009. Aside from sponsoring cultural events and housing a permanent exhibit of Lemko ethnography, the Ruska Bursa began to publish a bilingual Rusyn-Polish scholarly journal (*Richnyk Ruskoi Bursŷ*, 2005–present) initiated by the Lemko literary historian Olena Duć-Fajfer.

THE VATRA: A SYMBOL OF NATIONAL AND POLITICAL ADVOCACY

The name *vatra,* which means bonfire, has been used since 1983 to designate festivals organized by Lemko Rusyns anxious to promote their culture and identity within Polish society. Aside from the oldest and still largest Vatra Festival held annually in the Lemko Region (now in the village of Żdynia), two other *vatras* (at the village of Michałów in Lower Silesia and Ługi in Lubuskie) serve Lemko communities in western Poland. Aside from Lemkos of various national orientations, the *vatra* festivals attract a significant number of Poles who are interested in an "exotic" neighboring culture, as well as Poland's ethnic Ukrainians who come to celebrate a regional "branch" of their own culture. There are also several smaller *vatra* celebrations held each year in Lemko diaspora communities in western Poland and Canada; the largest of these take place in western Ukraine (at Monastyrys'ka in Galicia).

The *vatra* phenomenon actually derives from traditional practices connected with animal husbandry, especially in Subcarpathian Rus', where the tops of the highest mountains are tree-less fields (*polonyny*) used for centuries as pastures. The annual pasturage season was quite long, beginning sometime in late March or April (with the appearance of the first blades of grass) and lasting to early November. During those months there were three pasturage cycles—spring, summer, and fall—each lasting from 15 to 60 days. Cattle and sheep from owners in several villages were brought together and driven to the high mountain pastures (*polonyny*), where they would remain under the care of shepherds (*vivchar/iuhas/choban*) responsible to a specially selected head shepherd (*deputat/polonyn'osh/vatah/byrov do polonyny*).

Several customs arose in connection with the annual pasturage, beginning with a parting ceremony and the "march" to the mountain pasture (*polonyns'kyi khod*), and continuing with the festive opening of the shepherd's camp-site (*salash*), and the first lighting of the campfire (*vatra*) which was to remain lite (or at least smoldering) throughout the entire stay. When it was time to return home, the parting (*rozluchinnia*) from the campsite was preceded by putting out the *vatra* fire, which symbolized the close of one of the high mountain pasturing cycles or the end of the entire season. Upon arriving in the lowland villages, the shepherds returned the animals to their owners together with the cheeses they made during the summer. Highland mountain pasturing in the *polonyna* is still practiced today, although it is only in Ukraine's Subcarpathian Rus'/Transcarpathia where some of the rituals surrounding the departure and return are still maintained.

Despite the achievements of the Lemko Society (Stovaryshŷnia), the Ruska Bursa, and other organizations promoting Lemko-Rusyn culture and language, there are still several matters which continue to cloud relations with Polish society. The first of these is the memory of the Vistula Operation of 1947 and its disastrous impact (see above, Chapter 24). Efforts by Lemko organizations (whether pro-Rusyn or pro-Ukrainian) to obtain a formal apology from the Polish government have not been successful, nor have attempts to regain property lost by families after their deportation from their Carpathian villages.

The attraction of Polish assimilation

An even more serious consequence of the forced deportation of 1947 and the dispersal of Lemko Rusyns to various parts of western Poland has been national assimilation. The vast majority of younger and now middle-aged people, whose parents or grandparents were or are Lemkos, have themselves become Poles. This reality was graphically revealed in the census of 2002, in which for the first time since World War II questions on national/ethnic identity and native language were asked on Polish census forms. Lemko cultural activists had assumed that there were anywhere from 35,000 to 60,000 Lemkos living in Poland. The 2002 census returns recorded, however, only 5,900 persons of Lemko-Rusyn national identity (with a slightly less number of Lemko mother tongue). A significant majority were living outside the historic homeland, especially in Lower Silesia (3,100) and the Lubuskie palatinate (800), with about 30 percent (1,700) residing in the Lemko Region itself.[12] A decade later the number of persons in Poland who identified themselves as Lemkos (either as their only, their first, or their second identity) had nearly doubled to 10,000.[13]

It is true that Lemko Rusyns exist and that they are officially recognized and receive support for cultural activity from the Polish government. And it is also true that the Lemkos have solicited sympathy among many Poles who, through television programs and other media coverage have learned about the "exotic" culture of a few Lemkos who still manage to live in one of Poland's most popular tourist destinations—the Beskyd and Bieszczady ranges of the Carpathians. The question remains, however, whether Lemko Rusyns, in whichever three regions of the country they live, can survive the overwhelming social pressure to assimilate fully with Polish society.

Other Carpatho-Rusyn communities in the wake of the revolutions of 1989

The political transformation in central Europe brought about by the revolutions of 1989 made possible the emergence of newly organized Carpatho-Rusyn communities in four countries—Ukraine, the Czech Republic, Hungary, and Romania—and the reinvigoration of the older diasporan communities in the former Yugoslavia (eventually Serbia and Croatia) and in North America (Canada and the United States).

Ukraine

The Lemko diaspora resettled in historic eastern Galicia (Soviet Ukraine's oblasts of L'viv, Ternopil', and Ivano-Frankivs'k) eventually took advantage of the positive changes in the political atmosphere of the Soviet Union brought about by Mikhail Gorbachev. In May 1989, activists in L'viv formed the Lemko Society/Tovarystvo "Lemkovyna" under the leadership of the long-time postwar cultural and civic activist, Petro Kohut. This was followed by Lemko Region societies set up in the early 1990s in Ternopil' and Ivano-Frankivs'k for those respective oblasts, as well as numerous district (*raiony*) organizations throughout those three western Ukrainian oblasts as well as in other parts of eastern and southern Ukraine, including the capital Kyiv, where Lemkos lived.

The fall of the Soviet Union in late 1991 and the creation of independent Ukraine encouraged activists to form larger umbrella organizations, such as the First All-Ukrainian Congress of Lemkos/Pershyi Vseukraïns'kyi Konhres Lemkiv (1992) and the First Congress of the World Federation of Lemkos (1993), eventually comprised of Ukrainian-oriented Lemko organizations in seven countries of Europe and North America.

The basic goal of all these district (*raion*), regional (*oblast*), national (*vseukraïns'kyi*), and world organizations was to promote through a wide variety of cultural activities (concerts, conferences, summer Vatra festivals, art and ethnographic exhibits, publications) knowledge about the Lemko past and to create mechanisms to pass on the ancestral heritage to their offspring born in different parts of Ukraine far from the Carpathian homeland which they never knew nor even visited. These varied cultural activities have taken place in oblast centers (L'viv, Ternopil', Ivano-Frankivs'k), the national capital of Kyiv, and in smaller towns where Lemkos make up a significant percentage of the inhabitants. The most prominent of these is the town of Monastyrys'ka in southern Ternopil' oblast, which is the site of the largest annual Vatra festival and home to a Lemko Museum.

Throughout the 1990s, Lemko organization leaders grappled with the identity question. On the one hand, they all agreed that Lemkos had distinct speech and cultural characteristics, sometimes differing greatly from those of the rest of Ukraine. On the other hand, they argued that Lemkos are a branch of the Ukrainian nationality. Older activists (Petro Kohut, Ivan Krasovs'kyi) hoped to find some kind of compromise with the Carpatho-Rusyn revival taking place in Ukraine and neighboring countries; others succeeded in having all resolutions by national and world Lemkos congresses include a condemnation of "political Rusynism" and of any ideas that Carpatho-Rusyns (including Lemkos) comprise a distinct nationality. The identity dilemma was resolved in 1997, when, at the Second World Congress of Lemkos held in L'viv, all participants agreed to rename their representative umbrella organization the World Federation of Ukrainian Lemko Organizations/Svitova federatsiia ukraïns'kykh lemkivs'kykh ob'iednan'.

Aside from cultural activity, the Lemko Regional Society in Ternopil' headed by Oleksandr Venhrynovych engaged in civic and political work with the goal to convince the government of Ukraine that it recognize the deportation of Lemkos in 1944–1946 as something that did not occur voluntarily. If the authorities were to recognize that the deportation was carried out forcibly and was, therefore, a "crime" (*zlochyn*), Ukraine's Lemkos would have the right to moral and "material compensation" as well as "the right to return to the ancestral homeland [the Lemko Region in present-day Poland]."[1] The numerous interventions on this matter with Ukraine's authorities since 2001 have not produced any positive results.

While it is true that since 1989 and especially since 1991 there has been a wide range of Lemko cultural activity in independent Ukraine, such efforts at cultural preservation have had, in the end, an unintended opposite result—assimilation. During the more than four decades of the Soviet era (1944–1989), there were no formal structures (schools) other than a few folk ensembles that accepted, let alone promoted, Lemko cultural values and linguistic distinctiveness. Therefore, Ukrainian-born descendants of postwar resettled Lemkos could, at best, acquire only at home a passive knowledge of the language and culture of their ancestors. When it was finally possible in the late Gorbachev era to begin publicly promoting Lemko culture, most of the younger descendants of Lemko resettlers had by that time adopted a Ukrainian national identity and used Ukrainian as their daily language.

Most Ukrainian-oriented Lemko activists would likely not describe this development as assimilation, since Lemkos, they would argue, are a branch of Ukrainians. In the end, the efforts to preserve Lemko regional cultural attributes within the framework of a Ukrainian national identity have not succeeded. Even some pro-Ukrainian cultural activists have lamented the reality of "Ukrainian" assimilation:

> The generation [of Lemkos] born 'at home' [in the Lemko Region] have already forgotten their Lemko speech and for the most part speak a Lemko-Ukrainian mixed jargon. The generation born in Ukraine understands Lemko but cannot speak it, and, to be honest, does not want to. After all, they have no one to speak with. Before long Lemkos [in Ukraine] will no longer exist as an ethnic group.[2]

Czech Republic

Carpatho-Rusyns living in the Czech Republic have very diverse origins. One group comprises the children of state functionaries and other Czechs (small-scale businesspersons and farmers) who worked in Subcarpathian Rus' when it was part of interwar Czechoslovakia, but who were forced to leave the country's far eastern province when it was annexed to Hungary in 1938–39. Other "returnees" are the offspring of mixed Czech-Rusyn marriages from the interwar period; still others are family members of soldiers from Subcarpathian Rus', who served during World War II in the First Czechoslovak Army Corps and who, according to the Czechoslovak-Soviet Treaty of 1945, were given the option to live in postwar Czechoslovakia. Yet another group includes the large number of Carpatho-Rusyns from the Prešov Region, who in the immediate postwar years found work in the factories of northern Moravia and Silesia.

In the early 1990s, there were a few Carpatho-Rusyns still alive, who as young adults had settled permanently in Prague and other towns in Bohemia and Moravia during the 1920s and 1930s, when Subcarpathian Rus' was part of Czechoslovakia. The best known of them was Ivan Parkanyi, who since the early 1920s served as advisor for Subcarpathian affairs in the Office of the President of Czechoslovakia. After 1989, Parkanyi, who by then was in his nineties, caused a minor sensation among Czech journalists, who wrote about him in awe as a kind of living historic artifact. Even after the collapse of the first Czechoslovak republic in 1938, Parkanyi remained in the service of the presidential office until his retirement in 1952. This meant that he had the unique experience of having served four presidents: the democratic founders of the republic, Tomáš G. Masaryk and Edvard Beneš, the post-Munich puppet of Nazi Germany, Emil Hacha, and the Communist Klement Gottwald. Aside from his remarkable civil service career, Parkanyi was instrumental in creating in 1931 the first Greek Catholic parish to serve his countrymen then living in the Czechoslovak capital, Prague. (The parish church, within the Klementinum complex in the very heart of the city, became in 1968 the cathedral seat of the Greek Catholic Exarchate of the Czech Republic.)

In 1990, within a few months of Czechoslovakia's anti-Communist Velvet Revolution, the Society of Friends of Subcarpathian Rus'/Společnost přátel

Podkarpatské Rusi was established in Prague. Although the society included a few Carpatho-Rusyns, most of its members were ethnic Czechs born in Subcarpathian Rus' of parents who had worked as civil servants for the interwar Czechoslovak regime or had made often successful careers as entrepreneurs and small businessmen in the country's far eastern province. After the return of Hungarian rule and their forced evacuation in 1938–39, these people went back to Bohemia and Moravia, where their young children were raised and educated in a Czech environment.

For nearly half a century after World War II, the subject of Subcarpathian Rus', even its very name, was taboo in Communist Czechoslovakia. This is because the country's closest ally, the Soviet Union, had "reunited" the area with its "true" ancestral homeland, Ukraine, after a "thousand years of occupation" by foreign powers, one of the most recent being interwar "bourgeois Czechoslovakia." Consequently, the postwar Communist regime was not interested in remembering the "exploitive" nature of its predecessor, the interwar republic in Subcarpathian Rus'. But in the liberal post-1989 political atmosphere, these Subcarpathian-born Czechs could recall their youth and speak openly with nostalgic fondness of the first Czechoslovak republic under its beloved founder, Tomáš G. Masaryk, as a state of three Slavic peoples: Czechs, Slovaks, and Carpatho-Rusyns.

The leading force behind the Society of Friends of Subcarpathian Rus' was the well-known Czech journalist and anti-Communist dissident poet Jaromír Hořec. Under his leadership for over a decade, the Society published a Czech-language, quarterly magazine (*Podkarpatská Rus*, 1991–present) and a series of booklets, and it sponsored lectures and exhibits, all with the goal to inform its members and to remind the Czech public-at-large that their country had once included Subcarpathian Rus' within its borders. The society's cultural activity was made possible through public grants from the Czech government and, in particular, from the city of Prague as part of the latter's program to assist the many minority groups living in the post-Communist country's dynamic capital.

In 1995, the Society of Friends of Subcarpathian Rus' became a member of the World Congress of Rusyns, and gradually it tried to draw Carpatho-Rusyns as well as Czechs into its ranks. Among the first achievements in that regard was to cooperate closely with the Czech Republic's only Carpatho-Rusyn folk ensemble, Skejušan. This group, based in the Czech town of Chomutov, was made up of Carpatho-Rusyns and their offspring from the Banat region in west-central Romania (primarily from the village of Scăiuș), who were resettled to northern Bohemia just after World War II (see above, Chapter 25).

A much larger group of Carpatho-Rusyns in the Czech Republic were people in search of employment, who arrived in the 1990s from independent Ukraine's Transcarpathian oblast. Some had temporary work visas, but many more had no legal status, so that their numbers have been difficult to determine. There could have been, however, at any one time in the 1990s as many as 50,000 of these Transcarpathian guest workers.[3] The malcs among them found jobs, mostly in Prague, on construction sites, the females in restaurants, hotels, and other service industries. Because of their temporary resident status, the vast majority of these recent workers from Transcarpathia have had no time for participation in any "Czech" organization, let alone one like the Society of Friends of Subcarpathian Rus', which is dominated by nostalgically minded older folk concerned with a lost past. Moreover, these Soviet-educated Transcarpathians for the most part have no awareness of, or interest in, the idea of a distinct Carpatho-Rusyn people. In effect, they are simply workers from Ukraine who describe themselves— and are considered by Czech society—as Ukrainians. Not counting the guest workers, there may be an estimated 10,000 Carpatho-Rusyns in the Czech Republic; however, the census of 2001 recorded only 1,100.[4]

There are few successful Transcarpathian businesspeople who have become permanent residents in the Czech Republic and have "discovered" their Carpatho-Rusyn identity. Some even play a leading role in the Society of Friends of Subcarpathian Rus'. The presence of these recent arrivals from Transcarpathia has not, however, been welcomed by all of the older Czech activists, especially in the society's branch in Brno which, as a result, separated in 2010 from the main organization in Prague. The distance between older "local" members and the post-1989 newer arrivals from Transcarpathia—something that today characterizes Carpatho-Rusyn community life in the Czech Republic—is an even more prominent and problematic feature of another new organized community, that in Hungary.

Hungary

Within the present-day boundaries of Hungary, one might speak of two Carpatho-Rusyn communities. One is made up of individuals living in rural areas in the northeastern part of the country. Several villages there became home to Carpatho-Rusyns in the early eighteenth century; this occured in the context of the general resettlement of the lowland plains of Hungary following the departure of the Ottoman Turks. As residents for over two centuries, these Carpatho-Rusyns can be considered the "indigenous" population of certain villages in today's northeastern Hungary. In the course of the nineteenth century, however, almost all the inhabitants of these villages (who had numbered about 26,000 in the 1840s), while retaining their Eastern-rite Greek Catholic faith, were magyarized or in some cases slovakized.[5] Consequently, by the second half of the twentieth century, there were only two villages (Komlóska and Múcsony) where some inhabitants, mostly of the older generation, still spoke their local Rusyn dialect. Ironically, even these villages were classified as "Slovak" during the era of Communist rule in Hungary and were provided with Slovak-language elementary schools.

The other Carpatho-Rusyn community in present-day Hungary is based largely in Budapest, the capital of the country, which since the second half of the nineteenth century has attracted a certain number of Carpatho-Rusyns interested in making new careers and improving their economic status. Most of the Carpatho-Rusyn newcomers who settled in Budapest during the decades before World War I quickly assimilated and adopted the Magyar nationality. Ironically, the state's magyarization program in the second half of the nineteenth century and the magyarization of the Greek Catholic Eparchy of Hajdúdorog in the eastern part of the country were both implemented and/or instigated primarily by magyarized Rusyns living in Budapest.

A century later, in the 1990s, a few young Carpatho-Rusyns from rural northeastern Hungary settled in Budapest; the largest number, however, is comprised of newcomers from post-Communist Transcarpathia. Unlike the working-class temporary laborers from Transcarpathia who have gone to Prague, the smaller number of Transcarpathians who in the last two decades immigrated to Budapest and its immediate environs are made up primarily of professionally trained physicians, engineers, musicians, and artists. Moreover, many of these Transcarpathians had a clear sense of their national identity, whether as Carpatho-Rusyns or as Ukrainians. By the outset of the twenty-first century, the majority of Carpatho-Rusyns in and around Budapest comprised recent arrivals from post-Communist Transcarpathia.

In 1991, a handful of young activists from the village of Komlóska in northeastern Hungary, led by an aspiring musician and poet Gábor Hattinger, founded the Organization of Rusyns in Hungary/Organizatsiia Rusynov v Madiarsku. The organization quickly moved its headquarters to Budapest, where it managed to receive funding from the Hungarian government as part of its program of support for the country's national minorities. The new organization began publishing a bilingual newsletter in Rusyn and Hungarian (*Rusynskŷi zhyvot*, 1994–99); it joined the World Congress of Rusyns (1994); and its chairman Hattinger was made director of a Rusyn-language program (Rondo) within the framework of Hungary's state-owned radio broadcasting service for national minorities.

The status of Hungary's Carpatho-Rusyn community changed dramatically as a result of a law passed by the Hungarian parliament in 1993, which provided for a system of self-government for communities comprised of national minorities. The law required that the government draw up a list of officially recognized minorities that would be eligible for self-government. Among the 14 official nationalities on the list were both Rusyns and Ukrainians. It is interesting to note that most of the 1,100 Rusyns and 5,100 Ukrainians recorded in Hungary's 2001 census were recent arrivals from Transcarpathia.[6]

The 1993 law stipulated that a minority self-government could be established in a village, or even in a district of a large city, as long as 20 to 25 percent of the inhabitants requested one. From 1994, when the first Rusyn minority self-government was established (in the village of Múcsony), the number rose steadily to 9 (1998), then to 32 (2003), and by a decade later more than doubled to 72 (2013). Nearly half of the minority self-governments (35) are in northeastern Hungary, although of these only 14 are in traditional Rusyn villages; that is, in places where in the nineteenth century a significant number of inhabitants identified as Rusyns in decennial censuses (see Map 33). No less than 25 Rusyn minority self-governments are in the country's capital region, whether in Budapest itself (in 15 of its 27 districts) or in the surrounding Pest county. The people who form these self-governments are individuals who migrated to the capital region from villages in northeastern Hungary or, more likely, who arrived during the last two decades from Ukraine's Transcarpathian oblast (historic Subcarpathian Rus').

To coordinate the individual self-governments, there is a separate capital city administration for the 15 Rusyn minority governments in Budapest. More important, a statewide Administration for Rusyn Self-Government/Derzhavnoe samouriadovania menshynŷ rusynuv, established in 1998 with its own building in Budapest, acts as a spokesperson for all 72 Rusyn minority self-goverments in any negotiations with the Hungarian authorities. The entire self-government administrative structure is funded by the Hungarian government, which also provides grants for projects proposed by individual self-governments, such as publications (including the monthly magazine *Rusyns'kŷi svit*, 2003–present), public lectures, scholarly conferences, exhibits, concerts, and elementary school classes in Rusyn.

By the late 1990s, it was becoming increasingly obvious that there were concrete advantages to be gained by declaring oneself a member of a national minority in Hungary. Since the criteria for self-identification have from the outset been rather liberal, the system is susceptible to abuse and, as critics observe, has become a haven for those interested in personal gain, or so-called ethno-business. While many individuals legitimately rediscovered their ancestral Carpatho-Rusyn roots, there were also some, including ethnic Magyars, who suddenly became Carpatho-Rusyns for possible personal gain. Nevertheless, the various cultural and nationality conscious-raising activities of the self-governments have had a noticeable impact. Within the last decade the number of persons in Hungary declaring Rusyn as their nationality has increased well over threefold: from 1,098 (in 2001) to 3,882 (in 2011).[7]

The differing origins of the Carpatho-Rusyns in Hungary have contributed to the formation of two rival and at times antagonistic factions: (1) those who reside or whose origins are in villages in northeastern Hungary; and (2) recent immigrants from Transcarpathia. The ongoing rivalry between the two factions is also reflected in the so-called language question. Should a fifth variant of the Rusyn literary language be created; in other words, should there be a literary standard specifically for Hungary? And, if so, what should it be: a standard based on the spoken dialects of some village in Hungary (Komlóska or Múcsony); or a literary form based on dialects spoken by the immigrants from Transcarpathia? These questions remained unresolved.

Despite internal controversies, some of the Rusyn minority self-government communities, especially those in Budapest and Vác, have been quite successful in propagating Carpatho-Rusyn culture among the larger Hungarian public. Also of importance was the Department of Ukrainian and Rusyn Philology, established in 1992 at the university-level School of Higher Education in Nyíregyháza. For over a decade under its founding director, the

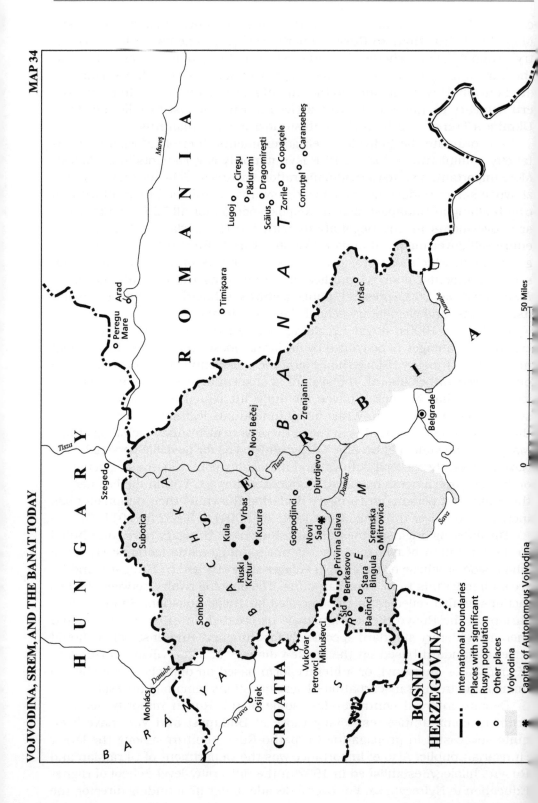

MAP 34

VOJVODINA, SREM, AND THE BANAT TODAY

International boundaries

Places with significant
Rusyn population

Other places

Vojvodina

Capital of Autonomous Vojvodina

50 Miles

0

Hungarian linguist István Udvari, the department sponsored research and publications on a variety of Carpatho-Rusyn topics. But after the untimely death of its founder, the Nyíregyháza university department effectively ceased functioning in 2012. The experience of Nyíregyháza reveals the fragility and tenuousness of the Carpatho-Rusyn movement in Hungary, often dependent on the lifespan of a dynamic and productive individual who may have no adequate successor. The community in Hungary remains numerically small, and with at best two Rusyn-language school classes it seems unable to attract younger generations to its ranks.

Romania

It took more than a decade after the revolution of 1989 before the first and only specifically Carpatho-Rusyn organization was formed in Romania. In the year 2000, the Cultural Society of Rusyns in Romania/Kulturne tovarystvo Rusyniv Romanii was set up at the initiative of Georgii Firtsak. Romania's post-1989 democratically elected national parliament adopted a provision that each national minority group living in the country should have at least one deputy. The new cultural society helped its chairman Firtsak to be elected in December 2000 as Romania's Rusyn parliamentary deputy.

Since that time, the Cultural Society of Rusyns in Romania receives governmental funding for its cultural activity, which is carried out by five branches throughout the country. In 2003 the society was accepted as Romania's representative in the World Congress of Rusyns, which five years later held its congress in the Romanian town of Sighet. Despite the enthusiasm of deputy Firtsak and his supporters, including a few Greek Catholic priests, the Cultural Society of Rusyns in Romania has not been able to have any widespread impact among the estimated 35,600 Carpatho-Rusyns in the Maramureş Region, who, whether actively or passively, continue to identify as Ukrainians. Consequently, in the national census of 2002, a mere 257 persons in Romania identified as Rusyns.[8]

Yugoslavia—Serbia and Croatia

The Rusyns/Rusnaks in the Vojvodina and Srem regions of former Yugoslavia continue to function as a viable community, although one where the rivalry between pro-Rusyn and pro-Ukrainian activists that character-ized community life before the revolutions of 1989 still continues. While one faction established in Ruski Kerestur the Rusyn Cultural Foundation/Ruska matka in 1990, its rival followed suit the same year by setting up in Novi Sad the Union of Rusyns and Ukrainians in Serbia/Soiuz Rusnatsokh i Ukraïntsokh Serbii.

The rivalry between the two organizations—the Rusyn-oriented Matka and the Ukrainian-oriented Soiuz—was complicated by the larger Yugoslav political situation. When the reduced Yugoslav federation (Serbia and Montenegro), headed by the Serbian nationalist Slobodan Milošević, refused to accept the secession of four republics in 1991, a full-scale war broke out. The initial phase of the conflict was between Serbia and Croatia, and one of the main battle lines was near the town of Vukovar; that is, precisely where Croatia's Rusyns lived. Vukovar itself was largely destroyed, including the headquarters of Croatia's own earlier established Union of Rusyns and Ukrainians, while Rusyn inhabitants in two nearby villages (Petrovci and Mikluševci) were forced to evacuate the dangerous battle zone.

The larger Rusyn/Rusnak community in the Vojvodina was not directly affected by the fighting, but the new head of the Rusyn Cultural Foundation and director of the influential Ruske Slovo Publishing House, Nataliia Dudash, was drawn into the political conflict after her appointment as vice-minister of culture in the Milošević regime. The appointment seemed at first to enhance the status of Vojvodina's Rusyns, but Dudash made the unwise decision to support Milošević until he was overthrown in 2000. His political demise opened the way for the pro-Ukrainian orientation led by Professor Iuliian Tamash to denounce the entire Rusyn movement for its alleged association (which was certainly the case with Dudash, who by then had fled the country) with the discredited political leader Milošević, who was eventually put on trial at the International Court in The Hague on charges of committing or abetting crimes against humanity. Consequently, for the next several years, supporters of the Ukrainian orientation came to dominate most state-supported Rusyn-language institutions in the Vojvodina.

The final demise of the Yugoslav federation and the fall of Milošević changed the status of the Vojvodinian-Srem Rusyns. Serbia was now an independent state, and it restored to the Vojvodina the autonomous status that it had before 1989. The autonomous government of the Vojvodina proceeded quickly to enhance the status of the region's various nationalities. In 2002, Vojvodina's regional parliament responded to Serbia's new constitution, whose provisions on rights for national minorities called for each minority to be governed by its own elected national council. Each national council was granted an annual budget and allowed to decide for itself how the allotted funds are to be used in the fields of education, culture, the media, and language use in the public sphere. To assist the national council in determining its policies and spending priorities, the regional government also created (in 2008) an Institute for the Culture of Vojvodina's Rusyns.

Both Rusyns and Ukrainians are recognized as distinct nationalities in Serbia's Vojvodina; therefore, each has its own national council. The pro-Ukrainian Rusyns are not, however, part of the Ukrainian National Council (comprised of descendents of pre-World War I immigrants from Galicia), but rather of the Rusyn National Council. The result is ongoing tension between the pro-Rusyn and pro-Ukrainian deputies for influence within Vojvodina's Rusyn National Council.

The much smaller Rusyn community in independent Croatia (2,300 in 2001) reconstituted itself after the end of the Croatian-Serbian war.[9] Ever since the 1970s, the small community in what was then the socialist republic of Croatia in Yugoslavia had its own civic and cultural organization called the Union of Rusyns and Ukrainians of Croatia/Soiuz Rusinokh a Ukraïntsokh Horvatskei. This Ukrainian-oriented organization survived the Yugoslav civil war and continued to exist in independent Croatia. Rusyn-oriented activists, mostly teachers who were displeased with the Ukrainian orientation of the Union of Rusyns and Ukrainians, formed their own Rusnak Society/Druzhtvo Rusnak in 2003. One of the society's main goals has been to convince the Croatian authorities that Carpatho-Rusyns are a people distinct from Ukrainians, and that in Croatia Rusyn cultural and educational institutions should be supported in their own right and not as a component of Ukrainian or Rusyn-Ukrainian organizations.

The controversies between the pro-Rusyn and pro-Ukrainian orientations in the former Yugoslavia subsided somewhat after political stability was restored in newly independent Serbia and Croatia. The main problem facing the Rusyn communities in both countries remains the sharp decline in numbers. The brutal and destructive wars of the 1990s and their negative impact on Vojvodina's economy increased further the trend toward emigration that had begun already in the previous decade. Instead of seeking temporary employment in West Germany, many Vojvodinian Rusyn families decided to leave—and for the most part permanently—for Canada. Permanent emigration abroad, combined with the out-migration of young people to nearby cities where they have tended to assimilate with the larger Serbian society, are two factors which have had a decisive and negative demographic impact. For example, if in 1981 there were 19,300 Rusyns in Serbia's Vojvodina, by 2012 their number declined by 26 percent to 14,200. Analogous figures for Croatia during this same period showed a decline of 30 percent, from 3,300 to 2,300.[10]

The United States

The revolutions of 1989 also had profound, if indirect, impact on Carpatho-Rusyns in North America. After over a half-century of separation—which was the result of World War II and the subsequent restrictions against contacts with the West imposed by Communist rule—Rusyn Americans were finally able to reconnect with families and friends in the European homeland of their parents and grandparents. The discovery after 1989 that Carpatho-Rusyns actually still existed in central Europe galvanized an increasing number of Americans of Rusyn ancestral heritage to rediscover—or more likely to discover for the first time—that they no longer needed to associate their ancestral heritage with an existing country and, therefore, identify as Slovak, or Russian, or Polish, or Ukrainian, but rather with what their ancestral heritage actually was—Carpatho-Rusyn.

Alongside the already existing Carpatho-Rusyn Research Center, which comprised a few academics engaged since the mid-1970s in scholarly and popular educational activity, there arose several grassroots membership organizations, the largest of which has been the Carpatho-Rusyn Society. Founded in 1994 with a base in Pittsburgh, Pennsylvania, the society under the dynamic direction of John Righetti established 11 branches throughout the United States. Through these branches it has sponsored lectures, participated in cultural festivals, promoted contacts through the media (including a Carpatho-Rusyn radio program and bimonthly magazine, *The New Rusyn Times*, 1994–present), and organized annual study tours to the main areas of Carpathian Rus' (the Lemko Region, the Prešov Region, and Subcarpathian Rus').

The revival of organized community life resulted in the first steps toward public recognition of Carpatho-Rusyns as a distinct people by the larger American society. Through the efforts of the Carpatho-Rusyn Research Center, the United States Bureau of the Census for the first time in history (before World War I it did use the vague term *Ruthenian*) included the category *Carpatho-Rusyn* in its ancestry question on the 1990 decennial census. Although fewer than 13,000 persons identified as Carpatho-Rusyn, Ruthenian, or Lemko, the very fact of their inclusion in the census indicated that they were recognized as a distinct people in the United States.[11] Entries on Carpatho-Rusyns also appeared in several encyclopedias of America's ethnic groups,[12] and in 1996 the Library of Congress devised a new classification (separate from Ukrainian) for books published in the Rusyn language.

Canada

The Carpatho-Rusyn community in Canada has also experienced somewhat of a revival. The Lemko Association, dating back to its establishment in Canada in 1929, had by the end of the twentieth century became moribund. At the same time, however, Canada became a destination for the Vojvodinian Rusyns fleeing war torn Yugoslavia. Beginning in the mid-1990s and continuing for at least a decade, emigration to Canada has resulted in the presence of about 160 families (an estimated 800 persons) concentrated primarily in the provinces of Ontario (Kitchener-Waterloo area) and Saskatchewan (North Brattleford).[13] The first generation of what has been called "an intellectual migration" has managed to establish a somewhat vibrant community characterized by social gatherings, language classes for children, and periodical publications (*Rusnatsi u shvetse*, 2002–present; *Saskachevansk ruski hlasnŷk/Saskatchewan Ruthenian Messenger*, 2007–present) in the Vojvodinian-Rusyn language.

In the wake of the changes in the European homeland brought about by the revolutions of 1989, Carpatho-Rusyns in the United States and Canada have renewed the kind of public advocacy work that had characterized their communities during the quarter century between the close of World War I (1918) and the end of World War II (1945). Their advocacy has been both political and cultural in nature and has been implemented at both the organizational and individual level. For example, Carpatho-Rusyns from North America have played an increasingly prominent role in the work of the World Congress of Rusyns since its establishment in 1991.

Responding to the programmatic goals of the World Congress, delegations of Carpatho-Rusyns from the United States and Canada initiated meetings in

Washington, D.C., with embassies of all countries where Carpatho-Rusyns live as well as with diplomatic representatives from the European Union and the Vatican. The issues of most concern have been: (1) the refusal of Ukraine to recognize Carpatho-Rusyns as a distinct nationality; (2) the slovakization policies of the Greek Catholic Eparchy of Prešov; (3) the reluctance of the government of Slovakia—when it was under the Mečiar regime—to promote adequate support for Carpatho-Rusyn cultural and educational institutions in the Prešov Region; and (4) the reluctance of the government of Poland to issue an apology for the forced deportation of Lemkos during the 1947 Vistula Operation and to assist them in regaining lost property. Some of these concerns have been brought to the attention of the United States government and congressional leaders, as well as to the parliamentary office of Ukraine's Ombudsman in Kiev.

Direct assistance from American and Canadian Rusyns to the Carpatho-Rusyn homeland in Europe began in the 1990s and consisted of humanitarian aid and funding for cultural and educational activity. Several tons of medical supplies and equipment were sent to hospitals in Transcarpathia and funds were distributed to assist educational projects among the Vojvodinian Rusyns in war-torn Yugoslavia. Publications were sent to the new Rusyn-language university departments in Prešov, Cracow, and Nyíregyháza, as were funds to support research projects and conferences at those institutions. Among the leading donors in this regard was Steven Chepa, a merchant banker of Carpatho-Rusyn ancestry in Canada, whose contributions have included the establishment of the World Academy of Rusyn Culture (2002), a fellowship in Carpatho-Rusyn Studies at the University of Toronto (primarily for scholars from the European homeland), and the annual Aleksander Dukhnovych Prize (1997) for the best literary work written in the Rusyn language. Of particular importance is the Rusyn Sunday School Program begun in Ukraine's Transcarpathian region (Subcarpathian Rus'), whose funding has come exclusively from organizations and individuals (of Rusyn and non-Rusyn origin) in North America.

In retrospect, it is certainly clear that the revolutions of 1989 and the subsequent collapse of the Soviet Union made possible new and ongoing contacts among Carpatho-Rusyns in every country where they live, whether in Europe or North America. It is also clear that these mutually beneficial contacts have enhanced the vitality and quality of what since 1989 has come to be known as the "third" Carpatho-Rusyn national awakening.

Carpathian Rus'—real or imagined?

Chapter 1 proposed the subject of this book to be an historic territory in the heart of central Europe known as Carpathian Rus'. The defining char-acteristic of that territory was that its majority population, at least until the mid-twentieth century, comprised an East Slavic people known by various names derived from the territorial and ethnic concept, *Rus'*. For reasons also outlined in Chapter 1, that people was referred to throughout the book as Carpatho-Rusyns.

Carpathian Rus': a reality or an idea?

But what about Carpathian Rus' and Carpatho-Rusyns today and in the immediate future? Is Carpathian Rus' a reality, or is it only an idea; that is, something contemporary theorists of nationalism like to refer to as an "imagined community"?[1] Perhaps it would be fair to say that Carpathian Rus' is both. And as for the Carpatho-Rusyn people? Their status within the real and the imagined Carpathian Rus' differs quite markedly.

At first glance there is nothing much left to Carpathian Rus' today. The historic territory that stretched from the Poprad River in the west to the headwaters of the Tisza River in the east is divided between four countries—Poland, Slovakia, Ukraine, and Romania. Moreover, the population living in this territory has changed radically. Most of the inhabitants whose parents and grandparents may have identified as Carpatho-Rusyns in the past are now likely to identify with another nationality, whether Slovak, Polish, or Ukrainian. Since World War II, there has been an influx of other peoples into various parts of Carpathian Rus', in particular Ukrainians and Russians into Subcarpathian Rus'/Transcarpathia and Poles into the Lemko Region. The result is that at the outset of the twenty-first century there were only about 56,000 persons in the Carpathian homeland who identified themselves as Carpatho-Rusyns (by nationality or language).[2] That is only a tiny fraction of the nearly two million people who inhabit Carpathian Rus'. Granted, these numbers reflect official census data, and it is common knowledge that even in the best of circumstances—which is certainly not the case in present-day

Carpathian Rus'—statistics on questions of identity are highly suspect and unreliable.

This leads us to the question of the "other" Carpathian Rus'; that is, Carpathian Rus' as an idea. It is perhaps not an exaggeration to say that nationalities are themselves the result of an idea made real. In other words, they are the result of concepts about identity formulated by individual intellectuals or state authorities which are then accepted by a group of people as a legitimate mechanism for self-identity. Modern history has also taught us that the eventual acceptance by a people of a common national identity may be achieved through voluntary or involuntary means. In one sense, the entire history of Carpatho-Rusyns since the nineteenth century has been the story of how states and intellectual leaders have manipulated the nationality and closely related language question to suit their own political needs and/ or personal tastes.

These questions have been particularly prominent in Carpathian Rus' during periods that scholars have characterized as the "national awakening." The first of these national awakenings took place in Carpathian Rus' during Austro-Hungarian times between the years 1848 and 1868, and the second during the interwar period (especially in Czechoslovakia) between 1919 and 1938. We have seen that there has clearly been a third national awakening since the revolutions of 1989. What, if anything, makes this third national awakening any different from the first two, and does it promise to make the *idea* of Carpathian Rus' more of a *reality*?

Carpathian Rus' beyond Carpathian Rus'

One of the most striking aspects of the post-1989 national revival has been its all-Rusyn or interregional context. For the first time since the political divisions put in place after World War I, Carpatho-Rusyns from every country have been meeting periodically and, to a large degree, coordinating their cultural activity. In the past, Carpatho-Rusyns from one region may have cooperated with those in another region, such as in 1918–1919, when Rusyn-American immigrants in the United States played an active role in homeland politics and when Lemko Rusyns from old Austrian Galicia tried to unite with their brethren south of the mountains in historic Hungary. These and other efforts were limited, however, both in geographic scope and in time, usually lasting no more than a few months.

Recent Rusyn interregional cooperation was initiated at the First World Congress of Rusyns in 1991, and since then at meetings of the congress's executive, the World Council, held three to four times annually between the full congress, which itself convenes every two years. Carpatho-Rusyns from various countries also collaborate on several concrete projects, such as language codification, publications, exhibits, theatrical performances, and student exchanges. These projects and periodic meetings afford writers, scholars, and other cultural activists the opportunity to interact personally, to exchange ideas, and to realize that their own aspirations are similar to those of Carpatho-Rusyns in other countries, from whom they can learn and work in solidarity for the achievement of common and specific goals. In short, the present Carpatho-Rusyn national revival has broken out of the provincial-minded mode that had characterized it during the two previous revivals in the second half of the nineteenth century and the interwar years of the twentieth century.

Modern technology has made interregional cooperation much easier, as texts and other communications are readily transmitted by telephone, e-mail, and computer disk. The automobile has made possible more frequent physical contact between activists from the various Rusyn-inhabited regions, the farthest from each other being the Lemko Region in Poland and the Vojvodina in Yugoslavia, which are separated by a distance of some 400 kilometers.

To be sure, interregional communication is possible because of the profound change in the international political climate. For over four decades following World War II, the Communist regimes which ruled the region restricted the flow of traffic across heavily guarded borders and actively discouraged contacts among Carpatho-Rusyns. The Revolutions of 1989 and the collapse of the Soviet Union in 1991 have opened—or in some cases literally torn down—borders, especially among those countries which sought, and eventually achieved, membership in the European Union.

The striving toward European integration has also brought Carpatho-Rusyns as a group to the attention of institutions such as the Conference on Security and Cooperation in Europe (CSCE) and the Council of Europe. Decrees issued by these bodies, which called for "unimpeded contacts" between individuals of the same nationality living in different states (CSCE Copenhagen Agreement of June 1990) proved to be of particular importance to the Carpatho-Rusyn movement.[3] In effect, Carpatho-Rusyns became the concern of other European countries and non-governmental organizations (NGOs), which argued that the right of an individual to decide one's own national identity and to self-expression in one's own language derives from the general principles of human rights that are considered today inalienable for all Europeans. The culmination of these developments came with the effective elimination of borders in 2004, when Poland, Slovakia, Hungary, Romania, and then Croatia (2013) became part of the European Union. In many ways, Carpatho-Rusyns now live in only two countries, the European Union (to which Serbia is a candidate) and Ukraine. The degree to which Ukraine can be gradually integrated into Europe will only work in favor of Carpatho-Rusyns still separated by at least one border.

Enemies as friends

One aspect in which the present Carpatho-Rusyn national revival is similar to previous revivals has to do with what might be called "internal enemies" or antagonistic rivals. To be sure, neither in the past nor in the present did or does every individual of Carpatho-Rusyn heritage believe that the ethnolinguistic group to which he or she belongs should function as a distinct nationality. For those who supported such a proposition, the "internal enemy" in the nineteenth century were the so-called Magyarones; that is, Carpatho-Rusyns who wanted at all costs to give up their Slavic heritage and become part of the Magyar state nationality. Later, during the interwar years of the twentieth century, large numbers of Carpatho-Rusyns believed that they were—and therefore they became—Russians and Ukrainians. As a corollary, "converts" to either a Russian and Ukrainian identity rejected the idea of a distinct Carpatho-Rusyn nationality. Today, it is only the pro-Ukrainians that remain the internal nemesis of Carpatho-Rusyns.

From the very outset of the present-day Carpatho-Rusyn national revival that began in 1989, local Ukrainian-oriented organizations and spokespeople rejected what they branded as "Rusyn separatism" and "political Rusynism." There was, however, a positive side to such criticism, based on the principle that new movements are able to focus better on specific goals when they are criticized from without. In other words, the Carpatho-Rusyn movement was actually helped by the pro-Ukrainians, since there is often no better way to convince an individual to define his or her frequently vague or passive sense of national identity—and, therefore, one's own existence—than if that identity is denied by someone else. In that sense, the phrase often repeated by pro-Ukrainian polemists, "There is not, and cannot be, a Rusyn language and people," helped to produce the opposite result—Carpatho-Rusyns who decisively opted to identify themselves as a distinct nationality.

A movement of women and young people

It is significant to note that the gender and socioeconomic composition of participants in the post-1989 Carpatho-Rusyn revival is much different from that which existed before. In earlier revivals, the leadership roles and articulate spokespeople were almost exclusively male. Since 1989, however, women have been conspicuously present at Rusyn World Congresses and at other international gatherings, on the editorial staff of the media, and in schools. Nor are they present simply as tokens or in subordinate positions. Rather, in every country where Carpatho-Rusyns live (except Ukraine) women function as directors of the leading Carpatho-Rusyn educational and cultural institutions. The visible presence of women in the Carpatho-Rusyn movement has occurred not because of any conscious effort at achieving gender balance (North American-style "political correctness" is not a social imperative in central Europe), but rather as a result of respect for individual talent and commitment to the national movement.

It is also perhaps not an exaggeration to describe the post-1989 Carpatho-Rusyn revival, at least at its beginnings, as a movement of youth, resembling in many ways a revolt of "sons against fathers." Ironically, the founder of the Society of Carpatho-Rusyns in Ukraine (Mykhailo I. Tomchanii) and the founder of the Rusyn Initiative Group in Czechoslovakia just after the Velvet Revolution (Aleksander Zozuliak, also the founding editor of *Narodnŷ novynkŷ* and *Rusyn*), were sons of the leading post-World War II Ukrainian writers in their respective countries (Mykhailo I. Tomchanii in Ukraine and Vasyl' Zozuliak in Slovakia). Both sons were raised and educated as Ukrainians and believed themselves to be such until the revolution of 1989, which served as a catalyst for the discovery of what they came to consider their true Carpatho-Rusyn heritage.

Analogously, the founding chairpersons of the first post-1989 Carpatho-Rusyn organizations in Poland, Ukraine, Slovakia, Hungary, and Yugoslavia were all between 32 and 45 years of age when, in the early 1990s, the present revival began. And, in contrast to leaders of previous Carpatho-Rusyn national revivals, who were often accused by their rivals as nationally retarded, not yet educated, and therefore, not conscious of their "true" Ukrainian or Russian identity, the post-1989 Carpatho-Rusyn national revival was mostly made up of leaders and spokespeople with a much different intellectual formation. They were educated in the Ukrainian language and themselves had identified as Ukrainian before at some point consciously rejecting that identity and "returning" to something they felt was closer to their true selves as embodied in a Carpatho-Rusyn identity.

Education and national self-confidence

Education is perhaps the most important of the factors that characterize the new Carpatho-Rusyn movement. Until the mid-twentieth century, nearly 90 percent of Carpatho-Rusyns were rural dwellers engaged in small-scale agriculture and related pursuits. Illiteracy ranged from 30 to 50 percent in various regions during the 1930s, with the remainder of the population having only a few years of attendance at elementary school. The policies of the interwar Czechoslovak regime, in particular, helped to raise educational levels, but it was the post-World War II Communist regimes that truly brought about an educational revolution. Along with the spread of education came industrialization that encouraged thousands of rural Carpatho-Rusyns to work in factories in nearby towns and cities, most especially in Slovakia and, to a lesser degree, in Ukraine's Transcarpathia.

As a result, most post-1989 Carpatho-Rusyn national activists have university degrees; they have spent most of their lives in urban areas, not villages; and they are fully comfortable functioning in modern industrialized societies. Of even greater contrast with the past is the fact that the present intellectual leadership now has as much of a nationality constituency living in towns as in villages. Regardless of where that constituency lives, nearly all its members have at least a senior high school (*gymnasium*) level of education and are, therefore, more easily able to understand the value of preserving the Carpatho-Rusyn heritage.

The very fact that a high proportion of the Carpatho-Rusyn population lives in towns has another advantage. This is related to the fact that the desire for cultural preservation often reflects a nostalgic longing on the part of urban dwellers to recapture a rural-based, allegedly pristine youth surrounded by loving grandparents. While in reality such a phenomenon is largely gone, it does remain an image that is perhaps stronger than ever in the mind. This does not mean, however, that present-day creative Carpatho-Rusyn intellectual leaders are satisfied with folk-dancing and with maintaining other forms of quaint but antiquated rural artifacts. In fact, the urban-based intelligentsia, with its higher level of education, has since 1989 been producing forms of Carpatho-Rusyn culture that include experimental theater, political satire, literature about the human condition in contemporary urban societies, and abstract art. Again, it is an irony of history that the Carpatho-Rusyn roots of the American artist and world renowned twentieth-century cultural icon Andy Warhol were discovered by activists in the Carpatho-Rusyn national revival, who managed in 1991 to create in the small town of Medzilaborce in Slovakia a large-scale Warhol Family Museum of Modern Art, complete with two kiosk-sized replicas of the artist's Campbell tomato soup cans that stand at the museum's entrance in stark contrast to the lush green of the surrounding Carpathian countryside.

But what does all this mean for the immediate and long-term future? Does the interregional aspect of the recent, "third" national revival, combined with possibilities offered by modern communication facilities, a favorable international environment in an increasingly regionally conscious Europe, and the existence of a gender-balanced and well-educated leadership and constituency guarantee the future survival of a distinct Carpatho-Rusyn nationality in the Carpathian homeland? Predictions are by their very nature problematic, but one thing is certain. Never before have Carpatho-Rusyns operated in a political and socioeconomic environment that has allowed, and, in the case of all states but one, encouraged the development of their distinct culture and language. In many ways, the future is in the hands of Carpatho-Rusyns and their leaders. Perhaps Carpathian Rus' the *idea* will once again become Carpathian Rus' the *reality*.

Notes

Chapter 1: Carpatho-Rusyns and the land of Carpathian Rus'

1 The official data in this table are drawn from national censuses carried out in 2011 and 2012 (or 2002 for Ukraine and 1990 for the United States) in all countries which listed Rusyns/Carpatho-Rusyns as a distinct category in questions on nationality/ancestry and language/mother tongue. For a discussion of Carpatho-Rusyns in national censuses and an explanation of the unofficial "informed estimates," see Paul Robert Magocsi, *The People from Nowhere* (Uzhhorod, 2006), p. 112n1; and Paul Robert Magocsi, *Our People: Carpatho-Rusyns and Their Descendants in North America*, 4th rev. ed. (Wauconda, Ill., 2005), pp. 12–13.

2 Data on language is available in the collective work *Rusyn'skŷi iazŷk*, ed. Paul Robert Magocsi, Najnowsze dzieje języków słowiańskich, Vol. XIV (Opole, 2004).

3 The settlements are listed in Magocsi, *Our People*, pp. 110–206; the criteria for determining what constitutes Carpathian Rus' by past and present scholars is discussed in Paul Robert Magocsi, "Mapping Stateless Peoples: The East Slavs of the Carpathians," *Canadian Slavonic Papers*, XXXIX, 3–4 (Edmonton, 1997), pp. 301–331.

4 In English the term *Hungarian* is often used to describe people who refer to themselves in their own language as Magyar (*magyarok*). This book will use the term *Magyar* to distinguish this particular ethnic group from others living in the historic Hungarian Kingdom. As residents/citizens of Hungary all the kingdom's inhabitants were technically "Hungarians," regardless whether their ethnicity/nationality be Magyar, Carpatho-Rusyn, Slovak, Romanian, etc.

5 To commemorate this geographical "discovery," a monument was erected in 1870 by the Austro-Hungarian authorities; a century later, as a kind of recommemoration of the original discovery, the then ruling Soviet authorities erected another monument. Today both monuments remain standing side by side, marking the geographic center of Europe.

Chapter 3: The Slavs and their arrival in the Carpathians

1 Bernard Lewis, *History—Remembered, Recovered, Invented* (Princeton, N.J., 1975), p. 59.

2 István Horvát, *Szittyiai történetek*, 2 vols. (Pozsony [Bratislava], 1806–1808), discussed in Louis J. Lekai, "Historiography in Hungary, 1790–1848," *Journal of Central European Affairs*, XIV, 1 (Boulder, Colo., 1954), pp. 3–18.

3 *Webster's Third New International Dictionary of the English Language* (Springfield, Mass., 1971), p. 1073.

Chapter 4: State formation in central Europe

1 The estimates are provided by István Fodor, *In Search of a New Homeland: The Pre-history of the Hungarian People and the Conquest* (Budapest, 1975), p. 284.

2 The first quote is by C. A. Macartney, *The Medieval Hungarian Historians: A Critical and Analytical Guide* (Cambridge, 1953), p. 54; the second by Martyn Rady, "The *Gesta Hungarorum* of Anonymous: The Anonymous Notary of King Béla: A Translation," *Slavonic and East European Review*, LXXXVII, 1 (London, 2009), p. 683.

3 *The Primary Chronicle: Laurentian Text,* translated by Horace G. Lunt, cited in Paul Robert Magocsi, *A History of Ukraine: The Land and Its Peoples*, 2nd rev. ed. (Toronto, Buffalo, and London, 2010), p. 51.

4 Cited in ibid., p. 60.

5 Cited in ibid., p. 66. This phrase has often been rendered in subsequent Russian and western European writings as "the mother of Russian cities," a formulation viewed by Ukrainians as a demeaning provocation. Kiev, after all, is not only *in* Ukraine but is the country's historic and cultural capital.

6 Typical of this widespread, though simplistic view in Ukrainian literature is the for- mulation: "Lev extended his domain into Transcarpathia, and Ukrainian rule in the Mukachiv region lasted for over 50 years." Vasyl Markus, "Hungary," in Volodymyr Kubijovyč, ed., *Encyclopedia of Ukraine*, Vol. II (Toronto, 1988), p. 275.

Chapter 5: Carpathian Rus' until the early 16th century

1 Peter F. Sugar, ed., *A History of Hungary* (Bloomington and Indianapolis, 1990), p. 27; Pál Engel, *The Realm of St. Stephen: A History of Medieval Hungary, 895–1526* (London and New York, 2001), p. 102.

2 Omelian Stavrovs'kyi, *Slovats'ko-pol's'ko-ukraïns'ke prykordonnia do 18 stolittia* (Bratislava and Prešov, 1967), pp. 82–89.

3 Ibid., pp. 70–77; Engel, *The Realm of St. Stephen*, p. 102.

4 Aleksei L. Petrov, *Medieval Carpathian Rus': The Oldest Documentation about the Carpatho-Rusyn Church and Eparchy* [1930] (New York, 1998), p. 81.

5 Ibid. p. 82.

6 Antal Hodinka, *A kárpátalji rutének lakóhelye, gazdaságuk és múltjuk* (Budapest, 1923), p. 20.

7 Zofia Szanter, "From Where Did the Lemkos Come?," in Paul Best and Jaroslaw Moklak, eds., *The Lemkos of Poland* (New Haven and Cracow, 2000), p. 94.

Chapter 6: The Reformation, the Counter-Reformation, and Carpathian Rus'

1 Oleksander Mytsiuk, *Narysy z sotsial'no-hospodars'koï istoriï Pidkarpats'koï Rusy,* Vol. II (Prague, 1938), pp. 35–36.

2 L'udovít Haraksim, *K sociál'nym a kultúrnym dejinám Ukrajincov na Slovensku do roku 1867* (Bratislava, 1961), p. 59.

3 Mytsiuk, *Narysy,* p. 36.

Chapter 7: The Habsburg restoration in Carpathian Rus'

1 Gábor Barta, et al., *History of Transylvania* (Budapest, 1994), p. 329.

2 Jean Bérenger, *La Hongrie des Habsbourg*, Vol. I: *de 1526 à 1790* (Rennes, 2010), p. 185.

3 One scholar has calculated that 2,115 men from Carpatho-Rusyn villages joined Rákóczi when he arrived in Subcarpathian Rus'. Ivan Hranchak, ed., *Narysy istoriia Zakarpattia*, Vol. I (Uzhhorod, 1993), p. 124.

4 Andrii Sash, "Narys sotsial'noï i hospodars'koï istoriï Shenborns'koï latyfundiï Mukachivs'ko-Chynadiïvs'koï v pershii polovyni XVIII st.," *Naukovŷi zbornŷk Tovarystva 'Prosvîta'*, IX (Uzhhorod, 1932), pp. 110–111.

Chapter 8: Habsburg reforms and their impact on Carpatho-Rusyns

1 Data drawn from the Rusyn and the Slovak texts of the *Urbarium* reproduced in A. L. Petrov, *Pervyi pechatnyi pamiatnik ugrorusskago nariechiia Urbar,* Materialy dlia istorii Ugorskoi Rusi, Vol. V, in *Sbornik otdieleniia russkago iazyka i slovesnosti Imperatorskoi akademii nauk*, Vol. LXXXIV, No. 2 (St. Petersburg, 1908), pp. 46–100.

2 Cited in Eduard Winter, *Byzanz und Rom im Kampf um die Ukraine 955–1939* (Leipzig, 1942), p. 129.

3 The data for the Mukachevo Eparchy is from the *Schematismus Ungvarensis, an. 1809–12,* cited in Oleksander Baran, *Iepyskop Andrei Bachyns'kyi i tserkovne vidrodzhennia na Zakarpatti* (Yorkton, Saskatchewan, 1963), p. 61; the data for the Prešov Eparchy is from Julius Kubinyi, *The History of the Prjašiv Eparchy* (Rome, 1970), p. 84.

4 *Ratio educationis 1777*, cited in Štefan Šutaj et al., *Key Issues of Slovak and Hungarian History* (Bratislava, 2011), p. 123.

5 Willibald Plöchl, *St. Barbara zu Wien,* Vol. I (Vienna, 1975), pp. 40–49.

6 From the author's introduction in verse, "Rukopys Mariiapovchans'koho varianta Hramatyky Arseniia Kotsaka, 1772–1778," first published in full in *Naukovyi zbirnyk Muzeiu ukraïns'koï kul'tury u Svydnyku*, Vol. XV, pt. 2: *pershodzherela* (Bratislava and Prešov, 1990), p. 75.

Chapter 9: The Revolution of 1848 and the Carpatho-Rusyn national awakening

1 Cited in Anton Spiesz and Dušan Čaplovič, *Illustrated Slovak History* (Wauconda, Ill., 2006), p. 103.

2 Cited in István Deák, *The Lawful Revolution: Louis Kossuth and the Hungarians, 1848–1849* (New York, 1979), p. 289.

3 From an article by V. Dobrianskyi [V. Dobránszky] in the newspaper *Budapesti Hiradó*, 27 June 1848, cited in L'udovít Haraksim, *K sociálnym a kultúrnym dejinám Ukrajincov na Slovensku do roku 1867* (Bratislava, 1961), p. 123.

4 *Slovanský sjezd v Praze 1848: sbírka dokumentů,* ed. Václav Žáček (Prague, 1958), p. 303.

5 D. [Aleksander Dukhnovych], "Sostoianie Rusynôv v Ouhorshchynî," *Zoria halytska*, No. 31 (L'viv, 1849).

6 "Vruchanie," in *Pozdravlenie rusynov na hod 1851* (Vienna, 1851), p. 69–70.

7 "Kratkaia biohrafiia Aleksandra Dukhnovycha, krŷloshana priashovskaho, ym samŷm napysannaia," in Oleksandr Dukhnovych, *Tvory,* Vol. III (Prešov, 1989), p. 405.

Chapter 10: Carpathian Rus' in Austria-Hungary, 1868–1914

1 Walter Allison Philips, "Austria-Hungary: History," in *Encyclopaedia Britannica,* Vol. III, 11th ed. (New York, 1910), p. 32.

2 "Holos radosty" (A Voice of Gladness), dedicated to Hryhorii Iakhymovych upon his appointment in 1860 as Greek Catholic metropolitan of Galicia, reprinted in Oleksandr Dukhnovych, *Tvory,* Vol. I (Prešov, 1968), p. 337.

3 Bogdan Horbal, *Działność polityczna Łemków na Łemkowszczyźnie, 1918–1921* (Wrocław, 1997), pp. 23–24.

4 Ibid., p. 27

5 Cited in C. A. Macartney, *The Habsburg Empire, 1790–1918* (New York, 1969), p. 560.

6 Data from the statistical table in Iurevyn, "Nashe rus'ke shkôl'nytstvo v desiatôm rotsî samostôinosty ChSR, *Uchytel',* X, 3–4 (Uzhhorod, 1929), p. 102.

7 Ivan G. Kolomiets, *Sotsial'no-ekonomicheskoe otnosheniia i obshchestvennoe dvizhenie v Zakarpat'e vo vtoroi polovine XIX stoletie,* Vol. II (Tomsk, 1962), p. 167.

8 Cited in Scotus Viator [R. W. Seton-Watson], *Racial Problems in Hungary* (London, 1908), p. 227.

9 Iurevyn, "Nashe rus'ke shkôl'nytstvo," p. 102.

10 S. A. [Agoshton Shtefan], *Görög katholikus szemle,* No. 19 (Uzhhorod, 1916)—cited in Paul Robert Magocsi, *The Shaping of a National Identity: Subcarpathian Rus', 1848–1948* (Cambridge, Mass., 1978), p. 74.

11 The statistical data varies greatly in secondary sources. The figures in this table (rounded off to the hundreths) are drawn from the work of the respected Hungarian demographers Elek Fényes, Pál Balogh, and others for the years 1840 through 1869, and from official Hungarian census reports for 1880 through 1910, as listed in Jan Húsek, *Národopisná hranice mezi Slováky a Karpatorusy* (Bratislava, 1925), pp. 463–465; C. A. Macartney, *Hungary and Her Successors: The Treaty of Trianon and Its Consequences, 1919–1937* (London, 1937), p. 33; Károly Kocsis, *Kárpátalja mai területének etnikai térképe/Ethnic Map of Present Territory of Transcarpathia (Subcarpathia)* (Budapest, 2001); Károly Kocsis, *Szlovákia mai területének etnikai térképe/Ethnic Map of Present Territory of Slovakia* (Budapest, 2000).

12 Jaromír Korčák, "Etnický vývoj československého Potisí," *Národnostní obzor,* II (Prague, 1933), p. 270.

13 Ivan Hranchak, ed., *Narysy istorii Zakarpattia,* Vol. I (Uzhhorod, 1993), p. 298.

14 Petro Smiian, *Revoliutsiinyi ta natsional'no-vyzvol'nyi rukh na Zakarpatti kintsie XIX –pochatku XX st.* (L'viv, 1965), p. 16.

15 Kolomiets, *Sotsial'no-ekonomicheskoe otnosheniia,* Vol. II, pp. 41–45; Vladimí Kuštek, "Obrazky ze Svaljavy," *Podkarpatská Rus,* XX, 4 (Prague, 2010), p. 5.

16 Ibid., pp. 10–37.

17 Hranchak, *Narysy,* p. 328; Smiian, *Revoliutsiinyi . . . rukh,* p. 15.

Chapter 11: Carpatho-Rusyn diasporas before World War I

1 Stefan Tomashivs'kyi, "Uhors'ki rusyny v s'vitli madiars'koï uriadovoï statystyky," *Zapysky Naukovoho tovarystva im. Shevchenka*, LVI, 6 (L'viv, 1903), p. 9.

2 *A magyar szent korona országaiank 1910. évi népszámlálása*, Magyar statisztikai közlemények, új sorozat, Vol. XLII (Budapest, 1912), pp. 177–183 and 470–477.

3 Paul Robert Magocsi, *Our People: Carpatho-Rusyns and Their Descendants in North America*, 4th rev. ed. (Wauconda, Ill., 2005), pp. 12–13.

4 Mark Wyman, *Round-Trip to America: The Immigrants Return to Europe, 1880–1930* (Ithaca, N.Y., 1993), pp. 9–12.

5 G. C. U. Membership Statistics, 1914, in James M. Evans, *Guide to the Amerikansky Russky Viestnik*, Vol. I (Fairview, N.J., 1979), pp. 425–426.

6 *A magyar . . . 1910. évi népszámlálása*, pp. 217 and 301. The estimated figures and their sources are discussed in Pavel Marek and Volodymyr Bureha, *Pravoslavní v Československu v letech 1918–1953* (Brno, 2008), p. 38.

Chapter 12: Carpathian Rus' during World War I, 1914–1918

1 Graydon A. Tunstall, *Blood on the Snow: The Carpathian Winter War of 1915* (Lawrence, Kan., 2010), p. 1.

2 Bogdan Horbal, *Lemko Studies: A Handbook* (New York, 2010), pp. 391–392.

3 Bogdan Horbal, "Vienna Trials," in *Encyclopedia of Rusyn History and Culture*, ed. Paul Robert Magocsi and Ivan Pop, 2nd rev. ed. (Toronto, 2005), p. 530.

4 Ivan Hranchak, ed., *Narysy istoriï Zakarpattia*, Vol. I (Uzhhorod, 1993), p. 379.

5 Cited in Mai Panchuk et al., *Zakarpattia v etnopolitychnomu vymiri* (Kiev, 2008), p. 184.

Chapter 13: The end of the old and the birth of a new order, 1918–1919

1 This phrase, originally used by Wilson in a May 1916 address to the League to Enforce Peace, was not included in the Fourteen-Point Declaration and was something that later the president stated he regretted having said. Cited in Joseph P. O'Grady, ed., *The Immigrants' Influence on Wilson's Peace Policies* (Lexington, Ky., 1967), p. 73.

2 Victor S. Mamatey, "The Slovaks and Carpatho-Ruthenians," in ibid., p. 249.

3 Cited in G. I. Žatkovič, *Otkrytie—Exposè a Podkarpatskoj Rusi* (Homestead, Pa., 1921), p. 1.

4 Data of the American Uhro-Rusin Commission reproduced in Joseph Danko, "Plebiscite of Carpatho-Ruthenians in the United States Recommending Union of Carpatho-Ruthenia with the Czechoslovak Republic," *Annals of the Ukrainian Academy of Arts and Sciences in the United States*, XI, 1–2 (New York, 1964–68), pp. 191–202.

5 From the questionnaire distributed by the Russka Narodna Rada, represented by the priest, Emilian Nevyts'kyi, reproduced in Zdeněk Peška and Josef Markov, "Příspěvek v ústavním dějinám Podkarpatské Rusi," *Bratislava*, V (Bratislava, 1931), p. 526.

Notes to pages 182–204

6 Cited from the proclamation, "A Magyarországi Rutének Néptanácsától/Ot Radŷ Uhro-rus'koho naroda", 10 December 1918, archive of the Carpato-Ruthenica Library, University of Toronto.

7 Resolution of the Khust National Council, cited in Ortoskop, *Derzhavni zmahannia Prykarpats'koï Ukraïny* (Vienna, 1924), p. 21.

8 Cited from the Czech and Rusyn texts of the resolutions adopted of the last day of the Central Rusyn National Council, Uzhhorod, 16 May 1919, reproduced in Peška and Markov, *Bratislava*, IV (1931), pp. 419 and 421.

9 Ibid.

10 *The Origin of the Lems, Slavs of Danubian Provenance: Memorandum to the Peace Conference Concerning Their National Claims*, signed by Anthony Beskid and Dimitry Sobin for the National Council of the Carpathian Russians at Prešov, 20 April 1919, p. 23.

11 Title of a map prepared by the Rand McNally Company in the United States.

12 *Traité entre les Principales Puissances Alliées et Associées et la Tchécoslovaquie* (Paris, 1919), Article 10, p. 26.

13 "Demographic Losses of the Kingdom of Hungary Due to World War I," in Piotr Eberhardt, *Ethnic Group and Population Changes in Twentieth-Century Central-Eastern Europe* (Armonk, N.Y., and London, 2003), p. 291.

Chapter 14: Subcarpathian Rus' in interwar Czechoslovakia, 1919–1938

1 Avhustyn Voloshyn, *Spomyny* (Uzhhorod, 1923), p. 94.

2 *Traité entre les Principales Puissances Alliées et Associées et la Tchécoslovaquie* (Paris, 1919), Article 10, p. 26.

3 See below, Chapter 23, Table 23.1.

4 *Traité*, p. 26.

5 Zdeněk Peška, "Podkarpatská Rus," in *Slovník veřejného práva československého*, Vol. III (Brno, 1934), p. 109.

6 "Memorandum do antanta, shto Uhro-rusynŷ ne khotiat odorvatysia ot Uhorshchynŷ," Budapest, 5 August 1919, in *Proklamatsiia do uhro-rus'koho naroda* (Budapest, 1919), pp. 35–51.

7 *Statistický lexikon obcí v Republice československé . . . na základě výsledků sčítání lidu z 15. února 1921*, Vol. IV: *Podkarpatská Rus* (Prague, 1928), pp. 10, 25, and 45.

8 First pronounced on 20 November 1920, the day the Treaty of Trianon was submitted to the Hungarian parliament. *Papers and Documents Relating to the Foreign Relations of Hungary*, Vol. I (Budapest, 1939), p. 988.

9 Paul Robert Magocsi, *The Shaping of a National Identity: Subcarpathian Rus', 1848–1948* (Cambridge, Mass., 1978), p. 206.

10 Ibid., p. 355.

11 Paul Robert Magocsi, *A History of Ukraine: The Land and Its Peoples*, 2nd rev. ed. (Toronto, 2010), pp. 648–649.

12 Ibid.

13 Data extracted from Table 65 in Branislav Šprocha and Pavol Tišliar, *Populačný vývoj Podkarpatskej Rusi*, Vol. I (Bratislava, 2009), p. 196.

14 For an explanation of statistical data, see the section on Czechs in Chapter 18.

15 Ievhen Iu. Pelens'kyi, "Shkil'nytstvo. Kul'turno-osvitnie zhyttia," in *Karpats'ka Ukraïna* (L'viv, 1939), pp. 125–127.

16 Magocsi, *Shaping of a National Identity*, pp. 224–225.

17 Šprocha and Tišliar, *Populačný vývoj*, Vol. II, pp. 74 and 84. Hungarian statistics for 1910 indicate that 54 percent of the inhabitants of what became Subcarpathian Rus' were illiterate. Those statistics, however, indicated a person's knowledge of Hungarian language; in that case, nearly 90 percent of Carpatho-Rusyns were "illiterate." Václav Drahný and František Drahný, *Podkarpatská Rus, její přírodní a zemědělské poměry* (Prague, 1921), p. 39. Citing Hungarian statistics, one Soviet scholar suggested that 74 percent of the Carpatho-Rusyn population was illiterate in 1900. Ivan G. Kolomiets, *Sotsial'no-ékonomicheskoe otnosheniia i obshchestvennoe dvizhenie v Zakarpat'e vo vtoroi polovine XIX stoletiia*, Vol. II (Tomsk, 1962), p. 244.

18 *Školství na Podkarpatské Rusi v přítomnosti* (Prague, 1932); Ievhen Iu. Pelens'kyi, "Shkil'nytstvo. Kul'turno-osvitnie zhyttia," in *Karpats'ka Ukraïna* (L'viv, 1939), pp. 125–127.

19 *Iak zakladaty y vesty chyt. 'Prosvita'?* (undated pamphlet), p. 2.

20 Paul Robert Magocsi, "The Nationalist Intelligentsia and the Peasantry in Twentieth-Century Subcarpathian Rus'," in his *Of the Making of Nationalities There Is No End*, Vol. I (New York, 1999), pp. 198–200.

21 The idea of a renaissance or revival comes from the well-informed Czech scholar at the time who was referring to literary culture in the broadest sense: Antonín Hartl, *Literární obrození podkarpatských rusinů v letech 1920–1930* (Prague, 1930), and *Die literarische Renaissance der Karpatoruthenen* (Prague, 1932).

22 *Statistický lexikon . . . 1921*, p. 45; *Statistický lexikon obcí v Republice československé . . . na základě výsledků sčítání lidu z 1. prosince 1930*, Vol. IV: *Země podkarpatoruská* (Prague, 1937), pp. xvi-xvii.

23 The first phrase of the quote comes from an editorial in *Nedîlia* (Uzhhorod), 26 April 1936; the second from the conclusion to a ten-part series of articles authored by an Honest Rusyn: Chestnyi Rusyn, "Panrusyzm i rusynizm," *Nedîlia*, 8 November 1936.

Chapter 15: The Prešov Region in interwar Slovakia, 1919–1938

1 Jurko Lažo, *Russkomu narodu na Slovensku* (Vyšný Svidník, 1924), p. 44.

2 The data refers only to Spish, Sharysh, and Zemplyn counties, but not to the western part of Ung county (also in the Prešov Region). Ivan G. Kolomiets, *Sotsial'no-ékonomicheskoe otnosheniia i obshchestvennoe dvizhenie v Zakarpat'e vo vtoroi polovine XIX stoletiia*, Vol. II (Tomsk, 1962), p. 199.

3 Ivan Vanat, "Shkil'ne pytannia na Priashivshchyni pid chas domiunkhens'koï respubliky," *Duklia*, XIV, 5 (Prešov, 1966), p. 63.

4 Cited in ibid.

5 *Soznam miest na Slovensku dl'a popisu l'udu z r. 1919* (Bratislava, 1919).

6 *Statistický lexikon obcí v Republike československej . . . na základe výsledků sčítania l'udu z 15. února 1921*, Vol. III: *Slovensko* (Prague, 1927), p. 160; Jan Húsek, *Národopisná hranice mezi Slováky a Karpatorusy* (Bratislava, 1925), pp. 463–464.

7 *Slovenská politika* (Bratislava), 2 September 1928, cited in Ivan Bajcura, *Ukrajinská otázka ČSSR* (Košice, 1967), p. 44.

8 Cited in Vanat, "Shkil'ne pytannia," pp. 61–62.

9 The phrase, which may have been apocryphal in nature, nonetheless was believed by many Carpatho-Rusyns. Cited in Ivan Bajcura, *Ukrajinská otázka v ČSSR* (Košice, 1967), p. 44n57.

10 Ivan Vanat, *Narysy novitn'oï istoriï ukraïntsiv Skhidnoï Slovachchyny*, Vol. I: *1918–1938* (Bratislava, 1979), pp. 136–148 and 211–214.

11 Ibid., pp. 218–221.

12 Ivan Vanat, "Shkil'na sprava na Priashivshchyni pid chas domiunkhens'koï Chekhoslovachchyny," in *Z mynuloho i suchasnoho ukraïntsiv Chekhoslovachchyny*, Pedahohichnyi zbirnyk, No. 3 (Bratislava, 1973), pp. 174–180.

13 From the opening statement by Chairman Metod M. Bella, at the Tenth Congress of the Slovak League, 8 June 1934, cited in Peter Švorc, *Krajinská hranica medzi Slovenskom a Podkarpatskou Rusou v medzivojnovom období, 1919–1939* (Prešov, 2003), p. 307.

14 Cited in ibid., p. 308.

15 Ján Ruman, *Otázka slovensko-rusínskeho pomeru na východnom Slovensku* (Košice, 1935), p. 34.

16 Róbert Ivan, *Obnova Pravoslávia na území Slovenska v 20. storočí* (Prešov, 2007), p. 56.

17 *Russkoe slovo* (Prešov), 30 August 1924.

18 Aleksandr Iv. Sedlak, *Grammatika russkago iazyka dlia narodnykh shkol Eparkhii Priashevskoi* (Prešov, 1920); Ivan F. Kyzak, *Bukvar dlia narodnýkh shkol Eparkhii Priashevskoi* (Prague and Prešov, 1921).

19 Fedor V. Dufanets, "Obshchestvo im. A. V. Dukhnovicha," in Ivan S. Shelpetskii, ed., *Priashevshchina: istoriko-literaturnyi sbornik* (Prague, 1948), pp. 293–297.

Chapter 16: The Lemko Region in interwar Poland, 1919–1938

1 Poland's 1921 census data did not list Ukrainian as separate from Rusyn in the language category; Orthodox was not listed because very few adherents existed before 1926. Główny Urząd Statystyczny, *Skorowidz miejscowości Rzeczypospolitej polskiej*, Vols. XII and XIII (Warsaw, 1924). The census data for 1931 and the figures for 1935/1936 (from archival records in Przemyśl relating to the Lemko Apostolic Administration) are drawn from tables in studies by Anna Krochmal and Krzystof Z. Nowakowski in Jerzy Czajkowski, ed., *Łemkowie w historii i kulturze Karpat*, Vol. I (Rzeszów, 1992), pp. 290–291 and 333.

2 N. A. Tsyliak, "Lemkovska emyhratsyia v Kanadi," *Karpatorusskyi kalendar Lemko-Soiuza na 1937* (New York, 1936), pp. 93–95.

3 Anna Krochmal, "Stosunki między grekokatolikami i prawosławnymi na Łemkowszczyźnie w latach 1926–1939," in Czajkowski, ed., *Łemkowie w historii*, p. 290.

4 Jarosław Moklak, "Ukraiński ruch narodowy na Łemkowszczyźnie kulturalno-oświatowe i gospodarcze," in *Krakowskie Zeszyty Ukrainoznawcze*, Vols. II–IV (Cracow 1995), p. 342.

5 Ivan Rusenko, *Výbrane* (Krynica and Legnica, 2010), p. 39.

Chapter 17: Carpatho-Rusyn diasporas during the interwar years, 1919–1938

1 In 1910, there were 15,000 Rusyns in the Vojvodina; the first Yugoslav census of 1921 recorded 21,748. Janko Ramach, *Rusnatsi u iuzhnei Uhorskei, 1745–1918* (Novi Sad, 2007), p. 333.

2 Jelena Perkovich, "Rusnatsi u istoriinei khvil'ki," *Ruske slovo* (Novi Sad), 5 December 2008, p. 10.

3 Statute of the Rusyn National Enlightenment Society, cited in Diura Latiak, "Vydavatel'na dïial'nosts Ruskoho narodnoho prosvitnoho druzhtva, 1919–1941," *Studia Ruthenica*, Vol. II (Novi Sad, 1990–91), p. 126.

4 Branislav Šprocha and Pavol Tišliar, *Populačný vývoj Podkarpatskej Rusi*, Vol. I (Bratislava, 2009), p. 196.

5 Paul Robert Magocsi, *Our People: Carpatho-Rusyns and Their Descendants in North America*, 4th rev. ed. (Wauconda, Ill., 2005), p. 15.

6 *Opportunity Realized: The Greek Catholic Union's First One Hundred Years, 1882–1992* (Beaver, Pa., 1994), p. 95.

Chapter 18: Other peoples in Subcarpathian Rus'

1 *Statistický lexikon obcí v Republice československé . . . na základě výsledků sčítání lidu z 15. února 1921*, Vol. IV: *Podkarpatská Rus* (Prague, 1928); *Statistický lexikon obcí v Republice československé . . . na základě výsledků sčítání lidu z 1. prosince 1930*, Vol. IV: *Země podkarpatoruská* (Prague, 1937).

2 Ildikó Orosz and István Csernicskó, *The Hungarians in Transcarpathia* (Budapest: Tinta Publishers, 1999), pp. 24–26.

3 The statistical data in this paragraph comes from the Czechoslovak census of 1930, cited in Jiři Sláma, "Die Parlamentswahlen im Jahre 1935 in Karpatorussland," *Bohemia*, XXIX, 1 (Munich, 1988), p. 38.

4 František Chmelař, "Několik úvah o školství v Zemi podkarpatoruské," in František Stojan, *Representační sborník veškerého školství na Podkarpatské Rusi* (Prešov, 1938), p. 4.

5 Cited in C. A. Macartney, *Hungary and Her Successors: The Treaty of Trianon and Its Consequences, 1919–1937* (London, New York, and Toronto, 1937), p. 183.

6 Statistical chart in Károly Kocsis, *Ethnic Map of the Present Territory of Transcarpathia (Subcarpathia)* (Budapest, 2001).

7 The figures in this paragraph are drawn from Yeshayahu A. Jelinek, *The Carpathian Diaspora: The Jews of Subcarpathian Rus' and Mukachevo, 1848–1948* (New York, 2007), p. 13.

8 According to the 1910 Hungarian census, only 51.9 percent of Jews could read and write. Branislav Šprocha and Pavol Tišliar, *Populačný vývoj Podkarpatskej Rusi*, Vol. I (Bratislava, 2009), p. 81.

9 These figures refer to persons of "Israelite" religion drawn from census returns cited in note 1.

10 Ibid.

11 In effect, there are census data on the number of persons who responded *židovská* (Jewish) on the nationality question (91,255) and *israelské* (Israelite) on the reli-

gious question (102,542). The difference between the two figures is explained by the fact that a certain number of Jews identified their nationality with the state in which they associated and felt most comfortable. In the 1930 census, among persons of Jewish religion who did not identify with the *židovská* (Jewish) nationality were 5,870 who identified as Magyars, 811 as "Czechoslovaks," and 708 as Rusyns. Ibid.

12 If, in 1921, 67 percent of Jewish students attended schools with Rusyn as the language of instruction, by 1932 that percentage decreased to 22. By contrast, the same period saw Jewish attendance at schools with Czech (or in some cases Slovak) as the language of instruction, from 2 to 58 percent. Friedmann, "Židovská národní menšina na Podkarpatské Rusi," *Národnostní obzor,* IV (Prague, 1934), p. 273.

13 Ibid.

14 Cited in Aryeh Sole, "Jews in Subcarpathian Ruthenia, 1918–1938," in *The Jews in Czechoslovakia,* Vol. I (Philadelphia and New York: Jewish Publication Society of America/Society for the Czechoslovak Jews, 1968), p. 148.

15 For example, in the 1935 elections to the Czechoslovak parliament, 51.3 percent of Jewish voters in Subcarpathian Rus' voted for the Communist party. Sláma, "Die Parlamentswahlen," p. 44.

16 See Allan L. Nadler, "The War on Modernity of Hayyim Elazar Shapira of Munkacz," *Modern Judaism,* XIV, 3 (Baltimore, 1994), pp. 233–264.

17 Earlier Hungarian censuses, whose "nationality" data was based on mother tongue, recorded 27,100 (1900) and 33,700 (1910) Germans. This anomaly of so large a number is explained by the fact that many Jews were recorded as Germans, since a large proportion of them (62 percent in 1910) indicated that their mother tongue was German. Friedmann, "Židovská národní menšina," p. 270.

18 Sláma, "Die Parlamentswahlen," p. 38.

19 Fedir Kula, *Nimets'ki shkoly na Zakarpatti/Deutsche Schulen in Transkarpatien* (Uzhhorod: Patent, 1998), pp. 8–17.

20 Ievhen Iu. Pelens'kyi, "Shkil'nytstvo. Kul'turno-osvitnie zhyttia," in *Karpats'ka Ukraïna* (L'viv, 1939), p. 125.

21 Data extracted from statistics listed above in note 1.

22 Despite the lack of information on this matter in official Czechoslovak census reports, one demographer has deduced the following: 9,477 Czechs in Subcarpathian Rus' in 1921, and 20,719 in 1930. Vladimír Srb, "Obyvatelstvo Podkarpatské Rusi," *Demografie,* No. 3 (Prague, 1999), p. 214.

23 Stojan, *Representační sborník,* p. 4.

Chapter 19: Autonomous Subcarpathian Rus' and Carpatho-Ukraine, 1938–1939

1 "Rezoliutsiï ukhvaleni na zasidanni holovnoï upravy Pershoï rus'koï (Ukraïns'koï) Tsentral'noï Rady v Uzhhorodi dnia 29. V. 1938," *Nova svoboda* (Uzhhorod), 15 June 1938.

2 "Cheskaia shkol'naia politika na Podk. Rusi," *Russkii vistnyk,* 16 October 1938.

3 Speech of Premier Brodii in Uzhhorod, 12 October 1938, cited in ibid.

4 Cited in Petro Stercho, *Karpato-ukraïns'ka derzhava* (Toronto, 1965), p. 91.

5 *Dnevnik* (Prague), 15 December 1938.

6 "Kabelagrammy pereslannyia Karpatorusskim Soiuzam, 6. IX. 1938," reprinted in ibid.

7 Telegram from the Carpatho-Ukrainian delegation abroad, cited in Petro Stercho, *Diplomacy of Double Morality: Europe's Crossroads in Carpatho-Ukraine, 1919–1939* (New York, 1971), p. 259.

8 *Nastup* (Khust), 17 January 1939.

9 Complete voting results by village are given in Stercho, *Karpato-ukraïns'ka derzhava*, pp. 242–252.

10 A phrase used for the title of one of the most impartial accounts, by the English journalist Michael Winch, *Republic for a Day: An Eye-Witness Account of the Carpatho-Ukraine Incident* (London, 1939).

Chapter 20: Carpathian Rus' during World War II, 1939–1944

1 Andrej Dudáš, *Rusínska otázka a jej úzadie* (Buenos Aires, 1971), p. 25.

2 Peter Koval', "Otázka slovensko-rusínskych etnických hraníc v čase formovania slovenskej štátnosti," in Martin Pekár and Richard Pavlovič, eds., *Slovensko medzi 14. marcom 1939 a salzburskýmy rokovaniami* (Prešov, 2007), p. 122n30.

3 Cited in Loránt Tilkovsky, *Revízió és nemzetiségpolitika Magyarországon 1938–1941* (Budapest, 1967), p. 218.

4 During the second half of 1939 and early 1940, the government organized the shipment of another 940 railway cars of corn to Subcarpathian Rus'. Zsigmond Perényi and Aleksander Yl'nytskii, *Odnorochna robota madiarskoho pravytel'stva za narod Podkarpatia* (Uzhhorod, 1940), pp. 6 and 26.

5 Speech of the governmental commissar for Subcarpathia, Miklós Kozma, inaugurating the Subcarpathian Scholarly Society, 26 January 1941, cited in *Zoria/Hajnal*, I, 1–2 (Uzhhorod, 1941), p. 8.

6 *Reabilitovani istoriieiu: Zakarpats'ka oblast'*, Vol. I (Uzhhorod, 2003), p. 55.

7 Yeshayahu A. Jelinek, *The Carpathian Diaspora: The Jews of Subcarpathian Rus' and Mukachevo, 1848–1948* (New York, 2007), pp. 308–309.

Chapter 21: Carpathian Rus' in transition, 1944–1945

1 In July 1943, the unit had 2,441 soldiers, of whom 72 percent were Carpatho-Rusyns; one year later the unit's size increased to 12,922 soldiers of whom 25 percent (3,177) were Carpatho-Rusyns. Ivan Vanat, "Zakarpats'ki ukraïns'ki v chekholoslovats'komu viis'ku v SRSR," in *Shliakhom do voli/Naukovyi zbirnyk Muzeiu ukraïns'koï kul'tury u Svydnyku*, II (Svidník and Prešov, 1966), pp. 193–199.

2 *Karpatorusskyi kalendar Lemko-Soiuza na 1944* (Yonkers, N.Y., 1944), p. 16.

3 "Rezoliutsiia 1-oï konferentsiï KPZU, 19.XI. 1944," in *Shliakhom Zhovtnia: zbirnyk dokumentiv*, Vol. IV (Uzhhorod, 1965), doc. 41, p. 62.

4 "Manifest Pershoho Z'ïzdu Narodnykh Komitetiv pro vozz'iednannia Zakarpats'koï Ukraïny z Radians'koiu Ukraïnoiu, 26. XI.1944," in ibid., doc. 51, p. 80.

5 National Council of the Transcarpathian Ukraine to the Official Delegate of the Czechoslovak Government, 30. IX. 1944, in F. Nemec and V. Moudry, *The Soviet Seizure of Subcarpathian Ruthenia* (Toronto, 1955), doc. 34, p. 263.

6 Memoirs of the Czechoslovak minister in Moscow, Zdeněk Fierlinger, *V službách ČSR: paměti z druhého zahraničního odboje,* Vol. II (Prague, 1948), p. 452.

7 Letter of Stalin to Beneš, dated 23 January 1945, reprinted in ibid., p. 558.

8 T. V. Vikhrova, "Osoblyvosti etnichnoï kul'tury lemkiv na Luhanshchyni," in Luhans'kyi oblasnyi kraieznavchyi muzei, Seriia: Kraieznavchi zapysky, Vol. VI: *Tradytsiino-pobutova kul'tura Luhanshchyny: zbirnyk naukovykh statei* (Luhans'k, 2013), p. 403.

9 The figures calculated by students of this problem vary; some suggesting 95,000 people from the Lemko Region (including all the Sanok district) went to Ukraine in 1945–1946 preceded by 5,000 in 1939–1940, while an estimated 30,000 to 35,000 remained behind. See Roman Drozd, "Lemkos and the Resettlement Action to Soviet Ukraine, 1944–1946," and Yurii Kramar, "The Deportation of Ukrainians from the Lemko Region, 1944–1947," in Paul Best and Jaroslaw Moklak, eds., *The Lemko Region, 1939–1947: War, Occupation, and Deportation* (New Haven and Cracow, 2002), esp. pp. 89 and 99.

10 Ivan Pop, "Optatsiia," in *Encyclopedia of Rusyn History and Culture*, ed. Paul Robert Magocsi and Ivan Pop, 2nd rev. ed. (Toronto, 2005), pp. 362–363.

Chapter 22: Subcarpathian Rus'/Transcarpathia in the Soviet Union, 1945–1991

1 Ivan Pop, *Dějiny Podkarpatské Rusi v datech* (Prague, 2005), p. 447.

2 Mykhailo M. Boldyzhar et. al., *Narysy istorïi Zakarpattia,* Vol. III (Uzhhorod, 2003), p. 117.

3 Ibid., pp. 124 and 605.

4 Ibid., p. 120.

5 Ibid., p. 148.

6 Cited from the statistical chart in Mai Panchuk et al., *Zakarpattia v etnopolitychnomu vymiri* (Kiev, 2008), p. 648.

7 Boldyzhar, *Narysy,* Vol. III, p. 538.

8 Peter Jordan and Mladen Klemenčić, eds., *Transcarpathia—Bridgehead or Periphery?* (Frankfurt am Main, 2004), p. 65; Hennadii V. Pavlenko, *Nimtsi na Zakarpatt* (Uzhhorod, 1995), p. 39.

9 The figures, which vary greatly, are discussed in Yeshayahu A. Jelinek, *The Carpathian Diaspora: The Jews of Subcarpathian Rus' and Mukachevo, 1848–1948* (New York, 2007), p. 328.

10 Jordan and Klemenčić, *Transcarpathia,* p. 65.

11 Pavlenko, *Nimtsi na Zakarpatti,* p. 41.

12 Boldyzhar, *Narysy,* Vol. III, pp. 547–549.

13 I. H. Shul'ha, "Rozvytok Radians'koho Zakarpattia," in *Velykyi Zhovten' a rozkvit vozz'iednanoho Zakarpattia* (Uzhhorod, 1970), p. 476.

14 A. V. Popovych, "Rol' radians'koho kinomystetstva v politychnomu vykhovanni trudiashchykh Zakarpattia," in ibid., p. 491.

15 Data from a statistical chart in Paul Robert Magocsi, *The Shaping of a National Identity: Subcarpathian Rus', 1848–1948* (Cambridge, Mass., 1978), p. 266.

16 Words of the associate editor of Transcarpathian Ukraine's official newspaper *Zakarpats'ka Ukraïna,* cited in Boldyzhar, *Narysy,* Vol. III, p. 62.

17 Mykola P. Makara in ibid., p. 607.

Chapter 23: The Prešov Region in postwar and Communist Czechoslovakia, 1945–1989

1 Vremennii Narodnŷi Komitet priashevskikh i russkikh ukraintsev, letter dated 29 November 1944, reprinted in Ivan Vanat, *Materialy do istoriï Ukraïns'koï Narodnoï Rady Priashivshyny* (Prešov, 2001), doc. 3, p. 18.

2 Protokol Pershoho z'ïzdu delehativ vid ukraïns'kykh sil i okruhiv Priashivshyny, dated 1 March 1945, in ibid., document 7, p. 38.

3 Ibid., p. 39.

4 "Memuary Nikity Sergeevicha Khrushchova," *Voprosy istorii*, Nos. 7–8 (Moscow, 1991), pp. 88–89.

5 Juraj Briškár, "Rusko-ukrajinská sekcia Demokratickej strany," in Mykhailo Rychalka, ed., *Zhovten' i ukraïns'ka kul'tura* (Prešov, 1968), p. 520.

6 Ibid.

7 Marián Gajdoš and Stanislav Konečný, *Postavenie Rusínov-Ukrajincov na Slovensku v rokoch 1848–1953* (Prague, 1994), pp. 26–29.

8 Vasyl' Kapishovs'kyi, "Ekonomichni peredumovy rozvytku ukraïns'koï kul'tury v ChSSR," in Rychalka, *Zhovten' i ukraïns'ka kul'tura*, p. 488.

9 There is much discrepancy in the figures. Traditionally, historians like Ivan Vanat, *Volyns'ka aktsiia* (Prešov, 2001), p. 41, have argued that most (96.8 percent) of the approximately 12,400 *optanty* who resettled in Soviet Ukraine were "Prešov Region Ukrainians" (i.e., Carpatho-Rusyns). Recent research has shown that about 65 percent were Carpatho-Rusyns, 20 percent were Slovaks, 10 percent "real" Russians and Ukrainians (i.e., post-World War I émigrés from Russia and Ukraine), and the remaining 5 percent Czechs, Magyars, Poles, Jews, and Roma/Gypsies. Michal Šmigel, "Reoptacia rusínskeho obyvatel'stva z Ukrajiny na Slovensko v rokoch, 1993–1998," in *Etnologia Actualis Slovaca*, No. 5 (Trnava, 2004), p. 136.

10 This 63 percent figure represents the average in the three counties (*okresy*) most heavily inhabited by Carpatho-Rusyns: Bardejov (66.5 percent), Humenné (53.4 percent), and Prešov (69.9 percent). Ivan Bajcura, *Ukrajinská otázka v ČSSR* (Košice, 1967), p. 141.

11 The statistics on this matter vary. These are taken from a report by the government representative of the Slovak Office for Church Affairs (SLÚC), cited in Atanáz Mandzák, "Štátny úrad pre veci cirkevné a Akcia 'P'," in Jaroslav Coranič et al., eds., *Cirkev v okovách totalitného režimu* (Prešov, 2010), p. 110.

12 Ibid.

13 Cited in Bajcura, *Ukrajinská otázka*, p. 132.

14 Cited in Ivan Humenyk, "KSUT-u—desiat' rokiv," *Duklia*, IX, 3 (Prešov, 1961), p. 6.

15 Ivan Bajcura, *Cesta k internácionalnej jednote* (Bratislava, 1982), pp. 5–6.

16 From a radio report, cited in the newspaper *Nove zhyttia* (Prešov), 23 March 1968.

17 See above, note 8.

18 Bronislav Sprocha and Pavol Tišliar, *Demografický obraz Slovenska v sčítaniach l'udu 1919–1940* (Brno, 2012), p. 155; Károly Kocsis, *Szlovákia mai területének etnikai térképe* (Budapest, 2000); Marián Gajdoš, ed., *Vývoj a postavenie ukrajin-skej národnosti na Slovensku v období výstavby socializmu* (Košice, 1989), pp. 36, 46, and 89; *Preliminary Results of the Population Census: Czech and Slovak Federal Republic, 3 March 1991* (Prague, 1991), pp. 30–31 and 38–39. The first figure for the year 1940 reflects the boundaries of Slovakia before the annexation of territory

by Hungary in late March 1939; the second figure reflects the boundaries of Slovakia after its loss of territory.

19 Pavel Uram, "Vývoj ukrajinského školstva v rokoch 1948–1953," in Rychalka, ed., *Zhovten' i ukraïns'ka kul'tura*, p. 523.

20 Michael Lacko, "The Re-establishment of the Greek Catholic Church in Czechoslovakia," *Slovak Studies*, XI: Historica, No. 8 (Cleveland and Rome, 1971), pp. 166–171.

21 Ibid., pp. 164–165.

22 Stepan Bunganych, "V chomu sprava?," *Nove zhyttia*, 20 April 1968; and Ivan Siika, "Hyne nasha kul'tura?," ibid., 27 April 1968.

23 Gajdoš, *Vývoj a postavenie*, p. 156.

24 See note 18.

25 Pavel Maču, "National Assimilation: The Case of the Rusyn-Ukrainians of Czechoslovakia," *East Central Europe*, II, 2 (Pittsburgh, 1975), p. 109n30.

26 A. Kovač, "Postavenie občanov ukrajinskej národnosti v Československu do druhej svetovej vojny," in Michal Čorný, ed., *Socialistickou cestou k národnostnej rovnoprávnosti* (Bratislava, 1975), p. 55.

27 Maču, "National Assimilation," p. 109.

28 Marián Gajdoš, Stanislav Konečný, and Mikuláš Mušinka, *Rusíni/ukrajinci v zrkadle polstoročia: niektoré aspekty ich vývoja na Slovensku po roku 1945* (Prešov and Uzhhorod, 1999), p. 93.

Chapter 24: The Lemko Region and Lemko Rusyns in Communist Poland, 1945–1989

1 Paul Robert Magocsi, *Historical Atlas of Central Europe*, 2nd rev. ed. (Seattle, 2002), p. 192.

2 Piotr Eberhardt, *Ethnic Groups and Population Changes in Twentieth-Century Central-Eastern Europe* (Armonk, N.Y., and London, 2003), pp. 141–142.

3 Pawel Przybylski, "60. rocznica akcji 'Wisła'," *Magury' 07* (Warsaw, 2007), p. 14.

4 Ibid., p. 14n3.

5 Jerzy Starzyński, *Szlakiem niestniejących wsi łemkowski* (Warsaw, 2006), pp. 9–74.

6 The estimate that approximately 30 percent of all Jaworzno internees were Lemkos (specifically 1,161 out of 3,871) is based on a detailed study of the camp by K. Miroszewski as discussed in ibid., p. 17n15.

7 The figures for Lower Silesia are found in ibid., p. 18; on the Florynka deportees, see Jarosław Zwoliński and Jarosław Merena, *Na Łemkowszczyźnie: Florynka (nasze seło)* (Koszalin, 1999), pp. 143 and 153.

8 Tomasz Kalbarczyk, "Powrót Łemków," *Biuletyn Instytutu Pamięci Narodowej*, No. 1–2 [48–49] (Warsaw, 2005), p. 76.

9 Cited in Bohdan R. Bociurkiw, "The Suppression of the Greek Catholic Church in Postwar Soviet Union and Poland," in Dennis J. Dunn, ed., *Religion and Nationalism in Central Europe and the Soviet Union* (Boulder, Co., and London, 1987), p. 106.

10 From a pastoral letter by the Apostolic Administrator, Aleksander Malinovskii, cited in Krzystof Z. Nowakowski, "Administracja Apostolska Łemkowszczyzny w latach 1939–1947," in Stanisław Stępeń, ed., *Polska-Ukraina 1000 lat sąsiedztwa*, Vol. II (Przemyśl, 1996), p. 235.

11 Zbigniew Wojewoda, *Zarys historii kościoła greckokatolickiego w Polsce w latach 1944–1989* (Cracow, 1994), pp. 66–67.

12 The figures regarding Volhynia remain a source of great controversy and animosity. Depending on the national orientation of a given author, the number of victims could at least be 80,000 for the Poles and 20,000 Ukrainians. The more measured estimates cited here are from Timothy Snyder, "The Causes of Ukrainian-Polish Ethnic Cleansing 1943," *Past and Present,* No. 179 (Oxford, 2003), pp. 202 and 224.

13 Aleksander Sław, "O kwestii ukraińskiej w Polsce," *Nowe Drogi,* XII, 8 (Warsaw, 1958), cited in Bogdan Horbal, *Lemko Studies: A Handbook* (New York, 2010), p. 447.

Chapter 25: Carpatho-Rusyn diasporas old and new, 1945–1989

1 Cited in Roman Kabachii, "Ostanni iz . . . Lemkiv?," *Homin Ukraïny* (Toronto), 24 September 2013, p. 12.

2 Aleksander Mušinka, "Lemkovia, presidleni z Rumunska do Čiech a na Moravu," in Stefan Dudra et al., eds., *Łemkowie, Bojkowie, Rusini—historia, współczesność, kultura materialna i duchowa* (Legnica and Zielona Góra, 2007), p. 263.

3 Mykola Mušinka, "Bojkovia, presidleni z Rumunska do západných Čiech," in ibid., pp. 269–271.

4 Mykhailo Zan, "Problemy etnichnoï, movnoï ta konfesiinoï identychnosti ukraïntsiv u povitakh Maramuresh ta Satu Mare (Rumuniia)," *Narodna tvorchist' ta etnohrafiia,* LIII, 2 (Kiev, 2009), p. 30.

5 Miron Zhirosh, *Bachvansko-srimski rusnatsi doma i u shvetse, 1745–1991,* Vol. I (Novi Sad, 1997), p. 454.

6 *Opportunity Realized: The Greek Catholic Union's First One Hundred Years* (Beaver, Pa., 1994), p. 242.

Chapter 26: The Revolutions of 1989

1 Declaration of the Carpatho-Rusyns Concerning Restoration of the Transcarpathian Oblast to the Status of an Autonomous Republic," *Carpatho-Rusyn American,* XIV, 1 (Pittsburgh, 1991), pp. 4–5.

2 Cited in Petr God'mash and Sergei God'mash, *Istoriia respubliki Podkarpatskaia Rus'* (Uzhhorod, 2008), p. 491.

3 Mai Panchuk et al., *Zakarpattia v etnopolitychnomu vymiri* (Kiev, 2008), p. 661.

Chapter 27: Post-Communist Transcarpathia—Ukraine

1 The texts of the "official" and four alternative proposals were printed in the Regional Assembly's official organ, *Novyny Zakarpattia* (Uzhhorod), 1, 22, and 27 February 1992.

2 Petr God'mash and Sergei God'mash, *Istoriia respubliki Podkarpatskaia Rus'* (Uzhhorod, 2008), pp. 498–500.

3 Among representative titles from these years are: Iurii Baleha, "Rusynstvo: ideolohy i pokrovyteli [Rusynism: Its Ideologues and Protectors]", *Dzvin,* LII, 5

(L'viv, 1991), pp. 96–109; Iurii Baleha and Iosyf Sirka, *Khto my ie i chyï my dity?* *polemika z prof. P. R. Magochi* [Who Are We and Our Descendants?: A Polemic with Professor P. R. Magocsi] (Kiev, 1991); Stepan Hostyniak, *Pro 'chetvertyi' skh-idnoslov'ians'kyi narod ta pro placheni vyhadky i nisenitnytsi kupky komediantiv* [About the So-Called Fourth East Slavic People and the Paid Fantasies and Stu-pidities of a Group of Comedians] (Prešov, 1992); Oleksa Myshanych, *Politychne rusynstvo i shcho za nym* [Political Rusynism and What's Behind It] (Uzhhorod, 1993).

4 Full text in Julian Galloway, "Stalinism or Tsarism in Present-Day Ukraine?," *Car-patho-Rusyn American*, XX, 1 (Fairfax, Va., 1997), p. 3.

5 Decree of the Russian imperial minister of the interior, Count Petr Valuev, 18 July 1863, cited in Paul Robert Magocsi, *A History of Ukraine: The Land and Its Peoples*, 2nd rev. ed. (Toronto, 2010), p. 393.

6 The only published source for this data appears in a publication of the Transcar-pathian Regional Office of Ukraine's State Committee of Statistical Data, *Natsion-al'nyi sklad naselennia ta ioho movni oznaky: statystychnyi biuleten'* (Uzhhorod, 2003), p. 62.

7 http://www.ohchr.org/english/bodies/cerd/docs/CERD.C.UKR.CO.18.pdf.

8 http://www. state.gov/g/drl/rls/hrrpt/2003/27871.htm.

9 Letter from John McCain, U.S. Senate, dated 6 June 2005, reproduced in Viktor Haburchak, Mikulaš Popovič, and Elaine Rusinko, *Rusyns in Ukraine* (copy of an MS Power Point presentation in the author's possession).

10 Minutes of the 1,785th meeting of the Committee on the Elimination of Racial Dis-crimination (CERD), 17 August 2006, cited in Mikhailo Feisa, *The New Serbia and its Ruthenian Minority* (Novi Sad, 2010), p. 125.

11 http://news.uzhgorod.ua/novosti/20432.

12 "Deklaratsiia assotsiatsii rusinskikh organizatsii Zakarpat'ia 'Soim Podkarpatskikh Rusinov', 15 dekabria 2007 g.," http://rusinpresent.narod.ru/62praz.htm.

13 "Memorandum 2-ho Ievropeis'koho Kongresu Pidkarpats'kykh Rusyniv pro pryiniattia Aktu proholoshennia vidnovlennia rusyns'koï derzhavnosti, Muk-achevo, 25 zhovtnia 2008 r.," *Karpats'ka Ukraïna* (Uzhhorod), 1 November 2008, p. 2.

14 Ibid.

15 Pavlo Robert Magochii and Steven Chepa, "Vidkrytyi lyst-zaiava pro vidmezhu-vannia vid ekstremizmu v karpatorusyns'komu rusi," *Krytyka*, XII, 7–8 [129–130] (Kiev, 2008), p. 21.

16 Mykhailo M. Boldyzhar et. al., *Narysy istoriï Zakarpattia*, Vol. III (Uzhhorod, 2003) p. 76.

17 Oleksandr O. Malets', *Etnopolitychni ta etnokul'turni protsesy na Zakarpatti 40–80 kh rr. XX st.* (Uzhhorod, 2004), p. 41.

18 Ibid., p. 108.

19 Mikhail Rushchak and Valerii Padiak, *Sistema khoziaistvovaniia v Zakarpatsko oblasti v 1991–2004 godakh* (Uzhhorod, 2004), p. 34.

20 Valerii Padiak, *Vozrodzhinia rusyns'koho oshkolovania na Podkarpats'kii Rusy* (Uzh horod, 2008), p. 11; Valerii Padiak, *Rusyns'ka shkola: vidrodzhennia narodnoï osv ity* (Uzhhorod, 2013), p. 10.

Chapter 28: The Post-Communist Prešov Region and the Lemko Region—Slovakia and Poland

1 Of the total 32,408 persons in the census report, the exact breakdown was: 16,937 Rusyns; 13,847 Ukrainians; and 1,624 Russians. *Preliminary Results of the Population Census: Czech and Slovak Federal Republic, 3 March 1991* (Prague, 1991), pp. 30–31.

2 These gross figures do not reveal interesting internal complexities. Included in the 49,099 who claimed Rusyn as their mother tongue were 27,868 "Slovaks"; 16,269 Carpatho-Rusyns; and 4,549 "Ukrainians." On the other hand, only 2,198 "Slovaks" and 122 Carpatho-Rusyns said that their mother tongue was Ukrainian. See the detailed table in Marián Gajdoš et al., *Rusíni/Ukrajinci na Slovensku na konci 20. storočia* (Prešov, 2001), p. 27.

3 In its first year of power (1995), the Mečiar government reduced the subsidy for Carpatho-Rusyn organizations to 1.6 million crowns (down from 6 million in 1994) and for Ukrainian organizations to 3.7 million crowns (down from 6.8 million in 1994). Marián Gajdoš and Stanislav Konečný, "Rusínska a ukrajinská menšina v národnostnej politike Slovenska po roku 1989," in Štefan Šutaj, ed., *Národnostná politika na Slovensku po roku 1989* (Prešov, 2005), pp. 112–113.

4 Anna Kuzmiakova et al., *Nasha dvadtsiat'richna put': zbirnyk dokumentiv prysviachenĝi 20 richnitsi iestvovaniu Rusyn'skoi obrodŷ* (Prešov, 2010), pp. 15–19.

5 The leading Slovak press organs of the time—with the exception of the former Communist and leftist-oriented daily newspapers which reported about "protests against codification," *Pravda* (Bratislava), 27 January 1995—accepted the new reality and each reported in its 28 January issue that "the Rusyn language is codified": *Narodna obrana, Smena, Slovenská republika, Sme* (all published in the country's capital Bratislava).

6 Pavlo Robert Magochii, "Priashivs'ka hreko-katolyts'ka tserkva?," in *Kovcheh: naukovyi zbirnyk*, No. 4 (L'viv, 2003), p. 172.

7 During this same period, the number of persons declaring Ukrainian nationality declined from 13,847 (1991) to 10,814 (2001). *Slovenský štatisticky úrad: obyvatel'stvo SR podl'a národnosti—sčítanie 2011, 2001, 1991*.

8 Ibid.

9 Council of Europe, *Report Submitted by Ukraine on Implementation of the Provisions of the Framework Convention for the Protection of Nationalities* (Received on 2 November 1999), p. 13.

10 Table 2: Central Government's Subsidies for Poland's Minorities in 2000, 2003, and 2006, in Bogdan Horbal, "Contested by Whom? Lemko Rusyns in the Post-Communist World," *Europa Ethnica*, LXV, 1–2 (Vienna, 2008), p. 48.

11 Table 4: Teaching of Lemko in Elementary Schools and Gymnasiums: 1997/1998–2004/2005, in ibid., p. 50.

12 The actual figures recorded were a total of 5,863 Lemkos living in Lower Silesia (3,084), Lubuskie (791), and the Lemko Region—Little Poland and Subcarpathia palatinates (1,731). www.stat.gov.pl—Table 35: Ludność według deklarowanej narodowości oraz obywatelstwa i województw w 2002 roku, pp. 220–221.

13 The preliminary reports contain only general figures: 6,000 persons having indicated Lemko as their only identity, the rest Lemko in combination with a Polish identity. Główny Urząd Statystyczny, *Narodowy Spis Powszechny Ludności i Mieszkań 2011: raport z wyników* (Warsaw, 2012), p. 106.

Chapter 29: Other Carpatho-Rusyn communities in the wake of the revolutions of 1989

1 Oleksandr Venhrynovych, "Lemky v Ukraïni," *Naukovyi zbirnyk Muzeiu ukrains'koï kul'tury*, Vol. XXVII: *Istoriia ta kul'tura Lemkivshchyny* (Svidník, 2013), p. 404.

2 Ihor Duda, *Lemkivs'kyi slovnyk* (Ternopil', 2011), p. 3.

3 The numbers declined somewhat in the first decade of the twenty-first century, although there were still an estimated 60,000 to 70,000 from both Transcarpathia and Galicia. H. Novotná, "Současná ukrajinská pracovní migrace a její integrace," in O. Šrajerová, ed., *Migrace, tolerance, integrace*, Vol. II (Opava and Prague, 2005), p. 307.

4 *Zpráva o situaci národnostních menšin v České republice za rok 2003* (Prague, 2004), p. 107.

5 László Sasvári, "Ortodoxok és görög katolikusok együttélése Észak-Magyarországon a 18–19. században," in *Interetnikus kapcsolatok Északkelet-Magyarországon* (Miskolc, 1984), p. 155.

6 *Központi Statisztikai Hivatal*, "A 2001. évi népszámlálási adatok összefoglaló táblázata," p. 1.

7 "Sviatochna besïda zamistytelia derzhtainyka Dr. Chaby Latortsoï," *Rusyns'kŷi svit/Ruszin Világ*, X [101] (Budapest, 2013), p. 6.

8 The total number of persons identifying as Ukrainian was 61,098, of whom 35,583 were in the Maramureş Region (Maramureş and Satu Mare counties). Intitutul Naţional de Statistică, *Recensământul Populaţiei şi locuinţelor 18 marţie 2002*, Vol. IV.

9 Nada Bajić, "Rusini u Hrvatskoj," *Hrvatska Revija*, VII, 4 (Zagreb, 2007), p. 64.

10 Miron Zhirosh, *Bachvansko-srimski rusnatsi doma i u shvetse, 1745–1991*, Vol. I (Novi Sad, 1997), p. 454; "Etnički sastav stanovištva Vojevodine: Popis 2002. godine," table reprinted in Mikhailo Feisa, *The New Serbia and Its Ruthenian Minority* (Novi Sad and Kucura, 2010), p. 190.

11 These figures represent a statistical sample, since the ancestry question only appeared on the so-called long form, sent to only 20 percent of American households. The actual total was 12,966 persons who classified themselves in one of five categories: Carpatho-Rusyn (7,316), Ruthenian (3,776), Rusyn (1,357), Carpathian (286), and Lemko (231). Susan J. Lapham, "Ancestry Reporting in the 1990 Census: Towards the 2000 Census," based on the U.S. Department of Commerce Bureau of the Census, SJLPAA93—Appendix A: Ancestry Code List with Estimates of Each Group, 1990.

12 *Harvard Encyclopedia of American Ethnic Groups* (Cambridge, Mass., 1980); Yale University's *Encyclopedia of World Cultures*, Vol. I: *North America* (Boston, 1991); *Gale Encyclopedia of Multicultural America*, Vol. I (Detroit, 1995); Macmillan's *American Immigrant Cultures: Builders of a Nation*, Vol. I (New York, 1997), among others, as well as two editions of a volume titled, *The Carpatho-Rusyn Americans*, in Chelsea House Publishers "The Peoples of North America Series" (Philadelphia, 1989 and 2001).

13 Miron Ziros, "Migration of Rusyns to Canada, 1991–2007," *Rusnatsi u shvetse*, VIII, 2 (Kitchener, Ont., 2009), p. 25; G. Koliesar, "Rusnatsi u Sivernej Ameriki: kel'o nas iest u Kanadi i Ameriki?," ibid., X, 1 (Kitchener, Ont., 2011), pp. 17–18.

Chapter 30: Carpathian Rus'—real or imagined?

1 Benedict Anderson, *Imagined Communities: Reflections on the Origin and Spread of Nationalism*, 3rd rev. ed. (New York, 1991).

2 This figure differs from others given in this book, in particular in Chapter 1, Table 1.1. The explanation is that the number in question—56,047—is based only on 2001–2002 census data for Carpatho-Rusyns living only in those parts of four countries that encompass historic Carpathian Rus': 44,141 persons in Slovakia—the Prešov kraj and Košice kraj (excluding the cities of Bardejov, Humenné, Košice, Michalovce, Poprad, Prešov, and Vranov); 10,100 in Ukraine—the Transcarpathian oblast; 1,731 in Poland—the Małopolskie (791) and Podkarpackie (147) palatinates; and 75 in Romania—the Maramureş (56) and Satu Mare (19) districts/judeţe. Data drawn from Štatistický úrad Slovenskej republiky—obdor štatistiký obyvateľstva, "Obyvateľstvo s rusínskym materinským jazykom . . . v obciach Prešovského a Košického kraja: z údajov zo sčítania . . . v roku 2001"; Derzhavnyi komitet statystyky—Zakarpats'ke oblasne upravlinnia, *Natsional'nyi sklad naselennia ta ioho movni oznaky za pidsumkamy pershoho Vseukraïns'koho perepysu naselennia 2001 roku* (Uzhhorod, 2003), pp. 62–70; Główny Urząd Statystyczny, *Narodowy Spis Powszechny Ludności i Mieszkań, 21. V—8.VI.2002*, Table 35: Ludność według deklarowanej narodowości oraz obywatelstwa i województw, pp. 220–221, www. stat.gov.pl; Mykhailo Zan, "Problemy etnichnoï, movnoï ta konfesiinoï identychnosti ukraïntsiv u povitakh Maramuresh ta Satu Mare (Rumuniia)," *Narodna tvorchist' ta etnohrafiia*, LIII, 2 (Kiev, 2009), pp. 33–36.

3 "Document of the Copenhagen Meeting of the Human Dimension of the CSCE, 5–29 June 1990," in Tom Trier, ed., *Focus on Rusyns: International Colloquium on the Rusyns of East Central Europe* (Copenhagen, 1999), p. 89.

For further reading

The following guide is intended to direct interested readers to published materials about the subjects discussed in this book. This is not a comprehensive bibliography, but rather a briefly annotated discussion of books, chapters, and journal articles which may assist those hoping to find more information about specific aspects of Carpathian Rus' and Carpatho-Rusyns. The emphasis is on English-language materials, although some of the most important studies on specific topics written in other languages are also noted, in particular studies published during the last few decades that are based on new research and on heretofore inaccessible archival sources.

The first section is devoted to reference works and general studies. The order of the subsequent sections reflects the general chronological sequence used in this book.

1. Reference works and general studies
   a. Encyclopedias and bibliographies
   b. General histories
   c. General church histories
   d. Other peoples—general surveys
   e. General studies of ruling states

2. Prehistoric times to the sixteenth century

3. The seventeenth and early eighteenth centuries

4. The reform era and Habsburg rule, 1770s to 1847

5. The Revolution of 1848 to the end of World War I

6. The interwar years, 1919–1938

7. International crises and World War II, 1938–1945

8. The Communist era, 1945–1989

9. The revolutions of 1989 and their aftermath

1. Reference works and general studies

a. Encyclopedias and bibliographies

There are a few encyclopedias which deal either with Carpathian Rus' as a whole or with one or more of its regions. *The Encyclopedia of Rusyn History and Culture*, 2nd revised and expanded edition, eds. Paul Robert Magocsi and Ivan Pop (Toronto, Buffalo, and London: University of Toronto Press, 2005), contains over 1,100 alphabetically arranged entries about individuals, organizations, and events in all regions of Carpathian Rus' as well as about the Vojvodina and the diaspora communities in North America. The Ukrainian-language edition of this work is enhanced by over 1,500 illustrations which do not appear in the English edition: *Entsyklopediia istoriï i kul'tury karpats'kykh rusyniv*, ed. Pavlo Robert Magochii and Ivan Pop (Uzhhorod: Vyd-vo V. Padiaka, 2010).

Two other encyclopedias focus on specific regions of Carpathian Rus' and include entries on individuals, events, and geographic places. For Subcarpathian Rus', see the Russian-language work by Ivan Pop, *Éntsiklopediia Podkarpatskoi Rusi*, 2nd revised ed. (Uzhhorod: Karpato-russkii étnologicheskii issledovatel'skii tsentr v SShA, 2006); for the Prešov region there is the Ukrainian-language volume by Fedir Kovach, *Kraieznavchyi slovnyk Rusyniv-Ukraïntsiv: Priashivshchyna* (Prešov: Soiuz Rusyniv-Ukraïntsiv Slovats'koï Respubliky, 1999).

The aforementioned encyclopedias include brief bibliographies following many of their entries. There are, however, several comprehensive bibliographies that provide unannotated lists of older literature: Nykolai Lelekach and Ivan Haraida, compilers, *Zahal'na bibliohrafiia Podkarpatia* (Uzhhorod: Podkarpatskoe obshchestvo nauk, 1944; reprinted: Uzhhorod: Vyd-vo V. Padiaka, 2000), for publications that appeared before World War II; and Paul Robert Magocsi, *The Shaping of a National Identity: Subcarpathian Rus', 1848–1948* (Cambridge, Mass., and London: Harvard University Press, 1978), pp. 465–485, for older works as well as those published up to the 1970s. Both these bibliographies focus on Subcarpathian Rus' and, in part, the Prešov Region. For more comprehensive and up-to-date listings, specifically on the Prešov Region, see the bibliography in Paul Robert Magocsi, *The Rusyns of Slovakia: An Historical Survey* (New York: Columbia University Press/East European Monographs, 1993), pp. 141–170.

Unannotated bibliographies for other Carpatho-Rusyn-inhabited lands and communities include: for the Lemko Region, Tadeusz Zagórzański, *Łemkowie i Łemkowszczyzna: materiały do bibliografii* (Warsaw: SKPB, 1984); for the Vojvodina, Vida Zaremski et al., *Bibliografia Rusnacoch u Jugoslaviji, 1918–1980*, Vol. II (Novi Sad: Biblioteka Matice srpske, 1990); and for North America, Paul Robert Magocsi, *Our People: Carpatho-Rusyns and Their Descendants in North America*, 4th revised edition (Wauconda, Ill.: Bolchazy-Carducci Publishers, 2005), pp. 207–215. There is also a comprehensive bibliography for works dealing with linguistic issues and the language question in Paul Robert Magocsi, ed., *Rusyn'skŷi iazŷk*, Najnowsze dzieje języków słowiańskich, Vol. XIV, 2nd revised printing (Opole: Uniwersytet Opolski—Instytut Filologii Polskiej, 2004/2007), pp. 427–469. Finally, there is a five-volume annotated bibliography of works published since 1975 in a wide variety of languages about all subjects and all regions of Carpathian Rus' and North America: Paul Robert Magocsi, *Carpatho-Rusyn Studies: An Annotated Bibliography*, Vol. I: *1975–1984* (New York and London: Garland Publishers, 1988); Vol. II: *1985–1994* (New York: Columbia University Press/East European Monographs, 1998); Vol. III: *1995–1999* (New York: Columbia University Press/East European Monographs, 2006); Vol. IV: *2000–2004* (New York: Columbia University Press/East European Monographs, 2011); and Vol. V: *2005–2009* (New York: Columbia University Press/East European Monographs, 2012).

The best introduction to the development of historical writings about Carpatho-Rusyns in Subcarpathian Rus', the Prešov Region, the Lemko Region, Vojvodina, and the United States is the entry "Historiography" by Ivan Pop, Bogdan Horbal, and Paul Robert Magocsi, in *Encyclopedia of Rusyn History and Culture*, 2nd edition, pp. 169–185. Much greater detail, with full bibliographical references, is found in Paul Robert Magocsi, "An Historiographical Guide to Subcarpathian Rus'," *Austrian History Yearbook*, IX–X (Houston, 1973–1974), pp. 201–265, reprinted with revisions in Paul Robert Magocsi, *Of the Making of Nationalities There Is No End*, Vol. II (New York: Columbia University Press/East European Monographs, 1999), pp. 323–408, which is supplemented with two essays covering publications for the years 1975 through 1994 in ibid., pp. 409–485. For the Lemko Region (including the Lemko diasporas wherever they are found), there is the monumental survey of writings about all aspects of the territory and its inhabitants in Bogdan Horbal, *Lemko Studies: A Handbook* (New York: Columbia University Press/East European Monographs, 2010).

b. General histories

There is only one general history that covers all of Carpathian Rus' and other lands inhabited by Carpatho-Rusyns from earliest times to the present—the popular volume by Paul Robert Magocsi, *The People from Nowhere: An Illustrated History of Carpatho-Rusyns* (Uzhhorod: Vyd-vo V. Padiaka, 2006); editions in Croatian (Uzhhorod: Naklada V. Paďaka, 2009), Czech (2014), Hungarian (2014), Polish (2014), Romanian (Uzhhorod: Editura lui V. Padeac, 2007), Rusyn (Uzhhorod: Vŷd-vo V. Padiaka, 2007), Slovak (Prešov: Rusín a L'udové novinŷ, 2007), Ukrainian (Uzhhorod: Vyd-vo V. Padiaka, 2007), and Vojvodinian Rusyn (Novi Sad and Uzhhorod: NVU Ruske slovo/Vyd-vo V. Padiaka, 2009). Other general histories, none of which are in English, focus on one or two regions of Carpathian Rus', although in most cases they are somewhat limited in their chronological span. Subcarpathian Rus' and the Prešov Region are often treated together, since until 1945 they functioned as one territorial unit. Still useful is the French-language introductory survey by the Swiss geographer Aldo Dami, *La Ruthénie subcarpathique* (Geneva-Annemasse: Les Éditions de Mont-Blanc, 1944), which covers the period up to World War II. Greater chronological coverage, from prehistoric times to the end of the twentieth century, is provided in a multivolume collective work in Ukrainian by former Soviet Marxist and post-Marxist historians under the editorship of Ivan Hranchak and Mykhailo Boldyzhar: *Narysy istorii Zakarpattia,* 3 vols. (Uzhhorod: Uzhhorods'kyi derzhavnyi universytet/ Zakarpats'ka oblasna derzhavna administratsiia, 1993–2003). Subcarpathian Rus' is also the focus of historical surveys in Czech and Slovak by Ivan Pop, *Podkarpatská Rus* (Prague: Nakladatelství Libri, 2005), and *Malé dejiny Rusínov* (Bratislava: Združenie inteligencia rusínov Slovenska, 2010); particularly useful is his Czech-language historical chronology, with appended lists of all rulers and administrators of the several states that ruled Subcarpathian Rus' from the medieval period to the present: Ivan Pop, *Dějiny Podkarpatské Rusi v datech* (Prague: Nakladatelství Libri, 2005).

Two other regions, whether alone or together, have general histories. For Carpatho-Rusyns in the Prešov Region, see Paul Robert Magocsi, *The Rusyns of Slovakia: An Historical Survey* (New York: Columbia University Press/East European Monographs, 1993), and the Slovak scholar Stanislav Konečný's excellent Rusyn-language volume: Stanïslav Koniechni, *Kapitoly z istorii Rusyniv na Sloven'sku* (Prešov: Rusyn i Narodný novynký, 2009). On the Lemko Region there are two older popular historical surveys: by the Ukrainian-oriented Iuliian Tarnovych, *Iliustrovana istoriia Lemkivshchyny* (L'viv: Vyd-vo Na storozhi, 1936; repr. New York: Vyd-vo Kultura, 1964, and L'viv: Instytut narodoznavstva NAN Ukraïny, 1998), and by the Lemko-Rusyn-oriented Ioann Polianskii, writing under the pseudonym I. F. Lemkyn, *Lemkovyna: A History of the Lemko Region of the Carpathian Mountains* (Higganum, Conn.: Carpathian Institute and Lemko Association, 2012). Although not intended as such, the bibliographical guide by Bogdan Horbal, *Lemko Studies: A Handbook* (New York: Columbia University Press/East European Monographs, 2010), provides an excellent, profusely documented general history of the Lemko Region from earliest prehistoric times to the present, including Lemko-Rusyn communities in the North American diaspora. Ukrainian scholars understand the Lemkos as an ethnographic group of Ukrainians living on both slopes of the mountains; that is, Carpatho-Rusyns in the Lemko Region proper and in the Prešov Region. The best example of this approach is the relatively detailed historical survey by Ivan Hvat and Oleksander Baran, "Istoriia," in Bohdan O. Strumins'kyi, ed., *Lemkivshchyna: zemlia—liudy—istoriia—kul'tura,* Vol. I (New York, Paris, Sydney, and Toronto: Naukove tovarystvo im. Shevchenka, 1988) pp. 149–376.

There are also general histories of Carpatho-Rusyn diasporan communities. For the Vojvodina and Srem, there is the pro-Rusyn interpretation in Fedor Labozh, *Istoriia rusinokh Bachkei, Srimu i Slavonii 1745–1918* (Vukovar: Soiuz rusinokh i ukraintsokh Horvatskei, 1979), and the pro-Ukrainian interpretation in Ianko Ramach, *Kratka istorii rusnatsokh* (Nov Sad: Hrekokatolïtska parokhiia sv. Petra i Pavla, 1993); both volumes only cover the period to the end of World War I. For the United States and Canada, see Paul Robert Magocsi, *Our People: Carpatho-Rusyns and Their Descendants in North America*, 4th rev. ed. (Wauconda, Ill.: Bolchazy-Carducci Publishers, 2005), and his more popular *Carpatho-Rusyn Americans*, 2nd rev. ed. (Philadelphia: Chelsea House Publishers, 2001).

c. General church histories

Because of the historic importance of religion among Carpatho-Rusyns, in particular Eastern-rite Christianity, general histories of the church provide an insight not only into religious but also more broadly cultural and political developments. For an overview of all Uniate/Greek Catholic churches in central Europe, including the position of Carpatho-Rusyns within that world, see Paul Robert Magocsi, "Greek Catholics: Historical Background," in Stéphanie Mahieu and Vlad Naumescu, eds., *Churches In-between: Greek Catholic Churches in Postsocialist Europe* (Berlin: Lit Verlag, 2008), pp. 35–44.

For a specific focus on Carpathian Rus', there are three survey histories of church life from the Middle Ages until the second half of the twentieth century, all written from the Byzantine/Greek Catholic perspective: John Slivka, *The History of the Greek Rite Catholics in Pannonia, Hungary, Czechoslovakia, and Podkarpatska Rus', 863–1949* (Brooklyn, N.Y.: p. a., 1974); Basil Boysak, *The Fate of the Holy Union in Carpatho-Ukraine* (Toronto and New York: n.p., 1963); and Athanasius B. Pekar, *The History of the Church in Carpathian Rus'* (New York: Columbia University Press/East European Monographs, 1992)—actually a translation, with revisions, of a Ukrainian-language work: Atanasii V. Pekar, *Narysy istoriï tserkvy Zakarpattia*, Analecta OSBM, Series II, Sectio I, Vol. XXII (Rome, 1967), reprinted in 1997 together with a second volume (but only in Ukrainian) in the series Analecta OSBM, Series II, Sectio I, Vol. I (Rome and L'viv: Vyd-vo otsiv Vasyliian Misioner, 1997). The histories by Boysak and Pekar deal with the Mukachevo Eparchy and the other jurisdictions which derived from the "mother eparchy": the Prešov Eparchy, Hajdúdorog Eparchy, and the Byzantine Ruthenian Church in the United States. There are also general surveys of three eparchies in Europe; two are written from the Greek Catholic perspective: Julius Kubinyi, *The History of the Prjašiv [Prešov] Eparchy* (Rome: Ukraïns'kyi katolyts'kyi universytet, 1970), and Tamás Véghseõ and Szilveszter Terdik, ". . . You Have Foreseen All of My Paths . . .: Byzantine Rite Catholics in Hungary* (Strasbourg: Éditions du Signe, 2012); the third is a Russian-language history of the Eparchy of Mukachevo written from the Orthodox perspective by Vasilii (Pronin), *Istoriia pravoslavnoi tserkvi na Zakarpat'e* (Mukachevo: Ukrainskaia pravoslavnaia tserkov', 2009).

d. Other peoples—general surveys

Peoples other than Rusyns have lived within historic Carpathian Rus', especially—although not only—in its towns and small cities. Useful introductions to the evolution of most of these "other" peoples, with emphasis on their relationship to Carpatho-Rusyns, are found in Paul Robert Magocsi and Ivan Pop, eds., *The Encyclopedia of Rusyn History and Culture*, 2nd revised ed. (Toronto, Buffalo, and London: University of Toronto Press, 2005): "Bulgarians," p. 53; "Czechs," pp. 83–87; "Germans," pp. 135–136; "Gypsies/ Roma," pp. 156–158; "Jews," pp. 217–222; "Magyars/Hungarians," pp. 314–316; "Poles," pp. 387–389; "Romanians," pp. 418–419; "Russians," pp. 429–431; "Slovaks," pp. 464–467; "Ukrainians," pp. 511–514; and "Vlach colonization" and "Vlachs," pp. 532–533.

There is an extensive body of literature on the Magyars of Subcarpathian Rus', but it deals only with their development in the twentieth century; see below, Section 6. The interwar years, 1919–1938; and Section 8. The Communist era, 1945–1989. The Jews of Subcarpathian Rus', who inhabited both small villages as well as larger towns and cities, where they at times comprised as high as 30 to 50 percent of the inhabitants, are the subject of several general surveys. These include an introductory popular survey by Herman Dicker, *Piety and Perseverance: Jews from the Carpathian Mountains* (New York: Sepher-Hermon Press, 1981), and the shorter but more scholarly surveys by Livia Rothkirchen, "Deep-Rooted Yet Alien: Some Aspects of the History of the Jews in Subcarpathian Ruthenia," *Yad Vashem Studies*, XII (Jerusalem, 1977), pp. 147–191; and Alexander Baran, "Jewish-Ukrainian Relations in Transcarpathia," in Peter J. Potichnyj and Howard Aster, eds., *Ukrainian-Jewish Relations in Historical Perspective* (Edmonton: Canadian Institute of Ukrainian Studies, 1988), pp. 159–171. By far the most comprehensive study is Yeshayahu A. Jelinek, *The Carpathian Diaspora: The Jews of Subcarpathian Rus' and Mukachevo, 1848–1948* (New York: Columbia University Press/East European Monographs, 2007). For studies on specific periods, see below, Section 6: The interwar years, 1919–1938; and Section 7: International crisis and World War II, 1938–1945.

As for other peoples living within Carpathian Rus', the only study available in English deals with Poles, specifically those who after World War II were settled in the largely depopulated Lemko-Rusyn village of Wisłok: Christopher M. Hann, *A Village without Solidarity: Polish Peasants in Years of Crisis* (New Haven and London: Yale University Press, 1985). Certain peoples in Subcarpathian Rus' have general studies about them, although all are written in the language of the group being described. On the Germans, see Nikolaus G. Kozauer, *Die Karpaten-Ukraine zwischen den beiden Weltkriegen unter besonderer Berücksichtigung der deutschen Bevölkerung* (Esslingen am Neckar: Bruno Langer Verlag, 1979); and Georg Melika, *Die Deutschen der Transkarpatien-Ukraine: Entstehung, Entwicklung ihrer Siedlungen, und Lebensweise im multietnischen Raum* (Marburg: N. G. Elwert Verlag, 2002); on the Romanians, see Ion M. Botoş, *La nord de Tisa în "România mică"* (Cluj-Napoca: Editura Pragoş Vodă, 2006); on the Russians, see A. E. Lugovoi, *Rossiiane v zhizni Zakarpat'ia: istoriia i sovremennost'* (Uzhhorod: Kievskii slavisticheskii universitet, Zakarpatskaia filiia, 2003); and on the Slovaks, see Zdenka Bolerácová, *História a kultúra Slovákov na Zakarpatskej Ukrajine* (Uzhhorod: Vyd-vo Mystecka Linija, 2006).

e General studies of ruling states

Readers interested in Carpathian Rus' may need to consult basic historical surveys that deal with states which ruled all or part of Carpathian Rus'
from medieval times to the present. There are several English-language
histories of Hungary. Among the best of these are the older but still reliable volume by C. A. Macartney, *Hungary: A Short History* (Chicago: Aldine
Publishing, 1962); the multi-authored systematic survey edited by Peter F.
Sugar, Péter Hanák, and Tibor Frank, *A History of Hungary* (Bloomington
and Indianapolis: Indiana University Press, 1990); and the somewhat
provocative book by Paul Lendvai, *A History of Hungary: A Thousand Years
of Victory in Defeat* (Princeton, N.J.: Princeton University Press, 2003).
For Poland, which ruled the Lemko Region until the late eighteenth cen-
tury and then again since 1918, an unconventional introductory survey is
Norman Davies, *God's Playground: A History of Poland,* 2 vols. (New York:
Columbia University Press, 1982); the older but still reliable *Cambridge
History of Poland,* 2 vols. (Cambridge: Cambridge University Press, 1950–
1951), ed. by R. Dyboski, O. Halecki, J. H. Penson, and W. F. Reddaway; and
two volumes in the multi-volume History of East-Central Europe, Vol. IV:
Daniel Stone, *The Polish-Lithuanian State, 1386–1795* (Seattle and London:
University of Washington Press, 2001), and Vol. VII: Piotr Wandycz, *The
Lands of Partitioned Poland, 1795–1918* (Seattle and London: University of
Washington Press, 1974; reprinted with corrections, 1984).

For the semi-independent Ottoman vassal state of Transylvania, which
played an especially important role in Subcarpathian Rus' during the sixteenth and seventeenth centuries, there are useful introductory histories from both the Hungarian perspective: Gábor Barta et al., *History of
Transylvania* (Budapest: Akadémiai Kiadó, 1994); and from the Romanian
perspective: Constantin C. Giurescu, *Transylvania in the History of Romania:
An Historical Outline* (London: Garnstone Press, 1969). Of the several histories of Austria-Hungary, in particular during the period 1772 to 1918, when
it ruled all of Carpathian Rus', the most authoritative are: Robert A. Kann,
A History of the Habsburg Empire, 1526–1918 (Berkeley, Los Angeles, and
London: University of California Press, 1974); Carlisle A. Macartney, *The
Habsburg Empire, 1790–1918* (New York: Macmillan, 1969); and, with par-
ticular emphasis on the area of the empire that surrounded and included
Carpathian Rus': Robert A. Kann and Zdeněk V. David, *The Peoples of the
Eastern Habsburg Lands, 1526–1918* (Seattle and London: University of
Washington Press, 1984).

For states that ruled various parts of Carpathian Rus' in the twentieth
century, there are several general histories. Among the more reliable are:
Victor S. Mamatey and Rademír Luža, eds., *A History of the Czechoslovak
Republic, 1918–1948* (Princeton, N.J.: Princeton University Press, 1973); and
for Slovakia, both before and during the entire twentieth century: Stanislav
J. Kirschbaum, *A History of Slovakia* (New York: St. Martin's Press, 1995);
and Anton Spiesz, *Illustrated Slovak History* (Wauconda, Ill.: Bolchazy-

Carducci Publishers, 2006). Although the Soviet Union may have ruled one part of Carpathian Rus' for less than half a century (1945–1991), it had a profound impact on the political and socioeconomic life of what was called Transcarpathia (historic Subcarpathian Rus'), as well as on post-1945 neighboring countries where Carpatho-Rusyns lived: Poland, Czechoslovakia, and Romania. In order to understand better the larger context for developments in Soviet-ruled Transcarpathia and the neighboring satellite countries, one should consult general histories of the Soviet Union. There are several, among which the best is the general survey by Ronald Grigor Suny, *The Soviet Experiment: Russia, the USSR, and the Successor States*, 2nd ed. (Oxford and New York: Oxford University Press, 2011); and, for the time frame when Transcarpathia/Subcarpathian Rus' was an integral part of the Soviet Union: John L.H. Keep, *Last of the Empires: A History of the Soviet Union, 1945–1991* (Oxford and New York: Oxford University Press, 1995).

Ukraine has also ruled the largest region of Carpathian Rus', Transcarpathia/Subcarpathian Rus', but only since that country gained its independence in 1991. From the Ukrainian national perspective, all of Carpathian Rus' and its inhabitants, referred to as "Carpatho-Ukrainians," are considered part of the Ukrainian ethnos and figure as part of the Ukrainian national narrative. Therefore, the entire history of Carpathian Rus', referred to as Carpatho-Ukraine, and especially its relationship to the rest of Ukraine is treated in general histories of the country. For the Ukrainian national perspective, see Orest Subtelny, *Ukraine: A History* (Toronto, Buffalo, and London: University of Toronto Press, 1988; 4th edition, 2009); for the multicultural approach, which includes several sections devoted specifically to Subcarpathian Rus'/Transcarpathia, see Paul Robert Magocsi, *A History of Ukraine: The Land and Its Peoples*, 2nd revised and expanded ed. (Toronto, Buffalo, and London: University of Toronto Press, 2010).

2. Prehistoric times to the 16th century

The literature in English on Carpathian Rus' during the prehistoric period and for much of the Middle Ages through the sixteenth century is very limited. For prehistoric times, the best albeit brief survey is the entry by Ivan Pop, "Archeological Settlements," in Paul Robert Magocsi and Ivan Pop, eds. *Encyclopedia of Rusyn History and Culture*, 2nd revised ed. (Toronto, Buffalo, and London: University of Toronto Press, 2005), pp. 7–9. There is a large body of published research in various Slavic languages on specific archeological periods. The best overall summary of this research covering the period "one million years before the Common Era (BCE) to the tenth century of the Common Era (CE)" is the comprehensive Ukrainian-language monograph by Viacheslav Kotigoroshko, *Verkhnie Potyssia v davnynu* (Uzhhorod Vyd-vo Karpaty, 2008), and the earlier multi-volume Slovak-language work by Branislav Varsik, *Osídlenie Košickej kotliny s osobitným zreteľom na celé východné Slovensko a horné Potisie*, 3 vols. (Bratislava: Veda/Slovenská akadémie vied, 1964–77).

Aspects of the millennium before the Common Era (BCE), which draw on archeological data from the Danubian Basin (including the Upper Tisza Region), are treated in monographs by Nándor Kalicz, *Clay Gods: The Neolithic Period and Copper Age in Hungary* (Budapest: Corvina Press, 1980); Miklós Szabó, *The Celtic Heritage in Hungary* (Budapest: Corvina Press, 1971); and in two essays by Marek Olędzki: "La Tène Culture in the Upper Tisza Basin," *Etnographisch-archaologische Zeitschrift*, XLI, 4 (Berlin, 2000), pp. 507–530, and "'Anarti' and 'Anartophracti': Transcarpathian Cultural and Settlement Relations of the Celts," in H. Dobrzanska et al., eds., *Celts on the Margin: Studies in European Cultural Interaction* (Cracow, 2005), pp. 145–152. Works that look at specific invaders from the east and south who settled in eastern Hungary and interacted with Carpathian Rus', from the Dacians in the first century CE and later Germanic and Turkic peoples, include chapters by András Mócsy, Gábor Vékony, Erdre Tóth, and István Bóna in Gábor Barta et al., *History of Transylvania* (Budapest: Akadémiai Kiadó, 1994), pp. 17–102; István Bóna, *The Dawn of the Dark Ages: The Gepids and the Lombards in the Danubian Basin* (Budapest: Corvina Press, 1976); E. A. Thompson, *A History of Attila and the Huns* (Oxford: Oxford University Press, 1948); and András Pálóczi Horváth, *Pechenegs, Cumans, Iasians: Steppe Peoples in Medieval Hungary* (Budapest: Corvina Press, 1989).

Because Carpatho-Rusyns are part of the Slavic branch of Indo-European peoples, the appearance of Slavs in the Carpathians beginning in the fifth and sixth centuries CE is of particular interest. There are several English-language monographs on the early Slavic peoples in general, which at best touch only tangentially on Carpathian Rus'. Among the best of these are: Zdeněk Váňa, *The World of the Ancient Slavs* (Detroit: Wayne State University Press, 1983), and the more recent work of Paul M. Barford, *The Early Slavs: Culture and Society in Early Medieval Eastern Europe* (Ithaca, N.Y.: Cornell University Press, 2001).

The ninth-century Slavic state known as Greater Moravia, whose farthest eastern sphere of influence reached Carpathian Rus' on both the southern as well as northern slopes of the mountains, is of particular importance to historians of Carpatho-Rusyn cultural and religious life. This is because many scholars believe that the "Apostles to the Slavs," Cyril and Methodius, brought in the early 860s Christianity directly or through their disciples to the Carpatho-Rusyns. For general works on this topic, which do not touch directly on Carpathian Rus', see Francis Dvornik, *Byzantine Missions among the Slavs: SS. Constantine-Cyril and Methodius* (New Brunswick, N.J.: Rutgers University Press, 1970); and Anthony-Emil N. Tachiaos, *Cyril and Methodius of Thessalonica: The Acculturation of the Slavs* (Crestwood, N.Y.: St. Vladimir's Seminary Press, 2001). For the impact of Cyril and Methodius in Carpathian Rus', see Michael Lacko, "The Cyrilo-Methodian Mission in Slovakia," *Slovak Studies*, I (Rome, 1961), pp. 23–49.

The introduction of Christianity according to the Eastern rite from Byzantium and the timing of its appearance in Carpathian Rus' and adjacent territories is not only connected with the 863 mission of Cyril and Methodius to the West Slavs. Byzantine diplomats and missionaries had even earlier, in the mid-tenth century, succeeded in converting some Magyar tribes, so that the spread of Eastern-rite Christianity was in part related to the expansion of Hungary northward to the foothills and crests of the Carpathian Mountains. This matter is discussed by Gyula Moravcsik, "The Role of the Byzantine Church in Medieval Hungary," *American Slavic and East European Review*, VI [18–19] (New York, 1947), pp. 134–151. The most detailed study of the Eastern-rite presence in the northeastern regions of the Hungarian Kingdom, with particular emphasis on monasteries in and adjacent to Carpathian Rus', is found in the wide-ranging and informative, although somewhat controversial Slovak-language monograph by Jozafát V. Timkovič [Vladimirus de juxta Hornad], *Dejiny gréckokatolíkov Podkarpatska 9.-18. storočie* (Košice: p.a., 2004).

This early period is also associated with the White Croats, an Iranian-led confederation of tribes who were eventually slavicized and who, in part, inhabited Carpathian Rus' roughly from the sixth to tenth centuries. The White Croats are given specific attention in Francis Dvornik, *The Making of Central and Eastern Europe* (London: Polish Research Centre, 1949; reprinted 1974), esp. pp. 268–304; and in the detailed report of the tenth-century Byzantine emperor Constantine VII, which has been translated into English with extensive editorial notes: Constantine Porphyrogenitus, *De Administrando Imperii*, 2 vols., translated and edited by Gyula Moravcsik, R. J. H. Jenkins, Francis Dvornik, and Bernard Lewis (London and Washington, D.C.: University of London/Athlone Press/Dumbarton Oaks Center for Byzantine Studies, 1962–67).

Carpathian Rus' again figures, although peripherally, in studies dealing with the arrival of Magyars in the Danubian Basin in the late ninth century. The controversial Hungarian medieval chronicle, which refers specifically to the "conquest" of Carpathian Rus' and its Prince Laborets', has been translated into English by Martyn Rady, "The *Gesta Hungarorum* of Anonymous," *Slavonic and East European Review*, LXXXVII, 4 (London, 2009), pp. 681–727. The best discussion of the early centuries of Magyar rule in what later became the Hungarian Kingdom is Pál Engel, *The Realm of St Stephen: A History of Medieval Hungary, 895–1526* (London and New York: I. B. Tauris Publishers, 2001).

The efforts of scholars to explain developments in those regions of Carpathian Rus' south of the mountains which eventually became part of the Hungarian Kingdom have given rise to several problematic historical questions, ranging from the earliest appearance of the Rus' in the Carpathian region, to the alleged eleventh-century "principality" called Marchia Ruthenorum/Rus'ka Kraina, and to the arrival of the fourteenth-century "Prince of Mukachevo," Fedor Koriatovych. These and other questions are analyzed in great detail—and for the most part dismissed as mythology—by the pre-revolutionary Russian historian Aleksei L. Petrov, *Medieval Carpathian Rus': The Oldest Documentation about the Carpatho-Rusyn Church and Eparchy* (New York: Columbia University Press/East European Monographs, 1998).

Several of these controversial questions—the origins, settlement, and "erroneous teachings" about the political history of Carpatho-Rusyns—are treated in Alexander Bonkáló, *The Rusyns* (New York: Columbia University Press/East European Monographs, 1990), esp. pp. 5–31 and 40–59; and Antony Hodinka, "The Home of the Ruthenian People," *Oxford Hungarian Review*, I, 1 (Oxford, 1922), pp. 51–77. The most comprehensive discussion of the medieval period through the sixteenth century remains two Ukrainian-language monographs: Oleksander Mytsiuk, *Narysy z sotsiial'no-hospodars'koï istoriï b. Uhors'koï nyni Pidkarpats'koï Rusy*, Vol. I: *do druhoï chverty XVI v.* (Uzhhorod: p.a., 1936; reprinted Uzhhorod: Vyd-vo Zakarpattia, 2003)—with an extended résumé in French; and Omelian Stavrovs'kyi, *Slovats'ko-pol's'ko-ukraïns'ke prykordonnia do 18 stolittia* (Bratislava and Prešov: Slovats'ke pedahohichne vyd-vo, Viddil ukraïns'koï literatury, 1967).

3. The 17th and early 18th centuries

The best introduction to this period, especially for Subcarpathian Rus', which for much of this time was part of the Principality of Transylvania, is by Katalin Péter and Ágnes R. Várkonyi, who in two chapters trace seventeenth-century developments during the reigns of Gábor Bethlen and various princes of the Rákóczi family, culminating in the "war for independence" led by Prince Ferenc II Rákóczi: Gábor Barta et al., *History of Transylvania* (Budapest: Akadémiai Kiadó, 1994), pp. 301–411. The literature on this period that deals specifically with Carpathian Rus' is very limited. For a discussion of the significant socioeconomic and demographic changes caused largely by the destructive Habsburg-Transylvanian-Ottoman military conflicts and the accompanying spread of disease, see the Ukrainian-language works of Oleksander Mytsiuk (esp. Vol. II, 1938) and Omelian Stavrovs'kyi mentioned in the previous Section 2. The Stavrovs'kyi volume does, in part, deal as well with developments north of the Carpathians, in the Lemko Region. Otherwise, the only discussion in English on that region which provides at least a brief historical narrative about the major developments in this period is Bogdan Horbal, *Lemko Studies: A Handbook* (New York: Columbia University Press/East European Monographs, 2010), esp. pp. 346–370.

There is, however, a body of literature in English that is devoted to religious affairs, in particular the church union at Uzhhorod, which in 1646 brought into being the Uniate (later renamed Greek Catholic) Church. Two of the previously mentioned general histories of the church (see Section, part c) devote some attention to the background and consequences of the Union of Uzhhorod. Athanasius B. Pekar, *The History of the Church in Carpathian Rus'* (New York: Columbia University Press/East European Monographs, 1992), esp. pp. 18–61, is concerned primarily with the organizational structure and status of the new church entity during the seventeenth and eighteenth centuries, while Basil Boysak, *The Fate of the Holy Union in Carpatho-Ukraine* (Toronto and New York: n.p., 1963), esp. pp. 17–95, puts greater emphasis on the theological and ideological relationship of the Uniates to the body they joined—the Catholic Church of Rome. The most detailed account of the church union among the Carpatho-Rusyns of Hungary, including their interaction with the surrounding Orthodox, Protestant, and Roman Catholic worlds, is by Michael Lacko, *The Union of Užhorod* (Cleveland and Rome: Slovak Institute, 1966).

For an interpretive account of the long-term significance of the Uniate/ Greek Catholic Church and how it reflects certain characteristics of Car- patho-Rusyn society, see Paul Robert Magocsi, "Adaptation without Assim- ilation: The Genius of the Greco-Catholic Eparchy of Mukachevo," *Logos*, XXXVII, 1–4 (Ottawa, 1999), pp. 269–282—reprinted in Paul Robert Magocsi, *Of the Making of Nationalities There Is No End*, Vol. II (New York: Columbia University Press/East European Monographs, 1999), pp. 194–204. Consider- ing the importance of the clergy in Carpatho-Rusyn society, the institutions created to educate prospective priests both within and beyond Carpathian Rus' are important not only for their clerical and educational function but for the region's cultural development as a whole. The earliest of these insti- tutions, all of which are connected to the Uniate or larger Catholic world, are discussed in the bilingual Rusyn (Roman alphabet)-English survey by Vasilij Shereghy and Vasilij Pekar, *Vospitanije podkarpato-ruskoho svjaščenstva/The Training of the Carpatho-Ruthenian Clergy* (Pittsburgh, Pa.: n.p., 1951), esp. pp. 14–45 and 73–105.

The earliest period of the Uniate Church's development and its first hier- archs, including the influential Bishop Decamelis, is the subject of stud- ies by István Baán, "Greek-Speaking Hierarchs on a Ruthenian See: The Diocese of Munkács (Mukačeve) in the Subcarpathian Region at the End of the 17th Century," in Giovanna Brogi Bercoff and Giulia Lami, eds., *Ukraine's Re-integration and Europe: A Historical, Historiographical, and Politically Urgent Issue* (Alessandria: Edizioni dell'Orso, 2005), pp. 97–107; Athanasius B. Pekar, "Tribute to Bishop Joseph J. De Camillis, OSBM (1641- 1706)," *Analecta OSBM*, Series II, Section II, Vol. XII [XVIII], 1–4 (Rome, 1985), pp. 374–418; and Paul R. Magocsi and Bohdan Strumins'kyj, "The First Carpatho-Ruthenian Printed Book," *Harvard Library Bulletin*, XXV, 3 (Cambridge, Mass., 1977), pp. 292–309. The careers of the bishops from the Ol'shavs'kyi family, especially Mykhaïl Emmanuïl Ol'shavs'kyi, who reigned during the first three-quarters of the eighteenth century, when the Uniate Eparchy of Mukachevo was jurisdictionally subordinate to the Roman Catholic bishop of Eger, are the focus of attention in three works: I. M Kondratovič, "The Olšavsky Bishops and Their Activity," *Slovak Studies*, II (Rome, 1963), pp. 179–198; Michael Lacko, "The Pastoral Activity of Manuel Michael Olšavsky, Bishop of Mukačevo," *Orientalia Christiana Periodica* XXVII, 1 (Rome, 1961), pp. 150–161; and Basil Boysak, *Ecumenism and Manuel Michael Olshavsky, Bishop of Mukachevo, 1743-1767* (Montreal University of Montreal, Faculty of Theology, 1967).

To be sure, not all Carpatho-Rusyn Orthodox accepted the idea of church union. Among the greatest opponents of the "hated Uniates" was a passion ate and talented polemicist, who is the subject of two studies by Luca Calvi: "Jerusalem versus Rome in the Works of Mykhajlo Rosvyhuvs'kyj-Andrella," in Wolf Moskovich et al., *Jerusalem in Slavic Culture*, special issue of *Jews and Slavs*, Vol. VI (Jerusalem and Ljubljana, 1999), pp. 251–262, and Luca Calvi, "Some Remarks on Mykhajlo Rosvyhuvs'kyi and His Works," *Slavica*, XXX (Debrecen, 2000), pp. 223–236; and Andrii Danylenko, "Polemics without Polemics: Myxajlo Andrella in Ruthenian (Ukrainian) Literary Space," *Studia Slavica Hungarica*, LIII, 1 (Budapest, 2008), pp. 123–146.

The above-mentioned studies all deal with the new Uniate/Greek Catholic Church serving Carpatho-Rusyns in the Hungarian Kingdom. For the Lemko Region, there are no specific works in English on the introduction of Uniatism, which came about as a result of the earlier church union completed at Brest in 1596. The general literature on this topic is extensive and includes two major studies: the older, now classic work by Oscar Halecki, *From Florence to Brest, 1439–1596* (Rome: Sacrum Poloniae Millennium, 1958; reprinted Hamden, Conn., 1968); and the more recent and wide-ranging monograph by Borys A. Gudziak, *Crisis and Reform: The Kyivan Metropolitanate, the Patriarch of Constantinople, and the Genesis of the Union of Brest* (Cambridge, Mass.: Ukrainian Research Institute, Harvard University, 1998).

4. The reform era and Habsburg rule, 1770s to 1847

The wide-ranging reforms implemented by the Habsburg Empire which had a profound impact on socioeconomic developments in Carpathian Rus' are treated in great detail in the second volume of the Ukrainian-language monograph (with an extensive résumé in French) by Oleksander Mytsiuk, *Narysy z sotsiial'no-hospodars'koï istoriï b. Uhors'koï nyni Pidkarpats'koï Rusy*, Vol. II (Prague: p.a., 1938; reprinted Uzhhorod: Vyd-vo Zakarpattia, 2003). Demographic questions, specifically in the ethnically mixed Rusyn-Hungarian county of Sobolch/Szabolcs, are discussed in István Udvari, "Rusyns in Hungary and the Hungarian Kingdom," in Paul Robert Magocsi, ed., *The Persistence of Regional Cultures: Rusyns and Ukrainians in Their Carpathian Homeland and Abroad* (New York: Columbia University Press/ East European Monographs, 1993), pp. 105–138.

Most of the available English-language literature for this period deals with cultural matters, including the earliest interest shown by the local intelligentsia in questions related to Carpatho-Rusyn nationality and identity. Two studies which focus on Carpatho-Rusyn lands in the Hungarian Kingdom from the 1770s to 1840s are: Paul Robert Magocsi, *The Shaping of a National Identity: Subcarpathian Rus', 1848–1948* (Cambridge, Mass.: Harvard University Press, 1978), esp. pp. 21–41; and Elaine Rusinko, *Straddling Borders: Literature and Identity in Subcarpathian Rus'* (Toronto, Buffalo, and London: University of Toronto Press, 2003), pp. 64–110. There are also a few articles which describe the views and activity of individual national activists, whose concern at the time was to determine the relationship of

Carpathian Rus' to the larger East Slavic ("Russian") world and the degree to which liturgical Church Slavonic was an appropriate medium for use as a literary language. On ties with Russia as seen through the prism of the literary works of a leading ecclesiastical figure, Bishop Hryhorii Tarkovych, see Elaine Rusinko, "Between Russia and Hungary: Foundations of Literature and National Identity in Subcarpathian Rus'," *Slavonic and East European Review*, LXXIV, 3 (London, 1996), pp. 421–444; on Church Slavonic and the local Rusyn vernacular, see two studies by Andrii Danylenko: "Between the Vernacular and Slaveno-Rusyn: the *Huklyvyj Chronicle* and the Eighteenth-Century Rusyn Literary Language," *Slavia Orientalis*, LIX, 1 (Cracow, 2009), pp. 53–74 and "Myxajlo Lučkaj—A Dissident Forerunner of Literary Rusyn?," *Slavonic and East European Review*, LXXXVI, 2 (London, 2009), pp. 201–226.

5. The Revolution of 1848 to the end of World War I

A useful introductory survey to developments in Carpathian Rus' during the second half of the "long," or historic nineteenth century, with particular emphasis on the national awakening and subsequent assimilation, is found in Paul Robert Magocsi, *The Shaping of National Identity: Subcarpathian Rus', 1848–1948* (Cambridge, Mass.: Harvard University Press, 1978), pp. 42–75. The same period is covered in more detail in two studies: the German-language monograph, also with emphasis on the nationality question, by Ivan Žeguc, *Die nationalpolitischen Bestrebungen der Karpato-Ruthenen 1848–1914* (Wiesbaden: Otto Harrassowitz, 1965); and the monumental Russian-language volumes which, although written from a Soviet Marxist perspective, are nonetheless rich in data, especially about socioeconomic developments: Ivan G. Kolomiets, *Sotsial'no-èkonomicheskie otnosheniia i obshchestvennoe dvizhenie v Zakarpat'e vo vtoroi polovine XIX stoletiia*, 2 vols. (Tomsk: Izd. Tomskogo universiteta, 1961–62).

Cultural matters related to the Carpatho-Rusyn national awakening that began in 1848, especially the role of belletrists in creating and propagating a national identity, are given extensive attention in two chapters in Elaine Rusinko, *Straddling Borders: Literature and Identity in Subcarpathian Rus'* (Toronto, Buffalo, and London: University of Toronto Press, 2003), esp. pp. 111–295. The "national awakener of Carpatho-Rusyns," Aleksander Dukhnovych, is given much attention in the above mentioned monograph as well as in three other studies: Elaine Rusinko, "Aleksander Dukhnovych and the Origin of Modern Drama in Subcarpathian Rus'," in Aleksander Dukhnovych, *Virtue Is More Important Than Riches: A Play in Three Acts* (New York: Columbia University Press/East European Monographs, 1994), pp. xi–xl; Michael Moser, "Did Alexander Dukhnovych Strive to Create a Rusyn Literary Language?," in Paul Best and Stanisław Stępień, eds., *Does a Fourth Rus' Exist?: Concerning Cultural Identity in the Carpathian Region* (Przemyśl and Higganum, Conn.: South-Eastern Research Institute in Przemyśl, 2009), pp. 63–80; and the unpublished doctoral dissertation by Julianna Dranichak, "Aleksander Dukhnovich and the Carpatho-Russian National

Cultural Movement" (State University of New York at Binghamton, 1979), which, although dated, is still useful for biographical data. The most comprehensive biography of this seminal figure (although without any discussion of his important contributions to church life) remains the Ukrainian-language introduction to the three-volume anthology of Dukhnovych's writings: Olena Rudlovchak, "Oleksandr Dukhnovych: zhyttia i diial'nist'," in Oleksandr Dukhnovych, *Tvory*, Vol. I (Bratislava and Prešov: Slovats'ke pedahohichne vyd-vo, Viddil ukraïns'koï literatury, 1968), pp. 15–168.

The last stage of the national revival during the late 1860s and 1870s was followed by increased state-sponsored magyarization. The general char-acter of that phenomenon is described in great detail by the pre-World War I British scholar sympathetic to the Hungary's Slavs and Romanians, Robert W. Seton-Watson, writing under the pseudonym Scotus Victor, *Racial Problems in Hungary* (London: Constable, 1908; reprinted New York: Howard Fertig, 1972), esp. pp. 59–89 and 205–233; and by the Hungarian civic activist and former minister for nationalities in early postwar Hungary, Oscar Jászi, *The Dissolution of the Habsburg Monarchy* (Chicago: University of Chicago Press, 1929; reprinted, 1961), esp. pp. 298–343. For the impact of magyariza-tion and assimilation of Carpatho-Rusyns, in particular the group's secu-lar and clerical elite, see Maria Mayer, *The Rusyns of Hungary: Political and Social Developments, 1860–1910* (New York: Columbia University Press/East European Monographs, 1997); Maria Mayer, "Some Aspects of the Development of the National Movement amongst the Ruthenes of Hungary (Subcarpathian Ruthenia), 1899–1914," in Keith Hitchens, ed., *Studies in East European Social History*, Vol. I (Leiden: E. J. Brill, 1977), pp. 177–191; and Paul Robert Magocsi, "Rusyn Organizations, Political Parties, and Interest Groups, 1848–1914," in his *Of the Making of Nationalities There Is No End*, Vol. I (New York: Columbia University Press/East European Monographs, 1999), pp. 112–123.

The success of the magyarization policy, to which many Carpatho-Rusyn intellectuals willingly contributed, was symbolized by the creation of a new Hungarian-language-oriented Greek Catholic eparchial jurisdiction. The developments leading up to and culminating in the eparchy's establishment are surveyed in the attractively illustrated history by Tamás Véghseő and Szilveszter Terdik, ". . . You Have Foreseen All of My Paths . . .: Byzantine Rite Catholics in Hungary* (Strasbourg: Éditions du Signe, 2012), esp. pp. 6–51; and in specialized studies by James Niessen, "Hungarians and Romanians in Habsburg and Vatican Diplomacy: The Creation of the Diocese of Hajdúdorog in 1912," *The Catholic Historical Review*, LXXX, 2 (Washington, D.C., 1994), pp. 238–257; and Bertalan Pusztai, "Discursive Tactics and Political Identity: Shaping Hungarian Greek Catholic Identity at the Turn of the Nineteenth and Twentieth Centuries," *National Identities*, VII, 2 (Abington, Eng., 2005), pp. 117–131. These and related topics are discussed in detail in a Hungarian-language monograph based on a wide selection of archival sources: József Botlik, *Egestas Subcarpathica: adalékok az Északkeleti Felvidék és Kárpátalja 19–20. századi történetéhez* (Budapest: Hatodik Síp Alapítvány, 2000), esp. pp. 11–134, which covers the period 1872 to 1919.

All the aforementioned studies deal with those parts of Carpathian Rus' (the Prešov Region and Subcarpathian Rus') that were in the Hungarian Kingdom. On the Lemko Region north of the Carpathians, which at the time was part of the Austrian province of Galicia, the only English-language discussion is a short chapter in Bogdan Horbal, *Lemko Studies: A Handbook* (New York: Columbia University Press/East European Monographs, 2010), pp. 371–384. The most comprehensive coverage of the Lemko Region during this period is the monumental Polish-language study by Helena Duć-Fajfer, *Literatura łemkowska w drugiej połowie XIX i na początku XX wieku* (Cracow: Polska Akademia Umiejętności, 2001).

There is a major study on socioeconomic, cultural, religious, and civic life of the Vojvodinian Rusyns by Ianko Ramach, *Rusnatsi u iuzhnei Uhorskei, 1745–1918* (Novi Sad: Vojvođanska akademija nauka i umetnosti, 2007). Although this work is only in Vojvodinian Rusyn, a shorter study that covers some of the issues from the nineteenth century are discussed by the same author in Janko Ramač, "The Religious and National Identity of the Ruthenians in the Eparchy of Križevci," in Hans-Christian Maner and Norbert Spannenberger, eds., *Konfessionelle Identität und Nationsbildung* (Stuttgart: Franz Steiner Verlag, 2007), pp. 199–209.

It is the Carpatho-Rusyns in the United States who have received extensive treatment. At a time when the vast majority of the immigrants arrived between the 1880s and the outbreak of World War I, there was not much of a distinction between Carpatho-Rusyns from Austrian Galicia (the Lemko Region) and the Hungarian Kingdom (the Prešov Region and Subcarpathian Rus'), since at least before 1914 they functioned together as a single community, which included as well other East Slavic immigrants from the rest of Galicia who only in America gradually adopted a Ukrainian national identity.

The demographic composition of the arriving immigrants is provided in a sociological study by Richard Renoff, "Carpatho-Ruthenian Resources and Assimilation, 1880–1924," *Review Journal of Philosophy and Social Science*, II, 1 (Meerut, India, 1977), pp. 53–78. For general surveys of developments among Carpatho-Rusyns in the United States before World War I, see especially the various sections in the chapters on migration, settlement patterns, and economic, religious, and organizational life in Paul Robert Magocsi, *Our People: Carpatho-Rusyns and Their Descendants in North America*, 4th rev. ed. (Wauconda, Ill.: Bolchazy-Carducci Publishers, 2005) and Walter C. Warzeski, *Byzantine Rite Rusins in Carpatho-Ruthenia and America* (Pittsburgh, Pa.: Byzantine Seminary Press, 1971), esp. pp. 95–128. For the Ukrainian perspective on this same period, see A. Pekar, "Historical Background of the Carpatho-Ruthenians in America," *Ukraïns'kyi istoryk*, XIII, 1–4 (New York, Toronto, and Munich, 1976), pp. 87–102 and XIV, 1–2 (1977), pp. 70–84; Alexander Baran, "Carpatho-Ukrainian Emigration 1870–1914," in Jaroslav Rozumnyj, ed., *New Soil—Old Roots: The Ukrainian Experience in Canada* (Winnipeg: Ukrainian Academy of Arts and Sciences, 1983), pp. 252–275; Myron B. Kuropas, *The Ukrainian Americans: Roots and Aspirations, 1884–1954* (Toronto, Buffalo, and London: University of Toronto

Press, 1991), esp. pp. 16–125; and Myron Kuropas, *Ukrainian-American Citadel: The First One Hundred Years of the Ukrainian National Association* (Boulder, Colo.: East European Monographs, 1996), esp. pp. 1–136.

Surveys that focus on specific communities both before and after World War I include: Walter C. Warzeski, "The Rusyn Community in Pennsylvania," in John E. Bodnar, ed., *The Ethnic Experience in Pennsylvania* (Lewisburg, Pa.: Bucknell University Press, 1973), pp. 175–215; William Duly, *The Rusyns of Minnesota* [Minneapolis: n.p., 1993]; Lorle Porter, *The Immigrant Cocoon: Central Europeans in the Cambridge, Ohio Coalfields* (New Concord, Ohio: n.p., 1994); and Robert Zecker, "'The Same People as Over Here': The Fluidity of Slovak and Rusyn Identity in Philadelphia," in Elaine Rusinko, ed., *Committing Community* (New York: Columbia University Press/East European Monographs, 2009), pp. 313–341.

Mutual benefit societies, or fraternal brotherhoods, were extremely important to the physical welfare of the early immigrants, the vast majority of whom were unskilled and semi-skilled laborers. The oldest and largest of the Carpatho-Rusyn fraternal societies is discussed in a comprehensive history that devotes several chapters to the pre-1914 period: *Opportunity Realized: The Greek Catholic Union's First One Hundred Years, 1892–1992* (Beaver, Pa.: Greek Catholic Union of the USA, 1994), esp. pp. 3–58. For the oldest Rusyn-American newspaper, which was published by the Greek Catholic Union, there is a comprehensive bibliographical guide; the titles of the articles themselves provide an excellent insight into the daily life of the community during those early years: James M. Evans, *Guide to the Amerikansky Russky Viestnik*, Vol. I: *1894–1914* (Fairview, N.J.: Carpatho-Rusyn Research Center, 1979). For a broader perspective that looks at a wider range of brotherhood societies, see Richard Custer, "The Influence of Clergy and Fraternal Organizations on the Development of Ethnonational Identity among Rusyn Immigrants to Pennsylvania," in Bogdan Horbal, Patricia A. Krafcik, and Elaine Rusinko, eds., *Carpatho-Rusyns and Their Neighbors* (Fairfax, Va.: Eastern Christian Publications, 2006), pp. 43–106.

Much attention has been given to the various churches—Greek Catholic and Orthodox—which effectively defined the Carpatho-Rusyn communities in the United States. Many authors who describe the religious world of Rusyn Americans are sympathetic to one or the other competing churches. For the Greek Catholic perspective, see John Slivka, *Historical Mirror: Sources of the Rusin and Hungarian Greek Rite Catholics in the United States of America, 1884–1963* (Brooklyn, N.Y.: n.p., 1978), esp. pp. 1–110; Stephen C. Gulovich, "The Rusin Exarchate in the United States," *The Eastern Churches Quarterly*, VI (London, 1946), pp. 459–485; and John T. Sekellik, "Catholic Ruthenians of the Byzantine Rite in the United States of America," *Diakonia*, XXV, 1 (Scranton, Pa., 1992), pp. 19–60. Much less partisan are studies on this period by Constantin Simon, "The First Years of Ruthenian Church Life in America," *Orientalia Christiana Periodica*, LX, 1 (Rome, 1994), pp. 187–232; Bohdan Procko, "The Establishment of the Ruthenian Church in the United States, 1884–1907," *Pennsylvania History*, XLII, 2 (Bloomsburg, Pa.,

1975), pp. 137–154; and Bohdan P. Procko, "Soter Ortynsky: First Ruthenian Bishop in the United States, 1907–1916," *Catholic Historical Review*, LVIII, 4 (Washington, D.C., 1973), pp. 513–533.

Greek Catholic-Orthodox relations, more specifically the growth of the latter at the expense of the former and the interaction between developments in the United States and Europe, both the Carpathian Rusyn homeland and the tsarist Russian Empire, are discussed at length in: Keith P. Dyrud, *The Quest for the Rusyn Soul: The Politics of Religion and Culture in Eastern Europe and in America, 1890–World War I* (Philadelphia: Balch Institute, 1992); Konstantin Simon, *The Ruthenian Emigration in the United States of America: The Earliest Years, 1884–1894* (Rome: Pontificum Institutum Orientale, 1988); Constantine Simon, "In Europe and America: The Ruthenians between Catholicism and Orthodoxy on the Eve of Emigration," *Orientalia Christiana Periodica*, LIX, 1 (Rome, 1993), pp. 169–210; and John S. Custer, "Byzantine Rite Slavs in Philadelphia, 1886–1916," *Records of the American Catholic Historical Society of Philadelphia*, CIV, 1–4 (Philadelphia, 1993), pp. 31–57.

Particular attention has been given to the disaffected Greek Catholic priest who began the return-to-Orthodoxy movement: Keith S. Russin, "Father Alexis G. Toth and the Wilkes-Barre Litigations," *St. Vladimir's Theological Quarterly*, XVI, 3 (Crestwood-Tuckahoe, N.Y., 1972), pp. 128–149; James Jorgeson, "Father Alexis Toth and the Transition of the Greek Catholic Community in Minneapolis to the Russian Orthodox Church," *St. Vladimir's Theological Quarterly*, XXXII, 2 (Crestwood-Tuckahoe, N.Y., 1988), pp. 119–137; and Michael Palij, "Early Ukrainian Immigration to the United States and the Conversion of the Ukrainian Catholic Parish in Minneapolis to Russian Orthodoxy," *Journal of Ukrainian Studies*, VIII, 2 (Toronto, 1983), pp. 13–37.

On the Hungarian government's response to the dangers posed by "their" immigrant subjects who converted to the religion of a political rival, the tsarist Russian Empire, see the chapter, "Rusyns in the United States at the Outset of the Twentieth Century," in Maria Mayer, *The Rusyns of Hungary: Political and Social Developments, 1860–1910* (New York: Columbia University Press/East European Monographs, 1997), pp. 190–231. Father Toth's own views on these matters are found in several volumes of his writings, translated and edited by George Soldatow: Archpriest Alexis Toth, *Letters, Articles, Papers, and Sermons*, 4 vols. (Chilliwack, British Columbia and Minneapolis: Synaxis Press/AARDM Press, 1978–88); *The Writings of St. Alexis Toth, Confessor and Defender of Orthodoxy in America* (Minneapolis: AARDM Press, 1994); and *The Orthodox Church in America and Other Writings by St. Alexis* (Minneapolis: AARDM Press, 1996).

General histories of Orthodoxy in the United States also inevitably deal with the pre-World War I Rusyn-American communities. The first Orthodox jurisdiction to which they were drawn was the Russian Orthodox Diocese of Alaska and the Aleutian Islands, later renamed the Russian Orthodox Greek Catholic Church of North America. Introductory histories of this institution, with brief references to Rusyn Americans, include: John H. Erickson,

Orthodox Christians in America: A Short History (Oxford: Oxford University Press, 2008); and Thomas E. Fitzgerald, *The Orthodox Church* (Westport, Conn.: Greenwood Press, 1995); and the older but more comprehensive collective work: Constance J. Tarasar and John H. Erickson, eds., *Orthodox America, 1794–1976: Development of the Orthodox Church in America* (Syosset, N.Y.: Orthodox Church in America, 1975), esp. pp. 27–172.

Several major World War I military campaigns and battles between tsarist Russian and imperial German and Austro-Hungarian forces took place in or near Carpathian Rus'. The standard account about all campaigns in this part of Europe remains that by Norman Stone, *The Eastern Front, 1914–1917* (New York: Charles Scribner's Sons, 1975). Recently, two monographs have focused specifically on campaigns in the Carpathians: Graydon A. Tunstall, *Blood on the Snow: The Carpathian Winter War of 1915* (Lawrence, Kan.: University Press of Kansas, 2010) and Richard L. DiNardo, *Breakthrough: the Gorlice-Tarnow Campaign, 1915* (Santa Barbara, Calif.: Praeger, 2010). As for the impact of the war on the local population, an early example of an eyewitness report which is particularly critical of the Austro-Hungarian military authorities is Dimitrii A. Markoff, *Belgium of the East* (Wilkes-Barre, Pa.: Peter G. Kohanik, 1920).

6. The interwar years, 1919–1938

There is an extensive literature on the interwar years, which coincides with the period of Czechoslovak rule in Carpatho-Rusyn lands south of the mountains (Subcarpathian Rus' and the Prešov Region) and Polish rule north of the mountains (the Lemko Region). Because specifically Subcarpathian Rus' formed during this period a distinct geopolitical unit with a theoretically autonomous status within Czechoslovakia as called for in the post-World War I international peace agreements, it has received the most attention.

Still the best introductory overview to this period is the chapter on "Ruthenia" in C. A. Macartney, *Hungary and Her Successors: The Treaty of Trianon and Its Consequences, 1919–1937* (Oxford: Oxford University Press, 1937), pp. 200–250. Also useful is the booklet by Walter K. Hanak, *The Subcarpathian-Ruthenian Question, 1918–1945* (Munhall, Pa.: Bishop Basil Takach Carpatho-Russian Historical Society, 1962). Much more detail on various aspects of the nationality question and the relations of Subcarpathian Rus' with the Czechoslovak central government are found in Paul Robert Magocsi, *The Shaping of a National Identity: Subcarpathian Rus', 1848–1948* (Cambridge, Mass.: Harvard University Press, 1978), esp. pp. 105–233 and 282–336; and Peter G. Stercho, *Diplomacy of Double Morality: Europe's Crossroads in Carpatho-Ukraine, 1919–1939* (New York: Carpathian Research Institute, 1971), esp. pp. 39–106.

For developments in the Prešov Region during the interwar Czechoslovak period, see Paul Robert Magocsi, *The Rusyns of Slovakia: An Historical Survey* (New York: Columbia University Press/East European Monographs, 1993), pp. 58–86. The most detailed accounts about the Prešov Region's Carpatho-

Rusyns remains the Ukrainian-language monograph by Ivan Vanat, *Narysy novitn'oï istoriï ukraïntsiv Skhidnoï Slovachchyny*, Vol. I: *1918–1938*, 2nd ed. (Bratislava and Prešov: Slovats'ke pedahohichne vyd-vo, Viddil ukraïns'koï literatury, 1990), and on the influential Greek Catholic Church, the Slovak-language detailed history by Jaroslav Coranič, *Dejiny Gréckokatolíckej cirkvi na Slovensku v rokoch 1918–1939* (Prešov: Vyd-vo Prešovskej university, 2013).

Some of the political actors from this period have left short accounts of the "Czechoslovak period," which are helpful in understanding a particular national orientation. The accounts are in the form of articles or book chapters by the following figures: the influential Subcarpathian cultural and civic leader, Augustyn Vološin, "Carpathian Ruthenia," *The Slavonic and East European Review*, XIII (London, 1934–35), pp. 372–378; Hungary's official responsible for the short-lived experiment in autonomy—Rus'ka Kraina, Oscar Jászi, "The Problem of Sub-Carpathian Ruthenia," in Robert J. Kerner, ed., *Czechoslovakia* (Berkeley and Los Angeles: University of California Press, 1949), pp. 193–215; the Magyar political leader and senator from Subcarpathian Rus', Charles J. Hokky, *Ruthenia, Spearhead toward the West* (Gainesville, Fla.: Danubian Research and Information Center, 1966); the pro-Hungarian Rusyn cultural activist and scholar, Alexander Bonkáló, *The Rusyns* (New York: Columbia University Press/East European Monographs, 1990), esp. the chapter entitled "Czech Occupation," pp. 32–39; the Prague-based representative of autonomous Carpatho-Ukraine, Vincent Shandor, *Carpatho-Ukraine in the Twentieth Century: A Political and Legal History* (Cambridge, Mass.: Harvard University Press/Ukrainian Research Institute, 1997), esp. pp. 3–66; and the Czechoslovak officials, František Nemec and Vladimir Moudry, *The Soviet Seizure of Subcarpathian Ruthenia* (Toronto: William B. Anderson, 1955), esp. pp. 30–46.

Subcarpathian Rus' also came to the attention of scholars throughout Europe, who wrote studies that focused primarily, or exclusively, on the interwar years. These works, appeared in various languages, including books by two French specialists on eastern Europe: René Martel, *La Ruthénie subcarpathique* (Paris: Paul Hartmann, 1935) and Jean Mousset, *Les villes de la Russie subcarpathique, 1919–1938* (Paris: Librairie Droz/Institut d'études slaves, 1938); by the specialist on minority rights from what was then Nazi Germany, Hans Ballreich, *Karpathenrussland: ein Kapitel tschechischen Nationalitätenrechts und tschechischen Nationalitätenpolitik* (Heidelberg: Carl Winter's Universitätsbuchhandlung, 1938); and in works sponsored by Soviet Ukraine's Institute of Marxism-Leninism: Oleksander Badan, *Zakarpats'ka Ukraïna: sotsiial'no-ekonomichnyi narys* (Kharkiv: Derzavne vyd-vo Ukraïny, 1929) and by Poland's Ministry of Foreign Affairs: Zygmunt Zawadowski, *Ruś Podkarpacka i jej stanowisko prawno-polityczne* (Warsaw: Zakłady Graficzne Straszewiczów, 1931).

More recently there have appeared several volumes that make use of heretofore restricted archival materials made accessible to scholars in post-Communist central and eastern Europe. The best and most compre hensive of these, written in the various languages of the region, are by József Botlik, *Közigazgatás és nemzetiségi politika Kárpátalján*, Vol. I: *1918–1945* (Nyíregyháza: Nyíregyházi Főiskola, Ukrán és Ruszin Filológiai Tanszék, 2005); Andrei Pushkash, *Tsivilizatsiia ili varvarstvo: Zakarpat'e 1918–1945* (Moscow: Izd-vo Evropa, 2006); Kirill Shevchenko, *Rusiny i mezhvoennaia Chekhoslovakiia: k istorii étnokul'turnoi inzhenerii* (Moscow: Modest Kolerov, 2006); Peter Švorc, *Zaklatá zem: Podkarpatská Rus, 1918–1946* (Prague: Nakladatelství Lidové Noviny, 2006); and two multi-authored volumes: Ivan Hranchak, ed., *Narysy istoriï Zakarpattia*, Vol. II: *1918–1945* (Uzhhorod: Vyd-vo Zakarpattia, 1995); and Mykola Vegesh and Csilla Fedinec, eds., *Zakarpattia 1919–2009 rokiv: istoriia, polityka, kul'tura* (Uzhhorod: Lira, 2010). Greater attention to the Prešov Region is found in Peter Švorc, *Krajinská hranica medzi Slovenskem a Podkarpatskou Rusou, 1919–1939* (Prešov: Universum, 2003), and to all three parts of Carpathian Rus'—Subcarpathian Rus', the Prešov Region, and the Lemko Region—in Kirill V. Shevchenko, *Slavianskaia atlantida: Karpatskaia Rus' i rusiny v XIX—pervoi polovine XX vv.* (Moscow: Regnum, 2011).

Specific aspects of interwar Subcarpathian Rus' are the subject of three essays by Paul Robert Magocsi: "The Rusyn Decision to Unite with Czechoslovakia," "Magyars and Carpatho-Rusyns in Czechoslovakia," and "The Nationalist Intelligentsia and the Peasantry in Twentieth-Century Subcarpathian Rus'," in Paul Robert Magocsi, *Of the Making of Nationalities There Is No End*, Vol. I (New York: Columbia University Press/East European Monographs, 1999), pp. 124–219. The manner in which literary works from various national and linguistic orientations helped to define and instill in Carpatho-Rusyns a national identity is discussed in Elaine Rusinko, *Straddling Borders: Literature and Identity in Subcarpathian Rus'* (Toronto, Buffalo, and London: University of Toronto Press, 2003), esp. pp. 296–406.

A major preoccupation among civic, cultural, educational, and religious activists during the interwar years was the so-called language question. This was because decisions about an appropriate literary language were intimately bound up with the Carpatho-Rusyn nationality question. A useful introduction to this topic is Paul R. Magocsi, "The Language Question Among the Subcarpathian Rusyns," in Riccardo Picchio and Harvey Goldblatt, eds., *Aspects of the Slavic Language Question*, Vol. II: *East Slavic* (New Haven: Yale Concilium on International and Area Studies, 1984), pp. 49–64—reprinted separately under the same title (Fairview, N.J., 1979 and 1987) and in a revised updated version under the title "The Rusyn Language Revisited," *International Journal of the Sociology of Language*, No. 120 (Berlin and New York, 1996), pp. 63–84—reprinted in Paul Robert Magocsi, *Of the Making of Nationalities There Is No End*, Vol. I (New York: Columbia University Press/ East European Monographs, 1999), pp. 86–111. The classic study on this topic appeared in Czech by František Tichý, *Vývoj současného spisovného jazyka na Podkarpatské Rusi* (Prague: Orbis/Nákladem Sboru pro výzkum Slovenska a Podkarpatské Rusi, 1938), although the focus in this work is only on Subcarpathian Rus' and, in part, the Prešov Region, from the sixteenth to mid-twentieth century. Only one study surveys developments related to language and nationality in all parts of Carpathian Rus' as well as among Rusyns in the Vojvodina, the German-language monograph by Marc Stegherr, *Das Russinische: kulturhistorische und soziolinguistische Aspekte* (Munich: Verlag Otto Sagner, 2003).

Church life and its relationship to the nationality and social questions in interwar Subcarpathian Rus' are discussed in several studies. Particular emphasis is given to the revival of Orthodoxy, although the basic liter-ature available in English is by authors who approach the subject from a Greek Catholic perspective: Basil Boysak, *The Fate of the Holy Union in Carpatho-Ukraine* (Toronto and New York: n.p., 1963), esp. pp. 179–210; and Athanasius B. Pekar, *The History of the Church in Carpathian Rus'* (New York: Columbia University Press/East European Monographs, 1992), pp. 107–140. On the influential role of émigré monks from the former Russian Empire who promoted Orthodoxy from their monastery and its very productive publica-tion facilities in eastern Slovakia, see Martin Fedor Ziac, "From Ladomirová to Jordanville: Changing Perceptions of Rusyn Identity," in Elaine Rusinko, ed., *Committing Community: Carpatho-Rusyn Studies as an Emerging Scholarly Discipline* (New York: Columbia University Press/East European Monographs, 2009), pp. 299–312.

There are also studies on the most prominent interwar Greek Catholic bishop of the Eparchy of Mukachevo in Subcarpathian Rus': A. Pekar, "Bishop Peter Gebey: Champion of the Holy Union," *Analecta Ordinis S. Basilii Magni,* Series II, Sectio II, Vol. IV [X], 1–2 (Rome, 1963), pp. 293–326; and a study in the form of a biography which discusses the Vatican's interest in the Eastern-rite Catholic Church in central and eastern Europe, in par-ticular Subcarpathian Rus': Constantin Simon, "The Life of Feodor (George Theodore) Romzha, 1911–1947," *Diakonia,* XXXIII, 2 and 3 (Scranton, 2000), pp. 123–152 and 215–250—reprinted in Constantin Simon, *Russicum: Pioneers and Witnesses of the Struggle for Christian Unity in Eastern Europe* (Rome: Opere Religiose Russe, 2001), pp. 136–181.

Other aspects of interwar Subcarpathian Rus' for which there is liter-ature include the activity of certain national minorities. On the Magyars and their relations at the time with Carpatho-Rusyns, see the sections writ-ten by Csilla Fedinec in Nándor Bárdi, Csilla Fedinec, and László Szarka, eds., *Minority Hungarian Communities in the Twentieth Century* (New York and Boulder, Colo.: Columbia University Press/East European Monographs, 2011), pp. 62–65 and 207–214; and Paul Robert Magocsi, "Magyars and Carpatho-Rusyns in Czechoslovakia," in his *Of the Making of Nationalities There Is No End,* Vol. I (New York: Columbia University Press/East European Monographs, 1999), pp. 147–187. There is as well a comprehensive encyclo-pedia-like historical chronology focusing specifically on Magyars in interwar Subcarpathian Rus'; although it is in Hungarian, readers may nonetheless be able to access the rich data related to events, provincial governmental administrations, and maps: Csilla Fedinec, *A kárpátaljai magyarság történet kronológiája 1918–1944* (Galánta/Dunaszerdahely: Fórum Intézet, 2002).

Literature in English is more extensive on the Jews. Aside from the discussion of the interwar years in several general surveys about Jews in Subcarpathian Rus' mentioned above (Section 1. Reference works and general studies: d. Other peoples), the Czechoslovak period is dealt with in several more specific studies. The best general overviews of this period are in Yeshayahu A. Jelinek, *The Carpathian Diaspora: The Jews of Subcarpathian Rus' and Mukachevo, 1848–1948* (New York: Columbia University Press/ East European Monographs, 2007), esp. pp. 113–224; and in the earlier survey by Aryeh Sole, "Subcarpathian Ruthenia, 1918–1938," in *The Jews of Czechoslovakia: Historical Studies and Surveys,* Vol. I (Philadelphia and New York: Jewish Publication Society of America/Society for the History of Czechoslovak Jews, 1968), pp. 125–154. Details on specific aspects of Jewish life during this period are found in Aryeh Sole, "Modern Hebrew Education in Subcarpathian Ruthenia," in ibid., Vol. II (1971), pp. 401–439; Allan L. Nadler, "The War on Modernity of R. Hayyim Elazar Shapira of Munkacz," *Modern Judaism,* XIV, 3 (Baltimore, 1994), pp. 233–264; and Yeshayahu A. Jelinek, "Jewish Youth in Carpatho-Rus': Between Hope and Despair, 1920–1938," *Shvut,* No. 7 [23] (Tel Aviv, 1998), pp. 147–165.

Finally, Czechoslovak rule in Subcarpathian Rus' drew the attention of several writers (journalists, belletrists) from various parts of Europe and North America who visited the region in the 1920s and 1930s and left their impressions. Many of these writings can help modern-day researchers to acquire a better insight into daily life and the attitudes of the inhabitants toward the Czechoslovak government, their own socioeconomic plight, their own leaders, and their neighbors of a different nationality and/or religion.

Among the earliest of these accounts is by the Englishman Henry Baerlein, *Over the Hills of Ruthenia* (London: Leonard Parsons, 1923), and his later account, *In Czechoslovakia's Hinterland* (London: Hutchinson, 1938), as well as the chapter titled "The Little Land of the Ruthenes," the travel account by the American Robert Medill McBride, *Romantic Czechoslovakia* (New York: Robert M. McBride, 1930), pp. 172–202. Valuable for the photographs as much as for the text are: Erskine Caldwell, *North of the Danube,* with photographs by the renowned Margaret Bourke-White (New York: Viking Press, 1939), esp. pp. 9–40; and J. B. Heisler and J. E. Mellon, *Under the Carpathians: Home of a Forgotten People* (London: Lindsay Drummond, 1946). Perhaps the most profound insights into Subcarpathian life during the interwar years are found in the writings of the Czech Ivan Olbracht, two of whose novels are translated into English: *Nikola the Outlaw* (Evanston, Ill.: Northwestern University Press, 2001), about the Carpatho-Rusyn folk hero Nykola Shuhai; and *The Sorrowful Eyes of Hannah Karajich* (Budapest, London, and New York: Central European University Press, 1999), about the challenges to traditional Orthodox Hasidic Jewish life in a small mountain village.

Historic literature about the Lemko Region during the interwar years is less extensive than that about other parts of Carpathian Rus'. There is an introductory survey in several short chapters covering the years 1918 to

1939 in Bogdan Horbal, *Lemko Studies: A Handbook* (New York: Columbia University Press/East European Monographs, 2010), pp. 394–405; as well as a more comprehensive monograph by Jarosław Mokłak, *The Lemko Region in the Second Polish Republic: Political and Interdenominational Issues, 1918–1939* (Cracow: Jagiellonian University Press, 2013).

Certain aspects of the interwar period have been given greater attention, in particular the political activity of Lemko Rusyns at the close of World War I and the creation of two "independent republics." An introduction to this phenomenon is found in Paul Robert Magocsi, "The Lemko Rusyn Republic (1918–1920) and Political Thought in Western Rus'-Ukraine," in his *Of the Making of Nationalities There Is No End*, Vol. I (New York: Columbia University Press/East European Monographs, 1999), pp. 303–315; a much more detailed discussion is in the Polish-language volume by Bogdan Horbal, *Działalność polityczna Łemków na Łemkowszczyźnie 1918–1921* (Wrocław: Wyd-wo Arboretum, 1997).

Lemko-Rusyn political thought, the nationality question, and the policy of the Polish government toward the group are treated in several essays: Jarosław Moklak, "The Political Situation of the Ruthenians of the Lemko Region before the Outbreak of World War II," and Wojciech Rojek, "The Position Taken by Provincial Authorities of the Second Polish Republic Concerning the Lemko Question towards the End of the Inter-war Period," in Paul Best and Jaroslaw Moklak, eds., *The Lemko Region, 1939–1947 War, Occupation, and Deportation* (Cracow and New Haven: Carpatho-Slavic Studies Group, 2002), pp. 19–38; and by Paul Best and Jaroslaw Moklak in a collected work of which they are the editors: *The Lemkos: Articles and Essays*, 2nd revised ed. (Cracow and Higganum, Conn.: Carpathian Institute, 2013), pp. 35–42 and 69–74. The aforementioned volume also includes essays on the position of interwar Poland's Ukrainian political parties toward the Lemkos, by Oleksandr Zaitsev (pp. 233–242), and on pro-Ukrainian Lemko social and political institutions, by Jarosław Mokłak, Stanisław Nabywaniec, and Damien Knutel with an excellent overview of Greek Catholicism and Orthodoxy among Lemkos (pp. 295–332) Jarosław Mokłak on the Orthodox movement (pp. 131–145); Paul J. Best on the Greek Catholic Apostolic Administration (pp. 269–274), and Anna Krochmal on Protestant "sects" (pp. 145–156). On religious matters, see also Inna Poyizdnyk, "Attempts of the Greek Catholic Church and its Clergy to Influence the Formation of National Identity in the Lemko Region," in Paul Best and Stanisław Stępień, eds., *Does a Fourth Rus' Exist?: Concerning Cultural Identity in the Carpathian Region* (Przemyśl and Higganum, Conn. South-Eastern Research Institute in Przemyśl, 2009), pp. 157–165.

There is very little literature on the heavily magyarized Carpatho-Rusyn communities in post-Trianon interwar Hungary. A good introduction to this topic is by Bertalan Pusztai, "Discoursing Boundaries: Hungarian Greek Catholic Identity Creation in the Inter-War Period," in Marko Lamberg, ed. *Shaping Ethnic Identities* (Helsinki: East-West Books, 2007), pp. 35–68 Also of use is the interwar section found in Tamás Véghseő and Szilveszter

Terdik, ". . . *You Have Foreseen All of My Paths . . .: Byzantine Rite Catholics in Hungary* (Strasbourg: Éditions du Signe, 2012), esp. pp. 52–74.

Material on Carpatho-Rusyn communities in North America during the interwar years is somewhat better developed. For general introductions to this period, see the appropriate chapters in Walter C. Warzeski, *Byzantine Rite Rusins in Carpatho-Ruthenia and America* (Pittsburgh, Pa.: Byzantine Seminary Press, 1971), esp. pp. 194–244; and in Paul Robert Magocsi, *Our People: Carpatho-Rusyns and Their Descendants in North America*, 4th revised ed. (Wauconda, Ill.: Bolchazy-Carducci Publishers, 2005).

Specific attention is given to immigrants from the Lemko Region in the chapter, "Emigration," in Bogdan Horbal, *Lemko Studies: A Handbook* (New York: Columbia University Press/East European Monographs, 2010), pp. 279–302. Emphasis on Lemkos who went to Canada instead of the United States in the late 1920s is found in Paul Robert Magocsi, "Carpatho-Rusyns in Canada," in his *Of the Making of Nationalities There Is No End*, Vol. I (New York: Columbia University Press/East European Monographs, 1999), pp. 446–466; and in the more polemical and apologetically leftist-oriented book by Michael Lucas, *From the Carpathian Mountains to Canada* (Toronto: Society of Carpatho-Russian Canadians, [2010?]), esp. pp. 8–17. For a more general history of the communities during the interwar years in both the United States and Canada, viewed through the prism of their largest organization, see *50th Anniversary Almanac of the Lemko Association of the USA and Canada* (Yonkers, N.Y.: Lemko Association, 1979), esp. pp. 1–18.

Studies on more specific topics include those which provide varied perspectives on the role that Rusyn Americans played in influencing political developments in Carpathian Rus' at the close of World War I: Victor S. Mamatey, "The Slovaks and Carpatho-Ruthenians," in Joseph P. O'Grady, ed., *The Immigrant's Influence on Wilson's Peace Policies* (Lewisburg: University of Kentucky Press, 1967), pp. 224–249; Joseph Danko, "Plebiscite of Carpatho-Ruthenians in the United States Recommending Union of Carpatho-Ruthenia with Czechoslovakia," *Annals of the Ukrainian Academy of Sciences in the United States*, XI, 1–2 (New York, 1964), pp. 184–207; and Paul Robert Magocsi, "The Political Activity of Rusyn-American Immigrants in North America in 1918," in his *Of the Making of Nationalities There Is No End*, Vol. I (New York: Columbia University Press/East European Monographs, 1999), pp. 430–445.

The interwar period was also a time when the Rusyn-American community was most culturally vibrant. Aspects of that vibrancy are discussed in two essays by Paul Robert Magocsi, "The Carpatho-Rusyn Press" and "Rusyn-American Ethnic Literature," in ibid., pp. 416–429 and 503–520; by Elaine Rusinko, "From the *Staryi krai* to the New World: Rusyn-American Literature," in Elaine Rusinko, ed., *Committing Community: Carpatho-Rusyn Studies as an Emerging Scholarly Discipline* (New York: Columbia University Press/East European Monographs, 2009), pp. 273–291; and can be gleaned from article titles listed in the annotated guide to the most widely read community newspaper at the time: Robert A. Karlovich, ed., *Guide to the*

Amerikansky Russky Viestnik, Vol. II: *1915–1929* (New York: Columbia University Press/East European Monographs, 2000).

It is the religious question, however, which has generated the most interest in writings dealing with Rusyn-Americans during the interwar years. The main issues at that time concerned the marital status of Greek Catholic priests and ownership of church property. For a detailed introduction to this problem, see Joseph A. Loya, "'Cum Data Fuerit' Fallout: The Celibacy Crisis in the Byzantine Catholic Church, 1930–1940," *Records of the American Catholic Historical Society of Philadelphia,* LVI, 3–4 (Philadelphia, 1995), pp. 149–174. Many of the numerous petitions, counter-petitions, and other documents related to these problems are found in John Slivka, *Historical Mirror: Sources of the Rusin and Hungarian Greek Rite Catholics in the United States of America, 1884–1963* (Brooklyn, N.Y.: p.a., 1978), esp. pp. 127–303. The secular mutual benefit/fraternal societies played an active role either criticizing or defending the position of the Greek Catholic hierarchy which was required to enforce the *Cum Data Furit* decree. The activity of the church's main protagonist both before and after 1929, when the controversial Vatican decree was issued, is surveyed in *Opportunity Realized: The Greek Catholic Union's First One Hundred Years, 1892–1992* (Beaver, Pa.: Greek Catholic Union, 1994), pp. 59–126.

One result of the controversy initiated in 1929 was the creation by disaffected Rusyn-American Greek Catholics of a new Orthodox church jurisdiction. The manner in which this came about is discussed in two histories of the church: Jaroslav Roman, "The Establishment of the American Carpatho-Russian Orthodox Greek Catholic Diocese in 1938: A Major Return to Orthodoxy," *St. Vladimir's Theological Quarterly,* XX, 3 (Tuckahoe-Crestwood, N.Y., 1976), pp. 132–160, and Lawrence Barriger, *Glory to Jesus Christ: A History of the American Carpatho-Russian Orthodox Greek Catholic Diocese* (Brookline, Mass.: Holy Cross Orthodox Press, 2000), esp. pp. 23–83; and in a biography of its first bishop: Lawrence Barriger, *Good Victory: Metropolitan Orestes Chornock and the American Carpatho-Russian Orthodox Greek Catholic Diocese* (Brookline, Mass.: Holy Cross Orthodox Press, 1985). The internal controversies which began to divide this body soon after its formation are reviewed through the prism of the parish that was designated the first episcopal seat: Richard Renoff, "The New 'Carpatho-Russian' Diocese and Other Conflicts in the Rusyn Community of Bridgeport," in Bogdan Horbal, Patricia A. Krafcik, and Elaine Rusinko, eds., *Carpatho-Rusyns and Their Neighbors* (Fairfax, Va.: Eastern Christian Publications, 2006), pp. 377–404.

7. International crises and World War II, 1938–1945

This period begins with the establishment in October 1938 of the long-awaited autonomy in Subcarpathian Rus'. Although lasting less than half a year, the province, which was renamed Carpatho-Ukraine, is of special interest to authors of a pro-Ukrainian national persuasion. The best example of this approach to appear in English is the comprehensive study by Petro

Stercho, *Diplomacy of Double Morality: Europe's Crossroads in Carpatho-Ukraine, 1919–1939* (New York: Carpathian Research Institute, 1971). More recently, publicists and scholars in post-1991 independent Ukraine, in par-ticular in the Transcarpathian oblast, have transformed the few months of Carpatho-Ukraine (October 1938–March 1939) into a praiseworthy exam-ple of early Ukrainian statehood. Of the numerous recent studies on this topic—all written in Ukrainian—most are by Mykola Vegesh, among which is a comprehensive encyclopedia-like volume devoted exclusively to Carpatho-Ukraine in 1938–1939: Mykola M. Vegesh, ed., *Vony boronyly Karpats'ku Ukraïnu: narysy istoriï natsional'no-vyzvol'noï borot'by zakarpats'kykh ukraïn-tsiv* (Uzhhorod: Vyd-vo Karpaty, 2002). For a more critical view of the exclu-sively Ukrainian perspective on Carpatho-Ukraine, see Paul Robert Magocsi: "The Nationality Problem in Subcarpathian Rus', 1938–1939: A Reappraisal," in his *Of the Making of Nationalities There Is No End,* Vol. I (New York: Columbia University Press/East European Monographs, 1999), pp. 220–234; and Christian Ganzer, "'Ukrainian Piedmont' or Merely a 'Republic for a Day'?: Carpatho-Ukraine 1938–1939," in Paul Best and Stanisław Stępień, eds., *Does a Fourth Rus' Exist?: Concerning Cultural Identity in the Carpathian Region* (Przemyśl and Higganum, Conn.: South-Eastern Research Institute in Przemyśl, 2009), pp. 167–178.

There are some memoir-like accounts of the Carpatho-Ukraine phe-nomenon by participants in the government, including its prime minister Julian Revay, "The March to Liberation of Carpatho-Ukraine," *The Ukrainian Quarterly,* X, 3 (New York, 1954), pp. 227–234; and its representative to the Czechoslovak central government in Prague, Vincent Shandor, *Carpatho-Ukraine in the Twentieth Century: A Political and Legal History* (Cambridge, Mass.: Harvard University Press/Ukrainian Research Institute, 1997), esp. pp. 67–189, whose account also includes a description of the Hungarian invasion and its new administrative structure (pp. 193–260). Much more bal-anced is an account by a well-informed British journalist, Michael Winch, *Republic for a Day: An Eyewitness Account of the Carpatho-Ukraine Incident* (London: Robert Hale, 1939). For an insight into how these few months were viewed by Ukrainians, who hoped that changes in Europe might bring them an independent state, see the recollections of two Ukrainian émi-grés, based at the time in Prague and New York City, who went to east-ern Czechoslovakia to cover these events: Mykola Galagan, "My Last Days in Carpatho-Ukraine," *The Trident,* III, 7–8, 9, and 10 (New York, 1939), pp. 18–31, 32–40, and 33–40; and Eugene Skotzko, "Mecca to Carpatho-Ukraine," *The Trident,* III, 3 (New York, 1939), pp. 6–22.

Much more critical of the Carpatho-Ukrainian experience is an account by the distinguished American diplomat posted in Czechoslovakia's capital at the time: George F. Kennan, "Reports on Conditions in Ruthenia, written in March 1939," in his *From Prague After Munich: Diplomatic Papers, 1938–1940* (Princeton, N.J.: Princeton University Press, 1968), pp. 58–93. The Czech perspective may be seen in František Nemec and Vladimir Moudry, *The Soviet Seizure of Subcarpathian Ruthenia* (Toronto: William B. Anderson,

1955), esp. pp. 47–57; and Theodore Procházka, "Some Aspects of Carpatho-Ukrainian History in Post-Munich Czechoslovakia," in Miloslav Rechcigl, Jr., *Czechoslovakia Past and Present*, Vol. I (The Hague: Mouton, 1968), pp. 107–114. The experience of the large Jewish community during these few months is discussed by Raz Segal, "Imported Violence: Carpatho-Ruthenians and Jews in Carpatho-Ukraine, October 1938–March 1939," in *Polin*, Vol. XXVI, ed. Yohanan Petrovsky-Shtern and Antony Polansky (Oxford and Portland, Ore.: Littman Library of Jewish Civilization, 2014), pp. 313–336.

The return of Hungarian rule to Subcarpathian Rus', which was implemented in two stages (November 1938 and March 1939), has, with the exception of a short chapter in Vincent Shandor's memoir-like account (see above in this section), no serious studies in English. It is only recently that this period has attracted the attention of scholars in Europe. Among the most comprehensive works include the Hungarian-language monograph by József Botlik, *Közigazgatás és nemzetiségi politika Kárpátalján*, Vol. II: *A Magyarországhoz történt visszatérés után 1939–1945* (Nyíregyháza: Nyíregyházi Főiskola, Ukrán és Ruszin Filológiai Tanszék, 2005); and a Ukrainian-language study focusing primarily on administrative aspects of the province under Hungarian rule, by Ihor Mazurok, *Pravove stanovyshche Zakarpattia u 1939–1944 rr.* (Mukachevo: Vyd-vo Karpats'ka Vezha, 2010). The evolution of a Carpatho-Rusyn (called Uhro-Rusyn) national orientation during the period of Hungarian rule is for the first time given serious attention through an analysis of cultural institutions and literary works, which the author considers to be the birth of "Rusyn modernism": by Elaine Rusinko, *Straddling Borders: Literature and Identity in Subcarpathian Rus'* (Toronto, Buffalo, and London: University of Toronto Press, 2003), esp. pp. 407–442.

There is one aspect of Hungarian rule in Subcarpathian Rus' that has received extensive attention: the destruction of the region's Jews during the Holocaust. For a brief introduction to this topic, see Randolph L. Braham, "The Destruction of the Jews of Carpatho-Ruthenia," in Randolph L. Braham, ed., *Hungarian-Jewish Studies* (New York: World Federation of Hungarian Jews, 1966), pp. 223–233. The most comprehensive discussion o this topic is the section on "The Holocaust Period" in Yeshayahu A. Jelinek *The Carpathian Diaspora: The Jews of Subcarpathian Rus' and Mukachevo 1848–1948* (New York: Columbia University Press/East Europear Monographs, 2007), pp. 227–321.

More specific aspects of Subcarpathia's Holocaust are the subject o shorter studies by Judit Fejes, "On the History of the Mass Deportations from Carpatho-Ruthenia in 1941," in Randolph L. Braham and Attila Pók *The Holocaust in Hungary Fifty Years Later* (Boulder, Colo., and New York Social Science Monographs/Columbia University Press, 1997), pp. 305–328 László Karsai, "Jewish Deportations in Carpatho-Ruthenia in 1944," *Acta Historica*, CI (Szeged, 1995), pp. 38–47; and the provocative discussion by Raz Segal, "Becoming Bystanders: Carpatho-Ruthenians, Jews, and the Politics of Narcissism in Subcarpathian Rus'," *Holocaust Studies*, XVI, 1–2 (London, 2010), pp. 129–156.

The Holocaust also figures prominently in studies of individual Jewish communities. Some of these are scholarly in approach, such as Raz Segal, "The Jews of Huszt between the World Wars and in the Holocaust," in *Yalkut Moreshet*, No. 4 (Tel Aviv, 2006), pp. 80–119; and Raz Segal, *Days of Ruin: The Jews of Munkács during the Holocaust* (Jerusalem: Yad Vashem, 2013). Others are memoir-like commemorative essays brought together in so-called memorial books devoted to specific Jewish communities. Even more than the scholarly studies, the memorial books describe the idyllic and often idealized years of interwar Czechoslovak rule in contrast to Hungarian rule during World War II, when, with Nazi German assistance, the deportation of Jews from Subcarpathian Rus' was carried out. Among such sources in English are: Yitzchak Kasnett, *The World That Was,* Section IIIa: *Hungary/Romania: A Study of the Life and Torah Consciousness in the Cities and Villages of Transcarpathia, the Carpathian Mountains, and Budapest* (Cleveland Heights, Ohio: Hebrew Academy of Cleveland, 1999), esp. pp. 94–216—on Jewish communities in Mukachevo, Sighet, and Ruscova/Rus'kova; Zvi Mendel, ed., *Chust and Vicinity: A Memorial Book of the Community*, 2 vols. (Rehovot, Israel: Organization of Chust and Vicinity, 2002); Hugo Gryn, with Naomi Gryn, *Chasing Shadows* (New York and London: Viking, 2000)—on the city of Berehovo; Joseph Eden (Eincig), *The Jews of Kaszony, Subcarpathia* (New York: p.a., 1988); Heimus fin Bistine [Alexander Kraus], *Our Village: Who Sleeps in My Little Bed Now?* (London and Tel Aviv: p.a., 1996)—on the village of Bushtyno; Susan Slyomovics, "Rebbele Mordkhele's Pilgrimage in New York City, Tel Aviv, and Carpathian Ruthenia," in Jack Kugelmass, ed., *Going Home,* special issue of the *YIVO Annual*, Vol. XXI (Evanston, Ill. and New York: Northwestern University Press/YIVO Institute, 1992), pp. 369–394; and Milada Nagy, ed., *Nagyszőlős, the Center of the World/Nagyszőlős, a világ közepe/ Sevliush, tsentr svita* (Budapest: Aposztróf Kiadó, 2009), about the town of Vynohradovo, formerly Nagyszőlős/Sevliush.

Among the few studies about those Subcarpathian Jews who survived the Holocaust, who returned to their homeland after World War II (by then Soviet Transcarpathia), and who soon after emigrated to postwar Czechoslovakia and/or Israel, are: Yeshayahu A. Jelinek, "Carpatho-Rus' Jewry: The Last Czechoslovakian Chapter, 1944–1949," *Shvut*, No. 1–2 [17–18] (Tel Aviv, 1995), pp. 265–295; and Mikhail Mitsel, "The Activity of 'the Joint' in Mukachevo in 1944–1945 and the Soviet Attitude toward it in 1953," *Jews in Russia and Eastern Europe*, I [58] (Jerusalem, 2007), pp. 5–39.

The literature in English on Carpatho-Rusyns in the Prešov Region, which was part of the Slovak state allied to Nazi Germany during World War II, is limited to one short essay by Paul Robert Magocsi, "Rusyns and the Slovak State," in his *Of the Making of Nationalities There Is No End*, Vol. I (New York: Columbia University Press/East European Monographs, 1999), pp. 235–241. The most detailed study on this period, although written from a pro-Ukrainian Marxist perspective, is the Ukrainian-language monograph by Ivan Vanat, *Narysy novitn'oï istoriï ukraïntsiv Skhidnoï Slovachchyny*, Vol. II: *vere-*

sen' 1938 r.—liutyi 1948 r. (Bratislava and Prešov: Slovats'ke pedahohichne vyd-vo, Viddil ukraïns'koï literatury, 1985), esp. pp. 79–178.

Somewhat more developed is the literature on Lemko Rusyns during the World War II period, a time when Poland ceased to exist and the Lemko Region was incorporated into Nazi Germany. A useful introduction is in Bogdan Horbal, *Lemko Studies: A Handbook* (New York: Columbia University Press/East European Monographs, 2010), esp. pp. 406–418. A few essays in a volume edited by Paul Best and Jaroslaw Moklak, *The Lemko Region, 1939–1947: War, Occupation, and Deportation* (Cracow and New Haven: Carpatho-Slavic Studies Group, 2002), deal in part with the World War II period in the Lemko Region, in particular the activity of the Polish underground (by Ihor Ilyushyn, pp. 119–126), Nazi repression (by Marian Zgórniak, pp. 127–130), the Greek Catholic Church (by Stanisław Stępień, pp. 183–198), and the school system (by Oleh Pavlyshyn, pp. 229–234). The Jewish experience is discussed in the recollections of a Holocaust survivor from a Lemko-Rusyn village: Samuel Oliner, *Restless Memories: Recollections of the Holocaust Years* (Berkeley, Calif.: Judith L. Magnes Museum, 1979), and his *Narrow Escapes: Childhood Memories of the Holocaust and Their Legacy* (St. Paul, Minn.: Paragon House, 2000).

The last major aspect of the World War II period concerns the arrival of Soviet troops in September 1944 and the establishment of a pro-Communist transitional administration, which prepared the annexation of what was by that time called Transcarpathian Ukraine (former Subcarpathian Rus') to the Soviet Union. A detailed account of these developments, together with numerous documents, is given by two Czechoslovak officials, one of whom was the representative in the region charged with securing its return to postwar Czechoslovakia: František Nemec and Vladimir Moudry, *The Soviet Seizure of Subcarpathian Ruthenia* (Toronto: William B. Anderson, 1955). The annexation/"reunification"/seizure of Subcarpathian Rus'/Transcarpathian Ukraine to the Soviet Union, which formally took place in June 1945, remains a topic of great controversy. There are monographs focusing solely on this topic in several languages and from differing political persuasions: the "officially approved" Soviet Marxist view, by Ivan F. Evseev, *Narodnye komitety Zakarpatskoi Ukrainy—organy gosudarstvennoi vlasti, 1944–1945* (Moscow: Gosudarstvennoe izd. iuridicheskoi literatury, 1954); the Ukrainian émigré nationalist view, by Vasyl Markus, *L'incorporation de l'Ukraine subcarpathique à l'Ukraine soviétique, 1944–1945* (Louvain: Centre ukrainien d'études en Belgique, 1956); and assessments from the post-Communist era, whether from the perspective of the political center in Moscow: Valentina Mar'ina, *Zakarpatskaia Ukraina (Podkarpatskaia Rus') v politike Benesha i Stalina* (Moscow: Novyi khronograf, 2003); or from the perspective of local developments in the region itself: Mykola P. Makara, *Zakarpats'ka Ukraïna: shliakh do vozz'iednannia, dosvid rozvytku, zhovten 1944-sichen' 1946 rr.* (Uzhhorod: Uzhhorods'kyi derzhavnyi universytet, 1995), and Mykhailo Boldyzhar and Oleksander Hrin, *Zakarpats'ka Ukraïna: der zhavno-pravovyi status i diial'nist', kinets' 1944 r.—pochatok 1946 r.* (Uzhhorod Polychka Karpats'koho kraia, 1999).

8. The Communist era, 1945–1989

The literature in English on the nearly half-century when Carpathian Rus' was ruled by Communist regimes in the Soviet Union and its neighboring satellite countries is generally limited. With regard to the largest territorial component, Soviet Transcarpathia (historical Subcarpathian Rus'), there are no general overviews of this period in English. It is only in the last decade, when scholars from the region have been "liberated" from government-imposed ideological guidelines, and when archival resources have become more accessible, that scholars from the region have published informative surveys on Soviet rule in Transcarpathia. These are in the form of collective works, the best of which is the Ukrainian-language *Narysy istoriï Zakarpattia*, Vol. III: *1946–1991*, edited by Mykhailo M. Boldyzhar et al. (Uzhhorod: Hosprozrakhunkovyi red.-vyd. viddil upravlinnia u spravakh presy ta infor-matsiï, 2003); and the Ukrainian and Hungarian editions of *Zakarpattia 1919–2009 rokiv: istoriia, polityka, kul'tura*, edited by Mykola Vegesh and Csilla Fedinec (Uzhhorod: Lira, 2010), esp. pp. 245–425/*Kárpátalja 1919–2009: történelem, politika, kultúra*, edited by Csilla Fedinec and Mykola Vegesh (Budapest: Argumentum/MTA Etnikai-nemzeti Kisebbségkutató Intézet, 2010), esp. pp. 209–376.

A few aspects of Soviet Transcarpathia have received attention in English-language works. For an overview of the social and cultural transformation of the region during the first few years of Soviet rule, see Paul Robert Magocsi, *The Shaping of a National Identity: Subcarpathian Rus', 1848–1948* (Cambridge, Mass.: Harvard University Press, 1978), esp. pp. 255–268. One aspect of Soviet cultural policy is discussed by Valerii Padiak, "The Reduction of the Status of the Rusyn Language to That of a Ukrainian Dialect as Part of the Language Policy of the USSR . . . after the Annexation of Subcarpathian Rus'," in Paul Best and Stanisław Stępień, eds., *Does a Fourth Rus' Exist?: Concerning Cultural Identity in the Carpathian Region* (Przemyśl and Higganum: South-Eastern Research Institute in Przemyśl, 2009), pp. 81–88. A unique insight into Soviet rule in Transcarpathia is found in the memoirs of an American citizen and resident of Uzhhorod who, because of a combination of odd circumstances, spent all her adult life in the region: Mary Halász, *From America with Love: Memoirs of an American Immigrant in the Soviet Union* (New York: Columbia University Press/East European Monographs, 2000).

The policies of the Soviet Union, which were followed by its satellite countries, led to the liquidation of the Greek Catholic Church between 1946 and 1950 in Poland, Czechoslovakia, and Romania. For a general description of the abolition of that institution in those countries and the subsequent implication for Carpatho-Rusyn society, see Serge Keleher, *Passion and Resurrection: The Greek Catholic Church in Soviet Ukraine, 1939–1989* (L'viv: Stauropegion, 1993), esp. pp. 39–81; and Paul Robert Magocsi, "Religion and Identity in the Carpathians: Eastern Christians in Poland and Czechoslovakia," in his *Of the Making of Nationalities There Is No End*,

Vol. I (New York: Columbia University Press/East European Monographs, 1999), pp. 60–85. For emphasis specifically on Soviet Transcarpathia (Subcarpathian Rus'), see Athanasius B. Pekar, *The History of the Church in Carpathian Rus'* (New York: Columbia University Press/East European Monographs, 1992), esp. pp. 144–161; and Michael Lacko, "The Forced Liquidation of the Union of Užhorod," *Slovak Studies,* I (Rome, 1961), esp. pp. 146–157.

The difficult status of the Magyar minority in Transcarpathia, in particular during the early years of Soviet rule, is discussed in two studies by Steven Bela Vardy: "Soviet Nationality Policy in Carpatho-Ukraine since World War II: The Hungarians of Subcarpathia," *Hungarian Studies Review,* XVI, 1–2 (Toronto, 1989), pp. 67–91, and "The Hungarians of the Carpatho-Ukraine: From Czechoslovak to Soviet Rule," in Stephen Borsody, ed., *The Hungarians: A Divided Nation* (New Haven: Yale Center for International and Area Studies, 1988), pp. 209–227. On their changing fate during the last years of Soviet rule, see Paul Robert Magocsi, "The Hungarians in Transcarpathia/Subcarpathian Rus'," in his *Of the Making of Nationalities There Is No End,* Vol. I (New York: Columbia University Press/East European Monographs, 1999), pp. 290–302; and Csilla Fedinec, "The Soviet Union Case Study," in Nándor Bárdi, Csilla Fedinec, and László Szarka, eds., *Minority Hungarian Communities in the Twentieth Century* (New York and Boulder, Colo.: Columbia University Press/Social Science Monographs, 2011), pp. 413–419.

The situation of Carpatho-Rusyns living in the Prešov Region during Czechoslovakia's Communist era has received more attention. For a general overview of the period, see Paul Robert Magocsi, *The Rusyns of Slovakia An Historical Survey* (New York: Columbia University Press/East European Monographs, 1993), esp. pp. 98–114. Much greater detail, with emphasis on the suppression, partial renewal, and resuppression of Carpatho-Rusyns as a distinct nationality, is found in Paul Robert Magocsi, "National Assimilation: The Case of the Rusyn-Ukrainians of Czechoslovakia," in his *Of the Making of Nationalities There Is No End,* Vol. I (New York: Columbia University Press/East European Monographs, 1999), pp. 242–289. The Ukrainian perspective on this same period, as seen through the prism of belles lettres and Communist cultural policies, is provided in Josef Sirka *The Development of Ukrainian Literature in Czechoslovakia, 1945–197?* (Frankfurt/Main, Bern, and Las Vegas: Peter Lang, 1978).

A few other topics from this period have received special attention. The immediate postwar years, which marked a transitional period before full Communist rule when a Ukrainian national orientation was being formulated but not yet fully implemented, are the subject of three studies: Mykola Mushynka, "The Postwar Development of Lemkos of the Prešov Region 1945–1947," in Paul Best and Jarosław Moklak, eds., *The Lemko Region 1939–1947: War, Occupation and Deportation* (Cracow and New Haven Carpatho-Slavic Studies Group, 2002), pp. 235–243; Stanislav Konečný "Rusyns in Slovakia and the Church Question after WWII, 1945–1947," in ihid., pp. 245–251; and Marián Gajdoš, "The Ukrainian National Council of Priaševčina (The Prešov Region), 1945–1951," in Paul Best and Stanisław Stępień, eds., *Does a Fourth Rus' Exist?: Concerning Cultural Identity in the Carpathian Region* (Przemyśl and Higganum: South-Eastern Research Institute in Przemyśl, 2009), pp. 197–211.

Following the Soviet practice in western Ukraine (including Transcarpathia), the Greek Catholic Church as embodied in the Eparchy of Prešov was abolished in Czechoslovakia in 1950. The process through which this took place is discussed in Michael Lacko, "The Forced Liquidation of the Union of Užhorod," *Slovak Studies*, I (Rome, 1961), esp. pp. 158–185; and Marián Gajdoš and Stanislav Konečný, "Political Aspects of 'Action P' in East Slovakia in the Year of 1950," in *Urbs-Provincia-Orbis: . . . in honorem O. R. Halaga editae* (Košice: Slovenská akadémia vied, Spoločenskovedný ústav, 1993), pp. 177–186. The subsequent relations between the legal Orthodox and illegal Greek Catholics is discussed in Andrew Sorokowski, "Ukrainian Catholics and Orthodox in Czechoslovakia," *Religion in Communist Lands*, XV, 1 (Kent, Eng., 1987), pp. 54–68.

The re-legalization of the Greek Catholic Church and the brief revival of a Carpatho-Rusyn identity was connected with the efforts in Czechoslovakia to reform Communist rule during the so-called Prague Spring of 1968. An overall view of these developments, approached from a Ukrainian perspective, is found in Grey Hodnett and Peter J. Potichnyj, *The Ukraine and the Czechoslovak Crisis* (Canberra: Australian National University, Department of Political Science, 1970). The fate of the church and its justifiable restoration as a Slovak-oriented institution is discussed in Michael Lacko, "The Re-establishment of the Greek Catholic Church in Czechoslovakia," *Slovak Studies*, XI (Rome, 1976), pp. 159–189. For a view of these same events from a Ukrainian perspective that is critical of "slovakization," see *The Tragedy of the Greek Catholic Church in Czechoslovakia* (New York: Carpathian Alliance, 1971); and Athanasius B. Pekar, "Restoration of the Greek Catholic Church in Czechoslovakia," *Ukrainian Quarterly*, XXIX, 3 (New York, 1973), pp. 282–296.

For the Lemko Region during the era of Communist rule in Poland, the best general survey, with extensive references to existing literature in a wide variety of languages, is Bogdan Horbal, *Lemko Studies: A Handbook* (New York: Columbia University Press/East European Monographs, 2010), esp. pp. 419–459. Particular emphasis has been given to the deportations carried out between late 1944 and 1947, which removed the Carpatho-Rusyn population from the Lemko Region. For a general introduction to these events, which also included the deportation of Ukrainians from neighboring areas in post-World War II eastern Poland, see Bohdan Kordan, "Making Borders Stick: Population Transfer and Resettlement in the Trans-Curzon Territories, 1944–1949," *International Migration Review*, XXXI, 3 (Staten Is., N.Y., 1997), pp. 704–720; Tadeusz Piotrowski, "Akcja 'Wisła'—Operation 'Vistula': Background and Assessment," *Polish Review*, XLIII, 2 (New York, 1998), pp. 219–238; and Marek Jasiak, "Overcoming Ukrainian Resistance:

The Deportation of Ukrainians within Poland in 1947," in Philip Ther and Ana Siljak, eds., *Redrawing Nations: Ethnic Cleansing in East-Central Europe, 1944–1948* (Lanham, Boulder, New York, and Oxford: Rowman and Littlefield, 2001), pp. 173–194. On the deportation process specifically from the Lemko Region, and the initial experience of the Lemkos in their new places of resettlement, see the essays by Eugeniusz Misilo, Roman Drozd, Yurii Kramar, Michal Wawrzonek, Czesław Brzoza, and Jan Pisulinski, in Paul Best and Jarosław Moklak, eds., *The Lemko Region, 1939–1947: War, Occupation, and Deportation* (Cracow and New Haven: Carpatho-Slavic Studies Group, 2002), pp. 75–117 and 137–148. Related to the deportations of 1947 was the presence of the underground Ukrainian Insurgent Army (UPA) against which the Polish government was fighting. For conflicting views on the question whether the Lemko-Rusyn population was in support of, or opposed to, the UPA, see the essays by Peter Potichnyj and Bogdan Horbal in ibid., pp. 149–181.

The other issue that is the subject of study concerns the abolition of the Greek Catholic Church in Poland, something that impacted not only the Lemko Region but also Lemko Rusyns who were resettled to other parts of the country. For a general overview of the reconfiguration of the Greek Catholic and Orthodox churches, including their relationship to Lemko Rusyns, see Andrew Sorokowski, "Ukrainian Catholics and Orthodox in Poland," *Religion in Communist Lands*, XIV, 3 (Kent, Eng., 1986), pp. 244–261—reprinted in the Harvard University Ukrainian Studies Fund Millennium Series (Cambridge, Mass., 1988); and Paul Robert Magocsi, "Religion and Identity in the Carpathians: Eastern Christians in Poland and Czechoslovakia," in his *Of the Making of Nationalities There Is No End*, Vol. I (New York: Columbia University Press/East European Monographs, 1999), pp. 60–85. On the Greek Catholics specifically in the Lemko Region before their deportation, see Stanisław Stępień, "The Greek Catholic Church in the Lemko Region in WWII and Its Liquidation, 1939–1947," and Mariusz Rynca, "The Liquidation of the Structure of the Greek Catholic Church in the Lemko Region," in Paul Best and Jarosław Moklak, *The Lemko Region, 1939–1947: War, Occupation, and Deportation* (Cracow and New Haven: Carpatho-Slavic Studies Group, 2002), pp. 183–206; and the graphic depiction of individual church buildings throughout the Lemko Region in Oleh Wolodymyr Iwanusiw/Oleh Volodymyr Ivanusiv, *Church in Ruins/Tserkva v ruïni* (St. Catherines, Ont.: St. Sophia Religious Association of Ukrainian Catholics in Canada, 1987), esp. pp. 25–124.

The dispersal of Lemkos from their homeland, their resettlement in western Poland, and the resultant national assimilation that they experienced are the subject of numerous studies, most of which are in Polish. The best of these works are by Andrzej Kwilecki, *Łemkowie: zagadnienie migracji i asymilacji* (Warsaw: Państwowe Wyd-wo Naukowe, 1974); and Kazimierz Pudło, *Łemkowie: proces wrastania w środowisko Dolnego Śląska, 1947–1985* (Wrocław: Polskie Towarzystwo Ludoznawcze, 1987). On the efforts of Lemkos to maintain their distinct identity, whether in western Poland or in scattered rcturnee communities in the Carpathian homeland, see Paul Best, "The Rusnak-Lemko Mountaineers and the National Question in People's Poland," *Connecticut Review*, IX, 2 (Hartford, 1976), pp. 74–81; Paul Robert Magocsi, "Nation-Building or Nation Destroying?: Lemkos, Poles, and Ukrainians in Contemporary Poland" (1988), in his *Of the Making of Nationalities There Is No End*, Vol. I (New York: Columbia University Press/East European Monographs, 1999), pp. 316–331; and the memoir-like account of a Lemko growing up in western Poland during the Communist era: Jaroslav Hunka [Iaroslav Horoshchak], "The Lemkos Today," *Carpatho-Rusyn American*, X, 4 (Cambridge, Minn., 1987), pp. 4–8. A recent study that speculates on the possible positive aspect of the postwar deportations is Rosa Lehmann, "From Ethnic Cleansing to Affirmative Action: Exploring Poland's Struggle with its Ukrainian Minority (1944–89)," *Nations and Nationalism*, XVI, 2 (Oxford, 2010), pp. 285–307; Lehmann's article, which is a summary of a doctoral dissertation on sociological problems in the Lemko Region, prompted criticism by Chris Hann, "Does Ethnic Cleansing Work?: The Case of Twentieth Century Poland," *Cambridge Anthropology*, XXIX, 1 (Cambridge, 2009), pp. 1–25.

Carpatho-Rusyns in North America during the period from the 1940s through 1980 are treated in only a limited number of publications. The activity of the community's largest secular organizations during these years is covered in the general organizational histories: *Opportunity Realized: The Greek Catholic Union's First One Hundred Years, 1892–1992* (Beaver, Pa.: Greek Catholic Union of the USA, 1994), esp. pp. 126–243; *50th Anniversary Almanac of the Lemko Association of the USA and Canada* (Yonkers, N.Y.: Lemko Association, 1979), esp. pp. 19–62; and Michael Lucas, *From the Carpathian Mountains to Canada: History of the Carpatho-Russians in Canada* (Toronto: Society of Carpatho-Russian Canadians, 2010), esp. pp. 18–105.

The phenomenon of widespread assimilation and loss of traditional culture and language that characterized Rusyn-American society in the 1950s and 1960s is examined through the activity of the Greek Catholic Union in the context of "other Slovak" organizations in Howard F. Stein, "An Ethnohistory of Slovak-American Religious and Fraternal Associations: A Study in Cultural Meaning, Group Identity, and Social Institutions," *Slovakia*, XXIX [63–64] (Havertown, Pa., 1980–81), pp. 53–101. Emphasis on church life and its influence on the Rusyn-American community during these decades is surveyed in Walter C. Warzeski, *Byzantine Rite Rusyns in Carpatho-Ruthenia and America* (Pittsburgh, Pa.: Byzantine Catholic Seminary Press, 1971), esp. pp. 245–271; and Lawrence Barriger, *Glory to Jesus Christ: A History of the American Carpatho-Russian Orthodox Diocese* (Brookline, Mass.: Holy Cross Orthodox Press, 2000), esp. pp. 84–115.

The Carpatho-Rusyn community, most especially in the United States, experienced an ethnic revival in the 1970s, which is outlined in Paul Robert Magocsi, "Made or Re-Made in America? Nationality and Identity Formation among Carpatho-Rusyn Immigrants and Their Descendants," in his *Of the Making of Nationalities There Is No End,* Vol. I (New York: Columbia University Press/East European Monographs, 1999), pp. 467–482; and in a history of the main organization that engineered the revival: Patricia A. Krafcik and Elaine Rusinko, eds., *Carpatho-Rusyn Research Center: The First Quarter Century* (Ocala, Fla.: Carpatho-Rusyn Research Center, 2004). Various aspects of the revival, including Carpatho-Rusyn interaction with other Slavic immigrant groups (in particular Ukrainians and Slovaks) and the relationship of ethnicity to church structures, are debated in several articles with commentaries by a variety of authors in Paul Robert Magocsi, *Of the Making of Nationalities There Is No End,* Vol. II (New York: Columbia University Press/East European Monographs, 1999), pp. 11–112 and 205–215.

9. The revolutions of 1989 and their aftermath

The enormous political, socioeconomic, and cultural transformation of Carpatho-Rusyn society brought about by the revolutions of 1989, the end of Communist rule, and the collapse of the Soviet Union are topics treated in several studies, which for the most part focus on specific countries. The best introduction to the socioeconomic and geopolitical status of Ukraine's Transcarpathia (historic Subcarpathian Rus') after 1989 is Peter Jordan and Mladen Klemenčić, eds., *Transcarpathia—Bridgehead or Periphery?: Geopolitical and Economic Aspects of a Ukrainian Region* (Frankfurt am Main: Peter Lang, 2004).

Three topics have received more attention: the economy, politics, and cross-border relations. On the new market economy in Transcarpathia and how it has worked out in both urban and rural settings, see Christos Kalantaridis, "Globalization and Entrepreneurial Response in Post-Socialist Transformation: A Case Study from Transcarpathia, Ukraine," *European Planning Studies,* VIII, 3 (Carfax, Eng., 2000), pp. 285–299; Jennifer A. Dickinson, "Gender, Work, and Economic Restructuring in a Transcarpathian (Ukrainian) Village," *Nationalities Papers,* XXXIII, 3 (Basingstoke, Eng., 2005), pp. 387–401; and Kateryna Sochka, "Challenges and Perspectives for the Entrepreneurship Development in Transcarpathian Rural Areas," in *Rehional'ni studiï: Naukovyi zbirnyk,* No. 4 (Uzhhorod, 2004), pp. 18–26.

The political changes in the region within a post-Communist independent Ukraine are discussed in Judy Batt, "Transcarpathia: Peripheral Region at the 'Centre of Europe'," in Judy Batt and Kataryna Wolchuk, eds., *Region State, and Identity in Central and Eastern Europe* (London and Portland Ore.: Frank Cass, 2002), pp. 155–177; and Kimitaka Matsuzato, "Elites and the Party System of Zakarpattya Oblast': Relations among Levels of Party Systems in Ukraine," *Europe-Asia Studies,* LIV, 8 (Glasgow, 2002), pp. 1267–1300. The geopolitical function of Carpathian Rus', which is only one part (but geographically the central part) of the Carpathian Euroregion set up in 1993, is the subject of a series, titled "Carpathian Euroregion: Prospects and Challenges," which contains the papers given at periodic workshops sponsored by foreign policy advisory agencies in Slovakia and Ukraine (Transcarpathia): No. 1: *Role of the Carpathian Euroregion in Strengthening Security and Stability in Central and Eastern Europe* (Prešov and Uzhhorod: Slovak Foreign Policy Association/Strategies Studies Foundation, 2001); No. 2: *Role of the Carpathian Euroregion in Confronting its Minority Agenda* (Prešov and Uzhhorod: Slovak Foreign Policy Association/Strategies Studies Foundation, 2001); No. 3: *Carpathian Euroregion: Prospects for Economic Trans-border Co-operation* (Prešov and Uzhhorod: Slovak Foreign Policy Association/Strategies Studies Foundation, 2001); and No. 4: *Role of the Carpathian Euroregion in Mitigating the Possible Negative Effects of Schengen* (Prešov and Uzhhorod: Slovak Foreign Policy Association/Strategies Studies Foundation, 2001).

Particular attention has been given to the interaction between the various peoples living within the Carpathian Euroregion, whether those living on either side of the international boundaries of the member states: Giuseppe Vedovato, "The Carpathian Euroregion as a Means for Reducing Possible Tensions between Ethnic Communities," *Rivisti di Studi Politici Internazionali,* LXIII, 4 (Rome, 1996), pp. 498–504; and Istvan Madi, "Carpatho-Ukraine," in Tuomas Forsberg, ed., *Contested Territory: Border Disputes at the Edge of the Former Soviet Empire* (Aldershot, Eng.: Edward Elgar, 1995), pp. 128–142; or those within Transcarpathia itself: Tom Trier, *Minorities in Transcarpathia* (Flensburg, Germany: European Centre for Minority Issues, 1998); Tom Trier, *Inter-Ethnic Relations in Transcarpathian Ukraine* (Flensburg, Germany: European Centre for Minority Issues, 1999); Tatiana Joukova, "The Ethnographic and Ethno-Social Processes in the Transcarpathian Region," in Albina Nećak Lük, George Muskens, and Sonja Novak Lukanovič, eds., *Managing the Mix Thereafter: Comparative Research and Mixed Communities in Three Independent Successor States* (Ljubljana: Institute for Ethnic Studies, 2000), pp. 65–86; and Oksana Chmouliar and Vasyl Bedzir, "Demographic and Ethnic Structure of Uzhhorod," in ibid., pp. 130–152.

There are also studies devoted to two of Transcarpathia's "other peoples" in the post-Communist era. On the Gypsies/Roma, see the European Roma Rights Centre report compiled by Claude Kahn, *The Misery of Law: The Rights of Roma in the Transcarpathian Region of Ukraine* (Budapest: European Roma Rights Centre, 1997). On the Magyars, see the general description, with an emphasis on demography, education, and group maintenance, as outlined in the *Report on the Situation of Hungarians in Ukraine* (Budapest: Government Office for Hungarian Minorities, 1998); in Ildikó Orosz and István Csernicskó, *The Hungarians of Transcarpathia* (Budapest: Tinta Publishers, 1999); and a study on religion and changing national identities among Transcarpathia's Magyars: Bertalan Pusztai, "Collision of Identities," *Acta Ethnografica Hungarica,* XLII, 1–2 (Budapest, 1997), pp. 149–163.

It is, however, the revival of a Carpatho-Rusyn identity and the efforts of the group to be recognized as a distinct nationality in post-Communist central Europe that has received the most attention in writings by observers and participants from both within and outside Carpathian Rus'. For a general introduction to the phenomenon, see two essays by Paul Robert Magocsi: "The Birth of a New Nation or the Return of an Old Problem?: The Rusyns of East-Central Europe" and "A New Slavic Nationality?: The Rusyns of East-Central Europe," in his *Of the Making of Nationalities There Is No End*, Vol. I (New York: Columbia University Press/East European Monographs, 1999), pp. 332–360 and 361–375. Other works which look at developments in most or all of the countries where a national revival has taken place include: Natalya Belitser, Dagmar Kusa, and Kazimierz Krzysztofek, "Human Rights and Minority Issues: The Ruthenian Communities in Poland, Slovakia, and Ukraine," in Margriet Drent et al., eds., *Towards Shared Security: 7-Nation Perspectives* (Groningen, Netherlands: Centre of European Security Studies, 2001), pp. 36–50; and essays by Paul Robert Magocsi, Robert Rothstein, Elaine Rusinko, and Brian Požun that assess the achievements of the Carpatho-Rusyn movement over the ten-year period 1995 to 2005, in Elaine Rusinko, ed., *Committing Community: Carpatho-Rusyn Studies as an Emerging Scholarly Discipline* (New York: Columbia University Press/ East European Monographs, 2009), pp. 3–58 and 345–396. Some scholars have compared the recent Carpatho-Rusyn revival to similar movements among other stateless peoples in central Europe: Magdalena Dembinska, "Adapting to Changing Contexts of Choice: The Nation-Building Strategies of Unrecognized Silesians and Rusyns," *Canadian Journal of Political Science*, XLI, 4 (2008), pp. 915–934; and Agnieszka Barszczewska, "Ethnic Identity Persistence in 19th and 20th Century East-Central Europe: the Carpatho-Rusyns Versus the Moldavian Csángós," *Danubian Carpatica*, Vol. I [48] Munich, 2007), pp. 307–319—a summary of a comprehensive Polish-language monograph by the same author: *Mołdawscy Csángó a Rusini karpaccy, 1867–1947* (Warsaw: Wyd-wo Trio, Collegium Civitas, 2012).

Because Carpatho-Rusyns had been officially designated as Ukrainians by Communist regimes throughout the region after 1945, and because the vast majority (almost three-quarters) live in Ukraine, many studies have focused on the evolution of the movement since 1989 in Transcarpathia. For the few that are in English, see Yaroslav Pylynskyi, *Rising Ethnic Self-awareness: Carpathian Rusins—Birth of a New Nation or a Political Game?* (Kiev and Copenhagen: Danish-Ukrainian Society, 1998); and Taras Kuzio, "The Rusyn Question in Ukraine: Sorting Out Fact from Fiction," *Canadian Review of Studies in Nationalism*, XXXII (Charlottetown, Prince Edward Is., 2005), pp. 1–15.

It is the Lemko Rusyns of Poland, however, who have received the most attention. The best introductory overview since 1989, with particular emphasis on Polish state policy toward the group, is by Bogdan Horbal, "Contested by Whom?: Lemko Rusyns in the Post-Communist World," *Europa Ethnica*, LXV, 1–2 (Vienna, 2008), pp. 45–58. The most detailed discussion of the post-1989 civic and political status of the Lemko Rusyns is the extensive Polish-language monograph by Leszek Filipiak, *Społeczno-polityczna sytuacja Łemków w III RP* (Toruń: Wyd-wo Adam Marszałek, 2013). On the specific question of maintenance of group identity, see Zdzisław Mach, *Symbols, Conflict, and Identity* (Albany, N.Y.: State University of New York Press, 1993), esp. pp. 231–241; Marek Dziewierski, "Space as the Value Felt to Be Accepted: The Case of the Lemkos," in Wojciech Świątkiewicz, ed., *Region and Regionalism: Culture and Social Order* (Katowice: Wyd-wo Uniwersytetu Śląskiego, 1995), pp. 105–114; Bożena Pactwa, "Religion and Ethnic-National Identity of Lemkos," in Marek S. Szczepański, ed., *Ethnic Minorities and Ethnic Majority* (Katowice: Wyd-wo Uniwersytetu Śląskiego, 1997), pp. 333–349; Susan Y. Mihalasky, "Lemkos View Poland and Poles," *Nationalities Papers*, XXV, 4 (Oxford, 1997), pp. 683–697; Susyn Mihalasky, "Rebuilding a Shattered Community: The Lemkos after the 'Akcja Wisła'," in Elaine Rusinko, ed., *Committing Community: Carpatho-Rusyn Studies as an Emerging Scholarly Discipline* (New York: Columbia University Press/East European Monographs, 2009), pp. 61–82; Christopher Hann, "Ethnicity in the New Civil Society: Lemko-Ukrainians in Poland," in László Kürti and Juliet Langman, eds., *Beyond Borders: Remaking Cultural Identities in the New East and Central Europe* (Boulder, Colo.: Westview Press, 1997), pp. 17–38; and Christopher Hann, "Peripheral Populations and the Dilemmas of Multiculturalism: The Lemkos and the Lazi Revisited," in Bogdan Horbal, Patricia A. Krafcik, and Elaine Rusinko, eds., *Carpatho-Rusyns and Their Neighbors: Essays in Honor of Paul Robert Magocsi* (Fairfax, Va.: Eastern Christian Publications, 2006), pp. 185–202.

The Carpatho-Rusyn revival in Slovakia is the subject of several studies: Stanislav Kužel, "Circumstance-Based National Identities: The Case of the So-Called Rusyns-Ukrainians in North-East Slovakia," in Zdeněk Uherek, ed., *Ethnic Studies and the Urbanized Space in Social Anthropological Reflections*, Prague Occasional Papers in Ethnography, No. 5 (Prague: Institute of Ethnology, Academy of Sciences of the Czech Repoblic, 1998), pp. 48–60; two essays by Patricia A. Krafcik, "The Power of a Newspaper: *Narodnŷ novynkŷ*," and "'But We Never Were Ukrainian!': The Struggle of Slovakia's Rusyns to Assert Their Identity," in Elaine Rusinko, ed., *Committing Community* (New York: Columbia University Press/East European Monographs, 2009), pp. 83–95 and 131–140; Anna Plíšková: "Practical Spheres of the Rusyn Language in Slovakia," *Studia Slavica Hungaricae*, LIII, 1 (Budapest, 2008), pp. 95–115—reprinted in Paul Best and Stanisław Stępień, eds., *Does a Fourth Rus' Exist?: Concerning Cultural Identity in the Carpathian Region* (Przemyśl and Higganum, Conn.: South-Eastern Research Institute in Przemyśl, 2009), pp. 89–113; and Anna Plishkova, "The Language of Slovakia's Rusyns in Religion and Education," in Bogdan Horbal, Patricia A. Krafcik, and Elaine Rusinko, eds., *Carpatho-Rusyns and Their Neighbors* (Fairfax, Va.: Eastern Christian Publications, 2006), pp. 349–265. The manner in which the figure of the American artist and cultural icon Andy Warhol has been used by activists in Slovakia to promote a Carpatho-Rusyn identity is explored in great detail in Elaine Rusinko, *"We Are All Warhol's Children": Andy and the Rusyns*, The Carl Beck Papers, No. 2204 (Pittsburgh: Center for Russian and East European Studies, University of Pittsburgh, 2012).

The community in the Vojvodina, especially the changes implemented by the post-Yugoslav independent Serbia, are discussed in Mikhailo Feisa, *The New Serbia and Its Ruthenian Minority* (Novi Sad and Kucura: Prometej/Kulturno-prosvetno drushtvo DOK, 2010); and the descriptive catalogue of civic and cultural organizations: Jelena Perković, ed., *The Ruthenians in Serbia: Bulletin* (Ruski Krstur: National Council of the Rusyn National Minority/Institute for Culture of the Vojvodinian Ruthenians, 2009).

One aspect of the national revival touched on in the above studies is the language question and its role both symbolically (as an enhancement to national pride and a distinct identity) and practically (as an instrument of communication, whether in the media, churches, cultural institutions, and most especially schools). General introductions to the language question in all regions where Carpatho-Rusyns live include: Paul Robert Magocsi, "The Rusyn Language Question Revisited," in his *Of the Making of Nationalities There Is No End*, Vol. I (New York: Columbia University Press/East European Monographs, 1999), pp. 86–111; and Nadiya Kushko, "Literary Standards of the Rusyn Language: The Historical Context and Contemporary Situation," *Slavic and East European Journal*, LI, 1 (Lexington, Ky., 2007), pp. 111–132. The most comprehensive coverage of this topic for all regions remains the Rusyn-language multi-authored collection dealing with both sociolinguistic as well as purely linguistic matters: Paul Robert Magocsi, ed., *Rusyns'kŷ iazyk*, Modern History of the Slavonic Languages, Vol. XIV, 2nd rev. ed (Opole: Uniwersytet Opolski, Instytut Filologii Polskiej, 2007); and the German-language monograph by Marc Stegherr, *Das Russinische: kulturhi storische und soziolinguistische Aspekte* (Munich: Verlag Otto Sagner, 2003). For a focus on particular regions, see Paul Robert Magocsi, ed., *A New Slavic Language Is Born: The Rusyn Literary Language of Slovakia* (New York: Columbia University Press/East European Monographs, 1996); Anna Plishkova, *Language and National Identity: Rusyns South of the Carpathians* (New York: Columbia University Press/East European Monographs, 2009); Juraj Vaňko, "The Rusyn Language in Slovakia: Between a Rock and a Hard Place," *International Journal of the Sociology of Language*, No. 183 (Berlin and New York, 2007), pp. 75–96; and, for the Lemko Rusyns, the Polish-language monograph by Małgorzata Misiak, *Łemkowie: w kręgu badań nad mniejszościami etnolingwistycznymi w Europie* (Wrocław: Wyd-wo Uniwersytetu Wrocławskiego, 2006).

History and literary works have traditionally been important components of nationalist ideology. The role of history is discussed by Ewa Michna, "The Rusyn's History Is More Beautiful Than the Ukrainian's: Using History in the Processes of Legitimization of National Aspiration by Carpatho-Rusyn Ethnic Leaders in Transcarpathian Ukraine," *Studia Slavica et Balcanica Petropolitana*, No. 1 [7] (St. Petersburg, 2010), pp. 89–108. Literary works both as a reflection of—and instrument for—creating a national identity is the subject of four studies by Elaine Rusinko: "Straddling the Past and Future," in her *Straddling Borders: Literature and Identity in Subcarpathian Rus'* (Toronto, Buffalo, and London: University of Toronto Press, 2003);

pp. 443 465; "Carpatho-Rusyns and Their Literature," "Rusyn Literature in Transcarpathia: A Cohesive or Divisive Force?," and "From Ukrainian to Rusyn in Literature: The Case of Vladŷmŷr Fedŷnŷshŷnets'," in Elaine Rusinko, ed., *Committing Community* (New York: University of Toronto Press, 2009), pp. 33–51, 96–118, and 160–172. See also Helena Dúć-Fajfer, "The Axiology of Ethnic Space in Lemko Cultural Texts," in *Does a Fourth Rus' Exist?* (Przemyśl and Higganum, Conn.: South-Eastern Research Institute in Przemyśl, 2009), pp. 45–61. For more modern forms of communication, which are being used by post-1989 Carpatho-Rusyn individuals and organizations to propagate the national idea (i.e., radio, television, film, the Internet), see Patricia A. Krafcik, "Carpatho-Rusyns: Depiction and Self-Depiction in Cinema," and Brian J. Požun, "Rusyn Media in the Context of Minority Language Media Studies," in Elaine Rusinko, ed., *Committing Community* (New York: Columbia University Press/East European Monographs, 2009), pp. 233–248 and 368–393.

In part, the success of the present-day Carpatho-Rusyn national movement depends on access to state funding, the amount of which is often determined by the numerical size of the group. That determination is usually based on decennial census data. How Carpatho-Rusyns have managed—or not managed—to be represented in census questionnaires is analyzed, especially in the problematic case of Ukraine, by Dominique Arel, "Interpreting 'Nationality' and 'Language' in the 2001 Ukrainian Census," *Post-Soviet Affairs*, XVIII, 3 (Palm Beach, Fla., 2002), pp. 213–249; and Jennifer A. Dickinson, "Documenting Identity: Census Categories and Rusyn Self-Determination in the 2001 Ukrainian Census," in Elaine Rusinko, ed., *Committing Community* (New York: Columbia University Press/East European Monographs, 2009), pp. 225–232.

The role of individual intellectual leaders in providing theoretical and practical direction to national movements is generally accepted by scholars as a basic characteristic of the phenomenon of nationalism. There already exists a literature on the post-1989 Carpatho-Rusyn intelligentsia. The most comprehensive of these works is the Polish-language monograph by the Jagiellonian University sociologist Ewa Michna, *Kwestie etniczno-narodowościowe na pograniczu Słowiańszczyzny wschodniej i zachodniej: ruch rusiński na Słowacji, Ukrainie i w Polsce* (Cracow: Polska Akademia Umiejętności, 2004); one aspect of this monumental work is summed up in her article, "Methods Used by Carpatho-Rusyn Leaders to Legitimize Their National Aspirations in Slovakia, Ukraine, and Poland," in Paul Best and Stanisław Stępień, eds., *Does a Fourth Rus' Exist?* (Przemyśl and Higganum, Conn.: South-Eastern Research Institute in Przemyśl, 2009), pp. 215–226.

Carpatho-Rusyn activists have also come to the attention of scholars in Germany, the United States, and Canada. Among the first to turn his attention to this subject was the social anthropologist Christopher Hann: "Intellectuals, Ethnic Groups, and Nations: The Late-Twentieth-Century Cases," in Sukumar Periwal, ed., *Notions of Nationalism* (Budapest, London, and New York: Central European University Press, 1995), pp. 106–128; "On

Nation(alitie)s in General, and One Potential Nation(ality) in Particular," in Paul Robert Magocsi, *Of the Making of Nationalities There Is No End*, Vol. I (New York: Columbia University Press/East European Monographs, 1999), pp. xiii-xxxvii; "All Kulturvölker Now? Social Anthropological Reflections on the German-American Tradition," in Richard G. Fox and Barbara J. King, eds., *Anthropology Beyond Culture* (Oxford and New York: Berg, 2000), pp. 259–276; and "From Ethnographic Group to Sub-Sub-Ethnicity: Lemko-Rusyn-Ukrainians in Postsocialist Poland," in Elaine Rusinko, ed., *Committing Community* (New York: Columbia University Press/East European Monographs, 2009), pp. 175–188. The view of historians and political scientists on this topic include: Raymond A. Smith, "Indigenous and Diaspora Elites and the Return of Carpatho-Ruthenian Nationalism, 1989–1992," *Harvard Ukrainian Studies*, XXI, 1–2 (Cambridge, Mass., 1997), pp. 141–161; Martin Fedor Ziac, "Professors and Politics: The Role of Paul Robert Magocsi in the Modern Carpatho-Rusyn Revival," *East European Quarterly*, XXXV, 2 (Boulder, Colo., 2001), pp. 213–232; and Taras Kuzio, Alexander J. Motyl, George G. Grabowicz, Serhii Plokhy, and Dominique Arel, "The Scholar, Historian, and Public Advocate: The Academic Contributions of Paul Robert Magocsi," *Nationalities Papers*, XXXIX, 1 (Basingstoke, Eng., 2011), pp. 95–134.

The opinions of Carpatho-Rusyn leaders themselves are also available, including civic activists from Poland (Andrzej Kopcza), Slovakia (Vasyl' Turok), Hungary (Gabriel Hattinger), Ukraine (Ivan M. Turianytsia), and the former Yugoslavia/Vojvodina (Mikhailo Varga), in Tom Trier, ed., *Focus on the Rusyns: An International Colloquium* (Copenhagen: Danish Cultural Institute, 1999). The views of intellectual spokespeople often take the form of an historical excursus on the particular area of Carpathian Rus' that they "represent": see Olena Duć-Fajfer, "The Lemkos of Poland"; Ljubomir Medješi, "The Problem of Cultural Borders in the History of Ethnic Groups: The Yugoslav Rusyns"; and Paul Robert Magocsi, "Made or Re-Made in America?: Nationality and Identity Formation among Carpatho-Rusyn Immigrants and Their Descendants," in Paul Robert Magocsi, ed., *The Persistence of Regional Cultures: Rusyns and Ukrainians in Their Carpathian Homeland and Abroad* (New York: Columbia University Press/East European Monographs, 1993), pp. 83–104 and 139–178. This same volume also includes studies by Oleksa V. Myšanyč from Transcarpathia (pp. 7–52) and Mykola Mušynka from Slovakia (pp. 53–82), who promote the Ukrainian viewpoint that denies the existence of Carpatho-Rusyns as a distinct nationality. For that interpretation, see also Oleksa Myshanych, "Political Ruthenianism—A Ukrainian Problem," *The Ukrainian Quarterly*, LIII, 3 (New York, 1997), pp. 234–243.

Other publications which reflect the views of intellectual activists in the post-1989 Carpatho-Rusyn movement include those by the writer from Ukraine's Transcarpathia Volodymyr Fedynyšynec', *Our Peaceful Rusyn Way: Two Essays* (Prešov: Rusynska obroda, 1992); by the academic and publicist from Serbia Mikhajlo Fejsa, "Vojvodina Rusyns/Ruthenians: Proof That a Fourth Rus' Does Exist," in Paul Best and Stanisław Stępień, eds.

Does a Fourth Rus' Exist? (Przemyśl and Higganum, Conn.: South-Eastern Research Institute in Przemyśl, 2009), pp. 229–238; and by the American scholar from Canada, Paul Robert Magocsi: "Speeches and Debates," in his *Of the Making of Nationalities There Is No End,* Vol. II (New York: Columbia University Press/East European Monographs, 1999), esp. pp. 3–297, which includes the programmatic addresses at the first four World Congresses of Rusyns: "The Scholar as Nation-Builder, or as Advisor and Advocate," *Nationalities Papers,* XXXVI, 5 (Basingstoke, Eng., 2008), pp. 881–892; and "The Fourth Rus': A New Reality in a New Europe," in Paul Best and Stanisław Stępień, eds., *Does a Fourth Rus' Exist?* (Przemyśl and Higganum, Conn.: South-Eastern Research Institute in Przemyśl, 2009), pp. 11–24.

Illustration Sources and Credits

Index

A

Aba/Abadé clan, 61, 63
Abov-Torna/Turna county, 185,186, 193
Abov/Abaúj county, 57, 83, 84, 87, 100, 182, 193–194, 219
Adalbert Erdeli/Béla Erdélyi, 256
Administration for Rusyn Self-Government in Hungary, 399
Adrianople, Battle of, 45
Adriatic Sea, 63
Adriatic-Balkan peoples, 26
Adventists. See Seventh-Day Adventists
Aegean Sea, 17, 38
Africa, 21
Agrarian Party, 201, 260, 266
Agriculture, 12–13, 27, 59, 60, 93, 143, 144, 149, 202–203, 236, 255–257 passim, 310, 325
Aleksevych, Andrii, 265
Aleksovych, Vintsent, 122
Alexander Dukhnovych Theater, 382
Alexis, Saint. See Toth, Alexis
Alföld culture, 15
Allegheny, Pennsylvania, 375
Allied and Associated Powers (in World War I), 169, 175, 176, 179, 187, 335
Allied Powers (in World War II), 292, 301
All-Ukrainian Congress of Lemkos, 393
Álmos, 41, 43

Alphabet: Cyrillic, 2, 37, 85, 123, 140, 174, 387; Glagolitic, 36; Latin/Roman (latynyka), 174
Alps, 12, 19, 50, 77
America, 145, 154, 156–160, 163, 165, 177, 197, 225, 236, 244, 341, 352, 354. See also North America; South America; United States
American Carpatho-Russian Central Conference (Pittsburgh), 293
American Carpatho-Russian Orthodox Greek Catholic Diocese, 245–246, 352
American National Council of Uhro-Rusyns (Homestead, Pa.), 177, 178
Americanization, 159, 351
Americans, 112, 162, 177–178, 221, 244, 246–247, 250–251, 292–293, 301, 350–354, 373, 403
Amerikanskii russkii viestnik (newspaper), 158, 244, plate 34
Anartii, 18, 19, 21
Anatolia, 70
Andrella, Mykhail Orosvygovs'kyi, 82
Andrew/András, 61
Anjou/Angevin dynasty, 61, 65
Annales Hildesheimensis, 55
Anonymous, 45
Antes, 28, 35
Anthems. See National anthems/hymns
Anti-Normanists, 49–50
Anti-Semitism, 289
Anti-Trinitarians/Socinians, 77
Antonii (Khrapovitskii), 209

Architecture, 94, 146, 202–203, 305
Ardanovo, 18
Argentina: Carpatho-Rusyns in, 204, 236
Aristov, Fedor F., 132
Armenians, 109
Árpád dynasty, 61
Árpád Line, 291, 294
Árpád, 42, 43, 146, plate 8
Art (Painting and Sculpture), 85, 207, 256, 267, 345, 412
Art Nouveau/Secessionism, 203
Asdings, 18, 22
Ashkenazim Jews, 257
Asia, 23, 29, 33, 35, 41, 47
Assimilation, 5, 93, 105, 116, 134, 136, 137, 141, 143, 154, 174, 243, 328, 333–334, 340, 381, 384, 385, 391, 394. *See also* Magyarization; Slovakization; Ukrainianization
Association of Lemko Culture, 388
Athos, The Holy Mount, 209
Attila, 23–24
Auschwitz-Birkenau, 289
Ausgleich/Compromise of 1867, 129, 136
Australia, 1, 198; Carpatho-Rusyns in, 1
Austria/Österreich, 50, 55, 270–271, 311, 365
Austria-Hungary, 7, 115, 126, 132, 138, 145, 146, 174–175, 179, 183, 184, 203, 255, 259, 317, 379
Austrian (Habsburg) Army, 119
Austrian Empire, 87–93, 96, 101, 107–111, 113, 118, 122, 125, 128, 129, 222
Austrians, 115
Austro-Germans, 109, 118
Austro-Hungarian Army, 169–173, 176, 186
Austro-Hungarian Dual Monarchy. *See* Austria-Hungary
Austro-Hungarian Empire. *See* Austria-Hungary
Autonomist Agricultural Union, 201, 225, 269
Autonomy, 112, 115, 127, 135, 175, 177–178, 181, 182, 189, 193–195, 197, 251, 269–278, 285–286, 287, 323, 330, 348, 350, 361–365, 371, 398–399, 402
Avar Kaganate, 29, 31
Avars, 18, 28–29, 31, 35, 45
Azov, Sea of, 50

B

Babila, Daniel, 104
Babjak, Ján, 384
Bacha, Iurii, 332, 366
Bachka region, 94, 95, 151, 153, 154, 243, 281, 287, 348
Bachka-Srem Rusyns. *See* Vojvodinian-Srem Rusyns
Bachka/Bács-Bodrog county, 95, 153, 242
Bachyns'kyi, Andrei, 100, 138, plate 19
Bachyns'kyi, Edmund, 270, plate 43
Bačinci, 153
Baiko Sisters, 345
Baius, Vasyl', 70, 96
Bajda, Piotr, xx
Balkans, 60, 104, 111, 132, 154, 162, 169, 312
Baloga, Viktor, 368
Balogh, Pál, 416n.11
Balogh-Beéry, László, 199
Baltic Sea, 7, 46, 47, 50, 279
Baltimore, Maryland, 247, 251, 422, 455
Baludians'kyi, Mykhail, 103
Bamberg, 92
Banat region, 11, 241, 346, 347; Carpatho-Rusyns in, 7, 11, 151–153, 154, 346-347
Bandera, Stepan, 292
Banderites/Banderovtsi, 292
Banja Luka, 151
Bantlin Brothers Corporation, 148
Baptists, 374–376
Barabolia, Marko, 213, 216
Barbareum, 101–102
Barbizon, 207
Bardejov/Bartfeld, 6, 59, 65, 151, 170, 227, 333, 386
Bartne, 171
Bartók, Béla, 147

Basilian monasteries. *See* Monasteries
Basilian Order, 146, 212, 315
Basque Land, 2
Báthory, Sophia, 84
Bavaria, 93
Bazylovych, Ioanykii, 101
Becherov, 163, 227
Béla IV, 48, 57, 59
Belarus, 26, 47, 78, 184, 281, 308
Belarusan language, 2, 386
Belarusans/Belorussians, 3, 41, 104,
    133, 184, 185, 301, 324, 335
Belgians, 112
Belgium, 108, 386; Carpatho-Rusyns
    in, 204, 224
Belgrade, 23, 305
Belorussian Soviet Socialist Republic,
    301
Belz, Issachar Dov Rokeah, 261
Beneš, Edvard, 191, 193, 200, 292,
    293, 297–300, 322, 323, 325, 395
Bercsényi, Miklós, 90, 92
Bereg county, 48, 49, 57, 64, 81, 82,
    84, 87, 90, 123, 146, 148, 149,
    156, 165, 173, 174, 182, 183, 185,
    186, 193, 194, 203, 257, 263, 375
Bereghy, Albert, 199
Beregvar, 146, plate 29
Berehovo/Beregszász, 21, 59, 141,
    146, 149, 213, 255, 256, 266, 273,
    278, 461
Berezhany castle, 90
Berkasovo, 153
Berlin 170, 274, 278
Besida (magazine), 358
Beskyd, Antonii, 136, 138, 181, 195,
    220, 229, 231, 251, plate 42
Beskyd, Konstantyn, 220
Beskyd, Nykolai, 220, 230, 231
Beskidek Pass, 11
Beskyds (mountain range), 7, 11, 198,
    391
Bessarabia, 313
Bets, Ivan, 90
Biała River, 11, 238
Bidermann, Hermann, 49, 55
Biecz land, 67
Biennale of Lemko-Rusyn Culture
    (Krynica), 387
Bieszczady (mountain range), 11, 391

Bihar region, 55
Bil'ak, Vasil, 332
Bila Tserkva, 18, 21, 318
Bilŷ khorvatŷ, *see* White Croats
Bindas, Diura, 242–243, plate 59
Birchak, Volodomyr, 212, 265
Black Sea, 19, 21, 23, 47
Blechnarka, 15
Bliakhy, 3
Blitzkrieg, 279
Bobul's'kyi, Antonii, 207
Bodenehr, Gabriel, plate 17
Bodaki, 171
Bohemia, 111, 202, 209, 219, 263,
    265, 266, 271, 275, 346-347;
    Carpatho-Rusyns in, 224, 395
Bohemian Brethren, 77
Boian Choral Society, 206
Boii, 19
Boiko: ethnonym, 3, 5; ethnographic
    group, 366, 388
Bokshai, Emilian, 213
Bokshai, Iosyp, 207
Bolesław I Piast, 46
Bolshevik Revolution of 1917, 176,
    209, 265, 306, 312
Bolshevik Russia, 187, 227
Bolsheviks, 175, 176, 181, 187, 189,
    299
Bon'ko, Mykhailo, 284
Bondra, Peter, 346
Bonkáló, Sándor/Aleksander, 138,
    443, 452
Borkaniuk, Oleksa, 318
Borsa, 61
Borshosh-Kumiats'kyi, Iulii, 207, 213
Borshov/Borsova county, 57
Borzha/Vary castle, 57
Borzhava River, 11
Bosnia, 33, 109, 151, 167, 169, 357
Bosnia-Herzegovina, 33, 109, 167,
    169, 357
Bosporus, 33
Botar River, 19, 21, plate 4a
Boukvar' iazyka slaven'ska, 85
Bradach, Ioann, 100
Brashchaiko, Iulii, 184, 186, 217
Brashchaiko, Mykhailo, 184, 186,
    217

Bratislava/Pozsony/Pressburg, 56, 89, 108, 119, 123, 186, 220, 225, 276, 283, 284, 288, 305, 313, 315, 323, 326, 330, 383, 384
Bratislava: Greek Catholic Eparchy of, 384
Bratslav (palatinate), 183
Brazil: Carpatho-Rusyns (Lemkos) in, 236
Breshko-Breshkovskaia, Ekaterina, 265
Brest-Litovsk, Treaty of, 176
Brest, 79. *See also* Union of Brest
Brevis notitia Fundationis Theodori Koriatovits, 103
Brezhnev, Leonid, 294
Brigands/Brigandage, 65, 69–70, 90, 96
British Bible Society, 376
British Commonwealth, 198
British Isles, 19
Brittany, 19
Brno, 318, 397, 417, 418, 425
Brodii, Andrei, 201, 270, 271, 286, 288, 314, plates 43 and 67
Brovdi, Ivan, plate 7
Bronze Age, 17, plate 4a
Brusilov, Aleksei, 170
Bucharest, plate 102
Buda, 73
Budapest, 14, 26, 42, 135, 138, 148, 162, 170, 174, 182, 196, 199, 223, 273, 285–286, 305, 317, 397–399, 414–418, 421, 423, 425, 430, 439, 441, 443, 445, 447, 455, 461, 463, 469, 471, 473
Buffalo Bill, 147
Buh River, 234
Bükk culture, 15
Bukovina , 109, 121, 122, 125, 133, 163, 175, 177, 179, 212, 222, 265, 313
Bulgaria, 21, 36, 37, 169, 270
Bulgarian Empire, 31, 33, 35, 37, 39, 41
Bulgars, 28, 29, 36, 41
Bunjevač, 349
Burebista, 21
Bursa (student dormitory), 134, 237, 389, 390, plate 25

Bushtyno/Buzhchyns'kyi Handal, 259
Byzantine Ruthenian Catholic Church, 40, 82, 250, 351. *See also* Ruthenian Catholic Church: in the United States
Byzantine/East Roman Empire, 33, 35, 36, 71, 85
Byzantium, 33, 35–37, 208
Byzantsii, Iurii, 100

C

Čabiny, 383
California, 351
Calvin, John, 76, 374
Calvinism/Calvinists. *See* Reformed Calvinism/Calvinists
Canada, 1, 185, 198, 366; Carpatho-Rusyns in, 1, 204, 224, 236, 244, 246, 360, 361, 386, 390, 403–405
Čapek, Karel, 267
Caraffa, Antonio, 89
Caransebeş, 153
Carpathian Mountains, 3, 5, 7, 11, 15, 17, 21, 24, 26, 29, 31, 35, 38, 42, 45, 46, 53, 55, 57, 59, 60, 63, 65, 86, 101, 126, 185, 279, 291, 311, 336, 343
Carpathian Plainchant, 246
Carpathian Sich Organization for National Defense, 274, 277, 278
Carpathian Slavs, 29, 40
Carpathian Winter War (*Karpathenkrieg*), 170–171
Carpathian/Spish Germans, 9, 57, 381
Carpatho-Russia, 5, 177
Carpatho-Russian: ethnonym, 3, 132, 312
Carpatho-Russian Autonomous Council for National Liberation (KRASNO), 285
Carpatho-Russian Autonomous Republic, 297
Carpatho-Russian Congress (Munhall, Pa.), 350
Carpatho-Russian Eagle Society/ Obshchestvo "Karpatorusskii orel", 207

Carpatho-Russian Eastern Orthodox Church, 209, 210, 211
Carpatho-Russian Liberation Committee (Kiev), 163
Carpatho-Russian National Congress (New York City), 247
Carpatho-Russian Orthodox Greek Catholic Diocese of the Eastern Rite, 245
Carpatho-Russian Section of the International Worker's Order, 247
Carpatho-Russian Union (New York City), 269
Carpatho-Russian Workers' Party, 201
Carpatho-Rusyn: ethnonym, 3, 404, 413n.1
Carpatho-Rusyn American (magazine), 352, 354
Carpatho-Rusyn Research Center (New York, N.Y.), 354, 403
Carpatho-Rusyn Society (Pittsburgh, Pa.), 403-404
Carpatho-Rusyns beyond Carpathian Rus'. *See* Argentina; Australia; Belgium; Brazil; Canada; Croatia; Czech Republic; France; Germany; Hungary; Poland; Romania (*see* Banat); Russia; Serbia (*see* Vojvodina); Ukraine; United States; Uruguay
Carpatho-Ruthenia, 5
Carpatho-Ruthenian: ethnonym, 3
Carpatho-Ukraine, 195, 274–278, 299, 315 (name) 5, 275, 276
Carpatho-Ukrainian: ethnonym, 3
Carpi, 18, 22
Casimir III Piast, 67
Caspian Sea, 24
Catalans, 214, (language) 386
Catholic Church. *See* Greek Catholic Church; Roman Catholic Church
Caucasus Mountains, 275
Ceauçescu, Nicolae, 357
Celebacy, 86, 160, 235, 245, 247–251
Celtic peoples, 18, 26, 50
Celts, 18–19, 28, 36
Census of population: Croatia (Rusyns) 402–403; Czech Republic (Carpatho-Rusyns) 397; Czechoslovakia/Subcarpathian

Rus' (Carpatho-Rusyns) 194, 221–222, 253, (Czechs) 204, 222, 253, 266, (Germans) 253, 263, 422n.17, (Jews) 222, 253, 257, 259, 421n.11, 422n.17, (Magyars) 199, 253, 255, (Orthodox) 207, (Roma/Gypsies) 253, 264, (Romanians) 253, 264, (Slovaks) 222, 253, 264; Hungarian Kingdom (Carpatho-Rusyns) 143, (Orthodox) 165; Hungary (Carpatho-Rusyns) 397–399, (Ukrainians) 398; Poland/Lemko Region (Greek Catholics) 234, (Lemko Rusyns) 234, 391, 429n.12 and n.13, 431n.2, (Orthodox) 234, (Ukrainians) 234; Romania/Maramureş (Carpatho-Rusyns) 401, 431n.2, (Ukrainians) 430n.8; Serbia/Vojvodina (Rusyns) 403, 421n.1; Slovakia/Prešov Region (Carpatho-Rusyns) 329, 380, 384–385, 429n.1 and 2, 431n.2, plates 97, 98, (Russians) 329, 380, 429n.1, (Ukrainians) 329, 380, 385, 429n.1 and 2; Ukraine/Transcarpathia (Carpatho-Rusyns) 367–368, 431n.2; United States (Carpatho-Rusyns) 404, 430n.11
Central Powers, 169, 176
Central Russian National Council (Khust), 275–276
Central Rusyn National Council (Uzhhorod), 187, 189, 193, 196, 220, 269, plate 41
Čertižné, 126, 225
Chaloupecký, Václav, 55
Chamberlain, Neville, 271
Charlemagne, 31
Charleroi, Pensylvania, plate 60
Charles I/Károly Robert Anjou, 61, 63
Charles VI Habsburg, 92
Chepa, Steven, 405, 428
Chepets', Vasyl', 70
Chernecha Hora, 64
Chernihiv (palatinate), 183
Chmel'ová/Komlōša, 227
Chomutov, 347, 396
Chop, 266, 305
Chopei, Laslo, 140

Chornock, Orestes, 245, 246
Chornoholova, 148
Chranilović, Jovan, 242
Christian Democratic Party, 201
Christianity, 36, 37–41, 73–76, 103,
    123, 124; Eastern-rite, 2, 9, 35,
    37–41, 46, 51, 60, 67, 70–71, 76,
    82, 83, 85, 86, 99, 132, 137, 138,
    146, 160, 185, 208, 228, 235, 245,
    247–251, 315, 330, 351, 354, 373,
    374, 377; Roman-rite, 9, 35, 37,
    46, 76, 85, 86, 99, 157, 159, 161,
    245, 325, 351, 374, 377. *See also*
    Greek Catholic Church; Orthodox
    Church; Protestantism/Protestants;
    Roman Catholic Church
Chrysostom, Saint John, 85
Chuchka, Pavlo, 366
Church of St. Barbara (Vienna), 102
Church Slavonic language, 37, 104,
    132, 135, 138, 214, 215, 217, 230,
    331, 351, 372, 376, 384
Church Union, 78–86. *See also* Union
    of Brest; Union of Uzhhorod
Churchill, Winston, 301
Chynadiievo, 92, 93
Chŷrnianskii/Czyrniański, Emilian,
    134
Čičvan, 63
Cinema/Film, 147, 266, 267, 316,
    473
Cireşu/Cheresne, 347
Cities. *See* Urbanization
Cleveland, Ohio, 84, 246
Cody, William Frederick/Buffalo Bill,
    147
Cold War, 351, 352, 354
Collectivization, 309, 325, 336, 358
Columbia University, 352
Comecon, 355
Comintern. *See* Communist
    International
Commercial Academy (Mukachevo),
    256, 275
Commission for Scholarly Research
    on [Poland's] Eastern Lands, 238
Committee for the Defense of the
    Eastern Rite, 245
Committee for the Elimination of
    Racial Discrimination, 368

Committee on National Education, 388
Common Era, 19, 28, 43, 50
Common Russian (*obshcherusskii*)
    language, 212, 230; nationality,
    235
Communism: ideology and rule, 216,
    247, 316, 318, 327, 336, 341, 351,
    352, 370, 371, 373, 376, 379, 397,
    403, 411
Communist International (Comintern),
    312, 313, 347
Communist Party, 301, 305; of
    Czechoslovakia, 256, 313, 321–325
    passim, 329, 332, 356; in Poland,
    283, 312, 336; in Slovakia, 225,
    326, 330, 332; Subcarpathian
    branch of, 201, 205, 260, 294–297
    passim, 307, 312–313; of the
    Soviet Union, 310, 355, 357, 362;
    of Transcarpathian Ukraine, 294–
    295, 307–309; of Ukraine, 307,
    322, 357; of Yugoslavia, 348, 350,
    357
Confederation of Bar, 95–96
Conference on Security and
    Cooperation in Europe (CSCE), 409
Congress of People's Committees
    of Transcarpathian Ukraine
    (Mukachevo), 295–296, 299, 321,
    plate 74
Congress of Soviets, 306
Congress of the Rusyn Language,
    386–387, plate 93
Congress of the World Federation of
    Lemkos, 393
Congress of Vienna, 108
Connecticut, 156, 244, 245, 376
Conrad, bishop of Salzburg, 55
Constantine I, 33
Constantine/Cyril, Saint, 37–41, 86,
    plate 7
Constantinople, 33, 36, 47, 70, 71,
    79, 82; Ecumenical Patriarchate of,
    85, 208, 209, 211, 246, 276
Copăcele/Kopachele, 153, 347
Copper Age, 17
Cornish, 19
Cornuţel/Kornutsel, 347
Cossacks, 95, 127. *See also* Don
    Cossacks; Zaporozhian Cossacks

Costoboci, 18, 21
Council for Mutual Economic Aid, 355
Council of Czechoslovak Rusyns, 331
Council of Europe, 368, 388, 409
Council of Trent , 77
Counter-Reformation, 73, 77, 99
Cracow 14, 35, 46, 67, 69, 79, 96, 134, 233, 281, 282, 317, 387, 389, 405
Crimea, 19, 28, 365, 369
Crimean Tatars, 75
Croatia, 1, 3, 409; Carpatho-Rusyns in, 153, 361, 367, 402–403
Croats/Croatians, 28, 31, 102, 109, 119, 242, 349; in the United States, 162, 177
Crown of St. Stephen, 113, 285, 288
Csáky, Pál, 381
CSCE. *See* Conference on Security and Cooperation in Europe
Cultural Society of Rusyns in Romania, 401
Cultural Union of Ukrainian Workers–KSUT (Prešov), 327, 330, 332, 346, 359
Cum Data Fuerit (decree), 249–250
Cum Deo pro Patria et Libertate, 91
Cumans, 56-57
Curzon Line, 301
Cyril, Saint. *See* Constantine/Cyril, Saint
Cyrillic. *See* Alphabet: Cyrillic
Czarna, plate 84
Czech and Slovak Federal Republic/Czecho-Slovakia, 356, 360, 361, 379–380, 381, 382
Czech language, 77, 204, 260, 266, 271, 275, 276, 334, 422n.12
Czech Republic, 1, 35, 368, 371, 381; Carpatho-Rusyns in, 361, 395–397; Greek Catholic Exarchate of, 395
Czech Socialist Republic, 379
Czecho-Slovak state, 178, 189, 194, 275
Czecho-Slovak-Rusyn Republic, 187
Czechoslovak: ethnonym, 115, 221, 222; in Subcarpathian Rus', 253, 276, 278, 328
Czechoslovak Army Brigade/Corps, 291, 294, 304, 318, 395, plate 73

Czechoslovak Army, 182, 187, 274, 277, 278
Czechoslovak Autocephalous Orthodox Church, 326
Czechoslovak Orthodox Church, 209
Czechoslovak-Soviet Treaty (1945), 300, 301, 305
Czechoslovakia, 7, 50, 138, 191–231 passim, 253–278 passim, 298, 313, 315 321–334 passim, 366; Carpatho-Rusyns in, 346-347, 395–396
Czechs, 29, 109, 121, 177, 178, 191, 198, 200, 221, 225, 230, 298, 300, 303, 329, 332, 379, 381, 396; in Subcarpathian Rus', 202–204, 207, 253, 261, 265–267, 273, 303–304, 379, 395, 396, 422n.22; in Ukraine (Volhynia), 324; in the United States, 177
Czerteż, 17
Czudar family, 63

D

Dacia/Dacians, 18, 19, 21–22, 24
Ďačov, 100
Damaskin (Grdanička), 210
Danube River 19, 21–24, 29, 31, 35, 41, 45, 51, 53, 56, 71, 89, 94, 107, 153, 281
Danubian Slavs, 29, 31
Danubian/Carpathian Basin, 7, 42, 43, 56, 108, 119, 187
Danzig, 301
Dazhboh, 27
De Ruget family. *See* Drugeth family
Debrecen, 119, 445
Decamillis, Joseph, 84, 85, plate 13
Decebal, 21
Deladier, Pierre, 271
Demjanovics, Emil, 138
Demko, Kálmán, 138
Demko, Mykhailo, plate 43
Democratic Party of Slovakia, 323
Demokraticheskii golos (newspaper), 323
Department of Rusyn Language and Literature (Prešov), 349

Department of Ukrainian and Rusyn
  Philology (Cracow), 399
Department of Ukrainian Language
  and Literature (Prešov), 327, 383
Deportation/Resettlement of
  populations, 5, 172–173, 289, 301–
  304, 324, 335–338, 390–391, 394,
  405, 424n.9, 425n.9
Derzhavnoe samouriadovania
  menshynŷ rusynuv (Hungary), 399
Diakovo, 15, 21, plate 4a
Diet: of Galicia, 131; of the Hungarian
  Kingdom, 61, 65, 66, 73, 91,
  108, 116, 118; of Poland, 67; of
  Subcarpathian Rus'/Carpatho-
  Ukraine, 270, 275, 276; of
  Slovakia, 278, 283, 284
Dilove, 13
Djurdjevo, 153
Długie, 163
DNA, 26
Dnieper River, 41, 47, 48, 50
Dobrians'kyi, Adol'f, 120–127 passim,
  135, 138, 139, 140, 223, 229, 319,
  plate 21
Dobrians'kyi, Viktor, 120, 122
Dobrians'kyi Society/Obshchestvo
  Dobrianskago (Bratislava), 284
Dobrodîtel' prevŷshaet' bohatstvo, 124
Dobron, 309
Dolynai, Mykola, plate 43
Dolyniane, 3, plate 2
Don Cossacks, 210
Don River, 196, 210, 275
Donbas region, 303
Donets'k, 343
Donskii, Ivan, 283
Donskii, Mykhal, 283, 341
Dosifej (Vasić), 209, 210
Dovbush, Oleksa, 96
Dovhe, 90
Dózsa, György, 66
Dragomireşti, 347
Dragula, Nykolai, 296
Drahomanov, Mykhailo, 132
Dramatychnŷi kruzhok, 133
Drang nach Osten, 303
Drovniak, Epifanii, 337
Drugeth, György III, 78
Drugeth, János X, 83

Drugeth, Jean, 63
Drugeth, Philippe, 63
Drugeth family, 63, 65, 81–83
Družhno vpered (magazine), 327
Druzhtvo Rusnak, 403
Dubček, Alexander, 329, 331, 332
Dubno, 163
Duć-Fajfer, Olena, xx, 388, 389
Dudáš, Andrej, 284
Dudash, Nataliia, 402
Dudyns'kyi, Mykhaïl, 103
Dukhnovych, Aleksander, 51, 105,
  121, 124-125, 127, 132, 139, 196,
  197, 198, 215, 223, 229, 230, 317,
  319, 360, plate 22
Dukhnovych Society/Obshchestvo im.
  A. Dukhnovicha (Prešov), 229, 230,
  plate 51; (Uzhhorod), 206, 212,
  216, 284, 288, 316, plates 47, 49
Dukla/Dukl'a Pass, 11, 119, 170,
  171, 233; Battle of, 294, 321
Dukla Ukrainian Song and Dance
  Ensemble (PULS), 327, 346, 382
Dumen, 276
Dunajec River, 170
Durych, Jaroslav, 267
Dutch language, 386
Dux Ruizorum, 55, 56
Dvorčak, Viktor, 223
Dvorce, 266
Dyida, 17
Dzubay, Alexander, 157
Dzurinda, Mikuláš, 381

E

Ea Semper (decree), 245, 248–249,
  251
East Galicia, 109, 122, 134, 173, 281,
  286, 299, 303, 315, 345, 393
East Germany, 356
East Prussia, 303
East Roman Empire. *See* Byzantine/
  East Roman Empire
East Slavs, 2, 3, 5, 9, 40–41, 50, 78,
  85, 104, 122, 124, 131, 132, 133,
  135, 185, 212, 288, 298, 303, 312,
  314, 317, 321, 325, 329, 352, 354,
  359, 366, 367, 371, 407
Eastern Brethren/Skhidni braty, 376

Eastern Carpathian Offensive, 293, 294
Eastern Orthodox. *See* Orthodox
  Church/Orthodoxy
Eastern Question, 169
Eastern rite. *See* Christianity:
  Eastern-rite
Eastern Slovak Republic, 223
Eastern Slovaks (Slovjaks), 223, 334
Economic life/Economy, 12, 93–94,
  144–149, 156, 201–204, 224, 236,
  244, 258, 259, 263, 264, 286–287,
  309–310, 333, 350, 370–371, 390
Education and Schools, 78, 100–103,
  105, 116, 122–123, 125, 140–141,
  204–205, 220–221, 225, 227, 229,
  231, 234, 239, 244, 256, 259–260,
  263–264 passim, 275, 282, 284,
  317, 323, 328–329, 332, 334, 349,
  378, 383, 385, 388–389, 399, 401,
  404–405, 411, plate 96
Egán, Ede, 149
Eger, 83–84, 100, 103
Egry, Ferenc, 256
Egypt, 19, 25
Elijah, Saint, 39
Emerich, 55, 56
Emese, 43
Emigration. *See* Carpatho-Rusyns
  beyond Carpathian Rus'
Eneolithic Age, 17
England, 19, 76, 96, 154
Enlightenment, the, 100–101, 113
Enlightenment Society. *See*
  Prosvita Society; Rusyn National
  Enlightenment Society/Zaria
  Cultural Enlightenment Union
Entente powers, 167
Eolithic period, 15
Erdeli, Adalbert/Erdély, Béla, 207, 256
Estonia, 47
Esztergom, 83
Etelköz, 41
Etruscans, 19
European Congress of Subcarpathian
  Rusyns, 369
European Council, 388
European Parliament, 365
European Union, 178, 369, 381–382,
  405, 409
Evangelical Baptists. *See* Baptists

Evangelical Christians, 376
Executive Committee of Emigrant
  Ruthenians (Budapest), 199

F

Farynych, Aleksei, 230
Fedchenkov, Veniamin, 209
Fedor, Pavel S., 230, 276
Fedoronko, Joseph, 177
Fedynyshynets', Volodymyr, 378
Felvidék, 42, 200
Fentsyk, Ievhenii, 139
Fentsyk, Shtefan/Stepan, 196, 201,
  251, 269, 270, 271, 285, 286, 288,
  314
Fényes, Elek, 117, 416n. 11
Ferdinand I Habsburg, 75
Ferenc I Rákóczi, 87
Ferenc II Rákóczi, 43, 89, 91–92, plate
  14
Fiala, Václav, 267
Filevïch, Ivan A., 132
Film. *See* Cinema/Film
Finnic peoples/tribes, 47, 49, 50
Finno-Ugric peoples, 9, 117
Firtsak, Georgii, 401
Firtsak, Iulii , 135, 149
Florynka, 181, 190, 235, 337
Fogorashii-Berezhanyn, Ioann/Ivan,
  104, 105
Foltyń, František, 267
Fontański, Henryk, 388
Fourteen-Point Declaration, 175,
  417n.1
Fourth Ukrainian Front, 293, 295
Fragner, Jaroslav, 203
France, 108, 113, 129, 299;
  Carpatho-Rusyns in, 204, 224, 375
Francis I Habsburg, 108
Franconia, 92, 93
Frankish Kingdom, 55
Franko, Ivan, 132–133, 317
Frantsev, Vladimir A., 132
Frantsuk, Ivan, 375
Franz Ferdinand Habsburg, 167, 169
Franz Joseph I Habsburg, 119, 122
Free Christians, 374–377
Free Enterprise Party, 260
Freiwald, Jindřich, 203, plate 46

French Empire, 108
French language, 113, 214
French Revolution of 1789, 108, 109, 112, 113, 195
Frič, Martin, 267
Frideshovo, 93, 148
Friendship Society for Subcarpathian Rus' (Bratislava), 267
Friesland, 2, 50
Frisians, 2, 50
Friulian Mark, 55
Frýdek-Místek, 346

G

Gaganets, Iosyf, 121
Gagatko, Andrei, 201, 212, 265
Galago district (Uzhhorod), 202
Galicia, 43, 90, 95, 96, 101, 109, 121, 122, 125, 129–134 passim, 137, 147, 148, 169–173 passim, 177, 179, 184, 186, 190, 209, 212, 222, 239, 276, 313, 343, 408. *See also* East Galicia
Galicia/L'viv, Greek Catholic Archeparchy/Metropolitanate of, 101, 282
Galicia-Volhynia (Lodomeria), Kingdom of, 122
Galician Diet. *See* Diet: of Galicia
Galician Question, 190
Galician Rus', 48, 55, 78, 132, 301
Galician Russian Benevolent Society, 163
Galish-Lovachka, 19, plate 5
Gánovce, 17
Gáti, József, 256
Gaul, 50
Gdańsk, 301
Gebei, Petro, 182
Gemer county, 83, 84
General Motors Corporation, 178
Generalgouvernement, 281, 282
Gepidia/Gepid Kingdom, 24, 29
Gepids, 18
German Army, 169, 171; Wehrmacht, 291, 293–294
German Cultural Union, 263
German language, 77, 109, 113, 123, 214, 263

German National Council (Khust), 263
German Party, 263, 277
Germanic peoples, 9, 22–24, 26, 28, 29, 33, 36, 45, 50, 57, 60, 303
Germans, 9, 117, 230, 270–271, 335, 336; in Czechoslovakia, 191, 271; in Habsburg Austria, 102; in the Hungarian Kingdom, 57, 59, 422n.17; in the Prešov Region, 7, 374; in Subcarpathian Rus' (*Sasy, Shvabŷ*), 6, 7, 93, 94, 201, 253, 263, 373, (deported from) 311. *See also* Austro-Germans; Carpathian Germans; Spish Germans
Germany, xx, 35, 55, 148, 154, 167, 169–171 passim, 176, 200, 291, 300, 301, 303, 311, 336, 337, 365, 387. *See also* East Germany; Nazi Germany; West Germany
Gerovskii, Aleksei, 163, 251, 269
Gerovskii, Georgii, 163
Gesta Hungarorum, 43, 45
Gestapo, 283
Getae, 18
Gładysz family, 69
Gładyszów, 15
Glagolitic. *See* Alphabet
Gočár, Josef, 203
Goidych, Pavel, 227–229, 283, 284, 326, 330, plate 52
Golden Bull, 61
Good Soldier Švejk, The, 174
Gorazd (Matej Pavlik), 209
Gorbachev, Mikhail S., 310, 355–358 passim, 362, 393, 394
Gorlice (city), 6, 134, 171, 172, 237, 322, 387, 389; (district), 95, 233, 238; Battle of, 171, 173
Görög katholikus szemle (newspaper), 140
Gorzów Wielkopolski, 388
Goths, 23
Gottwald, Klement, 323, 325, 395
Grab, 163
Grabar, Emilian, 126
Grabar, Igor, 126
Grand Duchy of Lithuania. *See* Lithuania
Graz, 173, plate 38

Great Britain, 113, 167, 169, 187, 271, 276, 279, 292, 299, 301
Great Famine/Holodomor, 307
Great Poland/Wielkopolska, 46
Great Russians, 104, 222. *See also* Russians
Greater Germany, 281. *See also* Nazi Germany
Greater Moravia/Moravian Empire, 31, 33, 35–37, 40, 41, 45
Greater Ukraine/*Soborna Ukraïna*, 184, 185, 274
Greece, 21, 31, 35, 37, 163, 169
Greek Catholic Church/Greek Catholicism, 2, 9, 82, 92, 100, 120, 134, 138, 140, 144, 157, 160–161, 195, 207, 211–212, 216, 228–229, 234, 236, 241, 245–251, 255, 258, 273, 284, 315–316, 325–326, 328–329, 334, 338–339, 348, 371–373, 375, 377, 384, 397. *See also* Byzantine Ruthenian Catholic Church; Galicia/L'viv, Greek Catholic Eparchy/Metropolitanate of; Czech Republic, Greek Catholic Eparchate of; Kyiv-Halych, Ukrainian Greek Catholic Major Archdiocese of; Hajdúdorog, Greek Catholic Eparchy of; Križevci, Eparchy of; Lemko Apostolic Administration; Mukachevo, Greek Catholic Eparchy of; Parma, Greek Catholic Eparchy of; Passaic, Greek Catholic Eparchy of; Pittsburgh, Greek Catholic Exarchate/Eparchy of; Prešov, Greek Catholic Eparchy of; Przemyśl, Greek Catholic Eparchy of; Uniate Church/Uniates; Van Nuys, Greek Catholic Eparchy of
Greek Catholic Union (Sojedinenije) of Rusyn Brotherhoods, 158, 162, 177, 178, 244, 352, plate 61
Greek language, 35, 37, 214
Greeks, 19, 38, 39, 154
Green Mountains, 11
Gregorian: calendar, 85, 86, 174, 235; mass, 85
Gregorian, Guilbrandt, plate 29
Grendzha-Dons'kyi, Vasyl', 207, 213

Grillparzer, Franz, 117
Grybów, 233
Gulag, 289, 309, 315, 318, 336, 346, 376, plate 71
Gulf of Finland, 47
György II Rákóczi, 87
Györke, István, 376
Gypsies. *See* Roma/Gypsies

H

Habsburg Austria, 87–92 passim, 96, 108, 113. *See also* Habsburg Empire
Habsburg dynasty, 75, 91, 97–99, 107–109, 111, 119, 179
Habsburg Empire xviii, 91, 94, 95, 97, 99, 104, 111, 120, 121, 127, 132, 136, 161, 173, 175, 177, 179, 190, 191, 194, 257
Habsburg-Lorraine dynasty, 107
Habura, 225
Hacha, Emil, 395
Hadrian II, pope, 37
Haidamaks, 95
Hajdúdorog, Greek Catholic Eparchy of, 139, 241, 398
Halle an der Saale, xx
Halstatt culture, 18
Hamilton, Ontario, 236, 246
Hańczowa, 15
Hangya Cooperative Society (Uzhhorod), 286, 288
Hann, Christopher, xx
Haraida, Ivan, 287
Harvard University, 50, 114
Hašek, Jaroslav, 174
Hasidim, 9, 257–261 passim
Hattinger, Gábor, 398, 474
Havel, Václav, 356, 380
Hazelton, Pennsylvania, 156
Hebrew language, 37, 214, 260
Helgi/Oleg, 50
Hellenic culture, 35
Henlein, Konrad, 263, 269
Heraclius, 31
Herder, Johann Gottfried von, 113, 117, 214
Heruls, 24
Highlands Program, 149

Hildesheim Chronicle, 55
Hirka, Ján, 331, 384
Historia Carpato-Ruthenorum, 104
Historical memory and mythology,
    24–26, 40, 42–45, 49–51, 55–56,
    64–65, 145–147, 299–300, 312,
    314, 317–319, 366–367, 396, 407–
    408, 414n.6
Hitler, Adolf, 251, 263, 270–271, 277–
    283 passim, 289, 291, 292, 299
Hladick, Victor, 177, 246
Hlas východu (newspaper), 266
Hlinka, Andrej, 224
Hnatink, Volodymyr, 133
Hodermarskyi, Iosyf 84
Hodinka, Antal/Hodynka, Antonii, 83,
    137
Hoffman, Eduard, 147
Hokky, Károly, 256
Hollósy, Simon, 146
Holmgård, 47, 48
Holocaust, 289, 311, 335
Holodomor/Great Famine, 307
Holos Rusyna, 385
Holovatii, Fedor, 65
Holy Mount Athos. *See* Athos
Holy Roman Empire, 91, 107, 108
Holzhandels Corporation, 148
Home Army/Armia Krajowa, 283, 292
Homer, 25
Homestead, Pennsylvania, 156, 177
Honfoglalás, 42
Honveds/*Honvédség*. *See* Hungarian
    National Guard
Hopko, Vasyl', 330–331
Horbal, Bogdan xx
Hořec, Jaromír, 396
Horiany, 78
Hornád River, 17
Horniak, Adal'bert/Geiza, 283
Hornïtsa/Highland, 153, 390
Horodyshche (hill-forts), 17, 57
Horoshchak, Iaroslav (Iaroslav
    Hunka), 339–340
Horthy, Miklós, 286, plate 69
Horvát, István, 25
Hötzendorf, Conrad von, 170
Hrabar, Emanuïl, 139
Hrabar, Konstantyn, 195, 217, 270,
    plate 42

*Hramatika bachvan'sko-ruskei
    beshedi*, 243
Hroerkr/Riuryk, 50
Hromosiak, Nykolai, 235
Hrushevs'kyi, Mykhailo, 55
Hrushovo, 71, 81
Hryb, Ivan, plate 93
Humenné, 6, 63, 65, 78, 148, 170,
    174, 224, 238, 333, plate 37
*Humillium promemoria de ortu,
    progressu et in Hungaria incolatu
    gentis Ruthenicae*, 103
Hungarian Army, 221, 278, 288,
    293–294
Hungarian Diet. *See* Diet: of the
    Hungarian Kingdom
Hungarian Kingdom, 43, 53–66, 82,
    85, 89, 105–118 passim, 122, 125,
    133, 134, 135, 136–149 passim,
    158, 161, 174, 177, 179, 208, 221,
    223, 245, 246
Hungarian language, 109,116, 119,
    123, 137–141 passim, 145, 174,
    216, 220, 256, 260, 261, 285, 312,
    419n.17
Hungarian National Guard
    (*Honvédség*), 119, 144, 169, 171
Hungarian National Party, 256
Hungarian National Theater
    (Budapest), 147
Hungarian plain, 7, 153, 154, 156,
    236
Hungarian Revolution of 1848–1849.
    See Revolution of 1848
Hungarian Rus', 122, 133, 209
Hungarian Soviet Republic, 187, 221
Hungarian Theater (Mukachevo), plate
    62
Hungarians: residents of the
    Hungarian Kingdom, 111, 114,
    115, 118, 313, 413n.4. *See also*
    Magyars
Hungary, 1, 9, 42, 56, 139, 178, 179,
    182, 187, 189-190, 199-200, 210,
    216, 228, 241-242, 255, 257, 270,
    273, 274, 278, 281, 285-289, 291,
    299, 304, 310, 311, 355, 356, 362,
    366, 368, 371, 375, 397–401, 409,
    411, 413n.4 (*see also* Austria-
    Hungary); Carpatho-Rusyns in

post-Trianon, 190, 241–242, 361, 367, 386, 387, 393, 397–401
Hunka, Iaroslav, 339
Hunnic Empire, 24
Huns, 22, 23–24, 28
Hunyadi, János, 43
Hus, Jan, 76
Husák, Gustav, 332
Hutsul: ethnonym, 3, 5; ethnographic group, 5, 182, 186, 366, 388
Hutsul region, 182, 186
Hutsul Republic, 181, 186–187

I

Iablochyn monastery, 163
Iablunets'/Tatar Pass, 11, 148
Iabur, Vasyl', 383
Ianyts'kyi, Aleksander, 122
Iar' (magazine), 284
Iarylo, 27
Iasynia 148, 181, 186
Iazychiie (macaronic jargon), 135, 215
Iceland, 47
Identity question. *See* Nationality/ Identity question
Igor, 50
Ihnatkov, Iurii, 139
Illés-Illyasevits, József/Illeish-Illiashevych, Iosyf, 137, 138
Illinois, 156, 244
Il'nytsia, plate 96
Il'nyts'kyi, Aleksander, 273, 286
Immigration. *See* Carpatho-Rusyns beyond Carpathian Rus'
Industry/Industrialization, 18–19, 21, 93–94, 114, 147–149, 154, 201–202, 310, 333, 334, 350, 370, 411
Ingvar/Igor, 50
Initiative Group of Czecho-Slovakia's Rusyn-Ukrainians for Reconstruction/Initsiatyvna hrupa rusyniv-ukraïntsiv ChSSR za perebudovu (Prešov), 359
Innsbruck, 139
Institute for Publishing Textbooks (Vojvodina), 349
Institute for Rusyn Language and Culture (Prešov), 383

Institute for the Culture of Vojvodina's Rusyns (Novi Sad), 402
International Socialist Party, 260
Ireland, 154
Ireland, John, 159–160
Irinej (Cirić), 210
Irish, 19, 40, 159, 214
Irliava, 309
Iron Age, 18
Iron Curtain, 358, 382
Irredentism, 190, 199–200, 251, 273
Irshava 202, 259
Islam, 70–71
Isonso River, 171
Israel, 260, 261
Istanbul, 85
Italians, 109, 154
Italy, 63, 109, 119, 167, 169, 171, 271, 279
Iurchakevych, Mykhaïl, 181
Iushchenko, Viktor, 368, 389
Ivano-Frankivs'k (city), 394; (oblast), 343, 393
Ivanov, Nikolai, 170
Iwonicz-Zdrój, 147
Iza, 209, 210
Izby, 95

J

Jagiellonian dynasty, 77, 78
Jagiełłonian University, 134, 282
Jakubany, 100
Jakusics, György, 83
Janowski, Maciej, xx
Japan, 167
Jarabina, 346
Jaśliska, 70
Jasło, (city), 6, 134; (district), 233, 238; (land), 67
Jászi, Oszkár, 182
Jaworzno, 337, 426n.6
Jazyges, 22
Jehovah's Witnesses, 374–376
Jelačić, Josip, 119
Jerusalem, 38
Jesuit Order (Society of Jesus)/ Jesuits, 77, 78, 79, 84, 89, 99, 102
Jesus Christ, 258

Jewish: ethnonym and religion, 222, 259, 421n.11
Jewish Party, 261
Jews, 9, 99, 109, 134, 144, 154, 191, 222, 326, 335, 388, 422n.17; in the Prešov Region, 284, (resettled from) 425n.9; in Subcarpathian Rus', 6, 201, 202, 204, 253, 255, 257–263, (deported) 289, 311, 421n.11 and 12, plate 72
Jogaila, 78
John the Baptist, Saint, 39
Joseph I Habsburg, 91
Joseph II Habsburg, 97, 99, 108, 109
Josip (Cvijević), 210
Julian Calendar, 79, 85, 179
Julius Caesar, 50

K

Kabaliuk, Aleksei, 165, 210, 211
Kachkovs'kyi Society/Obshchestvo im. M. Kachkovskoho, 133, 134, 237, plate 26
Kachmarchŷk, Iaroslav, 190, plate 39
Kadlec, Karel, 298, 300
Kakania, 111
Kalinov, plate 73
Kamienka, 346
Kamins'kyi, Iosyf, 286
Kanko castle, 57
Karabelesh, Andrii, 207, 213
Karaman, Vasilii/Vasyl', 276, 285
Karchmarchŷk, Iaroslav, 235
Karl I Habsburg, 179
Karlowitz/Karlovci, Treaty of, 89
Károlyi, Mihály, 179, 182, 186, 187
Karpathenkrieg, 170
Karpatskaia pravda (newspaper), 313
Karpatskii krai (journal), 207, 213
Karpatskii sviet (journal), 207, 213
Kashubia, 2
Käsmark, 57
Katekhisis dlia naouki Ouhorouskim liudem, 85, plate 13
Kazakhstan, 29
Kenez, 59
Kercha, Igor, 378
Kerestur. See Ruski Kerestur
Kežmarok/Käsmark, 57

Khazar Kaganate/Khazaria, 47
Kherson (oblast), 343
Khlīb dushy, 124
Khomiak, Miroslava, 388
Khrapovitskii, Antonii, 209
Khrushchev, Nikita, 310, 322
Khust, 185, 203, 210, 273, 275–278, 294, 297, 372, 373, plate 46
Khŷliak, Dmytrii, 235
Khŷliak, Vladymir, 96, 135
Kielce, 283
Kiev (city), 48, 50, 179, 317, 328, 362, 363, 365, 366, 368, 393, 405; (palatinate), 183
Kievan Rus', 33, 40–41, 46, 48–51, 56, 59, 64, 78, 132, 212
Kingdom of Two Sicilies, 63
Kipchaks/Polovtsians, 56
Kiresh/Kress culture, 17
Kitchener, Ontario, 404
Klementinum, 395
Kliurcharky, 375
Klochurak, Stepan, 182, 186
Klotilda Corporation, 148, 202, plate 30
Klympush, Dmytro, 274
Knyzhytsia chytalnaia dlia nachynaiushchykh, 105
Koblyna, 144
Kobylets'ka Poliana, 376
Kochish, Evgenii, 243
Kochish, Mikola, 349
Kohut, Petro 345, 393, 394, plate 85
Kokovs'kyi, Frants, 237
Kollár, Adam František, 103
Kolomatskii, Vladimir, 203
Komańcza/Komancha, 181
Komarów, 169
Komlóska 397, 398, 399
Konstanz, 148
Kontratovych, Irynei, 273, 315
Kopcha, Andrei, 358, 388, plate 88
Kopystians'kyi, Mykhail, 79
Koriatovych, Fedor, 51, 64, 103–104, plate 10
Korláth, Endre, 256
Korolevo 15, 57
Košice (city), 173, 223, 333, 383; (župa/district), 220
Košice, Greek Catholic Eparchy of, 384

Kosovo, 348, 357
Kossei, Pavlu, plate 43
Kossuth, Lajos, 117, 118, 119
Kostel'nik, Havriïl/Gabor, 154, 243, 315, 349, plate 32
Kotsak, Arsenii, 104
Kotsylovs'kyi, Iosafat, 235
Kotsylovskii, Petro, 131
Kovner Palace, 289
KOVO, 245
Kozma, Miklós, 286, 423
Krafcik, Patricia A., xx, 352
Krainiak, Frantishek, 384
Krainiaky, 3
Kralík, František, 266
Kralyts'kyi, Anatolii, 139
Krasne Pole, Battle of, 278
Krasný Brod/Krasnŷi Brid, 71, 170, 333. *See also* Monasteries: at Krasnŷi Brid
Krasovs'kyi, Ivan, 345, 394, plate 85
Kravchuk, Leonid, 363
Krempna, 171
Križevci, Greek Catholic Eparchy of, 348
Krosno (city), 6; (district), 233, 236, 238
Krupka, František, 203, plate 45
Krynica, 282, 345, 387, plate 56
Krynica-Zdrój, 147, 337
KSUT. *See* Cultural Union of Ukrainian Workers
Kuba, Ludvík, 267
Kubiiovych, Volodymyr, 282
Kuchma, Leonid, 367
Kucura, 95, 153, 348
Kugel, Hayim/Chaim, 260, 261
Kula, 153
Kulaks, 309, 319
Kulturne tovarystvo Rusyniv Romaniï, 401
Kul'turnyi soiuz ukraïns'kykh trudiashchykh Chekhoslovachchyny. *See* Cultural Union of Ukrainian Workers
Kun, Béla, 187, 221, 260
Kupalo, 27, 39
Kurtiak, Ivan, 201
Kurucz, 81, 87, 89, 91
Kurylovych, Volodymyr, 131

Kushko, Nadiya, xx
Kushtanovytsia culture, 18
Kutka, Ioann, 101
Kutka-Kutkafalvy, Miklós/Nykolai, 138
Kvasovo, 57
Kychera Song and Dance Ensemble, 387
Kyiv-Halych, Ukrainian Greek Catholic Major Archdiocese of, 372
Kymak, Viktor, 139
Kyzak, Ivan, 230

L

La Tène culture, 19
Labanc, 81
Laborec River, 11
Laborets'/Loborc, 45, 51
Lada, 27
Ladomirová, 209. *See also* Monasteries: at Ladomirová
Lamprechtsas, 59
Langdorf, 59
Language question, 109, 124–125, 131, 135, 184, 212–217, 229–230, 287–288, 313, 386–387, 399
Latin language, 35, 37, 109, 116, 214, 215
Latin rite. *See* Christianity: Roman rite
Latinization, 35, 37, 109, 116, 214, 215, 236, 325
Latorica Company, 203
Latorytsia River, 11, 263
Latynyka, 174
Lavrincová, Magdalena, 308
Lavrivskii/Lawrowski, Iuliian, 134
Lazho, Iurko, 220, 227
League for the Liberation of Carpatho-Russia (New York City), 177
League of Nations, 199
Lechfeld, Battle of , 45
Legnica, 337, 358, 387
Leib, Michael, 146
Lemberg. *See* L'viv/Lemberg
Lemkivska storinka, 341
Lemko (newspaper), 135, plate 27
Lemko: ethnonym, 3, 5, 115, 135, 238, 367, 404

Lemko Apostolic Administration, 238, 239, 282, 283, 338
Lemko Association/Lemko/ Lemkovskii soiuz: in Canada, 404; in Poland, 237, 239, 282; in the United States, 246–247, 293, 352
Lemko Commission (L'viv), 237
Lemko Cultural and Enlightenment Society (Montevideo), 236
Lemko Museum (Monastyrys'ka), 394
Lemko Region Affairs Committee (Warsaw), 239
Lemko Region, 6–7, 11, 12, 15, 17, 19, 29, 37, 46, 65, 67–70, 79, 81, 95–96, 101–102, 131–134, 137, 147, 161, 170–172, 179, 181, 187, 189, 190, 198, 208, 216, 233–239, 244, 246, 281–283, 293, 301–303, 335–342, 345, 387–391, 395, 407, plates 1, 36
Lemko Republic, 181, 190, 235
Lemko-Rusyn language. *See* Rusyn language
Lemko-Rusyn Philology Program (Cracow), 389
Lemko Rusyns/Lemkos, 5, 6, 29, 69, 70, 95–96, 115, 129, 131–134, 181, 185, 189, 190, 198, 366, 408; deported, 172–173, 301–303, 336–338, 424n.9, plates 76, 81; in Bosnia, 151; in Canada, 236, 244, 246, 390; in Nazi Germany, 281–283; in Poland, 216, 233–239, 301–303, 335–342, (deported from) 301–303 and 336, (resettled within) 337, 338, 358, 382, 387–391, 426n.6, 429n.12 and n.13; in South America, 236; in Ukraine, 1, 343–345, 390, 393–395; in the United States, 161, 162, 177, 185, 236, 246–247, 352, 430n.11
Lemko Society/Stovaryshŷnia Lemkiv (Legnica), 387–390, plate 88
Lemko Worker's and Peasant's Committee (Gorlice), 322
Lemkovyna, 238, 341, 345, 393
Lemkovyna Choir, 345
Lenin, Vladimir, plate 94
Leningrad, 127, 317
Leopold I Habsburg, 84

Lesko, 233, 234
Leszczycki, Stanisław, 239
Leszczyny, 70
Leutschau. *See* Levoče
Lev Danylovych
Levente (youth organization), 288
Levoča/Leutschau, 57
Lewis, Bernard, 25
Lex Apponyi, 141
Liberal Party, 136
Liberal/Neolog Jews, 257
Library of Congress, xx
Liebscher, Adolf , 203
Limanowa, 170
Lintur, Petro, 297
Lipovljani, 151
Liszt, Franz, 147
Literature (belles lettres), 135, 207, 230, 237–238, 267
Lithuania: Grand Duchy of, 64, 78, 79; Soviet Socialist Republic, 301. *See also* Poland-Lithuania/Polish-Lithuanian Commonwealth
Lithuanians, 78, 301, 335
Little Entente, 200, 210
Little Poland/Małopolska, 46
Little Russians (*Malorosy*), 104, 183, 222, 298, 367
Loborc. *See* Laborets'
Lodii, Petro, 103
Lodomeria. *See* Galicia-Volhynia (Lodomeria), Kingdom of
Lokota, Ivan, 313, 318
Łom Operation, 274
Lombardy-Venetia, 109
London, 118, 147, 289, 292–293, 297, 299
Longobards, 24
Łosie, 147, plate 57
Louis XIV Bourbon, 91
Louis/Lajos of Anjou, 63
Lower Silesia, 337, 387, 390, 391
Lubin, 337
Lublin, 78, 335
Lubuskie, 387, 390, 391
Luchkai, Mykhaïl, 104
Ługi, 390
Lugoj, 153, 347
Luhans'k, 343
Lupkov/Łupków Pass, 148, 170

Lusatia, 29, 35
Lusatian culture, 18
Lusatian Sorbs, 29
Luther, Martin, 76–77, 373
Lutheranism/Evangelical Lutherans, 9, 76–77, 99, 100, 373–374
Luxembourg, House of, 63
Luxemburgisch language, 214
Lyteraturna nedīlia (journal), 287
L'viv/Lemberg/Lwów (city), 43, 121, 131, 133, 134, 148, 170, 171, 179, 315, 345, plate 100
L'viv (oblast), 343

M

Macartney, Carlisle A., 136, 257
Macedonia 357
Macedonian language, 38
Mach, Šaňo, 283
Magocsi, Paul Robert, xix, 198, 366
Magyar Athletic Club (Uzhhorod), 256
Magyarization, 126, 136–143 passim, 154, 163, 174, 220, 223, 227, 241, 384, 397, 398
Magyarones, 228, 410
Magyars, 9, 41–46, 90, 91, 102, 105, 109, 111, 116–117, 119, 124, 135, 138, 140, 141, 146, 174, 185, 190, 222, 413n.4; in Slovakia, 191, 273, 381, (resettled from) 425n.9; in Subcarpathian Rus'/Transcarpathia, 6, 7, 13, 94, 191, 199–200, 201, 202, 253, 255–257, 271, 273, 286, (deported from) 311, 362, 373–376; in the United States, 154, 156, 157, 162
Mainz, 92
Makovytsia, 63, 81
Maksimenko, Vitalii, 227
Maksym (Sandovych), Saint, 172
Mala Kopania, 21, plates 3 and 46
Malcov, 100, 122
Małopolska, 46
Malorosy. See Little Russians
Malynovs'kyi, Oleksander, 282
Mamatey, Victor S., 177
Manailo, Fedor, 207
Manitoba, 246
Mányoki, Adam, plate 14

Maramorosh/Máramaros county, 57, 81, 82, 84, 90, 92, 99, 100, 123, 148, 151, 165, 173, 182, 185, 186, 187, 190, 193, 194, 220, 241, 257, 346, 347
Maramorosh-Sighet: (city) *see* Sighet; (trials), 165, 210
Maramureş Region, 6, 181, 216, 241, 281, 305, 347-348, 401
Marchia Ruthenorum, 55, 56
Maria Theresa, 97–100 passim, 102, 103, 108
Máriapócs, 94, 241
Markus, Vasyl, 295, 296
Markush, Aleksander, 207
Marxists, 145
Masaryk, Tomáš Garrigue, 193, 194, 221, 298, 395, 396
Mastsiukh, Vasyl', 238
Matica slovenská. *See* Slovak Cultural/National Foundation
Matola/Rudolf, 377
Matsyns'kyi, Ivan, 332
Matthias/Mátyás Corvinus, 65
Max Planck Institute, xx
Mazovia, 46
McCain, John, 368
Mečiar, Vladimír, 381, 405, 429
Mediterranean Sea, 19
Medzilaborce, 171, 224, 225, 294, 333, 360, 361, 412
Mehmed II, 71
Mekhlis, Lev, 294
Methodius, Saint, 37–41, 86, plate 7
Metternich, Prince Clemens von, 108
Mezník, Jaroslav, 270
Michalovce (city), 333; Orthodox Eparchy of, 326
Michalów, 390
Middle Ages, 35, 76, 103, 107, 109, 148, 359
Middle Atlantic states, 156
Middle East, 21, 47, 167
Mid-European Union, 178
Międzybrodzie, 17
Mieszko I Piast, 46
Miklósy, István, 174
Mikluševci, 153, 348, 402
Milošević, Slobodan, 401, 402

Miloslavskii, Petr, 265
Minneapolis, Minnesota, 160, plate 35b
Minorites (monastic order), 101
Minsk, 260
Mohács, Battle of, 73
Moisiuk, Ivan, 198
Mojmír I , 35
Mokryi, Volodymyr, 366
Molchan, Mykhaïl, 139
Moldavia, 63, 71
Molotov–Ribbentrop Pact, 279, 282
Monasteries, 99, 100, 163; at Hrushovo (St. Michael the Archangel) 71, 81; at Krasnŷi Brid (Descent of the Holy Spirit) 64, 71, 81, 104, 170; at Ladomirová (St. Job) 227; on Mount Athos, 163, 209; at Mukachevo (St. Nicholas) 64, 71, 104, plate 12; at Máriapócs (St. Basil the Great) 94, 241; at Pochaïv (St. Job) 163, 209, 227; at Uglia, 71
Monastyrys'ka, 390, 394
Mondok, Ivan, 313
Mondych, Olena Shinali, 207
Mongolo-Tatar invasion, 56
Monk's Hill, 64, 103, plate 12
Montenegro, 169, 357, 401
Morava River, 35
Moravia, 202, 209, 219, 263, 265, 266, 271, 275; Carpatho-Rusyns in, 224, 333, 346–347, 395. See also Greater Moravia
Moravians, 41
Morocco, 19
Moscow, 126, 211, 246, 282, 297, 299, 306–310 passim, 312, 317, 331, 355, 362, 376
Moscow Patriarchate. See Russian Orthodox Church—Moscow Patriarchate
Moskali (Russians), 126, 127
Mount Athos. See Athos, The Holy Mount
Múcsony, 397, 398, 399
Mudri, Mikhailo, 242
Muhi, 57
Mukachevo/Munkács, xix, 141, 146–149 passim, 182, 199, 202,
203, 255, 256, 259, 260, 261, 263, 264, 273, 275, 278, 289, 295-297 passim, 311, 315, 369, 375, 376, plates 7, 62, 74
Mukachevo castle, 43, 87, 89, 90, 146, plates 9, 17
Mukachevo, Eparchy of, 40, 83; Greek Catholic/Uniate Eparchy of, 83, 85, 100, 101, 103, 137, 138, 139, 149, 199, 211, 228, 315, 372, plates 18-20; Orthodox Eparchy of, 71, 316
Mukachevo Commercial Academy, 256, 275
Mukachevo-Chynadiievo estate, 92, 93
Mukachevo-Prešov, Carpatho-Russian Eparchy of, 210–211
Munhall, Pennsylvania, 350–351, plates 61, 101
Munich, 274
Munich Crisis/Pact, 251, 263, 270–271, 273, 279, 283, 292, 294, 299, 305, 323, 395
Munkach/Munkács/Munkatsch. See Mukachevo
Munkácsy, Mihály, 146
Muscophiles, 283
Muscovy, Grand Duchy/Tsardom of , 64, 78–79
Museum of Lemko Culture (Zyndranowa), 387
Museum of Rusyn Culture (Prešov), 383
Museum of the Lemko Region (Sanok) 237
Museum of Ukrainian Culture (Svidník), 327, 346, 383
Mushynka, Mykola, 332, 366
Music, 85, 147, 195–198, 206, 237, 246, 266, 319, 345
Musil, Robert, 111
Mussolini, Benito, 271, 279
Muszyna, 69
Muszyna Estate, 69
Myshanych, Oleksa, 366
Mŷshkovskii, Tyt, 134
Mythology. See Historical memory and mythology
Mytrak, Aleksander, 125, 139

N

Nadezhdin, Nikolai, 105
Nădlac/Velykŷi Lak, 153
Nagybánya School of Painting, 146
Nagyoroszi, 56
Nagyszőllős. *See* Sevliush
Napoleon Bonaparte, 108, 113
Narodna pedagogika, 124
Narodnaia gazeta (newspaper), 220
Narodni kalendar, 349
Narodnŷ novynkŷ (newspaper), 359,
    411
Narodnŷi Dom, 133
Nash Lemko (newspaper), 237
Nashe slovo (newspaper), 341
National anthems/hymns, 124, 195–
    198, 297, 319
National Czechoslovak Tourist Club,
    267
National Hockey League, 346
Nationalism, 109, 111–115, 126, 175,
    195
Nationality/Identity question, 49,
    113–114; among Carpatho-Rusyns,
    13, 51, 104–105, 114, 131–134,
    143, 157, 184–185, 212–213, 225,
    229, 235, 282, 284, 295, 312–314,
    321, 326–329, 336, 341, 345–348,
    354, 358–359, 366–369, 371–372,
    380, 388, 394, 397, 407–410, plate
    95 (in the United States) 161–162,
    246, 351–352, 403; among Jews,
    259; among Magyars, 116–117,
    135; among Slovaks, 223; among
    Ukrainians, 184, 367; among
    Vojvodinian Rusyns, 243, 348–350,
    402–403. *See also* Magyarization;
    Slovakization; Ukrainianization
Nauka (newspaper), 139, 140, 185
Naukovŷi zbornyk (journal), 185, 206
Nawojowski family, 69
Nazi Germany, 9, 216, 239, 263, 270–
    271, 273, 274, 278-284 passim,
    288, 292, 293, 299, 301, 311, 315,
    337, 389, 395
Nečas, Jaromír, 266
Nedīlia/Negyelya (newspaper), 140,
    174, 213
Nedzel'skii, Evgenii, 265

Neisse River, 301, 303
Nelipyno, plate 49
Němec, František, 294
Neolithic period, 15
Neolog Jews, 9, 257
Neo-Slavism, 132
Netherlands, 50
Neumann, Johann Balthazar, 94
Neumann, Stanislav, 267
Nevyts'ka, Iryna, 230
Nevyts'ke castle, 18, 57, plate 9
Nevyts'kyi, Emilian, 184, 185, 417n.5
New Jersey, 353
New Rome, 36
New Rusyn Times, The (magazine), 404
New York (city), xx, 177, 247, 269;
    (state), 156, 244, 246, 353
New York Public Library, xx
Nialab castle, 57
Niaradii, Dionisii, 228
Nicholas I Romanov, 119, 126
Nicholas II Romanov, 163, 171
Nieznajowa, 171
Nikola Šuhaj loupežník (novel), 267
Niš, 209
NKVD, 295
Nobility, 203; in Hungary, 53, 59–66,
    90–92 passim, 116, 287; in Poland,
    67–70, 95
Normanists, 49–50
Norsemen, 47
North America 1, 37, 47, 50, 83, 100,
    145, 159, 161, 163, 184, 198, 241,
    243, 245–248, 251, 350, 351, 361,
    366, 367, 378, 393, 403–405
North Brattleford, Saskatchewan, 404
North Sea, 19, 50
Norwegians, 40
Nova dumka (journal), 349
Nova Subocka, 151
Nova svoboda (newspaper), 277
Novak, Shtefan/István, 228
Nove zhyttia (newspaper), 327, 330
Novgorod, 47–48
Novi Sad, 242, 349, 401
Novo-Klynovo, 19
Novoe vremia (newspaper), 284
Nowy Sącz (city), 6, 134, 172;
    (district), 233, 238
Nowy Targ (district), 181, 233, 238

Nyíregyháza, 241, 399, 401, 405
Nyírség culture, 17
Nykyfor (Epifanii Drovniak), 337, plate 83
Nyzhnia Hrabivnytsia, 93
Nyzhnyi Verets'kyi, 174

O

Ob'iednannia Lemkiv v Pol'shchi, 389
Oblastna rada. *See* Transcarpathian Regional Assembly
obshcherusskii. See Common Russian language/nationality
Obshchestvo "Karpatorusskii orel", 207
Obshchestvo im. A. Dukhnovicha. *See* Dukhnovych Society
Oder River, 301, 303
Oder-Neisse Line, 303, 336
Odoacer, 50–51
Odrekhivs'kyi, Vasyl, 345
Odrekhivs'kyi, Volodymyr, 345
Odrzechowa, 134
Ohio, 156, 244, 246, 351
Olaf I Tryggvason, 40
Olashyn, Vasyl', plate 10
Olbracht, Ivan (Kamil Zeman), 258
Old Ruthenians (*starorusyny*), 131–135 passim, 139, 184, 237, 282
Olearov, Nikolai, 243
Oleg, 50
Ol'shavs'kyi, Mykhaïl Manuïl, 100
Ol'shavs'kyi, Symeon, 100
Ondava River, 11
Ongvar/Ungohrad/Ungvar, 45
Onogurs, 18, 29, 41
Ontario, 236, 246, 404
Opryshky. See Brigands/Brigandage
Optanty, 324, 345–346, 425n.9
Oradea, Greek Catholic Eparchy of, 139
Orange Revolution, 368, 369
Organization of Rusyns in Hungary/ Organizatsiia Rusynov v Madiarsku, 398
Organization of Ukrainian Nationalists (OUN), 235, 238, 274, 277, 292
Orlai, Ivan S., 103, 105
Orlov, 333

Orosvygovs'kyi, Mykhail, 82
Oroszfalva/Oroszvár, 56
Orthodox Church/Orthodoxy, 9, 73, 76, 79, 81–82, 84, 95, 96, 99–100, 132, 159, 161, 163, 165, 172, 207–211, 216, 227–228, 236–237, 245–246, 258, 265, 276, 297, 315, 325–326, 330, 338, 348, 372, 373, 377. *See also* American Carpatho-Russian Orthodox Greek Catholic Diocese; Carpatho-Russian Eastern Orthodox Church; Constantinople, Ecumenical Patriarchate of; Czechoslovak (Autocephalous) Orthodox Church; Michalovce, Orthodox Eparchy of; Mukachevo, Orthodox Eparchy of; Orthodox Church in America; Polish Autocephalous Orthodox Church; Prešov, Orthodox Eparchy of; Przemyśl, Orthodox Eparchy of; Russian Orthodox Church Abroad/in Exile; Russian Orthodox Church—Moscow Patriarchate; Russian Orthodox Eparchy of the Aleutian Islands and Alaska/in North America; Serbian Orthodox Church/Patriarchate; Warsaw-Chełm, Orthodox Eparchy of
Orthodox Church in America, 351
Orthodox Jews, 9, 146, 257, 260, 261
Ortynsky, Soter, 162
Osława River, 3, 11
Ost Mark, 55
Ostrava, 346
Ostrogoths, 23, 24
Osturňa, 238
Otomani culture, 17
Ottoman Empire, 64, 73, 75, 87, 89, 91, 111, 167, 169
Ottomans/Ottoman Turks 60, 70–71, 73, 75, 89, 91, 94, 107, 169, 397
OUN. *See* Organization of Ukrainian Nationalists

P

Pacific Ocean, 212, 229
Padiak, Valerii. *See* Valerii Padiak Publishing House

Pădureni, 347
Paganism, 27–28, 38–39
Painting. *See* Art (Painting and Sculpture)
Pakostov, 100
Palanok, 43, 147
Palestine, 201, 260, 261
Palota Pass, 11
Pan'kevych, Ivan, 212, 216, 265
Pan'ko, Iurii, 383, plate 93
Pankovych, Shtefan, 137, 139
Pannonia 24, 35, 45, 53, 92
Pannonian Slavs, 29, 31
Pan-Slavism, 104, 120, 139, 140, 162
Papp, Antal/Antonii, 137, 174, 199, 228
Papp, Gyula, plate 63
Paris, 146, 187, 193, 300
Paris Peace Conference, 189, 190, 199, 200, 241, 270, 281, 298
Parkanyi, Ivan, 395, plate 43
Parliament: of Habsburg Austria, 118, 131; of Czechoslovakia, 191, 201, 220, 266, 274, 300, 318, 322; of Hungary, 119, 120, 135, 138, 223, 285–286; of Poland, 233; of Romania, 401, plate 103; of Slovakia, 283, 284, 381; of Ukraine, 357, 362, 363, 365
Parma, 109
Parma, Greek Catholic Eparchy of, 351
Paskevich, Ivan, 119
Passaic, Greek Catholic Eparchy of, 351
Pastelii, Ioann, 101
Pásztély, István/Pastelii, Shtefan, 137
Pásztély, János, 137
Pataky, Ferenc, 289
Patrick, Saint, 40
Pauliuc, Dragoș, 198
Pavlik, Matej. *See* Gorazd
Pavlovych, Aleksander, 103, 139, 319, 360
Pavlovych, Andrei, 103
Pax Romana, 21, 22, 31, 33, 35, 36, 60
Peasantry, 65, 69–70, 90, 97–99, 116, 119, 135, 143–144, 151, 154, 236, 309

Pechenegs, 41
Pécs University, 285
Pedagogical University in Cracow, 389
Pelesh, Iuliian, 134
Peloponese, 31
Pennsylvania 156, 158, 160, 177, 178, 193, 244, 246, 350, 351, 352, 375, 403
People from Nowhere, The, xvii–xviii
People's Guard/Gwardia Ludowa, 283
Perechyn, 148, 202
Peregu Mare/Velykŷi Pereg, 153
Perényi, Zsigmond, 286–287
Perényi family, 63, 92, 144
Perun, 27, 39
Pest, 118–119, 135, 399
Pesti Hírlap (newspaper), 116
Peter I Romanov, 91
Petki, P., plate 95
Petra Society (Prešov), 228
Petrov, Aleksei L., 64, 132
Petrov, Ivan, 293
Petrovai, Vasyl', plate 93
Petrovci, 153, 348, 402
Petrovtsi, Ivan, 378
Petrovych, Petro, 63
Petrus/Peter, 63
Philadelphia, Pensylvania, 178, 251
Piast dynasty, 46, 67
Pidhoriany, 93
Pieradzka, Krystyna, 239
P'ieshchak, Ivan, 270, 271, plate 43
Piłsudski, Józef, 233
Pittsburgh, Greek Catholic Exarchate/Eparchy of, 245, 351
Pittsburgh, Pensylvania, 156, 162, 177, 245, 293, 403
Pittsburgh Agreement, 178
"Plan for Resolving the Problem of Ukrainians-Rusyns," 367, 368
Plast (scouts), 216
Plicka, Karel, 267
Ploteny, Nándor, 147
Pochaïv. *See* Monasteries: at Pochaïv
Podiaremnaia Rus', 132
Podkarpatská Rus, 193, 275, 300
Podkarpatska Rus' (journal), 213, 396
Podkarpatské hlasy (newspaper), 266
Podlachia, 163
Podolia, 64

Pogodin, Mikhail, 105
Pogroms, 258
Poland, 17, 82, 208, 233–239 passim,
    299, 313, 335–342 passim, 355,
    360, 366, 367, 386–391 passim,
    407, 409, 411
Poland-Lithuania/Polish-Lithuanian
    Commonwealth, 78, 79, 95, 96,
    183, 233
Poles, 9, 109, 114, 115, 131, 179,
    335, 339, 390, 425n.9, 427n.13;
    in the Lemko Region, 407; in the
    United States, 154, 157, 177
Polianskii, Ioann, 238, 283, plate 54
Polianskii, Petro, 135
Polish Army, 181, 279
Polish Autocephalous Orthodox
    Church, 172, 208, 238, 338
Polish Kingdom, 67, 78, 79
Polish language, 134
Polish United Worker's Party, 336
Political Rusynism, 366, 394, 410
Polovtsians. *See* Kipchaks
Pomerania, 301, 337, 338, 343
Popov, Aleksandr, 265
Popov, Mikhail, 210
Popovec, Iaroslav, 384
Popovych, Mikhail, 213
Poprad River, 7, 11, 212, 220, 229,
    271, 407
Poráč, 100
Poroshkovo, 148
Portugal, 371
Positivism, 25
Potoky, plate 16
Potsdam Conference, 301
Pozdravlenie Rusynov, 124, plate 23
Poznań, 46
Pozsony. *See* Bratislava
Prague 14, 50, 120, 121, 146, 191,
    193–196 passim, 199–202 passim,
    205, 220, 223, 228, 256, 260,
    265, 266, 267, 269–278 passim,
    283, 288, 299, 300, 305, 315,
    317, 356, 371, 374, 395–397
    passim
Prague, Patriarchate of, 209
Prague Spring, 329-331, 379
Pravoslavnaia Karpatskaia Rus'
    (newspaper), 227

Prešov (city), 59, 90, 101, 105, 107,
    119, 121, 124, 125, 137, 141, 153,
    156, 159, 160, 174, 181, 182, 189,
    225, 227, 230, 238, 270, 283, 284,
    321, 322, 326, 327, 330, 333, 359,
    372, 382, 383, 385, 387, plates 51,
    53
Prešov, Greek Catholic Eparchy of,
    101, 120, 122, 137, 138, 225, 228,
    325, 331, 372, 384, 405, plate 78
Prešov, Orthodox Eparchy of, 326
Prešov Literary Society, 124
Prešov Region, 5, 6, 7, 11, 12, 65, 69,
    70, 75, 81, 83, 87, 100, 101, 102,
    107, 109, 122, 125, 126, 129, 133,
    137, 151, 163, 169, 170, 177, 178,
    181, 185, 186, 187, 198, 208–210
    passim, 216, 219–231, 241, 269,
    271, 276, 281, 283-285, 308, 313,
    321–334, 345-347 passim, 374,
    377, 379–385
Prešov University. *See* University of
    Prešov
Pressburg. *See* Bratislava
Priashevshchina (newspaper), 323,
    327, plate 79
Priashevskaia Rus' (newspaper), 284
*Primary Chronicle. See Rus' Primary
    Chronicle*
Princeton University, 114
Printing and Publishing, 77, 84, 101,
    105, 124, 125, 127, 139–140, 207,
    212–213, 227, 237, 242, 244–245,
    287, 316, 327, 341, 349, 378, 384,
    388, 396, 404, 405
Pripet River, 26, 28
Pritsak, Omeljan, 50
Prnjavor, 151
Procyk, Judson, 250
Progressive Jews, 9
Prosvita Society/Tovarystvo
    "Prosvita": in Austrian Galicia,
    134; in the Lemko Region, 134,
    237; in the Prešov Region, 230;
    in Subcarpathian Rus', 206, 213,
    288, 316, plate 48
Prosvitni dom (Ruski Kerestur), 242,
    plates 58, 87
Protestantism/Protestants, 9, 75–77,
    79, 81, 99, 100, 255, 373–377.

See also Anti-Trinitarians;
Baptists; Bohemian Brethren;
Free Christians; Lutheranism/
Evangelical Lutheranism; Reformed
Calvinism; Seventh-Day Adventists;
Worldwide Church of God
Provisional National Council of Prešov
and Russian [sic] Ukrainians, 322
Prussia, 96, 108, 129, 303
Przemyśl (city), 35, 39, 48, 70, 102,
134, 301; siege of, 170, 171
Przemyśl, Greek Catholic Eparchy of,
79-81, 101, 120, 122, 137, 138,
225, 228, 235, 236, 238, 325, 331,
372, 384, 405
Przemyśl, Orthodox Eparchy of, 79,
101
Przemyśl-Novy Sącz, Orthodox
Eparchy of, 338
Pułaski, Casimir/Kazimierz, 95
PULS, 382
Pushkin, Aleksander, 317
Pynta, Ivan, 90, 96
Pysh, Simeon, 246

R

Rácz, Demeter/ Rats', Dymytrii, 94,
plate 12
Rada Powiatowa, 131
Rakhiv, 172, 202, 276, plate 77a
Rákóczi family, 87, 90, 92, 94. See
also Ferenc I and II Rákóczi;
György II Rákóczi; Zsigmond I
Rákóczi
Rakoshyno, 376
Rakovs'kyi, Ioann, 139
Rastislav, 35
Ratio educationis, 102
Recovered Lands/Zieme Odzyskane,
303, 335, 340
Red Army. See Soviet/Red Army
Red Ruthenia, 67
Reformation, 75–77, 375
Reformed Calvinism/Calvinists, 9,
76–77, 81, 89, 99, 255, 373–375
Reformed/Progressive (Neolog) Jews, 9
Reichsrat (Vienna), 131
Reichstag (Vienna), 118
Reinfuss, Roman, 239

Reményi, Ede, 147
Remety. See Turï Remety
Rémy, Saint, 40
Resettlement. See Deportation/
Resettlement of populations
Return to Greek Catholicism, 330, 372
Return-to-Orthodoxy movement, 86,
159, 162, 163, 207, 211, 277–278,
236, 325
Revai, Iuliian, 217, 270, plate 43
Revolution of 1848, 107, 118–121,
125, 127, 129, 143, 215
Revolutions of 1989, 216, 354, 355–
362, 366, 378, 379, 384, 386, 404,
409, 425n.9
Rhine River, 19, 22, 24, 31
Rhineland, 94
Richnyk Ruskoi Bursŷ (journal), 389
Righetti, John, xx, 37, 403
Rika River, 11
Rishko, Mykola, 275
Riuryk, 50
Rivne, 324, 345
Robin Hood, 96
Rodez, 50
Rohach, Ivan, 274
Roikovych, Dionisii, 285
Rokovyna, 144
Roma/Gypsies, 6, 109, 349; in
Slovakia, 381; in Subcarpathian
Rus', 253, 264
Roman Catholic Church/Roman
Catholicism, 9, 67, 73, 76–82
passim, 92, 96, 99, 100, 158–160,
235, 246, 247, 255, 263, 283, 315,
338, 339
Roman Empire, 19–25, 33, 36, 50,
51, 73. See also Byzantine/East
Roman Empire; Holy Roman
Empire; West Roman Empire
Roman rite. See Christianity: Roman
Rite
Romance peoples, 1, 9, 26, 59
Romania, 1, 9, 21, 73, 109, 120, 153,
163, 190, 241, 306, 313, 347-348,
356-357, 401, 407, 409; Carpatho-
Rusyns in, 190, 241, 305–306,
347–348, 361, 367, 401, 407, 409.
See also Banat; Maramureş
Region

Romanian Army, 186, 187
Romanian language, 2
Romanians, 9, 102, 109, 117–119
    passim, 154, 187, 413n.4; in
    Subcarpathian Rus', 149, 253,
    264, 310
Romans, 39
Rome 19, 21, 24, 33, 36, 37, 50, 77,
    79, 82, 83, 86, 100, 146, 160, 161,
    208, 246–251 passim, 314, 315,
    348
Romzha, Teodor, 315, 454
Rondo, 398
Rongyos Gárda, 274
Roosevelt, Franklin D., 301
"Roots" movement, 352
Ropa River, 11, 15
Ropica Górna, 171
Ros' River, 50
Roskovics, Ignácz/Roshkovych,
    Ignatii, 137
Rostyslav, 48
Rosvygovo, 259
Röszler, Richard, plate 62
Royal Hungary, 73–75, 81, 84, 87, 89,
    90, 92
Rozgonyi family, 63
Rozstajne, 171
Rozsypal, Antonín, 195, plate 42
Rudne, 345
Ruga, 23
Rukh–People's Movement of Ukraine,
    357
Rus', 46–47, 49–51, 55, 103, 122,
    132, 133, 171, 184, 185, 228,
    246, 317, 340. See also Galician
    Rus'; Hungarian Rus'; Kievan Rus';
    Marchia Ruthenorum; Rus' Land;
    Subcarpathian Rus'; Varangian Rus'
Rus': ethnonym and identity, 3, 5,
    49–51, 104, 134, 184–185, 247,
    313, 407
Rus': religious faith, 51, 100, 143,
    229
Ruś Czerwona (palatinate), 67
Rus' Club (Prešov), 229, plate 51
Rus' Land. See Rus'ka Kraina
Rus'/ruskii language, 132, 137, 244,
    328
Rus' March. See Marchia Ruthenorum

Rus' National Center (Prešov), 229,
    plate 51; (Uzhhorod) plate 47
Rus' National Republic, 181, 190
Rus' Primary Chronicle, 49, 183
Rus' Sports Club, 207
Rus'-Ukraine, 185
Ruscova/Ruskova River, 7, 11, 347
Ruscovce, 56
Rusenko, Ivan, 198, 237–238, plate 55
Rusinia, 5
Ruska Bursa. See Bursa
Rus'ka Kraina/Rus' Land, 55, 138,
    195, 196. See also Soviet Rus'ka
    Kraina
Ruska matka, 358, 401
Rus'ka molodezh (journal), 287
Ruská Vol'a, 353
Ruska/Rusyn Bursa. See Bursa
Ruske slovo (newspaper), 349
Ruske Slovo Publishers, 349, 402
Ruski kalendar, 242
Ruski Kerestur, 95, 153, 228, 242,
    348, 349, 350, 358, 401, plates 33,
    58, 86, 87
Ruski novini (newspaper), 242
Ruskii language, 132
Ruskýi/rus'kŷi language, 206, 227, 244
Rusnak: ethnonym, 3, 5, 95, 104,
    135, 184, 222–224, 229, 242, 312,
    324, 326, 328, 367
Rusnak, Nykolai, 228
Rusnak Society, 403
Rusnats'kyi svit (journal), 378
Rusnatsi u shvetse (magazine), 404,
    430
Russell, Charles Taze, 375
Russia, 40, 113, 140, 184, 185, 299,
    300, 318
Russian/russkii: ethnonym, 3, 115,
    243, 321, 323, 326, 328, 352
Russian Army (tsarist), 121, 124, 126,
    169–173
Russian Civil War, 176, 181, 298
Russian Days, 230
Russian Empire, 95–96, 103, 125,
    126, 163, 165, 184, 222, 260, 265
Russian language, 2, 125, 126, 132,
    135, 139, 140, 206, 215, 216, 227,
    229, 311, 313, 317, 323, 326, 327,
    328, 346, 376

Russian National Autonomist Party, 201, 269

Russian National Party (Prešov Region), 220, 225, 229

Russian Orthodox Catholic Mutual Aid Society, 162

Russian Orthodox Church Abroad/in Exile, 208, 209, 227

Russian Orthodox Church—Moscow Patriarchate, 211, 227, 297, 315, 316, 326, 372, 377

Russian Orthodox Eparchy of the Aleutian Islands and Alaska/in North America, 159, 161, 163, 246, 351

Russian Peasant Organization, 235, 237

Russian War Relief, 293

Russian-Ukrainian Central National Council, 269, 270

Russians, 3, 5, 40, 41, 104, 114, 115, 125–126, 133, 184, 185, 352, 354, 410; in Czechoslovakia, 222, 324; in the Prešov Region, 209, 380–381, (resettled from) 429n.1, 429n.9; in Soviet Transcarpathia, 312, 319, 407; in Subcarpathian Rus', 209, 212, 264–265; in the United States, 157, 162, 177, 352

Russka zaria (newspaper), 243

Russkii narodnyi golos (newspaper), 213

Russkoe slovo (newspaper), 228, 229

Russophiles/Russophilism, 124–126 passim, 132–139 passim, 139, 163, 177, 184, 206, 212, 220, 229, 230, 235–238 passim, 243, 246, 251, 271, 273–277 passim, 282, 284, 288, 296, 316, 326–328, 352, 367

Rusyn/*rus'kŷi*/*rus'ka*: ethnonym, 3, 5, 135, 161, 174, 184, 225, 229, 235, 243, 312, 313, 324, 326, 328, 331, 351, 367, 380, 382, 413n.1

Rusyn (magazine), 359, 385, 411

Rusyn Academy, 122

Rusyn Americans. *See* United States: Carpatho-Rusyns in

Rusyn Cultural Foundation/Ruska matka (Ruski Kerestur), 358, 401, 402

Rusyn District, 123. *See also* Uzhhorod District

Rusyn language/vernacular, 99, 121–125 passim, 135, 140, 141, 174, 213–216, 220, 225, 228, 229, 285, (Uhro-Rusyn) 287, 312, 313, 317, 331, 341, 351, 359–361 passim, 367, 368, 376–388 passim, 394–395, 405, 422n.12, 429n.5. *See also* Vojvodinian Rusyn language

Rusyn National Assembly, 182

Rusyn National Center/Prosvitni Dom (Ruski Kerestur), plates 58, 87

Rusyn National Committee (Prešov), 225

Rusyn National Council (Vojvodina), 402

Rusyn National Enlightenment Society/Ruske narodne prosvitne druzhtvo (Novi Sad), 242–243, 287

Rusyn National Union, 162

Rusyn Renaissance Society/ Rusyns'ka obroda (Prešov Region), 359, 382, 383

Rusyn Sunday School Program (Transcarpathia), 405

Rusynophiles/Rusynophilism, 216, 229, 246, 270, 273, 288, 365, 389, 402–403

Rusyns-Ukrainians, 186, 380

Rusynskŷi zhyvot (magazine), 398

Ruteni, 50

Rutenois, 50

Ruthenia, 5, 67

Ruthenian Catholic Church: in the United States, 245–251 passim; in Ukraine, 372

Ruthenian: church rite, 248–250, 372; ethnonym, 3, 161, 183, 350, 351, 404

Ruthenians, 102, 258; in Bukovina, 121, 122, 125, 132; in Galicia, 121, 122, 125, 127, 131, 132, 133, 135, 157, 179; in the Hungarian Kingdom, 122, 125, 132, 145; in the United States, 157, 158, 161, 163, 177, 238, 246, 430n.11. *See also* Old Ruthenians

Rymanów, 147

S

Sabinov, 333
Sabol, Sevastiian (Zoreslav), 230
Sabov, Feofan, 210, 211
Sabov, Ievmenii, 140, 216
Sabov, Kyryl, 139
Sabov, Orest/Szabo, Oreszt, 137, 138
Sabov, Simeon, 182
Sacred Congregation for the Propagation of the Faith (Vatican), 247, 248, 249
Sącz land, 67
Sajó River, 57
Salonika, 37
Sambir, 148
Samosh-Diakovo culture, 15
Samovol's'kyi, Edmund, 137
San River 5, 17, 35, 39, 48, 67, 170, 171, 179, 233–235, 281, 282, 301
Sandovych, Maksym, 165, 172
Sanok (city), 6, 17, 67, 134, 148, 170, 172, 181, 237, 282, 301, 338; (land), 67; (district), 233, 238
Sarajevo, 169
Sardinia, 129
Šariš/Sáros county. *See* Sharysh county
Sarmatians, 18, 28
Sarých, Mykhail, 165
Sas-Iavorskŷi, Valerii/Sas-Jaworski, Walery, 134
Sashalmi, Endre, xx
Saskachevanski ruski hlasnŷk (magazine), 404
Saskatchewan, 404
Satu Mare/Szatmár, 55, 261
Sava River, 71, 89, 94
Savatij (Antonín Jindřich Vrabec), 209–211
Savka, Andrii, 70
Saxons, 57
Saxony, 76
Scăiuş/Skeiush, 153, 396
Scandinavia, 47, 50, 154
Scandinavians, 26, 47, 49–50
Scholarship, 43, 45, 101, 103–105, 206, 238–239, 349, 383–387 passim

Schönborn, Friedrich Karl von, 92, plate 15
Schönborn, Lothar Franz von, 92
Schönborn family, 92–94, 144, 146, 148, 203, 257, 263, plate 29
School of Higher Education (Nyíregyháza), 399
Schools. *See* Education and Schools
Scots, 19
Scranton Resolution, 178
Scranton, Pennsylvania, 156, 178, 193
Sculpture. *See* Art (Painting and Sculpture)
Scythians, 18, 28, 35
Secretariat for Human Rights of the National Parliament of Ukraine (Kiev), 368
Section for the Development of Lemko Culture (Warsaw), 341
Securitate, 357
Segal, Raz, xx
Sejm Krajowy, 131
Sejm. *See* Diet: of Poland
Sembratovych, Iosyf, 134
Sembratovych, Silvester Cardinal, 134
Semenovych, Petro, 375
Senko, 96
Serafim (Ivanović), 210
Serbia, 1, 3, 43, 357, 401-403, 409; Carpatho-Rusyns in, *see* Vojvodinian-Srem Rusyns
Serbia-Montenegro, 357
Serbian Orthodox Church/Patriarch-ate, 208–211, 276, 297, 316
Serbs, 28, 102, 109, 119, 208, 209, 210, 211, 242, 349; in Subcarpathian Rus', 210
Seredne, 57, 78
Serfdom/Serfs, 61, 66, 69, 82, 90, 91 92, 95, 97–99, 100, 116, 119, 143, 151
Seventh-Day Adventists, 374, 376
Sevliush/Nagyszőllős, 147
Shapira, Hayim/Chaim Elazar, 261
Sharysh/Šariš/Sáros county, 57, 82, 83, 84, 87, 90, 101, 123, 156, 173, 182, 185, 186, 193, 194, 219, 223
Shchavnyts'kyi, Mykhaïl, 103
Shcherbyts'kyi, Volodymyr, 357

Shelestovo, 93
Shelukhyn, Scrlill, 50
Shevchenko, Taras, 317
Shmaida, Mykhailo, 332
Sholtes, Iosyf, 122
Sholtys, 59
Shtefan, Agoshton, 182, 187
Shtefan, Avhustyn, 275
Shuhai, Mykola, 258, 267
Shvabs/Swabians, 93, 263, plate 65
Shvetlosts (journal), 349
Siberia, 120, 310, 311
Šid, 153, 348
Sieniawska, Elżbieta, 90
Sienieński family, 69
Sighet/Sighetul Marmaţiei, 141, 148,
    165, 170, 186, 190, 257, 305, 348,
    401
Sigismund Luxembourg, 63, 64
Sigtuna, 47
Silesia, 29, 35, 57, 202, 204, 301,
    337, 338, 343, 346, 387, 388, 390,
    391, 395
Silesians, 29
Sil'vai, Ivan, 126, 139, 319
Simko, Antonii, 283
Singidunum, 23
Şiria, 120
Skejušan Ensemble, 396
Skotar Pass, 148, 170
Slaveno-Rusyn language, 215
Slavia Orthodoxa, 9
Slavia Romana, 9
Slavic Congress (Prague), 120, 121–
    122
Slavknyha Publishing House (Prešov),
    323, 327
Slavonia, 94, 151, 153
Slavonic language, 37
Slavonski Brod, 151
Slavophiles, 104
Sław, Aleksander, 341
Slovak: ethnonym, 328
Slovak Communist Party. *See*
    Communist Party: in Slovakia
Slovak Cultural/National
    Foundation/Matica slovenská, 137,
    223, 331
Slovak Diet. *See* Diet: of the Slovak
    State

Slovak Greek Catholic Church, 384
Slovak language, 2, 223, 225, 227,
    334, 384, 397, 422n.11
Slovak League/Slovenská liga, 225,
    227
Slovak National Council, 223
Slovak National Museum, 383
Slovak Soviet Republic, 221
Slovakia, 1, 9, 43, 56, 83, 143, 208,
    216, 219–231 passim, 318, 367,
    368, 371, 379–385 passim, 386,
    409, 411
Slovakization, 223, 328–329, 331,
    332, 334, 384, 385, 397, 405
Slovaks, 9, 90, 102, 109, 114, 117,
    119–121, 127, 136, 154, 177–178,
    191, 193, 198, 200, 219, 221–222,
    230, 283, 298, 300, 322, 329,
    331, 332, 354, 379, 381, 396,
    413n.4; in Canada, 331; in the
    Prešov Region, 7, 374, 381; in
    Subcarpathian Rus', 7, 253, 264,
    304; in the United States, 154,
    156, 157, 162, 177, 219, 225
Slovenes, 109, 242
Slovenia, 109, 357
Slovjaks. *See* Eastern Slovaks
Slovo naroda (newspaper), 230
SMERSH, 295
Smetana Society, 266
Snina, 281, 333
Soborna Ukraïna. *See* Greater
    Ukraine
Sobranije greko-katholičeskich
    cerkovnych bratstv. *See* United
    Societies (Sobranije)
Social-Democratic Party, 201, 260,
    261, 266
Society of Carpatho-Rusyns/
    Tovarystvo karpats'kykh rusyniv
    (Uzhhorod), 358, 362, 365, 410
Society of Friends of Subcarpathian
    Rus' (Prague), 395–397
Society of Jesus. *See* Jesuits
Socinians, 77
Soim podkarpatskykh Rusynov, 369
Soiuz Rusinokh a Ukraïntsokh
    Horvatskei (Vukovar), 349, 402, 403
Soiuz Rusnatsokh i Ukraïntsokh
    Serbii (Novi Sad), 401

Soiuz rusyniv-ukraïntsiv
  Chekhoslovachchyny (Prešov), 359
Sojedinenije greko-kaftoličeskich
  russkich bratstv. *See* Greek
  Catholic Union (Sojedinenije)
Sokol societies, 207
*Sokrashchennaia grammatika
  pis'mennago russkago iazyka*, 124
Solinka River, 3, 11
Solotvyno, 149, 259, 376, plate 64
Someş River, 45
Somme, Battle of, 171
Sorbian Mark, 55
Sotmar/Szatmár county, 64, 84
South America, 236
South Slavic Rusyns. *See* Vojvodinian-
  Srem Rusyns
Southern (Transylvanian)
  Carpathians, 153
Sova, Petr Petro, 276, 297
Soviet/Red Army, 211, 281, 291, 292,
  294, 299, 311, 315, 318, 321–323
  passim, 330, 331
Soviet Hungary. *See* Hungarian Soviet
  Republic
Soviet Rus'ka Kraina, 187, 260
Soviet Russia, 209
Soviet Transcarpathia, 304, 305–321,
  331, 346, 347, 358, 360, 361,
  362. *See also* Transcarpathia/
  Transcarpathian oblast
Soviet Ukraine, 197, 294, 299, 300,
  303, 305–320 passim, 343–346,
  361
Soviet Union, 9, 42, 126, 185, 299,
  305–320 passim, 360, 373, 409
Spain, 113
Spinka rabbinic dynasty
Spish/Spiš/Szepes county, 83, 84,
  100, 101, 123, 151, 182, 185, 186,
  193, 194, 219, 220
Spish German. *See* Carpathian/Spish
  Germans
Spišské Podhradie, 18
Spišský Štvrtok, 17
Společnost přátel Podkarpatské Rusi
  (Prague), 395
Sports, 206–207, 266
Spring of Nations, 127
Šramek, František, 203

Srem region, 3, 7, 94–95, 151, 153,
  154, 190, 242–243, 281, 343, 348
Srem/Szerem county, 95, 153, 242
Sremskii Karlovci, 209; Orthodox
  Metropolitanate of, 208
Sreznevskii, Izmail, 105
St. Athanasius Society (Prešov), 230
St. Barbara Church/Barbareum
  (Vienna), 101–102
St. Basil the Great Society (Uzhhorod),
  125, 137, 139, 140
St. Germain-en-Laye, Treaty of, 189,
  193, 194
St. John the Baptist Society (Prešov),
  125, 137, 384
St. Panteleimon Monastery, 163
St. Paul, Minnesota, 159
Stadnicki family, 69
Stadtkonvikt (Vienna), 102
Stalin, Joseph, 293, 299, 301, 306,
  316, 318, 322
Stalingrad, Battle of, 171, 291
Stanovo culture, 17
Stanyslaviv, 148
Stará L'ubovňa, 181, 184, 333
Staraia Ladoga, 47
Stari Vrbas, 243
Starukh, Mykhailo, 131
Stavrovs'kyi-Popradov, Iulii 139
Stebník, 70, 227
Štefánik, Milan, 298
Stefanovskii, Pavel, 341
Stephen I, Saint, 55, 56. *See also*
  Crown of St. Stephen
Stieber, Zdzisław, 239
Stoika, Aleksander, 213, 273
Stone Age, 15
Stovaryshŷnia Lemkiv. *See* Lemko
  Society
Stropkov, 63, 333
Stryboh, 27
Stryi, 148, 170
Stryps'kyi, Hiiador, 140, 195, 196
Studencheskii zhurnal (journal), 284
Studium Carpato-Ruthenorum
  (Prešov), xviii, xx, plate 99
Studium Ruthenum (L'viv), 103
Styria, 109, 173
Subcarpathia/Kárpátaljai, 5, 286,
  294

Subcarpathia, Eparchy of the Czechoslovak Orthodox Church, 209

Subcarpathian Agricultural Union, 201

Subcarpathian Barbizon, 207, 256

Subcarpathian Communist Party. *See* Communist Party: Subcarpathian branch of

Subcarpathian diet. *See* Diet: of Subcarpathian Rus'/Carpatho-Ukraine

Subcarpathian Hungarian Cultural Society, 256

Subcarpathian Hungarian Drama Patronage Society, 256

Subcarpathian Rus', 5, 43, 55, 109, 122, 133, 138, 143, 146, 149, 151, 191–217, 220, 253–278, 298–300, 313, 317, 373, 375, 390, 401, plate 2

Subcarpathian Rusyn Land, 195, 270

Subcarpathian Rusyn National Theater (Uzhhorod), 206, plate 50

Subcarpathian Scholarly Society (Uzhhorod), 287–288, 316, plate 70

Subcarpathian School of Painting/Barbizon, 207, 256

Subcarpathian Scout Federation, 256

Subcarpathian Territory/Kárpátaljai terület, 286

Subcarpathian Voivodeship/Kárpátaljai vajdaság, 285–289

Suçeava, 163

Sudeten German Party, 263, 269

Sudetenland, 271, 346

Sukhors'kyi, Andrii, 345

Suleiman I, 73

Šumiac, 100

Supreme Ruthenian Council (L'viv), 121

Supreme Soviet (Moscow), 306

Šuster, Rudolf, 381

Svaliava, 93, 149, 202, 203, 263, plate 45

Svaroh, 27

Svarozhych, 27

Svatopluk, 35

Sviatovit/Sventovyd, 27

Svidník, 170, 209, 227, 333, 383, plate 80

Svît newspaper), 125, plate 24

Svit D'itej/Children's World, 245

Svoboda, 266

Svoboda, Ludvík, 318

Svobodka, 266

Swabians. *See* Shvabs

Sweden, 47, 49

Świątkowa, 171

Swiss, 112, 148

Switzerland, 19, 76

Sydor, Dymytrii, 369, 377

Synod Abroad. *See* Russian Orthodox Church Abroad

Syria, 19

Szabó, Jenő/Sabov, Ievmenii, 137, 138

Szabó, Oreszt/Sabov, Orest, 137, 138, 182

Szabolcs, Ferenc, plate 63

Szabolcs county, 101

Szamos/Someş River, 45

Szamovolszky, Ödön /Samovol's'kyi, Edmund, 137

Szatmár county. *See* Sotmar county

Szczawnica, 147, 238

Széchenyi, István, 117

Szémán, István, 174

Szepes county. *See* Spish county

Szerém county, 95, 153, 242

Sziget-Satmar rabbinic dynasty, 261

Szlachta. *See* Nobility: in Poland

Szlachtowa, 17, 238

Szolyva Company, 148

Sztáray family, 92

T

Tachov, 347

Takach, Basil, 245

Tale of Bygone Years, The, 46

Talerhof/Thalerhof internment camp, 173, plate 38

Tamash, Iuliian, 402

Tarakhonych, Dmytro, 296

Tarasovych, Vasylii, 83

Tarna Mare, 347

Tarnovych-Beskyd, Iuliian, 237

Tarnów, Battle of, 171, 173

Tatar Pass, 148

Tatras, 276

Técső. *See* Tiachovo
Tehran Conference, 301
Teitelbaum, Joel, 261
Telegdi family, 63
Teleki, Pál, 285
Teleki family, 92, 144
Telgart, 100
Temesvár
Tenafly, New Jersey, 163
Tereblia River, 11
Teresva River, 11, 202
Ternavka, 347
Ternopil', 303, 343, 345, 393, 394
Teurisci, 18, 21
Teutonic Knights, 67
Teutsch-Au, 59
Thalerhof, 173
Theater, 133, 206, 216, 256, 287, 323
Thessalonika, 38
Thököly, Imre, 87, 89
Thomas, Johannes, 263
Thracians, 21
Tiachevo/Técső, 146
Timişoara, 347
Timko, Irinei, 198
Tiso, Jozef, 278, 283
Tisza, Kálmán, 136, 139
Tisza/Tysa River, 7, 45, 148, 151,
    153, 220, 271, 275, 305, 347, 407
Tisza-Danube plain, 24
Tito, Josef Broz, 348
Tkach, Joseph W., 377
Tomashivs'kyi, Stepan, 49, 133
Tomchanii, Mykhailo I., 411
Tomchanii, Mykhailo M., 358, 410
Topl'a River, 11
Torna county. *See* Turna county
Torontal, 95
Toronto, 236, 246
Torun'/Vyshkiv Pass, 11
Torysa River, 11
Toth, Alexis, 160–161, plate 35a
Tourism, 267, 391
Tovarystvo karpats'kykh rusyniv
    (Uzhhorod), 358
Tovt, Nykolai, 137
Transcarpathia/Transcarpathian
    oblast, 5, 43, 55, 109, 197,
    202–203, 305–319, 346, 355, 361,
    363–378, 390, 407, 411

Transcarpathian: "ethnonym", 320
Transcarpathian National Council,
    297, 305, 308, 314
Transcarpathian oblast. *See*
    Transcarpathia
Transcarpathian Regional Assembly/
    Oblasna rada, 197, 361, 363, 366,
    368, 369
Transcarpathian Ukraine, 197, 295–
    297, 300, 301, 313, 321, 322, 323,
    361
Transylvania, 21, 24, 42, 57, 73, 75,
    81–84 passim, 87, 89, 92, 109, 374
Transylvanian Carpathians, 153
Trebushany, 13
Tretiakov Gallery (Moscow), 126
Trianon, Treaty of, 189–190, 199–
    200, 418n. 8
Trianon Hungary, 190, 241
Tripartitum, 66
Trnava, 84–85, 425
Trojans, 25
Trokhanovskii, Iaroslav, 198
Trokhanovskii, Metodii, 237, plate 56
Trokhanovskii, Petro Murianka, 388
Trokhanovskii, Seman, 131
Tsibere, Pavel, 293
Tsurkanovich, Ilarion, 201, 212
Turï Remety, 148, 309
Turia Bystra, 148
Turia River, 148
Turianytsia, Ivan I., 296, 297, 309,
    plate 75
Turianytsia, Ivan M., 365
Turkey, 19, 70, 85
Turkic peoples/tribes, 41, 70
Turkish language, 386
Turna/Torna county, 83, 84, 101. *See*
    also Abov-Torna/Turna county
Turok, Vasyl', 359, plate 89
Tuscany, 109
Tylawa/Tŷliava, 171, 236
Tylicz/Tylič Pass, 11, 69
Tyrol, 109
Tysa River. *See* Tisza River

U

Uchytel's'kyi holos (journal), 213
Udavské, 224

Udvari, István, 401
Uglia/Uhlia (monastery), 71; (village) 309
Ugocha/Ugocsa county, 57, 66, 82, 84, 90, 92, 123, 182, 185, 186, 193, 194, 257, 347
Uhro-Rusinia, 189
Uhro-Rusyn: ethnonym, 3; language, *see* Rusyn language
Uhro-Rusyn National Council. *See* American National Council of Uhro-Rusyns
Uhro-Rusyn Political Party, 199
Uhro-Rusyn Theater (Uzhhorod), 287
Uhro-Rusyns, 177–178, 182, 199, 288, 298
Ukraine, 1, 9, 40, 50, 184, 300, 309, 318, 320, 363–378 passim, 386, 401, 411; Carpatho-Rusyns/ Lemkos in, 344–346, 390, 393–395
Ukrainian: ethnonym, 135, 183–185, 312, 321, 323, 326, 328, 367, 380
Ukrainian Autocephalous Orthodox Church, 372
Ukrainian Central Committee (Cracow), 282
Ukrainian Civic and Cultural Society (Warsaw), 340–341
Ukrainian Greek Catholic Major Archdiocese of Kyiv-Halych, 372
Ukrainian Insurgent Army (UPA), 291–292, 324–325, 326, 336, 339, plate 82
Ukrainian language, 2, 126, 134, 184, 206, 229, 275, 282, 313, 317, 328–329, 334, 339, 340, 346–349 passim, 372, 380, 383–386 passim, 411
Ukrainian Military Organization (UVO), 235
Ukrainian National Association (Jersey City, N.J.), 162
Ukrainian National Council (Vojvodina), 402
Ukrainian National Council of the Prešov Region, 321–323, 327, plate 79
Ukrainian National Republic, 183
Ukrainian National Theater (Prešov), 323, 327, 346

Ukrainian National Union (Khust), 277
Ukrainian Orthodox Church—Kiev Patriarhate, 372
Ukrainian Soviet Socialist Republic/ S.S.R., 183, 301, 305, 361. *See also* Soviet Ukraine
Ukrainian Writer's Union, 332
Ukrainianization, 312–313, 326–329, 332–333, 384–385, 394–395
Ukrainians, 3, 5, 40, 41, 109, 114, 115, 133, 179, 185, 292, 314, 339, 354, 360, 410, 427n.12; in Canada, 276, 367; in Croatia, 403; in the Czech Republic, 397, 430n.3; in Czechoslovakia, 222, 324; in Hungary, 398; in the Lemko Region, 282; in Poland, 228, 234–235, 274, (deported from) 303, 335–337, 390; in the Prešov Region, 380, 381, 383, 429n.1 and n.7; in Romania, 401, 430.n.8; in Soviet Transcarpathia, 312, 319, 365, 371, 407; in Subcarpathian Rus', 212, 215, 265, 274; in the United States, 156, 157, 162, 238, 239, 367; in the Vojvodina, 350, 402
Ukrainophiles/Ukrainophilism, 132–135, 134, 184, 206, 212, 216, 228, 230, 235, 237, 243, 270, 273–277 passim, 288, 316, 360, 389, 402–403, 410–411
Ukraïns'ka narodna rada Priashivshchiny (UNRP). *See* Ukrainian National Council of the Prešov Region
Ukraïns'ke sotsio-kul'turne tovarystvo (USKT). *See* Ukrainian Civic and Cultural Society
Ung/Uzh county, 81–84 passim, 90, 92, 94, 123, 148, 156, 173, 182, 185, 186, 193, 194, 257
Ungvár. *See* Uzhhorod
Unia. See Church Union
Uniate Church/Uniates, 79, 81–86, 95, 99–101
Uniates/Greek Catholics. *See* Greek Catholic Church/Greek Catholicism

Union of Brest, 79, 81, 86, 159, 246
Union of Carpathian Youth, 327
Union of Lemkos in Poland/
    Ob'iednannia Lemkiv v Pol'shchi,
    389
Union of Lublin, 78
Union of Russian Women, 230
Union of Russian Youth in Slovakia,
    227
Union of Rusyns and Ukrainians: in
    Croatia, 349, 402, 403; in Serbia,
    401
Union of Rusyns-Ukrainians of
    Czecho-Slovakia (Prešov), 359
Union of Uzhhorod, 82–84, 86, 100,
    159, 246, plate 11
Unitarians, 374
United Jewish Party, 261
United Nations, 351, 365, 366, 368
United Societies (Sobranije) of Greek
    Catholic Religion, 158, 177
United States, 1, 159, 185, 197,
    248–249, 318, 366, 375; Carpatho-
    Rusyns in, 1, 86, 145, 154–163,
    177–178, 187, 189, 204, 224,
    243–251, 276, 293, 298, 350–354,
    360, 361, 368, 373, 375–377, 386,
    403–405, 408
Unity of Subcarpathian Brothers, 375
University of L'viv, 123
University of Novi Sad, 349
University of Pennsylvania, 178
University of Prešov, xviii, xx, 382,
    383, plate 99
University of Toronto, xviii–xx, 366, 405
University of Trnava, 84
University of Uzhhorod, 317
UPA. See Ukrainian Insurgent Army
Upper Austria, 18
Upper Tisza Region, 15, 17, 18, 22, 29
Ural Mountains, 43
Urbanization, 59, 60, 310–311, 333–
    334, 411
Urbarium, 98–99, 415
Uruguay: Carpatho-Rusyns in, 236
USA. See United States
Uście Gorlickie, 15
USKT. See Ukrainian Civic and
    Cultural Society
Ustrzycki Górne, plate 81

Uzh county. See Ung county
Uzh River, 5, 146, 193, plate 9
Uzhhorod/Ungvár, 6, 45, 81, 83, 94,
    100, 101, 102, 120, 122, 123, 125,
    137, 141, 146, 148, 149, 189, 193,
    196, 202, 203, 255, 256, 257, 264,
    266, 273, 286, 287, 288, 305, 310,
    311, 313, 358, 369, plates 18, 20,
    41, 44, 47, 48, 50, 63, 65, 66, 70,
    94. See also Union of Uzhhorod;
    University of Uzhhorod
Uzhhorod castle, 83–84, 90, plate 11
Uzhhorod District, 123
Uzhhorod estate, 90, 92
Uzhok, plate 28
Uzhok Pass, 11, 148, 170, plate 31

V

Vác, 56, 399
Văgaş 347
Vajk, 45, 46
Valerii Padiak Publishing House
    (Uzhhorod), 378
Valyi, Ioann/John, 137, 160
Van Nuys, Greek Catholic Eparchy of,
    351
Vančura, Vladislav, 267
Vandals, 18
Varadka, 227
Varangian Rus'/Varangians, 47–48, 50
Vary castle, 57
Vatican, 86, 139, 247, 248–250
    passim, 405
Vatra: festivals, 341–342, 358, 389–
    390, 393, plate 84
Vel'ký Šariš, 18
Velvet Revolution, 356, 359, 379, 382,
    395
Velyki Lazy, 147
Velyki Luchky, 163
Velykyi Bychkiv, 148, 202, 375, plate
    30
Velykŷi Lak, 153
Velykyi Luh, 93
Velykŷi Pereg, 153
Venelin, Iurii, 105
Venhrynovych, Oleksandr, 394
Veniamin (Fedchenkov), 209
Verdun, Battle of, 171

Verets'kyi Pass, 42, 43, 90, 146, plate 8

Verkhovna Rada (Kiev), 357, 363, 365

Verkhovyna, 286

Verkhovyntsi/Highlanders, 3

Verkhratskyi, Ivan, 133

Vermont, 11, 376

Versailles, Treaty of, 270

Vienna, 14, 73, 75, 89, 91, 101, 102, 107, 108, 111, 118–123 passim, 125, 128, 129, 131, 134, 146, 148, 170, 173, 185, 273, 274, 276, 281, 300, 317

Vienna Award (1938) 273, 274, 276; (1940) 281

Vikings, 47

Világos, 120

Vişeu River, 7, 11, 241, 347

Visigoths, 18, 33

Vistula-Baltic Basin, 7

Vistula Operation/Akcja Wisła, 337, 390, 405, plate 81

Vistula River, 96, 279

Vistulans, 29

Vlach Law, 60, 61, 65, 66, 70

Vlachs/Volokhs, 59, 60, 65, 66, 69, 70

Vladimir (Rajić), 210

Vladimir/Volodymyr I, 40

Vladimirov. *See* Ladomirová

Vojta, Adolf, plate 62

Vojvodina, 3, 95, 109, 198, 216, 242–243, 315, 348–350, 386

Vojvodinian/Bachka-Srem Rusyns, 94–95, 132, 153–154, 198, 242–243, 281, 348–350, 358–359, 361, 367, 401–403

Vojvodinian Rusyn language, 153, 243, 315, 349, 350, 402

Volansky, John, 157

Volga River, 47

Volhynia, 209, 292, 303, 324, 343–346, 427n.12. *See also* Galicia-Volhynia

Volhynian Operation/Volynská akce, 324, 425n.9

Volksdeutscher, 270

Volodymyr I, 40

Volos, 27

Voloshyn, Avhustyn, 140, 182, 187, 193, 217, 270, 273–278 passim, 315, plate 68

Vrabec, Antonín Jindřich. *See* Savatij

Vrabel', Mykhaïl, 140

Vrbas, 153, 243

Vukovar, 348, 349, 402

Vylok, 90

Vynohradovo, 202, plate 3. *See also* Sevliush

Vysanyk, Mykhailo von, 122

Vyshova River, 241, 347

Vyslotskii, Dymytrii, 246, 247

Vyšný Svidník, 227. *See also* Svidník

W

Walachia, 71

Wallonia, 2

Warhol, Andy, xvii, 412

Warhol Family Museum of Modern Art, 412

Warsaw, 69, 179, 181, 233, 340

Warsaw Pact, 331

Warsaw-Chełm, Orthodox Eparchy of, 237

Warta River, 46

Washington, D.C., 248, 405

WASP/White Anglo-Saxon Protestant, 159

Watchtower Bible and Tract Society, 375

Waterloo, 404

Waterloo, Battle of, 108

Wehrmacht. *See* German Army

Weiss, Isaak/Eizik, 261

Weiss, Josef Meir, 259, 261

Welsh, 19

Werbőczi, István, 66, 75

West Germany, 347, 350, 403

West Roman Empire, 35, 50

West Slavs, 2, 9, 27

West Ukrainian National Republic, 179, 181, 183, 184, 186, 234

Western Bug River, 301

Western Christian Church. *See* Christianity: Roman-Rite; Protestantism/Protestants

White Croats, 18, 28–31, 37, 45, 69

White House (in Mukachevo), 94; (in Washington, D.C.), 178

Whites/White Russians, 176, 181

Wielkopolska, 46

Wietenberg culture, 17
Wilson, Woodrow, 298, 417n.1
Wincz, András, 291
Winnipeg, Manitoba, 246
Wisłok River, 3, 11, 19
Wisłoka River, 11
Wittenberg, 373
Władysław II Jagiełło, 78
Wołów, 337
Women, 230, 288–289, 309, 371, 397, 410
World Academy of Rusyn Culture (Toronto), 405
World Congress of Lemkos, 394
World Congress of Rusyns, 198, 360–361, 377, 396, 408, plates 91, 102
World Federation of Ukrainian Lemko Organizations, 389, 394
World War I, 139, 154, 161, 167–174, 175, 177, 183, 190, 234, 243, 298
World War II, 216, 239, 279–289, 291–294, 300, 326, 350
Worldwide Church of God, 377
Wrocław, 337
Würzburg, 92
Wycliffe, John, 76
Wysowa, 17
Wyszowadka, 163

Y

Yale University, 114
Yalta Conference, 301
Yiddish language, 9, 109, 257, 258, 261, 311, 386
Yidishe Shtime (newspaper), 261
Yidishe Tsaytung (newspaper), 261
Yonkers, New York, 246
Yugoslav Communist Party. See Communist Party: of Yugoslavia
Yugoslavia, 209, 357, 358, 360, 361, 386, 401-403, 411; Carpatho-Rusyn in, see Vojvodinian/Bachka-Srem Rusyns

Z

Zagranichnaia Rus', 132
Zagreb, 348, 430

Zahradka (magazine), 349
Zajíc, Josef, 266
Zakarpatia/Zakarpats'ka oblast. See Transcarpathia/Transcarpathian oblast
Zakarpats'ka pravda (newspaper), 316
Zápolyai, János, 75
Zaporozhian Cossacks, 183
Zaria Cultural and Enlightenment (National) Union of Yugoslav Rusyns (Stari Vrbas), 243, 287
Zatloukal, Jaroslav, 267
Závadka, 100
Zawadka Rymanowska, plate 26
Zbruch River, 96
Żdynia, 390
Żegiestów, 147
Žehra, 17
Zeman, Kamil, 258
Zemanchyk, Ivan, 103
Země podkarpatoruská, 270
Zemplín castle/hill-fort, 21
Zemplyn/Zemplén county, 57, 64, 66, 71, 82, 83, 84, 87, 101, 123, 156, 182, 185, 186, 193, 194, 219, 223, 224, 225
Zhatkovych, Gregory, 178, 187, 189, 194, 195, 293, 298, plate 40
Zhatkovych, Iurii, 140
Zhatkovych, Pavel, 178
Zhupan, Ievhen, 369
Zhupanat, 195
Zhydovs'kyi, Ivan, 270, 285
Zhydovs'kyi, Petro, 285, plate 43
Zhytomyr, 163
Zieme Odzyskane. See Recovered Lands
Zionism/Zionists, 260
Zoreslav. See Sabol, Sevastiian
Zoria/Hajnal (journal), 287
Zorile/Zgribeshti, 153, 347
Zozuliak, Aleksander, 359, 410, plate 90
Zozuliak, Vasyl', 308, 411
Zrínyi, Ilona, 43, 87
Zsidó néplap (newspaper), 261
Zsigmond I Rákóczi, 87
Zubryts'kyi, Dionisii, 230
Zyndranowa, 387

Plate 1. Mountain pasture in the Lemko Region.

Plate 2. A Dolyniane village in Subcarpathian Rus'. Photo by Oleksii Popov.

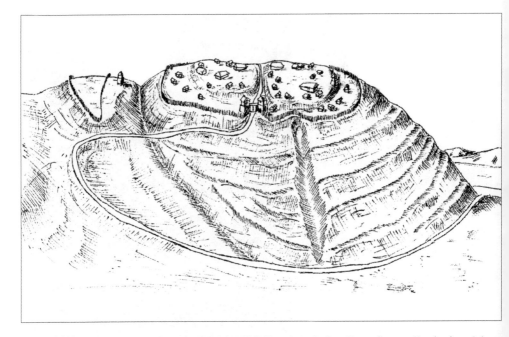

Plate 3. Reconstruction of the hill-fort (*horodyshche*) at Mala Kopania in the Tysa River valley near Vynohradovo, Subcarpathian Rus'.

a.

b.

Plate 4. Pre-historic artisan wares: a. vase, drinking cup, and dipper (late Bronze Age, circa 1000 BCE) found at Diakovo along the Botar River valley, Subcarpathian Rus'; b. ritual vessel in the shape of a lamb (outset of the Common Era) found at the Mala Kopania hill-fort, Subcarpathian Rus'.

Plate 5. Present-day view near Mukachevo, Subcarpathian Rus', of the Galish (204 meters) and Lovachka (306 meters) hill-ocks, site of Celtic settlements, 300–60 BCE.

Plate 6. Typical dwelling among the early Slavs, partly sunk into the ground

Plate 7. Ninth-century "Apostles to the Slavs," Saints Cyril and Methodius, sculpture by Ivan Brovdi erected 1999 in Mukachevo, Subcarpathian Rus'.

a.

b.

Plate 8. a. Rusyn-language book (1896) about Árpád, "founder of the fatherland"; b. annual celebration held before World War I at the obelisk atop the Verets'kyi pass where Árpád led the Magyar tribes into historic Hungary.

Plate 9.
Nevyts'kyi castle
overlooking
the Uzh River,
Subcarpathian Rus'.

Plate 10. Fourteenth-century Prince Fedor
Koriatovych, sculpture by Vasyl' Olashyn
erected 1996 in the upper courtyard of the
Mukachevo Castle, Subcarpathian Rus'.

Plate 11. Reconstruction of the Uzhhorod Castle with the church in the foreground where the Union of Uzhhorod took place in 1646.

Plate 12. Monastery of St. Nicholas on Monk's Hill just outside Mukachevo, residence in the foreground (1776–1772) designed by Demeter Rácz/Rats' and church (1798–1804).

Plate 13. Title page of the first printed book, *Catechism* (Trnava, 1698), commissioned by Bishop Joseph Decamelis.

Plate 14. Prince Ferenc II Rákóczi, painting by Ádám Mányoki (1708).

Plate 15. Prince Friedrich-Karl von Schönborn (1674–1746), lord of the Mukachevo-Chynadiievo estate.

Plate 16. Church of St. Paraskeva (1773) in the village of Potoky, Prešov Region.

Plate 17. Castle of Mukachevo/Munkács, woodcut (1720) by Gabriel Bodenehr.

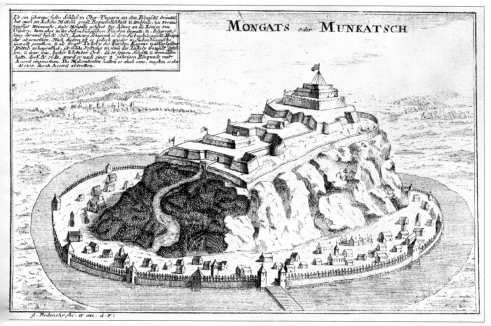

Plate 18. Pride of place given to Austria's empress, as a heavenly angel proclaims (in Latin): "Long Live Maria Theresa." Ceiling fresco in the Greek Catholic episcopal palace, Uzhhorod, 1780s.

Plate 19. Andrei Bachyns'kyi, bishop of the Greek Catholic Eparchy of Mukachevo, 1733–1809, woodcut (1804).

Plate 20. Greek Catholic cathedral church of the Eparchy of Mukachevo and episcopal residence, Uzhhorod, early 19th centur

Plate 21. Adol'f Dobrians'kyi (1817–1901), political and civic activist.

Plate 22. Aleksander Dukhnovych (1803–1865), "national awakener of the Carpatho-Rusyns."

Plate 23. Frontispiece and title page of the first Carpatho-Rusyn literary almanac (Vienna, 1851).

Plate 24. Masthead of the first Carpatho-Rusyn newspaper published in the homeland, *Svît* (The World, 1867–1871).

Plate 25. Ruska Bursa student residence (est. 1908), Gorlice, Lemko Region.

Plate 26. Kachkovs'kyi Society reading room in Zawadka Rymanowska, Lemko Region.

Plate 27. Masthead of the inaugural issue of the first Lemko-Rusyn newspaper, Lemko (1911–1913).

Plate 28. Carpatho-Rusyn mountain village, Uzhok, Subcarpathian Rus', early 20th century. Photo by Bohumil Vavroušek.

Plate 29. Schönborn family "hunting lodge" with 52 rooms to host European aristocrats, located north of Mukachevo alongside an artificial lake in the shape of the Austro-Hungarian Empire, architect Guilbrandt Gregorian, built 1890–1895.

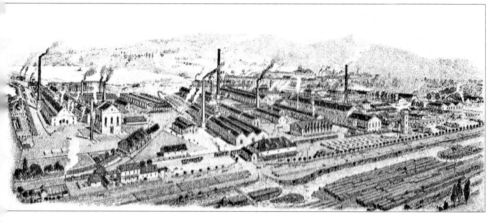

Plate 30. Klotilda factory complex at Velykyi Bychkiv, Subcarpathian Rus', 1890s.

Plate 31. Viaduct and tunnel leading to the Uzhok Pass, built by Hungarian State Railways, 1890s.

Plate 32. Havriïl/Gabor Kostel'nik (1886–1948), "father of the Vojvodinian Rusyn language."

Plate 33. Rusyn school in Ruski Kerestur, Vojvodina, built in 1913.

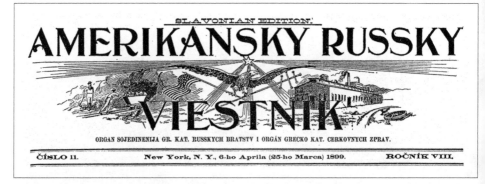

Plate 34. Masthead from 1899 of the *Amerikansky russky viestnik* (1892–1952), the oldest Rusyn-American newspaper.

a.

b.

Plate 35. a. Alexis Toth (1854–1909); b. St. Mary's Church, Minneapolis, Minnesota, where "the return to Orthodoxy" movement began.

Plate 36. Persecution of civilians by Austro-Hungarian troops, Lemko Region, 1914.

Plate 37. War damages during the Russian Army advance on Humenné, near the Prešov Region, 1915.

Plate 38. Deportation of Lemko-Rusyns to the Talerhof internment camp near Graz, 1914.

Plate 39. Iaroslav Kachmarchyk
(1884–1944), head of the Lemko-Rusyn
Republic.

Plate 40. Gregory Zhatkovych (1886–1967),
Rusyn-American activist and first governor of
Subcarpathian Rus'.

Plate 41. Delegates at the Central Rusyn National Council, which declared union with Czechoslovakia, Uzhhorod
Subcarpathian Rus', May 1919.

Plate 42. Antonín Rozsypal, Czech vice-governor, 1923–1927, and administrative president, 1928–1936; Antonii Beskyd, second governor, 1923–1933; and Konstantyn Hrabar, third governor, 1935–1938 of Subcarpathian Rus'.

Plate 43. Carpatho-Rusyn caucus, 1938, in the Czechoslovak parliament, senators and deputies from Subcarpathian Rus' and the Prešov Region: (seated) Stepan Fentsyk, Edmund Bachyns'kyi, Ivan Parkanyi—representative of the president's office, Pavlo Kossei, Andrei Brodii; (standing) Mykhailo Demko, Petro Zhydovs'kyi, Mykola Dolynai, Ivan P'ieshchak, Iuliian Revai.

Plate 44. Airplane approaching the Uzhhorod airport passing over the city's Masaryk Square, 1930.

Plate 45. Civic Center in Svaliava, architect František Krupka, built 1930.

Plate 46. Czechoslovak state housing complex ("Masaryk Colony") and *gymnasium* in Khust, architect Jindřich Freiwald, bui 1923–1926.

Plate 47. Rus' National Center, headquarters of the Dukhnovych Cultural and Enlightenment Society, Uzhhorod, built 1932.

Plate 48. National Center, headquarters of the Prosvita Cultural-Enlightenment Society, Uzhhorod, built 1928.

Plate 49. Dukhnovych Society branch reading room, meeting in the village school, Nelipynno, Subcarpathian Rus', ca. 1928.

Plate 50. Subcarpathian Rusyn National Theater, Uzhhorod, 1930s.

Plate 52. Pavel Goidych (1888–1960),
bishop of the Eparchy of Prešov, 1927–
1950, photographed at his episcopal
installation.

Plate 53. Greek Catholic
"Russian" gymnasium,
Prešov, opened in 1936.

Plate 54. Ioann Polianskii (1888–1978),
Lemko historian and chancellor,
1936–1941, of the Greek Catholic Lemko
Apostolic Administration.

Plate 55. Ivan Rusenko (1890-1960),
Lemko-Rusyn writer and cultural activist.

Plate 56. Lemko school children with their
teacher, Metodii Trokhanovskii, author of
the first Lemko Rusyn language textbooks,
Krynica, Lemko Region, early 1930s.

Plate 57. Cottage industry in the interwar Lemko Region,
grease wagon from the village of Łosie.

Plate 58. National Center, headquarters of the Rusyn National Enlightenment Society, Ruski Kerestur, Vojvodina.

Plate 59. Diura Bindas (1877–1950), Vojvodinian Rusyn cultural and civic activist.

Plate 60. Wedding of a Greek Catholic seminarian before ordination to the priesthood, Charleroi, Pennsylvania, 1922.

Plate 61. Headquarters and printshop, 1906 to 1987, of the Greek Catholic Union of Rusyn Brotherhoods in the United States, Munhall, Pennsylvania.

Plate 62. Hungarian Theater, Mukachevo, architects Adolf Voyta and Richárd Röszler, built 1896–1898.

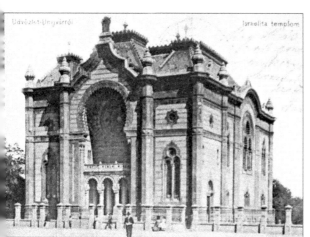

Plate 63. Orthodox Jewish synagogue, Uzhhorod, architects Gyula Papp and Ferenc Szabolcs, built 1904.

Plate 64. Jewish-owned store, Solotvyno, Subcarpathian Rus', early 1920s.

Plate 65. Swabian Street (reconstruction)—Austro-German inhabited section of Uzhhorod, late 19th century.

Plate 66. Czech-owned store of Eduard Flek, Uzhhorod, 1926.

Plate 67. Andrii Brodii (1895–1946), first prime minister of autonomous Subcarpathian Rus', October 1938.

Plate 68. Avhustyn Voloshyn (1874–1945), second prime minister of autonomous Subcarpathian Rus'/Carpatho-Ukraine, November 1938 – March 1939.

Plate 69. Propaganda poster to celebrate "the return" of Subcarpathian Rus' to Hungary, featuring Regent Miklós Horthy.

Plate 70. Administration and staff of the Subcarpathian Scholarly Society which functioned in Hungarion-ruled Uzhhorod, 1941–1944.

Plate 71. Young Carpatho-Rusyns who fled to the Soviet Union, 1939–1940, and were interned in the Soviet Gulag.

Plate 72. Jews being deported from a village somewhere between Khust and Irshava, Hungarian-ruled Subcarpathia, August 1941.

Plate 73. First Czechoslovak Army Corps crosses the border into Czechoslovakia near the Carpatho-Rusyn village of Kalínov, Prešov Region, 6 October 1944.

Plate 75. Ivan I. Turianytsia (1901–1955), first chairman of the National Council of Transcarpathian Ukraine, photographed 1944 as officer in the Czechoslovak Army Corps.

Plate 74. Scala movie house, Mukachevo, site of the Congress of People's Committees call for unification with the Soviet Union, 26 November 1944.

Plate 76. Resettlement of Lemko Rusyns from Poland to the Soviet Union, 1945–1946.

a.

).   c.

Plate 77. Soviet ideology as presented in a book about the "new" Transcarpathia, titled *The Achievements of Brotherhood* 1967): a. "A Child of the Soviet Five-Year Plan"—the paper processing mill in Rakhiv, late 1940s; b. "A home without a himney and windows without glass"—a Carpatho-Rusyn one-room dwelling in "bourgeois Czechoslovakia", 1937; c. "Chil-dren are healthy! Nevertheless, a visiting doctor has to make sure." The year is 1967.

Plate 78. The church council (sobor) proclaiming the liquidation of the Greek Catholic Eparchy of Prešov, 28 April 1950, under the slogans (in Slovak): "Slavs—heed the words of Saint Methodius—Beware of Rome" and "Rejoice in Peace unto You."

Plate 79. Masthead of *Priashevshchina*, the Russian-language organ (Prešov, 1945–1952) of the Ukrainian National Council of the Prešov Region.

Plate 80. Garment Factory named after the World War II Slovak partisan Captain Ján Nálepka, Svidník, built 1950s.

Plate 81. Deportation of Lemkos from the village of Ustrzyki Górne during the Vistula Operation, May 1947.

Plate 82. UPA (Ukrainian Insurgent Army) soldiers questioning a local resident in the Carpathians, 1947.

Plate 83. Nykyfor Krynytskii (1895–1968), world-renowned Lemko naive painter, after returning to his native town of Krynica, 1950s.

Plate 84. The second Lemko Vatra at Czarna, Lemko Region, June 1984.

Plate 85. Lemko diaspora cultural and civic activists in Soviet and independent Ukraine: Ivan Krasovs'kyi (1927–2014) and Petro Kohut (1919–2012).

Plate 86. The Petro Kuzmiak Rusyn *gymnasium* (senior high school) in Ruski Kerestur, Vojvodina, opened in 1977.

Plate 87. Main street in Ruski Kerestur, Vojvodina, early 1990s; the Rusyn National Center is on the left.

Plate 88. Founding chairman Andrei Kopcha (b. 1954) addressing the First Congress of the Lemko Society, Legnica, Poland, April 1989.

Plate 89. Vasyl' Turok (1940–2005), founding chairman of the World Congress of Rusyns.

Plate 90. Aleksander Zozuliak (b. 1953), civic and cultural activist in the Prešov Region.

Plate 91. Delegate from North America, Paul Robert Magocsi, addressing the opening session of the First World Congress of Rusyns, Medzilaborce, Czecho-Slovakia, March 1991.

Plate 92. Flyer urging residents of Ukraine's Transcarpathian region to vote in favor of autonomy in the December 1, 1991 referendum.

Plate 93. Writers and teachers Vasyl' Petrovai, Ian Hryb, and Professor Iurii Pan'ko at the First Congress of the Rusyn Language, Bardejovské Kúpele, Czecho-Slovakia, November 1992.

Plate 94. Statue of Lenin, symbol of Soviet rule, bring removed from a main square in Uzhhorod, August 1991.

Plate 95. The identity debate in Ukraine's Transcarpathia—Patient: "I was, Am, and Remain a Rusyn"; Nurse to doctor: "It's hopeless, even though he was given five liters of pure Ukrainian blood." Cartoon by P. Petki, Uzhhorod.

a.

b.

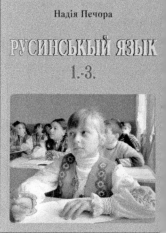

Plate 96. Rusyn School Program in Ukraine's Transcarpathia: a. class in the village of Il'nytsia, November 2008; b. languag textbook prepared for the program.

Plate 98. Bumper sticker urging inhabitants in the Prešov Region to indicate their nationality *Rusyn* and their religion *Greek Catholic* on Slovakia's 2011 census.

Plate 97. Flyer urging Carpatho-Rusyns to indicate their nationality and mother tongue as *Rusyn* on Slovakia's 2001 census form.

Plate 99. Teaching staff and graduates of the Studium Carpatho-Ruthenorum international summer school, Prešov University, June 2012.

Plate 100. Diaspora Lemkos in Ukraine at the consecration o their own parish church, L'viv, 1992.

Plate 101. National Headquarters (since 2004) of the Carpatho Rusyn Society of North America, Munhall, Pennsylvania.

Plate 102. Members of the World Council of the World Congress of Rusyns hosted by the speaker of the Romanian Parlia ment, Bucharest, March 2007.